PC HARDWARE
IN A NUTSHELL

A Desktop Quick Reference

PC HARDWARE
IN A NUTSHELL

A Desktop Quick Reference

Robert Bruce Thompson &
Barbara Fritchman Thompson

O'REILLY®

Beijing • Cambridge • Farnham • Köln • Paris • Sebastopol • Taipei • Tokyo

PC Hardware in a Nutshell

by Robert Bruce Thompson and Barbara Fritchman Thompson

Copyright © 2000 O'Reilly & Associates, Inc. All rights reserved.
Printed in the United States of America.

Published by O'Reilly & Associates, Inc., 101 Morris Street, Sebastopol, CA 95472.

Editor: Robert Denn

Production Editor: Colleen Gorman

Cover Designer: Hanna Dyer

Printing History:

October 2000:   First Edition.

Library of Congress Cataloging-in-Publication Data

Thompson, Robert Bruce.
    PC Hardware in a nutshell : a desktop quick reference / Robert Bruce Thompson,
    Barbara Fritchman Thompson.--1st ed. p. cm.
    ISBN 1-56592-599-8
    1. Microcomputers--Equipment and supplies. 2. Microcomputers--Upgrading.
        3. Microcomputers--Maintenance and repair. 4. Microcomputers--Purchasing.
        I. Thompson, Barbara Fritchman. II. Title.

TK7887.5 .T48 2000
621.39'16--dc21   00-062359

ISBN: 1-56592-599-8   [2/01]
[M]

To my agent, David L. Rogelberg.
No author could hope for a better colleague.

—Robert Bruce Thompson

To my parents, Richard Carl "Dutch" Fritchman
and Sankie Callahan Fritchman, who gave me
the opportunities and guidance
to help me succeed.

—Barbara Fritchman Thompson

Table of Contents

Foreword

My job is to persuade you to buy this book, or make you feel you've made the right choice if you've already bought it.

That's easy because there's not another book like this, and if you do much with computers you need a good reference work on hardware. Of course there are massively larger books on the subject, but that's just the point: most of the time you're not looking for a long essay on the subject, you need information, and reliable judgment, both of which Robert Bruce Thompson is highly—I am tempted to say uniquely—qualified to give.

I can say this with some authority. I've never actually met Robert Bruce Thompson face to face, but we've been friends for a couple of years. Such is the way with the modern Internet. I first "met" him in the dark days after BYTE Magazine suddenly and unexpectedly folded, and I continued my column on my web site. (Shameless self-promotion: *http://www.jerrypournelle.com.*) One of the features of both the web site and the column was reader mail, and there soon appeared a corps of regulars, all experts in one or another field, all articulate, and all very generous with their time and efforts. Robert Thompson stood out among these, and it was soon clear to me that he knew far more about computer hardware than I did. That was surprising: I've been in this business since 1978, and while no one can know everything, I thought I knew a good bit about nearly everything. I do, too, but Thompson knows more, both in depth and breadth, and that's astonishing.

He's pretty careful, too. Over the years I have found I agree with most of his conclusions, and when we disagree I have to rethink my position, because he's been right at least as often as I have been.

So. You have here a well-written book by someone who understands the subject. It's about computer hardware and nearly everyone needs a good, opinionated reference work on that subject, provided the opinions are sound, which in Thompson's case they certainly are. It's published by O'Reilly, which means it's well edited by editors who resist the temptation to become an unacknowledged collaborators. It's really the best book you'll find on this subject. And if that doesn't persuade you to buy this book, I doubt anything else I can say would.

—Jerry Pournelle

Preface

PC Hardware in a Nutshell. An oxymoron, as it turns out. When Robert started this project in late 1998, he planned to write a 300-page book in about five months. It soon became clear that the book would require about four times the work originally planned and end up much larger. Barbara joined the project early, at first as the researcher and later as the full co-author. After more than 18 months of working seven days a week, including last-minute re-writes to make everything as current as possible, the result is the book you are now holding. *"PC Hardware in a Coconut-shell*, more like," as our editor observed.

Robert decided to write this book because he couldn't find a good answer to what seemed to be a simple question. Robert, who has extensive PC experience, wanted to buy his first CD burner but didn't know much about them. He needed information about how to choose, install, configure, and use a CD burner. It would have been easy to check articles about CD burners in hardware-oriented magazines and enthusiast web sites, but Robert doesn't really trust them to provide accurate and unbiased information.

He next started checking the shelf of PC hardware books he owns. What he found in those books was lots of *interesting* information, but a surprising dearth of *useful* information. For example, one very popular title devoted only 4.5 of its 1500+ pages to CD-R and CD-RW, most of which described the history and low-level functioning of these devices. Advice on how to choose a CD burner? Advice on how to install it, configure it, use it, or troubleshoot it? Next to none. That same book devoted nearly 70 pages to a list of vendors—information easily accessible on the Web—so the shortage of information couldn't have been a result of page count constraints.

We were determined to write a book filled with useful information. You won't find tables of drive parameters for hundreds of obsolete disk drives, instructions on how to change the interleave by low-level formatting an XT hard drive, charts of keyboard scan codes, and so on. As interesting as those things might be, they fail the useful test. Pruning stuff that was merely interesting was painful, because we like to read interesting stuff as much as the next person. But we quickly found out why there's so much interesting and so little useful information in some PC hardware books. Interesting is quick and easy to write. Useful is slow and hard, because you actually have to *do* all the stuff.

We found numerous errors that were repeated nearly verbatim in more than one book—things that were clearly wrong, but that an author had simply repeated without verifying it rather than taking the time to check for himself. We're guilty of that at times, too. When we list the pinouts for a gameport, for example, we get that information from published sources. But surprisingly often, we found that these sources disagreed, and so were forced to check for ourselves.

And, boy, did we expend an incredible amount of time and effort checking things for ourselves. Rather than simply repeating what others have said about CD burners, for example, we decided to find out for ourselves. Doing that required building four computers—IDE/98, IDE/NT, SCSI/98, and SCSI/NT—and testing each configuration with different drive models by burning numerous CDs with each. About ten 14-hour days later, we finally had a handle on CD burners. All that work turned into just a few pages and some specific product recommendations.

We wouldn't have started this project unless we thought we could write a better PC hardware book. We think *PC Hardware in a Nutshell* meets that goal, and we hope you will too.

Audience

This book is intended for anyone who buys, builds, upgrades, or repairs PCs in a corporate, small-business, or home setting. If you want to buy a PC, this book tells you what to look for—and what to look out for. If you want to build a PC, this book explains, component-by-component, the key parts of a PC, describes the important characteristics of each, provides buying guidelines, lists recommended products (by brand name and model), and takes you step-by-step through building the PC. If you have an older PC, this book tells you what you need to know to upgrade it, as well as when it makes more sense simply to retire it to less demanding duties. Finally, if your PC breaks, this book tells you what you need to know to troubleshoot the problem and then choose and install replacement parts.

Organization

Each chapter of this book is devoted to one topic, and is self-supporting. The first two chapters provide an overview of PC hardware and standards, as well as detailed advice about buying, building, upgrading, and repairing PCs; describe the tools and software you'll need; explain basic procedures like installing expansion cards; and detail the tips and tricks we've learned during 20 years of working on PCs. These chapters include:

Chapter 1, *Fundamentals*
Chapter 2, *Working on PCs*

The second group of chapters covers the core components of any PC—motherboards, processors, and memory. These chapters take the form used throughout the rest of the book, beginning with brief background information about the component, followed by an explanation of the important characteristics, guidelines on choosing among competing products, instructions for installing and configuring the component, troubleshooting information, if applicable, and a final "Our Picks" section, where we list by name the products we actually use and recommend. This group includes the following chapters:

Chapter 3, *Motherboards*
Chapter 4, *Processors*
Chapter 5, *Memory*

The third group of chapters covers removable magnetic storage, including the pedestrian floppy disk drive, one of the few PC components that survives largely unchanged from the earliest days of PCs; "super-floppies" like the Iomega Zip and the Imation LS-120; removable hard disk drives like the Iomega Jaz and the Castlewood ORB; and tape drives, which remain the best choice for backing up data despite the arrival of new technologies. This group includes the following chapters:

Chapter 6, *Floppy Disk Drives*
Chapter 7, *Floppy Disk Drive Replacements*
Chapter 8, *Removable Hard Disk Drives*
Chapter 9, *Tape Drives*

The fourth group of chapters covers optical storage, an increasingly important component in modern PCs. We detail what you need to know to choose, install, configure, and use CD-ROM, CD-R, CD-RW, DVD-ROM, and DVD-RAM drives. This group includes the following chapters:

Chapter 10, *CD-ROM Drives*
Chapter 11, *CD-R and CD-RW Drives*
Chapter 12, *DVD Drives*

The fifth group of chapters covers ATAPI ("IDE") hard disk drives, which are ubiquitous in modern PCs, as well as SCSI models, which provide better performance at correspondingly higher prices. We explain the important characteristics of hard drives, provide guidelines for purchasing one, explain how to install, prepare, configure, and troubleshoot hard drives, and recommend specific models. This group includes the following chapters:

Chapter 13, *Hard Disk Interfaces*
Chapter 14, *Hard Disk Drives*

The sixth group of chapters covers sight and sound. We describe the important characteristics of video adapters, monitors, sound cards, and speakers, explain how to choose, install, configure and troubleshoot them, and recommend specific models for specific needs. We also include a brief introduction to MP3 and an explanation of how to use it. This group includes the following chapters:

Chapter 15, *Video Adapters*
Chapter 16, *Monitors*
Chapter 17, *Sound Cards*
Chapter 18, *Speakers and Headphones*

The seventh group of chapters covers input devices—keyboards, mice, and game controllers. We explain how they work, how to choose the best ones for your needs, and (as usual) how to install, configure, and troubleshoot them. Although which input devices you prefer is an intensely personal choice, we also recommend specific keyboards, mice, and game controllers that we've found suitable. This group includes the following chapters:

Chapter 19, *Keyboards*
Chapter 20, *Mice and Trackballs*
Chapter 21, *Game Controllers*

The eighth group of chapters covers three components—cases, PC power supplies, and backup power supplies—that receive little attention, but are important to system reliability and usability. We detail the important characteristics of each, provide guidelines for choosing the best case and power supplies for your system, and recommend specific models for different purposes. This group includes the following chapters:

Chapter 22, *Cases*
Chapter 23, *Power Supplies*
Chapter 24, *Backup Power Supplies*

The final group of chapters puts it all together, using case studies to explain, step-by-step, how to design systems appropriate for specific needs (and budgets), how to select and purchase components, and how to turn that pile of components into a working PC. This group includes the following chapters:

Chapter 25, *Designing a PC*
Chapter 26, *Building a PC*

Most chapters end with an "Our Picks" section, which tells you, specifically by brand name and model, what we use and recommend. We base these recommendations on our own experience, not after using the product for a day or a week, but after extensive day-in-day-out use under realistic conditions. If we say we found a particular CD burner to be durable, that means that we used that CD burner for months and burned a bunch of CDs with it. If we say a particular motherboard is stable, that means we used it in one of our own systems and found that it doesn't crash. If we say a particular monitor is the best we've used, it's because we sat in front of it for hours while writing this book. And so on.

The danger to this method, of course, is that PC hardware changes in Internet time. Components that were the hottest things on the market (or even preproduction engineering samples) when we started working with them became mainstream products by the time we went to press, and may even be discontinued by the time you read this book. That can't be helped, and it doesn't really matter anyway, because we focus throughout on important characteristics and guidelines, which don't change nearly as fast.

We recognize, though, that many people want specific advice by make and model—"Which motherboard/drive/monitor should I buy?" is one of the most common questions we get—so we've included that information. If we recommend a particular model of Intel motherboard or Seagate disk drive or Plextor CD burner, it's pretty safe to assume that the follow-on model will be as good or better. The computer industry is too competitive for companies to risk releasing bad products or resting on their laurels. But even good companies occasionally turn out dogs, and that's what our web site and newsletter are designed to address. Visit the web site regularly, or subscribe to the newsletter (or both) and we'll keep you posted on the latest stuff (contact information is available in the section "We'd Like to Hear from You" later in this preface).

Conventions

This book uses the following typographical conventions:

Italic
> Used for the names of files, directories, hostnames, domain names, URLs, and to emphasize new terms when they are first introduced.

`Constant width`
> Used to show the contents of files, command syntax, and the output from commands.

`Constant width-italic`
> Used in examples to show variables for which a context-specific substitution should be made. (The variable `filename`, for example, would be replaced by some actual filename.)

`[ option ]`
> When showing command syntax, we place optional parts of the command within brackets. For example, `ls  [-l]` means that the `-l` option is not required.

 This is an example of a Tip or Note. Tips suggest effective ways to accomplish common tasks or highlight important advice. Notes are short asides that convey supplemental information that may not be important to all readers.

 This is an example of a Warning. Warnings highlight dangerous procedures—those that may damage you, your hardware, or your data. Disregard warnings at your own peril.

Two kinds of bullets are used in many of the tables in this book. A closed, filled-in bullet (•) means that the category indicated applies to the column heading. An open bullet (○) means the category is not applicable to the column heading.

We'd Like to Hear from You

The information in this book has been tested and verified, but you may find that features have changed (or you may even find mistakes!). Please tell us about any errors you find, as well as your suggestions for improving future editions, by writing or calling:

O'Reilly & Associates, Inc.
101 Morris Street
Sebastopol, CA 95472
(800) 998-9938 (in the United States or Canada)
(707) 829-0515 (international/local)
(707) 829-0104 (fax)

There is a web site for the book, where we list examples, errata, and any additional information. You can access this page at:

http://www.oreilly.com/catalog/pchardnut/

To comment on the book or ask technical questions, send email to:

bookquestions@oreilly.com

For more information about our books, conferences, software, Resource Centers, and the O'Reilly Network, see our web site at:

http://www.oreilly.com

To contact one of the authors directly, send email to:

barbara@hardwareguys.com
robert@hardwareguys.com

We read all email we receive, but we cannot respond individually to requests for help in choosing hardware, resolving problems, and so on. But we do like to hear from readers.

We produce a free email newsletter that includes articles about new hardware and software we're testing, hardware tips and tricks we've discovered, useful industry news, and so on. To subscribe, send email (an empty message is fine) with the subject "subscribe" to:

pcn-subscribe@hardwareguys.com

We will not sell, rent, or otherwise disclose your email address to any third party unless forced to do so by a court order.

We also have a web site for the book, which includes updated hardware recommendations, buying guides, and articles, as well as errata, plans for future editions, and so on:

http://www.hardwareguys.com/pcn/pcn.html

Acknowledgments

In addition to the O'Reilly production staff, who are listed individually in the Colophon, we want to thank our technical reviewers, two of whom have themselves written books for O'Reilly: Matt Beland, David L. Farquhar (*Optimizing Windows for Games, Graphics and Multimedia*), Sam Kalat of Red Storm Entertainment, J. H. Ricketson, Roger G. Smith, Tom Syroid (*Outlook 2000 in a Nutshell*), and Shawn Wallbridge. These folks did yeoman duty in finding mistakes we made and in making numerous useful suggestions, all of which helped make this a better book. Many of our reviewers maintain personal web sites and are members of the informal Daynotes webring at *http://www.daynotes.com*.

We also want to thank our contacts at the hardware companies, who provided technical help, evaluation units, and other assistance. There are far too many to list individually, but they know who they are. Thanks, folks. We couldn't have done it without you.

The photographs in this book were shot with an Olympus D400-Z digital camera. We've used many different digital cameras, and have developed a strong preference for Olympus models. Their experience as a premier maker of film cameras shows clearly in the construction quality, picture quality, functionality, and ease-of-use of Olympus digital cameras.

Finally, we want to thank our editor, Robert J. Denn, and our publisher, Tim O'Reilly, both of whom contributed numerous useful comments and suggestions.

Thank you for buying *PC Hardware in a Nutshell*. We hope you enjoy reading it as much as we enjoyed writing it.

CHAPTER 1

Fundamentals

This chapter covers a mixed bag of important fundamental information about PCs, including how PCs are defined, an overview of PC components and technologies, a brief explanation of system resources, guidelines for building, buying, and upgrading PCs, smart buying practices, and suggestions as to what to do with old PCs.

PCs Defined

Who decides what is and what is not a PC? That question is not as trivial as it sounds, because there has never been (and probably never will be) an all-embracing *de jure* standard to define the PC. IBM created the *de facto* PC standard (and trademarked the name) when they shipped the first IBM Personal Computer in 1981. For more than five years, until their introduction of the ill-fated proprietary PS/2 line in 1987, IBM defined the PC standard. For a short time thereafter, some considered that Compaq defined the standard. But the days when any PC maker defined the PC standard are far in the past.

These days, Intel and Microsoft jointly define the *de facto* PC standard. In fact, a good working definition of a PC is a computer that uses an Intel or compatible processor *and* can run a Microsoft operating system. Any computer that meets both requirements—a so-called *Wintel* computer—is a PC. A computer that does not is not. Computers based on some Intel processors cannot run any Microsoft operating system, and thus are not PCs. Conversely, some computers with non-Intel processors can run Microsoft operating systems, but do not qualify as PCs. For example, DEC Alpha minicomputers running Windows NT 4 and handheld computers running Windows CE are not PCs.

The joint Intel/Microsoft standard, called the *PC 99 System Design Guide* (*PC 99*), is a book-length document that defines required, recommended, and optional (neither required nor recommended, but must meet the standard if included) characteristics for several classes of PCs, including *Basic PC 99* (further subdivided into *Consumer PC 99* and *Office PC 99*), *Workstation PC 99*, *Entertainment PC 99*, and

Mobile PC 99. These standards are *de facto* in the sense that system and peripheral makers are not required to comply with them to manufacture and sell their products. They might as well be *de jure* standards, however, because compliance is required to achieve such nearly mandatory certifications as inclusion on the Windows NT Hardware Compatibility List.

PC 99 is the latest in an evolution of documents that began in 1990 with the first MPC standard and continued with the PC 95, PC 97, and PC 98 revisions. *PC 99* was formalized in mid-1998, took partial effect in July, 1999 for systems to be delivered in Q4/99, and came into full effect on January 1, 2000. In some ways, *PC 99* is unrealistically far ahead of its time, for example, in recommending Device Bay and 1394 as standard storage interfaces. In other ways it's far behind, for example, in requiring only a 300 MHz processor and 32 MB of RAM for some configurations. Some portions are skewed to Intel CPUs (e.g., an L2 cache requirement was cut from 512 KB to 256 KB when Intel shipped Coppermine Pentium III CPUs with 256 KB L2 cache—probably not a coincidence) while many others are skewed toward Microsoft operating systems. Neither of those is surprising in the document that defines the Wintel standard. All of that said, PC 99 is an important document because it defines the future direction of PC development.

You can purchase *PC 99* in book form (Microsoft Press, 1998). You can view or download *PC 99 1.0* in Acrobat format (*http://developer.intel.com/design/desguide/*) or *PC 99a*—the final release of *PC 99*, with minor updates and corrections—in compiled HTML help format (*http://www.microsoft.com/hwdev/pc99.htm*). The PC Design Guide home page (*http://www.pcdesguide.org*) also contains links to these documents in various formats, as well as early beta versions of the *PC 2001 System Design Guide*.

If you've ever crawled around under a desk trying to read the tiny icons on port connectors, you'll appreciate one very visible manifestation of *PC 99* compliance—standard colors for port connectors, listed in Table 1-1. Nearly all PCs and peripherals shipped since Q4/99 use these colors.

Table 1-1: PC 99 Recommended Connector Color Codes

Connector	Color	Connector	Color
Analog VGA	Blue	PS/2-compatible keyboard	Purple
Audio Line-in	Light blue	PS/2-compatible mouse	Green
Audio Line-out	Lime	Serial	Teal/Turquoise
Digital monitor/flat panel	White	Speaker out/subwoofer	Orange
IEEE 1394	Grey	Right-to-left speaker	Brown
Microphone	Pink	USB	Black
MIDI/gameport	Gold	Video Out	Yellow
Parallel	Burgundy	SCSI, LAN, telephone, etc.	Not defined

PC Components and Technologies

The following sections provide a quick overview of the components and technologies used in modern PCs.

Hardware Components

One of the great strengths of the PC architecture is that it is extensible, allowing a great variety of components to be added, thereby permitting the PC to perform functions its designers may never have envisioned. However, most PCs include a more-or-less standard set of components, including the following:

Motherboard

> The *motherboard*, described in Chapter 3, *Motherboards*, is the heart of a PC. It serves as "Command Central" to coordinate the activities of the system. Its type largely determines system capabilities. Motherboards include the following components:

> *Chipset*

>> The chipset provides the intelligence of the motherboard and determines which processors, memory, and other components the motherboard can use. Most chipsets are divided physically and logically into two components. The *Northbridge* controls cache and main memory and manages the host bus and PCI expansion bus. The *Southbridge* manages the ISA bus, bridges the PCI and ISA buses, and incorporates a *Super I/O* controller, which provides serial and parallel ports, the IDE interface, and other I/O functions.

> *CPU slot(s) and/or socket(s)*

>> The type of CPU slot or socket determines which processors the motherboard can use. The most popular CPU connectors are Slot 1 (Pentium II/III and Celeron), Socket 370 (Pentium III and Celeron), Slot A (AMD Athlon), and the obsolescent Socket 7 (Pentium and K6-* processors). Some motherboards have two or more CPU connectors, allowing them to support multiple processors. A few motherboards have both Slot 1 and Socket 370 connectors, allowing them to support either type of CPU (but not both at once).

> *Voltage Regulator Module (VRM)*

>> VRMs supply clean, tightly regulated voltage to the CPU. Faster CPUs draw more current. Good VRMs are expensive, so some motherboard makers use the lowest-rated VRM suitable for the fastest CPU the motherboard is designed to support. Better VRMs allow a motherboard to accept faster future CPUs with only a BIOS upgrade.

> *Memory slots*

>> The type and number of memory slots (along with chipset limitations) determine the type and amount of memory you can install in a PC. All current systems accept 168-pin SDRAM DIMMs or Rambus RIMMs (or both). Older systems use 30- or 72-pin SIMMs.

> *Expansion bus slots*

>> The type and number of expansion bus slots determine the type and number of expansion cards you can add to the system. Most recent PCs include both PCI and ISA expansion slots, although the latest models have only PCI slots.

Integrated functions

Modern motherboards often include embedded features, such as video and sound (and, less commonly, LAN and SCSI interfaces), that were formerly provided by add-on expansion cards. The upsides to embedded components are reduced costs, better integration, and higher reliability. The downside is that it may be difficult or impossible to upgrade embedded components. Integrated motherboards are often ideally suited for casual users, but most readers of this book will avoid them and build *a la carte* from discrete components.

Processor

The *processor* or *CPU* (described in Chapter 4, *Processors*) is the engine that drives the PC. The CPU you use determines how fast the system runs and what operating systems and other software can run on it. Most PCs use processors from Intel (Pentium II/III or Celeron) or AMD (Athlon or K6-2/III). Processors vary in speed (300 MHz to 1,000 MHz), cost ($25 to $1,000+), physical connector (Socket 7, Socket 370, Slot 1, Slot 2, Slot A), efficiency at performing various functions, and in other respects. Although processors get much attention, the truth is that performance differences between the slowest and fastest current processors are relatively minor, little more than a factor of two.

Memory

A PC uses *Random Access Memory* (*RAM*), also called simply *memory*, to store the programs and data with which it is currently working. RAM is available in many different types, speeds, and physical packages. The amount and type of RAM a system can use depends on its chipset, the type and number of RAM slots available, and other factors. The optimum amount of RAM depends on the operating system you run, how many and which programs you run simultaneously, and other considerations. Typical new PCs may have from 32 MB—marginally adequate for some environments—to 128 MB, which is sufficient for most people. Adding RAM is often a cost-effective upgrade for older systems, which generally have woefully inadequate RAM to run modern operating systems and programs. Memory is described in Chapter 5, *Memory*.

Floppy disk drive

The humble *floppy disk drive* (*FDD*) was formerly used for everything from booting the PC to storing data to running programs to making backups, but has now been largely relegated to such infrequent uses as making emergency boot diskettes, loading updated device drivers, running diagnostics programs, or "sneakernetting" documents to other systems. Many people don't use their FDDs from one month to the next. The FDD has been officially declared a "legacy" device, and many PCs manufactured after mid-2000 will not have one. All of that said, the FDD remains important to millions of PC users because it is the only read/write removable storage device present on most current PCs. Chapter 6, *Floppy Disk Drives*, describes what you need to know about FDDs.

CD-ROM drive

CD-ROM drives began to appear on mainstream PCs in the early 90s, are now ubiquitous, and have remained generally unchanged except for improvements in speed and reliability. CD-ROMs store 600+ MB of data in read-only form, and, because they are both capacious and cheap to produce, are commonly used to distribute software and data. CD-ROM drives can also play CDs and multimedia discs, which makes them popular for listening to music and playing games. CD-ROM drives are detailed in Chapter 10, *CD-ROM Drives*. The chapters following that one cover other types of optical drives that are becoming common replacements for a CD-ROM drive. Chapter 11, *CD-R and CD-RW Drives* describes these devices, which allow you to make your own CDs. Chapter 12, *DVD Drives*, describes DVD-ROM, which are the follow-on to CD-ROM, and may be used to watch movies or access very large databases.

Hard disk drive

The *hard disk drive* (*HDD*) is the primary storage device on any PC. Unlike RAM, which retains data only while power remains applied, data written to an HDD remains stored there until you delete it. HDD space was formerly a scarce resource that users went to great lengths to conserve. Modern HDDs are so capacious (10 to 25+ GB) and so inexpensive (~$10/GB) that most people now regard disk space as essentially free. On the downside, modern HDDs can be difficult to install and configure, particularly in older systems, and their huge capacity makes some form of tape backup almost mandatory. Chapter 13, *Hard Disk Interfaces*, and Chapter 14, *Hard Disk Drives*, tell you everything you need to know about HDDs.

Video adapter

A *video adapter*, also called a *graphics adapter*, accepts video data from the computer and converts it into a form the monitor can display. In addition to image quality, the video adapter you use determines the sharpness, number of colors, and stability of the image your monitor displays. Most recent video adapters display text and simple graphics adequately, but video adapters vary greatly in their suitability for use with graphics-intense software, including games. Video adapters are covered in Chapter 15, *Video Adapters*.

Monitor

The monitor you use ultimately determines the quality of the video you see. Monitors are available in a wide variety of sizes, capabilities, features, and prices, and choosing the right one is not a trivial decision. Monitors are covered in Chapter 16, *Monitors*.

Sound adapter and speakers

All PCs can produce basic warning sounds and audible prompts using their built-in speakers, but for listening to audio CDs, playing games, watching DVDs with full surround sound, using the Internet to make free long-distance telephone calls, using voice-recognition software, and other PC audio functions, you'll need a sound card (or embedded motherboard sound adapter) and speakers or headphones. Sound cards are covered in Chapter 17, *Sound Cards*, and speakers in Chapter 18, *Speakers and Headphones*.

Keyboard and mouse

PCs use several types of devices to accept user input—keyboards for entering text; mice, trackballs, and other pointing devices for working in the Windows graphical environment; and game controllers for playing modern graphical computer games and simulations. These devices are covered in Chapter 19, *Keyboards*, Chapter 20, *Mice and Trackballs*, and Chapter 21, *Game Controllers*.

Case and power supply

The *case* (or *chassis*) is the outer shell that contains the PC and all internal peripheral devices. The *power supply* provides regulated power to all system components and cooling air flow to keep components from overheating. Cases are described in Chapter 22, *Cases*. Power supplies are covered in Chapter 23, *Power Supplies*. Chapter 24, *Backup Power Supplies*, tells you what you need to know about protecting the power that runs your PC.

Software Components

Many people think of a PC as comprising solely physical hardware, but hardware is just a useless pile of silicon, metal, and plastic unless you have software to make it do something. *Software* is a set of detailed instructions that allow a computer to perform a task or group of tasks. Software is usually categorized as being one of three types:

Applications programs

Applications programs are what most people think of when they hear the word software. These programs are designed to perform specific user-oriented tasks, such as creating a word processing document or spreadsheet, browsing the Web, reading and replying to email, managing your schedule, creating a presentation, or recovering a deleted file. Hundreds of thousands of applications programs are available, from comprehensive office suites like Microsoft Office, to vertical market packages like medical office billing software, to single purpose utilities like WinZip. Whatever you might want a computer to do for you, you can probably locate applications software that will do it.

Operating system

An *operating system* is software that manages the PC itself, providing such basic functions as the ability to write and read data from a disk or to display images on the monitor. A PC can run any of dozens of operating systems, including DOS, Windows 95/98, Windows NT, Windows 2000, Linux and other Unix variants, NetWare, BeOS, and many others. The operating system you use determines which applications programs you can run, which peripherals you can use (not all operating systems support all peripherals), which technologies are available to you (e.g., NT does not support Plug-N-Play or USB), and how reliable the system is. The vast majority of PCs run either Windows 95/98 or Windows NT, so those are the operating systems we focus on in this book.

Device drivers

We said that the operating system determines which peripherals you can use. That's true, but only indirectly. Operating systems themselves natively recognize only the most basic, standardized system components—things like memory, the system clock, and so on. *Device drivers* are small programs that work at a very low level to integrate support for other devices into the operating system. Using device drivers allows an operating system to be extensible, which means that support for new devices can be added incrementally, without updating the operating system itself. For example, if you install a new video card, installing a device driver for that video card allows the operating system to recognize it and use its full capabilities. Most operating systems include "vanilla" device drivers that allow devices to be used at less than their full capabilities (e.g., the standard VGA driver in Windows) until an appropriate driver can be installed. Most operating systems also include specific device driver support for common devices, such as popular video cards and printers, but these drivers are often old, slow, and do not take full advantage of hardware capabilities. In general, you should download the most recent device driver from the hardware manufacturer when you install new hardware.

Firmware Components and the PC BIOS

Firmware is a special class of software, so-called because it is more-or-less permanently stored on chips. Firmware is often referred to generically as a *BIOS* (*Basic Input/Output System*) because the only firmware contained in early PCs was the main system *ROM-BIOS* (*Read-Only Memory BIOS*). That's no longer true. Nearly every component in a modern PC contains its own firmware. Disk drives, SCSI host adapters, video cards, sound cards, keyboards, and most other devices contain firmware, and nowadays that firmware is seldom read-only.

Although few people do so, installing firmware updates is an important part of keeping a modern PC functioning at its best. For example, firmware for most CD writers is frequently updated to add support for new types of blank media.

The two most important pieces of firmware in a PC are the chipset and the main system BIOS. The chipset is the heart of the PC. Its capabilities determine such fundamental issues as which processors the motherboard supports, how data is communicated between processor and memory, and so on. The BIOS manages the basic configuration information stored in non-volatile CMOS memory, such as the list of installed devices, and controls many of the low-level configuration parameters that determine how the PC functions. Although the chipset is not updateable, the BIOS is in all modern PCs.

BIOS updates sometimes correct bugs, but BIOS code is so stable and well debugged (it has to be) that the purpose of most BIOS updates is to add support for new technologies. For example, many pre-1998 BIOS versions did not support hard disk drives larger than 8.4 GB. Installing an updated BIOS with Extended Interrupt 13 support allows the system to recognize and use larger hard disks. Another common reason for BIOS updates is to add support for new CPU types. For example, many Pentium II motherboards did not support Celerons, which use a different L2 caching method. Or a motherboard manufactured when the fastest Pentium II available was 350 MHz has no setting to allow using a Pentium II/400 or /450. Installing an updated BIOS fixes problems like these. Systems with Flash BIOS (which is to say, all modern systems) can be updated simply by downloading the new BIOS, booting the system to DOS, and running a special installer program.

Updating a flash BIOS is a nontrivial operation. Done incorrectly, it can render your PC incapable of booting. Read the detailed instructions supplied by the manufacturer before attempting to update your BIOS.

You configure BIOS options and chipset settings by running a special firmware program called CMOS Setup, which is usually invoked by pressing F1, F2, or Delete while the system is booting. Some systems allow the administrator to password-protect access to CMOS Setup, while others make CMOS Setup a "blind" option. For example, recent Intel motherboards by default display an Intel splash screen rather than the standard BIOS boot screen. To run CMOS Setup, press Esc when the splash screen appears to clear it, and then press F2 to enter BIOS Setup.

CMOS Setup programs vary at the discretion of the motherboard or system maker in terms of what they allow you to access and change. Some Setup programs provide essentially complete access to all settings, while others allow changing only some settings, and some provide no access to chipset options at all. Figure 1-1 shows the main screen of a typical BIOS setup program.

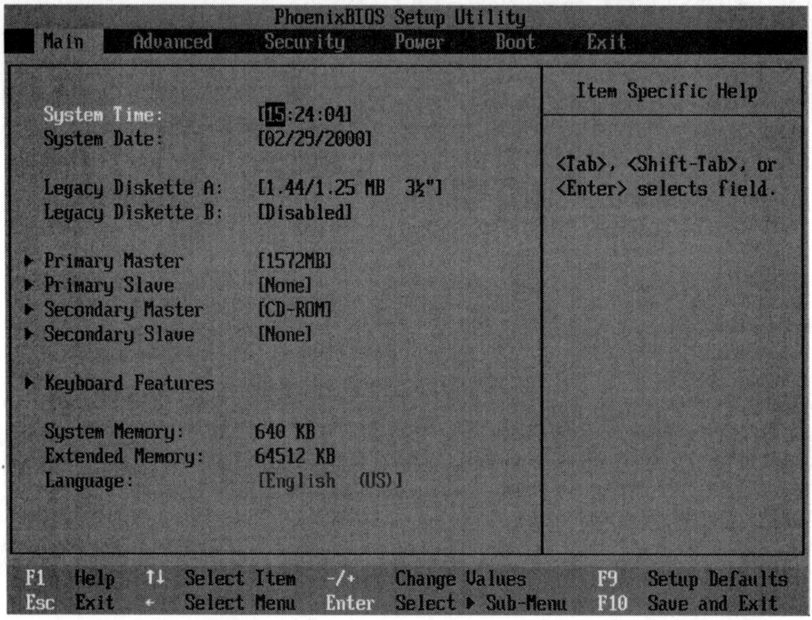

```
                        PhoenixBIOS Setup Utility
    Main     Advanced    Security    Power    Boot    Exit

                                                    Item Specific Help
      System Time:        [15:24:04]
      System Date:        [02/29/2000]
                                                 <Tab>, <Shift-Tab>, or
      Legacy Diskette A:  [1.44/1.25 MB  3½"]    <Enter> selects field.
      Legacy Diskette B:  [Disabled]

    ▶ Primary Master      [1572MB]
    ▶ Primary Slave       [None]
    ▶ Secondary Master    [CD-ROM]
    ▶ Secondary Slave     [None]

    ▶ Keyboard Features

      System Memory:      640 KB
      Extended Memory:    64512 KB
      Language:           [English  (US)]


    F1   Help    ↑↓  Select Item    -/+    Change Values    F9   Setup Defaults
    Esc  Exit    ←   Select Menu    Enter  Select ▶ Sub-Menu F10  Save and Exit
```

Figure 1-1: The Main page of the Phoenix BIOS Setup Utility

There are so many different chipsets, BIOS versions, and Setup utilities that covering BIOS and chipset options in detail would require writing a separate book. Fortunately, someone already has. Phil Croucher's superb *The BIOS Companion* (*http://www.electrocution.com/biosc.htm*) documents BIOS and chipset options in great detail, including some that even we don't understand. Every PC technician should own a copy of this book. Another very useful BIOS resource is Wim's BIOS Page (*http://www.ping.be/bios/*).

Technologies

Here are some important technologies pertinent to current and next-generation PCs, with a brief explanation of each:

ACPI

> *Advanced Configuration and Power Interface* (*ACPI*) is the current standard for configuring system components under PnP, monitoring the health of the system, and managing power usage. It replaces Intel's *Dynamic Power Management Architecture* (*DPMA*) and *Advanced Power Management* (*APM*). All current PCs and motherboards include at least partial ACPI support.

AGP

> *Accelerated Graphics Port* (*AGP*) is a dedicated video port connector that was introduced in 1997 by Intel and is now nearly ubiquitous. In theory, AGP improves video performance by removing it from the 33 MHz PCI bus and by allowing a video adapter to use main system memory. In practice, few applications saturate even a PCI video adapter, so the benefits of AGP are largely unrealized for now. AGP video cards do not fit PCI slots, or vice versa. AGP is fully supported only under Windows 98 and Windows 2000.

AMR

> *Audio-Modem Riser* (*AMR*) is an Intel initiative that defines a standard interface and connector that allow system and motherboard manufacturers to implement analog audio and modem functions inexpensively using chipset-based resources.

IAPC

> *Instantly Available PC* (*IAPC*) is an Intel initiative that defines power-saving modes that retain the ability to respond to programmed or external triggers, such as LAN activity (*Wake-on-LAN*, *WOL*) or an inbound telephone call (*Wake-on-Ring*, *WOR*).

PnP

> *Plug-N-Play* (*PnP*) is a joint Intel/Microsoft specification that allows computers and peripherals to configure themselves by negotiating for available system resources. Full implementation of PnP requires that the chipset, BIOS, operating system, and devices all be PnP-compliant. Ideally, adding a device in a PnP environment requires only physically installing the device. PnP then configures everything automatically, loading the appropriate driver and assigning non-conflicting resources (IRQ, I/O port, DMA, and memory space) to the device. In practice, PnP sometimes does not work properly. PnP is partially supported by early releases of Windows 95, and fully supported by Windows 95 OSR2+, Windows 98, and Windows 2000.

UDMA/66

> *Ultra DMA/66* (*UDMA/66*) is a new standard that supports IDE hard disk data transfer rates up to 66 MB/s, four times those supported under earlier *Programmed I/O* (*PIO*) modes, and twice that of UDMA/33. UDMA has low CPU utilization under heavy disk load (typically ~1.5%, versus 80% for PIO), and high-end UDMA drives approach low-end SCSI drives in raw performance. Current hard drives cannot saturate even a UDMA/33 interface, but high-performance IDE drives that ship in late 2000 will take advantage of

DMA/66, so it's worth having. UDMA/66 is supported by most current systems and motherboards, and by many current IDE drives. UDMA can be used with all versions of Windows 95/98, Windows NT 4, and Windows 2000, although configuring it is non-trivial in some of those environments.

USB

Universal Serial Bus (USB) is a general-purpose communications interface for connecting peripherals to PCs. The current USB 1.1 specification supports speeds up to 12 MB/s. USB 2.0, finalized in February 2000, is targeted to provide 480 MB/s. USB is royalty-free and strongly backed by Intel, which makes it likely to prevail over the competing, more expensive IEEE1394 "Firewire" standard. USB will ultimately replace low-speed "legacy" serial, parallel, keyboard, mouse, and floppy interfaces, and may also become the standard interface for mid-speed devices like video, network adapters, and optical drives. All current systems and motherboards include USB 1.1 ports, and an increasing number of peripherals are available in USB form. USB 1.1 is fully supported only under Windows 98 and Windows 2000.

As you might expect, Intel is the driving force behind most of these technologies. You can read more about the future direction of PCs at *http://developer.intel.com/technology/*.

System Resources

PCs have four types of system resources—Interrupt Request lines, DMA channels, I/O ports, and memory ranges. Many system components and peripherals require one or more of these resources, which raises the twin problems of resource availability and resource conflicts. Resource availability is particularly important with regard to IRQs, which are in high demand, and of which only 16 exist. Resource conflicts can occur when two devices are assigned the same resource, in which case one or both devices may not function, or may function unpredictably. Resource conflicts may occur even with plentiful resources, such as I/O ports, where many are available and only a few are in use.

A frequent cause of problems when building or upgrading PCs is a shortage of required resources or unintentional resource conflicts that occur when a new component is installed that was inadvertently configured to use a resource that is already in use. Two technologies, PCI and Plug-N-Play, used in conjunction with recent versions of Microsoft operating systems (Windows 95 OSR2, Windows 98, and Windows 2000), go a long way toward extending the availability of resources and preventing conflicts. Even in such an ideal environment, however, resource conflicts sometimes occur, particularly if you are using older "legacy" hardware. The following sections describe what you need to know about PC resources and how to manage them.

Interrupt ReQuest Line (IRQ)

When a component or peripheral, such as a network adapter or sound card, needs to get the CPU's attention, it does so by generating a signal on an *Interrupt ReQuest Line (IRQ)*. Table 1-2 lists IRQs and the devices that typically use them.

Table 1-2: 8/16/32-Bit ISA/PCI Standard IRQ Assignments

IRQ	Bus Type	Typically Used By
00	None	Non-Maskable Interrupt (NMI); system timer
01	None	Keyboard port
02	None	Programmable Interrupt Controller (PIC); cascade to IRQ 09
03	8/16-bit	Communications Port 2 (COM2:)
04	8/16-bit	Communications Port 1 (COM1:)
05	8/16-bit	Sound card; Printer Port (LPT2:)
06	8/16-bit	Floppy Disk Controller
07	8/16-bit	Printer Port (LPT1:)
08	None	System CMOS/real-time clock
09	8/16-bit	Redirected from IRQ 02; Network interface
10	16-bit	Network interface; USB host controller
11	16-bit	Video Adapter; SCSI host adapter
12	16-bit	PS/2 mouse port
13	None	Numeric Data Processor (math co-processor)
14	16-bit	Primary IDE interface
15	16-bit	Secondary IDE interface

An 8-bit ISA slot contains physical IRQ lines only for IRQ 03 through IRQ 07, because IRQ 00 and IRQ 01 are reserved for system functions. A 16-bit ISA slot contains physical IRQ lines for IRQs 03 through 07, 09 through 12, 14, and 15. IRQ 09 is mapped to IRQ 02, allowing 8-bit ISA cards to recognize IRQ 09 as IRQ 02. IRQs 00, 01, 02, 08, and 13 are not present in any slot, and so cannot be assigned to devices.

If the processor receives two or more interrupts simultaneously, it processes them in order of priority. On 8-bit systems (PCs and XTs), the lower-numbered IRQ always takes priority. That is, IRQ 00 is the highest priority and IRQ 07 is the lowest. 286 and higher systems use a second PIC to add a second set of eight IRQs, cascaded from IRQ2. That changes IRQ priority from the simple numerical order used by 8-bit systems. On 16-bit and higher systems, IRQ 00 is still the highest priority, followed by IRQ 01 and 02. But because IRQ 02 is the cascade IRQ, the IRQs that it supports—IRQ 08 through IRQ 15—are next in priority. IRQ 03 follows IRQ 15 in priority, and then in numerical order through IRQ 07, the lowest priority. Whenever possible, assign "important" devices to higher-priority IRQs. For example, if you have a serial mouse and a modem, assign the modem to COM2: (IRQ3) and the mouse to COM1: (IRQ4). Because the modem is on the higher-priority IRQ, it is serviced first if the modem and the mouse generate interrupts simultaneously.

ISA interrupts versus PCI interrupts

ISA and PCI handle interrupts very differently. ISA expansion cards are configured manually for IRQ, usually by setting a jumper, but sometimes by running a setup program. All ISA slots have all IRQ lines present, so it doesn't matter which card is placed in which slot. ISA cards use *edge-sensitive interrupts*, which means that an

Juggling ISA IRQs

Only IRQs 03, 04, 05, 06, 07, 09, 10, 11, 12, 14, and 15 are available. Six of those—03, 04, 06, 12, 14, and 15—are occupied by the serial ports, the floppy controller, the mouse, and the IDE interfaces on most ISA systems, leaving only 05, 07, 09, 10, and 11 available. If you require interrupt-based printing, you must allocate IRQ 07 to LPT1. If you have a sound card, it'll want IRQ 05. And so on. It's not surprising that many ISA systems have no free IRQs, and that allocating IRQs and resolving IRQ conflicts is a major issue for ISA systems.

If you find yourself out of IRQs on an ISA system, you may be able to reclaim one or more IRQs. Some cards and some systems allow using IRQ2 successfully, and some do not. If one or both of the serial ports is unused, disable it in BIOS to reclaim IRQ3 and/or IRQ4. If you have two serial devices that are never used at the same time (e.g., your modem and your Palm Pilot sync cradle), you can use a switch box to connect both to the same serial port and disable the other serial port. If there is no printer connected to the system, disable the printer port in BIOS (or configure it to a mode that does not use an IRQ) to free up IRQ 07. If you have only one IDE drive in the system, disable the secondary IDE interface in BIOS to reclaim IRQ 15. If you have two IDE drives, one on each interface, consider putting both drives on the primary IDE interface and disabling the secondary IDE interface to reclaim IRQ 15. Note, however, that putting some very old CD-ROM drives on the same IDE channel as the hard disk can seriously degrade hard disk performance.

ISA device asserts a voltage on one of the interrupt lines to generate an interrupt. That in turn means that ISA devices cannot share interrupts, because when the processor senses voltage on a particular interrupt line it has no way to determine which of multiple devices might be asserting that interrupt. For ISA slots and devices, the rule is simple: *two devices cannot share an IRQ if there is any possibility that those two devices may be used simultaneously.* In practice that means that you cannot assign the same IRQ to more than one ISA device.

PCI cards use *level-sensitive interrupts*, which means that different PCI devices can assert different voltages on the same physical interrupt line, allowing the processor to determine which device generated the interrupt. PCI cards and slots manage interrupts internally. A PCI bus normally supports a maximum of four PCI slots, numbered 1 through 4. Each PCI slot can access four interrupts, labeled INT#1 through INT#4 (or INT#A through INT#D). Ordinarily, INT#1/A is used by PCI Slot 1, INT#2/B by Slot 2, and so on.

AGP cards support only INT#1/A and INT#2/B, and share with PCI Slot 1. If a PCI Slot 5 exists, it shares with Slot 4. In either case, with slots that share resources, avoid installing cards in both slots if both cards require the same shared resource. If you must use both slots, install only cards that can share an IRQ. If you encounter a conflict on a PCI system, moving cards to different slots often solves the problem.

Bridging circuitry within the chipset allows additional PCI or other buses to be cascaded from the primary PCI bus. For example, the PCI-to-ISA bridge present in most current chipsets allows cascading an ISA bus from the primary PCI bus. One function of the bridging circuitry is to convert PCI interrupts to ISA interrupts when a PCI device needs to get the processor's attention. PCI interrupts do not correspond directly to ISA IRQs, although an INT# can be mapped to an IRQ via the PC's interrupt handler if the card using that INT# requires an IRQ. Some configuration firmware restricts mapping PCI interrupts to IRQ 09, 10, or 11 or Auto, while others allow mapping any INT# to any available IRQ.

In general, leave INT-IRQ mapping for all PCI slots set to Auto unless you have good reason to assign a specific IRQ. Sometimes a card with a dynamically mapped IRQ may work fine with some programs and not others. For example, many older games expect to find a sound card at IRQ 05. If you have a PCI/PnP sound card installed in PCI Slot 3, you can use INT-IRQ mapping to assign IRQ 05 to that slot and card, keeping the old games happy.

PCI expansion cards are normally assigned an IRQ dynamically, either by the BIOS or by Windows, depending on the version of Windows being used and the PCI/PnP configuration options in effect. On bridged PCI-ISA systems, ISA IRQs 0, 1, 2, 8, and 13 are reserved for critical system functions. Using the CMOS Setup PCI/PnP config- uration utility, IRQs 3 through 7, 9 through 12, 14, and 15 can be defined as belonging to either the PCI bus *or* the ISA bus, but not both. The terminology for this varies. Some utilities allow you to specify each IRQ as PCI/ISA PnP or Legacy ISA (or similar words). Others allow you to specify each IRQ as Level-Sensitive or Edge-Sensitive (or similar words). In either case, the effect is the same.

If you are installing a "legacy" card (i.e., a non-PnP ISA card), you can use static IRQ mappings to assign a specific IRQ, to that card. For example, if you install an old ISA sound card that requires IRQ 05, use the PCI/PnP configuration utility to set IRQ 05 for Legacy ISA or Edge-Sensitive, thereby reserving that IRQ for that card.

Do not confuse mapping PCI INT# interrupts to ISA IRQs with allo- cating IRQs to the ISA or PCI bus. The two are entirely unrelated. Use the former to "lock down" a PCI slot/card to a specific IRQ, for example, to allocate IRQ 05 to a PCI sound card. Use the latter to reserve IRQs for ISA devices, for example, to reserve IRQ 05 for an ISA sound card. Confusing these functions may cause lockups or other strange behavior. In general, the best way to prevent conflicts is to avoid installing ISA cards in PCI systems.

PCI Bus IRQ Steering

PCI Bus IRQ Steering is a function built into Windows 95 OSR2 or higher and Windows 98 (but not NT4 or Windows 2000). IRQ Steering allows Windows itself to assign IRQs to PCI devices. With earlier versions of Windows 95, the BIOS assigns IRQs to PCI devices, and Windows must accept the decisions made by the BIOS IRQ Steering. If Windows IRQ Steering is enabled, Windows can override those BIOS decisions, although it seldom does so. OSR2 disables IRQ Steering by default; Windows 98 enables it by default.

Windows IRQ Steering allows Windows to reassign PCI interrupts automatically to accommodate the inflexible requirements of ISA devices. For example, assume a PC with a BIOS that does not recognize non-PnP ISA cards (that is, IRQ Steering is not implemented in BIOS) is running Windows 98 with IRQ Steering disabled. The PC is properly configured with all PCI devices, and the BIOS has assigned IRQ 11 to a Creative SoundBlaster AudioPCI 128 sound card. You then open the case and install a 3Com 3C509 network adapter (a non-PnP ISA card), which is also config-ured for IRQ 11. When you restart the system, a conflict exists between the sound card on IRQ 11 and the network card, also on IRQ 11. If you enable Windows 98 IRQ Steering and restart the system, IRQ Steering takes the following actions during boot:

1. Detects that IRQ 11 is in use by the PCI sound card and the ISA network card.

2. Disables the PCI sound card.

3. Maps a free IRQ—one that is not being used by an ISA device—to a PCI inter-rupt and assigns an IRQ holder to it. If IRQ 10 is available, for example, PCI Steering may assign it to a PCI interrupt.

4. Reprograms the sound card to use IRQ 10.

5. Resets the IRQ mapping table to specify that IRQ 11 is now assigned to ISA and removes the PCI IRQ holder for IRQ 11.

When the system restarts, the sound card is now assigned to IRQ 10, the network card is still IRQ 11, and both devices work. Note that IRQ Steering does nothing that you cannot do for yourself. It simply automates the process of resolving IRQ conflicts when ISA devices are present in a PCI system.

To view the IRQ assignments made by IRQ Steering, right-click the My Computer icon, choose Properties, click the Device Manager tab, and double-click the Computer icon at the top of the tree to display the View Resources page of the Computer Properties dialog, shown in Figure 1-2. IRQs that IRQ Steering has assigned to PCI are flagged with an entry labeled "IRQ Holder for PCI Steering." This flag does not indicate that another device is assigned to the IRQ, but simply that IRQ Steering has reserved that IRQ for PCI, making it unavailable to ISA devices even if no PCI devices are currently using that IRQ.

IRQs that both the BIOS and Windows 98 have assigned to PCI are flagged twice. In Figure 1-2 IRQ Steering has assigned IRQ 10 as a PCI interrupt, which is being shared by a SCSI host adapter, a network adapter, and the USB host controller. Both BIOS IRQ Steering and Windows 98 IRQ Steering have assigned IRQ 10 to PCI. The Matrox video card on IRQ 11 is the only device assigned to that IRQ, and only BIOS IRQ Steering has assigned an IRQ Holder.

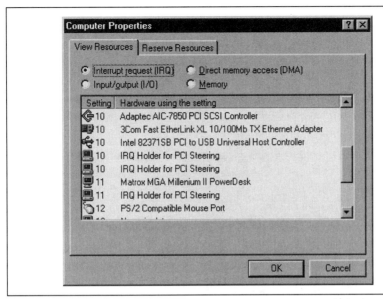

Figure 1-2: The View Resources page of the Computer Properties dialog

To view or change settings for IRQ Bus Steering itself, right-click the My Computer icon, choose Properties, and click the Device Manager tab. Double-click System Devices to expand the tree, and then double-click PCI Bus to display the PCI bus Properties dialog. Click the IRQ Steering tab to display the IRQ Steering page of the PCI bus properties dialog, shown in Figure 1-3.

The IRQ Routing Status pane at the bottom of the dialog displays the current status of IRQ Steering. Windows 98 enables IRQ Steering using the defaults shown. Leaving this checkbox marked means that Windows 98 manages IRQ Steering. To disable Windows 98 IRQ Steering and allow the BIOS to manage IRQ Steering, clear the Use IRQ Steering checkbox and restart the PC. If you do that, the DWindows Find New Hardware Wizard runs after the restart, locates the "new" devices, and installs drivers for them.

The "Get IRQ table..." checkboxes are a ranked priority list of the methods Windows can use to obtain the data it needs to manage IRQ Steering. Clearing one of these checkboxes causes Windows not to attempt that method. In Figure 1-3, Windows first attempts to obtain this data using the ACPI BIOS. That fails, so it next attempts to get the data using the MS Specification table, which also fails. The Protected Mode PCIBIOS 2.1 method is not checked, so Windows does not attempt to use that method. Finally, Windows attempts to get the data using a Real Mode PCIBIOS 2.1 call, which succeeds.

In general, leave IRQ Steering enabled. If problems occur with a PCI device being recognized or configured properly, take the following steps in order until the problem is resolved:

1. Clear the "Get IRQ table using ACPI BIOS" checkbox and restart the system.

2. Clear the "Get IRQ table using MS Specification table" checkbox and restart the system.

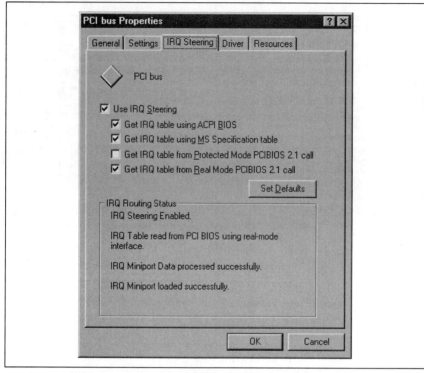

Figure 1-3: The IRQ Steering page of the PCI bus Properties dialog

3. Clear the "Get IRQ table using Real Mode PCIBIOS 2.1 call" checkbox, mark the "Get IRQ table using Protected Mode PCIBIOS 2.1 call" and restart the system.

4. Clear the "Use IRQ Steering" checkbox and restart the system to allow the BIOS to manage IRQ steering.

 If IRQ Steering cannot be enabled, the system BIOS may not support IRQ Steering (which is to say it will not allow Windows 98 IRQ Steering to change assignments) or the BIOS IRQ routing table may be missing or corrupt. In either case, contact the system or motherboard maker for an updated BIOS or additional assistance.

Direct Memory Access (DMA)

Direct Memory Access (DMA) is a means by which devices can exchange data with memory or with each other without requiring intervention by the processor. Standard DMA allows a device to exchange data with memory, but not with another device. *Bus mastering DMA* allows two devices to communicate directly with each other. The advantage of using DMA is that it reduces the load on the processor, allowing it to perform other tasks. There are even fewer DMA channels than IRQs—8 versus 16—but DMA channels are much less in demand than IRQs, so DMA channel availability is almost never an issue on ISA systems. Table 1-3 lists DMA channels and the uses to which they are typically put.

Table 1-3: Standard 16-Bit ISA DMA Channel Assignments

DMA	Bus Type	Transfers	Typically Used By
0	16-bit	8-bit	None
1	8/16-bit	8-bit	Some sound cards
2	8/16-bit	8-bit	Floppy disk controller
3	8/16-bit	8-bit	LPT1: in ECP mode
4	None	16-bit	DMA controller cascade
5	16-bit	16-bit	Some sound cards; ISA SCSI host adapter
6	16-bit	16-bit	ISA SCSI host adapter
7	16-bit	16-bit	Some sound cards; ISA SCSI host adapter

DMA 2 is used by nearly all systems for the floppy disk drive controller. Except DMA 4, which is a dedicated cascade channel, the other DMA channels are available for use with expansion cards. DMA 0 is almost never used because, although it appears only in 16-bit slots, it supports only 8-bit transfers. Most ISA sound cards require two DMA channels, with 8-bit sound using DMA 1 and 16-bit sound using DMA 5. Note that these DMA channels pertain only to ISA cards. PCI devices do not require one of these DMA channels to use DMA. For example, if you enable DMA transfer mode on one or both of the embedded PCI IDE controllers, you will find that they operate in DMA mode without occupying ISA DMA channels.

 The only time DMA conflicts are likely to arise is if you install an ISA sound card *and* an ISA SCSI host adapter. Nearly all ISA sound cards use both DMA 1 and DMA 5, and some ISA SCSI cards are configured by default to use DMA 5, which causes a conflict. The easy answer is to configure the SCSI host adapter to use DMA 6 or DMA 7. The better answer, as usual, is to avoid ISA cards whenever possible.

I/O Ports

Input/output ports (*I/O ports*) are ranges of addresses that function like mailboxes, allowing programs and components to exchange messages and data. An I/O port has a *base address*, which is the hexadecimal address of the first byte allocated to that I/O port, and a length, which is also expressed in hexadecimal. For example, many network adapters default to base address 300h and are 20h bytes (32 decimal bytes) long, and so occupy the range 300–31Fh.

There's no shortage of I/O ports, because thousands exist. We have never seen I/O port conflicts with PCI devices operating in a PnP environment, but I/O port conflicts commonly occur when two ISA devices are unintentionally assigned overlapping ranges. For example, another common base address for network adapters is 360h (range 360–37Fh). Unfortunately, that range overlaps the range of LPT1: (base address 378h), so setting a network card to 360h results in conflicts with the parallel port.

Memory Ranges

The original IBM PC used an 8088 processor, which supported up to 1 MB of physical memory, addressed as 16 64 KB segments. Memory locations are enumerated in hexadecimal, so the first segment includes the addresses 00000h through 0FFFFh (0 through 65,535 decimal) and the sixteenth includes the addresses F0000h through FFFFFh (983,040 through 1,048,575 decimal). The first ten of those segments—00000h through 9FFFFh—comprise the base 640 KB of memory addresses that are accessible by the operating system and programs. The last six segments—A0000h through FFFFF—comprise the 384 KB of upper memory addresses (the *Upper Memory Area* or *UMA*) reserved for system use. The first two UMA segments (A0000h through BFFFFh) are reserved for video memory. The second two UMA segments (C0000h through DFFFFh) are reserved address space for ROM BIOSes that reside on some adapters, such as video cards, SCSI host adapters, and network adapters. The final two UMA segments (E0000h through FFFFF) are reserved for the motherboard BIOS.

Modern processors use a flat (unsegmented) 32-bit address space, which allows them to access up to 4 GB (4,096 MB, or 4,294,967,296 bytes) of distinct memory addresses. That additional address space means that memory addresses are expressed as eight rather than five hexadecimal characters (e.g., addresses for the first MB are expressed as 00000000h through 000FFFFFh). Because few systems have anywhere near 4 GB of physical memory installed, huge ranges of unused memory addresses are available for assignment to devices that require memory ranges. Which of those ranges are used depends on how much physical memory is installed and which operating system you run.

Windows NT 4 uses address ranges from the UMA of the first megabyte (000A0000h through 000FFFFFh) for the original purposes of addressing video memory, adapter ROMs, and so on. It uses address ranges at the top of its address space, F0000000h and above (up near 4 GB) to provide additional memory ranges for which there is inadequate room in UMA. Windows 98 does the same, but also uses memory ranges immediately above the end of the range occupied by physical RAM.

Memory range conflicts are seldom a problem on modern computers running recent versions of Windows.

Viewing and Reserving System Resources

Windows 9X and Windows NT both provide convenient means to view the resources in use. Windows 98 also allows you to reserve resources manually for non-PnP ISA devices on systems with a BIOS that does not support IRQ Steering.

Viewing resources with Windows 9X

To view system resources with Windows 98, right-click My Computer, choose Properties, and click the Device Manager tab to display the System Properties dialog shown in Figure 1-4, which lists all installed devices. Clicking the + icon (or double-clicking a branch name) expands the list to show individual devices within that branch. If a problem exists with a device (a resource conflict, missing driver, etc.), Windows 98 automatically expands the branch that contains that device and flags the device with an alert icon.

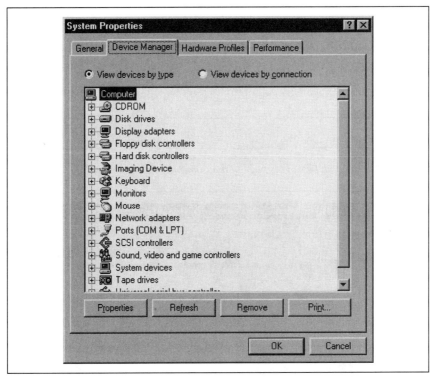

Figure 1-4: The Device Manager page of the System Properties dialog

To view a global list of resources, double-click the Computer branch to display the View Resources page of Computer Properties, shown in Figure 1-5. Choosing any of the four option buttons immediately displays a global list of assignments for that resource, allowing you to determine easily which resources are unassigned. Figure 1-5 shows that IRQ03, normally assigned to Communications Port (COM2), is available for use by a new device.

To view all resources being used by a particular device, expand the Device Manager tree (see Figure 1-4) and double-click the device name to display the Properties sheet for that device. Figure 1-6 shows the Properties sheet for a Matrox Millennium II video card. The Resource type pane displays all resources assigned to that device. If a resource conflict exists, Windows 98 displays a list of other devices using the same resource(s) in the Conflicting device list pane.

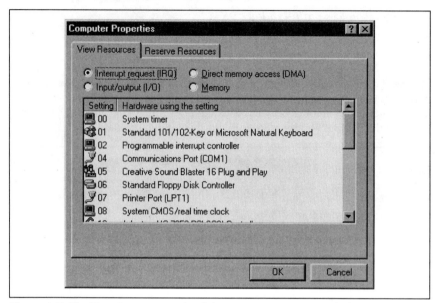

Figure 1-5: The View Resources page of the Computer Resources dialog

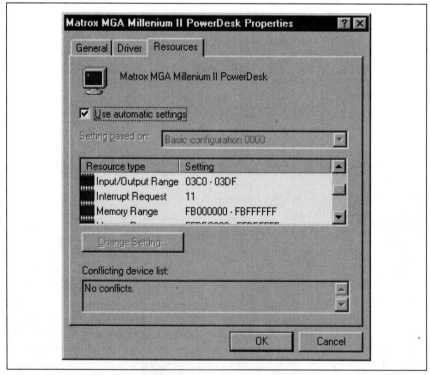

Figure 1-6: The Properties sheet for the Matrox Millenium II PowerDesk

Reserving resources with Windows 9X

If the system BIOS is up-to-date and all expansion cards are PnP-compliant, Windows 98 and PnP normally configure the system properly without further ado. However, if the system has an older BIOS and/or you need to install one or more cards that are not PnP-compliant, conflicts may occur because the BIOS and Windows cannot determine which resources those older cards need. For such situations, Windows allows you to specify manually which resources these older cards require, removing them from the pool of resources that Windows manages automatically.

To reserve resources, first examine the documentation and settings for the card to determine which resources (IRQ, DMA, I/O ports, and memory ranges) it requires. Display Device Manager and click the Reserve Resources tab to display the dialog shown in Figure 1-7. This dialog lists any resource reservations already in effect, allows you to modify existing reservations and to add new reservations. Mark one of the four option buttons to select the type of resource for which you want to add a reservation or view existing reservations.

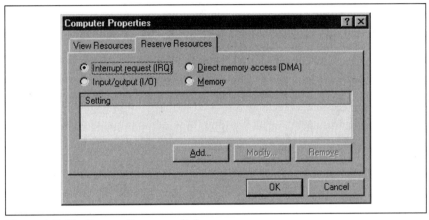

Figure 1-7: The Reserve Resources dialog

To add a resource reservation, click Add to display the Edit Resource Setting dialog, whose appearance varies depending on the type of resource you are adding a reservation for. Figure 1-8 shows the dialog for reserving an IRQ. Use the up and down arrows to specify a value for the resource to be reserved and click OK. You can reserve multiple resources in a single session by repeatedly selecting a resource type and adding reservations. When you finish reserving resources, click OK to store the resource reservations and then restart the system to put the changes into effect.

Device Manager initially displays reserved resources as System Reserved, as shown in Figure 1-9. However, once you restart the computer, that resource will no longer be displayed in Device Manager.

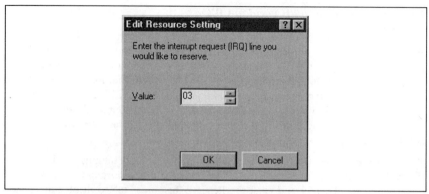

Figure 1-8: The Edit Resource Setting dialog

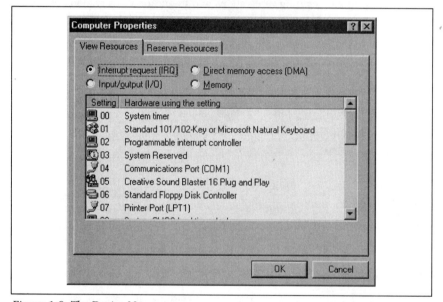

Figure 1-9: The Device Manager

 Be very careful when reserving resources. Windows 98 allows you to reserve any resource, including ones that are already in use. Reserving an in-use resource may disable the device that is currently using that resource. If that occurs, use Device Manager to remove the device, and then run the Add New Hardware Wizard from Control Panel to reinstall the device.

Viewing resources with Windows NT 4

Windows NT 4 has neither Device Manager nor PnP support beyond the minimum ability to recognize PCI PnP devices. Despite that, we actually experience fewer resource conflicts with PCI devices on Windows NT systems than on Windows 95/98 systems. With the sole exception of installing ISA PnP cards, such as a Sound-Blaster, Windows NT usually just works. However, if you are installing a legacy ISA card on a Windows NT system, you need to configure it to use resources that are not already in use.

To view existing resource allocations, choose Start → Programs → Administrative Tools (Common) → Windows NT Diagnostics, and display the Resources page, shown in Figure 1-10. Click the IRQ, I/O Port, DMA, or Memory button to display a global list of resources of the selected type.

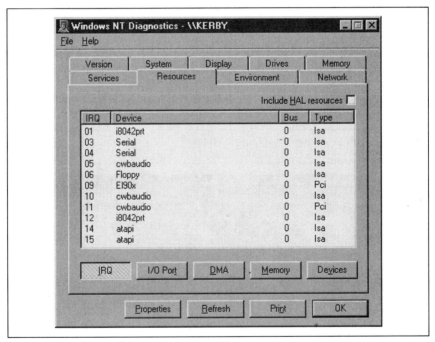

Figure 1-10: The Windows NT Diagnostics Resources page

Click the Devices button to display a list of installed devices, shown in Figure 1-11.

To view all resources allocated to a particular device, double-click that device to display the <device-name> Properties dialog, shown in Figure 1-12.

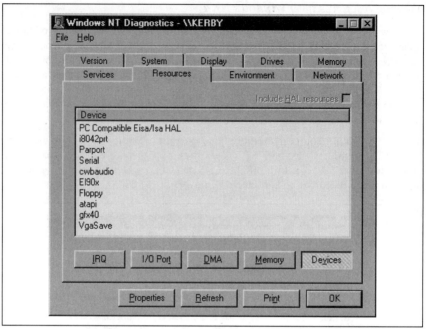

Figure 1-11: The Resources page Devices view

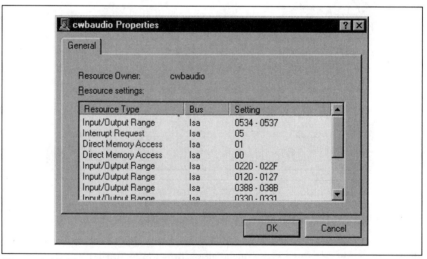

Figure 1-12: The <device-name> Properties dialog

Windows NT 4 has few problems with PCI PnP devices or non-PnP ISA devices, but does not detect PnP ISA devices. We first encountered this problem when installing a PnP ISA sound card. We physically installed the card, but when we attempted to install the drivers Setup could not locate the card. This problem, described in the Microsoft Knowledge Base article Q156344, can be resolved by installing the *Pnpisa.inf* file, which is located on the Windows NT 4 distribution CD in the *Drvlib\Pnpisa\i386* folder (right-click the filename and choose Install). Microsoft warns that this driver is unsupported and that you use it at your own risk.

Building or Buying a PC

The make-or-buy decision is a fundamental business school concept. Does it make more sense to make a particular item yourself or to just buy it? With entry-level PCs selling for well under $1000 and fully-equipped mainstream PCs for $1,500, you might wonder why anyone would bother to build a PC. After all, you can't save any money building one, can you? Well, yes you can. Quite a bit of money, in fact. But that's not the only reason to build a PC. Here are good reasons to do so:

Choice

When you buy a PC, you get a cookie-cutter computer. You may be able to choose such options as a larger hard drive, more memory, or a better monitor, but basically you get what the vendor decides to give you. And what you get is a matter of chance. High-volume direct vendors like Gateway and Dell often use multiple sources for components. Two supposedly identical systems ordered the same day may contain significantly different components, including such important differences as different motherboards or monitors with the same model number but made by different manufacturers. When you build a PC, you decide exactly what goes into it.

Component quality

Many computer vendors save money by using OEM versions of popular components. These may be identical to the retail version of that component, differing only in packaging. But OEM versions have several drawbacks. Many component vendors do not support OEM versions directly, instead referring you to the computer vendor. And OEM versions often differ significantly from the retail-boxed version. For example, Micron used the popular Intel SE440BX Seattle in many of its systems, but modified the Intel-supplied BIOS, which means that you cannot update your BIOS with a later version from the Intel web site. Instead, you must depend on Micron to provide an updated BIOS for your PC. Dell and other major makers sometimes use downgraded versions of popular products, for example, a big-name video card that runs at a lower clock rate than the retail version. This allows them to pay less for components and still gain the cachet from using the name-brand product.

Cost

PC manufacturers aren't in business for charitable reasons. They need to make a profit, and that means they need to sell computers for more than what they pay for the components and the labor to assemble them. Significantly more, in fact, because they also need to support such expensive operations as research and development departments, toll-free support numbers, and so on. But PC manufacturers get huge price breaks because they buy in very large volumes, right? Not always. The market for PC components is extremely efficient, with razor-thin margins throughout. A PC manufacturer may get the hard drive that costs you $150 for only $145, but they're not going to get it for $100. They may even have to pay $155, because PC manufacturers often have long-term contracts with suppliers. That can work either to the benefit or detriment of the PC maker. When the price of memory is plummeting, for example, a PC maker may have to pay twice as much as you do for memory. Conversely, when the price of memory skyrockets, you'll pay the spot price, while the PC maker may pay only half what you do because their memory suppliers are selling on a long-term contract price. Our rule of thumb is that, on average and all other things equal, you can probably build a mid-range PC yourself for about 75% of what a major manufacturer charges.

No bundled software

Most purchased PCs include Microsoft Windows 98, Microsoft Office, or other bundled software. If you don't need or want this software, building a PC allows you to avoid paying for it. You might think that the software has some value anyway, for example that you might be able to use it on one of your other systems or sell it to a friend. That turns out not to be the case. Under most license agreements, notably Microsoft's, you cannot legally transfer software from a newly purchased PC to another PC. That software is legally usable only on the PC that it was sold with. Note that, although OEM versions of Windows and Microsoft applications are often labeled "For sale only with a new PC," Microsoft takes a liberal view of what constitutes a new PC. Buying a hard drive or a motherboard may entitle you to buy an OEM version of the software you need at a greatly discounted price, less in fact than you'd pay for a retail upgrade version.

 OEM software is one of the best-kept secrets in the direct sales channel. It isn't advertised, and no one tells you about it unless you ask. If you buy a motherboard or hard disk and need this software, ask the vendor if he can supply it. The deals are often striking. For example, when we bought a motherboard for a new system in early 1999, we were offered a "Windows 98 Super Bundle" that included OEM copies of Windows 98 (full version, not upgrade), MS Works 98, Encarta 98, and Money 98. Total price? $49. As of June 2000, an OEM full version of Windows NT Workstation 4.0 with CD and manual sells for about $40. OEM full versions of Office 97 SBE sell for less than $100, and Office 2000 SBE for less than $150.

Warranty

The retail-boxed components you'll typically use in building your own PC include full manufacturer warranties which may run from two to five years or more, depending on the component. PC makers use OEM components that often include no manufacturer warranty to the end user. If something breaks, you're at the mercy of the PC maker to repair or replace it. We've heard from readers who bought PCs from makers who went out of business shortly thereafter. When a hard drive or video card failed six months later, they contacted the maker of the item, only to find that they had OEM components that were not under manufacturer warranty.

Experience

If you buy a computer, your experience with it consists of taking it out of the box and connecting the cables. If you build the computer, you know exactly what went into it, and you're in a much better position to resolve any problems that may occur.

Although there are many advantages to building a PC, there are some offsetting advantages to buying one instead, including:

Time

Building a PC takes time, not just the time actually needed to build it, but the time required to choose and order the components. If you're building your first PC, expect to spend at least a day selecting and ordering components and a weekend actually building it. Note that we maintain a frequently updated web site, *http://www.HardwareGuys.com*, that list our picks for the best components for various types of systems, from budget to high-end.

Integration

When you build a PC, you are responsible for making sure all components are compatible, locating and installing the necessary drivers, and so on. But this isn't as onerous as it may at first appear. With very few exceptions, PC components simply plug together and work, just as any VCR works with any television.

Component availability

If you absolutely need to have the latest, greatest CPU or whatever, you may have no choice but to buy a PC that includes it. Like any other business, component makers favor their major customers, who happen to be the large PC makers. When the AMD Athlon processor first shipped, for example, you couldn't buy a retail-boxed Athlon for love or money. If you wanted an Athlon, your only option was to buy a PC with an Athlon in it, because essentially 100% of Athlon production was going to the PC makers. If you're considering buying a PC for this reason, we suggest you think again. It's almost never worthwhile paying a significant premium for the latest and greatest, let alone buying an entire PC to get it.

Support

If you build a PC, you become Support Central for that PC. There's no single manufacturer to call, and it's up to you to figure out where the problem lies. If you isolate the problem to, say, the motherboard, you'll have to talk to the motherboard maker directly, assuming that they'll talk to you. Some will not, notably including Intel. You also may have to deal with multiple vendors all claiming that it must be the other guy's fault. Of course, just because you bought a packaged PC doesn't guarantee that the maker provides good tech support. Some makers, notably Dell, are famous for consistently excellent support. Others, like Gateway, are more variable in our experience, sometimes providing top-notch support and other times not. Some makers provide better support for corporate users than for individual buyers. Still other makers provide infamously bad support to all comers.

Bundled software

If you don't need bundled software, there's no sense in paying for it. But if you do want the software bundled with new PCs—typically Windows 98 and Microsoft Office 2000—you'll be hard pressed to find a full retail version for anything near as little as it actually costs you as part of a new PC purchase. On the other hand, as noted above, OEM versions of the software are often available at very low prices when you buy a disk drive or motherboard.

Upgrading a PC

Sometimes it's sensible to upgrade a PC. Other times, it's not. Whether it is economically feasible to upgrade a particular PC depends largely on how old the PC is, its existing configuration, and what you expect it to do.

PCs less than a year or two old are usually easy to upgrade. Components are readily available and sell at market prices. Necessary BIOS upgrades and firmware revisions are easy to obtain. PCs more than two or three years old are harder and more expensive to upgrade. Necessary components, particularly memory and BIOS upgrades, may be difficult or impossible to obtain. Even if you can obtain them, they may be unreasonably expensive. Upgrading one item often uncovers a serious bottleneck elsewhere, and so on. In general, restrict older PCs to minor upgrades such as adding a memory module or replacing a hard disk. If an older PC requires more than minor upgrades to meet your expected needs for the next year or so, it's probably not a good upgrade candidate.

The reason most people upgrade their PCs is to improve performance. The good news is that there are several relatively inexpensive upgrades that may yield noticeable performance increases. The bad news is that some are easier than others, and that doing all of them can easily cost as much or more than simply buying a new PC.

Processor

Upgrading the processor improves overall system performance. In general, upgrade only within the same generation, for example, a Pentium II/266 to a Celeron/500, or a Pentium 133 to a K6-2/400. Avoid upgrade kits that jump generations—e.g., kits to upgrade a 486 to Pentium or kits to upgrade a Pentium to Pentium II. These kits are usually expensive, provide limited performance improvements, and are often plagued with compatibility problems. If you upgrade within the same generation, you may have to upgrade your BIOS at the same time (usually a free download), and you may have to buy an adapter (for example, to install a Socket 370 Celeron in an older Slot 1 motherboard). In general, newer systems are easy to upgrade, and older systems are more difficult (or impossible) to upgrade. Upgrading processors is covered in Chapter 4. Cost: $30 to $200 (although you can spend much more). Difficulty: Easy to difficult, depending on the system and the processor.

L2 cache

Modern processors (Pentium II/III, Celeron, Athlon) have L2 cache built into the processor package. Older Socket 7 processors (Pentium, K6/K6-2) depend on discrete L2 cache that resides on the motherboard. On such systems, particularly if little or no L2 cache is already installed, adding L2 cache may provide a 10% to 25% boost in overall system performance. Upgrading L2 cache is covered in Chapter 3 and Chapter 5. Cost: $25 to $50. Difficulty: Easy to moderate, depending on the type of L2 cache the motherboard accepts.

Memory

If your PC does not have at least 16 MB (Windows 95/98) or 32 MB (Windows NT 4) of RAM, adding RAM is the most cost-effective upgrade you can make. Additional memory improves overall system performance, sometimes dramatically. However, many older systems do not cache memory above 64 MB (check the motherboard/chipset manual) which means that increasing memory beyond 64 MB can actually *decrease* performance, and that you may be sinking money into an obsolete form of memory that cannot be migrated later to a new system. Upgrading memory is covered in Chapter 5. Cost: $25 to $150 (varies with memory size and price). Difficulty: Usually easy, although physical access on some older systems is difficult.

CD-ROM

If you use your CD-ROM drive only for installing software and listening to music, even an original 1X model suffices. But if you use your CD-ROM drive for playing games, accessing large databases, or ripping audio CDs to MP3 format, you'll want a better drive. Recent 24X to 40X IDE models are inexpensive and easy to install. Upgrading CD-ROM drives is covered in Chapter 10. Cost: $50. Difficulty: Easy.

Hard disk

Modern hard disks are huge, fast, and inexpensive. Upgrading the hard disk not only provides additional storage space, but can dramatically increase performance if you run applications that access the disk frequently. Older systems cannot recognize large hard disks, but that problem can be gotten around by using a device driver (usually included with the new drive), by installing a BIOS upgrade, or by replacing the embedded IDE interface with an expansion card ($25 to $50) that supports large drives. Upgrading hard disks is covered in Chapter 13 and Chapter 14. Cost: $75 to $250. Difficulty: Easy, except for problems migrating existing programs and data.

Video adapter

Video adapter technology improves almost from month to month. Even so, if you use your system primarily for word processing, email, web browsing, and similar functions, you won't get much benefit from upgrading to a new video adapter. But if you play 3D games and your video card is more than a year or so old, upgrading to a more recent model can provide dramatic performance benefits. Upgrading video adapters is covered in Chapter 15. Cost: $50 to $200. Difficulty: Easy to moderate.

Monitor

Although CRT monitors are a mature technology, manufacturing improvements and other factors have resulted in dramatic price reductions on larger models. Not long ago, 15" monitors were the norm and 17" monitors sold for $750. Nowadays, decent 17" monitors cost $250 and 19" monitors $450. If you spend a lot of time in front of your PC, buying a bigger monitor may be the best upgrade you can make. Also, unlike most upgrades, a good monitor is a long-term asset. You can use it with your current system, your next system, and probably the next system after that. Upgrading monitors is covered in Chapter 16. Cost: $150 to $700. Difficulty: Easy.

Power supply

Although it may seem strange to include power supplies in the performance upgrade category, the fact is that many systems have inadequate power supplies, and replacing the original unit with a better unit can improve system performance and stability. Upgrading power supplies is covered in Chapter 23. Cost: $45 to $125. Difficulty: Easy.

Motherboard

The ultimate upgrade, of course, is to replace the motherboard, which in effect means building an entirely new PC. Before you undertake a motherboard upgrade, consider whether you might not do better to retire your current PC to other duties and buy or build a new system. If you do replace the motherboard, expect to pay $85 to $250 for the motherboard itself, but also plan to spend another $50 to $1,000 to replace processor, memory, and perhaps other components, depending on how much can be salvaged from the current system. Difficulty: Moderate to difficult if you have some experience working on PCs. Difficult if you don't.

Another reason to upgrade a PC is to add missing features. Here are some common feature upgrades:

CD writer

A CD writer allows you to burn your own CDs, which can subsequently be read in any recent CD-ROM drive. CD writers are popular for making archival backups and, of course, are used by many people to make pirated copies of data and audio CDs. Adding a CD writer is covered in Chapter 11. Cost: $150 to $400. Difficulty: Easy for IDE drives, easy to moderate for SCSI drives.

DVD-ROM drive

A DVD-ROM drive allows you to watch DVD movies on your PC and to access the increasing number of databases and games supplied on DVD. DVD-ROM drives can also read data and audio CDs, so they are becoming a popular replacement for CD-ROM drives. Adding a DVD-ROM drive is covered in Chapter 12. Cost: $85 to $250. Difficulty: Easy for IDE drives, easy to moderate for SCSI drives.

Tape drive

The downside of huge, cheap modern hard disks is that there is no practical means to back them up short of installing a tape drive. Tape drives store huge amounts of data—4 to 70 GB—on relatively inexpensive tape cartridges. Adding a tape drive is covered in Chapter 9, *Tape Drives*. Cost: $200 to $900. Difficulty: Easy for IDE drives, easy to moderate for SCSI drives.

Sound card and speakers

If you make no serious demands on the audio capabilities of your PC, the inexpensive sound card and speakers that probably came with it are usable. But PC audio hardware and applications are advancing faster than any component except video adapters, and there are a lot of fascinating new applications, including 3D gaming with positional audio, DVD playback, IP telephony, voice-recognition software, and so on. To use any of these new applications, you'll probably need to replace your sound card and perhaps your speakers. Adding a sound card and speakers is covered in Chapter 17 and Chapter 18. Cost: $50 to $400. Difficulty: Easy.

Game controller

Years ago, people bemoaned the fact that PC games were not up to the standards of arcade games or dedicated game machines like those from Sega, Sony, and others. Dramatic improvements in PC video and audio mean that nowadays the situation is exactly reversed. The best games run on PCs. But getting the most from those games requires adding dedicated game controller hardware. Adding a game controller is covered in Chapter 21. Cost: $10 to $150. Difficulty: Easy.

Smart Buying Practices

A decade ago, most computer products were bought in retail computer stores. Retail sales still make up a significant chunk of computer product sales—although the emphasis has shifted from computer specialty stores to mass market resellers like Best Buy and Costco—but the majority of computer products are now bought from direct resellers, via toll-free telephone number or the Web. Local brick-and-mortar retailers, with their high overheads, simply cannot match direct reseller prices and stay in business. Nor can they match direct reseller companies for breadth of selection or convenience. We frequently order components late in the evening. Early the next morning, our FedEx guy drops them on the front porch. All without our having to leave the house.

That said, there are some drawbacks to buying from direct resellers. You're dealing with an anonymous company, probably located far away. You need to know exactly what you want, and you need to understand the pitfalls of dealing with direct resellers. Most direct resellers are reputable, but some are not. Even reputable resellers differ greatly in their business practices, so it's important to understand the rules before you start playing the game. We've bought hundreds of thousands of dollars worth of products from direct vendors over the last decade or so, and have learned some things from that experience. Here are some guidelines to keep in mind:

Research the product

Make sure you know exactly what you're buying before you order it. For example, a hard disk may be available in two versions, each with the same model number but with sub-model numbers to designate different amounts of cache. Or you may find that a given hard disk maker manufactures two models of the same size that differ in both price and performance. Always compare using the exact manufacturer model number. Before you buy a product, research it on the manufacturer's web site and on the numerous independent web sites devoted to reviews. We use *http://www.reviewfinder.com* to locate reviews for specific products. We also maintain a partial list of review sites at *http://www.hardwareguys.com/links.html*.

Research the vendor

Vendors vary greatly. Some we trust implicitly, and others we wouldn't order from on a bet. Some are always reliable, others always unreliable, and still others seem to vary with the phases of the moon. You can check the reputation of a vendor with the Better Business Bureau. We also check *http://www. resellerratings.com*, which maintains a database of customer-reported experiences with hundreds of vendors.

Know the market price

The list price or Suggested Retail Price (SRP) published by the manufacturer is meaningless. Many computer products normally sell for a fraction of SRP, others sell for very near SRP, and for still others the manufacturer has no SRP, but instead publishes Estimated Selling Price (ESP). To do meaningful price comparisons, you need to know what different vendors actually charge for the product. Fortunately, there are many services that maintain frequently updated lists of what various vendors charge for particular products. Two such services we use are *http://www.pricewatch.com* and *http://www.pricescan.com*. These services may list 20 or more different vendors, and the prices for a particular item may vary dramatically. We tend to discard the top 25% and the bottom 25% and take an average of the middle 50% to decide what is a reasonable price for the item.

Understand retail-boxed versus OEM components

Many components are sold in both retail-boxed and OEM form. The core component is likely to be similar or identical in either case, but important details may vary. For example, Intel Celeron processors are available in retail-boxed versions that include a CPU cooling fan and a three-year Intel warranty. They are also available as OEM components (also called *tray packaging* or *white box*) that do not include the fan or the three-year warranty. OEM components are not intended for retail distribution, and the manufacturer may not provide any warranty to individual purchasers. Buying OEM components is fine, as long as you understand the differences and do not attempt to compare prices between retail-boxed and OEM.

Don't buy on price alone

As our all-time favorite unfortunately worded ad stated, "Don't be misled by price alone." The market for PCs and components is incredibly competitive and margins are razor-thin. If a vendor advertises a component for much less than other vendors, it may be a "loss leader." More likely, though, particularly if its prices on other items are similarly low, that vendor cuts corners somewhere, whether it be by using your money to float inventory, by shipping returned product as new, by charging excessive shipping fees, or, in the ultimate case, by taking your money and not shipping the product. If you always buy from the vendor with the rock-bottom price, you'll waste a lot of time hassling with returns of defective, used, or discontinued items and dealing with your credit card company when the vendor fails to deliver at all. Ultimately, you're also likely to spend more money than you would have by buying from a reputable vendor in the first place.

Determine the real price

The actual price you pay may vary significantly from the advertised price. When you compare prices, make sure to include all charges, particularly shipping charges. Reputable vendors tell you exactly how much the total charges will be. Less reputable vendors may forget to mention shipping charges, which may be very high. It's not unheard of for vendors to break out the full manufacturer pack into individual items. For example, if a retail-boxed hard drive includes mounting hardware, some vendors will quote a price for the bare drive without making it clear that they have removed the mounting hardware and charge separately for it. Also be careful when buying products that include a rebate from the maker. Some vendors quote the net price after rebate without making it clear that they are doing so.

Watch out for web pricing versus phone pricing

Some vendors charge more for an item ordered via their 800 number than they do for the same item ordered directly from their web site. Some others add a fixed processing fee to phone orders. One of our favorite vendors, *http://necxdirect.necx.com*, does this, adding a flat $25 processing fee to phone orders. These charges reflect the fact that taking orders on the web is much cheaper than doing so by phone, so this practice is likely to become much more common. But be careful. One of our readers desperately needed an $8 item that he could not find locally. He ended up paying about $68 for that item after the charges for overnight priority shipping and telephone order processing were added.

Don't be afraid to dicker

Most direct resellers are willing to sell for less than the price they advertise. All you need do is tell your chosen vendor that you'd really rather buy from them, but not at the price they're quoting. Use lower prices you find with the price comparison services as a wedge to get a better price. But remember that reputable vendors must charge more than scum-sucking, bottom-feeder vendors if they are to make a profit and stay in business. We generally try to beat down our chosen vendor a bit on price, but we don't expect them to match the rock-bottom prices that turn up on web searches.

Always pay by credit card

Using a credit card puts the credit card company on your side if there is a problem with your order. If the vendor ships the wrong product, defective product, or no product at all, you can invoke charge-back procedures to have the credit card company refund your money. Vendors who live and die on credit card orders cannot afford to upset credit card companies, and so tend to resolve such problems quickly. Even your threat to request a charge-back may cause a recalcitrant vendor to see reason.

Avoid vendors who place a surcharge on credit-card orders

Some vendors apply a surcharge, typically 3%, to their advertised prices if you pay by credit card. Surcharges violate credit card company contracts, so some vendors instead offer a similar discount for paying cash, which amounts to the same thing. Processing credit card transactions costs money, and we're sure that some such vendors are quite reputable, but our own experience with vendors that surcharge has not been good. We always suspect that their business practices result in a high percentage of charge-back requests, and so they discourage using credit cards.

Insist on a no-questions-asked money-back guarantee

Good vendors allow you to return a product for a full refund (often less shipping charges) within a stated period, typically 30 days. Buy only from such vendors. Note that nearly all vendors exclude some product categories, including notebook computers, monitors, printers, and opened software, either because their contracts with the manufacturer require them to do so or because some buyers commonly abuse return periods for these items, treating them as "30-day free rentals." Never buy from a vendor who uses the phrase, "All sales are final." That means exactly what it says.

Avoid vendors who charge restocking fees

Make sure to check carefully for any mention of restocking fees. Many vendors who trumpet a "no questions asked money-back guarantee" mention only in the fine print that they won't refund all your money. They charge a restocking fee on returns, and we've seen fees as high as 30% of the purchase price. These vendors love returns, because they make a lot more money if you return the product than if you keep it.

Get everything in writing

Don't accept verbal promises under any circumstances. Insist that the reseller confirm your order in writing, including any special terms or conditions, before charging your credit card or shipping the product. The fast turn-around of web-based and 800-number ordering makes postal mail largely useless for this purpose. We're not lawyers, and don't know the legal implications of email or faxed confirmations, but we've always used them and have never encountered a problem doing so. If a reseller balks at providing written confirmation of their policies, terms, and conditions, find another vendor. Most are happy to provide this information.

Keep organized records

File everything related to an order step-by-step, including a copy of the original advertisement, email, faxed, or written confirmations provided by the reseller, copies of your credit card receipt, a copy of the packing list and invoice, and so on. When we order by web, we print a copy of each page of the ordering process, and also use our web browser to save a copy of that page to the "never delete" folder in our data directory. We also jot down notes in our PIM regarding telephone conversations, including the date, time, telephone number and extension, person spoken to, purpose of the call, and so on. We print a copy of those to add to the folder for that order.

Accept no substitutes

Make it clear to the reseller that you expect them to ship the exact item you have ordered, not what they consider to be an "equivalent substitute." Require they provide written (or email) confirmation of the exact items they will ship, including manufacturer part numbers. Particularly when ordering a PC, leave no wiggle room. If the vendor has promised a Matrox G400 Max graphics card with 32 MB, for example, make sure that the component list includes that item by name and Matrox product number, rather than merely specifying "graphics card" or even "Matrox graphics card." Otherwise, you'll get less than you paid for. Count on it.

Verify the warranty

Ask about warranty terms. Some manufacturers provide the full specified warranty terms only for items purchased from authorized dealers in full retail packaging. For some products, the warranty period begins when the manufacturer ships the product to the distributor, which may be weeks or months before you actually receive the product. OEM products typically have much shorter warranties than retail-boxed products—sometimes as short as 90 days—and may be warranted only to the original distributor rather than to the final buyer. Better resellers may *endorse* the manufacturer warranty for some period on some products, often 30 to 90 days. That means that if the product fails, you can return the item to the reseller, who will ship you a replacement and take care of dealing with the manufacturer. Some resellers disclaim the manufacturer warranty, claiming that once they ship the item dealing with warranty claims is your problem, even if the product arrives DOA. We've encountered that problem a couple of times. Usually, mentioning phrases like "merchantability and fitness for a particular purpose" and "revocation of acceptance" leads them to see reason quickly. We usually demand the reseller ship us a new replacement product immediately and include a prepaid return shipping label if they want the dead item back. We don't accept or pay for dead merchandise under any circumstances, and neither should you.

Verify delivery terms

Direct resellers are required by law to ship products within the time period they promise. But that time period may be precise (e.g., ships within 24 hours) or vague (e.g., ships within three to six weeks). If the vendor cannot ship by the originally promised date, it must notify you in writing and specify another date by which the item will ship. If that occurs, you have the right to cancel your order without penalty. Be sure to make clear to the reseller that you expect the item to be delivered in a timely manner, and that time is of the essence for the transaction. Reputable vendors ship what they say they're going to ship when they say they're going to ship it. Unfortunately, some vendors have a nasty habit of taking your money and shipping whenever they get around to it. In a practice that borders on fraud, some vendors routinely report items as "in stock" when in fact they are not. Make it clear to the vendor that you do not authorize them to charge your credit card until the item actually ships, and that if you do not receive the item when promised you will cancel the order.

Don't expect problems to solve themselves

Even if you follow all of these guidelines, you may have a problem. Even the best resellers sometimes drop the ball. If that happens, don't expect the problem to go away by itself. If you encounter a problem, remain calm and notify the reseller first. Good resellers are anxious to resolve problems. Find out how the reseller wants to proceed, and follow their procedures, particularly for labeling returned merchandise with an RMA number. If things don't seem to be going as they should, explain to the vendor why you are dissatisfied, and tell them that you plan to request a charge-back from your credit card company. Finally, if the reseller is entirely recalcitrant and any aspect of the transaction (including, for example, a confirmation letter you wrote) took place via U.S. Postal Service, contact your postmaster about filing charges of mail fraud. That really gets a reseller's attention, but use it as a last resort.

Things to Do with Old PCs

So what do you do with an old PC that would cost too much to upgrade to current standards? We encounter that question frequently around here. We have everything from the latest multi-processor Intel boxes to creaking 386s. In fact, our original 1984-vintage IBM PC/XT died just last year, and it was doing useful work until its untimely demise. Here, in no particular order, are ten useful things to do with an old PC:

Give it to your spouse
> In many households, one spouse is a PC power user and the other is much less demanding. She works at home doing serious number crunching and plays Quake for relaxation, while he just checks his email periodically and uses the Web to keep up with the PGA Tour results. Or vice versa. He might be happier having an older system all to himself than he would be sharing the latest, fastest PC.

Give it to your kids
> Younger kids want to play educational games, some of which require a lot of PC, but many of which run just fine on a two- or three-year-old system. Older kids need word processing, web browsing, and email, but may also want to run games, some of which are quite demanding. Before you pass the old system on to the kids, consider doing one or more "$50 upgrades"—$50 for a faster processor, $50 to add RAM, $50 for a new video card, and, if necessary, $50 to replace the CD-ROM drive. Before you do much more than that, remember that you can buy or build a pretty competent PC nowadays for $500 or thereabouts, not including the monitor.

Give it to an elderly neighbor or relative
> An old Pentium system with a 15" monitor and 1 GB hard drive isn't a good upgrade candidate, but that doesn't mean it's useless. It's still more than good enough for web browsing, email, and light word processing, and there are many elderly people who would love to have such a machine. The stereotype that old people and computers don't mix is just wrong. One of our readers reports that his 103-year-old grandfather spends hours on the Web every day, and similar stories are common. If you ask around, what you find may surprise you. If you're going to do it, do it right. Strip the system down and re-install Windows, Internet Explorer, Outlook Express, and Office. Carry the system over, set it up for them, connect it to their phone line, and spend a couple of hours getting them started using it. Help them get connected to the Internet, and check back periodically to make sure they're having no problems.

Give it to your church, school, or library

Many non-profits are pathetically under-equipped with PCs. You may feel guilty about offering them what you consider to be an old, slow, and relatively useless computer, but utility is in the eye of the beholder. To someone running DOS applications on a 386—which many non-profits still do—your old Pentium may be a godsend, particularly if you're willing to spend some time helping them set it up and perhaps even network it to their other machines. Don't be surprised if a non-profit turns down your donation, though. Many of them have strict requirements for what they're willing to accept, probably because they've been deluged by people trying to dump old XTs and 286s for tax write-offs. If local non-profits aren't interested, contact the National Cristina Foundation (*http://www.cristina.org*). They accept anything from 486s up, including individual components.

Turn it into a resource server on your home network

If you don't have a home network yet, now may be a good time to set one up. For the small cost of a couple of network cards, some cables, and perhaps an inexpensive hub, you can share peripherals like large hard drives, tape drives, and printers among all the machines on the network. Better yet, you can use inexpensive proxy server or NAT software to share one Internet connection; Windows 98 even has Internet Connection Sharing built in. We've retired one of our old systems to duty as a network resource server. It has lots of disk space, the tape drive for system backups, and the Internet connection, which it shares with the rest of the network via the WinGate proxy server.

Use it to control your home automation and security system

Home automation, until recently the exclusive province of gear-heads, is becoming mainstream. Much still depends on obsolescent and unreliable X-10 technology, but other technologies are poised to make significant inroads. If you're not familiar with home automation, visit *http://www.home-automation.org* and check some of the web sites listed there. You might be surprised by what can be done, and an old PC can be quite useful as a central controller for a home automation system.

Use it to control your home telephone/voice mail/automated attendant system

If you work at home, consider installing a real telephone system and using your old PC to manage it. We both work at home, and have a Panasonic telephone system installed. We use an old 386sx system with a Talking Technologies BigmOuth card (alas, no longer available) to provide integrated automated attendant and voice mail functions. You can do the same to project a professional, "big company" image. As they say, "On the Internet, no one knows you're a dog."

Salvage it for swappers

You may think that 1.44 MB floppy, 1 GB hard disk, or 4X CD-ROM isn't worth much, and in one sense you're right. But if you have to troubleshoot your main system, just having a working spare of any type may save you a trip to the computer store. And that old ISA video card may be priceless if you need to install a flash BIOS update, because ISA video cards display the prompts and menus used by some flash BIOS update programs. PCI and AGP video cards do not display the prompts, forcing you to work blind.

Keep it on your desk

If you've never tried it, you might be surprised by how useful another PC on your desk can be, particularly if you network your home PCs. Windows and multitasking are great, but nothing beats having another monitor displaying a web page or other information while you work on your main PC. Robert takes this to an extreme, working surrounded by (currently) nine PCs, which share four monitors.

Install Linux

It's pretty obvious that Linux is no flash in the pan. Most people who read this book and are not running Linux now will be within a year, so it makes sense to get some experience with Linux starting now. Happily, Linux doesn't need much hardware. We've run it successfully on creaking 486 systems. It's fast on a Pentium, and it flies on older Pentium II and Celeron systems. Many people say Linux is less likely to have problems on newer hardware, and that's true to some extent. However, the problems that Linux has with older hardware are usually with unusual devices. So, although Linux may not support ancient tape drives or sound cards or network adapters, it's likely to work just fine with most of your older hardware. Our main Linux box at the moment is an elderly Gateway Pentium/133 with 64 MB of RAM, a 3 GB Western Digital hard disk, a Matrox Millennium video card, a 3Com 3C509 10BaseT Ethernet card, and a Conner/Seagate Travan TR-4 tape drive. Everything works for us. It probably will for you as well.

CHAPTER 2

Working on PCs

Popping the lid of a PPC for the first time can be pretty intimidating, but there's really no need for concern. There's nothing inside that will hurt you, other than sharp edges and those devilish solder points. There's also nothing inside that you're likely to damage, assuming you take the few simple precautions detailed in this chapter.

Some PCs—particularly those from office supply and electronics superstores—have seals that warn you the warranty is void if they're broken. This isn't so much to protect them against your ham-handedness as it is to ensure that you have to come back to them and pay their price for upgrades. We advise friends and clients to break such seals if they need to, do their own upgrades, and fight it out later if they have a problem that should be covered under warranty.

We've never heard of anyone being refused warranty service because of a broken seal, but there's always a first time. If you have a sealed PC that is still under warranty, the decision is yours. Note that hard disks are a special case. Breaking the seal on a hard disk does actually destroy it and will without question void the warranty.

Those issues aside, feel free to open your PC and tinker with it as you see fit. Far from forbidding you from working on your own PC, most mail-order and retail computer vendors actually expect you to do your own upgrades. As a matter of fact, most of them will try to talk you into doing your own warranty repairs so that they can avoid sending a technician to do them for you. The rest of this chapter explains the fundamentals you need to understand to start upgrading and repairing your PC.

Rules to Upgrade By

We've repaired, upgraded, and built hundreds of systems over the years, and learned a lot of lessons the hard way while doing it. Here are the rules we live by, some big, some small, and some more honored in the breach. We'll admit that we don't always take each of these steps when we're doing something simple like swapping a video card, but you won't go far wrong following them slavishly until you have enough experience to know when it's safe to depart from them.

Back everything up

Twice. Do a verify pass, if necessary, to make sure that what is on the backup tape matches what is on the disk drive. If you're connected to a network, copy at least your data and configuration files to a network drive. It's much easier to retrieve them from there than it is to recover from tape. If there's room on the network drive, create a temporary folder and copy the entire contents of the hard disk of the machine about to undergo surgery. About 99 times in 100 all of this will be wasted effort. The hundredth time—when everything that can go wrong does go wrong—will pay you back in spades for the other 99. If you don't have a tape drive, consider installing one as your first upgrade.

Make sure you have everything you need before you start

Have all of the hardware, software, and tools you'll need lined up and waiting. You don't want to have to stop in mid-upgrade to go off in search of a small Phillips screwdriver or to drive to the store to buy a cable. The first rule of upgrading says you won't find the screwdriver you need and the store will be closed. Make sure you have a boot disk with drivers for your CD-ROM drive, and test it before you start tearing things down. Create a new emergency repair diskette immediately before you start the upgrade. Make certain you have the distribution disks for the operating system, backup software, and any special drivers you need. If you're tearing down your only PC, download any drivers you will need, copy them to floppies, and unzip them if necessary *before* you take the computer apart. Just following that last piece of advice would have saved us many times from driving home to download a driver we needed when upgrading a computer at a friend's house.

Make sure you can get the answers you need

Read the manual first. A quick read-through often uncovers potential problems, hints, and tips that can make the upgrade much smoother. Check the web site for any new component you are installing. You'll often find FAQs (Frequently Asked Questions), Readme files, updated drivers, and other information that can make the difference between a trouble-free upgrade and a major mess. In fact, the quality of the web site that supports a component is a large factor in our purchase decision, and we suggest that you make it one in yours. Before we even consider buying a major component, we check the web site to verify that it is likely to have answers to any questions that may arise.

Make the technology work for you

You may have a choice between a slow manual way and a quick automatic way to accomplish a given task. The easy way may require spending a few bucks for a special-purpose utility program, but may save you hours of trial and error, manual labor, and aggravation. For example, if you are replacing a hard disk, you can move the contents of the existing disk to the new disk by spending hours doing a backup and restore, or you can buy a $15 utility program that does the same thing in a few minutes. Throughout the book, we point out utilities (many of them free) that we use to minimize manual trial-and-error work.

Record everything

During an upgrade, it's often important to be able to return to your starting point. If you've just spent an hour moving cables and changing DIP switches and jumpers, it's almost impossible to remember what went where originally. So, make sure to record each change as you make it. Some people like a visual record of what they're doing, and so use a Polaroid or digital camera to photograph the original state of the system and each change as they make it. We find that cumbersome, and prefer to use written or tape recorded notes.

The method we've settled on is to dictate the working details as we go along into a $30 Panasonic microcassette recorder—e.g., "pin 1 on the motherboard PS/2 keyboard connector is the red wire on the jack, with position 4 empty." Once we finish, we transfer important information—changes to jumpers and DIP switches, what components we've added and removed, etc.—to the written log book for that computer. Each time we buy or build a new computer, it gets its own log book with its name on the cover. We use the black-and-white speckled hard-bound composition books that Office Depot sells for a couple bucks.

Change one thing at a time

When upgrading multiple components, do so in phases. For example, to install a new video card and a new sound card, leave the old video card in place when you install the new sound card. Restart the computer and make sure the new sound card is working properly *before* you install the new video card. If you change only one thing at a time, any problems that occur are clearly a result of that change, and are relatively easy to track down and fix. If you swap multiple components simultaneously, resulting problems are harder to troubleshoot, because you're never certain whether the problem is caused by a bad or misconfigured new component, by a conflict between the new components, or by a conflict between one or more of the new components and one or more existing components.

Keep the PC plugged in while you work on it

Most PC user manuals tell you to unplug the PC before working on it. They say that not because it is good practice, but to minimize the risk of being sued if someone somehow electrocutes himself while working on one of their PCs. Disregard their advice. Every experienced technician we know leaves the PC plugged in while working on it, and for good reason. Doing so keeps the PC grounded, which minimizes the very real risk of static electricity destroying sensitive chips. Best practice is to plug the PC into a power strip or surge protector that is connected to the wall receptacle, but turn the power strip off. That grounds the PC to the building ground, but also ensures that no voltage can reach the PC while you're working on it.

Keep track of the screws and other small parts

Disassembling a PC yields an incredible number of screws and other small pieces. As you tear a PC down, organize these parts using an egg carton or old ice cube tray. As we can attest, one errant screw left on the floor can destroy a vacuum cleaner. Worse, one unnoticed screw can short out and destroy the motherboard and other components. The goal is to have all of the small parts reinstalled or accounted for when you reassemble the PC. Some people store the screws until they are needed by putting them back into the original component after removing it. This takes a bit longer, but does ensure that you use the proper screw for each component.

Use force when necessary, but use it cautiously

Many books tell you never to force anything, and that's good advice as far as goes. If doing something requires excessive force, chances are a part is misaligned, you have not removed a screw, or something similar. But sometimes there is no alternative to applying force judiciously. For example, drive power cables sometimes fit so tightly that the only way to get them off is to grab them with pliers and pull hard. Some combinations of expansion card and slot fit so tightly that you must press very hard to seat the card. If you encounter such a situation, ensure that everything is lined up and otherwise as it should be. Then use whatever force it takes to do the job, which may be substantial.

Check and recheck before you apply power

When an experienced PC technician does an upgrade, he does a quick scan of the entire PC before he performs the *smoke test* by applying power to the PC. Don't skip this step, and don't underestimate its importance. Most PCs that fail the smoke test do so because this step was ignored. Until you gain experience, it may take several minutes to verify that all is as it should be—all components secure, all cables connected properly, no tools or other metal parts shorting anything out, and so on. Once you are comfortable working inside PCs, this step takes 15 seconds, but that may be the most important 15 seconds of the whole upgrade.

Start small for the first boot

The moment of greatest danger comes when you power up the PC for the first time. Do what's necessary to minimize damage if the smoke test fails. If the system fails catastrophically—which happens from time to time no matter how careful you are—don't smoke more than you have to. For example, we finished building a server for which we'd bought four 128 MB DIMM memory modules and three hard disks. A new motherboard sometimes shorts out the first time it's powered up, so rather than installing the new DIMMs and hard drives before testing, we used an old 32 MB DIMM and an old hard disk to verify that the motherboard was good and all connections were right. Once we passed that hurdle, we installed the new DIMMs and hard disks. If the system had smoked, we'd have been out a motherboard, but our expensive new DIMMs and hard disks would be safe. We mentioned earlier another advantage to doing things this way. Limiting simultaneous changes makes it easier to get the hardware working properly. Starting small and adding components incrementally also helps you get Win9x Plug-N-Play configured more easily, particularly when you're installing "difficult" peripherals like sound cards, which want to grab every free resource in sight.

Don't throw the old stuff away

Don't discard the components you pull. With new hard disks costing only $10 per gigabyte, an old 1 GB hard disk may not seem worth keeping. But you may be glad you have it the next time you need to troubleshoot your system. Despite those correspondence school ads that show a technician using an oscilloscope to troubleshoot a PC, nobody really does it that way. In the real world, you troubleshoot PCs by swapping components. Keeping old components you pull during upgrades is a convenient (and free) way to accumulate the swappers you'll need later on to troubleshoot problems with this or another PC. Label them "known good," date them, and put them on the shelf.

Leave the cover off until you're sure everything works

An easy way to tell an experienced technician from a novice is to see when he reassembles the case. Experts wait until everything is installed and tested before putting the lid back on and securing the external cables. A novice installs the component, reassembles the case, reconnects all the cables, and *then* tests it. We watched one young woman do this several times before she caught on. The corollary to this rule is that you should *always* put the cover back on the case once the upgrade is complete and tested. Some believe that leaving the cover off improves cooling. Wrong. Cases do not depend on convection cooling, which is the only kind you get with the cover off. Cases are designed to direct cooling air across the major heat generating components, processors and drives, but this engineering is useless if you run the PC uncovered. Replace the cover to avoid overheating components.

Tools

It's worthwhile to assemble a toolkit that contains the hand tools and software utilities that you need to work on PCs. If you work on PCs only occasionally, you can get by with a fairly Spartan set of tools. If you work on PCs frequently, devote some time, effort, and money to assembling a reasonably complete set of hand tools and utilities. The following sections detail the components that we've found worth carrying in our tool kits.

Hand Tools

You don't need many tools for routine PC upgrades and repairs. We've successfully repaired PCs using only a Swiss Army Knife, but a more complete set of tools makes jobs easier. Putting together a dedicated PC toolkit and keeping it in a fixed location avoids the hassle of looking for a tool when what you really want to do is work on your PC.

Your first thought may be to buy one of those PC toolkits available from various sources, but we suggest you avoid them. Inexpensive kits available from most mail-order vendors contain shoddy tools and are not worth even their low price. The kits that are available from specialty catalogs like Specialized Products (*http://www.specializedproducts.com*) and Jensen (*http://www.jensentools.com*) are fine if you fix PCs for a living (and if your company buys the kit). Otherwise they're overkill and way too expensive.

Instead of buying any of the prepackaged kits, head for Sears and assemble your own PC toolkit. The basic tools you need for routine PC work cost under $50. Store these tools together, using a tool wrapper (available from auto parts stores) or a zipper case (available from Sears or specialty tool vendors). You can often buy sets of pliers, screwdrivers, and so forth for less than buying them each individually. We carry only the tools we need, so we usually buy the set, remove the ones we really wanted for our toolkit, and contribute the remainder to the general stock of tools around the house. Table 2-1 lists what we carry and recommend as a basic kit, with Sears part numbers in parentheses.

Table 2-1: A Basic PC Toolkit

Description	Description
Slotted screwdriver, 3/16" × 4" (41581)	Nutdriver, 1/4" (41971)
Slotted screwdriver, 1/4" × 4" (41583)	Nutdriver, 3/16" (41977)
Phillips screwdriver, #0 × 2 1/2" (41293)	Flashlight, mini MagLite or similar
Phillips screwdriver, #1 × 3" (41294)	Spare parts tube/organizer
Phillips screwdriver, #2 × 4" (41295)	Small brushes
Pliers, 4-1/2" long-nose mini-pliers (45173)	Band-Aids®

Even when we're not working on PCs, we always carry a Swiss Army Knife (we like the Victorinox CyberTool). If you don't routinely carry a knife, add a disposable snap-off razor blade, which is useful for opening blister-wrap packages, cutting cable ties, and so on. Also, although we prefer drivers with individual handles, you may prefer a handle with interchangeable bits. If so, get the Sears Craftsman 11-in-1 Screwdriver (41478), which includes five double-end bits and also serves as a 1/4" nutdriver.

If you work on PCs frequently or have special requirements, you may find useful the additions to the basic kit listed in Table 2-2. Depending on the types of PCs you work on, some of these tools may also be needed in the basic kit. For example, Compaq PCs use a lot of Torx fasteners.

Table 2-2: Supplemental Tools for the Basic PC Toolkit

Description	Source
Pliers, 4" diagonal mini-pliers (45178)	Sears
Torx driver, T10 (41473)	Sears
Torx driver, T15 (41474)	Sears
Screw starters (Phillips and slotted)	Sears
Wire stripper/crimper (82563)	Sears
Dental mirror	Drugstore
Hemostat	Drugstore
Spring-hook tool/parts retriever	Auto parts store
Digital voltmeter (DVM)	Radio Shack, specialty vendors

In addition to the tools themselves, a good toolkit contains several consumable items, including:

Alcohol

> PC components accumulate greasy brown residue, particularly if you smoke or if you heat with gas or oil. This residue attracts and holds dust, but can be removed with rubbing alcohol. Buy isopropanol (isopropyl alcohol), which

removes grease better than ethanol (ethyl alcohol), and carry a small screw-top bottle of it in your kit.

Swabs

Keep half a dozen Q-Tips® or foam swabs for cleaning mouse rollers, tape drive heads, and similar difficult-to-reach places. We prefer the foam swabs, which do not deposit stray bits of cotton.

Cotton balls

Carry a few of these as disposable cleaning aids. Moisten one with rubbing alcohol so that it is wet, but not dripping, and use it to clean larger components like disk drives. These things come in at least two sorts. In our experience, the ones intended for medical use (which are really cotton) leave fibers all over the place. The ones Barbara uses with her nail polish remover (which appear to be a man-made fiber) don't shed nearly as much.

Freon®

You can't get real Freon now because of the damage it supposedly does to the ozone layer, but everyone still calls the stuff you can buy Freon. We use Zero Residue Cleaner from Radio Shack. It comes in a pressurized spray can with a small tube that attaches to the nozzle and allows you to direct the spray. The stuff evaporates almost instantly, and does a good job of cleaning really dirty components. It's particularly useful for cleaning inaccessible things like the fan blades inside the power supply enclosure, which tend to get really filthy and are almost impossible to clean otherwise. It's also useful for cleaning the heads on floppy and tape drives. Just stick in the tube and give them a good squirt.

Canned air

Many technicians carry a can of compressed clean, dry air to blow out dust bunnies, to evaporate cleaner residue quickly, and so on. We've never felt that air was worth paying for, so we simply blow gently to accomplish the same thing. Try not to spray saliva on the components.

Two tools found in nearly every packaged PC toolkit should never be used:

DIP chip puller

A DIP (Dual Inline Pin) chip is an individual rectangular package with rows of pins perpendicular to the chip body running down each long side. In theory, you use these tools, which resemble ice tongs, by fitting the tabs at the end of each arm under the DIP chip and pulling up gently to remove the chip without bending the pins. In practice, you're almost certain to bend the pins when using one of these things, and you're as likely to pull the entire socket as just the chip. To remove a DIP chip, slide a small flat-blade screwdriver under one end and lever up *slightly*. Do the same on the other end of the chip and alternate ends until it pops free.

DIP chip inserter

By design, the pins on DIP chips never quite align with those in the socket—the opposing rows of pins are a bit further apart on the chip than on the socket so that the "spring" in the pins will ensure firm contact with the socket. These devices are intended to help you insert a DIP chip into a matching socket. In theory, a chip inserter gently squeezes those pins together so that they are aligned properly for insertion. In practice, it seldom works that way, and you end up squashing the pins flat and ruining the chip.

To insert a DIP chip into a socket, use one of the following methods, both of which work for us:

- Place the DIP chip flat on a table or other hard surface so that one row of pins is flush against the table top, and then *gently* press downward to bend all of the pins *slightly* inward toward the center of the chip. Repeat this process for the other side of the chip, alternating between sides to bend the two rows of pins gradually inward toward each other. Check frequently by putting the pins against the socket to determine when you have bent them inward enough to align directly with the socket. In theory, using this method eliminates the "spring action" built into the chip and should result in unreliable connections. In practice, chips we inserted this way have worked for years without problems.

- Without pre-bending the pins, and with the body of the chip at a slight angle, seat one row of pins partially into the socket. Then, using a pencil (or your finger) press gently on the other row of pins until they align with the socket and press down gently.

Be sure to orient DIP chips properly when inserting them. A DIP socket has a semicircular notch centered on one end. The DIP chip has a small printed or engraved circle on one end. To align the chip properly, seat the circle end of the chip in the notched end of the socket.

 The ubiquity of SIMM and DIMM memory modules nowadays means there aren't many socketed DIP chips in PCs. Your system may still have a few, however, and it's a good idea to reseat them every time you pop the cover. Do a quick scan of the motherboard and expansion cards, and just press down firmly with your thumb on each socketed chip you see. If the chip has begun to walk out of its socket, you'll feel it snap back into position as you press.

Software Tools

In addition to hand tools, your tool kit should have an assortment of floppy diskettes and CDs that contain reporting and diagnostic utilities and essential applications. The location of the kit can vary according to your own needs. If you have only one PC, keep all this stuff near it. If you work on many PCs, carry these items with you.

Essential utilities

The contents of your software toolkit depend greatly on how many PCs you maintain, which operating systems they run, and similar factors, but a good basic assortment includes the following essential utilities.

DOS boot diskette

Even if all your computers run Windows 95/98 or NT, the most important item in your software toolkit is a DOS boot disk with drivers for the CD-ROM drive. When the PC won't boot, this disk allows you to install or run diagnostic and repair utilities from a CD. Without it, you may be stymied because you can't access the CD-ROM drive, even to do something as basic as reinstalling the operating system. The Windows 9x emergency disk described later in this list fulfills this purpose. If you run only Windows NT, borrow someone's Windows 9x computer long enough to make a DOS boot disk. On this or another diskette, depending on free space, you'll want copies of several essential programs. At minimum, have matching versions of *fdisk* and *format*, and a text editor to modify configuration files.

DOS diagnostics

Years ago, PCs often came with CheckIt, QAPlus, AMIDiag, or a similar diagnostic utility. Now system vendors expect people to use the bundled Windows utilities. These are fine, as far as they go, but they don't go very far. Windows (particularly NT) isolates users and programs from the hardware, which makes it hard for a diagnostic utility to do its job. Also, Windows-based utilities are usable only if the computer boots. You can use these bundled utilities to do things like detecting a misconfigured component or an IRQ conflict on a bootable system, but that's not enough when you need detailed information or when the PC won't boot. For that, you need a DOS-based utility that provides comprehensive testing and reporting. Any of the following products will do the job. We use them all, but if you only get one, make it Touchstone CheckIt.

SiSoft Sandra (http://www.sisoftware.demon.co.uk/sandra/)

SiSoft Sandra is probably the most-used diagnostic program, not least because a free version can be downloaded from SiSoft. Although the free version is sufficient for most people's needs, SiSoft also sells the $29 Sandra Professional, which includes additional functionality and technical support.

Symantec Norton Utilities (NU) (http://www.norton.com/nu)

Almost since the first PCs shipped, most technicians have carried a copy of NU. Unfortunately, Norton recently discontinued the DOS version. Their current versions, *Norton Utilities for Windows NT* and *Norton Utilities 2000 for Windows 95/98*, are nice desktop extenders, but provide limited hardware diagnostics. Grab a copy of the DOS version if you can find one.

Touchstone CheckIt (http://www.checkit.com)

The best dedicated hardware diagnostic program is CheckIt, available in several versions. The $90 CheckIt Diagnostic Suite includes numerous supplemental utilities, comprehensive DOS diagnostics, and loopback plugs. The $45 CheckIt Portable Diagnostics includes only the DOS diagnostics and loopback plugs, which are all you really need. CheckIt is not as widely distributed as Norton, but is available from many major mail order vendors.

DOS diagnostics remain a popular shareware and public domain software category, although most are single-purpose products (e.g., a serial port tester) rather than general purpose diagnostics. If that's all you need, though, searching a shareware library like *http://www.shareware.com* using the string *diagnostic* may turn up a program that does the job for free.

Emergency Repair Diskette

Recent versions of Windows allow you to create an emergency disk that contains critical system configuration data, part or all of the registry, etc. Create or update this disk for a computer any time you make a significant change to it. Label and date the disk and store it near the computer or keep it with your tool kit. If you don't have a recent copy, do yourself a favor and make one right now. Use the following procedures to create an emergency disk:

Windows 95/98

From Control Panel, choose Add/Remove Programs. Display the Startup Disk page and click the Create Disk icon to create a Startup Disk. This disk is bootable and contains the drivers needed to access most IDE CD-ROM drives. You can use a Startup Disk created on any computer to start any other computer. Floppy disks have a way of getting lost or damaged, and you can't get far if you can't boot a problem PC, so we generally keep several copies of the Windows 98 SE Startup Disk distributed around our work areas, in our tool kits, and so on.

Windows NT 4.0 Emergency Repair Disk

Run \winnt\system32\rdisk.exe, choose Create Repair Disk, and follow the prompts. To update an existing disk, insert that disk and choose Update Repair Info. Note that the Emergency Repair Disk is not bootable. Repairing an NT installation requires a set of Windows NT boot floppies. If you have lost the set that came with Windows NT, you can recreate them by running *winnt32 /ox* from the distribution CD.

Windows 2000 Emergency Repair Disk

Run Start → Programs → Accessories → System Tools → Backup. With Backup running, click the Emergency Repair Disk icon to create the disk. In the resulting dialog, mark the "Also backup the registry..." checkbox to copy key system files to the repair directory on the hard disk. Like the NT ERD, the Windows 2000 ERD is not bootable. To repair Windows 2000, you must boot either from the distribution CD or the boot floppies.

Operating system distribution disks

You need the OS distribution disks to upgrade or replace the system hard disk. But you'll also need them frequently during routine upgrades because Windows often prompts for them to load drivers for a new device. If you've updated the operating system from the initial distribution version (e.g., by applying a Windows NT Service Pack), also keep the Service Pack or update CD handy.

With huge hard disks costing so little, we create a separate "distribution partition" on the hard disk of most systems we build. We copy the Windows distribution CD to this partition, along with service packs, the Office CD (and any other programs the system uses), the driver CDs for installed hardware, and so on. This has several benefits, including faster installation, the fact that you don't have to locate the CD when you change options or want to install additional modules, and the fact that you can if necessary completely rebuild the system using only a boot floppy to get started.

Backup utility

If you use a third-party backup utility, keep a copy of the distribution disk in your kit to make sure that you can restore backup tapes after reinstalling the operating system. Few things are more frustrating than getting a failed computer up again, having a good backup tape, but not having the software at hand that you need to restore it.

Anti-virus utility

If your system becomes infected by a virus, you will need to have a DOS-bootable, write-protected floppy disk and a recent version of an anti-virus utility. In fact, any time a system behaves strangely, a good first step is to run a quick virus scan. The DOS-bootable floppy allows you to boot cleanly and detect and remove a virus on a DOS or Windows 9x disk, or on a Windows NT disk that is formatted as FAT. Because you cannot access an NTFS volume after booting from a boot floppy, the only way to remove a virus from these volumes is to boot the system from the hard disk and run an anti-virus utility from a local hard disk or network drive. The big names in anti-virus utilities are McAfee VirusScan from Network Associates (*http://www.nai.com*), and Norton AntiVirus from Symantec (*http://www.symantec.com*). We've used both, and either is sufficient for the task.

CMOS save/restore utility

CMOS settings store the current configuration of a PC. These settings range from easily understood ones—current date/time, boot options, hard disk configuration, and so on—to ones like advanced chipset configuration that only system designers fully understand. Although you can manually record all of the settings on paper, there's a better way—a CMOS save/restore utility. These utilities save CMOS settings to a disk file, which you can later restore to recreate the settings in one step. CheckIt Diagnostics Suite includes such a utility. If you don't have CheckIt, download a dedicated CMOS save/restore utility. There are many free and shareware alternatives available. One that we've used is Benjamin Johnston's free CMOSViewer, which runs under Windows 9x and is available at *http://www.uq.net.au/~zzgajohn/cmos.html*. Numerous DOS products are available from shareware archives like *http://www.shareware.com*. Search for *CMOS*.

Most expansion cards, modems, and disk drives come with a driver CD. Just keeping them all straight is hard enough, let alone making sure that you have the correct and most recent driver for a particular component. When we buy or build a computer, we create a folder for it on a network drive. When we buy a component that comes with a floppy diskette or CD with drivers, we copy the contents of that disk to a subfolder of that folder. If you have a CD-R drive, use it to make a customized CD for each computer. Collect all the drivers and other miscellany in a folder and copy them to a CD for that system. Include a change log in the root directory. When you replace a component, note that in the change log and burn a new CD with the updated and new drivers. If there's room on the CD, also include the operating system, diagnostic tools, and so forth.

Supplemental utilities

Beyond essential utilities, we carry several supplemental utilities. These tools are nice to have, but not absolutely required. Rather than doing things you can't do without them, they save you time—sometimes a lot of time. If you work on PCs frequently, every one of these commercial utilities belongs in your bag. Each of them costs money, but unless your time is worth nothing an hour each pays for itself quickly—usually the first time you use it.

If you seldom work on PCs, these utilities probably aren't worth buying ahead of time. Instead, try to schedule your upgrades, and buy these as you need them. Note that most of these utilities are available in both inexpensive single user/single PC standard versions and much more expensive versions that are licensed to be used by a single technician on multiple PCs. The prices given are typical street prices for the standard versions.

Partition Magic

This $50 PowerQuest (*http://www.powerquest.com*) utility has saved us countless hours of extra work over the years. Before Partition Magic, the only way to change disk partitioning was to backup, delete the old partitions, create and format new partitions, and restore. In addition to taking hours, this process is perilous. More than once, we've been unable to restore a backup tape we made immediately before starting to repartition, even though that tape had passed a verify flawlessly. Partition Magic lets you repartition on the fly. It takes less time and is probably safer than the old backup-and-restore method. In fact, although PowerQuest recommends backing up before repartitioning, we confess that we seldom bother to backup our own systems before repartitioning. We've never lost any data doing it that way, but if you repartition without backing up and lose data, please don't send us any nasty messages. You have been warned.

DriveCopy

This $20 PowerQuest utility is the cheapest, easiest, and most reliable way we know to copy the contents of one hard disk to another, for example when you're replacing a hard disk. Using DriveCopy allows you to avoid the time-consuming process of backing up the old drive, installing the operating system on the new drive, and then doing a restore. Instead, you simply connect the new drive with the old drive still installed and use DriveCopy to replicate the entire contents of the old drive to the new. When you remove the old drive, the system boots from the new drive without further ado.

DriveImage

This PowerQuest utility is available in a $50 DriveImage version and a Drive-Image Pro version that is priced by user. DriveImage Pro is primarily a disk cloning product. It allows you to create an image of a master disk and then replicate that image to multiple hard disks—just the thing when you need to set up 100 identical workstations. It even has a SID editor, which allows you to get around the problem of Windows NT's unique SIDs. As a personal utility, DriveImage is useful for migrating programs and data between partitions and for disaster recovery. Unlike DriveCopy, DriveImage can copy individual partitions, can change the partition size after copying to the destination, and can automatically resize partitions to fit within a smaller drive. As useful as all this is, the really important thing about DriveImage is that it can create a compressed image of a partition. The image file typically occupies about a quarter of the space used on the source partition, and can be stored on another partition or on removable media. If disaster strikes, you can recover the image file automatically using the bootable recovery floppies that DriveImage creates for you. Any time we're about to do a significant software upgrade to a system, we run DriveImage first to create an image backup. That way, if the upgrade ends up causing a problem, we can immediately roll back the system to its original state.

 The best way we've found to organize and protect CDs is to lose the jewel cases and store the CDs in one of those zippered vinyl audio CD wallets you can buy for a few dollars at Circuit City and similar stores. They use plastic or Tyvek sleeves to protect the CDs, hold from a half dozen to two dozen CDs, and make it easy to find the one you want. If the CD has a serial number or init key on the original jewel case, make sure to record it on the CD, using a soft permanent marker on the *label* side.

We stock one of these wallets with essential CDs—Windows 95/98/NT/2000 distribution CDs, Office, various diagnostics, and so on—and always carry it with us. We also buy a CD wallet for each PC we buy or build. New PCs usually arrive with several CDs, and even video, sound, or modem cards are likely to come with their own CDs. Storing these CDs in one place, organized by the system they belong to, makes it much easier to locate the one you need.

DisplayMate

This $50 tool from Sonera Technologies (*http://www.displaymate.com*) does just one thing, but does it supremely well. It helps you optimize your video card and monitor. More than any other PC component, monitors can vary significantly between individual examples of the same model. We don't buy an expensive monitor without using DisplayMate to test it first, and neither should you. DisplayMate is also useful on an ongoing basis. Monitors change as they age. Using DisplayMate to tune them periodically results in the best possible picture. You can download a demo from the web site, which is sufficient for casual testing.

General Procedures

After you assemble a toolkit with the hand tools and utilities described in the preceding sections, you have everything you need to upgrade or repair a PC except the new components. Before you get started, take a few minutes to read through the following sections, which describe the common procedures and general knowledge you need to work on PCs. These sections describe the general tasks you perform almost any time you work on a computer—things like opening the case, setting jumpers and switches, manipulating cables, and adding or removing expansion cards. Instructions for specific tasks like replacing a motherboard, disk drive, or power supply are given in the relevant chapter.

Before You Open the Case

Although you may be raring to get in there and fix something, taking the time to prepare properly before you jump in pays big dividends later. Before you open the case, do the following:

Make sure it's not a software problem
> The old saying, "If all you have is a hammer, everything looks like a nail," is nowhere more true than with PC repairs. Just as surgeons are often accused of being too ready to cut, PC technicians are always too ready to pop the lid. Before you assume that hardware is causing the problem, make sure the problem isn't being caused by an application, by Windows itself, or by a virus. Use your hardware diagnostic utility and virus scanner *before* you assume the hardware is at fault and start disconnecting things.

Think things through
> Inexperienced technicians dive in willy-nilly without thinking things through first. Experienced ones first decide what is the most likely cause of the problem, what can be done to resolve it, in what order they should approach the repair, and what they'll need to complete it. Medical students have a saying, "when you hear thundering hooves, don't think about zebras." In context, that means that you should decide the most likely causes of the problem in approximate ranked order, decide which are easy to check for, and then eliminate the easy ones first. In order, check easy/likely, easy/unlikely, hard/likely, and finally hard/unlikely. Otherwise, you may find yourself tearing down a PC and removing the video card before you notice that someone unplugged the monitor.

Backup the hard disk(s)
> Every time you pop the cover of a PC, there's a small but ever-present risk that something that used to work won't work when you put everything together again. One of the wires in a cable may be hanging by a thread, or

the hard drive may be teetering on the edge of failure. Just opening the case may cause a marginal component to fail irreversibly. So, before you even think of doing PC surgery, make sure the hard drive is backed up.

Record CMOS settings

It's important to have a record of the CMOS settings before you open the case. Working on a PC doesn't normally affect CMOS settings, but some activities (such as flashing the BIOS, removing the battery, or shorting the CMOS clear jumper) can wipe out all settings. If that happens, you'll need to re-enter the settings, and you'd better have them available. Recording CMOS settings is particularly important when you're not replacing the motherboard, because they're the ones you'll continue to use. If you are replacing the motherboard, the only CMOS settings you need to record are those that specify the hard disk geometry. Even if you don't plan to do anything that might affect CMOS, use your CMOS save/restore utility to save these settings to a diskette before you open the case. If you don't have such a utility, download one or record the settings with pencil and paper.

Disconnect external cables

It may seem obvious, but you need to disconnect all external cables before you can move the PC itself to the operating room. Many PCs are under desks or otherwise make it difficult to see the rear panel. If necessary, get down on the floor and crawl behind the PC with a flashlight to make sure it isn't still tethered to something. We've dragged modems, keyboards, and mice off desks because we weren't paying attention, and we once came within inches of pulling a $2,000 monitor onto the floor. Check the cables or pay the price.

Set the monitor safely aside

Monitors are not only expensive and relatively fragile, but can cause serious injuries if the tube implodes. A monitor on the floor is an accident waiting to happen. If you're not taking the monitor to the work area, keep it on the desk out of harm's way. If you must put it on the floor, at least turn its face toward the wall.

Electrostatic Discharge (ESD) Precautions

You've probably been startled by a static electric shock on a dry winter day. T

his phenomenon—formally called *Electrostatic Discharge* (*ESD*)—can destroy sensitive PC components instantly. Just because you don't notice it doesn't mean it isn't there, either. Static potential must build to several thousand volts before you experience a shock, but levels of only a few hundred volts are hazardous for PCs. Worse, incremental damage may occur invisibly and is cumulative, so although any one zap may not kill a component outright, it will surely damage it and make it that much more prone to fail later on.

Although this may be off-putting, it's really no big deal. We've worked on hundreds of PCs over the years, and haven't damaged one yet, so far as we know. You can easily avoid problems with static electricity by following these rules:

- Don't wear rubber-soled shoes or synthetic clothing.

- Work in an uncarpeted area.

- Ground yourself to dissipate the static charge each time you are about to touch a PC component.

The first line of defense against static usually recommended is an *anti-static wrist strap*. One end wraps around your wrist. The other end may have alligator clips intended to connect to the PC case or power supply, or it may have a plug intended to fit a standard power receptacle. You can buy these things for a few dollars from most mail-order places. They are sometimes included with expensive chips like processors. We don't like these straps. They're awkward to work with, and—although we know it is safe—connecting a conductive strap to your wrist and then plugging it into the wall seems a bit *outré*.

We use a simpler method that protects sensitive components just as reliably, as long as you get in the habit of following it religiously. Leave the PC you're working on plugged in, which ensures that it is grounded. When you first sit down to work on the PC, and then each time you are about to touch a static-sensitive component, touch the chassis or power supply to dissipate the accumulated static charge. When we're working on a particularly sensitive or expensive component, like a CPU, we actually keep our left hand on the chassis the whole time we're in contact with the component. Note that ATX motherboards maintain constant low voltage, even when the system is turned off. For that reason, disconnect the power cord before working on an ATX system. Touching the power supply still works, however, as it provides an adequate sink for static charges.

Removing and Replacing the Cover

It sounds stupid, but it's not always immediately obvious how to get the cover off the chassis. We've worked on hundreds of different PCs from scores of manufacturers over the years, and we're still sometimes stumped. Manufacturers use an endless variety of fiendish ways to secure the cover to the chassis. Some were intended to allow tool-free access, others to prevent novice users from opening the case, and still others were apparently designed just to prove there was yet one more way to do it.

We have seen novice upgraders throw up their hands in despair, figuring that if they couldn't even get the case open they weren't destined to become PC technicians. Nothing could be further from the truth. It just sometimes takes a while to figure it out.

The most evil example we ever encountered was a mini-tower case that had no screws visible except those that secured the power supply. The cover appeared seamless and monolithic. The only clue was a two-inch long piece of silver "warranty void if removed" tape that wrapped from the top of the cover to one side, making it clear that the separation point was there. We tried everything we could think of to get that cover off. We pulled gently on the front of the case, thinking that perhaps it would pop off and reveal screws underneath. We pressed in gently on the side panels, thinking that perhaps they were secured by a spring latch or friction fit. Nothing worked.

Finally, we turned the thing upside down and examined the bottom. The bottom of computer cases is almost always unfinished metal, but this one was a finished beige material that looked just like the other parts of the cover. That seemed odd, so we examined the four rubber feet closely. They had what appeared to be center inserts, so we pried gently on one of these with our small screwdriver. Sure enough, it popped off and revealed a concealed screw within the rubber foot. Once we removed those four screws, the cover slid off easily, bottom first.

The moral is that what one person can assemble, another person can disassemble. It sometimes just takes determination, so keep trying. Obviously, your first resort should be the system manual, but manuals have a way of disappearing when you need them most. Fortunately, most cases don't use such convoluted methods. Standard systems generally use one of the following methods to secure the cover to the chassis:

Classic AT-style desktop cases

> These use five screws (one per corner and one at top center) that pass through the chassis and thread into receptacles on the inside of the cover. Don't confuse the screws that secure the power supply with those that secure the cover. Cover screws are located along the edge, while power supplies are normally secured by four screws in a square pattern located at the upper- and mid-left side of the rear panel as you are viewing it. On these systems, the cover comprises the top, front, and sides of the case, and slightly overhangs the rear of the chassis when installed properly. The lower edge of each side of the cover usually has a channel that fits a rail built into the chassis. Once you remove the screws, slide the cover a few inches towards the front and then lift it off. To install the cover, place it in position with a gap of a few inches between the back edge of the cover and the rear panel. Make sure that the channels in the bottom of each side panel are aligned with the chassis rail grooves and then slide the cover toward the rear of the PC until it seats. Be careful when installing or removing the cover not to snag the top center screw receptacle on any of the cables.

Recent AT-style and low-profile desktop cases

> These use three or more screws on the back of the case, which go through an overlapping lip on the cover and thread into the chassis itself. The removable part of the cover comprises the top and sides. To remove the cover, remove the screws from the back (make sure to remove only the cover screws, *not* the screws that secure the power supply), slide the cover back an inch or two, and then lift it clear. You may have to tilt the cover slightly by lifting the rear to allow it to come clear of the chassis. To reinstall the cover, place it over the chassis with an inch or two gap between the front edge of the cover and the rear of the front panel, then slide the cover forward. There is a lip around the sides and top of the cover that fits inside the front cover of the case. Usually, the top will fit easily if you've put the cover on correctly, but the sides may need to be pressed in before they will fit. Also note that there may be a lip or other retaining mechanism at the bottom edge of the cover which you may need to align before the cover will seat properly. Replace the screws from the back.

Tower and mini-tower cases

> These generally use three or four screws equally spaced down each side to secure the case. The covers on most of these system cases resemble those on recent AT-style and low-profile cases. The front of the cover at the top and on

both sides has an underbeveled lip that slides under the rear edge of the front bezel. The bottom edges of both side panels are channeled to fit guides that protrude vertically from the bottom of the chassis on each side. After removing the screws that secure it, remove the cover by sliding it far enough to the rear to clear the lips at the top and side front of the cover from the front panel bezel and then lifting it off.

Replacing the cover on one of these systems is often difficult because you must guide the lips on the top and both side panels of the cover under the front bezel while simultaneously making sure that the bottom of each side panel seats in the guides. The easiest way to do this is usually to lower the cover over the chassis a few inches back from its ultimate seated position. Then lift the rear of the cover an inch or two to angle the cover slightly. Make sure that the bottom edges of the cover seat in their channels, and then slide the cover toward the front while keeping the rear of the cover lifted an inch or two. Guide the top lip of the cover under the front bezel and then slowly lower the rear of the cover, making sure that the lips on the side panels slide under the sides of the front bezel.

Tool-free cases

Some of the easiest cases to work on are screwless, or nearly so. For example, one of our favorites, the Antec KS-288 (*http://www.antec-inc.com*) has only one thumbscrew, centered at the top of the back panel. After this thumb-screw is removed, the top panel slides off to the rear. That in turn frees both side panels, which simply lift off. Reassembling the case is just as easy, because it uses craftily designed triangular slots that make it easy to align things before dropping them into place. If properly designed, a tool-free case can be just as rigid as one that uses screws. Be careful, though, about buying a cheap tool-free case. We've seen some that are incredibly flimsy.

In addition to these standard case types, you may run into one of the following:

Clamshell cases

These cases are designed to allow quick access to the inside of the PC by removing only the top portion of the case, while the sides, front, and back remain fixed. These cases divide the top down the middle from front to back. To open them, you generally remove two or four screws, which may be located on the top of the case or at the top center of the back of the case. Once you remove these screws, the two parts of the top either swing up on hinges or can be removed completely. Although never very popular with PC vendors, clamshell cases are still made, and are sometimes encountered on low-volume custom-built systems.

Side panel cases

On these cases, all parts of the cover except the sides are semi-permanently attached. Each side panel is individually secured to the chassis using thumb-screws or screws along the rear and/or bottom of the case. To remove a side panel, loosen the screws securing it and slide the panel toward the rear and/ or bottom of the case, as necessary. The front and/or top of these panels is often secured using a lip that slides under an overhang on the top or rear panel. Depending on the case design, you may have to lift the panel slightly away from the chassis before it will slide clear. To reinstall the panel, reverse the process, guiding the lip into its matching channel until the panel slides easily back into the closed position and then reinsert thefs screws.

Managing Internal Cables and Connectors

When you pop the cover of a PC, the first thing you'll notice is cables all over the place. These cables carry power and signals between various subsystems and components of the PC. Making sure they're routed and connected properly is no small part of working on PCs.

The cables used in PCs terminate in a variety of connectors. By convention, every connector is considered either male or female. Many male connectors, also called *plugs*, have protruding pins, each of which maps to an individual wire in the cable. The corresponding female connector, also called a *jack*, has holes that match the pins on the mating male connector. Matching male and female connectors are joined to form the connection. Rather than using pins and holes, the connectors used on some cables (for example, modular telephone cables and 10BaseT Ethernet cables) use other methods to establish the connection. The connector that terminates a cable may mate with a connector on the end of another cable, or it may mate with a connector that is permanently affixed to a device, such as a hard disk or a circuit board. Such a permanently affixed connector is called a *socket*, and it may be male or female.

Some cables use individual wires joined to a connector. Only three cables of this sort are common in PCs—those used to supply power to the motherboard and drives, those that connect front-panel LEDs and switches to the motherboard, and those that connect audio-out on a CD-ROM drive to a sound card.

Most PC cables contain many individual wires packaged as a *ribbon cable*, so called because individually insulated conductors are arranged side-by-side in a flat array that resembles a ribbon. Ribbon cables provide a way to organize the wires required to connect devices like drives and controllers whose interfaces require many conductors. Ribbon cables are used primarily for low-voltage signals, although they are also used to conduct low voltage/low current power in some applications. Common ribbon cables range in size from the 10-wire cables used to extend embedded serial ports from the motherboard to the back panel, through 34-wire floppy drive cables, 40-wire IDE drive cables, to 50- and 68-wire SCSI cables. Ribbon cables are normally used only inside the case because their electrical characteristics cause them to generate considerable RF emissions, which can interfere with nearby electronic components.

System designers attempt to avoid two potential dangers with regard to PC cables. Most important is to prevent connecting a cable to the wrong device. For example, connecting a 12-volt power cable to a device that expects only 5 volts might have a catastrophic result. This goal is achieved by using unique connectors that physically prevent the cable from connecting to a device not designed to receive it. The second potential error is connecting the cable backward. Most PC cables prevent this by using unsymmetrical connectors that physically fit only if oriented correctly, a process called *keying*.

Two keying methods are commonly used for PC cables, either individually or in conjunction. The first uses mating connectors whose bodies connect only one way, and is used for all power cables and some ribbon cables. The second, used for most ribbon cables, blocks one or more holes on the female connector and leaves out the corresponding pin on the male connector. Such a ribbon cable can be installed only when oriented so that missing pins correspond to blocked holes.

An ideal PC cable therefore uses unambiguous keyed connectors. You can't connect these cables to the wrong thing because the connector only fits the right thing; you can't connect it backwards, because the connector only fits the right way. Fortunately, most of the really dangerous cables in PCs—the ones that could damage a component or the PC itself if they were misconnected—are of this sort. Power cables for disk drives and ATX motherboards, for example, fit only the correct devices and cannot be connected backwards.

Some PC cables, on the other hand, require careful attention. Their connectors may physically fit a component that they're not intended to connect to, and/or they may not be keyed, which means you can easily connect them backwards if you're not paying attention. Connecting one of these cables wrong usually won't damage anything, but the system may not work properly, either. The cables that link front panel switches and indicator LEDs to the motherboard are of this variety. So are the power cables for old-style AT motherboards, and connecting these wrong *can* destroy the motherboard.

Ribbon cable fundamentals

On first glance, ribbon cables appear to be dead standard. They're nearly all light gray nowadays, although you may encounter light blue, white, or rainbow ribbon cables on older systems. All of them use a contrasting colored stripe to indicate pin 1 (brown in the case of the rainbow cables). They use only two types of connectors (described later in this section) both of which are female and only one of which is commonly used nowadays. For a ribbon cable with a given number of wires, it might seem that the only distinguishing features are how long the cable is and whether it has connectors for two devices or just one. Problems may arise, however, if incompatible keying methods are used on the two connectors that need to mate.

Most ribbon cables use *header-pin connectors*, shown in Figure 2-1. Header-pin connectors are used on cables for hard drives, CD-ROM drives, tape drives, and similar components, as well as for connecting embedded motherboard ports to external rear panel jacks. The female header-pin connector on the cable has two parallel rows of holes that mate to a matching array of pins on the male connector on the motherboard or peripheral. On all but the least expensive drives and other peripherals, these pins are enclosed in a plastic socket designed to accept the female connector. On inexpensive motherboards and adapter cards, the male connector may be just a naked set of pins. Even high-quality motherboards and adapter cards often use naked pins for secondary connectors (like serial ports or feature connectors).

Some header-pin connectors, male and female, are not keyed. Others use connector body keying, pin/hole keying, or both. This diversity means that it is quite possible to find that you cannot use a particular header-pin cable for its intended purpose. For example, we recently installed a disk drive and attempted

Figure 2-1: A ribbon cable with a header-pin connector

to use the IDE cable supplied with the drive to connect that drive to the secondary IDE header pin connector on the motherboard. The motherboard end of that cable was keyed by a blocked hole, but the header-pin connector on the motherboard had all pins present, which prevented the cable from seating. Fortunately, the cable that came with the motherboard fit both the motherboard and the drive connectors properly, allowing us to complete the installation.

If you run into such a keying problem, there are three possible solutions.

Use an unkeyed cable

The IDE and other header-pin cables that most computer stores sell use connectors that use neither connector body nor pin/hole keying. You can use one of these cables of the proper size to connect any device, but the absence of all keying means that you must be especially careful not to connect it backwards.

Remove the key from the cable

If you don't have an unkeyed cable available, you may be able to remove the key from the existing cable. Most keyed cables use a small bit of plastic to block one of the holes. You may be able to use a needle to pry the block out far enough that you can extract it with your needlenose pliers. Alternatively, try pushing a pin into the block at an angle, then bending the top of the pin over and pulling both bent pin and block out with your pliers. If the key is a solid, integral part of the cable (which is rarely the case), you may be able to use a heated needle or pin to melt the key out of the hole far enough for the pin to seat.

Remove the offending pin

Sometimes you have no choice. If the stores are closed, the only cable you have uses pin/hole keying with a solid block that you can't get out, and you must connect that cable to a header-pin connector that has all pins present, you have to go with what you have. You can use diagonal cutters to nip off the pin that prevents you from connecting the cable. Obviously, this is drastic. If you nip the wrong pin, you'll destroy the motherboard or expansion card, or at least render that interface unusable. Before you cut, see if you can swap cables within the PC to come up with an unkeyed cable for the problem connector. If not, you can sometimes bend the offending pin *slightly*—enough to allow the female connector to partially seat. This may be good enough to use as a temporary connection until you can replace the cable. If all else fails and you need to cut the pin, before doing so align the keyed female connector with the pin array and verify just which pin needs to be cut. Also, check the manual for a detailed list of signal/pin assignments on that interface. The pin you are about to remove should be labeled No Connection or N/C in that list. Use the old carpenter's maxim here—measure twice and cut once.

Connector and keying issues aside, the most common mishap with header-pin connectors occurs when you install the cable offset by a column or a row. The socketed male connectors used on most drives make this impossible to do, but the male connectors used on most motherboards and expansion cards are an unsocketed double row of pins, making it very easy to install the connector with the pins and holes misaligned. Working in a dark PC, it's very easy to slide a connector onto a set of header pins and end up with an unconnected pair of pins at one end and an unconnected pair of holes at the other. It's just as easy to misalign the connector the other way, and end up with an entire row of pins and holes unconnected.

Card-edge connectors, also called *edge-card connectors*, form a connection by sliding the female cable connector onto a formed portion of a PC circuit board that has contacts laid down on the circuit card itself to serve as the male connector. Card-edge connectors were commonly used to connect 5.25" floppy drives, floppy interface tape drives, and old-style ST506/412 hard drives, but are seldom used anymore because the physical and electrical connection they provide is inferior to that provided by a header-pin connector.

Card-edge connectors should be keyed on the male (circuit board) side by the presence of an off-center slot, and on the female (cable) side by the presence of a matching insert in the connector body to prevent the cable from being installed backwards. However, many card-edge connectors on cables do not have this keying insert, which makes it easy to install the cable backwards. Some male card-edge connectors do not have the keying slot, which makes it impossible to connect a properly keyed cable to them.

The only common problem with card-edge connectors arises when you need to connect a keyed cable to a device that has no keying slot. Male connectors without a keying slot sometimes have a pre-notched area on the circuit board that you can break away with your long-nose pliers to allow the keyed cable to seat. If not, you may be able to use your pliers to remove the keying insert from the cable connector. If neither of these solutions is workable, the only solution is to replace the cable with an unkeyed version.

Locating pin 1

If you upgrade your system and it fails to boot or the new device doesn't work, chances are you connected a ribbon cable backwards. This can't happen if all connectors and cables are keyed, but nearly all systems have at least some unkeyed connectors. The good news is that connecting ribbon cables backwards almost never damages anything. We're tempted to say "never" without qualification, but there's a first time for everything. If this happens to you, go back and verify the connections for each cable. Better yet, verify them before you restart the system.

 One of the experienced PC technicians who reviewed this book tells us that he has "burned up" more than one floppy disk drive by installing the cable with the pins offset. We have frequently installed FDD cables reversed, offset, and in any other combination you can imagine (it always seems easier to seat a cable by feel rather than to remove the drive and do it right) with no worse result than the system failing to boot. The FDD cable carries only signal-level voltages, so we're not sure how offsetting pins could damage a drive, but we'll certainly be more careful in the future.

To avoid connecting a ribbon cable backwards, locate pin 1 on each device and then make sure that pin 1 on one device connects to pin 1 on the other. This is sometimes easier said than done. Nearly all ribbon cables use a colored stripe to indicate pin 1, so there's little chance of confusion there. However, not all devices label pin 1. Those that do usually use a silk screened numeral 1 on the circuit board itself. If pin 1 is not labeled numerically, you can sometimes determine which is pin 1 in one of the following ways:

- Instead of a numeral, some manufacturers print a small arrow or triangle to indicate pin 1.

- The layout of some circuit boards allows no space for a label near pin 1. On these boards, the manufacturer may instead number the last pin. For example, rather than labeling pin 1 on an IDE connector, the manufacturer may label pin 40 on the other side of the connector.

- If there is no indication of pin 1 on the front of the board, turn it over (this is tough for an installed motherboard) and examine the reverse side. Some manufacturers use round solder connections for all pins other than 1, and a square solder connection for pin 1.

- If all else fails, you can make an educated guess. Many disk drives place pin 1 closest to the power supply connector. On a motherboard, pin 1 is often the one closest to the memory or processor. We freely admit that we use this method on occasion to avoid having to remove a disk drive or motherboard to locate pin 1 with certainty. We've never damaged a component using this quick-and-dirty method, but we use it only for IDE drives, rear-panel port connectors, and other cables that do not carry power. Don't try this with SCSI, particularly differential SCSI.

Once you locate an unmarked or unclearly marked pin 1, use nail polish or some other permanent means to mark it so you won't have to repeat the process the next time.

Power supply cables

PC power supply cables are fully described in Chapter 23, *Power Supplies*.

Setting Jumpers and DIP Switches

Jumpers and DIP switches are two methods commonly used to set hardware options on PCs and peripherals. Although they look different, jumpers and DIP switches perform the same function—allowing you to make or break a single electrical connection, which is used to configure one aspect of a component. Jumper or switch settings may specify such things as the amount of installed memory, the base address, IRQ, and DMA assigned to a device, whether a particular function is enabled or disabled, and so on.

Older PCs and expansion cards often contain dozens of these devices and use them to set most or all configuration options. Newer PCs typically use fewer jumpers and DIP switches, and instead use the BIOS setup program to configure components. In fact, many recent motherboards (e.g., the Intel Pentium II boards) have only one jumper. You close this jumper when you first install the board to allow such static options as the speed of the installed processor to be configured or to perform such infrequent actions as updating the Flash BIOS. That jumper is then opened for routine operation.

More properly called a *jumper block*, a *jumper* is a small plastic block with embedded metal contacts that may be used to bridge two pins to form an electrical connection. When a jumper block bridges two pins, that connection is called *on, closed, shorted,* or *enabled*. When the jumper block is removed, that connection is called *off, open,* or *disabled*. The pins themselves are also called jumpers, usually abbreviated *JPx*, where *x* is a number that identifies the jumper.

Jumpers with more than two pins may be used to select among more than two states. One common arrangement, shown in Figure 2-2, is a jumper that contains a row of three pins, numbered 1, 2, and 3. You can select among three states by shorting pins 1 and 2, pins 2 and 3, or by removing the jumper block entirely. Note that you cannot bridge pins 1 and 3 because a jumper can be used to close only an adjacent pair of pins.

You can often use your fingers to install and remove isolated jumpers, but needle-nose pliers are usually the best tool. However, jumpers are sometimes clustered so tightly that even needle-nose pliers may be too large to grab just the jumper you want to work on. When this happens, use your hemostat. When you open a jumper, don't remove the jumper block entirely. Instead, install it on just one pin. This leaves the connection open, but ensures that a jumper block will be handy if you later need to close that connection.

Jumper blocks come in at least two sizes that are not interchangeable. Standard blocks are the largest and the most commonly used, and are usually black. Mini jumper blocks are used on some disk drives and boards that use surface-mount

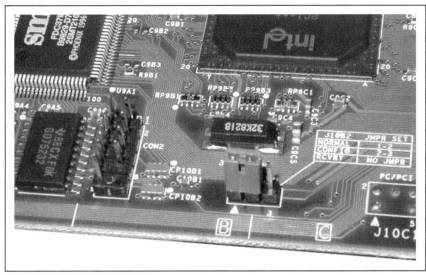

Figure 2-2: A typical 3-pin jumper (bottom center) set to close pins 1 and 2

components, and are often white or light blue. One of our technical reviewers reports that Quantum uses still a third size, which we'll deem "micro" jumper blocks, on some of their drive models. He reports that these tiny blocks disappear when dropped, cling like a burr to jumper pins, and are extremely hard to work with, even when using fine tweezers. New components always come with enough jumper blocks to configure them. If we remove one when configuring a device, we usually tape it to a convenient flat area on the device for possible future use. It's also a good idea to keep a few spares on hand, just in case you need to reconfigure a component from which someone has removed all the "surplus" jumper blocks. Any time you discard a board or disk drive, strip the jumper blocks from it first and store them in your parts tube.

A *DIP switch*, shown in Figure 2-3, is a small plastic block that contains one or more (usually four or eight) individual slide or rocker switches. Each of these individual switches performs the same function as a jumper block. Turning an individual switch on is equivalent to installing a jumper block, and turning it off is equivalent to removing the jumper block. DIP switches are labeled *SWx*, where *x* is a number that identifies the switch block. Each individual switch within the block is also numbered.

Figure 2-3: DIP switch (on and off)

The "on" position may be indicated by the word *On, Close, Short,* or *Enable* printed on one side of the switch, or by an arrow pointing to the on side. Turn on a rocker switch by depressing the side of the switch or the raised nub toward the on side. Turn on a slide switch by sliding the nub toward the on side.

Working with Expansion Cards

Expansion cards are circuit boards that you install in a PC to provide functions that the PC motherboard itself does not provide. For example, most motherboards don't include video circuitry. PCs built with such motherboards use a separate video adapter expansion card to provide it. Internal modems, sound cards, network adapters, and disk controllers are other commonly used expansion cards. Figure 2-4 shows a typical expansion card.

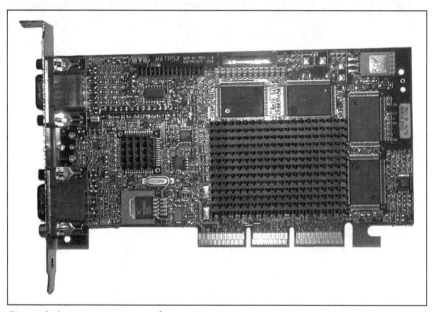

Figure 2-4: An expansion card

Each expansion card plugs into an *expansion slot* located on the motherboard or on a *riser card* that attaches to the motherboard. The rear panel of the PC chassis includes a cutout for each expansion slot, which provides external access to the card. The cutouts for vacant expansion slots are covered by thin metal *slot covers* that are secured to the chassis. These covers prevent dust from entering through the cutout and also preserve the cooling air flow provided by the power supply fan and any auxiliary fans installed in the system.

To install an expansion card, you remove the slot cover, which may be secured by a small screw or may simply be die-stamped into the surrounding metal. In the latter case, carefully twist off the slot cover using a screwdriver or your needle-nose pliers. If you need to replace the slot cover later, secure it to the chassis using a small screw that fits a notch in the top portion of the slot cover. The back of the expansion card forms a bracket that resembles a slot cover and is secured to the chassis in the same way. Depending on the purpose of the card, this bracket may contain connectors that allow you to connect external cables to the card.

 Cheap cases sometimes have slot covers that must be twisted off to be removed and are destroyed in the process. If you need to cover an open slot in such a case and don't have a spare slot cover, ask your local computer store, which probably has a stack of them in back.

Installing and removing expansion cards is by far the most common activity you'll perform when working on PCs. Even if you are not working on a particular expansion card, you must sometimes remove it to provide access to the section of the PC that you do need to work on. Installing and removing expansion cards may be hard or easy, depending on the quality of the case, the motherboard and the expansion card itself. High quality cases, motherboards, and expansion cards are built to tight tolerances, making expansion cards easy to insert and remove. Cheap cases, motherboards, and expansion cards have such loose tolerances that you must sometimes literally bend sheet metal to force them to fit.

People often ask whether it matters which card goes into which slot. Beyond the obvious—there are different kinds of expansion slots, and a card can be installed only in a slot of the same type—there are four considerations that determine the answer to this question:

Physical restrictions
Depending on the size of the card and the design of the motherboard and case, a given card may or may not physically fit a particular slot. For example, a protruding drive bay, memory module, or processor may prevent a slot from accepting a full-length card. If this occurs, you may have to juggle expansion cards, moving a shorter card from a full-length slot to a short slot and then using the freed-up full-length slot for the new expansion card. Also, even if a card physically fits a particular slot, a connector protruding from that card may interfere with another card, or there may not be enough room to route a cable to it.

Technical restrictions
There are several variables, including slot type, card type, BIOS, and operating system that determine whether a card is position sensitive. We'll describe the different bus and slot types in Chapter 3, *Motherboards*, but for now it's enough to know that ISA cards are not slot sensitive, but EISA cards (used in older servers) and PCI cards may be. For this reason, although it may not always be possible, it's good practice to reinstall a card into the same slot that you removed it from.

Electrical considerations
Although it is relatively uncommon nowadays, some combinations of motherboard and power supply can provide adequate power for power-hungry expansion cards like internal modems only if those cards are installed in the slots nearest the power supply. This was a common problem years ago, when

power supplies were less robust and cards required more power than they do now, but you are unlikely to experience this problem with modern equipment.

Interference considerations

Another problem that is much less common with recent equipment is that some expansion cards generate enough RF to interfere with cards in adjacent slots. Years ago, the manuals for some cards (notably some disk controllers, modems, and network adapters) described this problem, and suggested that their card be installed as far as possible from other cards. We haven't seen this sort of warning on a new card in years, but you may still encounter it if your system includes older cards.

Inserting expansion cards

To insert an expansion card, proceed as follows:

1. Remove the cover from the chassis and examine the motherboard to determine which expansion slots are free. Locate a free expansion slot of the type required by the expansion card (expansion slot types are detailed in Chapter 3). New PCs may have several types of expansion slots available, including ISA, PCI, combination ISA/PCI, and AGP. Older PCs may have other types of unused expansion slots, including VLB and EISA. If more than one slot of the proper type is free, you can reduce the likelihood of heat-related problems by choosing one that maintains spacing between the expansion cards rather than one that clusters the cards.

2. An access hole for each expansion slot is present on the rear of the chassis. For unoccupied slots, this hole is blocked by a thin metal slot cover secured by a screw that threads downward into the chassis. Determine which slot cover corresponds to the slot you chose. This may not be as simple as it sounds. Some types of expansion slots are offset, and the slot cover that appears to line up with that slot may not be the right one. You can verify which slot cover corresponds to a slot by aligning the expansion card itself with the slot and seeing which slot cover the card bracket matches.

3. Remove the screw that secures the slot cover, slide the slot cover out, and place it and the screw aside.

4. If an internal cable blocks access to the slot, gently move it aside or disconnect it temporarily, noting the proper connections so that you will know where to reconnect them.

5. Guide the expansion card gently into position, but do not yet seat it. Verify visually that the tongue on the bottom of the expansion card bracket will slide into the matching gap in the chassis and that the expansion card bus connector section aligns properly with the expansion slot.

6. When you are sure that everything is properly aligned, position your thumbs on the top edge of the card, with one thumb at each end of the expansion slot below the card, and press gently straight down on the top of the card until it is seated in the slot. Apply pressure centered on the expansion slot beneath the card, and avoid twisting or torquing the card. Some cards can be seated easily with little tactile feedback. Others require quite a bit of pressure and you can

feel them snap into place. Once you complete this step, the expansion card bracket should align properly with the screw hole in the chassis.

7. Replace the screw that secures the expansion card bracket, and replace any cables that you temporarily disconnected while installing the card. Connect any external cables required by the new card—don't tighten the thumbscrews quite yet—and give the system a quick once-over to make sure you haven't forgotten to do anything.

8. Turn on the PC and verify that the new card is recognized and that it functions as expected. Once you have done so, power the system down, replace the cover, and reconnect everything. Store the unused slot cover with your spares.

Removing expansion cards

To remove an expansion card, proceed as follows:

1. Remove the system cover and locate the expansion card to be removed. It's surprising how easy it is to remove the wrong card if you're not careful. No wonder surgeons occasionally get it wrong.

2. Once you're sure you've located the right card, disconnect any external cables connected to it. If the card has internal cables connected, disconnect those as well. You may also need to disconnect or reroute other unrelated cables temporarily to gain access to the card. If so, label those you disconnect.

3. Remove the screw that secures the card bracket, and place it safely aside.

4. Grasp the card firmly near both ends and pull straight up with moderate force. If the card will not release, *gently* rock it from front-to-back (*not* from side-to-side) to break the connection. Be careful when grasping the card. Some cards have sharp solder points that can cut you badly if you don't take precautions. If there's no safe place to grasp the card and you don't have a pair of heavy gloves handy, try using heavy corrugated cardboard between the card and your skin.

5. If you plan to save the card, place it in an anti-static bag for storage. If you are not installing a new expansion card in the vacated slot, install a slot cover to ensure proper air flow and replace the screw that secures the slot cover.

 You may encounter an expansion card that's seated so tightly that it appears to be welded to the motherboard. When this happens, it's tempting to gain some leverage by pressing upwards with your thumb on a connector on the back of the card bracket. Don't do it. The edges of the chassis against which the bracket sits are often razor sharp, and you may cut yourself badly when the card finally gives. Instead, loop two pieces of cord around the card to the front and rear of the slot itself, and use them to "walk" the card out of its slot. We've used shoelaces for this purpose when nothing else was at hand. For a card that's well and truly stuck, you may need a second pair of hands to apply downward pressure on the motherboard itself to prevent it from flexing too much and possibly cracking.

CHAPTER 3

Motherboards

The *motherboard* is the heart of a PC. Some manufacturers use the terms *system board*, *planar board*, *baseboard*, or *main board*, and Intel has recently begun calling their motherboards *desktop boards*. No matter what you call it, the motherboard defines the PC. It provides the common link to all other components inside the PC, including the CPU, memory, disk drives, video and sound adapters, keyboard, mouse, and other peripheral components. If you are building a PC, choosing the motherboard is the most important decision you will make and can be one of the most difficult. If you are upgrading a PC, replacing the motherboard is often the best and most cost-efficient means of doing so. This chapter describes the characteristics of motherboards, provides purchasing guidelines, and explains how to install and configure a motherboard.

Motherboard Characteristics

Several characteristics differentiate motherboards, including physical characteristics, which in combination are called the form factor; the chipset used, which defines the capabilities of the motherboard; the processors the motherboard supports; the BIOS it uses; and the internal and expansion buses that it supports. The following sections examine each of these factors.

Form Factor

Motherboards differ in size, shape, position of mounting holes, power supply connector type, and port types and locations. Together, these differences define the *form factor* of the motherboard. Form factor is a critical issue when you upgrade a system, because the replacement motherboard must physically fit the case and use the existing power supply connectors. Form factor doesn't matter when you're building a new PC. You simply select the best motherboard for your needs, and then buy a case that fits it. Many motherboard manufacturers build essentially identical motherboards in different form factors. Here are the form factors you may encounter:

AT, Baby AT (BAT), and LPX

All of these form factors are based on the motherboard used in the original 1984 IBM PC AT and are now obsolescent or, in the case of LPX, obsolete. Although it is still possible to buy AT and BAT motherboards, selection is limited (for example, Athlon motherboards are not available in these form factors) and most AT and BAT motherboards do not include the latest chipsets and other technologies. The only reason to purchase an AT or BAT motherboard is to upgrade an existing system without replacing the power supply and case, which is a minor savings. We recommend not purchasing a motherboard in any of these form factors.

ATX and variants

Nearly all current motherboards use the -ATX form factor, or one of its smaller variants, the miniATX, μATX, flexATX, and NLX. For a complete discussion of these form factors, including case and power supply issues, see Chapter 22, *Cases.*

Proprietary

Although it is much less common nowadays to find new systems that use proprietary motherboards, such boards were relatively common a few years ago, particularly in systems sold by major manufacturers like Compaq and IBM. A cynical observer might believe that the major manufacturers did this to lock customers in. In fact, it probably had more to do with the fact that the then-current Baby AT standard had reached the end of its useful life and the ATX standard had not yet become the obvious successor. To reduce manufacturing costs and increase reliability, manufacturers that had the in-house engineering talent to do so designed their own motherboards. Some of these are actually very elegantly designed. They all share one fatal flaw, however: they aren't standard. Any system that uses a proprietary motherboard form factor is effectively not upgradable.

Chipsets

Just as the motherboard defines a PC, the chipset defines a motherboard. The chipset determines the main characteristics of the motherboard—what processors it supports, what RAM types it can use, what bus types and speeds it supports, whether it supports current standards like AGP and USB, and so on.

There are scores of motherboard manufacturers, but only a handful of chipset manufacturers. This is true because designing a chipset requires significant engineering resources, but building a motherboard around that chipset is straightforward. Chipset manufacturers want motherboard manufacturers to buy their chipsets, so they provide detailed specifications and engineering drawings, which makes building motherboards more a matter of production than design.

Understanding chipset basics is important whether you are upgrading an existing PC or building a new one. If you are upgrading, understanding the chipset tells you what can and cannot be done within its limitations. It also helps you avoid useless or counterproductive upgrades. For example, the Intel 430TX Pentium chipset supports 256 MB RAM but caches only 64 MB, so adding more than 64 MB to a 430TX system can actually make it slower. If you are building or buying a new PC, its chipset is the most important factor in determining motherboard performance and future upgradability. Understanding the differences between competing chipsets lets you make rational decisions about which computer or motherboard to buy. Because chipsets are so important, we've devoted a great deal of space to explaining what you need to know about them.

CPU family support

Standard chipsets support only one CPU family—486 and similar fourth-generation CPUs, Pentium and compatible fifth-generation CPUs, or Pentium Pro/Pentium II/Pentium III/Celeron sixth-generation CPUs. This is true because processor families differ greatly in how they access and manage main memory, cache, and other major system components. For example, while fifth-generation CPUs use separate L2 cache memory on the motherboard, sixth-generation CPUs have L2 cache within the processor package or integrated on-die.

A given chipset may support most or all CPUs within a family, or may support only one of them. For example, some chipsets support both the Celeron and Pentium III sixth-generation CPUs, while others support only one or the other. Most chipsets designed for the Pentium also support compatible processors like the AMD K5 and K6 and the Cyrix 6x86 and 6x86MX, which were designed as pin-compatible, although using one of these CPUs may require different motherboard jumper settings and chipset CMOS parameters than those used for a genuine Pentium.

However, recent Pentium-compatible CPUs have sixth-generation features that are not supported by older chipsets, particularly Intel chipsets. Processors like the AMD K6-2/III and the Cyrix 6x86MX are sixth-generation internally, but physically fit fifth-generation motherboards. To encourage migration to the Pentium II, Intel stopped developing fifth-generation chipsets. Third-party chipset manufacturers, notably VIA, SiS, and ALi, took up the slack by introducing enhanced fifth-generation chipsets called Super Socket 7 chipsets. Using these chipsets allowed manufacturers to build motherboards that supported features not supported by Intel fifth-generation chipsets, like AGP.

CPU speed support

A chipset that supports a particular CPU may support all or only some of the speeds that that CPU is available in. In general, faster CPUs require faster chipsets, so you might imagine that a chipset rated to handle the fastest version of a particular CPU could also handle all slower versions of that CPU. That's not always the case, however. You configure a motherboard for a particular CPU speed using two settings, *memory bus speed* and *CPU multiplier.*

Memory bus speed

The speed at which the CPU communicates with system memory. Intel Pentium-class chipsets support Intel's official *memory bus* speeds of 50 MHz, 60 MHz, and 66 MHz. Third-party chipsets also support these standard speeds, and may also support other speeds, including 75 MHz, 83 MHz, 90 MHz, 95 MHz, 100 MHz, and 112 MHz. All sixth-generation chipsets support a 66 MHz memory bus speed, which is called *Front Side Bus* (*FSB*) speed on sixth-generation systems. Later versions may also support 100 MHz and 133 MHz, along with various intermediate speeds.

For many motherboards, including all Intel motherboards and most third-party motherboards, setting the memory bus speed also specifies the PCI bus speed. These motherboards, called *synchronous motherboards*, divide the memory bus speed by a fixed factor to determine PCI bus speed. For 50 MHz, 60 MHz, and 66 MHz memory bus speeds, the divisor is 2.0, which runs the PCI bus at 25 MHz, 30 MHz, and 33 MHz, respectively. For a 100 MHz bus, the divisor is 3.0, which runs the PCI bus at 33.3 MHz. For 133 MHz, the divisor is 4.0, which also runs the PCI bus at 33.3 MHz.

Some third-party motherboards, called *asynchronous motherboards*, allow memory bus speed and PCI bus speed to be set independently, usually by means of jumpers on the motherboard. They do this to allow using faster memory bus speeds while limiting PCI bus speeds to 33 MHz, which is the fastest reliable setting for the PCI bus. Otherwise, for example, setting the memory bus to 75 MHz would run the PCI bus at 37.5 MHz—too fast for reliability—and setting the memory bus to 83 MHz would run the PCI bus at a completely unusable 41.5 MHz.

CPU multiplier
Specifies the multiple of memory bus speed at which the CPU runs internally. Modern chipsets may support CPU multipliers from 1.5x to 10.0x or higher. For example, a 90 MHz Pentium CPU uses a 60 MHz memory bus speed and a 1.5x CPU multiplier, while a 733 MHz Pentium III uses a 133 MHz memory bus speed and a 5.5x CPU multiplier. All recent Intel CPUs have a locked multiplier, which means the only way to run them faster than their rated speed is to set the FSB for something above nominal. AMD CPUs are not multiplier locked.

You can generally determine the range of CPU speeds supported by a chipset and motherboard by examining the different memory bus speeds and CPU multipliers that it supports. For example, a typical Pentium motherboard may provide nominal memory bus speeds of 50, 60, and 66 MHz (actually, 50.0, 60.0, and 66.6 MHz), and CPU multipliers of 1.0, 1.5, 2.0, 2.5, and 3.0x. This motherboard will support Pentiums running at 75 MHz (50×1.5); 90 MHz (60×1.5); 100 MHz (66×1.5); 120 MHz (60×2.0); 133 MHz (66×2.0); 150 MHz (60×2.5); 166 MHz (66×2.5); and 200 MHz (66×3.0). The motherboard could also be configured for speeds for which no processors are available, e.g., 180 MHz (60×3.0x).

You may also have a choice of two or more speed/multiplier combinations to use. For example, you could install a 100 MHz CPU on this system board using either 66 MHz with a 1.5 multiplier or 50 MHz with a 2.0 multiplier. Generally, use the combination that uses the fastest memory bus speed, which provides faster performance. However, sometimes it makes sense to choose a slower memory bus speed. For example, you may install a 450 MHz CPU and memory that is allegedly rated for 100 MHz, but find that the system is unreliable using 100 MHz and 4.5x. Changing to 90 MHz and 5.0x may allow the system to run reliably at nearly the same performance level as the unreliable settings of 100 MHz and 4.5x.

Not all motherboards allow these two parameters to be set independently. Many boards, including Intel boards, allow you to set only CPU speed, which in turn selects a predetermined combination of memory bus speed and CPU multiplier. This is done to prevent *overclocking*, or running the CPU at higher than its rated speed, a practice that Intel naturally discourages. Intel's most recent boards have no user-accessible speed settings at all, depending on the CPU to identify itself to the motherboard and set the speed accordingly.

Some motherboards limit CPU speed by their choice of CPU sockets. For example, 166 MHz and faster Pentium CPUs do not physically fit Socket 5 motherboards, so although the chipset may support faster speeds, the socket prevents faster processors from being installed. Also note that the nominal speed of some Intel-compatible CPUs is inaccurate. This is not due to error, but because some manufacturers, notably Cyrix, label processors with *performance ratings* rather than actual speeds, intending to convey an approximate Pentium-equivalent performance level rather than the actual chip speed. For example, the Cyrix 6x86 PR166+ CPU supposedly provides performance similar to that of a 166 MHz Intel Pentium, but actually runs at 133 MHz, and should be jumpered accordingly. Running it at 166 MHz results in unreliable operation at best.

Multiple CPU support

Some chipsets support motherboard configurations with multiple CPU sockets. These chipsets coordinate operations between the multiple processors and memory, which is necessary but not sufficient to allow *symmetric multiprocessing* (*SMP*) operation. In addition to chipset support, SMP requires:

CPU SMP support
Non-Intel CPUs other than the AMD Athlon lack the necessary circuitry to support SMP. With minor exceptions, all current Intel CPUs support SMP. Intel says officially that Celerons do not support SMP, but as of Q2/2000, all shipping Celerons can in fact be used in a dual-CPU environment. That may soon change, however.

Operating system SMP support
DOS, Windows 3.x, and Windows 9X do not support SMP. Running one of these operating systems on an SMP PC uses only one of the CPUs. Windows NT/2000 supports SMP, as do some Intel-based Unix implementations, including Linux.

If you run an SMP-aware operating system and are buying a Pentium III motherboard, buy one that supports dual CPUs. The incremental cost is generally small, and the increased performance is significant. In particular, note that Intel's pricing strategy often makes buying two low- to mid-range CPUs less expensive than buying one top-of-the-line CPU. For example, in June 2000, the fastest Intel Pentium III shipping in quantity was the 733 MHz, at about $500, whereas the Pentium III/550 was widely available for about $230. In other words, a single-CPU motherboard with one 733 MHz Pentium III CPU cost about the same as a dual-CPU motherboard with two 550 MHz Pentium III CPUs. The dual-CPU motherboard will provide much better overall performance for most Windows NT/2000 and Linux users.

If you need to upgrade an existing single processor system to dual CPUs and the exact model CPU you currently use is no longer available, see the detailed Intel Processor Specification Update (*http:// developer.intel.com/design/processor/*) for a matrix of which currently available processors can be mixed and matched. In general, the safest course is to use two processors with identical S-Specs (Intel's identifying number for minor variations of a processor), but processors with different S-Specs can sometimes be used together in an SMP system, with some restrictions.

Memory and cache support

Chipsets vary significantly in the support they offer for memory and cache, as follows:

Maximum system memory
Every chipset places an absolute limit on the amount of RAM that it supports. For recent and current chipsets, this limit ranges from as low as 64 MB to as much as 4 GB or more. Chipsets also limit the number of memory sockets, which, in conjunction with available memory densities, may enforce a usable memory limit much lower than the theoretical limit.

Memory type
RAM is available in a bewildering array of form factors (e.g., SIMM, DIMM, RIMM), access types (e.g., FPM, EDO, SDRAM, RDRAM), logical types (e.g., registered, buffered), voltages, densities (e.g., 4M×72), error correction (parity, non-parity, or ECC) and so on. Different chipsets support different combinations of these characteristics. Some chipsets optimize their performance with one type of RAM at the expense of performance with other types, so make sure if your chipset supports different RAM types that you choose the type for which it is optimized. Most motherboards that support more than one type of RAM are "transition" motherboards—produced during a shift from one type of RAM to another—and are usually optimized for the earlier type of memory. For example, many motherboards that support both EDO SIMMs, EDO DIMMs, and SDRAM DIMMs are optimized for EDO. If in doubt, check the motherboard documentation.

Choose a chipset that supports the RAM characteristics you require. If you are buying RAM for an existing motherboard, make sure that RAM is of a type supported by the chipset. In the past, when memory cost $50 a megabyte, making sure that a replacement motherboard could use your existing RAM was a major issue. Nowadays, with RAM at about $1 per megabyte, this is a much less important issue.

Secondary (L2) cache size and type
Even the fastest standard memory is much too slow to keep pace with a modern CPU. To prevent the CPU from spending most of its time waiting for data to be read from main memory, modern chipsets support secondary (also called level 2 or L2) cache. L2 cache is a relatively small amount of very fast

(and expensive) memory that sits between the CPU and main memory, buffering requests. Sixth-generation CPUs like the Pentium III, Celeron, and Athlon embed L2 cache in the CPU package itself or actually place it on-die with the CPU. Fifth-generation CPUs, including the Pentium, and hybrid CPUs like the AMD K6 and Cyrix 6x86 depend on discrete cache installed on the motherboard.

Cache size

Most fifth-generation chipsets support 256 KB or 512 KB of L2 cache, although some support only 128 KB. All other things being equal, the larger the L2 cache, the faster the system will be. Many motherboards whose chipsets support 512 KB L2 cache have less than that installed. If you are doing a minor motherboard upgrade, such as replacing a 100 MHz Pentium with a 200 MHz Pentium, upgrading the cache at the same time is inexpensive and can increase performance noticeably, particularly if the system currently has little or no cache RAM installed. Size is not an issue for sixth-generation chipsets, which support the cache size embedded on the processor.

Cache type

Pentium-class chipsets support one or more cache types. In increasing order of performance and desirability, they are: *asynchronous, synchronous burst,* and *pipeline burst*. The policy that L2 cache uses to write data also differs. *Write-through cache* writes changes immediately to both the L2 cache and main memory to preserve coherence. With Write-back cache, the CPU writes changes to L2 cache, but not directly to main memory. This provides higher performance, at the expense of requiring additional circuitry to maintain coherence between main memory and L2 cache. Cache type is not an issue for sixth-generation chipsets, which support the cache type used by the processor.

Cacheable memory

Sixth-generation chipsets all support a cacheable memory area larger than the amount of memory that can be physically installed with current technology. Fifth-generation chipsets differ in the maximum amount of main memory they can support with the L2 cache. This figure is unrelated to the maximum amount of main memory that the chipset supports, but may vary with the amount of L2 cache installed. For example, the three Pentium-class chipsets that you are most likely to encounter are the Intel 430HX (Triton II); the 430VX (Triton III); and the current 430TX. The 430HX supports 512 MB main memory, all of which it can cache; the 430VX supports 128 MB, but can cache only 64 MB; the 430TX supports 256 MB, but can cache only 64 MB. Although the 430HX chipset itself can theoretically cache up to 512 MB of main memory, the amount that it can cache in practice depends on the amount of cache RAM installed on the motherboard. Most 430HX motherboards include the full amount of TAG RAM needed to cache 512 MB, but some do not. *Never* install more RAM on a motherboard than it can cache. Doing so can actually make the motherboard slower than it was before you added RAM.

Chipset buffers

One important duty of the chipset is to arbitrate transfer of data between the CPU, memory, and the local bus. Many factors determine how efficient such transfers are, including the quality of the chipset itself, the CPU type and speed, and the size and type of the L2 cache. Because many components are involved, which operate at widely different speeds, managing these transfers efficiently is critical to fast transfers and overall system performance.

When the CPU requests data from main memory, the chipset first determines if that data is already available in L2 cache. If so, it retrieves it from cache—which is much faster than main memory—and sends it to the CPU. If the data is not cached, the chipset retrieves it from main memory, sends it to the CPU, and also writes it to the cache (in case the CPU requests the same data in the near future). The timing of these transfers is controlled by the chipset, and some chipsets are better than others in any particular memory/cache/CPU environment.

Besides CPU-RAM transfers, the chipset also manages CPU-PCI transfers and PCI-RAM transfers. On systems with AGP video, the chipset also handles direct transfers between the CPU and the AGP video adapter. Nor are these transfers purely sequential. At any moment, the chipset may be arbitrating many transfers simultaneously. With many components doing different things at the same time and at different speeds, it's up to the chipset to juggle all of these conflicting demands for attention. One way it accommodates these demands is by using buffers to store data temporarily while other operations are in progress. Chipsets vary in the number of buffers they have available for various purposes, and how efficient those buffers are.

Memory timing

Because there is a huge disparity between CPU speed and main memory speed, the CPU must sometimes wait one or more clock cycles for memory to supply the data it requests. These enforced periods of CPU inactivity are called *wait states*, and the goal of any chipset is to minimize them. Wait states cannot be completely avoided, however, unless memory is fast enough to keep pace with the CPU, an impossible state of affairs given the extremely high cost of very fast memory and the absolute limitations on the speed of conventional memory. Using fast main memory and a large, fast, efficient L2 cache can minimize wait states, but can never completely eliminate them.

When L2 cache is temporarily unable to supply the data needed by the CPU, the chipset inserts a wait state—basically a command to the processor to twiddle its thumbs until the data it requested becomes available. Cache reads and writes data in 32-byte chunks called *lines*, but main memory is accessed in 64-bit (8-byte) increments, so it takes four separate memory read or write operations to transfer a cache line. The first operation is the slowest, because the memory address must be looked up and accessed before the first transfer can occur, a delay called *latency*. The next three transfers are much faster, because data is read from or written to sequential contiguous memory addresses based on the address used for the first transfer, eliminating latency.

These differing memory timings are specified in the form X-Y-Y-Y, where X is the number of clock cycles required for the first transfer (with latency) and Y the clock cycles required for the remaining transfers. This pattern varies according to the particular chipset, the memory bus speed, and the type of memory. For example, the Intel 430VX chipset using FPM RAM uses 5-3-3-3 timing at 60 MHz, and 6-3-3-3 timing at 66 MHz, while the later 430TX uses 4-3-3-3 and 5-3-3-3 respectively. With EDO RAM, the 430VX timings are 5-2-2-2 (60 MHz) and 6-2-2-2 (66 MHz), and the 430TX timings are 4-2-2-2 (60 MHz) and 5-2-2-2 (66 MHz). With BEDO or SDRAM, the 430VX 60/66 MHz and 430TX 60/66 MHz timings are 6-1-1-1/7-1-1-1 and 5-1-1-1/ 5-1-1-1, respectively.

Some BIOS chipset setup programs allow you to select only among predefined memory timings. For these setup programs, you choose a single memory timing setting. Other setup programs allow you to specify timing for the initial access independently of the timing for subsequent accesses. For these setup programs, you choose two separate settings. The first, in the form X-2-2-2, allows you to specify a value for X that sets timing for the initial access. The second, in the form 4-Y-Y-Y, allows you to specify a single value that will be used for all subsequent accesses. With either type of chipset setup program, choose the fastest timing supported by your chipset and memory.

Recent chipsets, including all sixth-generation chipsets, automatically detect the type, size, speed, and optimal timing settings for installed memory, and configure it accordingly, a process called *memory autodetection*. To do so, however, they require help from the memory itself. RAM that supports autodetection does so using a feature called *Serial Presence Detect* (*SPD*). SPD uses an EEPROM that is physically a part of the RAM module to store information about the type and configuration of that module. All current sixth-generation chipsets are optimized for SDRAM, except the Intel 820 and 840, which are optimized for RDRAM.

I/O bus support

The chipset determines what I/O bus standards the motherboard can support. The chipset manages the I/O buses, arbitrating data transfer between them, the CPU, and system memory. The chipset features determine which I/O buses the system supports, the speed at which the buses operate, and what additional related system features are supported. Depending on how you count, half a dozen or more I/O bus standards have been in common use since the first PCs. In order of their appearance, they include:

Industry Standard Architecture (ISA)
Used in 8-bit form in the PC and XT and 16-bit form in the PC/AT. Obsolete, but most current motherboards provide ISA slots for legacy cards. The latest "legacy-free" motherboards do not include ISA slots.

MicroChannel Architecture (MCA)
An IBM standard that never caught on. Obsolete.

Extended Industry Standard Architecture (EISA)
An open standard developed by Compaq and eight other PC makers (the so-called "Gang of Nine") to compete with the propriety MCA, but which achieved only limited acceptance, primarily in servers. Obsolete.

VESA Local Bus (VLB)
An open standard that was widely used in 486 systems, but whose technical shortcomings made it inappropriate for Pentium and later systems. Obsolete.

Peripheral Component Interconnect (PCI)
An open standard developed by Intel, used on late-model 486 systems and almost universally for Pentium and later systems. Older PCI systems use the PCI 2.0 standard, which limits upgrade possibilities. Newer systems use PCI 2.1, and the most recent use PCI 2.2.

Accelerated Graphics Port (AGP)
A dedicated I/O port used on late-model fifth-generation and most sixth-generation motherboards to provide high-performance graphics. Not technically a bus, because it supports only one device, but thought of as a bus because it is implemented as an expansion slot.

Most recent motherboards provide a mix of 16-bit ISA and PCI expansion slots, usually a few of each, and one shared ISA/PCI slot that can accept either type of expansion card. The chipset provides bridging functions between these I/O buses (the PCI–ISA bridge) and between I/O buses and other system buses, including the memory bus. The very latest motherboards have no ISA slots at all, and contain only PCI slots and perhaps an AGP slot.

Embedded feature support

The chipset also provides various embedded low-level system functions and features. Many low-level system functions, e.g., the Programmable Interrupt Controller (PIC), are well-standardized and have been so for years, so there is little choice among different chipsets on that basis. Chipset features differ not so much between competing chipset models as between generations. The following features are important when evaluating the upgradability of a motherboard that uses an older chipset:

ATA interface
Any modern motherboard provides an embedded dual-channel ATA/ATAPI interface, which supports a total of four ATA/ATAPI devices, two per channel. But not all embedded ATA interfaces are equal. All current motherboards support at least ATA/33, most support ATA/66, and some support the proposed ATA/100 standard, which is likely to be superceded by the forthcoming Serial ATA standard. Current hard disks cannot saturate even an ATA/33 interface, but choosing a chipset that supports at least ATA/66 makes future hard disk upgrades easier. If you are upgrading a system with an old motherboard, the chipset should support at least PIO-4 and *independent device timing*, which allows two dissimilar devices on one channel to both run at their optimal speed. If you are upgrading a system that uses an otherwise suitable older motherboard that does not support these features, you can disable the embedded ATA interface and install an ATA expansion card that supports recent ATA standards.

DMA controller and DMA mode support
Direct Memory Access (DMA) is a means to transfer data between devices without using the CPU as an intermediary, which can then increase system

performance. For example, a hard drive can use DMA to transfer data to and from memory without passing it through the CPU, allowing the CPU to do other things at the same time. DMA can be implemented using the DMA controller on the motherboard itself (called *first-party DMA*) or by using a DMA controller embedded on a device (called *third-party DMA* or *bus mastering DMA*). Newer chipsets typically provide additional DMA modes, faster DMA transfers, and DMA capability on all expansion slots.

Plug-N-Play (PnP) support

The PnP standard is closely linked to the PCI standard. Systems that have chipsets, BIOSes, peripherals, and operating systems that are PnP-aware recognize and configure installed hardware automatically, eliminating IRQ, I/O base address, and DMA resource conflicts. A system that uses a non-PnP chipset is too old to upgrade other than by a motherboard replacement.

Universal Serial Bus (USB) support

USB will eventually replace legacy I/O port standards, including serial, parallel, keyboard, and mouse ports. Most motherboards shipped since 1996 use chipsets that are USB 1.0 or 1.1-compliant. All current chipsets include USB support. None as yet support the USB 2.0 standard, which increases maximum data rates forty-fold to 480 MB/s. To use USB on an older system, install a $25 PCI USB card—the ADS Technologies USB Port (*http://www.adstech.com*) is one we've used successfully—or replace the motherboard with one whose chipset provides native USB support.

 Your motherboard may have "hidden" USB support. Most AT form factor motherboards made after 1996 have USB support, but only as sets of header pins on the motherboard. Using USB on these motherboards requires adding a port extender to route USB signals from the motherboard to the back panel. Such port extenders are readily available for $5 to $10 from motherboard makers and computer stores.

Accelerated Graphics Port (AGP) support

dAGP provides a fast, dedicated channel between the CPU and an AGP video adapter, moving video data off the memory bus. Because AGP is implemented as an expansion slot, any AGP-capable motherboard by definition uses an AGP-capable chipset and provides an AGP slot. But the AGP standard specifies different modes, including 1x, 2x, and 4x, not all of which are implemented in all chipsets. AGP 1x is obsolete, although you can use an AGP 2x or 4x adapter in an AGP 1x motherboard. Most current motherboards provide AGP 2x support, and the latest provide AGP 4x support, which is of questionable benefit. When you buy a motherboard, make sure it has support for at least AGP 2x mode.

Identifying chipsets

To make upgrade decisions based on chipset, you must identify which chipset you have. If you are buying a new motherboard, this is straightforward. The motherboard specifications always list the chipset. When you upgrade an existing system, determining which chipset it uses can be difficult. You can identify the chipset in one of the following ways:

- If you have the documentation for the system board or the PC, the chipset it uses will be listed in the detailed specifications. If you do not have the documentation, but can identify the make and model of the PC or motherboard, the manufacturer's web site should list the chipset it uses.

- Use a third-party diagnostics program like CheckIt (*http://www.checkit.com*) or SiSoft Sandra (*http://www.sisoft.co.uk*) to display system information. Figure 3-1 shows the results of running CheckIt 98 on an old Pentium/133 system. If you have no documentation, using a diagnostic utility is by far the easiest way to identify the chipset.

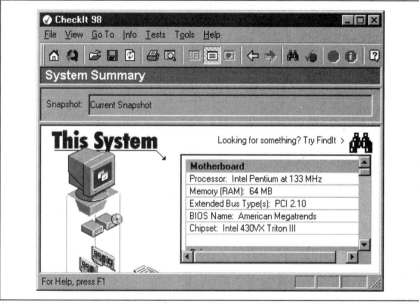

Figure 3-1: CheckIt 98 displays the chipset type (Intel 430VX Triton III) used by this elderly Pentium/133 motherboard

 Windows-based diagnostics programs either do not run or provide very limited functionality under Windows NT/2000, both of which limit access of applications to underlying hardware. If your system runs NT/2000, the best alternative is to boot DOS on it and run a DOS-based diagnostic utility.

- Identify the chipset visually by examining the motherboard. Most chipsets have two chips, although some have only one and a few have three or more. Look for relatively large, usually square chips that are labeled with the name of a chipset manufacturer—Intel, VIA, SiS, ALi, Opti, etc. Record the string of numbers and letters that identifies each such chip. Then visit that manufacturer's web site and search for those strings to determine which chipset, if any, those chips belong to. For example, if you locate an Intel chip labeled 82438VX, a quick check of the Intel web site tells you that that chip is part of an Intel 430VX chipset. (Intel calls most of its recent chipset models *PCIsets* or *AGPsets*.)

Fifth-generation chipsets

Systems that use Intel fifth-generation chipsets are now too old to be upgraded effectively at the CPU/motherboard level, although such systems can sometimes usefully be upgraded by adding memory, a faster hard disk, and so on. Systems based on late-model fifth-generation third-party Super Socket 7 chipsets, such as the VIA MVP3, are still marginally upgradable by replacing the existing processor with a faster model, although Socket 7 processors are becoming rarer and will likely disappear entirely by the end of 2000. Even if your system is technically upgradable, it's usually not cost-effective to do so. Instead, retire that system *in situ* to less demanding duties, and build a new system based on current technology.

Sixth-generation Intel and Intel-compatible chipset characteristics

Intel continued its chipset dominance into the sixth generation until they inexplicably stumbled by insisting on supporting only the outrageously expensive RDRAM in their 820 Camino chipset, which was intended as a direct replacement for the aging 440BX. Accordingly, Intel entered 2000 with a problematic group of chipset choices, including the underwhelming 810, the 810E, which is adequate for low-end applications and at least supports PC100 SDRAM, and the problem-plagued 820 and 840 chipsets. By prematurely ramping down production of the elderly but still-popular 440BX, Intel almost forced motherboard makers to turn to third-party chipset makers. VIA was waiting with their excellent Apollo Pro133A, which is everything that Intel should have provided in their 440BX follow-on, but did not.

Fortunately, Intel continues to provide several end-of-life sixth-generation chipsets, which are listed in Table 3-1. These obsolescent chipsets, notably the 440BX and its less capable cousin, the 440ZX, are still competent chipsets, although they lack such current features as support for PC133 SDRAM and the 133 MHz FSB, PCI 2.2, ATA/66, and so on. Many current motherboards are still manufactured using these chipsets. The chipsets listed in Table 3-1 will soon be superceded.

Table 3-1: Obsolescent Intel Sixth-Generation Chipset Characteristics

	440EX	440LX	440BX	440ZX	440ZX66	810
CPU Support						
Pentium II (66 FSB)	•	•	•	•	•	○
Pentium II (100 FSB)	○	○	•	•	○	•
Pentium III (100 FSB)	○	○	•	•	○	•
Pentium III (133 FSB)	○	○	○	○	○	○
Celeron	•	•	•	•	•	•
Number of CPUs	1	2	2	1	1	1

Table 3-1: Obsolescent Intel Sixth-Generation Chipset Characteristics (continued)

	440EX	440LX	440BX	440ZX	440ZX66	810
Host bus						
66 MHz	•	•	•	•	•	•
100 MHz	○	○	•	•	○	•
133 MHz	○	○	○	○	○	○
Memory Support						
EDO	256 MB	1 GB	○	○	○	○
PC66 SDRAM	256 MB	512 MB	1 GB	256 MB	256 MB	○
PC100 SDRAM	○	○	1 GB	256 MB	○	512 MB
PC133 SDRAM	○	○	○	○	○	○
VC133 SDRAM	○	○	○	○	○	○
RDRAM	○	○	○	○	○	○
ECC support	○	•	•	○	○	○
64/128/256 Mbit	•/○/○	•/○/○	•/○/○	•/○/○	•/○/○	•/•/○
EDO/SDRAM rows	4	6	8	4	4	4
RDRAM devices	○	○	○	○	○	○
Asynchronous setting	○	○	○	○	○	○
PCI						
PCI bus version	2.1	2.1	2.1	2.1	2.1	2.2
Concurrent PCI	•	•	•	•	•	•
Southbridge	PIIX4E	PIIX4	PIIX4E	PIIX4E	PIIX4E	82801
ATA support	33	33	33	33	33	33/66
AGP Support						
Integrated graphics	○	○	○	○	○	82810
1X	•	•	•	•	•	○
2X	•	•	•	•	•	○
4X	○	○	○	○	○	○

Table 3-2 lists the primary Intel desktop chipsets available as of Q1/00. Although Intel positions the 810e as a performance chipset, it is in fact simply an entry-level replacement for the obsolescent 810, which should be avoided. The ill-starred 820 and 840 chipsets are crippled by providing native support only for the hideously expensive RDRAM. Although both support standard SDRAM, they do so by means of the Memory Translator Hub (MTH), which reduces memory performance.

Table 3-2: Current Intel Sixth-Generation Chipset Characteristics, with the VIA PM601, Pro133, and Pro133A Chipsets Shown for Comparison

	Intel 810E	VIA PM601	Intel 820	Intel 840	VIA Pro133	VIA Pro133A
CPU Support						
Pentium II (66 FSB)	○	•	○	○	•	•
Pentium II (100 FSB)	•	•	•	○	•	•
Pentium III (100 FSB)	•	•	•	○	•	•

Table 3-2: Current Intel Sixth-Generation Chipset Characteristics, with the VIA PM601, Pro133, and Pro133A Chipsets Shown for Comparison (continued)

	Intel 810E	VIA PM601	Intel 820	Intel 840	VIA Pro133	VIA Pro133A
Pentium III (133 FSB)	•	•	•	•	•	•
Celeron	•	•	○	○	•	•
Number of CPUs	1	1	2	2	1	2
Host Bus						
66 MHz	•	•	○	○	•	•
100 MHz	•	•	•	○	•	•
133 MHz	•	•	•	•	•	•
Memory Support						
EDO	○	○	○	○	1.5 GB	1.5 GB
PC66 SDRAM	○	1 GB	○	○	1.5 GB	1.5 GB
PC100 SDRAM	512 MB	1 GB	512 MB	512 MB	1.5 GB	1.5 GB
PC133 SDRAM	○	1 GB	○	○	1.5 GB	1.5 GB
VC133 SDRAM	○	1 GB	○	○	1.5 GB	1.5 GB
RDRAM	○	○	1 GB	8 GB	○	○
Dual memory channel	○	○	○	•	○	○
ECC support	○	○	•	•	•	•
64/128/256 Mbit	•/•/○	•/•/○	•/•/•	•/•/•	•/•/•	•/•/•
EDO/SDRAM rows	4	4	2	2	4	4
RDRAM devices	○	○	32	32	○	○
Asynchronous setting	○	○	○	○	•	•
PCI						
PCI bus version	2.2	2.2	2.2	2.2	2.2	2.2
Concurrent PCI	•	•	•	•	•	•
Multiple PCI segments	○	○	○	•	○	○
Southbridge	82801	VT82C686A	82801	82801	VT82C596B VT82C686A	VT82C596B
ATA support	33/66	33/66/100	33/66	33/66	33/66	33/66
AGP Support						
Integrated graphics	82810E	Trident Blade3D	○	○	○	○
1X	○	○	•	•	•	•
2X	○	○	•	•	•	•
4X	○	○	•	•	○	•

Although the specifications for the PM601 chipset look good, it has not been widely adopted by motherboard manufacturers, most of whom have chosen the Intel 810E chipset instead. The 810e chipset is a reasonable choice for entry-level systems, but choosing a chipset for a mid-range or high-end system is problematic. Based on its specs, the VIA Apollo Pro133A appears to be the best choice, but our initial impressions are that the Pro133/133A offer few real advantages over the Intel 440BX other than their support for 133 MHz FSB Pentium III processors.

Even with the advantage of 133 MHz operation, the Pro133/133A tests little faster than the 100 MHz 440BX in many benchmarks. A 440BX overclocked to 133 MHz is substantially faster than the Pro133/133A in nearly every benchmark. This proves that the Intel chipset is inherently faster, which has historically been the case every time we have compared VIA and Intel chipsets. Support for AGP 4X and ATA/66 are nice checklist items, but neither has much real-world advantage with today's components. Also, the Apollo Pro133A is in relatively short supply, and has been the subject of an Intel lawsuit attempting to prevent its distribution. On balance, we think motherboards based on the Intel 440BX chipset remain the best choice until the Intel Solano 2 chipset arrives, although we don't think buying a Pro133A-based motherboard is necessarily a bad decision.

Table 3-3 lists the Intel desktop chipset roadmap for 2000. We do not yet have solid information about the 820e, 815, 815e, Timna, and Tehama chipsets. The obsolescent 440BX and 810 chipsets are to be discontinued in late summer 2000, as the 815 Solano and 815e Solano II chipsets become available. Intel announced in May 2000, that neither the 815 nor the 815e would support Mendocino-core Celerons, so motherboards using these chipsets will support only Coppermine-core Pentium III and Coppermine128-core Celeron processors. Although the 820 and 840 chipsets are both shown as being current throughout 2000, both have been problem-plagued, and are likely to disappear quietly as soon as Intel is able to ship their replacements. The Timna is scheduled to replace the Celeron at the very low-end, and is an integrated System on a Chip (SOC) processor that includes embedded graphics and chipset functions, similar to the earlier much-maligned Cyrix processors. Tehama is the chipset for the upcoming Willamette processor, which will probably become the Pentium IV.

Table 3-3: Intel Desktop Chipset Timetable for 2000

	Q1/00	*Q2/00*	*Q3/00*	*Q4/00*
440BX	•	•	•	○
i810	•	•	•	○
i810E	•	•	•	•
i820 (Camino)	•	•	•	•
i840 (Carmel)	•	•	•	•
i820E (Camino 2)	○	•	•	•
i815 (Solano)	○	•	•	•
i815e (Solano II)	○	•	•	•
Timna	○	○	•	•
Tehama (Willamette)	○	○	○	•

AMD Athlon chipset characteristics

Although the AMD Athlon processor itself is competitive with the Intel Pentium III in most respects, first-generation Athlon chipsets and motherboards, shipped from mid-1999 until Q2/00 and all based on the AMD-750 Irongate chipset, had enough problems and limitations that we could not recommend using the Athlon until better

Athlon chipsets and motherboards became available. The arrival in late Q1/00 of Athlon motherboards based on the VIA Apollo Pro KX133 chipset put some of those objections to rest. The KX133 is superior to the AMD-750 in many respects, although we still regard it as a late first-generation chipset rather than as a true second-generation chipset. The KX133 is by no means perfect, and was hampered initially by some compatibility issues and lack of drivers, but we now feel comfortable recommending KX133 motherboards for general use by those who prefer to use an Athlon processor rather than a Pentium III. Table 3-4 compares the first-generation AMD-750 chipset, which was not really intended to be used with shipping motherboards, to the VIA Apollo Pro KX133.

Table 3-4: AMD Athlon Chipset Characteristics

	AMD-750	VIA KX133
Processor Support		
Slot A/Socket A	•/○	•/○
FSB speed (MHz)	200	200
Number of CPUs	1	1
Memory Bus		
66 MHz	○	•
100 MHz	•	•
133 MHz	○	•
Memory Support		
PC66 SDRAM	○	○
PC100 SDRAM	768 MB	2 GB
PC133 SDRAM	○	2 GB
VC133 SDRAM	○	2 GB
DDR100 SDRAM	○	○
DDR133 SDRAM	○	○
ECC	•	•
64/128/256 Mbit	•/•/○	•/•/○
SDRAM rows	3	4
PCI		
PCI bus version	2.2	2.2
Concurrent PCI	•	•
Southbridge	AMD-756	VT82C686A
ATA support	33/66	33/66
AGP Support		
Integrated graphics	○	○
1X	•	•
2X	•	•
4X	○	•

In May 2000, AMD announced that they would not ship retail-boxed versions of their new Thunderbird-core Athlons in Slot A form. AMD will produce only limited numbers of Slot A Thunderbirds for the OEM market. We believe this decision is due to the recent discovery of timing problems with the KX133 chipset and Slot A Thunderbirds. The problem is apparently caused by the VIA chipset rather than the processor itself, because Slot A Thunderbirds operate properly in motherboards that use the AMD 750 chipset. The upshot is that owners of Slot A motherboards with either chipset will not be able to upgrade to the new-generation Athlon processors, except perhaps by using a Slocket adapter (none of which have yet been announced) to install Socket A processors in their Slot A motherboards.

The first true second-generation Athlon chipsets, the AMD-760 and 770, are scheduled to ship in Fall 2000. Relative to the 750, the 760 adds support for the 266 MHz FSB (double-pumped 133 MHz), ATA/100, and AGP 4X, and will also likely fix many of the nagging problems and incompatibilities that have plagued motherboards based on the 750 chipset. The AMD-770, sometimes called the AMD-760MP, should ship soon after the 760 and adds multiprocessor support. With the arrival of these chipsets, the Athlon should be able to compete on an equal footing with the Pentium III, and likely also with the Willamette/Pentium IV, which should ship at about the same time.

BIOS

By themselves, the processor, memory, chipset, and other motherboard components are a useless collection of silicon, plastic, and metal. None of them individually can do much without help from other components, and none of them knows how to talk to other components. Turning this random collection of parts into a functioning computer requires a BIOS, or Basic Input/Output System.

The BIOS is a real-mode program that is more or less permanently stored on a chip that resides on the motherboard. Originally, the BIOS was stored on a ROM (Read-Only Memory) chip, hence the term ROM BIOS. The only way to upgrade a ROM BIOS is to physically remove that chip and install a new one. Nowadays, the BIOS more likely resides on a *Programmable ROM (PROM)*, which allows the BIOS code to be updated without physically replacing the chip.

When power is applied to the system board, the CPU initializes. The final step in its hard-coded initialization routine is to jump to a predefined memory address and execute the program that it finds there. That address is the entry point for the BIOS code, so as the CPU finishes initializing, the BIOS code begins executing the system boot sequence. To begin, the BIOS initializes installed hardware and performs the power-on self test (POST). At the conclusion of the system boot sequence, the BIOS loads the operating system and passes control to it.

Once the operating system loads, the BIOS may also perform various low-level system services at the request of the operating system or applications. Operating systems like DOS and Windows 3.x depend relatively heavily on the BIOS to provide standardized basic services. But the BIOS is a slow real-mode program, so newer operating systems like Windows 95/98 and Windows NT/2000 depend less on BIOS services and more on drivers that access the hardware directly.

Most PCs contain several BIOSes. This discussion refers to the main system BIOS, but most network adapters, video adapters, and disk host adapters contain their own specialized BIOSes. When the system boots, the main BIOS detects the presence of these specialized BIOSes and loads them, allowing the PC to support that hardware by using the program routines contained on that BIOS. Using one of these BIOSes may be automatic or optional. For example, some SCSI host adapters contain a BIOS. If you load that BIOS at boot time, you can boot from a SCSI drive attached to that adapter. If you do not load that BIOS, you cannot boot from or access the SCSI device until the operating system loads the device drivers needed to recognize it.

One major function of the BIOS is to intermediate between the chipset, the CPU, and other major system components. Full implementation of some system-level features—things like USB, Plug-N-Play, Power Management, and AGP—requires support from both the chipset and the BIOS. If either lacks support for a feature, that feature is either unavailable or has limited functionality.

Most PCs and motherboards use BIOSes made by Phoenix, American Megatrends, Inc. (AMI), or Award (now a subsidiary of Phoenix). Some name-brand PCs like IBM and Compaq use a BIOS with that manufacturer's name on it, although that BIOS is usually a relabeled Phoenix, AMI, or Award BIOS, with or without minor modifications.

When you buy a new PC or motherboard, which BIOS it uses is relatively unimportant, certainly much less so than the chipset it uses. You can safely assume that the BIOS on any new PC or motherboard will support all or most of the chipset capabilities. There may be minor exceptions—for example, some early systems with USB ports came with BIOSes that did not support USB—but such exceptions are usually unimportant to the overall functioning of the system. Also, unlike the chipset, the BIOS in a modern PC can be upgraded easily to fix bugs and to support new hardware and additional features.

Processor Support

Motherboards are designed to accept a particular processor (CPU) or CPU family. Which CPUs a motherboard supports is determined by:

Chipset
Determines the CPU types the motherboard accepts. Non-Intel chipsets typically support a wide range of Intel and compatible CPUs. Officially, Intel chipsets support only Intel CPUs. In fact, compatible CPUs like the AMD K5/K6/K6-2, the Cyrix/IBM 6x86 (M1) and 6x86MX (M2), and the IDT WinChip run fine in motherboards with the appropriate Intel chipset. Also, although recent compatible CPUs can be installed in motherboards with older chipsets, those CPUs may not provide the highest performance of which they are capable, and some advanced features may not be supported by the chipset. The chipset also determines the fastest CPU that the motherboard can

support. Intermediate speeds may or may not be supported, depending on the configuration options available for the motherboard.

CPU voltages supplied

Early Pentium-class CPUs use 5 volts. Later ones use 3.3 volts or 2.8 volts, and most later Pentium-class CPUs use dual voltage, running the internal core logic at a lower voltage than the CPU components that interface with cache, main memory, and other external components. Early fifth-generation motherboards supplied a fixed voltage to the CPU. Later ones included a voltage regulator module (VRM) that allowed the motherboard to be configured to supply different voltages, according to the requirements of the CPU installed. Some non-Intel Socket 7 motherboards allow specifying Core voltage and I/O voltage separately, using very small increments. A motherboard like this can be tweaked to provide exactly the voltage required by a particular CPU. Sixth-generation CPUs may use 2.8 volts (e.g., Klamath-core Pentium II), 2.0 volts (e.g., Deschutes-core Pentium II), or 1.6 volts (most current sixth-generation processors). Sixth-generation motherboards automatically detect and supply the voltage required by the processor.

 Just because a motherboard supplies the nominal voltage used by a given processor does not mean that processor can be used with that motherboard. Available current is also an issue. For example, early versions of the Intel SE440BX Seattle motherboard provide the 2.0 volts used by Deschutes-core Pentium IIs and Katmai-core Pentium IIIs. But the VRM on early SE440BXs cannot supply the higher current required by the Pentium III. Attempting to run a Pentium III in the motherboard may damage both motherboard and processor.

Configuration options and memory bus speed

A motherboard may not support the necessary settings for bus speed and/or CPU multiplier for a particular CPU. For example, a motherboard that offers only 50, 60, and 66 MHz bus speeds will not properly support a CPU that uses a 75 MHz bus, although it may physically accept it, and a Pentium II motherboard that supports only 66 MHz FSB cannot use a Pentium II CPU that requires a 100 MHz FSB. In such cases, the processor will normally operate properly, but at some fraction of its rated speed.

Socket or slot

Determines which CPU packaging styles fit the motherboard. Table 3-5 lists the socket and slot types you may encounter. New motherboards are available for Socket 7 and Socket 8, both obsolete, Socket 370, Slot 1, Slot A, and Socket A. AMD's Slot A is physically identical to Intel's Slot 1, but electrically different. The same applies to AMD's Socket A versus Intel's Socket 370.

Table 3-5: Desktop Processor Sockets and Slots

	Pins	Arrangement	Voltage	Processors Supported
Socket 1	169	17×17 PGA	5	
Socket 2	238	19×19 PGA	5	486-SX; SX/2; DX; DX/2; DX/4

Table 3-5: Desktop Processor Sockets and Slots (continued)

	Pins	Arrangement	Voltage	Processors Supported
Socket 3	237	19×19 PGA	5/3.3	486-SX; SX/2; DX; DX/2; DX/4; 486 Pentium Overdrive
Socket 4	273	21×21 PGA	5	Pentium 60/66; Pentium 60/66 Overdrive
Socket 5	320	37×37 SPGA	3.3	Pentium 75–300; Pentium 75+ Overdrive
Socket 6	235	19×19 PGA	3.3	(Never used)
Socket 7	321	37×37 SPGA	VRM	Pentium 75–300; Pentium 75+ Overdrive
Socket 8	387	Dual SPGA	VRM	Pentium Pro
Socket 370	370	PPGA	VRM	PPGA Celeron, FC-PGA Pentium III
Slot 1	242	121×2	VRM	Pentium II, Celeron, Pentium III
Slot A	242	121×2	VRM	AMD Athlon (slotted version)
Socket A	462	37×37 SPGA	VRM	AMD Thunderbird/Duron (socketed)

Identifying the socket type on an existing motherboard may or may not be simple. Most sockets are labeled, although you may have to remove the CPU to see the label. If it isn't labeled, you can identify the socket type by referring to the manual, by examining the pin layout of the socket, or—sometimes ambiguously—by determining the CPU type currently installed. Motherboard upgradability varies by socket type, as follows:

Socket 1 through Socket 5

Any system that uses one of these is too old to upgrade. Replace the system.

Socket 7

Accepts third-generation Pentium (P55C) CPUs, also called Pentium/MMX, which use 2.8 volt core and 3.3 volt I/O components. Later model Socket 7 motherboards, especially Super Socket 7 motherboards, are marginally upgradable by installing a faster Socket 7 CPU, as long as those remain available. In general, the best advice for upgrading a Socket 7 system is not to do it. Replace the system.

Socket 8

Accepts only Pentium Pro CPUs, which are no longer made. Replace the system.

Socket 370

Accepts a *Plastic Pin Grid Array (PPGA)* Celeron or a *Flip Chip PGA (FC-PGA)* Coppermine-core Pentium III. Intel changed Socket 370 pinouts when they introduced the FC-PGA Pentium III. Earlier Socket 370 motherboards can accept only Celeron processors. The only direct upgrade available for these motherboards is replacing the existing Celeron with a faster Mendocino-core Celeron. Most Coppermine-compatible Socket 370 motherboards can be upgraded with a Mendocino-core Celeron, a Coppermine-core Celeron, or a Pentium III.

Although we've not used it, PowerLeap claims their Neo S370 PPGA to FC-PGA adapter allows some FC-PGA Pentium III and Celeron II processors to operate in some PPGA Socket 370 motherboards. The Neo S370 remaps FC-PGA pinouts to PPGA pinouts and converts the 2.0V used by PPGA processors to the 1.60/1.65V used by FC-PGA processors. This adapter works with only some motherboards, which are listed on the compatibility page (*http://www.powerleap.com*).

Slot 1

Accepts Pentium II, Pentium III, and/or Slot 1 Celeron CPUs. Most early Slot 1 motherboards can use either a Pentium II or a Celeron, but some support only one or the other. Later Slot 1 motherboards usually accept a Celeron, Pentium II, or Pentium III interchangeably, but again there are exceptions, which can sometimes be overcome by upgrading the BIOS. Within the limitations of the motherboard and BIOS, upgrade a Slot 1 motherboard by replacing a Celeron with a faster Celeron or Pentium III, or by replacing a Pentium II with a Pentium III. Some Slot 1 motherboards support only 66 MHz FSB CPUs. Others support both 66 MHz and 100 MHz FSB CPUs, and can be upgraded with any supported Celeron or Pentium III. However, upgrading from a 66 MHz FSB CPU to a 100 MHz FSB CPU may also require replacing existing RAM with PC100 or PC133 RAM. The most recent Slot 1 motherboards also support 133 MHz FSB processors, which is useful only for running a 133 MHz FSB Pentium III. Some Slot 1 motherboards have two CPU slots. If you run an SMP-capable operating system, you can significantly upgrade such a motherboard by adding a second CPU, which must be a Pentium II or Pentium III (Celerons do not support SMP), and should be closely similar or identical to the original CPU.

Various companies manufacture $20 slocket adapters, which adapt a Socket 370 processor to Slot 1. A popular use of slockets has been to run dual PPGA Celerons, a configuration that is officially unsupported by Intel, but with which many people have been successful. Running dual Slot 1 Celerons requires physical surgery on the CPUs themselves, but slockets allow using dual PPGA Celerons simply by setting jumpers on the slockets. Also, because Slot 1 Celerons are available only in the slower speeds and are more expensive than corresponding PPGA versions, it makes sense to upgrade a Slot 1 system by using a fast, cheap PPGA Celeron and a slocket. Note that first-generation slockets are incompatible with Coppermine-core Celeron and Pentium III processors.

Slot A

Accepts the AMD Athlon processor. The only upgrade available is a faster Slot A Athlon processor. Note, however, that early Slot A motherboards (those based on the AMD-750 Irongate chipset) may support only a limited range of

CPU speeds and are relatively poor upgrade candidates because of limitations in the chipset.

Socket A

Accepts second-generation AMD Athlon processors, based on the K75 Thunderbird core. As this is written in June 2000, we have not yet received samples of any Socket A motherboards based on the VIA KT133 chipset (a derivative of the KX133, formerly designated KZ133), so we cannot comment further. Production Socket A motherboards are likely to be upgradable by installing faster Socket A processors. AMD seems heavily committed to Socket A for its new generation Athlons, so upgrading should not be a problem.

Do not assume that a CPU is usable just because it fits the motherboard socket or slot. Some combinations are unambiguous. Pentium Pro processors, for example, fit only Socket 8 motherboards, which accept only Pentium Pro CPUs. Other combinations of CPU and socket/slot are ambiguous. The CPU may physically fit but work improperly or not at all. For example, although the Intel SE440BX motherboard physically accepts any Slot 1 CPU—Pentium II, Celeron, or Pentium III—it works only with Pentium II CPUs. The nearly identical SE440BX2 motherboard supports various Slot 1 CPUs, including Celerons and Pentium IIIs. Similarly, an FC-PGA Pentium III processor can be physically installed in any Socket 370 motherboard, but will simply not be recognized by any Socket 370 motherboard that does not explicitly support the Pentium III.

Bus Support

A *bus* is a shared linear pathway that connects multiple devices to provide a communication channel among them. Every bus provides access points to which devices can connect. Any device connected to the bus can communicate bidirectionally with other devices that are connected to that bus. A bus provides access points for three or more devices. A bus that connects only two devices is properly called a *port*. PC components—processor, cache, RAM, expansion cards, disks, and others—communicate using one or more of the multiple buses that exist in a modern PC. Recent PCs contain several bus types, all of which are coordinated by the chipset, as follows:

Processor bus

Also called the *host bus*, the *processor bus* is used by the processor to communicate with the chipset.

Memory bus

The *memory bus* connects the memory subsystem to the chipset and to the processor. Some systems use the same bus as both processor bus and memory bus. Systems that use sixth-generation processors like the Pentium III refer to the memory bus as the *Front Side Bus* or *FSB*. Early Pentium II and all Celeron processors use a 66 MHz FSB. Deschutes-core Pentium IIs and Katmai-core Pentium IIIs use a 100 MHz FSB. Coppermine-core Pentium IIIs use either a 100 MHz or 133 MHz FSB. Late model *Super Socket 7* motherboards with chipsets from VIA and others support AMD K-6 series processors at 100 MHz FSB. For most systems and most applications, increasing FSB speed provides only minor performance benefits.

Cache bus

Sixth-generation processors use a dedicated *cache bus* (also called the *Back Side Bus* or *BSB*) to access the integrated L2 cache. This bus may operate at full processor speed (e.g., Celeron and Coppermine-core Pentium III processors), or at some integer fraction of the processor speed (e.g., Katmai-core Pentium III and original Athlon processors). Fifth-generation processors, like Pentiums, do not have integrated L2 cache and do not use a BSB. Instead, they use the memory bus to communicate with external L2 cache memory.

Local I/O bus

The *local I/O bus* is a high-speed bus that connects high-performance peripherals like video adapters, disk adapters, and network adapters to the chipset, processor, and memory. Early 486 systems used *VESA Local Bus* (*VLB*), which literally extended processor leads to the expansion bus slots. This tight link between processor and VLB limited the number of VLB slots that could be supported and constrained the performance of those slots. VLB systems are no longer made and are poor upgrade candidates. Late 486 systems and all Pentium-class and higher systems use the *Peripheral Component Interconnect* (*PCI*) bus for this purpose. Technically, PCI is a *mezzanine bus* rather than a true local bus, because it isolates the processor electronically from PCI expansion slots. Isolating the processor from the PCI bus allows more PCI slots to be supported and removes performance constraints on the use of those slots. Any system or motherboard you buy today should provide PCI expansion slots in adequate number for your needs.

Standard I/O bus

Most current PCs contain legacy *Industry Standard Architecture* (*ISA*) expansion bus slots, a design that originated in 8-bit form in 1981 with the original IBM PC and was updated to 16-bit form with the 1984 introduction of the IBM AT. Originally, the presence of these legacy ISA slots was intended to allow using older ISA expansion cards in newer systems, and ISA slots may still be used in a pinch to connect slow peripherals like serial ports and parallel ports. However, the presence of legacy ISA devices in a system interferes with the ability of that system to configure itself under Plug-N-Play, and should be avoided if at all possible.

Accelerated Graphics Port (AGP)

Some recent PCs and motherboards include an *Accelerated Graphics Port* (*AGP*) slot designed to accept an AGP video card. Although AGP is sometimes called a bus, as the name indicates it is really a port, because it connects only two devices. Note that many motherboards with embedded video do not include an AGP slot. That means that upgrading the video adapter in that motherboard requires using a PCI video card, which is of little concern to most users, but may be of great concern to gamers and others for whom high video performance is important.

PC expansion buses differ in two respects that determine their performance:

Bus width

Every bus is actually two separate buses. The *address bus* specifies the locations (or addresses) from and to which data is to be transferred. The *data bus* carries the actual data between the devices connected to the bus. Data buses can be of different widths, all of which are multiples of one byte (or 8 bits). All other things being equal, a wide bus communicates data faster than a narrow bus because it communicates more bytes during each transfer cycle. The original IBM PC ISA bus is 8 bits wide; the AT ISA bus that appears in most systems is 16 bits wide; the VLB and PCI local buses are 32 bits wide; the memory, processor, and AGP buses on Pentium and later PCs are 64 bits wide. The width of the address bus and the data bus are independent. A wider address bus allows more memory locations to be accessed. For example, a 16-bit address bus can address 2^{16} or 65,536 memory locations, while a 32-bit address bus can address 2^{32} or 4,294,967,296 memory locations.

Bus speed

Buses transfer data during discrete *transfer cycles* or *clock cycles*. The clock speed of the bus determines how many transfer cycles occur each second, so a higher bus speed allows more data to be transferred per unit time. Most buses transfer one bit of data per data line per transfer cycle, so data transfer speed in bytes per second is the simple product of the bus width in bytes times the number of transfer cycles per second. For example, a PCI bus transfers 32 bits or 4 bytes during each cycle, and runs at 33.33 MHz, yielding throughput of (4 bytes/cycle × 33.3 million cycles/second) or 133.33 MB/s. The ISA bus requires two transfer cycles to move one byte, which halves its transfer speed relative to newer buses operating at the same speed. The AGP port running in 2x or 4x mode transfers two or four bits of data per data line per cycle, doubling or quadrupling its transfer rate relative to buses that transfer only one bit per data line per cycle. The original Athlon uses a 100 MHz FSB, but transfers two bits per data line per cycle, yielding an effective FSB speed of 200 MHz.

In combination, the product of bus width and bus speed determines the maximum theoretical bandwidth or throughput that the bus can provide. In practice, overhead prevents any bus from reaching its theoretical maximum. Also, some buses can run at other than their maximum speed, which further reduces throughput. Table 3-6 lists the theoretical throughput provided by common PC buses when running at the speed most commonly used in PCs.

Table 3-6: Width, Speed, and Throughput of Common PC Buses

Bus Type	Width (bits)	Speed (MHz)	Bits per line per cycle	Throughput (MB/s)
ISA (XT 8-bit)	8	8.33	1	8.33
ISA (AT 16-bit)	16	8.33	1	16.66
EISA	32	8.33	1	33.33
VLB	32	33.33	1	133.33
PCI	32	33.33	1	133.33
PCI (64-bit)	64	66.66	1	533.33
AGP x1	32	66.66	1	266.66
AGP x2	32	66.66	2	533.33
AGP x4	32	66.66	4	1,066.66

Although PCI 2.1 and 2.2 allow 64-bit transfers at 66.66 MHz, very few PCs implement widths greater than 32 bits or speeds higher than 33.33 MHz. One exception is AGP, which is a modified version of PCI that provides a dedicated high-speed interface for video adapters. All AGP transfers are 32 bits wide, but use the 66.66 MHz clock speed. The initial release of AGP transferred 1 bit per data line per clock cycle, yielding 266.66 MB/s throughput. AGP 2x mode, now widely available, uses special encoding to transfer 2 bits per data line per clock cycle, doubling throughput to 533.33 MB/s. AGP 4x mode is not widely available, but will double throughput again to 1,066.66 MB/s.

Various buses communicate at different widths and speeds, and using different protocols. But it's necessary for these buses to exchange data, which means that the system must have circuitry that translates between each incompatible pair of buses. This circuitry, called a *bridge*, is supplied with the chipset.

Northbridge (or North Bridge)
> The *Northbridge* provides bridge logic for the internal system buses that link the CPU to memory and cache and provide other core functions like PCI and power management. The Northbridge may be implemented as one or several discrete chips in the chipset.

Southbridge (or South Bridge)
> The *Southbridge* provides bridge logic for peripheral functions like ATA, mouse, keyboard, USB, and the Super I/O serial/parallel controller. The Southbridge is usually one chip, and a particular Southbridge may be bundled with different Northbridges to create different chipsets. For example the Intel PIIX4e PCI-to-ISA Interface Xcellerator Southbridge chip is used with minor variations on Intel chipsets that support Pentium II, Celeron, and Pentium III processors.

Choosing a Motherboard

You can sometimes upgrade a system cost effectively without replacing the motherboard, and the more recent the system, the more likely this is to be true. The easiest upgrade is always replacing a processor with a faster version of the same processor. Doing that may simply mean pulling the old processor and replacing it with the faster one, although a BIOS upgrade may also be needed. Alas, there is no guarantee that a given motherboard will support a faster version of the same processor, or that a required BIOS upgrade will be available, and the rapid advances in processors means that a faster version of the same processor may no longer be available. The next-easiest upgrade is to replace the processor with a later model from the same generation. For example, you may be able to replace a Pentium II/350 with a Pentium III/500 or /550 or, by using a slocket adapter, with a cheap, fast Celeron. When upgrading to a later model processor, a BIOS upgrade will almost always be needed, and you should check the motherboard manufacturer's web site carefully to determine which configurations are supported.

But it doesn't make sense to stretch an old motherboard too far. Just because you *can* upgrade a system without replacing the motherboard doesn't mean that you *should* do so. Motherboards are inexpensive, typically $75 to $150. Doing an in-place upgrade instead of replacing the motherboard leaves you with the limitations of the old motherboard and may limit the performance of the new processor. Before you decide to keep the motherboard, find out the costs and benefits of replacing it instead. Don't forget to factor in the supplementary benefits of a new motherboard—a better chipset and BIOS, support for the latest hard disk standards, etc. You might be surprised by the results.

Use the following guidelines when choosing a motherboard:

Decide which CPU to use
> The CPU you choose determines the type of motherboard you need. Choose an Intel Celeron (Socket 370), a Pentium III (Slot 1 or Socket 370), or an AMD Athlon (Slot A or Socket A) motherboard. Don't buy a Socket 7 motherboard. The availability of alternative processors, particularly the AMD K6-2, kept Socket 7 alive long after Intel departed that market, but Socket 7 is now dead. With fast Celeron processors available for $60, any price advantage previously enjoyed by Socket 7 is gone, and Socket 7 processors will see decreasing availability until they finally disappear, probably in late 2000. The future belongs to Slot 1/Socket 370 on the Intel side, and Slot A/Socket A on the AMD side. Any motherboard you choose should use one of those connectors.

Decide which chipset you want
> For a Socket 370 or Slot 1 entry-level motherboard, the Intel 810E chipset is a reasonable choice. For a general purpose Slot 1 motherboard, all of Intel's current chipsets have drawbacks. The 440BX and its derivatives are competent if aging chipsets, and do not support modern features like 133 MHz FSB and ATA 66. The 820 was designed for the hideously expensive RDRAM and, although it provides limited support for SDRAM, is not the best choice. Until new Intel chipsets arrive in H2, 2000, we recommend choosing a Slot 1 board based on the VIA Apollo Pro133A. For Athlon systems, there really isn't any choice. Although boards based on the obsolescent AMD-750 chipset may remain available, those based on the VIA KX133 chipset are the only ones worth buying.

Choose a board with flexible host bus speeds
> Motherboards for current Intel processors may support FSB settings of 66, 100, and/or 133 MHz. Ideally, choose a motherboard that supports all three settings for maximum flexibility. Otherwise, choose a motherboard that supports at least the settings you need now and expect to need for the life of the board—66 MHz for Celerons, 100 MHz for Katmai-based Pentium IIIs, and 100 or 133 MHz for Coppermine-based Pentium IIIs. All Athlon motherboards support a 100 MHz FSB (which uses DDR for an effective 200 MHz), but get a board with PC133 support for future upgradability. If you must buy a Socket 7 board for some reason, make sure it supports the host bus speed of your processor. Boards that offer a full range of host-bus speeds—from 66 MHz to 100 MHz or higher, ideally in small increments—give you the most flexibility. If you intend to overclock your system, make sure the motherboard offers multiple choices of host-bus speed (again, the smaller the increments, the better) and allows you to set CPU voltage, ideally over a wide range in 0.05 volt increments.

Make sure the board supports the type and amount of memory you need

What types of memory does the motherboard support, and how many memory slots are available? Two DIMM slots is marginal, three adequate, and four preferable. All current SDRAM-based boards support 128 MB unbuffered DIMMs, which provides 256 MB to 1 GB of RAM on a board with two to four memory slots. Not all boards support 256 MB registered DIMMs, which are quite expensive per MB, so plan accordingly. Ideally, for future upgradability, you want a board that supports PC133 SDRAM, even if the current CPU runs only at 100 MHz.

 Although you may be able to find a new motherboard that supports migrating existing memory from the old motherboard, it's usually not a good idea to do so unless that older memory is current—i.e., PC100 or PC133 SDRAM. Memory is cheap, and it seldom makes sense to base a new motherboard purchase decision on the ability to salvage a relatively small amount of old, slow memory.

Check documentation, support, and updates

Before you choose a brand or model of motherboard, check the documentation and support that's available for it, as well as the BIOS and driver updates available. Some people think that a motherboard that has many patches and updates available must be a bad motherboard. Not so. Frequent patch and update releases indicate that the manufacturer takes support seriously. We recommend to friends and clients that they give great weight to—and perhaps even base their buying decisions on—the quality of the web site that supports the motherboard.

Buy a motherboard with the proper form factor

If you are building a new system choose an ATX motherboard that best meets your needs, and then buy an ATX case and power supply to hold it. If you are upgrading an existing system that uses a BAT motherboard, choose a new BAT motherboard. *But,* before you worry too much about reusing the BAT case and power supply, consider that good quality ATX cases and power supplies are available for under $100. Most recent motherboards, including all AMD Athlon motherboards, are available only in ATX or one of its variants. You may be better off retiring the old case and buying a modern ATX case and motherboard.

The preceding issues are always important in choosing a motherboard. But there are many other motherboard characteristics to keep in mind. Each of them may be critical for some users and of little concern to others. These characteristics include:

Expansion slots

Any motherboard you buy will provide PCI (and possibly ISA) expansion slots, but motherboards differ in how many slots they provide. Three PCI slots is marginal, four adequate, and five or more preferable. Integrated motherboards—those with embedded video, sound, and/or LAN—can get by with fewer PCI slots. Using ISA slots should be avoided whenever possible, so the number of ISA slots is largely immaterial. Having an AGP slot (2X or 4X) is a definite plus, even if the motherboard includes embedded video. Many recent motherboards include an *Audio-Modem Riser (AMR)* slot, which is designed solely to allow system manufacturers to embed low-end audio and modem functions cheaply. Anyone reading this book will disdain AMR, instead installing discrete sound and/or modem support. The presence or absence of an AMR slot is therefore immaterial, except that it is much preferable that space occupied by an AMR slot instead be used by another PCI slot.

Warranty

It may seem strange to put something generally regarded as so important in a secondary category, but the truth is that warranty should not be a major issue for most users. Motherboards generally work or they don't. If a motherboard is going to fail, it will likely do so right out of the box or within a few days of use. In practical terms, the vendor's return policy is likely to be more important than the manufacturer's warranty policy. Look for a vendor who replaces DOA motherboards quickly, preferably by cross-shipping the replacement.

Ports, connectors, and front panel LEDs

Any new motherboard should provide at least two 16550A or better serial ports, one EPP/ECP parallel port, two USB ports, a keyboard port, and a mouse port. If you are upgrading an older system, you may need either to buy adapters separately for your keyboard and mouse or replace one or both of them. Also, depending on the motherboard and case, you may have to extend motherboard I/O ports to connectors mounted on expansion card brackets rather than on the back panel, which can make one or more expansion slots unusable. Make sure to ask which port connectors come with the motherboard. Many AT motherboards include a USB header, but the cable necessary to extend USB to the back panel may be a $10 option. Also check the documentation to determine how the header pins for front panel switches and indicators are arranged on the new motherboard. It's quite common to find that existing cables aren't long enough to reach the connectors on the new motherboard, or that the new motherboard uses different pin arrangements for particular connectors.

Embedded sound and video

Some motherboards include embedded sound cards and/or video adapters as standard or optional equipment. In the past, such motherboards were often designed for low-end systems, and used inexpensive and relatively incapable sound and video components. But nowadays many motherboards include "name brand" sound (e.g., SoundBlaster PCI) and video (e.g., nVidia), making them good choices around which to build a mainstream mid-range system. Such motherboards are normally priced $25 to $75 higher than a motherboard without the embedded peripherals, allowing you to save $50 to $100 by buying the integrated motherboard rather than separate components. If you buy such a motherboard, make sure that the embedded devices can be disabled if you later want to install a better sound or video card.

Power management and system management

We regard power management as a useless feature. It saves little power, and increases the wear and tear on the equipment. But if power management is an issue for you, make sure that the motherboard you buy supports at least

APM. The updated ACPI specification will eventually replace APM, but many people have reported problems with ACPI, including systems that go into a coma rather than going to sleep, requiring a hard reboot to recover. System management is usually unimportant outside a corporate environment. If system management is an issue for you, look for a motherboard that supports all or some of the following features: voltage monitoring, CPU and/or system temperature sensors, chassis intrusion alarm, and fan activity monitoring for one or more fans.

Wakeup functions

Again, these features are primarily of interest to corporate IS folks rather than individual users. But if wakeup functions are important to you, you can buy a motherboard that supports "Wake-on" some or all of the following: LAN activity, modem ring-in, keyboard/mouse activity, and real-time clock.

Jumperless (or single-jumper) configuration

Older-style motherboards are configured mostly by setting jumpers. Nearly all recent motherboards use fewer jumpers, depending instead on CMOS Setup to configure motherboard settings. A board that uses CMOS Setup is marginally easier to configure than one that uses jumpers.

Boot devices supported

Any motherboard supports booting from the hard drive or the floppy drive. Most modern motherboards also support booting from El Torito compliant CD-ROM drives and from floppy-replacement drives like the LS-120. If boot support is an issue for you, make sure the motherboard you buy supports booting from your preferred device. Also make sure that CMOS Setup allows you to specify a boot sequence that allows you to make your preferred device the primary boot device.

Minor or special purpose features

Motherboards attempt to differentiate themselves by including various minor features, such as IRDA port or additional fan power headers (at least one is needed for the CPU fan, but some motherboards include two or even three power headers to support supplemental fans).

Installing a Motherboard

Installing a motherboard for the first time intimidates most people, but it's really pretty easy if you do it by the numbers. Before you get started, prepare a well-lighted working area, ideally one with all-around access. The kitchen table (appropriately protected) usually works well. Have all tools and parts organized and ready to go. Open the box of each new component, verify contents against the manual or packing list to make sure no parts are missing, examine the components to ensure they appear undamaged, and do at least a quick read-through of the manual to familiarize yourself with the products.

Removing the Old Motherboard

If you are replacing a motherboard, you must remove the old motherboard before installing the new one. The exact steps vary according to the motherboard and case, but use the following general steps:

1. Power down the PC and all attached devices, Disconnect all external cables other than the power cord, noting which cable connects to which port. Then move the PC to your work area and remove the cover from the case. We can attest that one wayward case screw can destroy a vacuum cleaner, so put the screws safely aside. An old egg carton or ice cube tray makes a good parts organizer.

2. If the PC power cord is connected to an outlet strip, surge suppressor, or UPS, turn off the main power switch on that device, and turn off the main PC power switch as well. This removes power from the PC, but leaves the PC grounded.

 In most AT form factor power supplies and motherboards, turning off the PC power switch removes power from the motherboard. With newer ATX (and variants) power supplies and motherboards, turning off the main PC power switch leaves some power flowing to the motherboard, which supports features like *Wake-on-Ring (WOR)*, *Wake-on-LAN (WOL)*, and *Suspend to RAM (STR)*.

Although the voltage present is much too small to cause personal injury, working on a powered ATX motherboard may damage the motherboard, CPU, memory, or other components. Best practice when working on ATX motherboards is to use an outlet strip or other device to remove power from the PC entirely. If you must work on an ATX motherboard and have no such device, disconnect the power cord from the wall receptacle before beginning work. To avoid damaging components, touch the power supply to ground yourself before handling the motherboard, CPU, memory, or other static-sensitive components.

---

3. Note the position and orientation of each internal cable connected to an expansion card. If necessary, sketch or photograph the connections to make sure you can reconnect the cables as they were, and then remove those cables on the expansion card. Remove the expansion cards and set them aside, preferably on an anti-static surface, although a plain table top also works well. Alternatively, you may be able to leave the cables connected to the expansion cards and simply place the cards out of the way, perhaps balanced on top of the power supply.

4. Label and disconnect each cable that connects to the system board, including those to the power supply, to the front panel switches and LEDs, to back panel I/O ports, and to fans. When you complete this step, the motherboard should not have any obvious connections other than the mounting screws.

5. In most cases, the motherboard mounts directly to a fixed part of the chassis. In some cases, the motherboard mounts to a removable tray. If your motherboard uses a tray, remove the screws that secure the tray to the chassis and then lift the tray out carefully, watching for overlooked cable connections. Depending on the motherboard form factor, there may be from three to eight screws securing the motherboard to the chassis or tray. One or more screw

---

holes may be occupied by nylon spacers that snap in from the bottom of the motherboard and slide into slots in the chassis. If the motherboard is secured only by screws, remove all of them and then attempt to remove the motherboard by lifting gently straight up. If one or more nylon spacers are present (visible as small white nubs sticking up through screw holes), rather than lift the motherboard straight up, slide it gently a fraction of an inch toward the left side of the chassis and then lift straight up.

6. Place the old motherboard flat on a anti-static surface. Lacking that, put it on the table top. If you are salvaging the CPU or memory, ground yourself and remove those components. In any case, store the old motherboard in the anti-static bag that the new motherboard arrived in, once that bag is available.

Installing the New Motherboard

To install the motherboard, take the following steps, observing anti-static precautions throughout the process:

1. Touch the PC power supply to ground yourself, and then open the antistatic bag that contains the new motherboard. Remove the new motherboard from its anti-static bag, place the bag on a flat surface, and place the motherboard on top of the anti-static bag.

2. If you haven't done so already, read the motherboard manual to determine how to configure it. Verify each diagram in the manual against the actual motherboard to ensure that you can identify the important switches, jumpers, and connectors.

3. Configure the motherboard according to the instructions in the manual. Recent motherboards may use only one or a few configuration jumpers. Older technology motherboards, especially Socket 7 motherboards, may use many jumpers to set numerous options, including CPU speed, host bus speed, CPU voltage, etc. Make sure to get all of these jumpers set correctly, especially those that control voltage, before you apply power to the board.

4. After you have set all configuration jumpers properly, install the CPU and memory according to the instructions supplied with the motherboard and/or the components.

5. Determine how the motherboard mounts to the chassis. Old motherboards often used several snap-in nylon stand-off spacers and only a few screws to secure the motherboard. Modern motherboards use all or mostly screws, which secure to brass stand-off spacers. The important issue is whether a given hole location in the motherboard is designed to be grounded or not. If so, it will mount with a screw to a conductive brass stand-off spacer. If not, it will mount using a non-conductive nylon stand-off spacer. Using a conductive brass connector where an insulating nylon connector was intended can short out and destroy the motherboard. Using a nylon connector where a brass connector was intended can cause the motherboard to operate improperly or not at all, or to radiate excessive RFI. New motherboards come with a plastic bag that contains screws and stand-off spacers of the proper type. If yours does not and you are not sure which type is required, refer to the motherboard documentation or contact technical support.

6. Hold the motherboard over the chassis in the position that you will mount it. Typically all or all but one of the holes in the motherboard align with a stand-off spacer installed in the chassis. The motherboard is secured to the chassis by passing a screw through each of the motherboard screw holes and into the matching stand-off spacer. The final hole, usually the one nearest the back left corner of the motherboard, may use a slide-in spacer rather than a screw, which makes it easier to line up the motherboard with the other stand-off spacers. Most chassis have many more mounting holes than are needed to secure any particular motherboard. Visually align the holes actually present in the motherboard with the chassis to determine which subset of the chassis mounting holes will actually be used. If you are building a new system, thread brass stand-off spacers into the appropriate chassis mounting holes. If you are replacing a motherboard, spacers may already be mounted in most or all of the necessary locations. Add or relocate spacers as necessary to ensure that each hole in the motherboard has a matching spacer. Don't leave any motherboard mounting holes unused. Each of those mounting holes provides support for the motherboard at a key location. If you leave one or more of the mounting holes unsupported, the motherboard may crack later when you are pressing hard to seat an expansion card, CPU, or memory module.

 If you have a Slot 1 motherboard that uses an old-style retention mechanism that must be installed before the motherboard is mounted in the case, now is the time to install it. Most new-style retention mechanisms can be installed either before or after the motherboard is mounted, and many Slot 1 motherboards come with a folding retention mechanism already installed, which requires only raising the arms to vertical and locking them in place.

7. After you've installed all necessary stand-off spacers, slide the motherboard into position, aligning all holes with their matching spacers. Secure the motherboard using the screws provided with it, or the screws that secured the original motherboard.

8. Reconnect the cables, including power supply cable(s), ATA cable(s), floppy drive cable, the cables that link the motherboard to front panel switches and LEDs, and the cables that link the motherboard I/O ports to the back panel connectors.

9. Reinstall only the expansion cards needed to test the system (usually just the video card), reconnect any cables that connect to them, and then reconnect the external cables that link the system unit to the monitor, keyboard, mouse, and so on.

10. Verify that everything that needs to be connected is connected, that everything is connected to the right thing, and that you haven't left any tools where they might short something out.

11. Time for the smoke test. Turn on the monitor and then turn on power to the system unit. The BIOS boot screen should appear on your monitor. If no

video appears, or if you hear a beep sequence other than the normal single startup beep, you have something misconfigured. Turn off the power immediately (or just pull the power cord) and recheck all connections and settings you've made.

12. Once you're satisfied that the system is working properly, shut it down, remove power from it, reinstall any additional expansion cards, and restart the system.

13. When the system begins a normal boot sequence, press whatever key the BIOS boot screen prompts you to press to enter CMOS setup. If you have jumpered the motherboard in configuration mode, special CMOS Setup options (e.g., setting CPU speed or voltages) may be available now that will no longer be available once you rejumper the motherboard for normal operation. Configure and save the CMOS Setup options, and then turn off power to the system.

14. If necessary, rejumper the motherboard for normal operation and then restart the system. Verify proper system operation, particularly that the system recognizes the hard drive(s) you have installed. Once you are sure that the system is working as expected, shut it down, reinstall the case cover, restart the system, and begin installing your operating system and applications.

Configuring CMOS

Each time a system boots, the BIOS boot screen appears momentarily. While this screen is being displayed, pressing a designated key runs the CMOS Setup program, which resides in firmware. CMOS Setup is used to configure CMOS and chipset settings ranging from those as obvious as the Date and Time to those as obscure as memory timings and bus settings.

Recent Intel motherboards replace the standard BIOS boot screen with an Intel-logo splash screen. Display the standard BIOS boot screen on such systems by pressing the Escape key while the logo is visible.

To invoke CMOS Setup, you normally press F1 (AMI), Del (Award), or F2 (Phoenix). Other BIOS manufacturers use different keys, and some system and motherboard manufacturers modify a standard BIOS to use another key. The key that invokes CMOS Setup nearly always appears on the BIOS boot screen, but if your BIOS boot screen doesn't show that key, try Del, F1, F2, F10, Ctrl-Alt-S, or refer to the documentation.

The exact appearance of CMOS Setup and the available options depend on the chipset, the BIOS make and version, and changes made to the BIOS and CMOS Setup programs by manufacturers. For example, two motherboards may use the same chipset, processor, and BIOS, but one may give users complete freedom to configure chipset options, while the other allows users access to only some of the settings and uses hard-wired values for other settings.

All BIOSes default to a reasonable set of CMOS settings, one that allows the system to boot and function normally. Beyond that, it's up to you to choose settings to configure the system as you want it and to optimize its performance.

Some CMOS Setup options, the so-called basic settings, are pretty obvious—things like time and date, hard drive parameters, power management, boot sequence, and so on. Others, particularly those segregated as advanced settings and chipset settings, are anything but obvious. The brief help descriptions provided with them are usually not much help unless you already understand the issue. The primary rule here is *if you don't understand what an option is for, don't change it.*

That's easy to say, but it ignores the fact that accepting default settings for obscure options can result in a PC that performs significantly below its potential. PC and motherboard manufacturers differ in how "aggressive" they are in choosing default settings, particularly those for such things as memory timing and wait states. Those that tend toward slower, more conservative default settings say, with some justification, that they cannot predict what components (particularly what speed and quality of memory) a user will install. Choosing conservative settings allows them to be sure that the motherboard will at least work, if not optimally. Those who are more aggressive (often, PC vendors, who have control of which memory and other components will be installed) assume that users want the highest possible performance level and use components that support those aggressive settings.

The first place to look for detailed CMOS Setup instructions is in the manual that came with the computer or motherboard. Some manufacturers provide detailed explanations of general CMOS Setup and Chipset Setup options, but many cover only basic CMOS Setup options and ignore Chipset Setup completely. If that's the case with your manual, you may be able to download detailed instructions from the BIOS manufacturer's web site.

- AMI does not provide end-user documentation, leaving that to the computer and motherboard vendors that use their BIOS.

- Award Software (*http://www.award.com/docs/docs.htm*), now a part of Phoenix Technologies, provides very detailed documentation (down to the level of different documents for different chipsets) in HMTL and *.zip* format for CMOS Setup and Chipset Setup, POST codes, beep codes, and so on.

- Phoenix Technologies (*http://www.phoenix.com/support/#reference*) provides less detailed (but adequate) docs in the form of the *PhoenixBIOS 4.0 Setup Guide* and the *PhoenixBIOS Post and Beep Codes*, both of which are supplied in Adobe *.pdf* format.

Upgrading the System BIOS

When you upgrade an existing system without replacing the motherboard, the BIOS version it uses can be a critical issue. Some system features—notably support for large hard disks, high-speed transfer modes, and AGP—are BIOS-dependent, so an in-place upgrade often requires a BIOS upgrade as well. Fortunately, recent systems use a flash BIOS, which can be upgraded simply by downloading a later version of the BIOS to replace the existing BIOS.

Be extraordinarily careful when upgrading a flash BIOS. Before you proceed, make *absolutely* sure that the BIOS upgrade patch you are about to apply is the *exact* one required for the current BIOS. If you apply the wrong patch, you may render your system unbootable from the floppy drive, which makes it difficult or impossible to recover by reapplying the proper patch.

Upgrading a flash BIOS requires two files. The first is the upgraded BIOS itself in binary form. The second is the "flasher" program provided by the BIOS manufacturer, e.g., *awdflash.exe*. The exact steps you follow to upgrade a flash BIOS vary slightly according to the BIOS manufacturer and the version of the flasher program you are using, but the following steps are typical.

1. Before proceeding, record all current BIOS settings, either using pencil and paper or a utility program that writes BIOS settings to a disk file. If you have a UPS, connect the system to it for the duration of the BIOS update. Losing power during a BIOS update can result in a motherboard that is unusable and must be returned to the maker for repair.

2. Determine the manufacturer, version, date, and identifying string of the existing BIOS. You can do this by using a third-party diagnostics program like CheckIt, or by watching the BIOS screen that appears briefly each time the system boots. With most systems, pressing the Pause key halts the boot screen, allowing you to record the BIOS information at your leisure. With other systems, the Pause key does nothing, so you may have to reboot the system several times to record all the relevant information. It is important to record *exactly* what appears. Completely different BIOS versions are often differentiated by very minor changes in the BIOS identifying string.

3. Locate a flash BIOS patch file that is intended to upgrade the *exact* BIOS version you have. Close isn't good enough. Begin your search on the PC manufacturer's web site. If you can't find an appropriate BIOS update there, check Wim's BIOS Page at *http://www.ping.be/bios/*. While you are searching for the proper BIOS update file, keep the following points in mind:

   • Having a particular PC model is no guarantee that it uses the same BIOS as another PC with the same model number. High volume PC manufacturers often sell systems that use different motherboards under the same model designation, and the BIOS update file intended for one motherboard used in that model cannot be used to upgrade the same model with a different motherboard.

   • A particular motherboard and BIOS may be available in several versions that cannot use the same flash update file. For example, Micron produced several systems using the popular Intel SE440BX Seattle motherboard, but with a slightly customized BIOS. The SE440BX flash update available on the Intel web site can only be used to update an unaltered SE440BX, not the Micron version of that motherboard.

- Even a motherboard supplied directly by the manufacturer may have shipped in several revisions, which require different BIOS patches. For example, Robert's main system uses an EPoX KP6-BS dual-CPU motherboard, which was made in two versions, one with a 1 MB BIOS chip and the other with a 2 MB BIOS chip. The BIOS patches for these two versions are different and incompatible. Sometimes the only way to know for sure which BIOS patch you need is literally to take off the cover and examine the identifying numbers on the Flash BIOS chips themselves.

- BIOS patches are cumulative. That is, if your existing BIOS is version 4.003, you may find that the web site has versions 4.004, 4.005, and 4.006 available. You need not apply each of those patches sequentially. Instead, update your 4.003 BIOS directly to 4.006 in one step by applying the 4.006 patch to it.

- BIOS patch files are usually supplied in *.bin*, *.exe*, or *.zip* form. The *.bin* files can be used directly by the flasher utility. When run, the *.exe* files automatically extract the BIOS patch in *.bin* form. If the BIOS update is supplied as a *.zip* file, use WinZip or a similar zip utility to extract the *.bin* file

4. Download the BIOS flasher utility, either from the motherboard manufacturer's web site or directly from the BIOS manufacturer's web site. Note that some motherboard manufacturers supply BIOS updates as an archive file (*.zip* or *.exe*) that contains both the BIOS update *.bin* file and the flasher utility. These distributions sometimes take the form of an executable file that when run automatically creates a bootable floppy diskette and copies the *.bin* BIOS update file and the flasher utility to it.

5. Unless the BIOS update you've downloaded is one of those that automatically creates a boot floppy, format a bootable floppy disk. If you are using MS-DOS, Windows 3.x, or Windows 9X, use the command format a: /s to create the bootable floppy. If you are updating the BIOS on a system that runs Windows NT, Linux, or another non-DOS operating system, format a bootable DOS floppy on another computer. Copy the flasher utility and the *.bin* file to this floppy.

6. Enable flash BIOS update mode on your motherboard. To prevent viruses from altering the system BIOS, most motherboards have a jumper that must be set in one position to enable flash BIOS updates and in another position to re-enable normal system operation. Set this jumper to BIOS update mode.

7. Boot the system using the DOS boot floppy you created earlier. At the DOS prompt, type the command line specified in the documentation for your flasher utility. For example, the command to update an Abit BH-6 motherboard using the Award flasher and the *bh6_gy.bin* BIOS update file while saving a copy of the old BIOS and clearing the CMOS settings is *Awdflash bh6_gy.bin Oldbios.bin /cc*. *Oldbios.bin* specifies the filename that the old BIOS will be saved as, and the */cc* argument clears CMOS settings.

8. When the flash BIOS update completes, restart the system and enter BIOS setup mode. Depending on the BIOS manufacturer, the flasher version you use, and the command-line arguments you specified, the CMOS settings may or may not be cleared. Even if they aren't, it's always a good idea to clear and re-enter them after a flash BIOS update, and for many BIOS updates it's

mandatory. To do so, load the default BIOS settings and then enter the correct settings for time and date, hard disk type, etc. that you recorded in step 1. Once you have entered the correct settings for all values, restart the system again. It should display the updated BIOS version in the boot screen.

Although most recent systems use some variant of this method, some systems allow you to update the BIOS simply by copying a *.bin* file to a floppy diskette, which needn't be bootable, and restarting the system with that floppy in the drive. The obvious danger with this method is that you might unintentionally update your BIOS from a floppy disk that contains a hacked version. Accordingly, most recent systems require you to explicitly move a jumper to enable BIOS update mode.

Although updating a flash BIOS is a pretty intimidating operation the first time you try it—or the tenth time, for that matter—BIOS updates usually complete successfully if you do everything by the numbers. But if you accidentally apply the wrong patch or if the flash update process fails through no error of your own, the PC can end up non-bootable. If this happens, there may not be an easy way to recover. Depending on the BIOS, one of the following methods to recover from a failed flash BIOS update may be usable:

- Recent Award BIOSes have a small permanent boot-block BIOS. This portion of the BIOS is not overwritten during a flash update, and is sufficient to allow the computer to boot to a floppy disk. Unfortunately, this BIOS supports only the floppy disk and an ISA video card. If a flash update fails on a system with such a BIOS and a PCI or AGP video card, you can re-flash the BIOS by using another system to create a bootable floppy disk that contains the *awdflash.exe* utility and the proper BIOS *.bin* file, with an *Autoexec.bat* file that automatically executes the flasher utility with the proper command-line arguments. With a PCI video card, you will not be able to view the progress of the update, but once the update completes and you restart the system, everything should operate properly. With an ISA video card, you can view the update procedure as it occurs.

- The flash BIOS chip on some systems is socketed rather than soldered. If a failed flash BIOS update renders such a system unbootable, you can contact the system manufacturer to request a working BIOS chip. Most manufacturers will supply a replacement chip that contains the current version of the BIOS on request. Some even do so for no charge, although they often require that you return the original nonfunctional BIOS chip. If you can get a replacement BIOS chip, simply pull the original chip, replace it with the new chip, and restart the system.

- As a last resort, if you have an identical system that works, you can temporarily install the BIOS chip from the good system into the nonworking one and reboot that system using the good BIOS chip. Once the system boots, pull the good BIOS chip and replace it with the nonworking BIOS chip without powering down the system. Then, with the system still running, execute the flasher utility from diskette to reapply the flash BIOS update to the damaged BIOS chip. As a general rule, of course, removing and installing chips while the system is running is a good way to fry a motherboard. We've never tried this and can't guarantee that you won't fry your motherboard if you try it, but some people claim to have done it successfully.

Because a failed flash BIOS update may have such dire results, never flash a BIOS without first connecting the system to a UPS, if only temporarily while doing the update. The one time we violated that rule, sure enough, the lights flickered about five seconds after we started the update. Hoping against hope that the PC hadn't crashed—this update was one of those ones where the screen stays blank until the update is complete—we sat staring at the blank screen for another half hour before we admitted to ourselves that we'd probably just killed the motherboard. With our fingers crossed, we powered the system down and back up again, but, as expected, it was deader than King Tut. Unless your luck is better than ours, always use a UPS when flashing a BIOS.

Our Picks

In the past, we regarded performance as the least important aspect of a mother-board. Most mainstream boards used the 440BX chipset, and benchmarked within a few percent of each other in processor and memory performance. More important by far were issues like stability, reliability, construction quality, and driver support. As the 440BX begins to fade from the scene and new chipsets are introduced by Intel and others, performance may again become an issue, so we thought it worthwhile to devote some significant time and effort to benchmarking various boards and chipsets.

Table 3-7 and Table 3-8 show our benchmark results under Windows 98SE and Windows NT, respectively, using four Intel motherboards with three different chipsets and four different Intel Pentium III Coppermine processors, all running at the same speed. Unfortunately, we did not receive VIA Pro133A boards in time for detailed benchmark testing.

Table 3-7: SiSoft Sandra 2000.3.6.4 Benchmarks Under Windows 98 SE

Motherboard	Chipset	Pentium III	Dhrystone	Whetstone	CPU Memory	FPU Memory
Intel CA810E	810E	600	1616.0	802.8	211.4	223.6
Intel CA810E	810E	600EB	1617.0	803.0	212.2	223.4
Intel CC820	820	600EB	1617.0	803.0	203.6	234.8
Intel VC820	820	600EB	1617.0	803.0	359.2	457.8
Intel SE440BX2V	440BX	600E	1617.0	803.2	287.8	317.6

Table 3-8: SiSoft Sandra 2000.3.6.4 Benchmarks Under Windows NT 4 Workstation (SP6a)

Motherboard	Chipset	Pentium III	Dhrystone	Whetstone	CPU Memory	FPU Memory
Intel CA810E	810E	600	1621.0	805.0	211.8	214.0
Intel CA810E	810E	600EB	1622.2	805.2	212.2	214.2

Table 3-8: SiSoft Sandra 2000.3.6.4 Benchmarks Under Windows NT 4 Workstation (SP6a) (continued)

Motherboard	Chipset	Pentium III	Dhrystone	Whetstone	CPU Memory	FPU Memory
Intel CC820	820	600EB	1622.4	805.0	204.6	231.8
Intel VC820	820	600EB	1623.0	805.2	375.6	466.4
Intel SE440BX2V	440BX	600E	1624.0	806.0	302.4	331.4

We ran each benchmark test seven times, discarding the highest and lowest results and averaging the remaining five. We used an FC-PGA Pentium III/600 (100 MHz FSB) and an FC-PGA Pentium III/600EB (133 MHz FSB) in the CA810E, a Slot 1 Pentium III/600EB (133 MHz FSB) in the two 820-based boards, and a Slot 1 Pentium III/600E (100 MHz FSB) in the 440BX-based board. We tested all motherboards using one 64 MB Crucial PC133 SDRAM DIMM, except the VC820, for which we used one 64 MB Samsung PC800 RDRAM RIMM.

We also benchmarked the boards using various other standard benchmark tests, such as Ziff-Davis WinBench, which provided similar results. Clearly, there is little to choose between based on the processor benchmarks. Just as clearly, there are significant differences in memory performance. Under both operating systems, the VC820 with RDRAM far outpaces the others, and the 440BX is in strong second place. But we confess that we were unable during extensive actual use to notice any performance differences based on differences in memory benchmarks. The performance of the CA810E system and the VC820 system, for example, "felt" about the same to us.

So, with the proviso that chipsets and motherboards are in a state of flux, here are the motherboards we use and recommend as of June 2000:

Socket 7

None. Socket 7 is obsolete. The only remaining mainstream Socket 7 processors are the AMD K6 series, which are currently moribund, and will likely be discontinued as AMD ramps up Socket A Athlon production from mid-2000. Don't consider using Socket 7 for a new system. If you must buy a Socket 7 motherboard—e.g., to replace a failed motherboard in an older system—use an EPoX Socket 7 motherboard. EPoX makes the most stable Socket 7 motherboards we know of. Models are available in AT and ATX that accept SIMMs or DIMMs, although those that support SIMMs are becoming hard to find. (*http:// www.epox.com/html/english/products/motherboard/Default.htm*)

Socket 370

Intel CA810E. At $125, the CA810E is a good choice for building anything from value PCs to mainstream systems. Although its memory benchmarks are slower than those of other chipsets, we see little difference in real-world use. It supports all current PPGA and FC-PGA Socket 370 processors from inexpensive Celerons to (currently) the Pentium III/800, with support for faster CPUs added frequently via BIOS updates. It integrates Intel i752 video—which gamers sniff at but which provides good 2D performance and image quality and 3D performance adequate for casual gaming—and Creative SoundBlaster 128 PCI audio. If you need 100BaseT Ethernet, the $140 CA810EAL includes an embedded Intel 10/100

Ethernet adapter. The main drawback of the CA810e is that it has no AGP slot, which means video upgrades require using a PCI video card. Avoid the similarly named CA810, which is based on the older i810 chipset. Robert uses a CA810E in one of his two main systems. It triple-boots Windows 98SE, Windows NT 4 Workstation, and Windows 2000 Professional, all without problems. (*http://developer.intel.com/design/motherbd/ca2/ca2_ds.htm*)

Many Socket 370 boards are available that use chipsets other than the integrated 810E but we prefer Slot 1 boards for building systems for which we want to choose video and sound adapters separately. This also allows us to use either a Slot 1 processor or—by using a slocket adapter card—a Socket 370 processor. As Intel phases out Slot 1 and more Socket 370 boards become available based on chipsets like the Intel 815E Solano 2, we will likely shift to Socket 370. But for now Slot 1 motherboards are a viable and flexible solution, and are likely to remain so through at least 2002. Here are some of the Slot 1 boards we like:

Slot 1 (Intel 440BX chipset)

Intel SE440BX2V. Here's the downside. As an Intel board, the $120 SE440BX2V doesn't allow overclocking. It uses the venerable 440BX chipset, which means it doesn't support 133 MHz FSB, AGP 4X, or ATA/66. But none of those matter much. Performance differences between 100 MHz and 133 MHz FSB are minor, AGP 4X has no discernable advantage over AGP 2X, and current drives cannot saturate even ATA/33. On the upside, the SE440BX2V is a robust, stable, proven Slot 1 board suitable for building general-purpose systems. We have several systems here that use the SE440BX2V and its earlier variants, and have chosen the SE440BX2V for our standard benchmarking test-bed system. (*http://developer.intel.com/design/motherbd/se2/se2_ds.htm*)

Slot 1 (Intel 820 chipset)

Intel VC820. If you want the fastest Slot 1 motherboard available regardless of price, choose the $145 Intel VC820, whose memory performance simply annihilates every other board we've tested. Construction quality of Intel motherboards is the best we've seen, and the VC820 is no exception. We would recommend this board without qualification except that it requires RDRAM, which is currently five to eight times the price of SDRAM. Do not mistake the VC820 for its sibling, the problem-plagued and recently-recalled CC820, which uses SDRAM via the Memory Translator Hub (MTH) and has very poor memory performance. Note that getting top performance from the VC820 requires using PC800 RDRAM, which is even more expensive and difficult to find than PC600 or PC700 RDRAM. (*http://developer.intel.com/design/motherbd/vc/vc_ds.htm*)

Slot 1 (VIA Apollo Pro133A chipset)

AOpen AX64Pro. Although we prefer Intel chipsets, the VIA Apollo Pro133A is a first-class chipset and we would not hesitate to use a high-quality board based on it. Based on our preliminary impressions, the $120 AX64Pro is such a board. If not the fastest Pro133A board, it is not far behind the leaders in that respect, and has several offsetting advantages, including reasonable over-clocking support with a decent range of FSB and voltage settings. As is typical of AOpen products, construction quality is top-notch. Although, in our experience, boards based on non-Intel chipsets are never quite as stable as those that use Intel chipsets, the AX64Pro is a reasonably stable board. We'd choose this board if we were building an overclocked system, or one for a serious gamer. For general use, we'd stick with the Intel SE440BX2V. (*http://english. aopen.com/products/mb/ax64pro.htm*)

Slot 1 (dual CPU)

EPoX KP6-BS. The $160 440BX-based KP6-BS is our choice for a dual Slot 1 board. The KP6-BS supports any Slot 1 Pentium II/III processor that uses the 66 MHz or 100 MHz FSB, including 100 MHz Coppermines through the 750E MHz version. The board is well-built, well-supported, and has been completely stable in our testing. EPoX provides frequent BIOS updates, which is something that some manufacturers fail to do. EPoX also makes the similar $360 EP-BXB-S, which includes an embedded Adaptec U2W SCSI host adapter. Robert's main system uses a KP6-BS running dual Pentium III/550 processors. (*http://www.epox.com/html/english/products/motherboard/kp6-bs.htm*)

 If you need a slocket to adapt a Socket 370 CPU to a Slot 1 motherboard, get one that supports both PPGA Celeron and FC-PGA Pentium III CPUs, whose pinouts differ slightly. If possible, buy the slocket made by the motherboard manufacturer to ensure complete compatibility.

So much for motherboards that support Intel processors. If you want to jump aboard the AMD Athlon bandwagon now, avoid motherboards based on the aging AMD-750 chipset. Second-generation boards that use the VIA Apollo Pro KX133 with the 686A Southbridge are the way to go for now, at least until boards based on the VIA KT133 and AMD-760 chipsets arrive. Many manufacturers began shipping the KX133 motherboard in volume during H1, 2000, and they are now widely available. Because most are based on the VIA reference platform, these boards are more alike than different in most respects. But we have to pick one, so here's our choice:

Slot A

Asus K7V. This motherboard is the best of the current crop of first-generation Athlon boards based on the VIA Apollo KX133 chipset. It's fast, stable, and uses the premium 686A Southbridge rather than the less expensive 596B. At $150 or so, this motherboard is reasonably priced for its quality, which is up to the usual high standards of Asus. Until the AMD-760 chipset begins shipping in quantity in late 2000, this is the Athlon motherboard we'd choose for any purpose. Note, however, that this a large full-ATX board, which is difficult to install in some small cases. Asus also makes the similar K7V-RM, a microATX version of this board, with only three PCI slots. Note, however, that choosing a motherboard that uses the KX133 may restrict your processor upgrade options, as noted earlier. (*http://www.asus.com/Products/Motherboard/slota.html*)

Socket A

None yet. As we write this in June 2000, AMD is about to ship their second-generation Athlon processors, many of which will use Socket A rather than Slot A. Although we have not yet been able to obtain samples, we believe that Socket A to Slot A slocket adapters will soon be available to allow using a

Socket A CPU in a Slot A motherboard. See our web site for our recommendations, which will appear once we've had a chance to use some of these boards.

We constantly test and review new equipment. For the latest information about what we currently use, visit:

http://www.hardwareguys.com/picks/motherboards.html

CHAPTER 4

Processors

The *processor*, also called the *microprocessor* or *CPU* (for *Central Processing Unit*), is the brain of the PC. It performs all general computing tasks and coordinates tasks done by memory, video, disk storage, and other system components. The CPU is a very complex chip that resides directly on the motherboard of most PCs, but may instead reside on a daughtercard that connects to the motherboard via a dedicated specialized slot.

Processor Components

Modern processors have the following internal components:

Execution unit
   The core of the CPU, the *execution unit* processes instructions.

Branch predictor
   The *branch predictor* attempts to guess where the program will jump (or branch) next, allowing the *Prefetch and Decode Unit* to retrieve instructions and data in advance so that they will already be available when the CPU requests them.

Floating point unit
   The *floating point unit* (*FPU*) is a specialized logic unit optimized to perform non-integer numeric calculations much faster than the general-purpose logic unit can perform them.

Primary cache
   Also called *Level 1* or *L1 cache, primary cache* is a small amount of very fast memory that allows the CPU to retrieve data immediately, rather than waiting for slower main memory to respond. See Chapter 5, *Memory*.

Bus interfaces
   Bus interfaces are the pathways that connect the processor to memory and other components. For example, modern processors connect to memory via a dedicated bus called the *Frontside Bus* (*FSB* or *Host Bus*).

Processor Speed

The processor *clock* coordinates all CPU and memory operations by periodically generating a time reference signal called a *clock cycle* or *tick*. Clock frequency is specified in *MHz*, or millions of ticks per second, and determines how fast instructions execute. Some instructions require one tick, others multiple ticks, and some processors execute multiple instructions during one tick. Ticks per instruction varies according to processor architecture, its *instruction set*, and the specific instruction. *Complex Instruction Set Computer (CISC)* processors use complex instructions. Each requires many clock cycles to execute, but accomplishes a lot of work. *Reduced Instruction Set Computer (RISC)* processors use fewer, simpler instructions. Each takes few ticks but accomplishes relatively little work.

These differences in efficiency mean that one CPU cannot be directly compared with another purely on clock speed. A 450 MHz AMD K6-III, for example, may or may not be faster than a 450 MHz Intel Pentium III. The comparison is complicated because different CPUs have different strengths and weaknesses. For example, the K6-III provides integer performance comparable to the Pentium III at similar clock speeds, but the floating point performance of the K6-III is lower. The only safe use of direct clock speed comparisons is within a single family. An 800 MHz Pentium III, for example, is roughly 33% faster than a 600 MHz Pentium III, but even there the relationship is not absolutely linear. Also, even within a family, processors with similar names may differ substantially internally.

Processor Architecture

Clock speeds increase every year, but the laws of physics limit how fast CPUs can run. If designers depended only on faster clock speeds for better performance, CPU performance would have hit the wall years ago. Instead, designers have improved internal architectures while also increasing clock speeds. Recent CPUs run at 200 times the clock speed of the PC/XT's 8088, but provide 2,000 times the performance. Here are some major architectural improvements that have allowed CPUs to continue to get faster every year:

Wider data buses and registers
> For a given clock speed, the amount of work done depends on the amount of data processed in one operation. Early CPUs processed data in 4-bit (*nibble*) or 8-bit (*byte*) chunks, whereas current CPUs have larger registers (small but very fast "scratchpad" storage areas within the processor itself) and process 32 or 64 bits per operation.

Floating Point Units (FPU)
> All CPUs work well with integers, but processing floating point numbers to high precision on a general purpose CPU requires a huge number of operations. All modern CPUs include a dedicated FPU that handles floating point operations efficiently.

Pipelining
> Early CPUs took five ticks to process an instruction—one each to load the instruction, decode it, retrieve the data, execute the instruction, and write the result. Modern CPUs use *pipelining*, which dedicates a separate stage to each process and allows one full instruction to be executed per clock cycle.

Superscalar architecture

If one pipeline is good, more are better. Using multiple pipelines allows multiple instructions to be processed in parallel, an architecture called *superscalar.* A superscalar processor processes multiple instructions per tick.

Intel Processors

Intel now sells one fifth-generation processor, the *Pentium/MMX*, and several sixth-generation processors, including the *Pentium II*, *Pentium III*, and *Celeron*, all of which are variants of the original sixth-generation *Pentium Pro.* Although some earlier processor models remain available as niche products, only the Pentium III and Celeron variants are currently used in mainstream desktop systems. The following sections describe recent Intel processors.

Fifth Generation (Pentium, Pentium/MMX)

With the fifth generation, Intel abandoned *86 names and used Pentium, a name that could be trademarked. Intel produced three major sub-generations of Pentium:

P54

These earliest Pentium CPUs, first shipped in March, 1993, fit Socket 4 motherboards, use a 3.1 million transistor core, have 16 KB L1 cache, and use 5.0 volts for both core and I/O components. P54-based systems use a 60 or 66 MHz memory bus and a fixed 1.0 CPU multiplier to yield processor speeds of 60 or 66 MHz.

P54C

The so-called Classic Pentium CPUs, first shipped in October, 1994, fit Socket 5 motherboards, use a 3.3 million transistor core, have 16 KB L1 cache, and use 3.3 volts for both core and I/O components. P54C-based systems use a 60 or 66 MHz memory bus and CPU multipliers of 1.5, 2.0, 2.5, and 3.0x to yield processor speeds of 75, 90, 100, 120, 133, 150, 166, and 200 MHz.

P55C

The Pentium/MMX CPUs, first shipped in January 1997, fit Socket 7 mother-boards, use a 4.1 million transistor core, have a 32 KB L1 cache, improved branch prediction logic, and use 2.8 volt core and 3.3 volt I/O components. This so-called split-rail design runs the processor core itself at the lower 2.8V (to reduce heat production and allow higher speeds), while running the I/O components at 3.3V, which allows them to interface with standard external components designed for 3.3V processors. P55C-based systems use a 60 or 66 MHz memory bus and CPU multipliers of 2.5, 3.0, and 3.5x to yield processor speeds of 150, 166, 200, and 233 MHz.

Pentiums are CISC processors and, like 486s, use 32-bit operations internally. The Pentium doubles the 32-bit 486 data bus to 64 bits, allowing it to access memory eight bytes at a time. Pentiums use a *dual-pipelined superscalar* design that allows them to execute more instructions per tick than 486s. Pentiums execute integer instructions using the same five stages as 486s—Prefetch, Instruction Decode, Address Generate, Execute, and Write Back—but have two parallel integer pipelines (versus the 486's one) allowing them to execute two integer operations simultaneously. For equal clock speeds, Pentiums process integer instructions about twice as fast as 486s. Pentiums include an improved 80-bit FPU that is much more efficient than the 486 FPU. Pentiums also include a *Branch Target Buffer* to provide dynamic branch prediction, a process that greatly enhances instruction execution efficiency.

Where 486s have one 8 KB L1 cache (16 KB for the 486DX/4) that uses the inefficient *write-through* algorithm, P54 and P54C Pentiums have dual 8 KB L1 caches—one each for data and instructions—that use the more efficient *two-way set associative write back* algorithm. P55C Pentiums double L1 cache size to 16 KB, providing still more improvement.

The biggest changes from P54 to P54C were the reduction from 5V to 3.3V, which allows the CPU to run cooler, and the addition of CPU multipliers, which allow the CPU to run internally at some multiple of the bus speed. The P55C doubled L1 cache and incorporated two major architectural enhancements:

MMX

> Sometimes described as *MultiMedia eXtensions* or *Matrix Math eXtensions*, but Intel says that MMX stands for nothing. MMX is a set of 57 instructions dedicated to manipulating audio, video, and graphics data, which allows these operations to be performed much more efficiently than if they were calculated using the standard instruction set.

SIMD

> *Single Instruction, Multiple Data* (*SIMD*) allows one instruction to operate simultaneously on multiple sets of similar data.

Together, MMX and SIMD allow Pentiums to process eight bytes per clock cycle rather than one, which can dramatically improve performance, particularly graphics rendering.

Sixth Generation (Pentium Pro, Pentium II, Celeron, Pentium III)

Intel stuck with modified forms of the Pentium moniker like Pentium Pro and Pentium II for early sixth-generation processors, and began inventing new names like Celeron for some later models. But for the latest, the Pentium III, they've returned to the older style. Intel also manufactures processor variants for servers (the Pentium II/III Xeon), mobile systems, and so on, which are beyond the scope of this book. The following sections describe sixth-generation desktop Intel CPUs.

Pentium Pro

Intel's first sixth-generation CPU, the Pentium Pro, was introduced in November, 1995—along with the new 3.3 volt 387-pin Socket 8 motherboards required to accept it—and was discontinued in late 1998. Intel positioned the Pentium Pro for servers, where its support for four-way *Symmetric Multiprocessing* (*SMP*) versus the two-way SMP supported by the Pentium II ensured continuing sales until its replacement, the Pentium II Xeon, shipped in mid-1998. The Pentium Pro was available in 133, 150, 166, 180 and 200 MHz versions, was expensive to build, did not support MMX, and was optimized for efficient 32-bit operations at the expense of 16-bit Windows 95 performance. Although the Pentium Pro is discontinued, it was the first Intel sixth-generation processor, and introduced many important architectural improvements. Understanding the Pentium Pro *vis-à-vis* the Pentium helps understand current Intel CPU models. The two CPUs differ in the following major respects:

Secondary (L2) cache

Pentium L2 caches use a narrow (32-bit), slow (60 or 66 MHz memory bus speed) link between the processor's L1 cache and the L2 cache. Pentium Pro L2 cache is located on the CPU itself, and uses a 64-bit path running at full processor speed to link L1 to L2 cache. The CPU-to-L1 cache bus is the *Backside Bus* (*BSB*). The CPU-to-memory bus is the *Frontside Bus* (*FSB*). Together, BSB and FSB are called *Dual Independent Bus* (*DIB*) architecture. In effect, 256 KB of Pentium Pro L2 cache provides about the same performance boost as 2 MB or more of Pentium L2 cache.

Dynamic execution

The Pentium Pro uses a combination of techniques—including *branch prediction, data flow analysis,* and *speculative execution*—that collectively are referred to as *dynamic execution*. Using these techniques, the Pentium Pro uses clock cycles that the Pentium wastes.

Super-pipelining

A technique that allows the Pentium Pro to use *out-of-order instruction execution,* another method to avoid wasting clock cycles. A Pentium executes instructions first-come, first-served, which means that it waits for all required data to process an earlier instruction instead of processing a later instruction for which it already has all of the data. The Pentium Pro uses super-pipelining with three sections. The first, the *in-order front end,* decodes and issues instructions. The second, the *out-of-order core,* executes instructions in the most efficient order possible based on available data, regardless of the order in which it received the instructions. The third and final section, the *in-order retirement section,* receives and forwards the results of the second section.

CISC versus RISC core

Pentiums use a CISC core. The Pentium Pro, the first Intel CPU to use a RISC core, translates CISC instructions to RISC instructions and then uses RISC processing internally. Conversion adds overhead, but for pure 32-bit operations (e.g., Windows NT), the benefit of RISC conversion outweighs the drawbacks. For 16-bit operations (e.g., Windows 9X), the converse is true.

Pentium II family

In effect, a Pentium II family processor is a faster Pentium Pro with MMX added, and the following major changes:

L2 cache

Earlier members of the Pentium II processor family use discrete L2 cache *Static RAM* (*SRAM*) chips that operate at half CPU speed and reside within the CPU package but are not a part of the CPU itself. Some later members include L2 cache integrated onto the CPU substrate.

Packaging

Pentium Pros use the 387-pin *Dual Pattern Staggered Pin Grid Array (DP-SPGA) Socket 8*. Intel developed simplified alternative packaging methods for various members of the Pentium II family processors.

Improved 16-bit performance

Intel solved the Pentium Pro 16-bit performance problem in the Pentium II by substituting the Pentium segment descriptor cache, which processes 16-bit operations very efficiently, for the 32-bit optimized segment descriptor cache used by the Pentium Pro.

Current members of the Pentium II/III desktop family include:

Pentium II

First generation Pentium II processors shipped in 233, 266, 300, and 333 MHz versions with the 2.8V *Klamath core* and a 66 MHz FSB. In mid-1998, Intel shipped second generation Pentium II processors, based on the 2.0V *Deschutes core*, that ran at 350, 400, and 450 MHz, and used a 100 MHz FSB. Pentium II processors have 512 KB of L2 cache running at half CPU speed. Pentium II processors use a *Single Edge Contact Connector (SECC)* or SECC-2 cartridge, which contains the CPU and L2 cache. The SEC package mates with a *242-contact slot connector*, formerly known as *Slot 1* and now as the *SC242 socket*, which resembles a standard expansion slot. Excepting FSB speed and fab process, all Slot 1 Pentium II processors are functionally identical.

Celeron

Initially an inexpensive variant of the Pentium II, and, in later models, an inexpensive Pentium III. Klamath-based (*Covington core*) Celerons shipped in April, 1998 in 266 and 300 MHz versions without L2 cache. Performance was poor, so in fall 1998 Intel began shipping modified Deschutes-based (*Mendocino core*) Celerons with 128 KB L2 cache. The smaller Celeron L2 cache runs at full CPU speed, and provides L2 cache performance similar to that of the larger but slower Pentium II L2 cache for most applications. Mendocino (0.25μ) Celerons have been manufactured in 300A (to differentiate it from the cacheless 300), 333, 366, 400, 433, 466, 500, and 533 MHz versions, all of which use the 66 MHz FSB. Celerons are available in two form factors:

Single Edge Processor Package cartridge

All Celerons through 433 MHz were produced in *Single Edge Processor Package (SEPP)* cartridge form, which resembles the Pentium II SECC and SECC-2 packages, and is compatible with the Pentium II 242-contact slot. In mid-1999 Intel largely abandoned SEPP in favor of PPGA, but they continue to sell SEPP Celerons in 400 and 433 MHz varieties.

Plastic Pin Grid Array

As a cheaper alternative to SEPP, Intel developed the *Plastic Pin Grid Array* (also called *PPGA* or *Socket 370*), which resembles Socket 7 but accepts only 370-pin PPGA Celeron and *Flip-Chip PGA (FC-PGA)* Pentium III processors. All Mendocino and Coppermine core Celerons are manufactured in PPGA. The Celeron/466 was the first Celeron produced only in PPGA.

Celerons based on the 0.18μ, 1.6V Coppermine core Pentium III have just begun to ship in volume in 533A, 566, and 600 MHz versions as this is written in June 2000. These Celerons have half of the 256 KB on-die L2 cache disabled to bring L2 cache size to the Celeron standard, use a 4-way set associate L2 cache rather than the 8-way version used by the Coppermine core Pentium III, and use the 66 MHz FSB speed, but otherwise support the standard Coppermine core Pentium III features, including SSE, described later in this section. Because these new Celerons effectively *are* Pentium IIIs, some *may* be easy to overclock. For example, a Celeron/600 (66 MHz FSB) is effectively a down-rated Pentium III/900 (100 MHz FSB). We speculate that until yields improve Intel may recycle Coppermines that are unreliable at 100 MHz as 66 MHz Celerons. Our guess is the initial Coppermine Celerons will not be good overclockers, but that should change as production ramps up. However, this will be true only for the Celeron/566 and /600. Overclocking faster Celerons by running them with a 100 MHz FSB would cause them to run near, at, or over the 1 GHz mark, which appears to be the effective limit of the Coppermine core itself.

Pentium III (Katmai core)

Initial Pentium III variants use the *Katmai core*, essentially an enhanced Deschutes with the addition of 70 new *Streaming SIMD Extensions* (*SSE*)— formerly called *Katmai New Instructions* or *KNI* and known colloquially as *MMX/2*—that improve 3D graphics rendering and speech processing. They use the 0.25μ process, operate at 2.0V core voltage, use a 100 MHz FSB, incorporate 512 KB L2 cache running at half CPU speed, and support two-way SMP. Katmai-core processors are available in SECC-2 (Slot 1/SC242) and FC-PGA (Socket 370) packaging.

Pentium III (Coppermine core)

Later Pentium III variants use the Coppermine core, which is essentially a refined version of the Katmai core. Coppermine processors use the 0.18μ process, which reduces die size, heat production, and cost. They operate at nominal 1.6V core voltage (with faster versions requiring marginally higher voltage), are available at either 100 MHz or 133 MHz FSB, and (except the 1 GHz version) support SMP. Coppermine core processors are available in SECC-2 (Slot 1/SC242) and FC-PGA (Socket 370) packaging in both 100 and 133 MHz FSB variants. Finally, Coppermine also incorporates the following significant improvements in L2 cache implementation and buffering:

Advanced Transfer Cache

Advanced Transfer Cache (*ATC*) is how Intel summarizes the several important improvements in L2 cache implementation from Katmai to Coppermine. Although L2 cache size is reduced from 512 KB to 256 KB, it is now on-die (rather than discrete SRAM chips) and, like the Celeron, operates at full CPU speed rather than half. Bandwidth is also quadrupled, from the 64-bit bus used on Katmai and Mendocino core Celeron processors to a 256-bit bus. Finally, Coppermine uses an eight-way set associative cache, rather than the four-way set associative cache used by earlier Pentium III and Celeron processors. Migrating L2 cache on-die increased transistor count from just under 10 million for the Katmai to nearly 30 million for Coppermine, which may account for the reported early yield problems with the Coppermine.

Advanced System Buffering

Advanced System Buffering (*ASB*) is how Intel describes the increase from Pentium III Katmai and earlier processors to the Coppermine from four to six fill buffers, four to eight queue entry buffers, and one to four writeback buffers. The increased number of buffers was primarily intended to prevent bottlenecks with 133 MHz FSB Coppermines, but also benefits those running at 100 MHz.

Table 4-1 summarizes the important differences between Pentium III variants available as of June 2000. To differentiate processors with the same speed but different FSB or cache types, Intel uses the *E* suffix to indicate support for ATC and ASB, the *B* suffix to indicate 133 MHz FSB, and the *EB* suffix to indicate both. All processors faster than 600 MHz include both ATC and ASB. Note that A-step FC-PGA processors do not support SMP. B-step and higher FC-PGA processors support SMP.

Table 4-1: Intel Pentium III Variants as of June 2000

	1.0B GHz	933, 866, 800EB, 733, 667, 600EB, 533EB	850, 800, 750, 700, 650, 600E, 550E	850, 800, 750, 700, 650, 600, 550E, 500E	933, 866, 800, 733, 667, 600EB, 533EB	600B, 533B	600, 550, 500, 450
Package	SECC-2	SECC-2	SECC-2	FC-PGA	FC-PGA	SECC-2	SECC-2
Process	0.18μ	0.18μ	0.18μ	0.18μ	0.18μ	0.25μ	0.25μ
FSB	133 MHz	133 MHz	100 MHz	100 MHz	133 MHz	133 MHz	100 MHz
L2 cache	256 KB	256 KB	256 KB	256 KB	256 KB	512 KB	512 KB
SMP	No	Yes	Yes	Yes	Yes	Yes	Yes

 When Intel introduced the Pentium III in FC-PGA form, they changed Socket 370 pinouts. Those changes mean that, although an FC-PGA processor physically fits any Socket 370 motherboard, it will not run in motherboards designed for the Celeron/PPGA. Motherboards designed for FC-PGA processors are backward-compatible with PPGA Celeron processors.

Future Intel Processors

The recent story of Intel processors has been continuing incremental improvements and a shift in price strategy to reclaim the low-end market that Intel formerly ceded to its competitors. In the short term, that will continue, with the following developments expected in 2000 for Intel desktop processors:

Celeron

At the end of Q1/2000, the fastest shipping Celerons ran at 533 MHz, although Intel had just introduced the Celeron/533A, /566, and /600, all based on the Coppermine core. Throughout 2000, Intel will introduce faster Coppermine Celerons, with 633, 666, and 700 MHz versions scheduled for Q3 and Q4. Depending on various considerations, including technical, yield, competitive and other marketing issues, Intel may ship 733 and 766 MHz versions in Q4. The next-generation Celeron, code-named *Timna*, is scheduled to ship in H2, 2000. Timna includes integrated graphics, and will initially support SDRAM. A later version of Timna, scheduled for 2001, will support RDRAM. See Chapter 5, *Memory*, for an explanation of the pros and cons of RDRAM.

Pentium III

Intel originally planned to ramp up Pentium III Coppermine speeds much more slowly, with the 1 GHz version originally scheduled for introduction in late 2000. Competition from the AMD Athlon processor forced Intel to introduce faster Coppermines much earlier than planned. Intel shipped the 1 GHz Coppermine in very small quantities in March 2000 to match the announcement of the 1 GHz Athlon, but the 1 GHz Coppermine and its 850 and 866 MHz siblings are unlikely to be available in commercial quantities much before the fall of 2000. Expect no significant increases in clock speed throughout 2000, but greatly improved availability and reduced prices for Coppermines at 800 to 1,000 MHz as production ramps up and yields improve.

Willamette

The much-awaited processor code-named *Willamette*, which we expect to be officially designated the Pentium IV, is scheduled to ship in late 2000, initially at speeds greater than 1 GHz on a 0.18μ process, and in 2001 at speeds of 1.5 GHz or higher on a 0.13μ process. Willamette is both the first member of the Intel P7 family and the last Intel IA-32 (32-bit) processor. Preliminary specifications can be downloaded from *http://developer.intel.com/design/processor/wmtsdg.htm*.

In the long run, Intel processors from 2001 and forward will incorporate two technological changes:

Copper interconnect technology

Current processors use aluminum traces to interconnect components. It is now possible to build processors with copper interconnects, which allows smaller, closer traces for faster, cooler processors. Intel processors will not use copper interconnects until at least 2001.

IA-64

Current Intel processors use the IA-32 32-bit architecture that directly supports the classic x86 instruction set. Beginning in late 2000, Intel will gradually shift from IA-32 to the 64-bit IA-64 architecture that it has developed with Hewlett-Packard. IA-64 is expected to provide large increases in native CPU performance, but will offer backward compatibility with IA-32 code only via emulation, which means that IA-64 CPUs are likely to run older code slower than late-model IA-32 CPUs.

Intel-Compatible Processors

Although Intel has dominated the microprocessor market since its inception, there have always been Intel-compatible processors. The following sections describe the major alternative processors.

Advanced Micro Devices

Advanced Micro Devices (*http://www.amd.com*) has been manufacturing Intel-compatible processors for about 15 years, at first by producing second-source replicas of the Intel 286 and 386, and later by producing "improved" versions of the Intel 486 and Pentium processors, such as the 486/DX4-120 and the more-or-less Pentium-compatible K5.

Until recently, AMD processors were regarded by most people simply as cheaper, slower alternatives to mainstream Intel processors. In general, AMD processors had a reputation for good integer performance, poor floating point performance, and minor but nagging incompatibilities. The market dominance, technical superiority, and higher performance of Intel processors largely relegated AMD processors to use in low-end, mass-market computers. But all that changed when AMD shipped the Athlon.

Athlon

The AMD Athlon, which was originally code-named the K7 and began volume shipments in August, 1999, is the first Intel-compatible processor from any maker that can compete on an equal footing with mainstream Intel processors. First-generation Athlon processors match or exceed Katmai-core Pentium III processors in most respects, including (for the first time ever) floating point performance. Intel finally has a fight on its hands.

Although AMD represents the Athlon as the first seventh-generation processor, we regard the Athlon as essentially an enhanced sixth-generation processor. Athlon has, in theory, several advantages relative to the aging Intel sixth-generation architecture, including the ability to perform nine operations per clock cycle (versus five for the Pentium III); more integer pipelines (three versus two); more floating-point pipelines (three versus one); a much larger L1 cache (128 KB versus 32 KB); more full x86 decoders (three versus one); and a faster FSB (100 MHz double-pumped to 200 MHz versus 100/133 MHz). While all of those things are very nice, tests show that in practice the Athlon and Pentium III are pretty much dead even in both integer and floating point performance, with the Coppermine Pentium III perhaps a bit ahead, particularly at higher processor speeds where its faster L2 cache comes into play.

Although the first-generation Athlon is a very good processor, it has the following drawbacks:

Poor chipset and motherboard support
> Initial acceptance of the Athlon was hampered because the only chipset available was the AMD-750, which was originally intended as a technology demonstrator rather than as a production chipset. The VIA KX133 chipset,

originally planned to ship at the same time as the Athlon, was significantly delayed, and motherboards based on the KX133 began shipping in volume only in Q2/2000. Many motherboard manufacturers delayed introducing Athlon models, and the first Athlon motherboards were relatively primitive products compared to the polished products available for the Pentium III. In addition to indifferent quality, stability, compatibility, performance, and features, first-generation Athlon motherboards were in short supply and relatively expensive compared to comparable models for the Pentium III. We think this situation will gradually improve throughout 2000, although Socket A motherboards for second-generation Socket A Athlon processors are likely to be thin on the ground at first.

Fractional CPU-speed L2 cache

Like the Deschutes core Pentium II and the Katmai core Pentium III, the first Athlon processors shipped used L2 cache running at half CPU speed. Unlike Intel, which uses on-die L2 cache for the Coppermine Pentium IIIs, AMD continues to use discrete L2 cache chips, which they must buy from third parties. Athlon architecture allows running L2 cache at anything from a small fraction of CPU speed to full CPU speed. AMD has taken advantage of this as they have introduced faster and faster versions of the Athlon by reducing the speed of L2 cache relative to processor speed, allowing them to use less expensive L2 cache chips. 700 MHz and slower Athlons run L2 cache at 1/2 CPU speed; 750, 800, and 850 MHz Athlons run L2 cache at 2/5 CPU speed. 900 MHz and faster Athlons run L2 cache at 1/3 CPU speed. Unfortunately, compared to the full-speed Pentium III Coppermine L2 cache, the fractional CPU speed L2 cache used on fast Athlons decreases performance noticeably in some applications.

High power consumption

First-generation Athlon processors are power-hungry, with some original 0.25μ models consuming nearly 60 watts. In comparison, typical Intel processors use one-half to one-third that amount. High power consumption and the concomitant heat production has many implications, including possibly shorter component life and the requirement for improved system cooling and larger power supplies. In fact, for the Athlon, AMD took the unprecedented step of certifying power supplies for use with their processor.

Lack of SMP support

For now, no multiprocessor Athlon systems exist. Although the Athlon processor itself is SMP-capable (and in fact supports the superior point-to-point SMP method rather than Intel's shared bus method), no current Athlon chipset supports multiple CPUs. AMD recognizes this lack, however, and will address it by shipping the AMD-770 chipset in late 2000. However, because Intel owns MPS (Multiprocessor Specification) and is unlikely to license it to AMD, implementing an SMP Athlon system will require the operating system kernel support Athlon-specific SMP, which may or may not come to pass. So for the immediate future, if you need an SMP system the only choice is the Intel Pentium III.

With the exception of SMP support, these faults will be corrected in the forth-coming generation of Athlon CPUs. Like Intel, with its shift from Slot 1 to Socket

370 for low-end processors, AMD has recognized that producing cartridge-based slotted processors is needlessly expensive for the low-end, and makes it more difficult to compete in the value segment. Accordingly, AMD has developed a socket technology, analogous to Socket 370, which they call Socket A. Socket A is the future of AMD processors, and AMD will rapidly phase out Slot A during 2000. Although none are yet available, it is likely that slocket adapters will be made to allow using Socket A Athlon processors in Slot A motherboards. AMD expects to ship the following Athlon variants in H2/2000, all based on the enhanced K75 core. AMD says the code-names for these processors are based on the automobiles of the same name rather than the aircraft.

Duron

The *Duron*, code-named *Spitfire*, is planned for Socket A implementation only, and targeted at the value desktop market. The Duron is AMD's Celeron-killer, and with it AMD straddles a fine line between matching Celeron clock speeds and performance on the one hand, versus avoiding cannibalizing sales of their mainstream Athlon processors on the other. Accordingly, AMD will, at least initially, differentiate the Duron from the Athlon by limiting its clock speed and using a smaller and perhaps less efficient L2 cache. Based on a 0.18μ process using aluminum interconnects, the Duron is the first Athlon to use integrated, full-speed L2 cache, probably of 128 KB. Duron supports a 100 MHz DDR FSB, yielding an effective FSB of 200 MHz. As this is written in June 2000, Duron processors are sampling to motherboard and system vendors, but are not yet shipping into the retail channel. We expect Duron to begin shipping in June 2000, and to ship in volume during Q3/2000.

Thunderbird

Thunderbird, which may be formally named *Athlon Professional*, is planned initially for Socket A and Slot A implementation, and targeted at the mainstream desktop and entry-level workstation market, in direct competition with the Intel Pentium III and the forthcoming Pentium IV. The major differences from the Duron are that the Thunderbird has a larger full CPU-speed L2 cache—with 512 KB and possibly 1 MB versions expected—and that faster versions of the Thunderbird will likely be introduced before a Duron model operating at the same speed is released. The first Thunderbird processors will be based on a 0.18μ process using aluminum interconnects, but in late 2000 AMD will convert to a 0.18μ process with copper interconnects. As they shift to copper, AMD will phase out Slot A Thunderbird models, and shift entirely to Socket A. Thunderbird will almost certainly be AMD's last Slot A processor. We expect Thunderbird to ship in volume during Q3/2000.

Mustang

Mustang, which may be formally named *Athlon Ultra*, will be released only as a Socket A part, targeted at servers and high-performance workstations and desktops. Mustang is an enhanced version of Thunderbird, with reduced core size, lower power consumption, and large, full-speed, on-die L2 cache, probably 2 MB or more. Mustang will support a 133 MHz DDR FSB, yielding an effective FSB of 266 MHz. Mustang will use a 0.18μ process with copper interconnects from the start, and will require the AMD-760 chipset or better. SMP Mustang implementations will be possible when AMD releases the AMD-770 chipset, although operating system support will also be needed for a usable SMP system. We expect Mustang to begin shipping during Q4/2000.

Our take is that the first-generation Athlon is less suitable than a comparable Intel Pentium III or Celeron for most mainstream users. The second-generation Athlon, however, is likely to pose a serious threat to Intel's core processor business, assuming that the expected high-quality second-generation Athlon chipsets arrive on time and that AMD is able to deliver processors in quantity, neither of which is a sure thing.

Other AMD processors

In addition to their flagship Athlon line, AMD manufactures the following CPUs:

K6-2

Introduced in mid-1998, as of June 2000 the K6-2 remains available in 450, 475, 500, 533, and 550 MHz versions. K6-2 integer performance is close to that of a Celeron at the same clock speed, but floating point performance is noticeably inferior, and the processor is hampered by its dependence on the aging Socket 7 platform. Although still available, the K6-2 is now used only in low-end systems.

K6-III

The Socket 7 K6-III shipped in Q1/99 at 450 MHz, but the expected faster versions never materialized. As of June 2000, the K6-III remains available in 400 and 450 MHz versions, although it has been officially discontinued. The K6-III is designed to function in any K6-2 motherboard with only a BIOS update. It adds a 256 KB on-chip L2 cache, which addresses the long-standing problem of Socket 7 L2 cache being accessible only via the relatively slow memory bus. The K6-III also supports an L3 cache residing on the motherboard, which increases performance, but may introduce subtle problems with existing chipsets. K6-III integer performance generally matches the Celeron at the same clock speed. Floating point performance is improved relative to the K6-2, but is still inferior to Intel.

The introduction of Socket A Athlon processors sounds the death knell for the AMD K6-* line of processors, although they will remain available in mobile versions throughout 2000.

Other Alternative Processors

By late 1999, the market share of AMD and Intel for processors totaled literally near 100%, leaving only tiny niches for such CPU makers as Cyrix, Integrated Device Technology (IDT), and Rise. Even those niches comprised sales of processors less costly than the Intel Celeron and the AMD K6-* series. It's impossible to make a profit selling small numbers of $20 processors, so Cyrix, IDT, and Rise effectively departed the market, leaving Intel and AMD as the only mainstream processor makers.

Cyrix

Cyrix was best known as a manufacturer of inexpensive x86 processors that were used in mass-market PCs like those sold by Best Buy, Circuit City, and similar retailers. National Semiconductor, which owned Cyrix, sold it in 1999 to VIA Technologies, the chipset maker. VIA currently produces the VIA Cyrix III processor, which is aimed at the sub-$500 PC segment, but which is unlikely to survive competition from Intel and AMD even there. In the past, Cyrix has produced the following processors. Any system that uses one of these processors is a poor upgrade candidate.

6x86

The first Pentium-compatible processor shipped, the 6x86, like the P54C, runs a 3.3 volt core and supports 5.0 volt I/O. Usually thought of as fifth-generation, the 6x86 was really the first "hybrid" processor. It incorporates aspects of both fifth- and sixth-generation processors, and is closer internally to the Pentium Pro than the Pentium. Other than its very poor floating point performance, the 6x86 is a better processor than a Pentium.

Sex, Lies, and CPU Speeds

Because the 6x86 executes integer instructions faster than a Pentium at the same clock speed, Cyrix developed the *Performance Rating* or *PR* system, which rates processors by assigning them a PR number that corresponds to their approximate performance relative to the Intel Pentium, adding a "+" when the Cyrix CPU somewhat exceeds the performance of the closest Pentium model. For example, the PR150+ actually runs at 120 MHz, but (according to Cyrix, at least) is faster than a Pentium/150. Although it compared favorably to the Pentium in many respects, a combination of poor pricing, incompatibilities with existing motherboards, market timing, overheating problems, and questions about NT compatibility killed the 6x86.

MediaGX

In early 1997, Cyrix introduced the MediaGX, a "PC on a chip" that put the CPU, chipset, PCI interface, memory controller, I/O functions, video adapter, and sound card all in one two-chip package. The MediaGX provided decent if unexceptional performance at the lowest possible price, required a special motherboard, and became a dominant force in the very low-end consumer PC market. The MediaGX was available in 166 and 180 MHz versions. The MMX-enhanced MediaGX processor was available in 200, 233, 266, and 300 MHz versions.

6x86MX

In mid-1997, Cyrix countered the P55C Pentium/MMX with the 6x86MX, a dual-voltage (2.9v/3.3v) Socket 7 CPU that shared the basic architecture of the 6x86, but added MMX support, increased the unified L1 cache from 16 KB to 64 KB, added a better memory management unit, and slightly improved the

FPU. The 6x86MX quickly achieved widespread acceptance by providing integer performance comparable to the Pentium II and K6 at a lower price. The 6x86MX is available in PR166, 200, 233, and 266 versions. 6x86MX floating point performance remains inferior to AMD and much inferior to Intel.

MII

The MII is an enhanced 6x86MX that runs at higher clock speeds, and is available in PR300, 333, 350, and 400 versions, which provide integer performance comparable to that of a Celeron running at equivalent nominal speeds.

The most recent Cyrix processor, the VIA Cyrix III, is currently available in a PR500 model, which in fact provides integer performance comparable to an Intel Celeron/500. But, as has always been the case with Cyrix processors, floating point performance is anemic, so much so that in some comprehensive benchmarks the VIA Cyrix III/500 generates results that indicate it is slower than its actual clock speed, let alone its PR rating. For low-end systems that will run only standard productivity applications, where floating point performance is not an issue, the Socket 370-compatible Cyrix III can provide the basis for a very inexpensive system with reasonable performance.

Integrated Device Technology (IDT)

IDT, which sold its processor technology to VIA Technologies and departed the processor market in 1999, focused on selling its WinChip into the ultra-low-cost PC market and the Socket 7 upgrade market. Where late-model AMD and Cyrix Socket 7 processors worked only in late-model Socket 7 and Super 7 motherboards, WinChips worked in nearly any Socket 5 or 7 motherboard. We regret the departure of IDT from the market because, while the WinChip provided modest performance, using one was an easy way to double or triple the performance of an aging Pentium system at minimal cost. If you ever find a WinChip while salvaging an old system, hold onto it. It may come in handy if you ever need a cheap way to upgrade an old Pentium system, for which no other alternatives are available. IDT produced the following WinChip variants:

WinChip C6

The WinChip C6 shipped in December, 1997, and fits P54C Classic Pentium Socket 5 or P55C Pentium/MMX Socket 7 motherboards interchangeably. It uses the same voltage for core and I/O, and was available in various speeds and voltages, including: 200 MHz/3.3V (to replace P54C CPUs), 200 MHz/3.52 (to replace AMD K5 CPUs), 225 MHz/3.52V, and 240 MHz/3.52V.

WinChip 2

The WinChip 2 first shipped in November 1998. It added an AMD-compatible 100 MHz Super 7 bus, a new pipelined floating point unit, and 3DNow! instructions. It was available in either 3.3V or 3.52V form. It was shipped in 200 MHz (66 MHz bus; 3.0X) and 233 MHz (66 × 3.5X) versions that run at the nominal speed, and also in PR266 (100 × 2.33X, 233 MHz actual) and PR300 (100 × 2.5X, 250 MHz actual) versions.

Choosing a Processor

The processor you choose determines how fast the system runs, and how long it will provide subjectively adequate performance before you need to replace the processor or the system itself. Buying a processor just fast enough to meet current needs means that you'll have to upgrade in a few months. But processor pricing has a built-in law of diminishing returns. Spending twice as much on a processor doesn't buy twice the performance. In fact, you'll be lucky to get 25% more performance for twice the money. So although it's a mistake to buy too slow a processor, it's also a mistake to buy one that's too fast. Consider the following issues when choosing a processor:

Horizon

What kind of applications do you run and how long do you want the system to be usable without requiring an upgrade? If you run mostly standard productivity applications and don't upgrade them frequently, a low- to low/mid-range Celeron or Duron may still be fast enough a year or more after you buy it. If you run cutting-edge games or other demanding applications, buy a mid-high to high-end processor initially, and expect to replace it every six months to a year. But expect to pay a price for remaining on the bleeding edge.

Hassle

Do you mind upgrading your system frequently? If you don't mind replacing the processor every six months to a year, you can get most of the performance of a high-end system at minimal cost by replacing the processor frequently with the then-current low/mid-range processor.

Trade-offs

If you're working on a fixed budget, don't spend too much on the processor to the detriment of the rest of the system. You may be better off, for example, settling for a mid-range Celeron and spending the extra money on more memory, a faster hard disk, or a bigger monitor. A Celeron/500 with 128 MB RAM blows the doors off a Pentium III/1000 with 16 MB RAM every day of the week. Don't make yourself "processor poor."

Form factor

Keep form factor in mind when you're shopping for a processor, particularly if you're also buying a motherboard.

Socket 7

Don't consider buying a Socket 7 processor, except as an inexpensive (<$30) upgrade for an existing PC. Spending much more than that on Socket 7 is wasting money. Retire the old system to less demanding duties, and build or buy a new system instead.

Slot 1/Socket 370

Intel is de-emphasizing Slot 1 in favor of Socket 370, but that doesn't necessarily mean that Slot 1 is a bad choice. Because Intel originally positioned Socket 370 as a low-end solution, Socket 370 motherboards are more likely to incorporate low-end features like entry-level embedded video than are Slot 1 motherboards, and less likely to incorporate high-end features like dual-CPU support, embedded network adapters, and embedded SCSI adapters. If you have, or are buying, a Slot 1 motherboard, buying a Slot 1 processor may (or may not) be the best and most cost-effective choice. Slot 1 motherboards can also accept Socket 370 processors by using a slocket adapter, although there is no guarantee that a particular Socket 370 CPU will function with a given slocket in a given Slot 1 motherboard. In general, when using a Slot 1 motherboard, we prefer to install a Socket 370 processor using a slocket produced by the motherboard manufacturer.

Slot A/Socket A

Like Intel processors, AMD Athlon processors are available in slotted and socketed versions, which differ in physical characteristics but have identical electrical characteristics. The AMD situation is a bit less clear, however, for a couple of reasons. Whereas Intel originally intended Slot 1 and Socket 370 to co-exist, dividing broadly by product lines, with low-end processors using Socket 370 and high-end processors Slot 1, AMD intends Socket A as a direct replacement for Slot A. The likely result is that Slot A motherboards and processors will remain commonly available until Socket A processors and motherboards ship in volume, at which point the future availability of Slot A processors and motherboards becomes doubtful. Also, although we think it likely that slockets to adapt Socket A processors to Slot A motherboards will be produced, we don't know that for a fact, nor even that a particular Slot A motherboard will support Socket A processors. The generally primitive nature of Slot A motherboards, the relatively low volume in which they have sold, and the relatively short time for which they have been produced may mean that Socket A will simply replace Slot A more or less overnight. If that occurs, any money you have invested in Slot A components will be a sunk cost. In fact, the transition from Slot A to Socket A is one of the major reasons why we cannot yet recommend AMD Athlon processors for general use.

When upgrading a system, the existing motherboard determines upgradability, as follows:

486 motherboards

It is not cost-effective to upgrade 486 systems. Evergreen, Kingston, and others sell upgrade kits, which we suggest you avoid. The Kingston Turbo-Chip 133 is typical. It uses a 133 MHz 5x86 chip to boost performance to the level of a Pentium/75 at a cost of $75 or so, which is about what an entire used Pentium/75 system costs. Compatibility is always problematic, and we regard these kits as a waste of money. Upgrading the processor in a 486 is a sucker bet.

Socket 4 motherboards

The original P54 60 and 66 MHz Pentiums fit Socket 4 motherboards. Again, although upgrade processors are available for these systems, buying one is not a cost-effective upgrade. Replace the motherboard and install a modern processor.

Socket 5 and old Socket 7 motherboards

Socket 5 systems use Pentium P54C processors. Older Socket 7 systems use Pentium P55C processors. Either of these motherboards may be a reasonable

Can Two Slow Processors Beat One Fast One?

If you run an SMP-capable operating system like Windows NT or Linux, consider buying a dual-processor motherboard, even if you only install one processor initially. You'll find that for many applications a system with two slower processors is faster than a system with one faster processor. Intel's CPU pricing strategy means that you can buy two mid-range processors for less than the cost of one top-of-the-line processor. Although using two mid-range processors doesn't give you literally twice the speed of using one, such a system usually "feels" noticeably faster than a system with one high-end processor, particularly when running multiple demanding applications simultaneously.

Although Intel did not intend Celerons to support dual-processor operation, you can build a dual-Celeron system. Dual Socket 370 motherboards are hard to find, but you can use slockets to install two Socket 370 Celerons in a dual-CPU Slot 1 motherboard. Recent slockets support both PPGA and FC-PGA processors, and allow you to configure dual-CPU operation simply by setting jumpers. With two PPGA Celerons, two slockets, and a dual Slot 1 motherboard, you can build a very fast SMP system on the cheap.

candidate for a drop-in CPU upgrade, but the exact characteristics of the motherboard, especially the voltages it supports, determine which upgrade processors can be used with it. Installing an IDT WinChip 2 is usually the best solution for such systems. Do not attempt to do too much with these old motherboards. Upgrading a 75/133 MHz Pentium P54C system to a 66 MHz bus WinChip 2/233 is often a cost-effective upgrade. If you need something faster, buy a Slot 1 or Socket 370 board and a Celeron or Pentium III.

Recent Socket 7 motherboards

If your system has a recent Socket 7 board (particularly a Super7-compliant board), you have more alternatives, notably the AMD K6-2 and K6-III series of processors, to the extent that they remain available. Before you buy a new processor, make sure that the motherboard provides the necessary bus speed, multiplier, and voltage settings to support it, and that the processor manufacturer certifies your motherboard for use with that processor. You may also need a BIOS upgrade to enable all features of the new processor. Note that if you are upgrading from a 66 MHz bus processor to a 100 MHz bus processor, you may also need to replace your L2 cache with cache memory rated to run at 100 MHz.

Slot 1 motherboards

Pre-440BX motherboards are limited to the 66 MHz FSB, so the best upgrade alternative is a fast 66 MHz FSB Celeron. If the system currently uses a 233 or 266 MHz Pentium II, installing a 400 or 433 MHz Celeron provides a large performance boost at low cost, assuming that the BIOS upgrade needed to support the Celeron is available. If the motherboard uses the 440BX or later chipset, and if an updated BIOS is available, consider upgrading to a 100 MHz

FSB Pentium III. Note that upgrading from a 66 MHz FSB processor to one that uses the 100 MHz FSB requires using PC100 memory as well. Don't restrict yourself to Slot 1 processors, which are available only in limited types and speeds. Consider installing a PPGA or FC-PGA Socket 370 processor by using a slocket adapter. Before you buy a Socket 370 processor to upgrade a Slot 1 system, make sure that the motherboard and latest available BIOS support the processor you want to use.

Socket 370 motherboards

These motherboards are new enough that there are usually few upgrade options. Although you can install a faster Celeron, it is for now unlikely that the fastest available PPGA Celeron will be much faster than what is already installed. Note that two distinct versions of Socket 370 exist. The earlier version, designed to accept PPGA Celeron processors, is incompatible with FC-PGA Pentium III and Coppermine128-based Celeron processors. The later version supports any Socket 370 processor, including PPGA Celerons, Coppermine128 Celerons, and FC-PGA Pentium IIIs.

Although we've not used it, Powerleap claims their Neo S370 PPGA to FC-PGA adapter allows some FC-PGA Pentium III and Celeron II processors to operate in some PPGA Socket 370 motherboards. The Neo S370 remaps FC-PGA pinouts to PPGA pinouts and converts the 2.0V used by PPGA processors to the 1.60/1.65V used by FC-PGA processors. This adapter works with only some motherboards, which are listed on the compatibility page (*http://www.powerleap.com*).

Installing a Socketed Processor

Installing any socketed processor is a straightforward operation if you do things by the numbers. The most important thing to remember is that processors are particularly sensitive to static shock. Take great care to observe anti-static procedures while you are handling the processor. It's a good rule of thumb to always keep one hand in contact with the PC power supply while you handle the processor.

Socket 5, Socket 7, Socket 370, and Socket A motherboards have a *Zero Insertion Force (ZIF)* socket, which allows a chip with hundreds of pins to be seated easily. To install a new socketed processor, take the following steps:

1. If you are installing a new processor in an older system, before beginning work check to see if an updated BIOS is available for the system. The new processor may require a BIOS update to function at full capacity, or indeed to function at all. If a new BIOS is available, download it and update your PC as described in Chapter 3, *Motherboards*, before you install the new processor.

2. Move the PC or motherboard to a well-lit work area, preferably one with all-around access. Collect all of the tools, software, manuals, and upgrade components you need. Read through the processor documentation before proceeding.

3. To install a processor in a new motherboard, ground yourself, remove the motherboard from its packaging, and place it flat on the anti-static bag. If you are installing a new processor in an existing PC, you can probably do so without removing the motherboard, although you may have to reroute or temporarily disconnect cables to gain unobstructed access to the socket.

4. If a heat sink and cooling fan are not already installed on the processor, consider installing them before continuing. Some cooling devices are easy to install whether or not the processor is already in its socket. Some are easy to install on a loose processor, but difficult to install once the CPU is in the socket. Others are exactly the opposite. Installing some cooling devices, for example, blocks the ZIF lever, leaving you no choice but to install them after the processor is seated. If your cooling device appears to be easy to install either way, install it after the processor is in the socket. That makes it much easier to get the processor aligned and seated correctly. When you install the cooling device, don't forget to apply a dab of thermal grease if the documentation recommends it.

 When installing an FC-PGA Pentium III or FC-PGA Celeron processor, be sure the heat sink you use is designed specifically for the FC-PGA processor you are installing. The FC-PGA package places the actual microprocessor chip on top, where it comes into direct contact with the base of the heat sink. Although heat sinks designed for PPGA or Socket 7 processors may physically fit the FC-PGA processor, they may not make proper contact with the processor, and will almost certainly allow it to overheat. Worse, using the wrong heat sink may crack the FC-PGA processor, destroying it. Also note that different FC-PGA processors require different heat sinks. For example, a heat sink designed for a Celeron/533A does not provide adequate cooling for a Pentium III/933. Use the correct heat sink and fan for FC-PGA processors. You have been warned.

5. Refer to the processor documentation to determine the proper settings for bus speed, CPU multiplier, core voltage, and I/O voltage. Refer to the motherboard manual or manufacturer's web site to locate the configuration jumpers and to determine the jumper settings that match those required by the new processor. There are four settings you may have to make, all or any of which may not be present on a given motherboard. In particular, Socket 370 motherboards designed for PPGA Celeron processors may have only a single configuration jumper and allow the CPU speed to be configured in CMOS setup.

Bus speed

All Socket 5 and Socket 7 motherboards provide settings at least for 60 and 66 MHz. Some motherboards support higher bus speeds, including 75, 83, and 95 MHz, which are intended to allow "overclocking" the processor—running it faster than its rated speed. Don't use these settings unless you are sure you want to overclock the processor. New Super7 motherboards also support a 100 MHz bus speed, which is a standard speed for new Socket 7 processors. These motherboards may also include various overclocking settings, including 103, 112, and 124 MHz. Again, avoid using overclocking unless you are making an informed decision to do so.

 At least one processor, the AMD K6-2/333, was actually designed for the oddball 95 MHz speed (with a 3.5X multiplier). Most of those processors were bought by people intending to overclock them to 350 MHz on a 100 MHz bus.

CPU multiplier

The product of the bus speed and CPU multiplier determines how fast the processor runs. Note that some processors convert the chosen CPU multiplier internally to a different multiplier. Note also that some CPUs are named with a "performance rating" rather than their actual speed. When setting the bus speed and CPU multiplier, it is important to choose settings that run the processor at its actual rated speed rather than the labeled performance equivalent.

You can sometimes choose between two combinations of bus speed and CPU multiplier that have the same product. In this case, choose the combination of the higher bus speed and lower multiplier, so long as the higher bus speed is supported. For example, when installing a 300 MHz processor, you can choose 66 MHz/4.5X or 100 MHz/3.0X. Either setting runs the processor at 300 MHz, but the latter setting provides marginally faster performance by allowing data to be communicated faster between the CPU and the external L2 cache memory.

Voltage

Different processors require different voltages. Some processors operate on a single voltage, and others require different *Core* and *I/O* voltages. Old motherboards may support only one fixed voltage, and so may not be usable with recent low-voltage or dual-voltage CPUs. *Pay close attention to voltage, because installing a low-voltage CPU in a high-voltage motherboard may destroy the processor.* Adapters are available to allow installing newer low-voltage processors in older motherboards, but in that situation it is better in every respect simply to replace the motherboard.

Asynchronous PCI

Systems with a 60 or 66 MHz FSB run the PCI bus at half speed—30 MHz and 33 MHz respectively. Systems with a 100 MHz FSB run the PCI bus at one-third speed—33 MHz. Using these fixed divisors is called using synchronous PCI. But PCI devices are unreliable much above 33 MHz, and overclocking the system by using a 75, 83, or 95 MHz FSB on a synchronous motherboard causes the PCI bus to run at 37.5 MHz (marginal), 41.5 MHz (unusable), or 47.5 MHz (ridiculous). Super7 motherboards running at 95 MHz run the PCI bus at 31.67 MHz—safe but slow. At 83 MHz, most Super7 boards run the PCI bus at 41.5 MHz (unusably fast) or 20.75 MHz (unusably slow). Many motherboards designed to support overclocking include a jumper to set the PCI bus at 33 MHz regardless of the FSB speed, which is called *asynchronous PCI.*

6. Once you have set and verified all jumpers, lift the ZIF lever, which is located on one side of the socket, as far as it will go. If there is a processor in the socket, grasp it firmly and lift it free. It should come away without resistance. If it does not, verify that the ZIF lever is fully vertical before again attempting to remove the processor.

7. Locate pin 1 on the new processor, usually indicated by a dot or beveled edge on one corner of the processor, or by a missing pin on that corner. Locate pin 1 on the ZIF socket, which is usually indicated by a dot or beveled edge, and sometimes by a numeral 1 silk-screened onto the motherboard itself. Orient pin 1 on the new processor to pin 1 on the socket and then gently press the processor into the socket. The processor should seat fully with little or no resistance. If the processor does not seat easily, remove it, verify that the pins align correctly, and try to seat it again. Avoid excessive force when seating the processor. It's easy to bend pins, and straightening them is next to impossible.

8. Once the processor is fully seated, press the ZIF lever down until it is parallel to the edge of the socket. This locks the processor into the socket and makes electrical contact on all pins.

9. If you did not previously install the cooling device, do so now. Most heat sinks and fans clip directly to the processor or to the socket. Don't forget to use thermal compound to improve heat transfer between the processor and the cooling device. Attach the fan power cable to a motherboard fan power header, or to an available power supply connector, as appropriate.

10. Install the motherboard, if necessary, connect or reroute any cables you'd moved, do a quick visual once-over, reconnect the monitor, keyboard, and mouse, and then apply power to the system. The system should begin a normal boot sequence. If nothing (or something strange) happens, immediately turn the power off and re-verify all connections and settings.

11. Once the system boots normally, enter CMOS setup and make whatever changes, if any, the processor documentation recommends. Once the system is working normally, turn off the power, reinstall the chassis cover, return the PC to its working location, reconnect all cables, and restart the system.

Installing a Slotted Processor

Installing a Slot 1 or Slot A processor is in some ways easier than installing a socketed processor and in some ways harder. Intel manufactures processors for two similar but incompatible slots. The 242-pin connector, formerly called Slot 1, accepts slotted Celeron, Pentium II, and Pentium III processors. The 330-pin connector, formerly called Slot 2, accepts Xeon-class processors. These processors come in different physical packaging (SEC, SEC2, SEPP, etc.), each of which uses a different *retention mechanism.* For example, an SEC Pentium II and an SEPP Celeron both fit the same Slot 1, but use different and incompatible retention mechanisms.

To further complicate matters, Intel ships the same processor in different variants. For example, the retail boxed version of the Pentium II processor comes with an attached fan, while the OEM version of that processor does not. If you purchase an OEM processor with an attached fan, that package may or may not fit the standard retention mechanism (although it usually does fit). So, the first rule is to make sure that the retention mechanism accepts the processor. If you purchase a cooling device that does not fit the standard retention mechanism, it should be supplied with a mechanism that fits it. Thankfully, all retention mechanisms mount to the standard set of holes in Slot 1 motherboards.

To install a new slotted processor, take the following steps:

1. When installing a new processor in an older system, determine if a BIOS update is available, because the processor may require a later BIOS to support its new features. For example, the Intel SE440BX "Seattle" motherboard accepts any Slot 1 processor, including a Pentium III. But you must upgrade the BIOS to take advantage of the new Pentium III SSE instructions. Installing the Pentium III without upgrading the BIOS simply makes the Pentium III run like a faster Pentium II. If a new BIOS is available, download it and update your PC as described in Chapter 3.

2. Move the PC or motherboard to a well-lit work area, preferably one with all-around access. Collect all of the tools, software, manuals, and upgrade components you need. Read through the processor documentation before proceeding.

3. To install a processor in a new motherboard, ground yourself, remove the motherboard from its packaging, and place it flat on the anti-static bag. If you are installing a new processor in an existing PC that uses a compatible retention mechanism, you can probably do so without removing the motherboard, although you may have to reroute or disconnect cables to gain unobstructed access to the slot. If the retention mechanism needs to be replaced, e.g., when upgrading a Celeron system to a Pentium III, you may or may not have to remove the system board to replace the retention mechanism.

4. If it is not already installed, install the retention mechanism by following the instructions supplied with it or the motherboard. Standard retention mechanisms are notched at one end to match the notch in the Slot 1 connector on the motherboard. Align the retention mechanism and seat the four posts into the matching holes on the motherboard. Press down firmly until the retention mechanism seats. Each post has a sliding internal pin with a flat, circular, white, plastic top. Forcing that pin down into the post expands the bottom of the post on the far side of the motherboard, securing the post to the motherboard. Press down each of the pins until it snaps into place. Some newer Slot 1 motherboards come with the retention mechanism already installed, but with the vertical supports folded flat. If your motherboard is like this, lift the vertical supports until they snap into place.

5. If the cooling device is not already installed on the processor, install it now. Some processor packages also contain a supplementary support mechanism designed to secure the processor against the additional weight and vibration

of the cooling fan. If your package contains such a supplemental support, install it on the processor according to the instructions provided with it.

6. Refer to the processor documentation to determine the proper settings for bus speed and CPU multiplier. Refer to the motherboard manual or manufacturer web site to locate configuration jumpers and to determine the jumper settings that match those required by the new processor. Some boards have separate jumpers for FSB speed and CPU multiplier, others have jumpers for CPU speed only (which implicitly sets both FSB speed and CPU multiplier), and still others use "jumperless setup," which sets FSB and CPU multiplier options in CMOS Setup. Slot 1 processors do not require voltages to be set manually. All current Slot 1 processors use 3.3 volts for external I/O. Klamath-based processors use 2.8 volts internally, and Deschutes-based processors use 2.0 volts. Voltage setting is handled completely automatically via the Voltage ID (VID) pins on the processor itself.

7. Once you have made the necessary jumper changes, if any, install the processor, first removing the existing processor if necessary. The card-edge connector on Slot 1 processors has a keying notch that divides the connector about one-third of the way along its length. Align that notch with the corresponding key in the motherboard Slot 1 connector, align the edges of the processor with the vertical supports of the retention mechanism, and slide the processor into place. Press firmly until the processor seats firmly.

8. Attach the fan power cable to a motherboard fan power header.

9. Install the motherboard, if necessary, connect or reroute any cables you'd moved, do a quick visual once-over, reconnect the monitor, keyboard, and mouse, and then apply power to the system. The system should begin a normal boot sequence. If nothing (or something strange) happens, immediately turn the power off and re-verify all connections and settings.

10. Once the system boots normally, enter CMOS setup and make whatever changes, if any, the processor documentation recommends. Once the system is working normally, turn off the power, reinstall the chassis cover, return the PC to its working location, reconnect all cables, and restart the system.

A Word About Overclocking

Overclocking means running a processor faster than its designers intended it to be run, for example, by running a Celeron/366 processor at 550 MHz. The mechanics are easy enough. You simply set the memory bus speed and/or the CPU multiplier to higher than the correct value. All recent Intel processors are multiplier-locked, which means that changing FSB speed is the only way to overclock an Intel processor. AMD processors are not locked, and may be overclocked by altering FSB speed, CPU multiplier, or both.

Here's how it works. The Celeron/366 uses a 66 MHz FSB and a 5.5X multiplier ($66 \times 5.5 = 366$). Setting the FSB at 100 MHz runs the Celeron/366 at 550 MHz (100 $\times 5.5 = 550$). That usually works because most Celeron/366s use L2 cache chips fast enough to support 550 MHz operation, and the Mendocino core itself can operate at that speed. In effect, Intel sells a 550 MHz processor labeled at 366 MHz. Depending on the processor, overclocking may work, at least for a while.

But overclocking a processor risks subtle data corruption and may also dramatically shorten the life of the processor, particularly if it requires higher than nominal voltage to achieve the overclocked speed.

Overclockability varies by processor. Few IDT or Cyrix processors can be overclocked successfully, in effect because they already run at or near the limit of their cores and cache chips. Conversely, *some* AMD and Intel processors are easy to overclock, notably the slower versions of the Intel Celeron and Pentium III and the AMD Athlon. But not all processors can be overclocked, and you can't judge which are overclockable simply by model, because manufacturers sell different processors with the same model/speed designation. For example, all Pentium II/300 processors were not created equal. Some were based on the original 2.8V Klamath core and others on the 2.0V Deschutes core. Some used L2 cache chips rated for 450/225 MHz operation and others use chips that are not reliable much above 300/150 MHz. Finding subtle variations between supposedly identical processors is a subculture whose members discuss steppings and countries of origin like oenologists discuss vintages.

Interestingly, both Intel and AMD have begun to do what amounts to overclocking their own processors in an attempt to deliver processors with the fastest possible speed. Any processor core has a design voltage. For example, Katmai core Pentium IIIs are designed to run at 2.0V, and Coppermine core Pentium IIIs at 1.6V. Within reason, running a processor at higher than its design voltage allows it to run faster.

Overclocking is a phenomenon whose time has passed, if indeed it ever arrived. If you need higher performance, buy a faster processor. If despite these warnings you still want to overclock your processor, visit one of the enthusiast web sites like AnandTech (*http://www.anandtech.com*) for detailed instructions.

Our Picks

Although processor makers hate to admit it, the processor is actually a relatively minor factor in overall system performance. The difference in absolute processor performance between an $80 processor and an $800 processor may be a factor of two or less. Nor does buying an $800 processor make your system run twice as fast, because processor speed is only one element of system performance. Before you plunk down $800 for a processor, consider instead spending that extra money on more memory, a faster video card, a SCSI hard disk—or all of those. If you run Windows NT, Windows 2000, Linux, or another operating system that supports multiple processors, consider using two slower, inexpensive processors rather than one fast, expensive one.

Here are the processors we use and recommend:

Entry-level system
> **Intel Celeron.** No other current processor even comes close to providing the bang-for-the-buck ratio of the Celeron, although the Socket A Duron, due to ship in volume in mid-2000, may do so. Clock-for-clock, Celeron processors provide 90% to 100% of the performance of Pentium III or Athlon processors in most applications, but cost only a fraction the price. For an entry-level system, buy the least expensive PPGA Celeron available, at least until the

price of the FC-PGA Coppermine128 core Celerons drops and the Mendocino core Celerons are discontinued. When that happens, choose a Coppermine128-based "Celeron II." Note that Intel announced in May 2000 that their forthcoming 815 Solano and 815e Solano II chipsets, follow-ons to the 440BX chipset, will not support Mendocino-core Celeron processors. (*http://developer.intel.com/design/celeron/*)

Mainstream system

Intel Coppermine128 Celeron. We know that many will take issue with us here for not recommending the Intel Pentium III and/or the AMD Athlon, but the truth is that any reasonably priced Pentium III or Athlon provides only minimal performance benefits relative to the Celeron II, which even includes the vaunted SSE instruction set introduced with the Pentium III. For a mainstream system, buy the least expensive Coppermine128-core Celeron available.

High-performance system

Dual Intel Pentium III. If you run Windows NT/2000, Linux, or another SMP-capable operating system, we recommend using a dual processor system. In our experience, responsiveness in a multitasking environment is better with two low-end or mid-range Pentium III processors than with one faster processor. No one task runs as fast on the dual-CPU system as it would on the faster single processor, but the dual-CPU machine simply doesn't bog down. Robert runs a dual Pentium III/550 system as his main workstation, often with 30 or more background processes running and 20 windows open. He finds that the dual Pentium III/550 "feels" faster than an otherwise similar system that uses one 850 MHz processor. Of course, for the fastest possible system, install two of the fastest Pentium III processors you can afford.

We constantly test and review new equipment. For the latest information about what we currently use, visit:

http://www.hardwareguys.com/picks/processors.html

CHAPTER 5

Memory

A few years ago, this book could have covered memory in a page or two. All memory came as discrete chips, and there were only a few sizes and speeds available. You bought however many chips you needed, installed them, and that was that.

Dramatic CPU speed increases over the last few years have brought designers up against one hard fact. It's difficult to design faster CPUs, but it's even harder to build faster memory. Building *affordable* fast memory is harder still. Faster processors require faster memory, so engineers have come up with various methods to increase memory speeds. One result is that memory isn't a simple issue anymore. This chapter tells you what you need to know to make good decisions about buying memory when you build or upgrade a system.

Understanding Memory

This chapter focuses on general-purpose memory, where PCs store programs and data that are currently in use, the pipeline that supplies data to and receives results from the processor. General-purpose memory, called *read-write memory* or *Random Access Memory (RAM)*, must be readable-from and writable-to. Two types of RAM are used on modern PCs:

Dynamic RAM (DRAM)
> *Dynamic RAM* stores data for only a tiny fraction of a second before losing it. To maintain stored data, the system must constantly *refresh* DRAM, which exacts a performance penalty and limits its speed. Typical DRAM provides 60 nanoseconds (ns) access, but costs only a dollar per megabyte.

Static RAM (SRAM)
> *Static RAM* automatically maintains its contents as long as power is applied to it, without requiring refresh. SRAM is the fastest memory type available (typically 6 ns) but is very expensive and power-hungry.

PCs use a tiered memory architecture that takes advantage of these characteristics:

Main memory

The bulk of a PC's memory uses DRAM and is called *main memory*. It is large—typically 32 MB to 256 MB—but too slow to keep up with a modern CPU. Main memory is where the CPU stores programs and data that it will soon need. Main memory functions as a buffer between the CPU and disk and stores tens to hundreds of megabytes.

Cache memory

Cache memory is a small amount of fast SRAM that buffers access between the CPU and main memory.

Modern PCs have at least one, typically two, and sometimes three layers of cache memory:

Primary cache memory

Primary cache, also called *Level 1 cache* or *L1 cache*, is typically 16 to 128 KB of very fast memory on the same chip as the CPU itself. L1 cache size and efficiency are major factors in CPU performance. The amount and type of L1 cache is determined by the CPU you use, and cannot be upgraded.

Secondary cache memory

L1 cache is not large enough to eliminate the speed disparity between processors and main memory. *Secondary cache*, also called *Level 2 cache, L2 cache,* or (on Pentium-class motherboards) *external cache*, bridges that gap with a reasonable compromise between cost and performance. L2 cache resides on the motherboard of most Socket 7 systems—where it can be upgraded—but is a nonupgradable part of the CPU package (or of the CPU substrate itself) on Celeron, Pentium II/III, and AMD K6-III and Athlon systems.

Depending on its type, external L2 cache on Pentium-class motherboards may be upgraded as follows:

Discrete SRAM chips

Older motherboards often use individual socketed or soldered SRAM chips. If free sockets are available, you can expand L2 cache by adding SRAM and TAG chips of the appropriate number, type, and speed.

Cache on a Stick

Newer systems use *Cache on a Stick (COASt)* modules, also called *Card Edge Low Profile (CELP)* modules, which install in a socket that looks much like a PCI slot. COASt modules come in various types and speeds, so when upgrading be sure to purchase the correct type.

High-density surface-mount SRAM packages

Most current Super Socket 7 motherboards use surface-mount SRAM packages, which are not upgradable. Some motherboards have available sockets, and can be upgraded by adding the type of chips specified by the documentation.

Most Pentium motherboards have 256 or 512 KB of L2 cache, but inexpensive systems may have none. You can improve performance of such systems cheaply by installing 256 KB of L2 cache. Installing more than that usually yields diminishing returns, but may be worthwhile on a heavily loaded system running Windows NT or Linux.

 Some PCs and motherboards arrive with cache memory installed but disabled. Always check the Chipset Setup section of CMOS Setup to verify that L1 and L2 cache are both enabled.

Memory Access Methods

PC memory may use the following access methods:

Asynchronous
> *Asynchronous DRAM*, which was used in all PCs until recently, uses a window of fixed minimum duration to determine when operations may occur. If the CPU has transferred data while a window is open, and if a subsequent clock cycle occurs while that window remains open, the CPU cannot transfer additional data until the next window opens, thereby wasting that clock cycle. Asynchronous operation forces the CPU to conform to a fixed schedule for transferring data, rather than doing so whenever it wishes. Asynchronous DRAM is available in the following types:

> > *Fast Page Mode (FPM) DRAM*
> > FPM was commonly used on 486 and earlier systems, and may be installed in early Pentium systems. FPM is still sold, but is not supported by recent chipsets. Although you can migrate FPM from an old Socket 5 or 7 system to a new Socket 7 motherboard, that old memory will be small and slow. It's better simply to replace FPM with a more recent and faster type of memory. You may be able to install surplus FPM in your laser printer.

> > *Extended Data Out (EDO) DRAM*
> > EDO, also sometimes called Hyper Page Mode DRAM, is marginally faster than FPM, is still available in all common package types, and was commonly installed on new systems until late 1998. Purchasing EDO today makes sense only if you are adding memory to a system that currently has EDO installed. Even then, many systems allow EDO and SDRAM to co-exist, albeit with the SDRAM performing at the lower level of EDO, so it often makes sense to buy SDRAM even when upgrading an EDO system.

> > *Burst Extended Data Out (BEDO) DRAM*
> > BEDO slightly improved upon EDO, but never became popular due to the introduction of SDRAM. Do not buy BEDO unless your motherboard will use nothing else.

Synchronous
> *Synchronous DRAM* shares a common clock reference with the CPU. No window is needed because the CPU and memory are slaved together, allowing the CPU to transfer data to and from memory whenever it wishes to

do so, rather than requiring the CPU to await an arbitrary time window. Synchronous DRAM takes one of the following forms:

JEDEC Synchronous DRAM (SDRAM)

Ordinary SDRAM, sometimes called *PC66 SDRAM* to differentiate it from Intel *PC100 SDRAM*. PC66 SDRAM was formerly much less expensive than PC100 SDRAM, but PC100 SDRAM is now so dominant that PC66 SDRAM is difficult to find and may actually cost more than PC100 SDRAM. Because PC100 SDRAM can be used on any system running a 100 MHz or slower FSB, buying JEDEC SDRAM makes no sense, even for systems that run memory at 66 MHz. PC66 SDRAM salvaged from an older system can be used in any system that runs a 66 MHz FSB, including those running Celeron or older model Pentium II processors.

PC100 SDRAM

SDRAM that complies with the Intel PC100 specification, and is rated for use on a 100 MHz FSB. PC100 SDRAM is mainstream memory, and you should not consider buying anything slower. PC100 SDRAM is commonly available in two variants which vary only in CAS latency. CAS-3 PC100 SDRAM is the more common form, and is what you will receive if you do not specify otherwise. CAS-2 PC100 SDRAM has lower latency, is therefore slightly faster in a motherboard that can take advantage of it, and costs somewhat more.

PC133 SDRAM

Technically, PC133 SDRAM does not exist, because neither JEDEC nor Intel publishes a standard to define it. However, the informal PC133 specification to which memory manufacturers adhere defines SDRAM for the 133 MHz FSB speed featured in some new chipsets. PC133 SDRAM now costs little more than PC100 SDRAM, operates properly—although only at the lower speed—in nearly all systems that require PC100 SDRAM, and is usually the best choice when you're buying memory, even for a 66 MHz or 100 MHz FSB system.

Double Data Rate SDRAM (DDR-SDRAM)

DDR-SDRAM doubles the amount of data transferred per clock cycle, and thereby effectively doubles PC100/133 memory performance to 200/266 MHz. Although as of mid-2000 the latest high-performance video cards use DDR-SDRAM, and some new chipsets support using DDR-SDRAM for main system memory, the success of DDR-SDRAM is not guaranteed because no current Intel chipset supports it. That is likely to change, however, as Intel backs off from their ill-considered single-minded support for RDRAM and as DDR-SDRAM becomes mainstream in the AMD Athlon segment. Production of DDR-SDRAM will be ramping up throughout 2000, and by 2001, DDR-SDRAM is likely to be shipping in many mainstream systems. Although DDR-SDRAM has heretofore been strongly linked in most people's minds with the AMD Athlon, forthcoming Intel chipsets like the i815 Solano and the i815E Solano II support DDR-SDRAM. We expect DDR-SDRAM eventually to replace standard PC100 and PC133 SDRAM as the memory technology of choice for mainstream PCs.

Protocol-based DRAM

The preceding DRAM types use separate address, control, and data buses, each with many lines. Managing these wide parallel buses limits performance. Protocol-based DRAM instead uses a narrow, very fast channel with protocols that manage address, control, and data information. The following two standards for protocol-based DRAM exist:

Rambus DRAM

Formerly called *Direct Rambus RDRAM (DRDRAM)*, Rambus RDRAM is a proprietary RAM standard developed jointly by Intel and Rambus. The current RDRAM implementation supports 100 and 133 MHz FSB. The newest Intel chipsets, including the forthcoming Intel 850 "Tehama" chipset for the Willamette (Pentium IV), support RDRAM, so RDRAM is likely to play an increasingly large role in the memory market from mid-2000 onward. But RDRAM is as much as five to ten times more expensive than SDRAM, and its rollout has been delayed due to production problems and yield issues. More important, RDRAM doesn't address the real problem. Current systems are not throughput-bound, even with PC100 RAM. The bottleneck is memory latency, which RDRAM does not improve. In fact, RDRAM is inherently a high-latency technology, and increasing the number of RDRAM modules in a system also increases the already-high latency. Using more than two or three RDRAM modules increases latency to unacceptably high levels, as is evidenced by the fact that forthcoming server motherboards from Intel—certainly the biggest proponent of RDRAM outside Rambus itself—will not use RDRAM. Note that the high performance figures sometimes quoted for RDRAM are based on PC800 RDRAM rather than the PC600 or PC700 RDRAM which is used by most commercial RDRAM-based systems.

Synchronous Link DRAM (SLDRAM)

SLDRAM is an open, royalty-free protocol-based SDRAM standard that has several advantages relative to standard SDRAM and RDRAM and is backed by memory manufacturers. SLDRAM uses standard DRAM chips and operates on current bus designs, making it less expensive to produce than RDRAM. Because it is protocol-based, SLDRAM operates at higher bus speeds than SDRAM—currently 200 MHz, with higher speeds expected. Like DDR-SDRAM, SLDRAM activates operations on both rising and falling edges of the clock cycle, which doubles throughput to 400 MHz. Like SDRAM, SLDRAM uses a 64-bit channel. At 400 MHz, that yields throughput of 3.2 GB/s, twice that of PC800 RDRAM and four times that of PC100 SDRAM. The SLDRAM 200 MHz clock is half the speed of the fastest RDRAM clock (PC800 RDRAM actually runs a 400 MHz clock), which contributes to ease of design and production versus RDRAM. SLDRAM also provides faster memory timings (lower latency) relative to standard SDRAM and RDRAM. Because latency is the main bottleneck, the reduced latency of SLDRAM translates into real-world performance increases. Although SLDRAM is faster and cheaper than RDRAM, its success is not guaranteed. Current Intel chipsets do not support SLDRAM, which may cripple its ability to compete in the market. New chipsets from VIA, ALi, and SiS are likely to support SLDRAM, which may eventually force Intel to add SLDRAM support to its chipsets. Unless that happens, SLDRAM may wither on the vine.

Memory Packaging

Memory is available in various physical packaging. Roughly in order of their appearance, the major types of DRAM packaging include:

DIP (Dual Inline Pin Package)
> This package comprises a rectangular chip with a row of pins down each long side, making it resemble an insect. DIP was the most common DRAM package used in PCs through early 386 models. DIP chips were produced in Page Mode and Fast Page Mode, and are long obsolete. DIP packaging was also used for L2 cache memory on most 486 and some Pentium-class motherboards. DIP DRAM is useless nowadays.

SIPP (Single Inline Pin Package)
> This package turns a DIP chip on its side and extends all leads straight out one side parallel to the plane of the chip. SIPPs were intended to allow memory to be installed more densely, and were used in a few 386SX systems, but never caught on. SIPPs were produced in Page Mode and Fast Page Mode form, and are long obsolete.

SIMM (Single Inline Memory Module)
> This package mounts multiple individual DRAM DIP chips on a small circuit board with a card edge connector designed to fit a socket on the motherboard. Mainstream SIMMs have been manufactured in two form factors:

30-pin
> > These SIMMs were used in a few 286 systems, most 386 systems, and some 486 systems, and were produced in Page Mode and Fast Page Mode form. Although they are still available, 30-pin SIMMs are obsolete. If you tear down an old system, any 30-pin SIMMs you salvage are too small and too slow to be useful, but keep in mind that some laser printers use them.

72-pin
> > These SIMMs were used in some 386 systems, most 486 systems, and nearly all Pentium-class systems built before the advent of DIMMs. 72-pin SIMMs were produced in Fast Page Mode, EDO, and BEDO form. When tearing down old systems, 72-pin SIMMs may be worth salvaging, as they can be used to populate some current Socket 7 motherboards or to expand the memory in some laser printers.

DIMM (Dual Inline Memory Module)
> DIMMs are dual-side modules that use connectors on both sides of the circuit board. Standard DIMMs have 168 pins, but 100- and 144-pin DIMMs are also made. Only SDRAM and EDO are commonly packaged as DIMMs.

SODIMM (Small Outline DIMM)
> A special package used in notebook computers and on some video adapters.

RIMM

A Rambus RDRAM module. RIMM is a trade-name rather than an acronym. RIMMs are physically similar to standard SDRAM DIMMs, except that the keying notches are in different locations.

Banks Versus Rows

Memory *rows* and *banks* are easily confused. Rows are physical groups and banks are logical groups. A bank comprises one or more rows, the number depending on CPU address bus width and the width of the memory, which is closely associated with its form factor.

DIP

These are 1 bit wide, and require eight chips per row (nine, if parity is used). The number of rows per bank depends on the CPU. XT-class PCs, which use an 8-bit memory bus, require one row per bank. 286s (16-bit bus), require two rows per bank. 386s and 486s (32-bit bus) require four rows per bank.

30-pin SIMM

These are 8 bits wide. 286s require two modules (rows) per bank. 386s and 486s require four modules per bank. Pentiums (64-bit bus) require eight modules per bank.

72-pin SIMMs

These are 32 bits wide. 486s require one module per bank. Pentium and higher systems require two modules per bank.

168-pin DIMMs

These are 64 bits wide. One 168-pin DIMM always forms one bank.

168-pin RIMMs

Although RIMMs technically use a 16-bit communications channel, a single RIMM appears to the chipset as one bank.

You must install memory *at least* one full bank at a time. One DIMM equals one row equals one bank, period. One 72-pin SIMM equals one bank in 386s and 486s, and two SIMMs equal one bank in Pentiums. But older systems, particularly 486s, may interleave banks to improve performance, which requires installing *two* banks at a time.

 In a RIMM-based system, all memory slots must be populated, either with a RIMM module or with a terminator. For those used to working with standard memory, as we are, it's easy enough to forget this requirement. We spent an hour one day trying to figure out why a system we'd built just sat there beeping instead of booting. Turned out that we'd forgotten to install the terminator, which was buried deep in the motherboard packaging.

Parity and ECC Memory

Parity and Error Checking and Correction (ECC) memory use extra bits to store checksum information that can detect and sometimes correct memory errors.

Parity memory
> Uses nine bits per byte to provide simple error detection, so simple as to be useless on modern PCs. Most early DIP-based PCs required parity memory, and so used nine chips per row. SIMMs, which are much more reliable than DIPs, made parity unnecessary. The Intel Triton Pentium-class chipset and competing chipsets removed support for parity memory. Recent chipsets again support parity memory, but there is no good reason to use it.
>
> Although parity memory is still sold, buy it only if your computer requires it. Some computers do not allow mixing parity and nonparity modules. Before buying parity memory, verify which type is already installed and whether your chipset can mix parity with nonparity memory. Identify parity modules by counting the chips on the module. If that number is evenly divisible by three, it's a parity module. If nonparity memory is installed, or if parity memory is installed but your chipset allows mixing types, buy nonparity memory. Buy parity memory only if parity memory is already present and your chipset does not allow mixing types.

ECC memory
> An enhanced form of error checking memory that can detect and correct single- and multi-bit errors. ECC originated on mainframes, migrated to mini-computers, and is now common on PC servers.
>
> ECC memory requires five extra bits to protect an 8-bit byte, six to protect a 16-bit word, seven to protect a 32-bit word, and eight to protect a 64-bit word. A 72-bit wide DIMM supports either parity or ECC interchangeably. Chipsets that support 168-pin DIMMs usually also support ECC, although ECC is not always implemented in BIOS. If your BIOS supports it, you can use ECC by installing 72-bit DIMMs and enabling ECC in Chipset Setup. The downside is that 72-bit DIMMs cost about 12.5% more than standard 64-bit DIMMs, and enabling ECC reduces memory performance, typically about 3%. Use ECC only on servers when constant uptime is critical. Avoid parity and ECC memory for ordinary PCs.

How Much Memory Is Enough?

How much memory you need depends on the operating system and applications you use, how many windows you keep open, which background services and processes you run, and so on. Memory is more important than processor speed to system performance. Windows NT 4 runs much faster on a Celeron/300 with 64 MB than on a Pentium III/500 system with 16 MB.

Using a big swap/paging file cannot substitute for having enough RAM. Windows virtual memory allows you to run more and larger programs than fit into physical memory by temporarily swapping data from RAM to a disk file. When Windows swaps to disk, performance takes a major hit. If your hard disk clatters away every time you switch between running applications, that's a sure sign that heavy paging is going on and that your system needs more memory. RAM is cheap. Install enough of it to minimize use of the paging file.

To determine how much memory you need, choose the following category that best describes your usage pattern. If you fall between two, choose the higher. Note that newer versions of applications usually require more memory.

Light
> Web browsing, email, casual word processing and spreadsheets, checkbook management, and simple games; one or two windows open; particularly if using software one or two versions behind current releases.

Typical
> Applications listed for light, particularly current versions; three to five windows open; using more demanding applications, including casual database updates and queries, complex spreadsheets, light/moderate programming, mainstream games. File and print sharing in small workgroups or home networks.

Heavy
> Memory-intensive applications, e.g., Photoshop; speech/pattern-recognition software; many windows open; multiple background services; graphics-intensive games like Quake III; heavy programming, especially with an Integrated Development Environment (IDE) and doing frequent compiles and links; file and print sharing for large workgroups or departmental groups. Limited use as an application or database server.

Extreme
> Professional scientific, engineering, and statistical applications. Manipulating very large data sets. Use as a consolidated file, print, application, and database server.

Table 5-1 lists recommended memory by operating system and usage. These are *ad hoc* rules based on our experience, so your mileage may vary. If the category description matches your usage patterns closely, the middle of the listed range should work well. If you do only one or a few of the things listed for a category, the lower amount of memory in the range should be adequate. If you do several or all of the things in a category—particularly if you do them at the same time—install the maximum amount of memory listed for the range, or jump to the next higher category. Windows 9X is of questionable robustness for Heavy usage, let alone Extreme usage, so we do not provide recommendations for Windows 9X in Extreme usage.

Table 5-1: Recommended Memory by Operating System & Usage Pattern

Operating System	Light	Typical	Heavy	Extreme
Windows 95	12–24 MB	24–64 MB	64–128 MB	N/R
Windows 98	16–32 MB	32–64 MB	64–128 MB	N/R
Windows NT 4 Workstation	32–64 MB	64–128 MB	128–256 MB	384+ MB
Windows NT 4 Server	64–96 MB	96–256 MB	256–512 MB	768+ MB
Windows 2000 Professional	64–96 MB	96–192 MB	192–384 MB	512+ MB
Windows 2000 Server	96–128 MB	128–256 MB	256–512 MB	768+ MB
Linux (GUI workstation)	64–96 MB	96–128 MB	128–256 MB	384+ MB
Linux (Text-based server)	32–64 MB	64–96 MB	96–192 MB	256+ MB

Each operating system has a "sweet spot" that depends on the application mix. Adding memory increases performance until you reach the sweet spot, but adding more than that results in decreasing returns. For typical usage, we find the sweet spot for Windows 95 and 98 to be 64 MB; for Windows NT Workstation 4.0, 96 MB; for Windows NT Server 4.0, 128 MB; for Windows 2000 Professional, 128 MB; for Windows 2000 Server, 192 MB; for Linux used as a GUI workstation, 96 MB; and for Linux used in text-mode as a server, 64 MB. Your mileage may vary. In general, the best way to determine if you've reached the sweet spot for your own mix of applications and your personal working style is to keep an eye on how frequently the system pages out to the hard disk. If that happens frequently, you need more memory. If your system pages only occasionally, you probably have enough memory. Our rule is simple. If in doubt, always err on the side of having more memory rather than less.

Memory Selection Guidelines

The following sections provide guidelines for selecting memory for a new system or to upgrade an existing system. Follow these guidelines as closely as possible to ensure the memory you select functions optimally in your system.

When upgrading an older motherboard, it is sometimes impossible to match the installed memory. Some motherboards have 30-pin and 72-pin SIMM sockets, and many have both SIMM and DIMM sockets. If the installed memory occupies all available sockets of one type, you may have to add memory of a different type.

If so, consult the manual to determine supported configurations. For example, many 30/72-pin motherboards provide four 30-pin and two 72-pin sockets, but allow you to populate both 72-pin sockets only if no memory is installed in the 30-pin sockets. Similarly motherboards with both SIMM and DIMM sockets may allow using a DIMM only if one or more SIMM sockets are vacant or populated only with single-sided SIMMs.

Mixing memory types may degrade performance. Some chipsets run all memory at the speed of the slowest module. Others, including the 430HX and 430VX, run each bank at optimum speed. Mixed memory configurations are nonstandard and best avoided. Memory is cheap enough that it's often better to use all new memory.

Observe the following general guidelines when selecting memory:

- Verify your motherboard can cache the full amount of RAM you install. For example, the Intel 430TX chipset supports 256 MB RAM, but caches only 64 MB. Adding RAM beyond 64 MB actually decreases system performance. Some motherboards have insufficient cache installed to cache the full amount of cacheable RAM supported by the chipset. Some of these have sockets that you can fill with additional cache. The cacheable RAM area of Slot 1 systems is determined by the processor itself. The L2 cache present on Pentium II CPUs can cache a maximum of 512 MB of system memory.

- Purchase only name-brand memory, especially if you overclock your system. Motherboards vary in their tolerance for different brands of memory. Some motherboards accept and use nearly any compatible memory, but others are reliable only with some brands of memory. A name-brand memory module functions properly on nearly any motherboard designed to accept that module. We use only Crucial memory (*http://www.crucial.com*) in our systems, and have never had a problem with it.

- Don't attempt to save money by mixing newer memory with older memory. For example, if you buy two 32 MB PC100 SDRAM DIMMs for a system that currently has one 16 MB EDO DIMM installed, you may be tempted to use all three DIMMs for a system total of 80 MB rather than 64 MB. That's usually a mistake. Some systems accept mixed EDO and SDRAM memory, but most systems will run the newer, faster memory at the same speed as the slower old memory.

- Buy one larger capacity module in preference to two smaller ones of the same total capacity. This is particularly important with DIMM modules. Most motherboards have only two to four DIMM sockets, so buying smaller capacity DIMMs may later force you to replace existing memory when you want to add more memory to the system.

- Memory modules and sockets may use tin or gold contacts. Manufacturers often recommend using modules with the same contact metal as the sockets. In theory, mixing gold and tin can cause corrosion and other problems. In practice, we've never seen this happen.

DIMM/SDRAM Guidelines

DIMM memory is available in many more variants than SIMM memory, so be careful to buy DIMMs that match your requirements. Use these guidelines when choosing DIMM/SDRAM memory modules:

- Get the proper voltage. Most PC DIMMs are 3.3V. Some DIMMs, often called Macintosh DIMMs, use 5V. Some early DIMM-based PC motherboards use 5V DIMMs.

- DIMMs are available in EDO and SDRAM. If your system supports either, buy the SDRAM DIMMs for future flexibility.

- SDRAM DIMMs are available in *buffered* (also called *registered*) and *unbuffered* versions. Some motherboards accept only registered DIMMs, others accept only unbuffered DIMMs, and still others will accept either registered or unbuffered DIMMs, but do not allow mixing types.

- For SDRAM, buy nothing slower than PC100 modules, which are backward-compatible with systems that use PC66 memory. Consider buying PC133 modules, which cost little more than PC100 modules and function properly in most systems that use PC66 or PC100 memory. No formal PC133 specification yet exists, but current PC133 modules will almost certainly be compatible with forthcoming processors and motherboards that use a 133 MHz FSB.

- Don't mistake modules labeled "100 MHz" for true PC100 memory. PC100 memory supports 125 MHz (8 ns) operation, but 100 MHz (10 ns) memory is usable at FSB speeds no higher than 83 MHz. Some vendors label modules "LX" to indicate they work with the 66 MHz FSB 440LX chipset, and "BX" to indicate they work with the 100 MHz FSB 440BX chipset. "BX" modules *usually* run at

100 MHz FSB, but are not PC100 modules unless so labeled. PC133 memory is new, but expect some vendors to sell "133 MHz" DIMMs, hoping buyers will mistake them for PC133.

- Make sure DIMMs support Serial Presence Detect (SPD), a serial EEPROM that stores DIMM parameters—including memory type, size, speed, voltage, number of row and column addresses, and so forth—which can be read by the system BIOS at boot time and used to correctly configure memory. Some motherboards won't boot with non-SPD memory. Others boot, but with a warning message. Some vendors label SPD modules "EEPROM," but a module so labeled isn't necessarily SPD-compliant. Ask.

- Purchase modules with lower CAS Latency whenever possible. PC100 and PC133 DIMMs are available in CAS2 or CAS3 (sometimes shown as CL2 or CL3). CAS2 modules provide a small performance boost relative to CAS3 modules. More important, CAS2 modules have a bit more in reserve that allows them to function more reliably in overclocked or heavily loaded systems. CAS2 modules typically cost 2% or so more than CAS3.

- When upgrading an older system, determine if it requires 2-clock or 4-clock modules. Recent PCs use 4-clock memory, which is now ubiquitous. If your system requires 2-clock memory, you'll have to ask for it. It may be a special-order item, for which you will be charged a premium.

All 168-pin DIMMs use similar sockets, but both modules and sockets are keyed to prevent using the wrong type of DIMM. If there is such a thing as a "standard" PC DIMM, it would be a 3.3 volt, nonparity (x64), unbuffered, PC 100, CAS 3 SDRAM DIMM.

SIMM Guidelines

Use the following guidelines when choosing SIMM memory modules:

- Unless you are upgrading an older Socket 7 system that accepts only 72-pin SIMMs, buy only 168-pin DIMM memory. Many Socket 7 motherboards have both SIMM and DIMM sockets. Buying DIMMs for such a board makes more sense than buying obsolescent SIMMs. However, note that some early boards support DIMMs only with very slow memory timings.

- SIMMs are available in FPM and EDO. If your motherboard supports either type, buy EDO. Some motherboards support both FPM and EDO, but do not allow mixing types, either per bank or globally. Because FPM is obsolescent and demand for it is small, FPM often costs more than EDO. If FPM is installed and the motherboard does not allow mixing FPM with EDO, consider removing the FPM SIMMs and installing all EDO SIMMs.

- Don't assume the motherboard supports large SIMMs. Check the manufacturer's web site to determine the supported SIMM capacities and memory configurations. Older motherboards often support nothing larger than 16 MB SIMMs. Conversely, don't assume the motherboard cannot support larger SIMMs than those currently installed just because the manual says so. For example, one of our technical reviewers has a Compaq system whose manual lists 16 MB SIMMs as the largest supported. That was true when the manual was printed, because 32 MB SIMMs were not yet available. But that system uses 32 MB SIMMs without problems.

- Some motherboards, particularly those with four or more SIMM sockets, restrict the number of double-sided SIMMs that can be used or restrict the total number of SIMM sides that can be used. If your motherboard has such a limitation, verify that the combination of currently installed SIMMs and the SIMMs you plan to install does not exceed the limit.

Upgrading Memory in 386 Systems

It seldom makes sense to upgrade the memory in a 386. But if you have retired a 386 to some dedicated function such as a home automation controller, a telephone/voicemail system, or a fax server, you may find that adding memory allows it to serve that purpose a while longer. When upgrading memory in a 386, note the following issues:

- Install memory similar or identical to that already installed. Early 386s use individual DIP chips, but most 386s use 30-pin SIMMs. A very few 386s used SIPPs, and some late 386s use 72-pin SIMMs. 386 motherboards can often use more than one type, e.g., both 30-pin and 72-pin SIMMs.

- 386 motherboards are often fully populated with memory. If so, expanding memory requires removing existing memory and replacing it with larger capacity chips or modules.

- 386s use only FPM DRAM. You can install EDO DRAM if FPM memory is unavailable, but 386s treat EDO as FPM DRAM.

- Most 386s require parity memory.

- Add memory in full banks. Install 32 (nonparity) or 36 (parity) DIP chips per bank, four 30-pin SIMMs per bank, and one 72-pin SIMM per bank.

- Not all memory configurations are supported by all systems. For example, although a system may support either 256 KB SIMMs or 4 MB SIMMs, it may not be able to use both sizes simultaneously. The manual is the best source of information about supported memory configurations. If the manual is not available and you cannot locate detailed information about your motherboard on the Web, the best recourse is trial and error.

- Always install larger SIMMs in Bank 0, and smaller ones in higher banks. The chipset determines the largest SIMM the motherboard supports. Older 386s may support nothing larger than 1 MB, and many 386s support nothing larger than 4 MB. A system will ordinarily use a larger SIMM, but will recognize it as smaller than its true capacity.

- Most 386s use 70 ns memory, although many older 386s use 80 ns memory, and some late model 386s use 60 ns memory. Make sure new memory is at least as fast as existing memory. It does no harm to install faster memory, but neither does it provide any benefit. Determine memory speed by examining the identification number of the chip or module, which normally ends with a hyphen followed by a one- or two-digit number. The final number identifies the speed. For example, a 60 ns part may be identified as xxxxxxx-60, xxxxxxx-06, or xxxxxxx-6.

Upgrading Memory in 486 Systems

It is often cost-effective to upgrade memory on fast, late-model 486 systems. A 486-DX4/120, for example, runs Windows 95 as fast as any but the fastest Pentiums. If you use the system primarily for light duties—web browsing, email, word processing, and so on—a 486 may be enough CPU for the job. But most 486s have only 4 or 8 MB of RAM. That's marginal for Windows 3.1x and inadequate for Windows 95. Expanding the memory on such a system to 16 MB or 32 MB costs only $25 to $50 and dramatically improves its performance. When upgrading memory in a 486, note the following issues:

- Because 386s and 486s use a 32-bit memory bus and generally do not use the sophisticated caching schemes used by Pentium and later systems, memory upgrade issues and practices for 486 systems are similar to those for 386 systems, except that 486s do not use DIP packaging.

- Early 486s use 30-pin SIMMs and later ones use 72-pin SIMMs. Many 486 motherboards—particularly Pacific Rim models made during the transition from 30-pin to 72-pin modules—support both types of SIMMs, usually four rows of 30-pin SIMMs and two rows of 72-pin SIMMs. As with 386s, 30-pin SIMMs must be installed four per bank, and 72-pin SIMMs may be installed one per bank.

- Most ISA and VLB 486s use FPM memory, and may use parity or nonparity memory, depending on the chipset. Some systems require parity memory, but many can use either type. Most that accept either require that all installed memory be the same type. Some systems automatically disable parity if any nonparity is installed. If nonparity memory is unavailable, you can usually install parity memory in a system that does not support it, although it will be treated as nonparity memory.

- Most PCI 486s, particularly those with non-Intel chipsets, can use EDO memory, although they may have EDO or FPM memory installed. Some chipsets allow mixing EDO and FPM memory, although doing so often causes the EDO memory to perform at FPM levels. Some chipsets support either FPM or EDO memory, but not both simultaneously. In general, the safest course when upgrading one of these systems is to add whatever type of memory is already installed.

- Most 486s use 70 ns or 60 ns memory. Make sure the memory you install is at least as fast as that already installed.

Upgrading Memory in Pentium Pro and Pentium-Class Systems

Pentium Pro and P54C/P55C Pentium-class systems, including those with an AMD K6 or higher, are excellent candidates for a memory upgrade. When upgrading memory in a Pentium or Pentium Pro, note the following issues:

- Try to install memory identical to that already installed. Early Pentiums and most Pentium Pros use 72-pin SIMMs, but either type of system may use DIMMs in addition to or instead of SIMMs. Existing memory may be FPM,

EDO, or SDRAM. Many systems can use different memory types, e.g., FPM or EDO, but do not allow mixed types.

- Most such systems have nonparity memory installed. Some do not support parity memory. Pentium Pro systems often have parity memory installed, and may use ECC. Some systems support parity or nonparity memory, but do not allow mixed types. Others accept parity or nonparity RAM interchangeably, but disable parity if any nonparity modules are installed. For SIMM-based systems, count chips to determine memory type. For DIMM-based systems, locate the identification number on a module and check the manufacturer's documentation to determine its type.

- These systems use a 64-bit memory bus, and therefore require adding 72-pin SIMMs in pairs. DIMMs may be added individually.

- Most SIMM-based systems use 60 ns or 50 ns memory. Make sure new memory is at least as fast as that already installed. Early DIMM-based systems use FPM or EDO DIMMs, which you should match as closely as possible. Later DIMM-based systems may use JEDEC (PC66) SDRAM. You can use PC66 SDRAM, but it's better to buy PC100 SDRAM, which can be recycled later if you upgrade to a faster system.

Upgrading Memory in Pentium II/III and Celeron Systems

These systems are excellent candidates for memory upgrades. Early Pentium II systems often have only 16 MB RAM. In the price-sensitive consumer Celeron market, even a recently purchased system may have only 16 MB, and some Celeron systems have been sold with only 8 MB. Expanding memory to 32 MB or 64 MB is the most cost-effective upgrade you can make. When upgrading memory in one of these systems, note the following issues:

- Some early systems use EDO SIMMs or DIMMs, but most use 3.3 volt 168-pin unbuffered SDRAM DIMMs.

- Conserve DIMM sockets. A few motherboards have four DIMM sockets, most have three, and low-end systems have only two. If you have the choice, always install one larger DIMM rather than two smaller ones that total the same amount of memory.

- Most of these systems have nonparity memory installed, but can use either parity or nonparity DIMMs interchangeably. Unless you plan to install 256 MB or more, install nonparity DIMMs. We have been told that when using very large amounts of memory—256 to 384 MB or more—memory errors introduced by cosmic rays make it worthwhile to pay the additional cost for parity/ECC memory and accept the small performance hit that using ECC produces.

- As always, memory must always be added in full banks. These systems use a 64-bit memory bus, and therefore require adding 72-pin SIMMs in pairs. DIMMs may be added individually.

- Most SIMM-based systems use 60 ns or 50 ns memory. Make sure memory you add is at least as fast as the memory already installed. Early DIMM-based systems use FPM or EDO DIMMs, which you should match as closely as possible. Later DIMM-based systems may use JEDEC (PC66) SDRAM. You can install PC66 SDRAM, but it usually makes more sense to buy PC100 SDRAM for these systems, because it can be recycled later if you upgrade to a faster system.

Installing Memory

Installing a SIMM or DIMM module is straightforward. Most recent motherboards automatically detect installed memory modules regardless of the slot they occupy, but it is good practice to fill banks from the lowest numbered to the highest. For example, if the motherboard has three banks, fill Bank 1 only after Bank 0 is filled, and fill Bank 2 only after Banks 0 and 1 are filled.

Some motherboards require larger modules be installed in lower numbered banks. For example, if the motherboard has three DIMM sockets, Bank 0 is currently occupied by a 32 MB DIMM, and you are installing two 64 MB DIMMs, rather than simply installing the two new 64 MB DIMMs in Banks 1 and 2, you may need to remove the 32 MB DIMM from Bank 0, install the 64 MB DIMMs in Banks 0 and 1, and then reinstall the original 32 MB DIMM in Bank 2.

That rule is not invariable, though. A few motherboards require smaller modules be installed in the lower banks. Some motherboards don't care which module you install in which bank. Best practice is to check the manual before installing memory. If no documentation is available, experiment by moving modules around. If some or all of the memory is not recognized during the boot-time memory check or in CMOS Setup, try rearranging the modules. If all memory is recognized, you can safely assume that you have the modules installed correctly.

Installing and Removing SIMMs

To install a SIMM

Locate a free SIMM socket of the proper type (30- or 72-pin). One side of the SIMM has a notch that aligns with a matching post on the SIMM slot support bracket, which prevents the SIMM from being installed backward. Align the notch and then slide the contact edge of the SIMM into the SIMM slot at about a 45 degree angle. Once you have the SIMM aligned properly, maintain slight pressure toward the slot and pivot the SIMM upward toward the vertical until it snaps into place. Verify that the spring connectors on each side of the SIMM slot bracket have both snapped into the matching holes on the SIMM.

To remove a SIMM

Locate the spring connectors at the top of each side of the SIMM slot bracket and press both of them lightly at the same time while simultaneously pressing the SIMM gently away from the vertical. After the spring connectors release their grip on the SIMM, pivot the SIMM gently downward to about a 45 degree angle and then pull it gently out of the slot.

Installing and Removing DIMMs

To install a DIMM

Locate a free DIMM socket and pivot the ejector arms on each side of the socket as far as possible toward the horizontal. The contact edge of the DIMM module is keyed with notches that correspond to protuberances in the DIMM socket. Align the notches and slide the DIMM straight down into the socket. Position your thumbs on top of the DIMM at roughly one third of the way from each end and press down firmly. The DIMM slides (sometimes snaps) into the socket, which automatically pivots the ejector arms toward the vertical. If the ejector arms are not fully vertical, press them toward the DIMM until they lock into the vertical position. Note that some DIMM sockets have minor physical variations. If the DIMM does not fit easily into the socket, do not force it. Contact the vendor who supplied the DIMM for a replacement.

To remove a DIMM

Pivot both ejector arms simultaneously toward the horizontal position. The DIMM simply pops out.

Testing and Configuring Newly Installed Memory

After you install the new memory modules and verify that all is as it should be, apply power to the system. The memory self-test should increment up to the newly installed amount of memory. If it instead shows only the original amount of memory, the cause is almost always that you have not seated the new memory module completely. Power down, reseat the module, and try again.

If the memory check shows an amount of memory larger than the original amount but smaller than the expected new amount, the problem is almost always that the BIOS and/or chipset do not support memory modules of the size you've installed. If that occurs, you may need to do one or more of the following things to resolve the problem:

- Check the Chipset Setup portion of CMOS Setup to determine how memory is configured for the newly installed bank(s). Most recent chipsets and BIOSes automatically determine the correct size and configuration parameters for installed modules. But some chipsets, BIOSes, and memory modules do not implement SPD correctly. If this occurs, you may have to set the correct size manually, if indeed the module size you have installed is an available option.

- A limitation on maximum module size may be enforced by the chipset, the BIOS, or both. Before deciding you cannot use the larger module, check the motherboard manufacturer's web site for a BIOS update. If the restriction on module size is enforced by the BIOS but not by the chipset, you may find that a later BIOS revision adds support for the larger module.

- If all else fails, the only alternative may be to return the memory module (you did make sure you had the right to return an incompatible module, didn't you?) and obtain a smaller module.

Troubleshooting Memory Installation and Operation

Once installed and configured, memory seldom causes problems. When problems do occur, they may be as obvious as a failed RAM check at boot or as subtle as a few corrupted bits in a data file. The usual symptom of memory problems is blue-screen crashes of the operating system. Unfortunately, that occurs so often with Windows that it's of little use as a diagnostic aid. When troubleshooting memory problems, always:

- Use standard anti-static precautions. Ground yourself before you touch a memory module.

- Remove and reinstall all memory modules to ensure they are seated properly. While you're doing that, it's a good idea to clean the contacts on the memory module. Some people gently rub the contacts with a pencil eraser. We've done that ourselves, but memory manufacturers recommend against it because of possible damage to the contacts. Also, there is always the risk of a fragment from the eraser finding its way into the memory slot, where it can block one or more contacts. Better practice is to use a fresh dollar bill, which has just the right amount of abrasiveness to clean the contacts without damaging them.

 Although we have never used it, many people whom we respect recommend using Stabilant-22 (*http://www.stabilant.com/*), a liquid contact enhancer. You'll probably keel over from sticker shock when you see the price of this stuff, but a drop or two is all that's needed, and a tiny tube lasts most people for years.

- Before assuming memory is the problem, check all internal cables to ensure none is faulty or has come loose.

The next steps you should take depend on whether you have made any changes to memory recently.

When You Have Not Added Memory

If you suspect memory problems but have not added or reconfigured memory (or been inside the case), it's unlikely that the memory itself is causing the problem. Memory does simply die sometimes, and may be killed by electrical surges, but this is uncommon because the PC power supply itself does a good job of isolating memory and other system components from electrical damage. The most likely problem is a failing power supply. Try one or both of the following:

- If you have another system, install the suspect memory in it. If it runs there, the problem is almost certainly not the memory, but the power supply.

- If you have other memory, install it in the problem system. If it works, you can safely assume that the original memory is defective. More likely is that it will also fail, which strongly indicates power supply problems.

If you have neither another system nor additional memory, and if your system has more than one bank of memory installed, use binary elimination to determine which modules are bad. For example, if you have two modules installed (one per bank), simply remove one module to see if that cures the problem. If you have four identical modules installed (one per bank), designate them A, B, C, and D. Install only A and B and restart the system. If no problems occur, A and B are known good and the problem must lie with C and/or D. Remove B and substitute C. If no problems occur, you know that D is bad. If the system fails with A and C, you know that C is bad, but you don't know whether D is bad. Substitute D for C and restart the system to determine if D is good.

If you haven't enough banks to allow binary elimination, the best solution is to remove the modules, wrap them if possible in a static safe bag (the pink plastic that most components arrive in), and take them to a local computer store that has a memory tester.

 MS-DOS, Windows 3.x, and Windows 9X do not stress memory. If you install Windows NT or Linux, memory errors may appear on a PC that seemed stable. People often therefore assume that they did something while installing the new OS to cause the errors, but that is almost never the case. Such errors almost always indicate a real problem with physical memory. The memory was defective all along, but the more forgiving OS simply ignored the problem.

When Adding Memory

If you experience problems when adding memory, note the following:

- If a DIMM appears not to fit, there's good reason. DIMMs have two notches whose placement specifies 3.3V versus 5V and Buffered versus Unbuffered. If the DIMM notches don't match the socket protrusions, the DIMM is the wrong type.

- If the system displays a memory mismatch error the first time you restart, that usually indicates no real problem. Follow the prompts to enter Setup, select Save and Exit, and restart the system. The system should then recognize the new memory. Some systems require these extra steps to update CMOS.

- Verify the modules are installed in the proper order. Fill banks sequentially from lowest number to highest. Generally, install the largest module in Bank 0, the next largest in Bank 1, and so on. A few systems require the smallest module be in Bank 0 and larger modules sequentially in higher banks.

- If the system recognizes a newly installed module as half actual size and that module has chips on both sides, the system may recognize only single-banked or single-sided modules. Some systems limit the total number of "sides" that are recognized, so if you have some existing smaller modules installed, try removing them. The system may then recognize the double-side modules. If not, return those modules and replace them with single-side modules.

- A memory module may not be defective, but still be incompatible with your system. For example, many 486s treat 3-chip and 9-chip SIMMs differently, although they should theoretically be interchangeable. Some 486s use only 3-chip SIMMs or only 9-chip SIMMs. Others use either, but generate memory errors if you have both types installed.

- A memory module may not be defective, but still be incompatible with your current configuration. For example, if you install a CAS3 PC100 DIMM in a 100 MHz FSB Pentium II that is configured to use CAS2 timing, the system will almost certainly generate memory errors.

Our Picks

For maximum flexibility when building a new system or upgrading an existing one, we recommend whenever possible purchasing only PC133 SDRAM memory, even for motherboards that require only PC66 or PC100. Before you do so, however, verify on the motherboard manufacturer's web site that your motherboard functions properly with PC133 SDRAM. A few motherboards designed for PC66 or PC100 memory have problems with PC133.

We use and recommend only name-brand memory. Commodity memory may not work properly in a given motherboard. Even if it appears to work properly at first, you may later experience subtle problems attributable to the memory. Name-brand memory costs little more than commodity memory, and is definitely worth the small extra cost.

We have installed only Crucial Technologies memory (*http://www.crucial.com*) in the scores of systems we've built during the last 18 months, and have experienced no problems attributable to that memory. That's something we can't say for other brands of memory we've used, and certainly not for commodity memory. Another advantage to buying memory from Crucial is the memory locator page on their web site, which allows you to enter the manufacturer and model of your system or motherboard and returns a list of memory modules, with prices, that are certified to be compatible with that system or motherboard.

We constantly test and review new equipment. For the latest information about what we currently use, visit:

http://www.hardwareguys.com/picks/memory.html

CHAPTER 6

Floppy Disk Drives

The following four chapters cover standard floppy disk drives, high-capacity "super" floppy drives, removable hard drives, and tape drives, all of which are characterized as removable magnetic storage devices. These devices use media that can be swapped in and out of the drive, versus hard disk drives, whose media are a fixed part of the drives themselves. Although they are typically slower at accessing data than a hard disk—sometimes much slower—removable magnetic storage devices are useful because you can store an unlimited amount of data on additional cartridges, albeit with only a subset of the data available online at any one time. Because media are separate items, you can transfer data between computers that are not networked, if those computers are equipped with a compatible drive. Removable media also allow storing data off-site as protection against fire, theft, or other catastrophes.

A major drawback of removable magnetic storage is inherent: magnetic storage is less reliable than optical storage. Over time, zero bits and one bits stored as magnetic domains tend to become unreadable blurs. A less obvious drawback is the proprietary nature of most magnetic drives and media, and the continually changing standards. Try, for example, to read data written only five years ago to a proprietary DC600 tape drive. The original drive is dead, the manufacturer no longer exists, and the software used to write the data won't run on anything later than Windows 3.1. Even something as simple as reading data from a 5.25" floppy diskette can turn into a major undertaking. Accordingly, the most appropriate uses of these drives are to provide supplemental working storage, to transfer large amounts of data between computers, and to make backups. They are much less suitable for archiving data long-term.

Removable magnetic storage devices differ in many respects, including drive cost, storage capacity, and access time. Perhaps the most important difference is the cost of media, both per cartridge and per megabyte stored. When selecting a removable magnetic storage device, always keep in mind that media cost over the service life of the drive will likely greatly exceed the cost of the drive itself, particularly for drives that use proprietary, patented, and/or licensed media. Many of these drives are marketed on the King Gillette model of giving away the razor and selling the blades. The cost of those blades can really add up.

A *floppy disk drive* (*FDD*) is so called because it records data on a flexible circular plastic disk coated with ferrite or other magnetic medium. This plastic disk is enclosed within a protective sleeve or cartridge. This assembly is called a *floppy disk* or a *diskette*. FDDs have been manufactured to accept 8", 5.25", and 3.5" diskettes, although only the last is still in common use.

Diskette Types and Formats

Before a diskette can be used to store data, it must be prepared by formatting it, although many diskettes nowadays come preformatted. Formatting creates the physical tracks and sectors that the drive uses to store data (called *low-level* or *physical formatting*) and the logical structure used by the operating system to organize that data (called *logical* or *DOS formatting*). Unlike hard disks, which require two separate formatting passes, FDDs perform both physical and logical formatting in one step. Also unlike hard disks, diskettes do not need to be partitioned.'

 The Quick Format option available in Windows and later versions of DOS doesn't really format the diskette. It simply "zeros out" the File Allocation Tables and Root Directory entries, giving the appearance of a freshly formatted diskette, but using the original format. Because data on diskettes fades with time, your data will be much safer if you do an actual format, which does a surface test and refreshes the physical and logical format structure of the diskette. Use Quick Format only on diskettes that have recently had a full format done on them. You have been warned.

Format a diskette in Windows by right-clicking the drive icon in My Computer or Explorer, choosing Format, and marking the appropriate options. At the command line, format a diskette by typing the command `format a: /options`, where `a:` is the drive letter of the FDD, and `/options` controls how the disk will be formatted. The available options and the required syntax varies according to the version of DOS or Windows you use. Type `format /?` to display available formatting options. Which options are usable depends upon both the FDD type and the diskette type. Some FDDs accept only one type of diskette, while others accept two or more.

For about a decade, the 3.5" high density (HD) FDD has been standard. However, you may encounter older types of FDDs and diskettes when upgrading an old machine or salvaging data, so it's worth knowing something about these obsolescent and obsolete formats. Table 6-1 lists the various diskette formats that have been supported on the IBM platform over the years.

Table 6-1: Diskette Characteristics

	5.25" Formats			3.5" Formats		
	SSDD	DSDD	HD	DD	HD	ED
Formatted Capacity (KB)	160/180	320/360	1,200	720	1,440	2,880
Media Descriptor Byte	0xFE/ 0xFC	0xFF/ 0xFD	0xF9	0xF9	0xF0	0xF0
Bytes/Sector	512	512	512	512	512	512
Sectors/Track	8/9	8/9	15	9	18	36
Tracks/Side	40	40	80	80	80	80
Sides	1	2	2	2	2	2
Sectors/Disk	320/360	640/720	2,400	1,440	2,880	5,760
Available Sectors/Disk	313/351	630/708	2,371	1,426	2,847	5,726
Tracks/inch (TPI)	48/48	48/48	96	135	135	135
Track width (inch/mm)	.0118/ .300	.0118/ .300	.0061/ .155	.0045/ .115	.0045/ .115	.0045/ .115
Bits/inch (BPI)	5,876	5,876	9,646	8,717	17,434	34,868
Media formulation	Ferrite	Ferrite	Cobalt	Cobalt	Cobalt	Barium
Coercivity (Oersteds)	300/300	300/300	600	600	720	750
Sectors/Cluster	1	2	1	2	1	2
FAT type	12-bit	12-bit	12-bit	12-bit	12-bit	12-bit
FAT length (sectors)	1/2	1/2	7	3	9	9
Root directory (sectors)	4/4	7/7	14	7	14	15
Root directory entries	64/64	112/112	224	112	224	240

In addition to the standard formats described in Table 6-1, Microsoft uses the proprietary *DMF* (*Distribution Media Format*) for some of the distribution diskettes it supplies. DMF increases the capacity of a standard high-density 3.5" diskette by reducing the inter-sector gap to allow 21 sectors/track rather than the standard 18 sectors/track, thereby expanding capacity to a true 1.64 MB (usually called 1.68, 1.7, or 1.72 MB).

On most systems, you cannot read data from or write data to DMF diskettes directly, because DIR, DISKCOPY, and other standard disk utilities do not recognize DMF. In fact, attempting to use DISKCOPY to copy a DMF diskette not only yields an unreadable target diskette, but may actually damage the DMF source diskette. DMF diskettes are readable only by Setup and other Microsoft utilities designed to work with CAB files (the compressed Cabinet files used for software distribution), and by some third-party utilities such as WinZip (*http://www.winzip. com*), which allows you to extract data directly from compressed CAB files, and WinImage (*http://www.winimage.com*), which allows you to format and copy DMF diskettes directly.

Fortunately, most software is now distributed on CD, so DMF diskettes are less commonly used today than they were a few years ago. We say fortunately, because in our experience DMF diskettes are much more likely than standard 1.44 MB diskettes to generate read errors. We have frequently found DMF diskettes that were unreadable straight out of the box, and a DMF diskette that is several years old is very likely to be unreadable. A standard diskette was simply never intended to store that much data.

If you encounter an unreadable DMF diskette, we recommend using WinImage to attempt to extract the CAB files manually to the hard disk. If one FDD consistently generates read errors, the diskette may be readable on a different FDD, at least well enough to let you get the CAB files extracted.

Drive Types

As distinct from diskette types and formats, six drive types have been installed in PC-compatible systems:

5.25" 160/180 KB (SSDD)
  Single-Sided, Double-Density (SSDD) was the standard FDD in very early PC-class systems. These drives read and write only SSDD diskettes.

5.25" 320/360 KB (DSDD)
  Double-Sided, Double-Density (DSDD) was the standard FDD in PC-class systems, and often found as a second FDD in early AT and 386 systems. These drives read and write single-sided (160/180 KB) and double-sided (320/360 KB) formats.

5.25" 1.2 MB (HD)
  High-Density (HD)—this and all later formats are double-sided, but that part is no longer stated—is the standard FDD in 286, 386, and some early 486 systems, and often found as a second FDD in early systems with 3.5" primary FDDs. These drives read and write any 5.25" format. A diskette previously formatted or written to by a 5.25" DD drive and then written to by a 5.25" HD drive may not subsequently be reliably readable in any 5.25" DD drive.

3.5" 720 KB (DD)
  Double-Density (DD) is an interim standard, commonly found as a primary drive in early low-end 286 systems, and as a secondary drive in a few PC-class systems and many 286, 386, and 486 systems. These drives read and write only the 720 KB DD format.

3.5" 1.44 MB (HD)
  High-Density (HD) is the standard FDD on mainstream systems for the past decade. These drives read, write, and format any 3.5" HD or DD diskette.

3.5" 2.88 MB (ED)
  Extra Density (ED) is a failed standard, introduced by IBM and now effectively obsolete. ED diskettes are very expensive—typically $3 each versus $0.25 for a 1.44 MB diskette—which doomed the format. These drives are difficult to find new nowadays, but can read, write, and format any 3.5" diskette in any format.

It's worth noting that 5.25" drives and 3.5" drives use different methods for write-protecting diskettes. 5.25" diskettes have a write-enable notch. To write-protect a 5.25" diskette, cover that notch with opaque tape. 3.5" diskettes have a write-protect hole with a sliding shutter. To write-protect a 3.5" diskette, slide the shutter to uncover the hole.

FDD Interface and Cabling

The FDD interface and power requirements are completely standardized, as follows:

Controller
PC-class systems used a separate FDD controller card. XT- and AT-class systems and some early 386s used a combination HDD/FDD controller card. Current systems use an embedded FDD controller. These controllers differ only in their maximum data rate, which determines the FDD types they support. Early controllers run at 250 KB/s, which supports only 360 KB 5.25" FDDs and 720 KB 3.5" FDDs. Later controllers run at 500 KB/s, which supports any standard FDD, or at 1 MB/s, which is required for 2.88 MB 3.5" FDDs. Run BIOS Setup to determine which FDD types a given system supports.

 If you must install a higher capacity FDD than the controller supports—e.g., if you must salvage data from a hard drive in a system whose old 5.25" 360 KB FDD has failed and you have only a 3.5" HD FDD to replace it—you have two alternatives:

— Remove or disable the on-board FDD controller, and replace it with a third-party FDD controller that supports the higher capacity FDD.

— Lie to the old system about what type of FDD you are installing. For example, install a 1.44 MB FDD, but tell the system that it is a 360 KB or 720 KB FDD. All FDDs run at 300 RPM, except 5.25" 1.2 MB FDDs, which run at 360 RPM. That means that any ED, HD, or DD 3.5" FDD can emulate any lower-capacity 3.5" drive, as well as the 5.25" 360 KB FDD. Use blank DD diskettes, and format them in the new drive. Copy data to the floppies and then attempt to read them on another system. Some systems will happily read such oddities as a 3.5" 360 KB diskette, but others will simply return an "unknown media type" message. If the latter occurs, use BIOS Setup on the good system to reconfigure the FDD temporarily to the same settings as those on the older system.

Data cable
FDD data cables use a standard 34-pin pinout (see Table 6-2), but connectors vary. 5.25" drives use a card edge connector. 3.5" drives use a header pin connector. A standard FDD cable has at least three connectors, one for the FDD interface and two for drives. Most FDD cables have five connectors, with redundant header pin and card edge connectors at each of the two drive positions, allowing any type of FDD to be connected at either position.

Power

5.25" drives accept the larger Molex power connector. 3.5" drives accept the smaller Berg power connector. Chassis that permit a 3.5" drive to be installed in a 5.25" bay typically include a Molex-to-Berg adapter.

Table 6-2: Floppy Disk Drive Cable Pinouts

Pin #	Signal	Pin #	Signal
Odd pins (1–33)	Ground	20	Step pulse
2, 4, and 6	Not Used	22	Write Data
8	Index	24	Write Enable
10	Motor Enable A	26	Track 0
12	Drive Select B	28	Write Protect
14	Drive Select A	30	Read Data
16	Motor Enable B	32	Select Head 1
18	Direction (Stepper motor)	34	Disk Change

The BIOS identifies the drive as *A:* or *B:* based on how the drive is jumpered and by the cable position to which that drive connects. Older 5.25" drives have four *drive select (DS)* jumper positions, labeled DS0 through DS3 or DS1 through DS4. Later drives have only two settings, labeled DS0/DS1 or DS1/DS2. Many recent 3.5" drives are permanently set to the second DS position (DS1/DS2). The BIOS recognizes a drive set to the first DS position (DS0/DS1) as *A:* and a drive set to the second DS position (DS1/DS2) as *B:*, assuming that drive is connected to the controller with a straight-through cable.

But a standard two-drive FDD cable has wires 10 through 16 twisted between the first (middle) drive connector and the second (end) drive connector, which effectively reverses the jumper setting on the drive connected to the end connector. In other words, a drive that is jumpered as the second drive (DS1/DS2 or *B:*) and connected to the end connector is seen by the system as the first drive (DS0/DS1 or *A:*) because of the twist. Because many recent chipsets support only a single FDD, many recent FDD cables have only two connectors, one for the motherboard FDD interface, and the second for the single FDD. This cable has a twist, which means that a drive connected to it must be set to the second DS position if it is to be recognized as *A:*.

Use the following rules for connecting FDDs:

- To install one FDD in a system, standard practice is to jumper that drive as the second drive (DS1/DS2) and connect it to the end connector. Alternatively, you can jumper the drive as the first drive (DS0/DS1) and connect it to the middle connector. Either method allows the system to see that drive as *A:*.

- To install two FDDs in a system, jumper both drives as the second drive (DS1/DS2). Connect the *A:* drive to the end connector and the *B:* drive to the middle connector. (Note that the chipsets used in many recent systems support only one FDD.)

- Sometimes, cable constraints (length or available connector types) make it impossible to configure the drives as you want them. If this happens, check

BIOS Setup to see if it allows you to exchange *A:* and *B:*, overriding the drive designations made by DS jumper settings and cable position.

Working with FDDs

Keep the following issues in mind when working with FDDs:

Choosing

3.5" HD FDDs are $15 commodity items made by several manufacturers. We prefer the Teac FD235HF, but there is little difference between brands. Buy whatever is offered. 5.25" FDDs are still available new for $40 or so, but that won't last forever. If you need a 5.25" FDD to rescue data on old disks, get the drive now. If you patronize a local computer store, check there first. They may have a stack of old 5.25" FDDs they'd be happy to give away or sell cheaply.

Installing

5.25" FDDs require a 5.25" half-height, externally accessible drive bay. 3.5" FDDs can be installed in an externally-accessible 3.5" third-height bay, or, by using an adapter, in a 5.25" half-height bay. The BIOS automatically detects installed FDDs, but can determine type unambiguously only for 5.25" HD (1.2 MB) FDDs, which spin at 360 RPM rather than 300. For other drive types, older machines assume 360 KB or 720 KB and newer systems assume 1.44 MB. Use BIOS setup to confirm that the drive type is configured correctly.

Cabling

If you add or replace an FDD, also replace the cable, particularly if it is the original cable. Manufacturers often fold and crimp the FDD cable for improved cable routing and airflow. An old cable that has been so treated is no longer reliable, especially after you disturb it to install the new drive.

Change Line Support

All but the oldest FDD controllers use line 34 for Change Line Support. When the FDD door is opened, the FDD signals on line 34 to tell the system that the diskette may have been changed. If you install a 360 KB or 720 KB FDD, verify the Change Line setting, ordinarily set on the drive by a jumper labeled "Line 34" or "Change Line." If you install such a drive in a PC/XT-class system, leave the jumper open. On any later system, install a jumper block to connect line 34 and enable Change Line Support. Failing to do so and then writing to a diskette in that drive may destroy the data on that diskette by overwriting the FATs and root directory entries with data from the diskette that was formerly in the drive.

Cleaning

FDDs are used so little nowadays—an occasional boot or program install— that head wear and media accumulation isn't a problem. Dust needs to be removed periodically. You can buy special FDD cleaning kits, but we don't bother with them. Every few months (or when we open the case for other reasons) we vacuum out the drive and drench it down with Radio Shack Zero Residue cleaner or the equivalent.

Floppy Disk Drives

Repairing

Don't. Replace the drive. Modern 3.5" drives are so cheap that it makes no sense to repair one, and they are often sealed units without repair access anyway. Older 5.25" drives often are repairable, but the cost to do so exceeds the cost of a new drive.

Working with Obsolete Diskette Formats

If you've been computing for a long time, it's sometimes necessary to read a diskette written in an obsolete format. You may also need to format and write a diskette in an obsolete format, e.g., to create a boot diskette for an older system whose hard drive will not boot but still contains valuable data. If you find yourself in such a position, keep the following issues in mind:

- A 3.5" 1.44 MB FDD can read, write, and format 720 KB (DD) and 1.44 MB (HD) diskettes. 3.5" 2.88 MB (ED) diskettes are readable only by an ED drive. These are difficult to find new, so your only option may be to locate someone with an ED drive who is willing to allow you to use it to transfer your data.

- A 5.25" 1.2 MB FDD can read any 5.25" diskette written with an IBM format in any 360 KB or 1.2 MB drive. A problem may arise when you exchange 360 KB diskettes between 360 KB and 1.2 MB drives. 360 KB drives write a wider track than 1.2 MB drives, which cannot completely erase or format data put down by 360 KB drives. If a 360 KB drive formats or writes to a 360 KB diskette, a 1.2 MB drive can subsequently read, write, or format that diskette, but once that diskette has been written or formatted in the 1.2 MB drive, it will no longer be reliably readable in a 360 KB drive. This problem does not arise if the 360 KB diskette has never been written to in a 360 KB drive. Accordingly, if you need to write data with a 1.2 MB drive that must subsequently be read by a 360 KB drive, use blank 360 KB diskettes (bulk-erased, if necessary), and format them to 360 KB in the 1.2 MB drive.

- Old diskettes often have errors, either because the diskette has been physically abused or simply because the magnetic domains on the diskette have gradually faded with time. Reading data from a diskette that was last written five or more years ago is very likely to yield some read errors; one ten or more years old is almost certain to have multiple read errors, and may be completely unreadable. Using the diskette rescue utilities included with Norton Utilities for DOS (*http://www.symantec.com*) and SpinRite (*http://www.spinrite. com*) can often retrieve some or all of the data from a marginal diskette.

 If the data is critical, consider sending the diskette to one of the firms that specialize in data retrieval and advertise in the back of computer magazines. These services are not cheap and cannot guarantee that they will be able to salvage the data, but they do offer the best hope. If the data is important enough to pay a data retrieval firm to salvage, send the diskette to them without trying to salvage the data yourself first. Running one of the utilities mentioned previously may render what would have been salvageable data unreadable by the data retrieval company.

- You can generally install a newer FDD in an older system and use it to emulate an older FDD, with the following limitations:

  - The 5.25" 1.2 MB FDD spins at 360 RPM (versus 300 RPM for all other FDDs) and cannot be used in a system whose FDD controller supports only 360 KB FDDs.

  - You can install a 3.5" 1.44 MB FDD in nearly any 286 or later computer and some late-model XT clones, although the drive may be recognized only as 720 KB. If that occurs, use 720 KB (DD) diskettes in that drive. In theory, you should also be able to install a 3.5" FDD in a PC or XT-class system and use it as a 360 KB FDD. In practice, this works on some PC and XT-class systems, but not all. For reasons that are not clear to us, some old systems refuse to recognize the 3.5" drive at all. If that occurs, your only alternative is to locate an actual 5.25" 360 KB drive and use it to do the transfer.

 To use this method, you also have to temporarily reconfigure the 3.5" drive on the modern system to 360 KB in order to read and write 360 KB 3.5" diskettes. Some systems allow this, but others return a hardware error. Before you install the 3.5" FDD in the older system, check the newer system to make sure that it allows its 3.5" drive to run as a 360 KB 5.25" drive. To do so, run BIOS Setup on the newer machine, set the drive type to 360 KB 5.25", and restart the system. If the system does not return a hardware error, insert a blank 720 KB (DD) diskette into the drive and issue the command format a:. If the diskette formats successfully to 360 KB, that drive is usable for your purposes.

Salvaging Diskette Data

If a diskette is physically damaged, you may be able to salvage the data by removing the actual diskette medium from its protective sheath. For a 5.25" diskette, take the following steps, which we've used successfully more than once:

1. Use a razor blade or sharp knife to carefully trim about 1/8" (3 mm) from the bottom edge of the protective sheath of another diskette that you don't care about. The bottom edge is that nearest the drive door when the diskette is inserted into the drive.

2. Gently squeeze the two edges adjoining the trimmed edge toward the center to open a gap in the trimmed edge. Grasp the plastic medium and gently slide it out of the sheath, leaving the Tyvek inner liner in place. Discard the medium and save the sheath.

3. Repeat the first step on the damaged diskette, and then remove the medium, touching it as little as possible. Put your finger in the central hub hole and gently press the medium towards the trimmed edge. If you must grasp the

medium itself, do so only at the very edge. Be very careful not to bend or deform the medium while you are extracting it.

4. Gently slide the medium from the damaged diskette into the new sheath that you previously prepared, making sure that the medium is right-side up, fully inserted, and that the hub hole in the medium is centered in the hub hole on the sheath. Rotate the medium gently by using your finger in the hub hole to ensure that it turns easily.

5. Insert the patched diskette into the drive and attempt to access it. It's not necessary to tape or otherwise secure the trimmed edge. If you can access some or all of the data on the patched diskette, immediately copy it elsewhere and then discard the diskette.

Salvaging data from a 3.5" diskette is usually impossible. Any damage that renders the hard plastic shell unusable normally also destroys the medium that it contains. However, if recovering the data is critical, you can attempt the following process, which we've had much less luck with:

1. Locate a 3.5" diskette of the same type (DD, HD, or ED) as the damaged diskette that you are willing to destroy. Using a nail file or small screwdriver, gently pry the sliding metal shutter off the diskette and discard the shutter.

2. Gently pry open the shell. Remove and discard the medium, leaving the two Tyvek inner liners in place. Place the shell aside.

3. Repeat the first step on the damaged diskette, and then remove the medium, touching it as little as possible. If the medium is visibly damaged, as it probably will be, continuing is likely to be useless. However, we did once succeed in recovering some files from a medium that appeared to be severely damaged, so it may be worth the effort.

4. Place the medium from the damaged diskette into the new shell you prepared, making sure to orient the medium as it was in the original diskette, and snap the shell closed. Use your fingertip to make sure that the medium turns freely within the shell. Insert the repaired diskette into the drive (you need not replace the shutter first) and attempt to read the diskette.

Our Picks

Here are the floppy disk drives we actually use and recommend:

Floppy Disk Drive (3.5")
Any name-brand drive. These $15 drives are commodity items, and one is about as good as another. We use whatever make happens to be most readily available or cheapest, including (alphabetically) Mitsumi, NEC, Sony, Teac, Toshiba, and probably several others we've forgotten. We use Teac 235HF units by choice, but that's probably just from habit.

Floppy Disk Drive (5.25")
None. Although we keep one or two around on general principles, the 5.25" FDD is obsolete except to read old 5.25" diskettes, most of which were written so long ago that they are now probably unreadable. As of June 2000, new 5.25" FDDs are still manufactured and sold, but few vendors stock them and they are

becoming hard to find. If you need to read an old 5.25" diskette, contact your local computer store, which probably has a stack of 5.25" HD (1.2 MB) FDDs in the back room and will probably give you one for the asking.

We constantly test and review new equipment. For the latest information about what we currently use, visit:

http://www.hardwareguys.com/picks/remstore.html

CHAPTER 7

Floppy Disk Drive Replacements

Many vendors have tried and failed to establish a standard for an FDD replacement. All these so-called superfloppy drives suffer from some combination of non-standardization, incompatibility with standard diskettes, lack of boot support, expensive media, small installed base, lack of OEM acceptance, low reliability, and poor performance. The Iomega Zip Drive and, to a lesser extent, the Imation LS-120 have achieved some degree of acceptance. Others, such as the fast, 200 MB Sony HiFD and the Samsung Pro-FD have features that compare favorably to the Zip Drive and LS-120, but have not been adopted in significant numbers.

Table 7-1 lists the key characteristics of the Zip Drive and LS-120, with ADR NS8 tape, CD-R, and CD-RW shown for comparison. Note that CD-R blanks are not reusable. Costs are approximate and are current as of June 2000 and are shown in U.S. dollars.

Table 7-1: Key Characteristics of FDD Replacements, with OnStream ADR Tape, CD-R, and CD-RW Shown for Comparison

	Zip 100	*Zip 250*	*LS-120*	*ADR tape*	*CD-R*	*CD-RW*
Native capacity (MB)	100	250	120	~15,000	~ 650	~480–650
IDE/SCSI/ Parallel/USB	•/•/•/•	•/•/•/○	•/•/•/•	•/•/•/○	•/•/•/•	•/•/•/•
Rotation rate (RPM)	2,945	2,945	720	N/A	N/A	N/A
Average read access (ms)	39	39	112	Minutes	125–350	125–350
Sustained transfer (KB/sec)	225–1,400	400–2,400	~200	1,024–2,048	600–1,200	300–600
Drive cost	$75	$150	$100	$250–500	$100–300	$125–400
Media cost (per cartridge)	$8	$15	$18	$35	< $1.00	~$2.00

	Zip 100	Zip 250	LS-120	ADR tape	CD-R	CD-RW
Media cost (per gigabyte)	$80	$60	$150	$2.33	~$1.50	~$3.00
Bootable	•	•	•	○	•	•
Read/Write 1.44 MB?	○ / ○	○ / ○	• / •	○ / ○	○ / ○	○ / ○

Choosing a Floppy Disk Drive Replacement

Use the following guidelines when choosing a floppy drive replacement:

To exchange data bidirectionally with people or computers not on your network
> Buy a drive compatible with the media in use. LS-120 and Zip Drives cannot read or write each other's media. LS-120 drives are common on recent Compaq computers, but are seldom seen elsewhere. Zip Drives are by far the most commonly used superfloppy, so installing one allows you to exchange data with more people. The Zip Drive 250 can read and write both 100 and 250 MB media, and so offers the most flexibility. It also transfers data about twice as fast as the Zip Drive 100.

To send data to other people or computers, but will not receive data from them
> Do not buy a superfloppy. Buy a CD-Recordable (CD-R) or CD Rewritable (CD-RW) drive and a supply of inexpensive CD-R disks. Nearly everyone has a CD-ROM drive that can read the CDs you produce.

To use the drive to back up and/or archive data
> Do not buy a superfloppy. They are unsuited to this purpose because they are slow and use costly and relatively unreliable media. If backup is your primary need, buy a tape drive. If you need to archive data permanently, buy a CD-R or CD-RW drive and archive the data to CD-R disks. If you can afford only one drive, and if 650 MB is enough capacity to back up your important data, buy a CD-RW drive and a supply of CD-RW disks, which can be reused repeatedly.

We've installed one Zip 250 drive on our home network, which we use only to read Zip disks that people send us. We use tape drives for backup, and CD-R drives for archiving data or sending it to others. If you decide on a Zip Drive, keep the following issues in mind:

Click of Death (COD)
> Zip disks whose logical formatting is damaged cause the dreaded Click of Death. When this occurs, the drive repeatedly seeks unsuccessfully, making a characteristic COD clicking sound. This problem can usually be solved simply by using another disk. However, if the problem disk is physically damaged it generates the same clicking sound, but physically damages any drive you attempt to read it in. When they experience COD, many people immediately either attempt to read the disk in another drive—which simply destroys that drive as well—or attempt to read another disk in the damaged drive, which simply destroys yet another disk. A damaged drive literally has its heads ripped loose and a damaged disk has its edge shredded. Using a good disk in

a damaged drive destroys that disk, which will subsequently destroy any drive that attempts to access it. If you experience COD, always examine the disk carefully to determine if it is physically damaged before you do anything else. For details about COD, visit *http://www.grc.com/clickdeath.htm*. This page describes the COD in full detail and has a link to a free utility that you can use to test Zip and Jaz drives for this problem.

Choose your interface carefully

The Zip Drive 100 and the Zip Drive 250 are available in IDE, SCSI, parallel, and USB interfaces. An external parallel or SCSI unit provides the most flexibility. They can be carried from computer to computer along with the data— e.g., to download a large service pack using the T1 at work and then carry the drive home to install the service pack—and used to expand the disk storage available on older laptop systems with small hard drives.

IDE/ATAPI

The IDE/ATAPI version (Zip Insider) is fast, easy to install, and runs reliably. However, if you plan to use your Zip Drive for disaster recovery— which is not the best choice anyway—note that the Iomega IDE Zip drivers do not function under DOS. The SCSI and parallel drivers do, which means you can access data on a SCSI or parallel Zip Drive before Windows is reinstalled and running. We have had few problems when installing the ATAPI version as the Sole/Master on the Secondary ATA channel—the usual configuration on a system that has an existing Primary/Master hard disk and a Primary/Slave CD-ROM drive. We have experienced occasional problems installing the ATAPI version as a Slave on the Primary channel with a Primary/Master hard disk. If this happens, installing the Zip as Secondary/Master usually solves the problem. We have experienced more problems when installing an ATAPI Zip Drive as either Master or Slave on the Secondary ATA channel with a CD-ROM drive jumpered to the opposite. Some systems do not function properly with the CD-ROM as Master and the Zip as Slave, but work fine with the Zip as Master and the CD-ROM as Slave. Others work properly with the drives jumpered conversely. Some systems don't work properly either way, and the only option is to swap drives around between the Primary and Secondary channels, or to substitute a different CD-ROM drive.

SCSI

The SCSI version is fast and runs reliably. However, to use it you must install a SCSI adapter, which adds to the expense and complexity. Note that only the final device in a SCSI chain should be terminated, and SCSI Zip Drives are terminated by default on the assumption that they will be the only SCSI device installed. If you install a SCSI Zip Drive on an existing SCSI chain, turn off termination unless the Zip Drive is the final device on the chain. In that case, make sure to turn off termination on the device that was formerly the last device.

Parallel

These are much slower than the other versions, but can be used on any computer with an available parallel port. We have occasionally encountered incompatibilities with the parallel versions, including failure to recognize the drive and inability to access the drive other than in Safe Mode under Windows 95/98. If this occurs, check BIOS Setup to determine how the parallel port is configured. Setting the port to EPP or EPP/ECP (depending on your BIOS) may resolve the problem, and will allow the Zip Drive to operate at the highest possible speed, although that is still much slower than the other versions. If the port is already configured correctly, removing and then reinstalling the drivers sometimes cures the problem.

Parallel Zip Drives may also be problematic under Windows NT. Some Windows NT systems bluescreen at boot if a parallel Zip Drive is attached. If this occurs, remove the Iomega parallel port SCSI driver, change the parallel port mode (some NT systems work properly only if configured for Standard Parallel Port, while others seem to prefer EPP/ECP mode), and reinstall the Iomega parallel port SCSI driver.

Parallel Zip Drives may also cause conflicts with some printer drivers, notably those for HP inkjet printers. This problem is documented with workarounds on both the Iomega and HP web sites.

USB

The USB Zip Drive is officially supported on the Macintosh (it comes in a blue plastic case that matches the iMac) and on Windows 98, and seems to function properly in either of these environments. Although Windows 2000 putatively supports both USB and the Zip Drive, we have had numerous reports of problems in that environment. Presumably, these problems will be fixed by a later service pack or updated drivers for the Zip drive.

Always eject the disk properly

Although the Zip Drive has an eject button, using it risks damaging your data. Always eject the disk by selecting My Computer, highlighting the drive icon, and choosing Eject. Alternatively, use the Iomega icon on the desktop to eject the disk. If you have just written data to the disk, a period of several seconds must pass before Eject is enabled. During this period, data is being written to the disk, and using the Eject button on the drive may force an eject before the write is complete, which will trash your data.

Check frequently for updated drivers

Many Zip Drive problems can be solved by using the most current drivers, which Iomega updates frequently. Numerous strange things happen with Zip Drives using older drivers, e.g., exiting Excel97 SR1 causes the Zip disk to eject under some circumstances when using older drivers. If your Zip Drive begins behaving strangely, update your driver to the latest version before taking any other troubleshooting steps.

Our Picks

Here are the floppy disk drive replacements we actually use and recommend:

FDD replacement

None. There's little point to buying an FDD replacement unless you need to transfer moderately large files between systems that are not networked. For that, install the same type of FDD replacement that is installed on the other system. If neither system currently has an FDD replacement, install the Iomega Zip 250 for maximum capacity and compatibility with the large installed base of other Zip users. Better still, to transfer files between local systems, install a network. A simple network is relatively cheap and easy to set up, and provides much more functionality than using SneakerNet. If the systems aren't local to each other, install a CD-R(W) drive in each system. The drives are relatively inexpensive, and blank discs that cost from less than $1 (CD-R) to $1.50 to $3.00 (CD-RW) hold from two to six times more than a Zip disk.

We constantly test and review new equipment. For the latest information about what we currently use, visit:

http://www.hardwareguys.com/picks/remstore.html

CHAPTER 8

Removable Hard Disk Drives

Removable hard drives are an odd product category. They provide nearly the capacity and performance of an obsolescent hard disk, but in removable form. The availability of cheap, huge, fast hard disks and such technologies as CD-R(W) has made removable hard drives a niche product. They are typically used for such tasks as transferring huge image files and other pre-press materials to service bureaus, for booting one computer to multiple operating systems, or for making instantly accessible (and bootable) backups. For such specialized needs, they can be useful indeed, but most people are better served by standard hard drives and such writable technologies as CD-R(W) and tape.

Numerous companies, such as SyQuest, have entered and then departed this market, which makes the continuing availability of media (which is always proprietary) a concern. The two remaining products in this niche are the Iomega Jaz and the Castlewood ORB, detailed in Table 8-1. For now, the Jaz is the dominant product, particularly among service bureaus, but the Castlewood ORB is coming on strong.

Table 8-1: Key Characteristics of Removable Hard Drives

	Iomega Jaz 2 GB	Castlewood ORB
Nominal capacity	2,002 MB	2.2 GB
IDE/SCSI/Parallel/USB	○/●/●/○	●/●/●/●
Rotation rate	5,394 RPM	5,400 RPM
Average read/write access time	15.5/17.5 ms	15.5/17.5 ms
Sustained transfer rate (min/max)	4.9/8.7 MB/sec	6.8/12.2 MB/sec
Average spin-up/spin-down time	15/15 sec	12/6 sec
Full format/Quick format time	55 min/45 sec	33 min/0 sec
Estimated disk shelf life	10 years	20 years
Drive/Media Warranty	1 year/none	1 year/lifetime
Drive cost (bare)	~ $250	~ $200

Table 8-1: Key Characteristics of Removable Hard Drives (continued)

	Iomega Jaz 2 GB	*Castlewood ORB*
Media cost (per cartridge)	~ $85	~ $40
Media cost (per gigabyte)	~ $43	~ $18

If you think you need a Jaz or Orb, consider instead buying a chassis that converts a standard 3.5" hard drive into a removable drive. Such products as the $140 Kingston Data Express (*http://www.kingston.com/storage/dexpress*) are available for IDE and SCSI hard drives. They comprise a carrier into which a standard hard drive is inserted, and a chassis that installs in a standard 5.25" drive bay and accepts the drive carrier. If you need to move data between systems, you can purchase additional chassis separately. Likewise, if you need to use multiple hard drives, you can buy carriers separately. Antec also manufactures similar removable hard disk enclosures, called the DataSwap series (*http://www.antec-inc.com/product/datastorage/swap.html*). The advantage of these products is that they provide the capacity and performance of a standard hard drive because they *use* a standard hard drive. The disadvantage is that each "cartridge" comprises a carrier and a standard hard drive, which together cost substantially more than a Jaz or ORB cartridge, albeit while providing double or triple the performance and up to 25 times the capacity.

Our Picks

Here are the removable hard disk drives we actually use and recommend:

Removable hard disk drive

Castlewood ORB. Although the Iomega Jaz is better known, the ORB matches or exceeds it in every important respect, is less expensive, and uses much less expensive disks. Available in $180 (IDE) and $210 (Ultra SCSI) internal versions and $220 (Ultra SCSI) and $265 (USB) external versions, the ORB uses $40 cartridges that store 2.2 GB. Although the capacity of the ORB makes it less than ideal as a backup device, it can serve that purpose if you have a limited amount of data to back up, need a removable hard disk drive, and cannot also afford a tape drive. One exception: if you must transfer image files or other large pre-press materials, consider the Jaz drive if only because it is more common for service bureaus to have a Jaz drive than a Castlewood ORB. (*http://www.castlewood.com*)

We constantly test and review new equipment. For the latest information about what we currently use, visit:

http://www.hardwareguys.com/picks/remstore.html

CHAPTER 9

Tape Drives

Although the cost and capacity of other removable magnetic storage devices continues to improve, tape drives remain the best choice to back up data or to transfer very large amounts of data between systems. Tape drives provide a combination of high capacity, speed, low media cost, and reliability that no other technology can match. Three tape technologies compete for the standalone PC and small network market:

Quarter Inch Cartridge (QIC)

Originally developed in the early 1970s, two styles of QIC cartridges exist. The DC600 is physically larger and is now obsolescent. Recent QIC drives use DC2000 mini-cartridges, which are available in a wide variety of incompatible types and capacities. QIC drives use *serpentine recording*, which records many parallel tracks on each tape. The drive records data from the beginning to the end of the first track, reverses direction, writes data from the end to beginning of the second track, and so on, until all tracks have been written. This means that filling a tape may require fifty or more passes of the tape through the drive, which increases wear and tear on both drive and tape. Only the most recent QIC drives have the extra head required for *read-while-write*, which allows the drive to backup and compare data in one pass. Doing a compare on a single-head drive doubles the number of passes required, and extends backup time significantly.

Most current QIC drives use Travan technology, a combination of tape and drive technologies developed by 3M/Imation, and now implemented by many drive manufacturers. The new generation Travan-NS (Network Solution) drives provide read-while-write verification and *hardware compression*, which allows the drive itself to compress data as it writes it, rather than depending on compression performed by the backup software. Travan drives are relatively inexpensive, provide high capacity and performance, and are available in IDE,

SCSI, and parallel interfaces. The major practical drawback of Travan is the relatively high cost of tapes, typically $25 to $40, depending on capacity.

Digital Data Storage (DDS)

Often incorrectly called *Digital Audio Tape (DAT)*, DDS drives use helical-scan recording similar to that used by a VCR. The recording head rotates at an angle relative to tape movement and lays down a series of short diagonal tracks across the full width of the tape. This means that a DDS drive can theoretically fill a tape during one pass, although real-world drives may require several passes to do so. The lower tape speed and smaller number of passes means that DDS drives incur much less wear on both drive and tape during a backup pass, but the more complex tape path offsets this advantage somewhat. Nearly all DDS drives support read-while-write. DDS drives provide high capacity and performance, but are relatively expensive, and require a SCSI interface. The major advantage of DDS drives is that they use relatively inexpensive tapes, typically $3 to $15. DDS drives are most appropriate for servers that use a tape rotation scheme that requires many tapes.

Advanced Data Recording (ADR)

ADR is a proprietary technology developed by Phillips and currently available in the line of tape drives available from OnStream (*http://www.onstream. com*). ADR writes eight tracks simultaneously, which allows it to provide high throughput while running the tape very slowly, which in turn means ADR drives are quieter and minimize tape wear. For complete details on ADR, see *http://www.onstream.com/adr/index.html*.

Table 9-1 lists the three major tape technologies suitable for backing up stand-alone PCs and small networks. All figures are native, and do not include the 2:1 compression assumed by all tape manufacturers, which doubles capacities and transfer rates. Numerous other tape technologies (e.g., DDS-4, 8mm, DLT, and AIT) are available, but are quite expensive, targeted at large-scale networks, and beyond the scope of this book.

Table 9-1: Key Characteristics of Mainstream Tape Technologies for Typical Drive Models

	Travan			Digital Data Storage		OnStream	
	TR-4	NS8	NS20	DDS-2	DDS-3	ADR30	ADR50
Capacity (GB)	4	4	10	4	12	15	25
Transfer rate (MB/min)	30	36	60	46	70	60	120
IDE/SCSI/Parallel	•/•/•	•/•/○	•/•/○	○/•/○	○/•/○	•/•/•	○/•/○
Read-while-write?	○	•	•	•	•	○	○
HW compression?	○	•	•	•	•	○	○
Drive cost (U.S. $)	< 200	~ 250	400–700	600+	800+	250–400	600
Tape cost (U.S. $)	24	24	35	8	12	35	45
Tape cost/GB (U.S. $)	6.00	6.00	3.50	2.00	1.00	2.33	1.80

Choosing a Tape Drive

Consider the following issues when choosing a tape drive.

Capacity

The single most important consideration. Get a drive that can back up all data on one tape, allowing for some growth. If your data set exceeds the capacity of one tape, you may find that drive is no longer usable (if no one is available to change tapes during an overnight backup) or that it has suddenly become very expensive to use (because you must buy twice as many tapes). In such a case, the only alternative to replacing the drive is to use a backup scheme that mixes full and incremental or differential partial backups, which is riskier for your data.

Tape drive manufacturers arbitrarily rate their drives at double actual capacity, assuming that you will use software or hardware compression that effectively doubles the space available. The actual compression ratio you experience depends on the data mix (e.g., documents and spreadsheets compress well; executables, images, and archives much less so), the backup software you use, and sometimes on the speed of the computer where the drive resides. We find that real-world data sets typically compress at 1.5:1 to 1.7:1, so plan accordingly.

Speed

This may or may not be a critical factor, depending on your own environment and practices. If you have a limited backup window available, speed may be as important as capacity. If you can simply start a backup when you finish work for the day and allow it to run overnight, speed may be a minor factor.

Actual throughput depends on the drive mechanism, the interface, the speed of the computer in which the drive is installed, and the data set being backed up, but will likely be lower than the drive manufacturer advertises. Compression may also have a significant impact on throughput, for better or worse. For example, our Seagate TapeStor TR4 ATAPI drive is rated at 30 MB/min native and 60 MB/min compressed, but we actually get 20–22 MB/min native and 35–38 MB/min when using compression. Our OnStream DI30 ATAPI drive is rated at 60 MB/min native and 120 MB/min compressed. We actually get 45–50 MB/min native, but only 15–17 MB/min when using the bundled Echo software with compression turned on. Our Tecmar Travan NS20 SCSI drive is rated at 60 MB/min native and 120 MB/min compressed, but we actually get about 80 to 100 MB/min. These figures are for backing up local volumes. Backing up data across a network (10BaseT or 100BaseT) commonly cuts throughput by half or more due to operating system overhead, file system overhead, and network latency.

Media cost

Travan and OnStream ADR drives are constructed with loose tolerances, and are accordingly inexpensive, but require expensive tapes built to close tolerances. DDS drives, conversely, are expensive because they are built to tight tolerances, which allows them to use inexpensive, loose tolerance tapes. A typical tape rotation may require from 4 to 50 or more tapes. Tapes must be replaced periodically (on the schedule recommended by the drive and/or tape manufacturer—trying to stretch the lifetime of tapes is a foolish economy).

Tape drives have a realistic service life of perhaps two years with heavy use, and three or four years with moderate use (by which time the drive is likely no longer adequate for your needs anyway). Expect to spend from as much to several times as much as the cost of the drive to buy tapes over the drive's life.

Interface

Tape drives are commonly available in ATAPI/IDE, SCSI, and parallel interfaces.

ATAPI

ADR and Travan drives are available with ATAPI interfaces. ATAPI drives are typically less expensive than those using other interfaces, can use the ubiquitous IDE interface present on any modern motherboard, provide reasonably high throughput, and are easy to install. Choose an ATAPI drive for convenience, ease of installation, or when cost is an overriding issue.

SCSI

ADR, Travan, and DDS drives are available with SCSI interfaces. SCSI drives typically sell for at least a $50 to $100 premium over similar ATAPI models, require adding a $100+ SCSI interface card if the PC is not already so equipped, and are more complicated to install and configure than ATAPI models. SCSI drives typically provide much higher throughput and much lower CPU utilization than ATAPI models. The largest and most feature-laden drives are available only in SCSI. Most SCSI-only models are designed for use on servers, and are therefore better built and more reliable than ATAPI drives designed for the mass market. Choose a SCSI drive for highest capacity, performance, durability, and reliability. SCSI is the only option if there are no available ATAPI connections or if you require capacity and/or features available only in a SCSI model.

Parallel

These typically have half or less the throughput of ATAPI/IDE, but are a reasonable choice if you must use one drive to back up local data on multiple standalone PCs. On a small network, it is usually better to map a drive on the server where a tape drive resides for each local workstation volume and back up centrally to an ATAPI or SCSI drive. If you are considering a parallel drive because you have several standalone PCs that must be backed up, consider instead connecting those PCs with a simple network and using an internal server-based tape drive.

Cross-drive compatibility

Here's a dirty little secret that drive manufacturers don't talk much about. You might reasonably assume that a tape you created in one drive would be readable in a similar drive, but that's not always the case. In particular, we have found that some Travan TR-4 drives produce tapes that cannot be read by another drive, even one of the identical make and model. We have encountered the same problem on DDS drives, although it appears to be much less common with them. We do not yet have enough experience with Travan NS8/NS20 and OnStream ADR drives to judge.

Unless you use a tape drive to transfer large quantities of data between computers, this may seem a minor issue. It can be critical, however, if your computer is stolen or damaged by flood or fire. Even if your backup tapes are safely locked away, you may find that a replacement drive of the same model is unable to read them. If your data is important enough to warrant extreme precautions, buy two identical tape drives and verify that a tape written in either drive is readable by the other. Repeat this verification periodically, because drives do start marching to their own drummer as they age. Alternatively, consider backing up key data frequently to CD-R and verifying that the CD is readable.

Installing and Configuring a Tape Drive

External tape drives are "installed" simply by connecting them to the parallel or SCSI port, as appropriate, and connecting power. Internal tape drives are 3.5" or 5.25" half-height devices, and require the same physical installation steps as any other externally accessible drive. The exact configuration steps required differ between ATAPI and SCSI interfaces, as described in the following sections.

Some tape drive manufacturers, including Seagate, recommend installing the backup software *before* installing the tape drive. But do not *run* the backup software before the drive is installed and recognized by the computer and operating system, or you may find that you need to reinstall the backup software in order for it to recognize the drive. Microsoft Backup has burned us this way more than once. Conversely, some tape backup software—typically that bundled with a tape drive—refuses to install unless a tape drive that it supports is already installed. Read the manual for the tape drive *and* the backup software before you begin the installation.

Installing and Configuring an ATAPI Tape Drive

ATAPI tape drives are physically installed and configured just like any other ATAPI/IDE device: set the drive's Master/Slave jumper, secure the drive in an available drive bay using four screws to secure it, connect the data cable, aligning pin one on the drive connector with the colored stripe on the cable, and connect the power cable. Note the following issues when installing an ATAPI tape drive:

- Installing a tape drive on the same IDE channel as a hard disk risks data corruption. If the system has one hard disk, install it as the Primary Master and the tape drive on the Secondary channel. If the system has two hard disks, install both on the Primary channel, and install the tape drive on the Secondary channel. Do not install three ATA hard disks in a system with an ATAPI tape drive. If the system has an ATAPI CD-ROM drive, make that drive Secondary Master and the tape drive Secondary Slave. If the system has no ATAPI CD-ROM drive, make the tape drive Secondary Master.

- Some tape drives have configuration jumpers to enable such things as hardware compression, read-while-write, DMA/PIO mode, and emulation mode. If your drive has one or more of these jumpers, set them as follows:

Hardware compression

Ordinarily, enable this option to allow the drive itself to compress the data stream before recording it to tape. If you do enable this option, make sure to disable software compression in your backup utility. Leaving both enabled results in "churning" that can actually increase the size of the data being written to tape. Some backup utilities have a configuration checkbox that allows you to select hardware compression. We've never been entirely sure of the purpose of this checkbox, because hardware compression is (or should be) transparent to the backup application, but if your backup utility has such a checkbox, it's probably a good idea to mark it if you enable hardware compression on the drive.

 Although different drive models from a particular manufacturer may supposedly use compatible hardware compression, any tape made with hardware compression enabled may be unreadable except in the drive that wrote it. There is no guarantee that you will be able to read a hardware-compressed tape made on one drive with any other drive. Something as subtle as a minor difference in firmware revision may prevent reading a compressed tape even in a seemingly identical drive.

Read-while-write

If your drive has a jumper to enable read-while-write, doing so allows the drive to use its separate read head to read and verify data immediately after it is written, avoiding the need for a time-consuming second compare pass. Not all backup software supports this function. If your backup software does support it, you may need to enable support for it within the backup program.

DMA/PIO mode

Not all tape drives can operate in DMA mode, which increases throughput and reduces CPU utilization. If your drive is DMA-capable, it may have a jumper to configure the drive for DMA mode versus PIO mode. In general, if the tape drive is the only device on the ATA channel, or if the other device on that channel is also DMA-capable, enable DMA mode for the tape drive and enable DMA support for that channel in the operating system. If the tape drive shares the channel with a PIO-only device (e.g., an older CD-ROM drive), disable DMA mode for the tape drive or replace the other device with a DMA-capable device.

Emulation mode

Some tape drives can emulate other drives via a jumper setting that causes the drive to return incorrect identification data to the operating system. For example, our Tecmar Travan NS20 tape drive is jumpered by default to identify itself as a Wangtek Model 51000. Removing this jumper causes the drive to identify itself as a Tecmar Travan NS20. Using emulation allows a new drive model to be used with older software that does not support the new model. Set this jumper, if present, according to the manufacturer's instructions.

- Recent BIOSes allow setting boot sequence to first attempt booting from a CD-ROM drive. What this actually tells the system is to boot from the first ATAPI device. If an ATAPI tape drive is configured as Master (even on the Secondary Channel), a system so configured may attempt to boot from the tape drive, which causes the system to hang. You can avoid this problem by setting the CD-ROM drive to Secondary Master and the tape drive to Secondary Slave. This problem may also occur if the tape drive is the only device on the Secondary Channel, whether it is configured as Master or Slave. If you cannot correct the configuration or disable CD-ROM boot in BIOS, boot the system with no tape in the drive.

Installing and Configuring a SCSI Tape Drive

Installing and configuring a SCSI tape drive is more complicated. Rather than attempting to provide step-by-step instructions, which vary according to the specific drive and adapter, we've chosen to illustrate a typical installation using a Tecmar Travan NS20 drive and an Adaptec 2930 SCSI host adapter, both representative selections.

- If you have not already done so, install the SCSI host adapter. To do so, power down the system, remove the cover, and locate an available bus-mastering PCI slot. (Some older systems don't support bus-mastering on all slots. Bus-mastering slots are usually white or ivory; non-bus-mastering slots are brown or black.) Remove the slot cover for the selected slot, align the bus connector with the slot and press down firmly to seat the adapter. Use the screw that secured the slot cover to secure the adapter. If you have a spare drive activity indicator LED, connect it to J2 on the host adapter to indicate SCSI bus activity.

- The Adaptec host adapter supports *SCAM (SCSI Configured Auto-Magically)*— a kind of Plug-N-Play for SCSI that automatically configures SCSI ID and termination. (SCAM is described in Chapter 10, *CD-ROM Drives*, in the "Installing and Configuring a SCSI CD-ROM Drive" section). The Tecmar tape drive does not support SCAM, and so requires manually setting jumpers to assign SCSI ID.

  Like most manually configured SCSI devices, the Tecmar drive has three jumpers—ID0 (SCSI ID 1), ID1 (SCSI ID 2), and ID2 (SCSI ID 4)—to set SCSI IDs 0 through 7. Connecting no jumpers assigns SCSI ID 0. Connecting one jumper sets the SCSI ID associated with that jumper (e.g., ID1 assigns SCSI ID 2). Connecting two jumpers assigns the SCSI ID that is the sum of the two jumpers (e.g., ID0 and ID2 sums the SCSI IDs 1 and 4 to assign the SCSI ID 5). Connecting all three jumpers assigns SCSI ID 7. Like most SCSI tape drives, the Tecmar drive is jumpered to SCSI ID 4 by default, which is the recommended setting, and the one we use.

Avoid setting a tape drive to SCSI ID 0, 1, or 7. ID 0 is reserved by convention for a bootable hard drive, ID 1 for a second hard drive, and ID 7 for the host adapter.

- The Tecmar drive also requires setting termination manually. Exactly two devices must be terminated on each SCSI bus, and these devices must be those at each end of the bus, as follows:

  – If the SCSI adapter has only internal devices attached to it, the adapter itself and the final device on the internal SCSI chain must be terminated.

  – If the SCSI adapter has only external devices attached to it, the adapter itself and the final device on the external SCSI chain must be terminated.

  – If the SCSI adapter has both internal and external devices attached to it, the adapter must not be terminated. Instead, terminate the final internal device and the final external device attached to the SCSI chain.

  In this case, the Tecmar tape drive is the final device on the internal SCSI chain, which has no external devices, so the drive and the host adapter must both be terminated. We jumper pins 3 and 4 on the drive to terminate it. Adaptec host adapters, which we use and recommend exclusively, by default automatically detect terminated SCSI devices on the bus and set their own termination status accordingly, so no further action is required to configure termination properly for this setup. Note that a few internal SCSI cables have a built-in terminator at the end of the cable. If you use such a cable, make sure that termination is disabled on all drives connected to that cable.

 Most drives ship with termination power enabled, which is usually correct. If you have trouble accessing a tape drive, check the host adapter manual to determine if termination power should be disabled.

- Once you have resolved SCSI ID and termination issues and have the drive physically installed, the next step is to connect the cables. Most adapters are supplied with a standard two-device cable. If you need to connect more than two drives, replace the cable before proceeding. Otherwise, connect the cable to each drive, making sure to align pin 1 on the cable (indicated by a red stripe) with pin one on each device (indicated by a small number, triangle, or dot on the connector). For SCSI IDs, it doesn't matter which drive connects to which cable position, so mix and match drives and cable positions in what-ever way makes it easiest to route the cable. Just make sure that the physical last drive on the cable is the one that's terminated. Connect the power cable.

- After verifying all settings and connections, turn on any external SCSI device(s) first, and then turn on the PC. Ordinarily, the system should boot normally, but the SCSI tape drive may or may not be recognized, depending on the drive itself, your operating system and other factors. Before you configure the operating system to use the drive, some systems may require one or both of the following steps:

CMOS setup

On most systems, the PCI bus assigns IRQs and port addresses automatically. If your system requires setting PCI bus parameters manually, do so during the first restart, using the system or motherboard documentation for guidance. (If your system BIOS is capable of assigning IRQs automatically, there will usually be a CMOS Setup option worded something like "Plug-N-Play OS?" If that option is set to No, the PC BIOS assigns IRQs. If it is set to Yes, the BIOS allows the PnP-capable OS (Windows 9X/2000) to assign IRQs.)

SCSI setup

At boot time, the SCSI BIOS displays adapter and BIOS information and a list of installed SCSI devices. Ordinarily, the default settings are fine, but in some cases you may need to change settings to get the drive to work at all or to optimize its performance. If this is the case for your system, press whatever key sequence is needed to invoke the SCSI setup routine and make the necessary changes, as recommended by the documentation for the host adapter and/or drive.

If either or both of these steps are needed, restart the system after completing each. After you complete these steps, the system should boot normally and physically recognize the tape drive.

Configuring Windows 9X to Support a Tape Drive

Windows 9X does not really support *any* tape drives in the usual sense, although it may or may not recognize and display the name of an installed tape drive, depending on the drive and the version of Windows. Unlike most other devices, for which drivers are readily available and can be installed using the Add New Hardware Wizard, tape drives running under Windows 9X depend on device support built into the backup application itself. This is why, for example, the Windows 98 Microsoft Backup applet—an OEM version of Seagate Backup Exec— can use some tape drives and not others: the program itself contains drivers for the supported tape drives. All this really means is that you can't use unsupported drives with the built-in backup applet, not much loss for Windows 98, and no loss at all for Windows 95.

Recent versions of third-party Windows 9X backup applications include drivers for many recent-model tape drives. Most tape drives bundle a competent backup utility—often a special version of BackupExec or ARCserve—that contains the necessary drivers to support that drive under the operating systems intended to run them. You may, however, need to download drivers for a new tape drive either from the tape drive manufacturer (most of whom do not supply drivers) or from the backup software company, if one of the following is true:

- You have a previously purchased backup utility that does not contain drivers for the new drive.

- You have a backup utility that you want to continue to use that was originally bundled with a drive you are replacing and that backup utility has no support for the new drive.

- The backup application supplied with the new drive does not support the operating system you are using.

Before you purchase a tape drive for use with Windows 9X, verify that the backup application you intend to use has drivers for that tape drive.

Configuring Windows NT to Support a Tape Drive

Windows NT 4 recognizes some tape drives at install time, but does not recognize others, notably Travan drives. If you install a Travan drive at any time, or another drive after Windows NT is already installed, proceed as follows:

1. Select Start → Settings → Control Panel, and double-click Tape Devices. Windows scans the SCSI bus and/or ATA controllers to locate tape drives and (usually) displays the name of any connected tape device.

    - If the Devices page displays the tape drive name, Windows NT recognizes the drive, which it usually will for 4mm "DAT" drives and some other tape drives. View the Drivers page to determine which driver Windows NT is loading, and install an updated driver from the tape driver manufacturer if one is available. For example, many tape drive vendors supply an updated driver to replace the *4mmdat.sys* driver supplied with Windows NT 4. If the installed driver is appropriate, NT 4 is configured properly for your drive.

    - If the Devices page displays "(No tape device found)"—as it will for Travan drives—or if you need to install an updated driver for a supported drive, click the Drivers tab to display the Drivers page.

2. Click Add to display a list of available drivers by manufacturer and model. For a Travan drive, choose "(Standard tape drives)" in the Manufacturer pane, and "IDE (QIC-157) tape drive" in the Tape Devices pane (use this driver even if your Travan drive is SCSI). For a non-Travan drive, choose the appropriate maker in the Manufacturer pane and model in the Tape Devices pane. Once you have selected the correct manufacturer and tape device, click OK to install the driver. If the manufacturer and/or model of your tape drive is not displayed, click Have Disk, insert a driver disk supplied by the tape driver maker, and follow the prompts.

3. When prompted, insert the Windows NT distribution CD or enter another location where the driver files are located. If the driver files are already installed on your disk, Setup displays a prompt to ask if you want to use the existing files or reinstall the driver files. Always choose to reinstall unless you are certain that the driver already on the hard disk is more recent than the version you have. Once the driver files are copied, Windows NT displays the System Settings Change dialog to inform you that you must restart the computer before the changes take effect. Remove any diskettes or CDs from the drives and restart the system.

4. When the system restarts, redisplay the Tape Devices dialog and verify that the correct driver is loaded and that it is shown as running. At this point, Windows NT should recognize the tape drive. You can verify this by starting

Windows NT Backup or your third-party backup utility and verifying that the tape drive is shown as an available backup destination.

Care and Feeding of a Tape Drive

Tape drives and tape cartridges are surprisingly durable, but getting the best results requires following a few simple rules:

- *Clean the drive regularly.* The most frequent cause of tape drive problems is dirty read/write heads. Tape drive manufacturers typically recommend cleaning the drive monthly or after every 10 to 25 hours of use. It is also a good idea to clean the drive immediately after first using a new tape. Depending on how you use your drive and how clean your environment is, even that may be inadequate. Problems caused by dirty heads are not always immediately obvious, because tape drives use industrial-strength ECC methods that allow them to recover from most read and write errors. The first sign of dirty heads may simply be that backups begin taking longer than they should. If your environment is typical, it's probably not excessive to clean the tape drive weekly or before each full backup. Some drives can only be cleaned by using the recommended cleaning cartridge. Other drives allow you to vacuum or blow out the dust and then use a foam swab moistened with rubbing alcohol to clean the heads and rollers (cotton swabs can leave debris on the heads, and should be avoided). Having once watched a cleaning cartridge destroy the heads on a tape drive, we prefer the second method if the drive manufacturer lists it as a permissible method.

 Some tape drives, typically high-end models, keep track of how much the drive has been used since the last cleaning. For example, Robert's Tecmar TS3900i DDS-3 drive generates a warning message in Backup Exec when it is time to clean the drive. Running a cleaning cartridge through the drive clears and resets the timer, and the message disappears until the next time cleaning is due. We've been told that some tape drives simply refuse to operate if you ignore the warning messages too long, but we've never experienced that, simply because we've never risked allowing an expensive drive to go too long without cleaning.

- Avoid exposing tapes to magnetic fields. This should be obvious, but what may not be obvious is that stray magnetic fields from monitors and other peripherals can damage even tapes that are stored some distance from the source. We once found that tapes stored in a desk drawer had been damaged by the field from a monitor sitting on the desk surface above them. For DAT tapes, the only loss is the data stored on the tape, because DAT drives format tapes on the fly as they write the data. For Travan and ADR tapes, any damage is fatal to the tape. These tapes are formatted at the factory, and cannot be reformatted by the user. If you expose a Travan or ADR tape to a magnetic field strong enough to damage the data on it, that tape can no longer be used at all.

- Retension tapes frequently. Periodic retensioning is required by Travan and ADR tapes, but not by DAT tapes. Retensioning simply winds the tape out to the end and then back to the beginning. You should retension a tape before using it for the first time; if it has not been used for a month or more; if it has been shipped (or dropped); or if it has been exposed to a significant temperature change. As a rule of thumb, retension a tape used daily once a week, and one used weekly once a month.

- Store the tapes safely. Tapes are quite sensitive to their storage environment, and are happiest at the same levels of temperature and humidity that are comfortable for people. When a tape is not actually in the drive, always replace it in its sleeve or case to avoid dust. Never place a tape in direct sunlight. For safe storage on-site, use a fire safe. Make sure that safe is rated to store magnetic media. Less expensive fire safes are designed to protect paper, and allow internal temperatures to exceed levels safe for tapes. If the temperature or humidity differs greatly between the storage and use locations, always allow the tape an hour or two to reach equilibrium before using it.

- Replace tapes periodically. Tapes do not last forever. Each time you use a tape, the magnetic medium becomes more abraded and the substrate stretches. For best results, replace tapes every two years or 50 uses, whichever comes first. That is, replace a tape that is used daily at least every two months. Replace a weekly tape at least once a year. Replace a monthly tape every two years or more often. In addition to risking the data written to it, using an elderly, worn tape risks damaging the tape drive heads.

Troubleshooting Tape Drive Problems

Here, in rough order of frequency, are the most common problems and some things you can do to solve them:

Read/write errors

If you experience numerous read/write errors, noticeably slower performance, excessive initialization time, or tapes that eject themselves immediately after they are inserted, first suspect a dirty drive. Cleaning the drive as described in the preceding section usually cures such problems immediately. Retensioning tapes periodically also helps avoid this problem.

Configuration problems or incompatibilities with backup software or drivers

If the backup software doesn't recognize the drive, can't load the driver, or does not contain a driver for the drive, first make sure that the host adapter recognizes the drive as present at boot time. For SCSI, ensure the operating system recognizes the SCSI host adapter and download and install later drivers from the host adapter manufacturer's web site, if any are available. If you have recently installed a new version of your backup software, verify that it contains support for the tape drive, and download updated drivers for that drive if necessary. If your tape drive manufacturer provides downloadable firmware updates, download and install the latest recommended firmware for your drive.

SCSI communication problems

If the controller does not recognize the tape drive or the controller or system hangs at boot, the most likely cause is physical damage to or a configuration problem with the SCSI chain. First verify that the data and power cables are undamaged and fully connected to the drive. Verify that there are no SCSI ID conflicts and check termination, particularly if you have just added a new SCSI device to the chain. If everything appears correct and the problem persists, use the SCSI BIOS utility to make one or more of the following changes to the host adapter configuration: disable Sync Negotiation; disable Wide Negotiation; set the transfer rate to the lowest available value; enable Disconnect. In other words, slow things down until the drive functions properly. If none of this works, the most likely problem is a malfunctioning drive or controller. If other devices on that chain function properly, suspect the drive.

SCSI bus scan displays drive on all or most SCSI IDs

This is nearly always the result of assigning the tape drive the same SCSI ID as the host adapter. Reassigning the tape drive to an unused SCSI ID fixes the problem.

Our Picks

Here are the tape drives we actually use and recommend:

Inexpensive tape drive

OnStream DI-30. For backing up a standalone Windows 98 system or a small workgroup server, the $250 DI30 is hard to beat. It's fast, quiet, reliable, inexpensive, uses the ubiquitous IDE interface, and stores 15/30 GB on a $35 tape. Although it is probably too lightly built for routine use in demanding server applications (and has limited support for standard server backup programs anyway), it is suitable for typical backup duties on a standalone PC. Another benefit of the OnStream drive, particularly for individual users, is that it requires cleaning infrequently. One $35 OnStream cleaning cartridge does 30 cleanings, and OnStream recommends using it only every three months. That means one cleaning cartridge lasts 7.5 years, longer than the expected service life of the drive itself. (*http://www.onstream.com*)

Travan tape drive

Tecmar TS520 Travan NS20. For backing up a high-end workstation or a workgroup/departmental server, the $425 SCSI version of the Tecmar Travan NS20 is a superb choice when drive cost is more important than tape cost. It stores 10/20 GB on a $35 tape, supports read-while-write and hardware compression, and has a rated throughput of 60/120 MB/min. Barbara uses a SCSI TS520 on her main workstation (which is also a server) and gets 80 to 100 MB/min throughput with hardware compression. Tecmar also manufactures a $375 ATAPI TS520, which we have not tested. (*http://www.tecmar. com/product/travan/travan20/travan20.html*)

DDS3 tape drive

Tecmar TS3900i. This $850 DDS3 drive compares favorably in speed, capacity, and reliability to some tape drives that cost three or four times as much. The 3900i is an excellent choice for backing up a high-end workstation or for a workgroup/departmental server when tape cost is more important than drive cost. It stores 12/24 GB on a $12 tape, supports read-while-write and hardware compression, and has rated throughput of 70/140 MB/min. Robert uses a 3900i on his main workstation and gets 100 to 125 MB/min throughput with hardware compression. (*http://www.tecmar.com/product/4mm/3900/3900.html*)

We constantly test and review new equipment. For the latest information about what we currently use, visit:

http://www.hardwareguys.com/picks/remstore.html

CHAPTER 10

CD-ROM Drives

The following two chapters cover standard CD-ROM drives, CD-Recordable (CD-R) drives, and CD-Rewritable (CD-RW) drives, all of which store data on optical discs. Most drive manufacturers other than Seagate use the spelling "disk" for drives that use magnetic storage. By convention, all manufacturers use the spelling "disc" for drives that accept optical media.

Commercially produced discs record data as a series of microscopic pits and lands physically embossed on an aluminum substrate. Optical drives use a low-power laser to read data from those discs without physical contact between the head and the disc, which contributes to the high reliability and permanence of optical storage. Write-capable optical drives use higher-power lasers to record data on special discs. CD-Recordable (CD-R) records data permanently to the disc, and is also called Write-Once. CD-Rewritable (CD-RW) allows data that has been written to be erased or over-written, and is also called Write-Many.

 Many people are careful about the clear side of optical discs, but take less care with the label side. In fact, the clear side is a protective polycarbonate layer. Data actually resides on a thin aluminum substrate immediately beneath the label. Because the label is very fragile, it is the label side that deserves careful handling.

Compact Disc Fundamentals

Unlike magnetic storage devices, which store data on multiple concentric tracks, all CD formats store data on one physical track, which spirals continuously from the center to the outer edge of the recording area. All CD formats use 3,234-byte physical sectors, which allocate 882 bytes to control and error correction data, leaving 2,352 bytes available. Different CD formats use this space differently: audio CDs use the entire 2,352 bytes to store audio data; computer CDs use only 2,048 bytes to store user data, and allocate the remaining 304 bytes to store additional ECC and control data, including header data and synchronization data. (Audio CDs are addressable to within one second; computer CDs must be addressable by sector, or 1/75 second.) Sectors are grouped as logical numbered tracks, which are listed in the Table of Contents (TOC) for the disc, a special unnumbered track that is analogous to the File Allocation Table and root directory on a computer disk.

All current CD formats derive from the original CD-DA (Compact Disc–Digital Audio) format introduced in 1974 as a replacement for vinyl record albums. The following standards define the formats used for compact discs:

Red Book

The original CD standard, which defines Compact Disc–Digital Audio (CD-DA, the audio CD), a method that allows digital recording of 74 minutes of audio separated into tracks. Red Book also defines CD infrastructure, including disc dimensions, optical stylus, modulation and error correction standards, sub-code channels used for control and display, and the 16-bit Pulse Coded Modulation method used to store audio data. Red Book allows a CD to contain up to 99 tracks, each containing a single audio selection. Each sector contains 2,352 bytes of audio data, two 392-byte EDC/ECC layers, and 98 bytes of control data, which is divided into sub-codes (or sub-channels) identified as P through W. Control data allows jumping to the beginning of each track, and stores such information as track number, track time, and total time. All computer CD drives support the Red Book standard.

Yellow Book

Contains extensions to Red Book that define the Compact Disc–Read Only Memory (CD-ROM) standard, which allows CDs to store digital computer data. Yellow Book defines two sector structures for user data and the error detection codes (EDC) and error correction codes (ECC) used to ensure data integrity. Mode 1 is the common CD-ROM format, and segments the 2,352 available bytes as 12 bytes sync, 4 bytes header, 2,048 bytes user data, 4 bytes EDC, 8 bytes blank, 276 bytes ECC. Mode 2, which is never used, segments the 2,352 bytes as 12 bytes sync, 4 bytes header, and 2,336 bytes user data. All computer CD drives support the Yellow Book standard.

CD-ROM XA

The original Yellow Book standard defined a means to store computer data, but made no provision for audio or video data. sCD-ROM XA (Extended Architecture) extended Yellow Book with two new track types, which allow a CD to store compressed audio and/or video data mixed with computer data. Mode 2, Form 1 is used for computer data, and segments the available 2,352 bytes as 12 bytes sync, 4 bytes header, 8 bytes sub-header, 2,048 bytes user data, 4 bytes EDC, and 276 bytes ECC. Mode 2, Form 2 is used to store audio/video data, and use 12 bytes sync, 4 bytes header, 2,324 bytes user data, and 4 bytes EDC. The sub-header field describes sector contents, allowing Form 1 (data) sectors and Form 2 (audio/video) sectors to be interleaved within one track. CD-ROM/XA compliant drives can separate Form 1 computer data from Form 2 audio/video on-the-fly, delivering each to the appropriate destination for processing. The only CDs you are likely to find using CD-ROM XA formats are Kodak PhotoCD and VideoCD (both CD-i Bridge formats), the Karaoke-CD, and the Sony PlayStation CD.

Yellow Book defined the physical sector structure, but did not define logical file formats. This meant that early Yellow Book data CDs by necessity used proprietary files formats that were incompatible with each other. To address this problem, CD producers created the *ad hoc* High Sierra format, which was subsequently formalized almost without change by the ISO as ISO-9660. The strength of ISO-9660 was that it was universal—ISO-9660 discs are readable by nearly any operating system. The other side of that coin was that ISO-9660 achieved this universality by restricting choices to least common denominator—e.g., filenames limited to 8.3, which was supported by all operating systems. The constraints imposed by ISO-9660 mean that it is seldom used any more except where universal compatibility is more important than filesystem features—such things as huge tables of government data and other boring stuff. ISO-9660 is also still used occasionally to produce hybrid discs that are readable by both PCs and Macs. These discs use ISO-9660 formatting for the PC data and Mac HFS formatting for the Mac. But if the ISO-9660 format defined by CD-ROM XA is seldom used any more, it was at least a start.

Green Book

This extension of Yellow Book defines Compact Disc Interactive (CD-i). CD-i supports Mode 2, Form 2 audio, video, and picture data mixed with Mode 2, Form 1 computer data, which users can control interactively. CD-i CDs required a special CD-i player, which contained an embedded computer running a special operating system (OS/9, CD-RTOS), so CD-i tracks could not be played on normal CD-ROM drives. A hybrid format called CD Bridge defines a method for recording CD-i data on CD-ROM XA discs, allowing that data to be read by any CD-ROM XA drive. The only CD Bridge format still in common use is Kodak PhotoCD. The CD-i format achieved some popularity on dedicated CD-i players in the early- to mid-90s for games, educational programs, encyclopdiae, and so on, but is now obsolescent and being replaced by various flavors of DVD.

Orange Book

Defines standards for recordable CDs. Part I defines Compact Disc–Magneto-Optical (CD-MO); Part II, Compact Disc–Write Once (CD-WO, usually called CD-Recordable or CD-R); and Part III, Compact Disc–Erasable (CD-E, usually called CD-Rewritable or CD-RW).

Orange Book defines both single-session (Disc-At-Once, DAO) recording, and incremental multisession (Track-At-Once, TAO) recording. Multisession allows recording an initial session that does not fill the disc, and subsequently adding one or more additional sessions until the capacity of the disc has been reached. Each new session contains a Table of Contents that lists both the old and new information on the disc, so any CD-ROM drive or CD player used to read multisession discs must be capable of locating and using the last-recorded Table of Contents. Any recent CD-ROM drive and most recent CD players can read multisession discs, but older drives and players usually cannot. Unless, that is, you use your CD burner to "finalize" the session, which closes the disc to further recording sessions and writes a final Table of Contents that can be read by any CD drive or player. Even then, very old players may not be able to read the disc, because their lasers and data pickups are incapable of dealing with the color and low reflectivity and contrast of recordable media.

White Book

Defines the Video CD format, also known as Digital Video (DV), developed and promoted by Matsushita, JVC, Sony, and Phillips. Video CDs are a type of CD-ROM/XA bridge disc based on the Karaoke CD standard. They use MPEG-1 compression to store up to 70 minutes of full-screen, full-motion video with CD-quality audio, using CD-ROM/XA Mode 2 Form 2. They can be played on a dedicated Video CD player, a CD-i player with a Digital Video cartridge, or a PC with a CD-ROM/XA drive, an MPEG-1 decoder, and the necessary software. White Book is now obsolescent, and is being replaced by DVD.

Blue Book

Defines the Enhanced Music CD, also called CD-Extra or CD-Plus, which specifies a multisession format that stores mixed audio and data recorded as separate sessions to prevent standard CD players from attempting to "play" a data session. For compatibility with standard CD players, a Blue Book CD contains two sessions. The first session contains the audio tracks, and the second session a data track. A Blue Book CD stores a limited amount of data that is related to the audio, which comprises the major portion of the content on the CD. For example, a Blue Book CD of Johann Sebastian Bach's Brandenburg Concertos might include historical background and the score, while a Rock CD might include album notes and lyrics. Blue Book CDs can be played on any standard audio CD player (which sees a Blue Book CD as a standard CD-DA disc), on PCs with compliant CD-ROM drives, and on dedicated players.

CD-ROM drives are so well standardized and have become so ubiquitous that many treat them as commodity items. If all you use a CD-ROM drive for is playing music CDs, loading software, or other similarly undemanding duties, nearly any reasonably recent CD-ROM drive will do the job. If you need to replace a failed drive or buy a drive for a new system, simply buy an inexpensive 24X to 40X ATAPI drive. But if you put more demands on a drive, such as accessing databases, playing games directly from CD, or using the drive as a source to duplicate CDs, it's worth learning about the differences between currently available drives.

CD-ROM Drive Performance

Although CD-ROM drives differ in reliability, which standards they support, and numerous other respects, the most important issue for most buyers is performance. But performance is not accurately described by the simple transfer rate number that most manufacturers use to characterize drive performance. There are actually two important performance measures:

Data Transfer Rate

How fast the drive delivers sequential data to the interface. Data Transfer Rate (DTR) is determined by drive rotation speed, and is rated by a number followed by an X. All other things equal, a 32X drive delivers data at twice the speed of a 16X drive. But note that we have used 16X SCSI drives that transfer data faster than some 32X ATAPI drives, so it's a mistake to depend solely on X-rating. The specifications for some drives list only maximum burst transfer rate, which is always the advertised number, while others list sustained transfer rate, which is far more important to overall drive performance. Fast DTR is most important when you use the drive to transfer large files or many sequential smaller files, e.g., for gaming video.

Average Access

How fast the drive accesses random files located anywhere on the CD. Average access time is only loosely tied to DTR, is determined by the quality of the head actuator mechanism, and is rated in milliseconds (ms). Some inexpensive drives have very high nominal DTR ratings but relatively poor average access performance. To make matters more complicated, different manufacturers calculate average access using different methods, so you cannot necessarily compare figures from one manufacturer with those of another.

The following sections describe Data Transfer Rate and Average Access in detail.

Data Transfer Rates

CD-DA discs record music as a digital data stream. The analog music is examined or *sampled* 44,100 times per second (the *sampling rate*) using 16-bit samples, for a data rate of 88,200 bytes/s. Multiplied by two channels for stereo, that means the CD stores 176,400 bytes for each second of music. Each second's data is stored as 75 physical sectors, each of 2,352 bytes.

Music data need not be completely error free because an occasional flipped bit will be inaudible, which means that the entire 2,352 byte capacity of each physical sector can be used to store actual music data. The same is not true for computer data, for which every bit must be correct. Accordingly, CDs store computer data using 2,048 bytes/sector, with the remaining 304 bytes in each physical sector allocated to error detection and correction data. This means that a computer CD running at the same speed as an audio CD delivers ($75 \times 2,048$ bytes) per second, or 150 KB/s. This data rate is called 1X, and was the transfer rate supported by early CD-ROM drives.

Later CD-ROM drives transfer data at some integer multiple of this basic 150 KB/s 1X rate. Rather than designating drives by actual KB/s throughput, drive manufacturers use a multiple of the standard 1X rate. A 2X drive transfers (2×150 KB/s), or 300 KB/s, a 12X drive transfers data at 1,800 KB/s, and so on.

CLV Versus CAV Versus P-CAV

Unlike hard disks, which record data on a series of concentric tracks, CDs have only one track which spirals from the center of the CD out to the edge, much like a vinyl LP but in reverse. Because the portions of the track toward the center are shorter than those toward the edge, moving data under the head at a constant rate requires spinning the disc faster as the head moves from the center—where there is less data per revolution—to the edge, where there is more. If an audio CD spun at some compromise constant rate, the audio would sound like the Addams' Family's Lurch when the CD was playing the inner portion of the track, and like Alvin the chipmunk when it was playing the outer.

The solution to this is to change the disc rotation rate as the heads progress from the inner to the outer portions of the track. When you play an audio CD in a CD player (or in your computer's CD-ROM drive), the drive actually speeds up and slows down according to where the heads are currently reading. This technology is called *Constant Linear Velocity* (*CLV*).

All audio CD players drives use CLV. CLV is a good choice for audio for two reasons: first, the drive only need spin fast enough to deliver 150 KB/s. Second, music is inherently sequential. That is, music data is typically played from first to last, which requires only gradual changes in rotation speed. Early CD-ROM drives also used CLV, but it soon became apparent that CLV was not the best choice for data CDs, for two reasons: first, market demands meant that the speed of CD-ROM drives had to keep increasing, from 1X to 2X, 4X, 6X, 8X, and ultimately to 12X or 16X. Delivering data at 16X speeds requires spinning the disc much faster than for 1X audio. Second, data CDs are often accessed randomly, which means that the head may have to move quickly from the inner to the outer portion of the track, or vice versa. In order to maintain CLV with such rapid head moves, the drive motor was required to make radical changes in speed. Motors capable of doing this were large, power-hungry, loud, and expensive. That meant that 12X was the realistic limit for CLV CD-ROM drives, although a very few 16X CLV CD-ROM drives were made.

The solution to this problem was to implement *Constant Angular Velocity* (*CAV*), which is a fancy term for simply spinning the CD at a constant speed, allowing the data rate to vary according to which portion of the track is being read. The advantage to CAV is that the drive can use a relatively simple, inexpensive motor because that motor runs at a constant rate. The disadvantage is that the data rate varies according to what portion of the disc is being read, which is really no disadvantage at all for data CDs. Actually, CAV drives are also capable of running in CLV mode, which is why you can play an audio CD in any CD-ROM drive. But that's slow CLV. For delivering data, which is their true purpose, CAV drives run at a much higher, but constant speed.

Because the data rate on a CAV drive varies according to which portion of the track is being read, there's no single number that describes the drive's transfer rate. Accordingly, such drives are called *variable speed* or **-Max* (as in "32X Max") drives, and are rated using the fastest data transfer rate (that on the outer portion of the track). When this was written, 32X- and 40X-Max CD-ROM drives were commonplace, and 52X drives were available. The upshot is that a 40X Max drive may read the longer, outer portions of the track at 40X, but may read the shorter, inner portions of the track at only 17X, with an "average" speed for a full CD of 27X, and a somewhat lower rate for a partially full CD.

Finally, some drives use *Partial CAV* (*P-CAV*). A P-CAV drive, rather than using a constant rotation rate, changes between some small number of discrete rotation rates (typically two) according to which arbitrarily defined zone of the CD the head is currently reading. That is, a P-CAV drive may rotate at one rate when reading the outer half of the track, and at some higher rate when reading the inner half. The advantage of P-CAV drives is that they deliver data at a more nearly constant transfer rate than CAV drives.

TrueX Drives

TrueX drives are CLV drives with a difference. Conventional CD-ROM drives read data with one low-powered laser beam. TrueX drives use a diffractor to split a higher-powered laser beam into seven separate beams, which are directed at seven separate parts of the track simultaneously. Using a multi-beam detector array, a TrueX drive reads those seven signals and combines them into one high-speed data stream. The result is that a TrueX drive running at 9.5X CLV provides a data transfer rate equivalent to a conventional 52X drive. The leisurely 9.5X spin rate of a TrueX drive means that it is quiet in comparison to high-speed CAV drives, which spin at very high rates and are correspondingly loud.

There are some drawbacks to TrueX drives, however. First, like any CLV drive, a TrueX drive needs a robust (and expensive) drive motor to support the constant changes in rotation rate required by a CLV drive. Second, CLV drives typically have relatively poor random access performance, because the drive motor must constantly adjust and stabilize the spin rate as the head seeks across the disk. Third, during heavy random seeks, TrueX drives vibrate noticeably, which makes us wonder how durable the drive will prove in heavy-use environments. Fourth, the higher-powered laser used by TrueX drives can cause discs and the drive itself to become very warm during sustained operations. We suspect that the higher operating temperature of TrueX drives may have a deleterious effect on media, particularly CD-R discs, although we have no evidence to support that suspicion.

TrueX drives are based on technology developed by Zen Research (*http://www. zenresearch.com*) and are manufactured exclusively by Kenwood (*http://www. kenwoodtech.com*). In addition to the 52X SCSI unit, Kenwood also manufactures a 72X ATAPI unit, which we have not seen.

Average Access

Although it bears superficial resemblance to the hard drive rating with the same name, average access for a CLV CD-ROM drive is much more complex to calculate, and is subject to manipulation by drive manufacturers who wish to boost their performance figures. Hard drives spin at a constant rate, and average access is calculated as average seek time (the time required for the heads to move over the proper track) plus latency (the time required for the disk to spin the one half revolution that will be required on average to move the correct sector under the heads).

Average access for CLV CD-ROM drives was originally calculated using a similar 1/3 stroke method, assuming that the drive would be used mainly for reading large multimedia files. In about 1993, some manufacturers began substituting "random access" for 1/3 stroke testing. This method was subject to abuse, because manufacturers could define the size of the zone they used for testing. Some chose very small zones to boost their average access ratings, with the result that some drives were advertised with average access times under 60 ms. Worse still, some makers began promoting seek time as a performance measure. Seek time is a useless performance measure for a CLV drive, because it ignores the fact that a CLV drive needs to speed up or slow down the disc to the speed required for data to be read. This time required for this step—roughly analogous to latency, but subject to much wider variation—is determined by the quality of the motor used.

Newer drives, which use CAV, are less subject to these manipulation methods because the disc spins at a constant rate. However, manufacturers are still free to define the zone they use for random access testing, which means that you cannot safely compare different drives unless you know the testing method used to rate them. The upshot is that if you have an older CLV drive that has a very good average access rating, you should suspect that it is artificially inflated. A newer drive, even one with a substantially slower rated average access, will likely outperform the older drive by a significant margin. As a point of reference, the fastest CD-ROM drive currently on the market, the Plextor UltraPlex Wide, is rated at 85 ms average access. Testing that drive against inexpensive ATAPI drives that have faster published average access reveals that the Plextor is in fact much faster at retrieving random data from a CD. Therefore, take any published average access rating with a grain of salt and do your own testing if possible.

Choosing a CD-ROM Drive

Ordinarily, you will purchase a CD-ROM drive only when building a new system. CD-ROM drives seldom fail, and replacing your current CD-ROM drive seldom makes sense unless it is an elderly 1X or 2X unit. Even a 4X drive is adequate for most purposes, including all but the most CD-intensive games and multimedia applications, many of which are still optimized for least-common-denominator 4X drives. Consider the following issues when choosing a CD-ROM drive:

Data Transfer Rate

> For most applications, DTR is the most important performance characteristic of a CD-ROM drive. DTR is most important if you use the drive mainly for sequential data transfer, such as playing games or loading software. Unless you have very special needs, a $30 to $50 ATAPI 24X to 40X drive is more than sufficient for anything you need to do. Purchase one of the fast (52X+) drives only if you play games directly from CD or use other applications that really benefit from the higher DTR. Such applications are few and far between.

Average access time

> Average access time is important if you use the drive mainly for random access, such as searching databases. Although access time and DTR are not inextricably related—it is possible to build a drive with a fast actuator and a slow motor or vice versa—there is a fair degree of correlation. Typical inexpensive ATAPI drives may provide true 100 to 200 ms average access (although they are often marketed with inflated average access performance numbers), while high-end drives, particularly SCSI drives, may provide true 85 ms access. If you use databases heavily, go with a high-end drive for its improved average access. Otherwise, a typical ATAPI drive will do the job.

Buffer size

> Currently available drives have buffers ranging from 64 KB to 512 KB or more. All other things being equal, the drive with the larger buffer will provide higher performance. But all other things are seldom equal, and a drive with a smaller buffer from one manufacturer may outperform a drive from another manufacturer that has a larger buffer and otherwise identical specifications. We recommend treating buffer size as a minor issue when

choosing a drive. If a drive is available in two models differing only in buffer size, and the price difference is minor, go with the larger buffer. Otherwise, ignore buffer size.

Interface

CD-ROM drives are commonly available in ATAPI (IDE), SCSI, and parallel interfaces, with USB drives just beginning to appear. The vast majority of CD-ROM drives installed in systems or sold individually are ATAPI, which are inexpensive and adequate for nearly any application. Make sure any ATAPI drive you buy supports DMA (bus-mastering) transfer mode, which improves performance and greatly reduces CPU utilization. SCSI drives typically cost $25 to $50 more than equivalent ATAPI drives (in addition to the cost of the SCSI host adapter, if your system is not already so equipped). Choose an ATAPI drive unless the faster average access and higher sustained throughput typical of SCSI drives is a factor (such as for high-speed CD duplication) or unless the internal-only limitation of ATAPI is an issue.

Internal versus external

ATAPI drives are internal-only. Parallel and USB drives are external-only. SCSI drives are available in either form. External drives typically sell at a $50 premium over similar internal models. Choose an internal drive unless you have no externally accessible drive bays available or you need to share the drive among multiple PCs.

Mounting method

Nearly all modern CD-ROM drives use tray mounting. A few drives still use caddy mounting, in which each CD is more-or-less permanently inserted in a protective cartridge called a caddy. In theory, tray mounting has two drawbacks: the tray mechanism is more expensive and less reliable than the caddy mechanism, and the tray mechanism does nothing to protect CDs from dust and physical damage. In practice, caddies are expensive and more trouble than they're worth. Some drives use a slot mounting mechanism like that used by dash-mounted car CD players. This is in theory the best compromise, but few such drives are available, and we have had enough reports of problems with slot mounting mechanisms that we recommend avoiding them. Unless you have compelling reasons to do otherwise, choose a drive that uses tray mounting.

Formats and disc types supported

Which formats a CD-ROM drive supported was a major issue back when standards were still developing. Some drives, for example, did not read Kodak PhotoCD discs. Most current drives support all formats and disc types you are likely to need to read, with one exception: some drives still cannot read discs written on CD-Rewritable (CD-RW) media. Any drive you buy should support the following:

Formats

CD-DA, CD-ROM Mode 1; CD-ROM XA Mode 2, Form 1 and Form 2; Multisession (Photo-CD, CD-Extra, CD-RW, CD-R) Mode 1 & 2; CD UDF (variable packets)

Disc type
> ISO 9660-HFS; Rockridge; CD-I Bridge (PhotoCD, Video CD); CD-I; CD-I Ready, CD-Extra (CD-Plus); Enhanced CD; CD-R; CD-RW; CD+G; CD-Midi; CD-Text

Digital Audio Extraction (DAE)

If you will use the CD-ROM drive as a source drive for duplicating audio CDs to a CD-RW drive, make sure the drive supports DAE, which is required to copy audio digitally. All current CD-RW drives support DAE. Few CD-ROM drives shipped before mid-1998 fully support DAE, although some models offer partial DAE support. A typical DAE-capable ATAPI drive supports DAE at only a small fraction of its rated speed. For example, our Toshiba XM-6402B 32X ATAPI CD-ROM drive supports DAE at only about 6.8X (see Figure 10-1). Many pre-1999 DAE-capable ATAPI 24X to 36X drives support DAE at only 1X or 2X. High quality SCSI CD-ROM drives, such as the Plextor models, support DAE at or near their rated read speeds. Attempting to use DAE at a rate higher than the drive supports yields a "Rice Krispies" dupe—full of snaps, crackles, and pops (along with some hissing). If this occurs, the only solution short of replacing the CD-ROM drive is to set your CD-R drive to record at 2X or 1X.

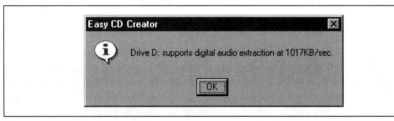

Figure 10-1: Using Adaptec Easy CD Creator to test a 32X Toshiba CD-ROM drive shows that it supports DAE at 1017 KB/s (~6.8X)

 Although they are less popular than they used to be, CD changers are still available. These drives allow you to insert from three to six individual CDs and access them individually, often either by one shared drive letter or by a separate drive letter for each CD. We have never had much luck with these devices, although some people swear by them. They are less popular than formerly because, with hard disk space at less than $10/GB, it's faster, cheaper, and easier just to copy multiple CDs to the hard drive.

We recommend steering clear of changers unless you need immediate access to multiple CDs that will not run when copied to the hard drive. If you need access to only two or three CDs, consider installing two or three ATAPI CD-ROM drives rather than a changer. If you must have a changer, make very sure that drivers are and will continue to be available for your operating system.

Installing and Configuring a CD-ROM Drive

External CD-ROM drives are "installed" simply by connecting them to the parallel or SCSI port, as appropriate, and connecting power. Internal CD-ROM drives are 5.25" half-height devices, and require the same physical installation steps as any other 5.25" externally accessible drive. The exact configuration steps required differ between ATAPI and SCSI interfaces, as described in the following sections.

Installing and Configuring an ATAPI CD-ROM Drive

ATAPI CD-ROM drives are installed just like any other ATAPI/IDE device. Other than physical installation, the only decisions you need make are whether to install the drive on the Primary or Secondary ATA interface and whether to jumper the drive as Sole, Master, or Slave. In general, use the following guidelines:

- On a system with one or two ATA hard drive(s) and one ATAPI CD-ROM drive, install the first hard drive as Primary Master (PM), the second hard drive, if present, as Primary Slave (PS), and the CD-ROM drive as Secondary Master (SM).

- On a system with three ATA hard drives and a CD-ROM drive, install the first two hard drives as PM and PS respectively, the third hard drive as SM, and the CD-ROM drive as Secondary Slave (SS).

- On a system with one or two ATA hard drives, an ATAPI CD-ROM drive, and an ATAPI tape drive, install the hard drive(s) as just described, the CD-ROM drive as SM, and the tape drive as SS.

- On a system with an ATA hard drive, an ATAPI CD-ROM drive, and an ATAPI CD writer, jumper the hard drive PM, the CD-ROM drive PS, and the CD writer SM. The goal is to have the CD writer on a different ATA channel than any drive that may be used as a source, including the CD-ROM drive and the hard drive.

- On a system with two ATA hard drives, an ATAPI CD-ROM drive, and an ATAPI CD writer, jumper the first hard drive PM, the CD-ROM drive PS, the second hard drive SM, and the CD writer SS. Recognize that attempting to create a CD from data on the second hard drive risks data corruption, because the second hard drive and the CD writer are on the same ATA channel.

- On a system with an ATA hard drive, an ATAPI CD-ROM drive, an ATAPI CD writer, and an ATAPI tape drive, jumper the hard drive PM, the CD-ROM drive PS, the CD writer SM, and the tape drive SS.

ATAPI CD-ROM drives require no special configuration steps to function. All recent operating systems, including Windows 95/98 and Windows NT, load ATAPI drivers and recognize ATAPI drives automatically.

Enabling Bus Mastering (DMA) Support

By default, ATAPI CD-ROM drives usually operate in Programmed I/O (PIO) mode rather than Direct Memory Access (DMA) mode, which is also called Bus Mastering mode. The fact that PIO mode limits DTR to 16.7 MB/s versus the 33.3 or 66.7 MB/s DTR available with DMA is unimportant, because no current CD-ROM drive even

Master/Slave Problems with ATAPI CD-ROM Drives

We occasionally receive reports of ATAPI CD-ROM drives that work properly when configured as Slave, but not when configured as Sole or Master, even when they are the only device on the channel. We have never encountered this situation in working with hundreds of systems and CD-ROM drives over the years. However, this has been reported to us often enough that we believe a problem may exist, although we do not have adequate information to determine what combination of controller, drive, operating system, and so on causes the problem.

In theory, any ATAPI CD-ROM drive can function as a master, slave, or sole drive on an ATA channel. That has been our experience. Many CD-ROM drives are designed to function properly as the only drive on a channel even when they're jumpered Slave. That's a matter of convenience, and to avoid support calls when a user forgets to change the default jumpering, which is almost always Slave. Configuring an ATAPI device as a Master-less Slave is not officially supported in the ATA/ATAPI specification, though.

We speculate that one possible cause of the confusion is that an ATA channel may be set to use bus mastering (DMA). If that's the case, making a non-DMA-capable CD-ROM drive the master might indeed cause problems, although we have not tried this configuration. A channel must run both devices either PIO or DMA, and the presence of a non-DMA device on the channel should make that channel revert to PIO, whatever the configuration settings happen to be. Most (but not all) currently shipping ATAPI CD-ROM drives are DMA-capable.

approaches the DTR limit of PIO mode. What is important is that PIO mode causes much higher CPU utilization than DMA mode. A typical ATAPI CD-ROM drive operating in PIO mode may occupy 80% or more of the CPU when the drive is being accessed heavily, while the same drive operating under the same conditions in DMA mode may occupy only 1% to 5% of CPU time.

Accordingly, enabling DMA mode is usually a good idea, but doing so requires that the BIOS, operating system, chipset, and CD-ROM drive itself support DMA mode. Most, but by no means all, recent ATAPI CD-ROM drives support DMA mode. Most motherboards of late Pentium vintage or later also support DMA mode on their embedded ATAPI interfaces. All versions of Windows 95/98, and Windows NT 4 with Service Pack 3 or later support DMA mode. The exact steps required to enable DMA mode differ according to your chipset and the exact version of Windows you are using, as follows:

Windows 95

> Identify the exact release of Windows 95 you are using by right-clicking My Computer and choosing Properties. The General page displays the minor version number, as follows:

> - 4.00.950 (Windows 95 Retail) or 4.00.950a (OEM Service Release 1): No DMA driver is supplied with these versions. If your computer uses an

Intel 430 or 440 chipset, download the Intel Windows 95 Bus Mastering IDE driver from *ftp://download.intel.com/design/pcisets/busmastr/ bmide_95.exe* and install it following the directions supplied with the driver. The Intel BM-IDE driver works directly with the chipset, and does not require a system BIOS that supports DMA. Many CDs supplied with motherboards contain the Intel BM-IDE driver. If the version you have is 3.01 or earlier, do not install it. Download and install version 3.02 or higher. If your computer uses a non-Intel chipset, visit the web page for the motherboard or chipset manufacturer to locate drivers.

– 4.00.950b (OSR 2/2.1) or 4.00.950c (OSR 2.5): A native DMA driver is supplied with these versions. Use that driver rather than the driver supplied by Intel or another chipset manufacturer. The Microsoft drivers require DMA support in BIOS, so you may need to flash your system BIOS to the latest version before installing the driver. Before installing the Microsoft driver, remove the Intel BM-IDE driver (if present) by running the BM-IDE installation program and choosing deinstall. To install the Microsoft driver, right-click My Computer, choose Properties, and then click the Device Manager tab. Locate the CD-ROM drive and double-click it to display the Properties sheet. Click the Settings tab and mark the DMA checkbox in the Options section. Close the dialog and reboot the system. Redisplay the Properties sheet for the drive after rebooting to verify that the checkbox remains marked and that DMA is enabled.

Windows 98

The original Windows 98 release and also Windows 98 SE are both identified as 4.10.1998, and both are supplied with a native DMA driver. To enable it, follow the same steps described for Windows 95 OSR 2 or higher. Note the following considerations for Windows 98 and DMA:

– On a clean install, we found that Windows 98 automatically determines whether the chipset, drives, and BIOS support DMA. If so, DMA is automatically enabled by default.

– On an upgrade install to a system running Windows 95 OSR1 or earlier, we found that Windows 98 Setup does not install DMA support, even if all required elements are present. If this occurs, you can enable DMA support by marking the DMA checkbox and restarting the system.

– On an upgrade install to a system running Windows 95 OSR2 or higher, we found that Windows 98 Setup enables DMA only if Windows 95 had the Microsoft DMA drivers installed and enabled. If the drivers were not installed, or if they were installed but DMA was not enabled, Windows 98 Setup installs using PIO mode. Again, you can enable DMA support manually by marking the DMA checkbox and restarting the system.

– Installing Windows 98 as an upgrade on a Windows 95 system running the Intel BM-IDE driver causes all sorts of IDE problems. The Intel BM-IDE driver version 3.01 has no uninstall option, but can be uninstalled using the version 3.02 or higher setup program. Before upgrading to Windows 98, run BM-IDE version 3.02 or higher and choose the deinstall option.

Windows NT 4

The early versions of Windows NT 4 have no DMA support. Microsoft began shipping a DMA driver with Service Pack 3, but we have had various problems with that driver. The driver supplied with Service Pack 4 or later seems to function properly. To enable DMA on a Windows NT 4 system, take the following steps:

- If you have not already done so, download and apply Service Pack 4 or later.

- Run *Dmacheck.exe* from the *\support\utils\i386* directory. The dialog indicates the present status of DMA on each ATA channel. Mark the DMA Enabled option button on the channel(s) you want to enable DMA for. Note that if a channel has two ATA devices connected, you should not enable DMA unless both devices are DMA-capable.

- Restart the computer and run *Dmacheck.exe* again. The channel(s) you enabled should still have the DMA Enabled option button marked. If that is not the case, either the ATA interface or one or more devices on the channel are not DMA-capable.

Installing and Configuring a SCSI CD-ROM Drive

Installing and configuring a SCSI drive is somewhat more involved. Rather than attempting to provide step-by-step instructions, which vary according to the specific drive and adapter, we've chosen to illustrate a typical installation using a Plextor UltraPlex 32X drive and an Adaptec 2930 SCSI host adapter, noting potential pitfalls along the way:

- If you have not already done so, the first step is to install the SCSI host adapter. To do so, power down the system, remove the cover, and locate an unused PCI expansion slot that supports bus-mastering. Many recent systems support bus-mastering on all available slots. Older systems may support bus-mastering on only some slots. In that case, the slots capable of bus-mastering are normally white or ivory, and those not capable of bus-mastering are brown or black. Remove the slot cover for the selected slot, align the bus connector with the slot and press down firmly to seat the adapter. Use the screw that secured the slot cover to secure the adapter. If you have a spare drive activity indicator LED, you can connect it to J2 on the host adapter (pins 1 and 2 if the cable has only two positions).

- Both the Plextor drive and the Adaptec host adapter fully support *SCAM (SCSI Configured Auto-Magically)*, a kind of Plug-N-Play for SCSI. Note the following issues when working with SCAM:

  - *SCAM-compliant* drives like the Plextor UltraPlex 32X allow a SCAM-compliant host adapter like the Adaptec 2930 to set the drive's SCSI ID and termination status automatically.

  - *SCAM-tolerant* drives report their SCSI ID and termination status to the adapter, but cannot reset SCSI ID or termination status automatically. Instead, you must change jumpers or switches on the drive manually to set SCSI ID and termination.

– *Non-SCAM* drives do not even report their current settings to the adapter, let alone allow the adapter to reset them automatically. When using non-SCAM devices, you must manually verify settings and change them as necessary. Note that enabling SCAM on the host adapter may cause your computer to hang if you connect a non-SCAM drive, because the adapter is unable to determine current settings for the non-SCAM device. If this occurs, use the Adaptec SCSISelect utility at boot time to disable SCAM on the adapter.

• If you are installing a non-SCAM adapter and/or drive, you must set SCSI IDs manually using the jumpers or switches on the adapter and drive. If the adapter supports seven devices (plus the adapter itself), the adapter is normally configured as SCSI ID 7 (the highest priority SCSI ID), leaving SCSI IDs 0 through 6 available for drives. ID 0 is normally reserved for the boot hard disk, and ID 1 for a secondary hard disk. A CD-ROM drive should normally be assigned to ID 2 or higher. If the host adapter is dedicated to devices other than hard drives, it is acceptable to assign ID 0 or ID 1 to the CD-ROM drive.

• If you are installing a non-SCAM adapter and/or drive, you may also need to terminate the SCSI bus manually. Exactly two devices must be terminated on each SCSI bus, and these devices must be those at each end of the bus, as follows:

– If the SCSI adapter has only internal devices attached to it, the adapter itself and the final device on the internal SCSI chain must be terminated.

– If the SCSI adapter has only external devices attached to it, the adapter itself and the final device on the external SCSI chain must be terminated.

– If the SCSI adapter has both internal and external devices attached to it, *do not* terminate the SCSI adapter itself. Instead, terminate the final device attached to the internal chain and the final device attached to the external chain.

Note that most recent SCSI host adapters, including the Adaptec 2930, can automatically detect the presence of terminated SCSI devices on the bus and automatically set their own termination status accordingly. On Adaptec models, which we recommend exclusively, this option can be enabled or disabled by using SCSISelect to set Host Adapter Termination to AutoTerm, which is the default setting. Also note that a few internal SCSI cables have a built-in terminator at the end of the cable. If you use such a cable, make sure that termination is disabled on all drives connected to that cable.

• Once you have resolved SCSI ID and termination issues and have the drive physically installed, the next step is to connect the cables. Most adapters are supplied with a standard two-device cable. If you need to connect more than two drives, replace the cable before proceeding. Otherwise, connect the cable to each drive, making sure to align pin 1 on the cable (indicated by a red stripe) with pin 1 on each device (indicated by a small number, triangle, or dot on the connector). It doesn't matter which drive connects to which cable position, so mix and match drives and cable positions in whatever way makes it easiest to route the cable. Also connect the power cable and the audio cable that links the CD-ROM drive to the appropriate connector on your sound card or motherboard.

- After verifying all settings and connections, turn on any external SCSI device(s) first, and then turn on the PC. Ordinarily, the system should boot normally, but the SCSI CD-ROM drive may or may not be recognized, depending on your operating system and other factors. Before you configure the operating system to use the drive, however, some systems may require that you complete one or both of the following steps:

   – CMOS Setup: on most systems, the PCI bus assigns IRQs and port addresses automatically. If your system requires setting PCI bus parameters manually, do so during the first restart, using the system or motherboard documentation for guidance.

   – SCSI Setup: the SCSI BIOS displays its own splash screen while initializing, which normally displays adapter and BIOS information and a list of installed SCSI devices. Ordinarily, the default settings are fine, but in some cases you may need to change settings to get the drive to work at all or to optimize its performance. If this is the case for your system, press whatever key sequence is needed to invoke the SCSI setup routine and make the necessary changes, as recommended by the documentation for the host adapter and/or drive.

   If either or both of these steps are needed, restart the system after completing each.

General SCSI CD-ROM Troubleshooting

If you have installed your SCSI host adapter and drive properly, and have installed the requisite drivers (described in the following sections) and your drive does not work, check the following items before proceeding to other troubleshooting steps:

- Is the host adapter installed in a bus-mastering PCI slot? Verify with the system or motherboard documentation that the chosen slot supports bus-mastering, or try another slot.

- Are all SCSI devices turned on, and were they turned on when you booted the system? The SCSI adapter recognizes only devices that are active when the system boots. If necessary, power down all SCSI devices, turn off the computer, turn the SCSI devices back on, and then turn the PC back on.

- Are all SCSI cables and power cables connected properly? Verify that the pin-1 orientation of all SCSI cables and devices is correct, and that the power cable is fully seated in each SCSI drive.

- Does each SCSI device on the bus, including the host adapter, have a unique SCSI ID, and is the bus terminated correctly? If not, correct the ID assignments and/or termination and restart the system.

- If SCAM is enabled on your host adapter, are you certain that all connected devices are SCAM-compliant (or at least SCAM-tolerant)? If not, either replace the non-SCAM device, or disable SCAM on the adapter and configure SCSI IDs and termination manually.

- Are you certain that you have installed all driver software that your adapter and/or devices require?

Windows 95/98 SCSI Driver Installation and Troubleshooting

Ordinarily, Windows 95/98 automatically detects installed SCSI host adapters and devices. If it does not, first verify that the hardware is installed and configured properly. If there is no apparent hardware problem, use the Add New Hardware Wizard to force installation of the necessary drivers for the new hardware.

To do so, open Control Panel (Start → Settings → Control Panel) and double-click Add New Hardware. Accept the default selection to allow Windows 95 to attempt to auto-detect the new hardware. If Windows 95 fails to detect the hardware, or locks up during the detection process, restart the system, re-invoke the Add New Hardware Wizard, and this time tell it that you want to select from a list. If you have a driver disk supplied by the manufacturer, choose the Have Disk option at the appropriate point in the process. Otherwise, use the lists of manufacturers and models displayed by the Add New Hardware Wizard to select the standard Windows 9X drivers for the installed devices. If no listed device exactly matches what is installed, you can sometimes select the most similar device that is listed. Ordinarily, the driver will load correctly and the device will be recognized. If problems occur, use the following method to resolve them:

1. Open Device Manager (Start → Settings → Control Panel → System → Device Manager). Locate the SCSI controller item in the list, and click the plus sign to its left to expand the listing. Your SCSI host adapter should be listed. If it is not and you have not yet installed drivers manually, exit device manager and install the drivers. If you have already attempted a manual installation and are certain that all hardware is properly installed and configured, contact the manufacturer or dealer for a replacement device.

2. If the device is listed, highlight it and click Properties to display the General page of the property sheet for the device. The Device Status section should state "This device is working properly." If it does not, the most likely causes are a resource conflict or a hardware problem. The Device usage section contains a list of stored hardware profiles. Make sure that the checkbox for current configuration (and any other configurations for which you want to use this device) is marked.

3. Click the Resources tab and examine the Conflicting device list section at the bottom, which should state, "No conflicts." If a conflicting device is listed, reconfigure one or both devices to eliminate the conflict.

4. After making any necessary changes to the General page and the Resources page, save your changes and restart the system. The device should be recognized properly. If it is not, contact the adapter manufacturer's technical support.

Windows NT 4 SCSI Driver Installation and Troubleshooting

After ensuring that the SCSI adapter and devices are installed and configured properly, restart Windows NT. Open Control Panel (Start → Settings → Control Panel), and double-click SCSI Adapters. Windows NT displays the SCSI Adapters dialog

Devices page, which shows installed SCSI (and IDE) adapters. Click Add to install the device drivers for the host adapter. Windows NT displays a "Creating driver list" progress bar as it builds the driver list, and then displays the Install Driver dialog, which contains a list of manufacturers in the left pane and a list of SCSI adapters for the selected manufacturer in the right pane. Select the manufacturer and adapter from these lists only if you do not have a more recent driver supplied by the manufacturer. If you have a driver disk, click Have Disk and follow the prompts. In either case, if drivers already exist on the system, you'll be asked whether you want to use the existing drivers or install new drivers. When so prompted, install the new drivers unless you have good reason to keep the old ones. After driver installation completes, restart the system to load the drivers. Ordinarily, the driver will load correctly and the device will be recognized. If problems occur, use the following methods to resolve them:

- Use Event Viewer (Start → Programs → Administrative Tools (Common) → Event Viewer) to view the System log, which contains a time-stamped list of errors. These messages are often terse and confusing, but may allow you to narrow down the problem.

- Use the SCSI Adapters utility (Start → Settings → Control Panel → SCSI Adapters) to verify that the SCSI driver was installed.

- Use Windows NT Diagnostics (Start → Programs → Administrative Tools (Common) → Windows NT Diagnostics) to verify the SCSI driver is running, the resources it is using, and whether there are any conflicts.

- Use the Devices utility (Start → Settings → Control Panel → Devices) to verify that the SCSI driver is listed as a supported device and that it is configured to start automatically when the system starts.

Changing CD-ROM Drive Letter Assignments

By default, all versions of Windows assign a CD-ROM drive the next available drive letter following those for any local volumes. If you subsequently install an additional hard disk or repartition your drive to create additional volumes, the letter assigned to the CD-ROM drive changes, which may confuse installed software that attempts to access the CD-ROM drive as the old letter. You can avoid this "musical chairs" reassignment of CD-ROM drive letters by manually assigning the CD-ROM drive a drive letter that is higher than the drive letter for any existing local or network volume. We use R: for the CD-ROM drive by long-standing habit, although there is something to be said for assigning it to Z:. To assign a different drive letter to the CD-ROM drive, proceed as follows:

Windows 95/98
Right-click the My Computer icon, choose Properties, and then click the Device Manager tab. Double-click the CD-ROM drive to display its Properties sheet, and then click the Settings tab. Use the spinner to assign an unused drive letter to the CD-ROM drive and then restart the system.

Windows NT 4
Start Disk Administrator (Start → Programs → Administrative Tools (Common) → Disk Administrator). Right-click the CD-ROM drive and mark the Assign Drive Letter option box. Use the drop-down list to assign the desired drive

letter and click OK. Windows NT displays a confirmation dialog. If you accept the change, the new drive letter becomes active immediately.

If you change the drive letter assignment for a CD-ROM drive, do so immediately after installing the drive or the operating system. If you use that drive under its original letter to install software, that software will later attempt to access the drive using the old drive letter.

Cleaning a CD-ROM Drive

The first symptom of a dirty drive is that you get read errors on a data CD or degraded sound from a music CD. If this happens, it is often because the CD itself is dirty or scratched, so try a different CD before assuming the drive is at fault. In theory, CD-ROM drives require little cleaning. They are reasonably well sealed against dust, and all recent drives incorporate a self-cleaning lens mechanism. That said, the fact is that CD-ROM drives accumulate dust and grime internally just like any other removable media drive. Caddy-load drives are less subject to this problem than tray-load drives, but all drives eventually become dirty.

For routine cleaning, simply wipe the external parts of the drive occasionally with a damp cloth. Many drive makers recommend using a drive cleaning kit every month or two, although we usually do so only when we begin getting read errors. To use these kits, which are available in wet and dry forms, you simply insert the cleaning disc and access the drive to spin the cleaning disc for a few seconds. For a particularly dirty drive, you may need to repeat the cleaning process several times. Most CD-ROM drive manufacturers discourage taking more extreme measures, so if you go beyond these routine cleaning steps, you are on your own and may void your warranty.

Caddy load drives can be cleaned more thoroughly by removing the drive from the chassis, vacuuming the interior gently (or using compressed air to blow it out), and then drenching it down with zero-residue cleaner. Tray-load drives may be more problematic, because the tray on some drives blocks access to the interior whether it is open or closed. If that is not the case on your drive, you can clean it using the same procedure as for a caddy-load drive. If the tray does block access when it is open, the only alternative is to disassemble the drive, if that is possible.

Some drives use a crimped sheet metal enclosure that cannot be removed without damaging the drive. Other drives have a removable metal bottom plate, usually secured by four screws. Removing that plate may provide adequate access to the drive interior for cleaning purposes. If not, do not attempt to disassemble the drive any further. Unless your time is worth nothing an hour, it's easier and cheaper just to replace the drive.

If you experience errors reading some CD discs, the problem may be dirty discs rather than a dirty drive. We usually clean discs by spraying them lightly with Windex® and gently drying them with a soft cloth. That method is frowned upon by some, but we've never damaged a disc by cleaning it that way. If you want to use an approved method, buy one of the commercial CD-ROM or CD Audio disc cleaners, which are readily available from computer and audio supply resellers.

Our Picks

Here are the CD-ROM drives we actually use and recommend:

ATAPI CD-ROM drive

Toshiba XM-6402B (32X) or Toshiba XM-6502/6602B (40X). For undemanding applications, or those where cost is an overriding issue we use a $50 ATAPI drive, usually one of these Toshiba models, although nearly any name-brand drive serves as well.

SCSI CD-ROM drive

Any Plextor model. We prefer SCSI drives for their greater performance and reliability, and in particular for their very low CPU utilization. In fact, we often install SCSI CD drives even in systems with ATA hard drives. The best SCSI CD-ROM drives, bar none, are made by Plextor. Most of the time, we use the $85 Plextor PX-32TSi UltraPleX 32X drive. It's much faster than ATAPI drives (including those with higher nominal speeds), supports 20 MB/s burst-mode UltraSCSI transfers, supports DAE at a true 24X, and is a superb source drive for duplicating CDs. When only the best will do, we install the $110 Plextor PX-40TSUWi UltraPleX Wide drive, a 40X Wide UltraSCSI (40 MB/s) drive which is simply the fastest CD-ROM drive we have ever used. Faster than the so-called 52X ATAPI drives. Faster, in fact, than some hard drives. In addition to being the fastest drives available, Plextor drives are also built like tanks.

We constantly test and review new equipment. For the latest information about what we currently use, visit:

http://www.hardwareguys.com/picks/optical.html

CHAPTER 11

CD-R and CD-RW Drives

CD Recordable (*CD-R*) and *CD Rewritable* (*CD-RW*) drives—collectively called CD writers or CD burners—are essentially CD-ROM drives with one difference: they have a more powerful laser that, in addition to reading discs, can *record* (also called *write* or *burn*) data to special CD media. The resulting CDs are readable, with some limitations, in any CD drive. CD writers can be used for many purposes, including duplicating commercial data and music CDs, transferring large amounts of data to anyone who has a CD-ROM drive, and archiving or backing up data. CD writers can use one or both of these media types:

CD-R discs

Record data permanently. Data written to a CD-R disc cannot subsequently be deleted, which may be an advantage or a drawback, depending on how you use the drive. If you partially fill a CD-R disc, you can add more data to it during a later session, but once that disc is full, no more data can be written to it. CD-R discs are cheap—less than a dollar each in bulk—and are a cost-effective means to archive data or to transfer large amounts of data to someone else. CD-R discs can be read in all but the oldest CD-ROM drives, and in most consumer CD players made in the last year or two.

CD-RW discs

Allow data to be erased. In fact, CD-RW was originally designated CD-Erasable (CD-E), but marketing folks decided that "erasable" had bad implications. A CD-RW disc can be used repeatedly, deleting old data to make room for new. CD-RW discs can be written and re-written at least 1,000 times. CD-RW discs are more expensive than CD-R discs—$1.50 to $3 each as of mid-2000—although their price is dropping fast. Because CD-RW discs are less reflective than CD-R discs and much less reflective than standard pressed CDs, only very recent CD-ROM drives can read them. Very few consumer CD players can read CD-RW discs, making them nearly useless for duplicating audio CDs.

CD writers come in two varieties:

CD-R drives

These drives can write CD-R discs, but not CD-RW discs, and can read standard CDs, CD-R discs, and (usually) CD-RW discs. CD-R drives are usually used in "batch mode" to copy standard audio and data CDs. They can also be used with packet-writing software, although their lack of rewritability makes them better suited to archiving data than backing it up. CD-R drives remain popular because they sell for $25 to $100 less than an equivalent CD-RW drive, and many people do not need a rewritable drive.

CD-RW drives

These drives can write CD-R and CD-RW discs, and can read any CD disc. The most common use for CD-RW drives is with packet-writing software, such as Adaptec's DirectCD, that allows the CD-RW drive to appear as a Windows drive letter and to function much like an enormous floppy diskette. For example, you can drag files over to the CD-RW drive icon and drop them to back up those files to the CD-RW disc, where they can also be readily retrieved using Explorer. When a disc is full, you can simply erase some or all existing files to make room for new ones

Choosing a CD Writer

Use the following guidelines when choosing a CD writer:

CD-R versus CD-RW

CD-RW drives are somewhat more expensive than CD-R drives. Decide between them based on how you will use the drive. For example, a CD-R model may write twice as fast as a CD-RW model that costs the same, and that higher write speed may be more useful to you on a daily basis than RW support that you will seldom use. If in doubt, buy a CD-RW drive unless you are certain that you will never need CD-RW.

Transfer rate

As with CD-ROM drives, throughput is rated in comparison to standard CD-DA (CD-Digital Audio), which transfers 150 KB/s, and is designated 1X. CD-R drives have two speeds. The lower refers to the write speed, and the higher to the read speed. An 8X/24X CD-R drive, for example, writes data at 1,200 KB/s and reads it at 3,600 KB/s. CD-RW drives have three speeds: the lowest refers to how fast data can be written to a CD-RW disc, the middle to how fast data can be written to a CD-R disc, and the highest to how fast the drive can read data.

If you will use the drive primarily for recording CD-R discs, look for a drive that provides 4X or higher write performance. Although they are considerably more expensive than 4X write drives, drives that provide 6X or 8X write are useful if you burn CDs frequently. 8X-certified media was initially two to three times more expensive than 4X media, but that differential is disappearing quickly. If you will use the drive frequently to create CD-RW discs, look for a drive with 4X rewrite. Otherwise, 2X rewrite is adequate for occasional CD-RW use. The read performance of the recorder is generally irrelevant, unless you will install it in a PC that has no CD-ROM drive.

Average access

The more powerful lasers required for burning CDs require heavier heads than standard CD-ROM drives, which in turn means that average access times are slower. For example, the Plextor 8/2/20 burner has an average access of 170 ms, twice that of Plextor CD-ROM drives. If you will use the burner primarily for duping CDs, average access is relatively unimportant. If you will use it heavily for reading CDs or for packet-mode access, average access time is more important. Current models range from about 140 ms to more than 300 ms average access. Buy a model with average access of 200 ms or less.

Interface

All other things being equal, creating CDs is less trouble prone if you use SCSI rather than ATAPI, and Windows NT rather than Windows 9X. SCSI burners typically cost $50 to $100 more than similar ATAPI models, in addition to the $100 or so a SCSI card costs if your system is not already so equipped. If you will use the burner infrequently and are willing to do nothing else on the computer while the CD is being made, an ATAPI model may suffice. Otherwise, get a SCSI model, particularly if you are running Windows 9X.

Buffer size

A large buffer helps avoid ruining CD-R discs due to buffer underruns, particularly if the drive is ATAPI and/or runs under Windows 9X. How large is large enough depends on the maximum write speed of the drive. For example, an 8X burner (which writes at 1,200 KB/s) with a 2 MB buffer can store about 1.7 seconds of data (2,048 KB/1,200 KB/s) when the drive is writing at maximum speed, and about 3.4 seconds of data when the drive is writing at 4X. In our experience with ATAPI CD-R drives running under Windows 9X, a 2 MB buffer is suitable for a 4X drive and a 4 MB buffer for an 8X drive. The superior ability of SCSI (particularly under Windows NT) to deliver an uninterrupted data stream means that it's safe to shade these numbers somewhat for SCSI CD-R drives on NT systems. In that situation, we're comfortable with a 1 MB buffer for a 4X drive, a 2 MB buffer for an 8X drive, and a 4 MB buffer for a 12X drive.

Packet-writing support

Not all drives support packet-mode operation. Make sure you buy one that does.

Supported formats and methods

Any burner you buy should support at least the following:

- Read-mode formats: CD-DA (Audio CD), CD-ROM, CD-ROM/XA, Audio-combined CD-ROM, CD-I, CD-I Ready, CD Bridge, Video CD, CD-Extra, CD-R (Orange Book Part II), and CD-RW (Orange Book Part III).

- Write-mode formats: CD-DA (Audio CD), CD-ROM, CD-ROM/XA, Audio-combined CD-ROM, CD-I, CD-I Ready, CD Bridge, Video CD, CD-Extra and CD-RW.

- Writing methods: Disc-at-Once, Session-at-Once, Track-at-Once, and multisession.

- Software bundle The software you use is as important as the CD-R hardware. Nearly all CD burners are bundled with various software, which is described in the following section.

CD Writer Software

By itself, a CD writer is a dumb device, which Windows recognizes as just another CD-ROM drive. Using the drive to burn CDs requires special application software to enable writing. Other than the drive itself, the most important element in obtaining fast, accurate burns is the software you use. Two major types of software are used with CD writers:

Premastering

> Used to create a CD in a continuous batch mode operation. Premastering software allows you to duplicate entire discs, sessions, or tracks, and is most frequently used to replicate audio and data CDs. You can also use premastering software to assemble custom audio CDs that comprise individual tracks from several audio CDs or to create CDs that contain your own data with a layout that you define. Adaptec Easy CD Creator is the most commonly bundled premastering software.

Packet-writing

> In addition to batch premastering, which all burners support, some burners support packet-writing mode. In simple terms, packet writing extends the Orange Book CD-R multisession specification. With early burners, you had to record the entire disc in one continuous operation. Orange Book Part II allowed keeping a volume open for multiple recording sessions. Packet writing goes further, allowing a session to remain open while adding discrete packets. Packet-writing software allows the drive to be addressed as just another Windows volume, much like a gigantic floppy disk. You can create, delete, and rename files and folders by using drag-and-drop or other standard Windows methods, including saving directly to the CD-R(W) disc from within applications such as Word. Adaptec DirectCD is the most commonly bundled packet-writing software.

Alas, the rapidly dropping price of CD burners has led some vendors to scrimp on the software bundle. Rather than include mainstream full-function packages, they instead supply simple, proprietary individual applets that perform basic functions. Although these applets are generally usable, you'll want one of the mainstream packages to get the most from your drive, so when comparing prices, include the cost of buying both a premastering application and a packet-writing application in the cost comparison. If your drive does come bundled with mainstream applications, always visit the software vendor's web site immediately to check for updates before you use the drive.

In addition to the third-party software that is supplied with the drive, do not overlook proprietary software. Some vendors, notably Plextor, supply a wide range of powerful and useful utilities with their drives. Although these utilities typically run only on that manufacturer's drive, they often provide enhanced capabilities not available in the third-party applications.

One of the most important and frequently overlooked aspects of CD burner software is firmware, which determines the capabilities and compatibility of the drive. Good drives allow user-installable firmware updates. Good makers supply firmware updates as necessary to keep their drives current with changing conditions and standards. For example, a newly introduced disc type may require a different laser power and write scheme than media supported by the existing firmware. If your drive's manufacturer makes the required update available, you can install it yourself and use that new media. If not, you're stuck with an increasingly obsolescent drive that may ultimately become unusable when the media it supports are no longer available. Note that most drives that do not support packet mode cannot be upgraded by a simple firmware update. Packet writing requires specific physical drive capabilities, and drives that do not have those capabilities will never support packet writing.

Installing and Configuring a CD Writer

In general, installing and configuring a CD writer requires the same steps detailed in the preceding chapter for CD-ROM drives. There are, however, some considerations peculiar to CD writers:

- For ATAPI writers, make sure the writer is on a different channel than the source device(s). On a typical PC with a hard drive, a CD-ROM drive, and the CD writer, make the hard drive Primary Master (PM), the CD-ROM drive Primary Slave (PS), and the CD writer Secondary Master (SM). This allows you to record CDs directly from CD-ROM or from an image stored on your hard drive. If the PC has a second hard drive, set that drive to Secondary Slave (SS), and do attempt to record CDs from it. If the PC has an ATAPI tape drive, set it as SS. Attempting to record from a source located on the same IDE channel as the writer almost always fails.

- If you have IDE bus mastering (DMA) drivers installed, remove them from the channel to which the writer connects, unless the drive manufacturer specifically recommends using DMA for its drive. We have frequently encountered problems with ATAPI writers on DMA-enabled channels, even when the writer was recognized by Windows 98 as a DMA-capable device.

- SCSI writers coexist well on a host adapter shared with low-demand devices or those that will not be used while a CD is being burned, but you *may* have problems if you connect the burner to the same SCSI bus that supports hard drives. We have several SCSI systems with hard drives and CD writers connected to the same SCSI bus, and have never encountered a problem with that configuration. But we have received enough reports from readers who have had problems putting a hard drive and writer on the same SCSI channel that we believe this may sometimes be an issue. It's okay for a writer to share with scanners, tape drives, Zip drives, and similar devices. But if you encounter problems sharing the channel between your hard drive and writer, install a second inexpensive SCSI host adapter to support the writer and other non-hard disk SCSI peripherals.

- When you install a SCSI burner, never depend on the SCSI drivers supplied with the operating system. The bundled drivers are fine for hard disks and low-demand peripherals, but often have bugs and missing features that cause problems with CD-R(W) drives. Download the latest drivers and ASPI files for your SCSI host adapter from the manufacturer's site.

- Writing CD-R discs—and particularly writing CD-RW discs—generates considerable heat. If possible, mount the CD writer above other drives to permit that heat to dissipate. A drive bay with unoccupied bays above and below it (particularly above it) is an ideal location. If you will frequently burn two or more CDs in quick sequence, install a drive cooler. PC Power & Cooling (*http:// www.pcpowercooling.com/*) makes the best ones.

- Some CD writer manufacturers recommend specific registry tweaks or configuration changes to the operating system to support their drives optimally. Although we would never discourage anyone from following the manufacturer's advice, our experience is that these changes have little benefit on high-end (fast CPU, lots of memory, SCSI, Windows NT) systems, but are worth implementing on low-end (slow CPU, minimal memory, ATAPI, Windows 9X) systems.

Burning CDs

The following sections condense our experience in burning a lot of CDs in various environments.

General CD Burning Guidelines

The process of burning CDs can be smooth and reliable or a complete nightmare. Which it is depends on the entire system you use to burn CDs—processor, memory, operating system, configuration settings, background processes, hard disk type and fragmentation level, source CD-ROM drive and the source CD itself, CD-R(W) drive, firmware revision, application software, and the blank discs themselves. In short, the process of burning CDs is a Black Art rather than a science.

That's less true now than it was even a couple of years ago, because systems are faster and CD burners are better. But it still pays to keep in mind that what counts is not just the CD burner or the blanks, but the entire system. Once you have the system working reliably, making even a minor change to one element can break it. For example, we once added an apparently innocuous Windows NT service to our main CD-R burning system. Suddenly, a system that was formerly rock-solid for burning CDs was no longer reliable. Removing the service cured the problem.

On a properly configured system, you can burn hundreds of CDs uneventfully. On a marginal system, even the slightest problem or anomaly can result in a ruined CD blank, called a "coaster." Making an occasional coaster is less aggravating now that blanks cost $1 each instead of $20 each, but it still wastes at least 10 minutes or so. So, no matter how good your system is, use the following guidelines to burn CDs reliably:

- Disable screensavers, schedulers, anti-virus utilities, and any other software or service that may interrupt the recording process. In particular, if your PC is configured to answer phone or fax calls, disable that for the duration of the burning session.

- When recording from a disk image (writing the source data to the hard drive as an intermediate step, rather than doing a direct CD-to-CD copy), defragment the disk drive before starting the burn.

- If your PC is on a network and is configured to share its disk or printer, disable sharing before attempting to burn a CD. If another user accesses your disk or printer while the CD is burning, the burn may fail.

- The first time you use your CD recorder (and subsequently each time you change recording method, media type, or any other factor), use test mode before actually burning a CD. Even changing to a different media lot may cause problems. Nominally identical discs may in fact be manufactured in different factories, and may have different recording characteristics. For example, one spindle we bought was 4X certified but we were able to record reliably at 8X to discs from that lot. The discs in another supposedly identical spindle could be burned reliably only at 4X. Back when blanks were relatively expensive, many people got in the habit of using "test and burn" mode routinely. Now that blanks are a buck each, we hardly ever use test mode. It doubles the time required and puts more wear and tear on the drive. An occasional coaster is a small price to pay for the time savings and reduced drive wear. But any time we do get a coaster, we immediately try to determine the cause, and use test mode until we've isolated and cured the problem.

- In the past, conventional wisdom was that making high quality reproductions of audio CDs required that both source drive and CD burner be SCSI. That's no longer true in that some very recent ATAPI CD-ROM drives are suitable as source drives for high-quality audio duping, but the ATAPI CD-ROM drives common in most PCs of 1998 or earlier vintage are likely not suitable source drives for doing high-quality audio dupes. If your CD-ROM drive is in the latter category, you can still do high-quality audio dupes by using your CD burner as both source drive and destination drive. Doing so requires that your CD copy utility support disc-to-image copying, whereby your burner reads the source CD, writes an image of that CD to your hard drive, and then uses that image as the source.

- If the data to be copied resides on a network drive, copy it to the local hard drive before attempting to burn the disc. Writing data from a network drive frequently yields a coaster, even on a 100BaseT network. Note that this caution applies only to writing CD-R discs, which is a synchronous (timing-critical) operation. We have frequently written CD-RW discs from data located on a network drive. Recording CD-RW discs in packet-writing mode is an asynchronous operation, so network delays have no effect on the integrity of the copy.

Making Copies of Copies

Although it surprises many people—it certainly surprised us—the CDs you make in your burner are not necessarily exact copies of the source CD. For audio CDs, this usually isn't a problem. An occasional dropped or flipped bit will probably be inaudible. But for data CDs, it can be a major problem. We found this out while playing with a new burner. We duped the original FrontPage CD, and were able to install FrontPage from the dupe. But when we duped the dupe and then tried to install from the second-generation copy, Setup returned file read errors. Doing a binary compare on those files told the sad truth: the files were identical on the original CD and the first-generation copy, but differed on the second-generation copy.

Remember that CDs depend heavily on error correction and detection code. All CD formats use 3,234-byte physical sectors, which allocate 2,352 bytes to data and the remainder to control and error correction data. Audio CDs use the entire 2,352 bytes for audio data. Yellow Book Mode 1 (data) CDs use only 2,048 bytes for data and allocate the remaining 304 bytes to another ECC layer. The problem arises because of the different ways that CD burners and software read and write Mode 1 data:

Raw mode

> The drive reads the entire 2,352 byte sector as a raw bit stream and writes that raw data to the destination device. Any data read errors in either the data segment or the ECC segment are written literally to the destination. Working in this mode, generational degradation can overwhelm the ability of ECC to correct errors and result in a CD that returns read errors or contains corrupted files. This may occur as early as a second-generation copy, and almost certainly after several generations.

Cooked mode

> The drive reads only the 2,048 byte data segment, using the ECC segment to verify the data and correct it if necessary. The drive then recalculates the proper ECC segment for that data segment and writes the original data segment with the new ECC segment to the destination disc.

This means it is impossible to ensure an exact copy of any CD that uses 2,352 byte data segments (audio CDs) or 2,336 byte data segments (Mode 2 data CDs) because those segments contain no sector-level ECC data. Fortunately, Mode 2 CDs are rare, and you can copy the common Mode 1 data CDs reliably by using cooked mode, assuming that your drive and software support it. To minimize copying problems, use the following guidelines:

- For Red Book (audio) CDs, use an original (pressed) CD as the source. There is no reliable way to make a copy of an audio CD that is itself a copy. When copying original source CDs, note that some drives disable some error-correcting features during digital audio extraction, or may use error correction only during DAE at 1X. Experiment to determine the optimum recording speed for best sound quality. Differences are subtle, particularly with recent drives and media, but they do exist. Some people swear you should always dupe audio CDs at 1X (or 2X or 4X), but the truth is that the optimum speed depends on the drive and media. Drive A may make the best dupes with Media A at 1X and with Media B at 4X, while Drive B may be exactly the opposite. Test with each drive and each time you change media.

- For Yellow Book Mode 2 data CDs, always use an original CD as the source. There is no reliable way to make a copy of a Mode 2 CD that is itself a copy. If you must copy a Mode 2 copy, do a file-by-file binary compare afterwards to verify the copy.

- For Yellow Book Mode 1 data CDs, either use the original CD as the source (using either raw or cooked mode), or use cooked mode when copying from a source CD that is itself a dupe. Also note that problems may arise if the source dupe was made in raw mode rather than cooked mode.

Creating a Bootable CD-R Disc

If your Windows 9X computer allows booting from CD, a bootable CD can be a useful emergency fallback. To create a boot CD with Adaptec Easy CD Creator, take the following steps:

1. Create a bootable diskette that contains the 16-bit CD-ROM device driver and *Mscdex.exe*. If you have a SCSI CD-ROM drive, you will also need to copy the driver for the SCSI host adapter. (Note that not all SCSI host adapters and motherboards permit booting from a SCSI CD-ROM.) Copy the files *Sys.com* and *Xcopy.exe* to the floppy. Also copy *Format.exe*, *Fdisk.exe*, and any other utilities you may need to recover from a hard disk problem. You may also add such things as keyboard drivers and other locale-specific files. If you have already created a Windows 98 Startup Disk, you may use that rather than creating another disk.

2. Using *Notepad.exe* or another ASCII text editor, create on the floppy the file *Config.sys*, and enter the following lines:

```
lastdrive=z
device=cd-rom driver name.sys /d:restore
```

   and any other real-mode drivers you need to access your hard disk or other system components, including the SCSI host adapter driver, if present.

3. Create on the floppy the file *Autoexec.bat*, and enter the following line:

```
mscdex.exe /d:restore /l:z
```

   and any other commands needed.

4. Start Adaptec Easy CD Creator, and add your hard disk's contents to the Data CD Layout screen. If the entire contents of your hard disk will not fit, select the most important directories, including all system directories, for this boot CD. You can create additional CDs to store the other directories.

5. From the File menu, choose CD Layout Properties, then Data Settings. Mark the Bootable CD checkbox. Then choose ISO 9660, click Properties, and choose Any MS-DOS 8+3 name.

6. Create the CD. When you are prompted, insert the bootable floppy you created in step one. The creation process places an image of this bootable floppy on the CD, allowing it to boot.

Restoring from a Bootable CD

To restore from a bootable CD, your motherboard must support booting from the CD. Most recent motherboards do. To set your system to boot from CD, run BIOS Setup and locate an option named "Boot Sequence" or something similar. That option will typically be set to something like "A:, C:, CD-ROM, SCSI" by default. Insert the bootable CD, change the boot sequence to make the CD-ROM the first boot device, and restart the system. The system will boot from the CD, which it will recognize as drive A:. (The actual FDD will become B:). From the A: prompt, type SYS C: to transfer the boot files to the hard drive. Once that process completes, change to the root directory of C: and type a:\xcopy a:*.* /s to restore all files and directories from the CD.

Creating an AutoRun CD-R Disc

At times it's useful to create a CD that when inserted in the drive automatically loads and runs a specified program or document. For example, you can distribute HTML content on a CD that automatically invokes the user's browser and loads *index.html.* The only thing necessary to enable AutoRun for program files is to put a properly formatted *AutoRun.inf* file in the root directory of that CD. *AutoRun.inf* is a plain ASCII text file with the following syntax:

```
[autorun]
Open=CmdLine
```

Inserting a CD that contains *Notepad.exe* and *Index.html* in the root directory and the following *AutoRun.inf:*

```
[autorun]
Open=notepad.exe index.html
```

causes Windows to AutoRun *Notepad.exe* and load *Index.html* into it. You can optionally specify a path before the program or document name. *AutoRun.inf* supports many more options, which are documented at *http://www.microsoft.com/ MSJ/0998/win320998top.htm.*

Unfortunately, AutoRun does not honor file associations, which makes it difficult to invoke the user's browser to run an HTML source file automatically. There are several workarounds for this problem, but the one we prefer is the small utility *Autohtml.exe,* developed by Mark Trescowthick and Ross Mack, which is available for download at *http://www.avdf.com/oct98/art_ot005.html.* That page includes full instructions for using the utility.

Repeatedly burning CDs while you are testing your custom *Autorun.inf* is time-consuming and wasteful. One alternative is to modify the registry to allow AutoRun to work on a floppy disk. As always, back up before making changes to the registry, and proceed with caution. To make this change, which works on Windows NT 4 and Windows 9X systems, run *Regedit.exe* and locate the value entry NoDriveTypeAutoRun, which resides in the key HKEY_CURRENT_USER\ Software\Microsoft\Windows\CurrentVersion\Policies\Explorer. Double-click the value entry to edit the value.

Windows actually stores a 4-byte value, but only the following binary digits of the first byte are meaningful. Those digits are used as a binary bitmap, as follows:

```
Bit  Type
0    DRIVE_UNKNOWN
1    DRIVE_NO_ROOT_DIR
2    DRIVE_REMOVABLE
3    DRIVE_FIXED
4    DRIVE_REMOTE
5    DRIVE_CDROM
6    DRIVE_RAMDISK
```

By default, this bit mask is set to 10010101 (95H), which disables AutoRun for removable drives, remote drives, and RAM disks. (1=disable Autorun; 0=enable it.) Change this bit mask to 10010001 (91H) to enable AutoRun for removable drives, including floppy diskette drives and Zip drives. Save the change and restart the computer. A floppy disk does not AutoRun when inserted because the floppy drive cannot notify Windows that the disk has been inserted. However, you can manually AutoRun that floppy by right-clicking on the drive icon and choosing AutoPlay.

Media Issues

There's been a lot of nonsense written about CD-R media. One person swears that gold/green discs are great and silver/blue discs worthless, and another says the opposite. The truth is that there are distinct differences in media, but no absolutes. Disc A may work perfectly in Drive A and not work at all in Drive B, and Disc B may work perfectly in Drive B and not at all in Drive A. Here are the differences.

Current CD-R blanks use one of these reflective layers:

Gold

> The metal used in early CD-R discs, and still commonly used in current production discs. The advantage of gold is that it is stable. The disadvantage is that 24K gold is expensive, even in the microscopically thin layers used in CD-R discs. As the price of CD-R discs continues to plummet, the cost of gold becomes an increasingly important factor, which has led some manufacturers to substitute silver.

Silver alloy

> The advantages of silver alloy relative to gold are that it is relatively inexpensive and actually has better reflective characteristics across a wide spectrum. The chief disadvantage of silver is that it corrodes. Even a tiny crack in the label layer can allow airborne pollutants, particularly sulfides, to gain access to and react with the silver layer. If this occurs, the CD become unreadable.

Most current CD-R blanks use one of these dyes (although to avoid patent infringement some disc manufactures use similar but not identical dyes):

Cyanine

> As the name indicates, this dye is cyan (bluish-green) in color. Used with a gold reflective layer, cyanine-based discs appear green on the clear side and gold on the label side (the so-called "green/gold" discs). Used with a silver reflective layer, cyanine disks appear light blue/silver. Cyanine was the first dye used to make CD-R discs, and quickly developed a reputation for stability problems. That has been overcome in current discs by using metal-stabilized cyanine. The advantage of cyanine is that it is more sensitive to light than other dyes, which means that cyanine discs tolerate a wider range of laser power settings, making them more likely to be compatible with any given drive and firmware revision. For example, a typical cyanine disc can be written with a laser power setting between 5.5 and 7.5 milliwatts, while a typical pthalocyanine disc requires 5.0 to 6.0 milliwatts. On the downside, accelerated aging tests show expected lifetimes for cyanine-based discs of "only" 50 years or so, significantly less than other dyes. In practical terms, no one 50 years from now will have a drive capable of reading any CD, so this matters little.

Pthalocyanine

This dye is a very pale yellow-green color, approaching colorless. With a gold reflective layer, discs appear gold/gold or greenish-gold/gold. With a silver layer, they appear light yellow-green/silver or even silver/silver. Because cyanine-based CD-R discs were protected by patent, other manufacturers developed alternative dyes, including pthalocyanine. The one thing to be said in favor of pthalocyanine is that its lower light sensitivity relative to cyanine gives it estimated archival stability of nearly 100 years. Lower light sensitivity also means that pthalocyanine-based CD-R discs are less likely to be compatible with any given CD-R drive, particularly an older model. All recent CD-R drives support pthalocyanine-based discs, and most older models can accommodate them with a firmware upgrade.

Azo

This dye is a deep blue color. Commonly available Azo discs, notably those from Verbatim, use a silver reflective layer, which gives the data side a very deep blue color. Azo is even less sensitive to light than pthalocyanine, which gives azo-based discs expected archival stability of more than 100 years, and makes drive support even more problematic than pthalocyanine. All recent CD-R drives support azo-based discs, and most older models can accommodate them with a firmware upgrade. Due to their insensitivity, some early azo-based discs did not support writing faster than 1X or 2X, but current azo-based discs are usable at high recording speeds.

There is no single answer to the question "Which is best?" There are numerous variables in the CD-R manufacturing process. The thickness and density of the dye layer varies, as does that of the reflective layer. Some manufacturers have begun using dyes that resemble those listed here, but have different characteristics. There is no way to tell by appearance alone which dye a disc uses. The physical groove structure of different CD-R blanks may differ to optimize that disc for different laser power, writing speeds and schemes. But the bottom line is that all CD-R blanks, including the no-name ones, are much better than they were a few years ago. The primary measure of CD-R disc quality, Block Error Rate (BLER) is much lower now than in the past.

But the real problem is that, although CD-R disc manufacturers make every effort to comply with strict Orange Book specifications, some CD writer manufacturers do not. The upshot is that different writers vary widely in which discs they can use successfully. In general, more compromises are made with inexpensive writers, which are typically much more media-sensitive than are more expensive models. A $350 Plextor burner is likely to work with just about any media you attempt to use. A $100 no-name ATAPI burner may be very choosy indeed about which blanks it is willing to write. Also, do not overlook the importance of keeping your drive firmware up-to-date. As disc manufacturers change formulations and new disc types come on the market, you may need to update your firmware to enable your drive to use those new blanks.

Your sole criterion should be which media work properly in your recorder. The best starting point is to use the disc(s) recommended by the drive manufacturer. Most manufacturers provide such a list on their web sites. Those lists are updated as new media types become available, and assume you have the latest firmware.

Whichever blanks you settle on, recognize that any CD-R disc should be treated more carefully than a pressed CD. In particular, avoid exposing blank or recorded CD-R discs to sunlight or heat unnecessarily. Leaving an unprotected CD-R disc on the dashboard of your car is a quick way to destroy it.

Finally, a few words about labeling. Drive and media manufacturers vary in what they recommend, and the best course is to follow those recommendations. However, there are some guidelines that are nearly universal:

- *Never* use a standard sticky label on a CD-R disc. The adhesive may damage the label side of the disc, causing it to degenerate rapidly and become unreadable. Also, the small weight of that label is sufficient to imbalance the disc in some high-speed players. At best, such an imbalance may cause read errors. At worst, it may destroy the disc or even the drive.

- The circular labels designed for CD-Rs are generally safe, but even they have been known to imbalance a disc if not applied perfectly centered. If you use such labels, never attempt to peel one off. Doing so may cause the top layer of the CD-R to separate, destroying the disc.

- Do not use a hard-tip marker, which may score the label layer. We usually label CD-R discs with a Sharpie® soft-tip permanent marker. Some sources recommend not using a permanent solvent-based pen because it may etch the label layer. Other sources, including some CD-R manufacturers *recommend* using a solvent-based permanent marker. Although we've never had a problem using the Sharpie®, for maximum safety choose your marker according to the recommendations of the disc manufacturer.

- When hand labeling is not neat enough, e.g., for discs you plan to distribute outside your company, consider using printable discs, which have a surface that may be printed with an inkjet and/or thermal printer. These are available in various types and background colors, and generally work well if you follow the manufacturers instructions carefully.

 What to do with the disc when you make a coaster? Do an Internet search for "cd-r" and "microwave." You'll find that microwaving coasters is a popular pastime. We've never had the nerve to do this, fearing for the safety of our microwave. If you try this, you're on your own.

Additional CD-RW Source Material

You can find additional information about CD writers and creating CDs at the following web sites:

http://www.fadden.com/cdrfaq/
> The home of Andy McFadden's CD-Recordable FAQ. Good information about all aspects of CD-R(W).

http://www.adaptec.com/support/faqs/cdrindex.html
> Adaptec's CD-R support page. Definitions, advice, step-by-step procedures, and troubleshooting help.

http://www.cd-info.com/index.html
> The CD Information Center. Industry news, articles, bibliography, links to manufacturer sites, and various FAQs.

Our Picks

Here are the CD-R and CD-RW drives we actually use and recommend:

ATAPI CD-R(W) drive
> **Plextor PX-W1210TA PlexWriter 12/10/32A.** In the past, we recommended ATAPI burners only when cost was the top priority. In early 2000, Plextor introduced the 8/4/32A, an ATAPI burner which we found as fast, robust, and reliable as any but the best Plextor SCSI burners. In July 2000, Plextor trumped their own ace when they shipped their $250 12/10/32A, which was both the fastest burner available (particularly for rewriting) and the most reliable. The 12/10/32A provides 12X write, 10X rewrite, and 32X read. This burner is the first we've seen that incorporates BURN-proof technology, licensed from Sanyo, which allows the drive to stop burning when the buffer empties and restart the burn once it again has data available. The result is that it's almost impossible to burn coasters with this drive. We verified this by starting a burn from an image on the hard disk and then running a disk defragmenter on that hard disk while the disc was being burned. The burn took longer than usual, but the resulting disc was perfect. If you're looking for an ATAPI burner, look no further than the Plextor 12/10/32A. It has proven extremely reliable under Windows 98, 2000, and NT, and is the first (and only) ATAPI burner that can compete on an equal footing with the best of the SCSI burners. (*http://www.plextor.com*)

SCSI CD-R(W) drive
> **Any Plextor model.** If you need a SCSI burner, once again, Plextor is the brand to buy. We prefer the $300 Plextor PX-W8220Ti PlexWriter 8/2/20 internal, an 8X write, 2X rewrite, 20X read unit. If you need 8X write but don't need rewrite, the $275 Plextor PX-R820Ti PlexWriter 8/20 is the best choice. If you don't need 8X write speed, buy the $240 Plextor PX-W4220Ti PlexWriter 4/2/20 CD-RW drive. Like all other Plextor products we have seen, these drives are solidly built and fast. Although we did not receive a unit in time for review, Plextor also manufactures the $330 PX-W12432Ti PlexWriter 12/4/32 for those who burn a lot of CDs or need the results very quickly. The best endorsement we can give to Plextor is that we have never made a coaster using a Plextor SCSI CD burner, including the time we accidentally used the PlexWriter 8/2/20 to burn at 8X on a disc certified only for 4X .

CD-R(W) software
> **Ahead Software Nero Burning ROM.** Adaptec Easy CD Creator is bundled with most CD writers, but just because it comes with your drive doesn't mean it's the best product to use. We've experienced numerous problems using Easy CD under Windows 2000, particularly when we also have DirectCD (Adaptecs

packet-writing program) loaded. Looking for better mastering software, we tried many competing products. The best we found was Nero, which is so much better than Easy CD that it's worth paying for separately. After burning more than a hundred CDs with Nero on different systems with different CD writers under Windows 98, NT, and 2000, we've found that Nero is faster than Easy CD, much less likely to burn coasters when using a marginal configuration, and able to copy source discs that Easy CD chokes on. Ahead also makes a companion packet-writing program called InCD, which we haven't yet tested. (*http://www.nero.com*)

CD-R(W) discs

Kodak. We recognize that, despite all we've said, many people still want a simple answer to the complex question of which CD-R(W) discs to buy. If you don't have the time or patience to do your own testing, we think Kodak CD-R(W) discs are the best bet. Kodak makes Ultima (silver alloy) CD-Rs in 74- and 80-minute lengths and Ultima Gold (pure gold) CD-Rs in 74-minute length. The only difference is the material used for the reflective layer, with Ultima discs being about ten cents cheaper per disc and somewhat less archivally stable than Gold Ultima discs. Several variants are available, including jewel-case packaging or bulk (spindle) packaging, discs with or without screen-printed log, thermal-printable, and inkjet-printable. Kodak manufactures their own discs and maintains very high quality-control standards. We've used Kodak CD-R and CD-RW media successfully in numerous CD-R(W) drives, including some that were very picky about which media they would accept. We've also tried Kodak's suggested field-expedient archival testing method—leaving a CD on the dashboard in the sun—and found that Kodak CD-R media are indeed more stable than the others we've tried under these extreme conditions. (*http://www.kodak.com/US/en/digital/cdr/*)

We constantly test and review new equipment. For the latest information about what we currently use, visit:

http://www.hardwareguys.com/picks/optical.html

CHAPTER 12

DVD Drives

DVD originally stood for *Digital Video Disc*, later for *Digital Versatile Disc* (yuck), and now officially stands for nothing at all. DVD is basically CD on steroids. Like a CD, a DVD stores data using tiny pits and lands embossed on a spiral track on an aluminized surface. But where CD-ROM uses a 780-nanometer (nm) infrared laser, DVD uses a 636-nm or 650-nm laser. Shorter wavelengths can resolve smaller pits, which enables pits (and tracks) to be spaced more closely. In conjunction with improved sector formatting, more efficient correction codes, tighter tolerances, and a somewhat larger recording area, this allows DVD to store seven times as much data—about 650 MB for CD-ROM versus about 4.7 GB for DVD.

One significant enhancement of DVD over CD is that DVD does away with the plethora of incompatible CD formats. Every DVD disc uses the same physical file structure, promoted by the Optical Storage Technology Association (OSTA), and called *Universal Disc Format* (*UDF*). This common physical format means that, in theory at least, any DVD drive or player can read any file on any DVD disc. Microsoft did not support UDF until Windows 98. This forced DVD content providers to adopt an interim standard called *UDF Bridge*, which combines UDF and the CD standard ISO 9660. Only Windows 95 OSR2 and later supports UDF Bridge, which forced DVD hardware manufacturers to include UDF Bridge support with their hardware in order to support pre-OSR2 Windows 95 versions.

DVD-ROM

Two types of DVD discs are produced commercially: DVD-Video discs, which store movies, and DVD-ROM discs, which store games, databases, and other computer data. All DVD-Video discs are also DVD-ROM discs, but not all DVD-ROM discs are DVD-Video discs. In effect, DVD-ROM discs correspond to CD-ROM discs, and DVD-Video discs correspond to CD-DA audio discs. DVD-Video discs can be played in DVD-Video players, which are increasingly common in home-theatre setups, or in a computer's DVD-ROM drive. DVD-ROM discs can be played only in a DVD-ROM drive. Like CDs, DVDs are produced commercially by a mechanical pressing process. The DVD-ROM standard is specified by ECMA-267 (*http://www.ecma.ch/stand/Ecma-267.htm*) and ECMA-268 (*http://www.ecma.ch/stand/Ecma-268.htm*).

DVD-ROM Types and Capacities

DVD-ROM discs are (or will be) available in numerous standardized types, most of which are uncommon or not used at all. Discs may be either of two physical sizes, and may have one or two sides, each of which may store data in a single or double layer. Like CDs, standard single-sided (SS) DVD-ROM discs are 1.2 mm thick. Double-sided (DS) discs are simply two thin (0.6 mm) discs glued back to back. Most DVD players and drives require manually flipping the disc to access the data on the other side. Each side may contain a single data layer (SL) or a double layer (DL). In the latter case, the top layer is semi-transparent, allowing the laser to read the second layer underneath it, at the expense of sacrificing some capacity from each layer. Double-sided mixed-layer (DS/ML) discs use a single data layer on one side and a double layer on the other, a compromise made necessary by the limitations of current DVD production methods. DS/DL discs are still a laboratory curiosity, and likely to remain so for some time. Table 12-1 lists the types available and the capacities of each DVD type. Capacities are always given in billions of bytes (10^9 bytes) rather than true gigabytes (2^{30} bytes), but always advertised as "GB" nonetheless.

Table 12-1: DVD-ROM Types and Capacities

Type	Diameter	Layers	Actual GB	Stated GB	Video
DVD-1	80 mm	SS/SL	1.36	1.45	0.5 hr
DVD-2	80 mm	SS/DL	2.47	2.65	~ 1.3
DVD-3	80 mm	DS/SL	2.72	2.9	~ 1.4
DVD-4	80 mm	DS/DL	4.95	5.3	~ 2.5
DVD-5	120 mm	SS/SL	4.38	4.7	~ 2.0
DVD-9	120 mm	SS/DL	7.95	8.5	~ 4.0
DVD-10	120 mm	DS/SL	8.75	9.4	~ 4.5
DVD-14	120 mm	DS/SL+DL	12.33	13.24	~ 6.5
DVD-18	120 mm	DS/DL	15.90	17	~ 8.0

DVD-ROM Speed

Like CD drives, DVD drives use the "X-factor" to specify throughput. Confusingly, DVD "X" has a different meaning than CD-ROM "X." A 1X CD drive transfers data at 150 KB/s (0.146 MB/s), but a 1X DVD drive transfers data at 11.08 million bits/sec (1.321 MB/s), or about nine times the 1X CD rate. In theory, then, the X-rating for a DVD drive when playing a CD disc would be about nine times its DVD rating. In practice, many 1X and 2X DVD drives spin CDs faster than DVDs, allowing CD X-ratings of 20X max for 1X DVD drives and 24X or 32X max for 2X DVD drives.

DVD-ROM drives have been sold with 1X, 2X, 4X, 4.8X, 5X, 6X, 8X, 10X, and 12X ratings, although the higher speed drives often cannot provide sustained throughput at the rated speed. Doing the math might lead you to believe that a 12X DVD drive would spin CDs at a 108X rating, but in fact this is not the case. All current DVD-ROM drives top out at 40X or so when playing CDs. DVD throughput faster than 1X is unimportant for movies, which always play at 1X, but does provide faster and smoother searching. High throughput is more important if you use the drive for playing games or for accessing encyclopediae, databases, and similar data.

As with CD drives, average access time is often not emphasized on DVD drives. The most common use of DVD drives is playing movies, which are sequential data, making both average access time and speeds higher than 1X unimportant. However, if you use a DVD drive to access databases or for other purposes where random access predominates, both average access time and throughput speed become more important.

Like CD-ROM drives, early DVD drives (and some current models) used CLV, spinning the disc more slowly on outer tracks and faster near the center. Some recent drives use CAV, spinning the disc at a constant speed and using a buffer to maintain a constant data rate for sequential applications like movies. A sure sign that a drive is CAV is if it lists "Max" in its speed rating.

Choosing a DVD-ROM Drive

Use the following guidelines when choosing a DVD-ROM drive:

- Get at least a third-generation (and preferably a fourth-generation) drive. DVD-ROM drive generations are primarily differentiated by speed, but secondarily by read compatibility. For watching movies, 1X is adequate, but faster drives make for smoother playback effects and faster searching. For playing games and accessing random data, one of the relatively inexpensive 4X to 6X drives is adequate, but faster is always better. At a minimum, make certain the drive will read at least DVD-ROM (DVD-5, -9, -10, -18), DVD-R, and the following CD formats: CD-DA, CD-ROM, CD-ROM XA, CD+(E)G, CD-Midi, CD-Text, CD-I, CD-I Bridge (Photo-CD and Video-CD), CD-R, CD-RW, Multi-session (Photo-CD, CD-Extra, CD-R, CD-RW). If possible, get a drive that will also read DVD-RAM (2.6 GB and 4.7 GB formats) and +RW discs.

- If you intend to watch movies or play games on your DVD-ROM drive, make sure to get a hardware MPEG-2 decoder board with your drive or use a video card that incorporates decoding hardware. Some early DVD-ROM discs used MPEG-1, but all current discs use MPEG-2 compression. MPEG can be processed in software, but software MPEG processing is generally unsatisfactory, even on a fast system. Consider a Pentium II/450 system an absolute minimum for software MPEG processing, and even then attempting to do anything else on the system at the same time will cause dropped frames. Even a Pentium III/600 cannot decompress MPEG with software at the full 30 frame/ sec rate. Hardware MPEG-2 decoder cards use one of two methods to handle the DVD video stream:

  - *Video overlay* (also called *analog overlay* or simply *overlay*) cards receive the analog VGA video stream from the video adapter, insert the DVD video data into this stream, and deliver it to the monitor. This means you must disconnect your monitor from your video adapter and connect it to the MPEG-2 decoder card. The advantages of this method are that it keeps high-volume DVD video data off the system bus and that it can be used with nearly any video card. The disadvantages are that the DVD video is often of low quality, that it is impossible to capture screen shots of DVD video (because that signal is injected into the video stream between the video adapter and the monitor), that the in-line MPEG card may limit the highest video resolution usable to something less than your monitor and video adapter support, and that inexpensive MPEG cards sometimes do odd things to your PC video (e.g., causing the monitor to drop certain colors). Most bundled MPEG decoder cards are of the video overlay type, including the Creative Labs DxR series and the Sigma Designs Hollywood series.

– *Video inlay* (also called *video port extension* (*VPE*), *VGA-inlay*, or simply *inlay*) cards inject the digital DVD video signal directly into the VGA adapter. The main advantages of this method are that it is usually somewhat easier to install and configure a video inlay card than a video overlay card, that the DVD video quality is often noticeably better, and that you can capture screenshots. The main disadvantages of video inlay are that it places a heavy load on the system bus and video adapter. Do not use a video inlay card unless you have a very capable video adapter, e.g., G400, TNT2, Voodoo 3, or better.

On balance, we prefer the video overlay method.

- Buy a drive kit that includes the DVD-ROM drive, the MPEG-2 decoder board, and the necessary software. Attempting to integrate components yourself can be an exercise in frustration.

- DVD-ROM drives are available in ATAPI and SCSI interfaces. Buy a SCSI version if at all possible. ATAPI drives are plagued by the throughput, concurrency, and other limitations of ATAPI, which become particularly noticeable with DVD. SCSI drives are typically smoother, less likely to drop frames at high frame rates, and place a much smaller load on the CPU.

DVD Writable and Rewritable

In addition to DVD-ROM drives, DVD writable and rewritable drives have begun to appear. Because of its high cost, it is clear that DVD-RW will remain a niche product, although it will continue to be used for DVD mastering and other specialized purposes. It is also clear that either DVD-RAM or +RW will become the mass-market DVD rewritable standard, but it is by no means certain which will ultimately triumph. Here are the various competing standards:

DVD-R and DVD-RW

DVD-R (Recordable) was the first recordable DVD standard. The first generation DVD-R drives, shipped by Pioneer in late 1997, cost $17,000 and stored 3.95 GB on an $80 write-once disc. Second generation Pioneer DVD-R drives, shipped in mid-1999, cost $5,000 and store 4.7 GB on a $50 write-once disc. The hideous cost of drives and media effectively limits DVD-R to premastering commercial DVD discs. DVD-R is well suited for this purpose because it provides the full 4.7 GB capacity of a standard DVD-ROM disc and because DVD-R discs are readable in most DVD-ROM drives and players. Both these requirements are critical for commercial DVD production, and neither is met by any competing recordable DVD standard.

DVD-RW (Rewritable) is a new Pioneer technology, based on DVD-R but using phase-change erasable media. DVD-RW was originally designated DVD-R/W and then briefly DVD-ER. Like DVD-R, DVD-RW will store 4.7 GB per disc and produce discs that are readable by most DVD-ROM drives and players, although the lower reflectivity of DVD-RW discs fools some DVD-ROM players into thinking they're reading a dual-layer disc. DVD-RW drives and media will initially be priced similarly to DVD-R, and will be used for similar purposes. Pioneer plans to ship DVD-RW drives in 2000.

Until now, DVD-R and DVD-RW have been the exclusive preserve of Pioneer. However, Ricoh, Sony, and Yamaha have announced they will begin making DVD-R(W) drives, and numerous mainstream media vendors have also announced they will produce DVD-R(W) media. Because there is nothing inherently more expensive about DVD-R(W) technology, it is possible that this broad-based support will reduce the price of drives and media dramatically, making DVD-R (and particularly DVD-RW) a viable competitor with other recordable DVD standards. For more information about DVD-R(W), see *http://www.pioneerusa.com/cd_dvd.html#dvdrec*. The DVD-R standard is specified by ECMA-279 (*http://www.ecma.ch/stand/Ecma-279.htm*).

DVD-RAM

The DVD-RAM (Random Access Memory) standard is backed by Hitachi, Matsushita (Panasonic), and Toshiba. First generation DVD-RAM drives, currently available for under $400, began shipping in mid-1998, and use a mix of phase-change and magneto-optical technology to record about 2.6 GB per side on rewritable media. These discs are not readable by older DVD players and drives, although some manufacturers are beginning to ship DVD-ROM drives that will read them. Next-generation Hitachi DVD-RAM drives, scheduled to ship in 2000, will read and write both the original 2.6 GB DVD-RAM media and the new 4.7 GB media.

Several DVD-RAM media types are available. Single-sided 2.6 GB media, which as of June, 2000 cost about $20, are available with or without a cartridge, and that cartridge may be Type 1 (sealed) or Type 2 (removable). Double-sided 5.2 GB media, which cost $25 to $35, are available only in sealed Type 1 cartridges. Using a cartridge raises two problems: first, because standard DVD players and drives cannot physically accommodate a cartridge, DVD-RAM discs enclosed in cartridges cannot be read on these devices. Second, once removed from their cartridge, single-sided DVD-RAM discs in Type 2 cartridges can no longer be reliably recorded, so doing so effectively turns them into write-once media.

The DVD-RAM standard is specified by ECMA-272 (*http://www.ecma.ch/stand/Ecma-272.htm*) and ECMA-273 (*http://www.ecma.ch/stand/Ecma-273.htm*).

+RW

Originally called DVD+RW, +RW is a competing rewritable standard backed by Hewlett-Packard, Mitsubishi Chemical, Philips, Ricoh, Sony, and Yamaha. Although its backers are members of the DVD Forum, the +RW standard is not recognized by that organization. Current +RW drives use phase-change rewritable technology to store 2.8 GB per side. The +RW group has announced that second-generation +RW drives, due in 2001, will expand capacity to 4.7 GB per side and support writing CD-R and CD-RW discs. First generation +RW drives read and write +RW media, and read CDs, DVDs, and DVD-R(W)s, but do not read DVD-RAM discs. Current DVD players and most DVD-ROM drives cannot read 2.8 GB +RW media, although the most recent Sony and Philips DVD-ROM drives can. Unfortunately for +RW backers, the three major DVD-ROM drive makers (Hitachi, Panasonic, and Toshiba) are all members of the DVD-RAM camp, and are unlikely to provide 2.8 GB +RW read compatibility even in their next generation of drives. However, formatting changes that will be made to 4.7 GB +RW media should mean that those discs will be readable in many standard DVD players and drives.

+RW backers claim two primary advantages for +RW relative to DVD-RAM: first, like CDs, +RW discs do not use a cartridge. This should ultimately translate into lower costs for drives and media, and allows +RW discs to physically fit standard drives. It also makes +RW drives a viable alternative for laptop systems, which the cartridge-based DVD-RAM drives are not. Second, +RW drives use CLV access for sequential data (like movies) and CAV access for random data, which allows higher performance.

As of June 2000, +RW drives had not begun shipping, and it appears the +RW faction may cede the rewritable DVD market to DVD-RAM by default. However, +RW is still officially in development, and actual products may yet ship. More information about +RW is available at *http://www.dvdrw.org/*. The +RW standard is specified by ECMA-274 (*http://www.ecma.ch/stand/Ecma-274.htm*).

MMVF
MMVF (Multimedia Video File), a standard proposed by NEC, stores 5.2 GB on a single-sided disc and has certain advantages for recording video. MMVF is backed only by NEC, and is unlikely to be a factor.

Read/Write Compatibility

Table 12-2 lists read/write compatibility between various types of optical drives and media. Note that read and write compatibilities are not absolute. For example, most (but not all) modern CD-ROM drives can read CD-RW media, and some (but not all) DVD-ROM drives can read DVD-RAM media. "R" means the drive will read the media. "R/W" means the drive will read and write the media. " ○ " means the drive will neither read nor write the media. "*" means at least some drive models will read and/or write some media types, but with limitations, which may be drive- or media-specific. "?" means unknown or not-yet-determined compatibility. Drives are in the top row; media types are in the left column.

Table 12-2: Drive and Media Compatibility

	CD	CD-R	CD-RW	DVD	DVD-R	DVD-RW	DVD-RAM	+RW
CD-DA	R	R	R	R	R	R	R	R
CD-ROM	R	R	R	R	R	R	R	R
CD-R	R	R/W	R/W	R	R	R	R	R
CD-RW	R	R	R/W	R	R	R	R	R

Table 12-2: Drive and Media Compatibility (continued)

	CD	CD-R	CD-RW	DVD	DVD-R	DVD-RW	DVD-RAM	+RW
DVD Video	○	○	○	R	R	R	R	R
DVD-ROM	○	○	○.	R	R	R	R	R
DVD-R	○	○	○	R*	R/W	R/W	R	R*
DVD-RW	○	○	○	R*	R	R/W	R*	R*
DVD-RAM	○	○	○	○	○	○	R/W	○
+RW	○	○	○	R*	?	?	○	R/W

 As of June, 2000, hybrid drives like the Toshiba SD-R1002 and the Ricoh MP9060A are shipping in volume. At $350 or so, these drives are both DVD-ROM readers and CD-R(W) writers. Expect similar drives from other manufacturers later in 2000.

Choosing a Writable DVD Drive

The fact that DVD-RAM drives have been shipping since mid-1998 while competing +RW drives have not yet begun shipping as of June, 2000 may give DVD-RAM an overwhelming lead in the race to establish a writable DVD standard. When we first examined this issue in mid-1999, we noted that so few DVD-RAM drives had been sold that this market-share advantage was illusory. However, that one-year head start is now a two-year head start, and it is beginning to seem that +RW may never see the light of day. Although +RW has some attractive advantages in theory—not least of which is that it does not require a cartridge—those advantages remain illusory in the absence of shipping +RW drives. If we needed a high capacity writable optical drive now, we would buy a Hitachi 2.6 GB DVD-RAM drive, or one of their new-generation 4.7 GB units once they become available. Otherwise, we'd wait for the market to decide the winner, which is unlikely to occur much before late 2000.

Installing and Configuring a DVD Drive

Installing and configuring a DVD-ROM drive or writable DVD drive requires the same steps detailed in Chapter 10, *CD-ROM Drives*, with the following exceptions:

- Windows 95B/98 and Windows 2000 support DVD drives. Windows NT 4 recognizes DVD drives only as standard CD-ROM drives.

- DVD drives use Region Coding, which restricts which DVD discs may be played in that drive. For example, a drive set to Region 1 (U.S. and Canada) can play only Region 1 discs, while a drive set to Region 2 (Europe) can play only Region 2 discs. By default, DVD Region is set to the installation location. The Region setting for the drive can be changed a limited number of times, typically five.

  Use Device Manager to change DVD Region setting under Windows 98/2000. Expand the listing for DVD/CD-ROM drives, double-click the entry for the DVD drive to display Properties, and then display the Advanced Settings page, shown in Figure 12-1. The line at the bottom of the dialog states how many more Region Code changes are allowed for this drive. Use the scrolling list to locate the country and click to highlight that country. Windows inserts the corresponding region in the New Region box. Click OK and confirm the warning dialog to reprogram the drive for the new region.

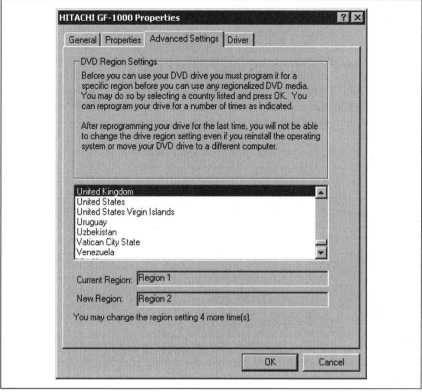

Figure 12-1: Use the Advanced Settings page of the drive Properties dialog to set the DVD Region Code

 Some DVD drives shipped before 1/1/2000 did not implement Region Code locking in hardware, instead using software and the registry to control the number of times the Region could be changed. If you have one of those drives and exceed the allowed number of Region changes, you can reset the counter by uninstalling the drive itself and the software that accesses it (e.g., a DVD player application), deleting all references to the drive and the software from the registry, and then reinstalling the drive and software. All DVD drives shipped on or after January 1, 2000, implement Region Code locking on a chip inside the drive itself, and cannot be reset short of returning them to the manufacturer.

Our Picks

When we originally researched DVD in 1999, we were unable to recommend either a DVD-ROM drive or a writable DVD drive. DVD-ROM drives were expensive and problematic. The competing incompatible DVD-RAM and +RW standards, with no sure winner, made buying a writable DVD drive risky. Since then, things have settled down. DVD-ROM drives are still more expensive than CD-ROM drives, but with careful shopping you can find a high-quality DVD-ROM drive for $90 to $125, and current model DVD-ROM drives substitute well for a CD-ROM drive. As of June, 2000, +RW drives *still* aren't shipping, leaving DVD-RAM the winner by default.

Here are the DVD drives we actually use and recommend:

ATAPI DVD-ROM drive

> **Hitachi GD-5000**. This $120 third-generation DVD-ROM drive reads DVDs at 8X with 120 ms access, and CD-ROMs at 40X with 90 ms access. The huge 512 KB buffer—most DVD-ROM drives have 128 KB buffers—ensures smooth playback under all circumstances. This drive reads everything we throw at it, including CD, CD-R, CD-RW, and all standard DVD formats from 4.7 GB to 17 GB. Hitachi DVD drives are used primarily by OEMs, and may be difficult to find at retail. If you have trouble locating a Hitachi DVD drive, another good choice is the $150 Toshiba SD-M1402. This drive reads DVDs at 12X with 95 ms access, and CDs at 40X with 80 ms access. It resembles the Hitachi drive in most respects except its smaller 128 KB buffer. (*http://www.hitachi.com/storage/products/dvd/dvdframe.html*)

SCSI DVD-ROM drive

> **Toshiba SD-M1401**. DVD-ROM is primarily a consumer-oriented technology, so relatively few drives are available in SCSI. Of those, the SD-M1401 is the best we know of. SCSI is usually a step ahead of ATAPI in performance, but in this case the M1401 SCSI drive is a step behind the M1402 ATAPI model. The M1401 is marginally slower than the ATAPI M1402, providing 10X DVD-ROM reads with 105 ms access, and 40X CD-ROM reads with 85 ms access. Although we are SCSI proponents, when it comes to DVD-ROM drives, we use ATAPI models. (*http://www.toshiba.com/taecdpd/products/features/SDM1401-Over.shtml*)

DVD-RAM drive

> **Hitachi GF-1000 or GF-1050**. If you need rewritable optical storage and CD-RW is too small, get one of these $350 2.6/5.2 GB DVD-RAM drives. These two models differ only in interface, with the GF-1000 using ATAPI and the GF-1050 SCSI-2. Both are rated for 1.38 MB/s write speed, but we find real-world throughput closer to 0.4 MB/s when copying many small files and 0.9 MB/s when copying a few large files. Although Hitachi does not sell these drives directly, they are available in relabeled kits from various manufacturers including Compaq and QPS. If you have difficulty locating the Hitachi models, another good choice is the Toshiba SD-W1111, which is comparable to the Hitachi drives in price, performance, and specifications, and uses the SCSI-2 interface. Robert's secondary main system has a GF-1000 installed, which he uses to archive all working data at the end of each work day. Unless you have

an urgent need for a large optical drive, we recommend waiting for one of the next-generation 4.7 GB DVD-RAM drives, which should ship by late 2000.

Combination DVD-ROM/CD-RW drive

Toshiba SD-R1002. We've never been big fans of combination devices. They seldom do the job as well as individual components, and are often more fragile. That said, if you need both DVD-ROM and CD-RW and are cramped for space, give this $285 ATAPI drive a look. It's not fast—4X CD-R and CD-RW writes, 4X DVD-ROM reads, and 24X CD-ROM reads—but it does put all the optical drive functions most people need into one drive. If we needed both functions, we'd prefer to install a $100 DVD-ROM drive and a $185 CD-RW drive, but this drive has the undeniable advantage of requiring only one drive bay and one ATA connector. (*http://www.toshiba.com/taecdpd/products/ features/SDR1002Kit-Over.shtml*)

We constantly test and review new equipment. For the latest information about what we currently use, visit:

http://www.hardwareguys.com/picks/optical.html

CHAPTER 13

Hard Disk Interfaces

The hard disk interface defines the physical and logical means by which the hard disk connects to the PC. In the 1980s, the most popular disk interfaces were ST506/412 and ESDI, which are now obsolete. These old drives use two ribbon cables (a 20-pin data cable and a 34-pin control cable), versus the single ribbon cable used by modern drives. Finding one of these old dual-cable drives in a PC by itself establishes that the computer is too old to be upgraded economically. A modern PC uses one or both of the following hard disk interfaces:

Integrated Drive Electronics (IDE)
> Pronounced as individual letters, IDE is the overwhelmingly dominant type of hard disk found in modern computers. Modern IDE hard disks are large, fast, standardized, well-supported by PCs, and relatively inexpensive.

Small Computer System Interface (SCSI)
> Usually pronounced *scuzzy* (but sometimes *sexy*), SCSI hard disks are usually used in servers and high-end workstations, where they provide two major advantages: improved performance relative to IDE in multitasking, multiuser environments, and the ability to daisy-chain many drives on one computer. SCSI interfaces are available in various sub-types, which have different physical and electrical interfaces and transfer rates. Modern SCSI hard disks are the largest, fastest disks available, although recently IDE hard disks have begun to approach SCSI in size and speed. Within the different SCSI flavors, interfaces are well defined and standardized, but configuring SCSI to work on a standard PC can be complicated.

SCSI disks are seldom used in standard PCs because they cost more than IDE disks with similar capacity and performance. For example, if an IDE hard disk costs $250, a similar model with a SCSI interface may cost $350 to $400. In addition to the higher cost of the drives themselves, using a SCSI disk requires installing a SCSI host adapter, which may add $75 to $250 to system cost. However, spending an extra $175 to $400 to install SCSI may increase system performance more than spending that same sum on a faster processor, so don't rule SCSI out. In our experience, the slowest SCSI hard disks outperform the fastest IDE disks, particularly under multi-tasking operating systems like Windows NT/2000 and Linux.

IDE

IDE, more properly called the *AT Attachment (ATA)* interface, is the means used by most computers to interface hard disks and other drives to the computer. You may or may not need to understand much about IDE to install and configure a hard drive, depending on how old your hardware is. The most recent drives, motherboards, and BIOSes handle the hard parts for you, automatically detecting and configuring the drive, interface, and BIOS for optimum performance. So, if all you're doing is installing a new IDE hard drive in a recent PC, you can safely skip this entire section and jump forward to the section on installing the drive.

If, however, you're upgrading an older system with a new drive or installing an older drive in a new system, keep reading. If any of the components is more than a couple of years old, you need to understand quite a bit about IDE, not just to configure the PC for optimum performance, but to ensure that your data is not corrupted by running data transfer rates higher than your hardware can safely support. Understanding the fundamentals of IDE also helps you make good decisions when you purchase drives, system boards, and add-on IDE interface cards.

Early hard disk interfaces used a separate hard disk and controller card, which limited throughput. In 1986, Compaq and Western Digital combined the hard disk and controller card into one unit, thereby inventing IDE. Early IDE drives used an expansion card called a paddle card, but this card was not really a disk controller. It simply provided an interface between the bus and the embedded disk controller on the hard drive itself.

IDE/ATA Data Transfer Modes

To understand ATA data transfer modes, it's necessary to understand something about how data is read from and written to the hard drive. Real mode operating systems like 16-bit Windows and DOS make read and write requests to the BIOS, which passes the command to the drive. Protected mode operating systems like Windows NT/2000 and Unix bypass the real mode BIOS and use their own protected mode I/O subsystems to accomplish the same purpose.

Data transfer commands are controlled by the BIOS or I/O subsystem, but execution speed—and therefore data transfer rate—is determined by the strobe frequency of the ATA interface hardware. The time needed to complete one full cycle, measured in nanoseconds (ns), is called the *cycle time* for the interface. A shorter cycle time allows more cycles to be completed in a given period, and therefore provides a higher data transfer rate. For example, a 600 ns cycle time yields 1.66 million cycles/second. Because each cycle transfers one word (16 bits or two bytes), a 600 ns cycle time translates to a data transfer rate of 3.33 MB/sec.

ATA supports two data transfer modes, called *Programmed Input/Output (PIO) Mode* and *Direct Memory Access (DMA) Mode*. Each of these has several sub-modes that use different cycle times and have different data transfer rates. When an ATA interface interrogates a modern drive with the *Identify Drive* command, the drive returns its model, geometry, and a list of the PIO and DMA modes it supports, allowing the interface, given proper BIOS support, to automatically configure the best settings for optimum drive performance. With an older drive, an older BIOS, or both, it's up to you to configure these settings yourself, so it's important to understand what they mean to avoid either crippling drive performance by choosing too slow a mode or risking your data by choosing one that's too fast for your hardware.

 Your operating system also determines whether an ATA hard disk is configured automatically for optimal performance. Windows 98 and Windows 2000 (usually) detect DMA-capable interfaces and drives and configure them automatically to operate in the more efficient DMA mode. Windows 95 and Windows NT 4 use the less efficient PIO mode by default, and must be configured manually to use DMA mode on hardware that supports it. Configuring DMA mode on ATA drives is described in Chapter 14, *Hard Disk Drives.*

Programmed Input/Output (PIO) modes

PIO is a means of data transfer that requires the CPU to intermediate data exchanges between the drive and memory. This dependence on the CPU places unnecessary demands on it and slows CPU performance under multitasking operating systems. Accordingly, modern drives and interfaces substitute DMA modes, described in the next section, to provide high-speed data transfer. PIO modes remain important, however, when connecting older drives to newer interfaces or vice versa. Table 13-1 lists PIO modes, not all of which are supported by all drives and all interfaces.

Table 13-1: ATA Programmed Input/Output (PIO) Modes

PIO Mode	Cycle Time	Transfer Rate	Revision
PIO-0	600 ns	3.3 MB/sec	ATA
PIO-1	383 ns	5.2 MB/sec	ATA
PIO-2	330 ns	8.3 MB/sec	ATA
PIO-3	180 ns	11.1 MB/sec	ATA-2
PIO-4	120 ns	13.3 MB/sec	ATA-2
PIO-5	90 ns	22.2 MB/sec	Never implemented

PIO Modes 0, 1, and 2 are not used on recent systems except to support older drives. Using PIO Modes 3 or 4 provides reasonably fast transfer rates, but requires that the drive support using the IORDY line for hardware flow control. If the interface delivers data faster than a PIO Mode 3 or 4 drive can accept it, the drive de-asserts IORDY to notify the interface to stop delivering data. Running a drive that does not support IORDY on an interface configured for PIO Mode 3 or 4 may appear to work, but risks corrupting data. If you are not certain· that your drive supports PIO Mode 3 or 4, configure the interface to use PIO Mode 2.

Direct Memory Access (DMA) Modes

DMA is a data transfer mode that allows bidirectional transfer of data between drives and memory without intervention from the processor. If you use a multitasking operating system like 32-bit Windows or Unix, using DMA mode increases performance by freeing the CPU to do other things while data is being transferred. DMA doesn't improve performance with single-tasking operating systems like DOS or 16-bit Windows, because the processor must wait until the transfer is complete before doing anything else. Table 13-2 lists DMA modes, not all of which are supported by all drives and all interfaces. Note ATA-3 introduced no new modes.

Table 13-2: ATA Direct Memory Access (DMA) Modes

DMA Mode	Cycle Time	Transfer Rate	Revision
Single Word Mode 0 (SDMA-0)	960 ns	2.1 MB/sec	ATA
Single Word Mode 1 (SDMA-1)	480 ns	4.2 MB/sec	ATA
Single Word Mode 2 (SDMA-2)	240 ns	8.3 MB/sec	ATA
Multiword Mode 0 (MDMA-0)	480 ns	4.2 MB/sec	ATA
Multiword Mode 1 (MDMA-1)	150 ns	13.3 MB/sec	ATA-2
Multiword Mode 2 (MDMA-2)	120 ns	16.6 MB/sec	ATA-2
Ultra-DMA Mode 0 (UDMA-0)	240 ns	16.6 MB/sec	ATA-4
Ultra-DMA Mode 1 (UDMA-1)	160 ns	25.0 MB/sec	ATA-4
Ultra-DMA Mode 2 (UDMA-2)	120 ns	33.3 MB/sec	ATA-4
Ultra-DMA Mode 3 (UDMA-3)	90 ns	44.4 MB/sec	ATA-5
Ultra-DMA Mode 4 (UDMA-4)	60 ns	66.7 MB/sec	ATA-5

The SDMA modes were made obsolete by ATA-3, and are useful only for older drives and interfaces. MDMA modes provide reasonable transfer rates, and are useful for drive/interface configurations that are ATA-2 compliant, but where the drive and/or interface is not Ultra-ATA compliant. Using UDMA modes requires that the drive, interface, BIOS, and operating system be Ultra-ATA compliant. MDMA-2 and UDMA-0 provide identical transfer rates, but MDMA-2 does not use hardware flow control, while UDMA-0 uses CRC error detection to prevent data corruption. Hardware that supports UDMA modes 3 and 4, also called UDMA/66, began shipping in early 1999, and are becoming standard on new systems in 2000. Installing a UDMA/66 drive on an older system requires adding a UDMA/66 interface card and using a special 80-wire, 40-pin ATA cable.

There are two ways to implement DMA. *First-party DMA*, also called *bus mastering DMA*, uses a DMA controller embedded in the device itself to arbitrate possession of the bus and data transfer. *Third-party DMA* instead depends on the DMA controller that resides on the motherboard. If the motherboard is of recent vintage, either first-party or third-party DMA can be used for high-speed DMA transfer modes.

A problem arises with older systems' boards, whose DMA controllers cannot support third-party DMA for fast DMA modes. DMA controllers on ISA motherboards are too slow to support ATA DMA. DMA controllers on VLB motherboards don't support third-party DMA at all. In either of these situations, the best solution is to replace the motherboard. The DMA controller on many PCI motherboards, including some relatively recent ones, supports third-party DMA, but only at lower rates. The solution here is to install a first-party (bus mastering) add-on ATA interface card that supports high-speed DMA.

 The CMD-640 and RZ-1000 PCI-to-IDE interfaces used on some older interface cards and motherboards have bugs that may corrupt data. These bugs are subtle, and may damage data for months before being noticed. For detailed information about this problem and utilities to test for it, download the file *eidete20.zip* (or later), which is available from numerous Internet ftp sites.

IDE/ATA Standards and Implementations

Although it was originally proprietary, the cost and performance advantages of IDE quickly made it the standard hard disk interface. By 1990, most computer systems came with IDE hard disks. A slew of acronyms and standards has arisen as IDE has proliferated, some meaningful and many that are just marketing hype. The formal ATA standards are maintained by *Technical Committee T13* of the National Committee *on* Information Technology Standards (NCITS), and may be viewed at *http://www.t13.org*. These standards include:

ATA

The original IDE specification, ATA defines a standard 40-pin interface that supports two hard disk devices on one cable.

ATAPI (ATA Packet Interface)

The first ATA standard supported only hard disks. Manufacturers soon realized that the ubiquity, high performance, and low cost of the IDE interface also made it ideal for non-disk devices like CD-ROM and tape drives. The ATAPI standard was developed to allow these non-disk devices to be connected to a standard ATA port. ATAPI hardware connects to and works with any standard IDE or EIDE port. Note that, although ATAPI devices connect to ATA ports, they are not ATA devices, and differ significantly from an ATA hard drive. This is not a problem with most motherboard IDE ports and IDE interface cards, but caching controllers and other intelligent interfaces must be explicitly ATAPI compliant to support ATAPI devices.

ATA-2

Advances in hard disk technology soon made it clear that the original ATA standard was too confining. Since the original standard was completed, several developments made it desirable to produce an updated version of the specification. That updated specification, ATA-2, adds faster PIO and DMA modes, improves Plug-N-Play support, and adds Logical Block Addressing (LBA).

ATA-3

Provided several minor improvements to the ATA-2 standard, including: enhanced reliability, especially for PIO-4, better power management, and the incorporation of *Self Monitoring Analysis and Reporting Technology* (*SMART*), which allows the drive to warn the operating system of impending problems. ATA-3 did not add any PIO or DMA modes faster than those defined in ATA-2.

ATA/ATAPI-4

The current revision of the ATA standard. ATA-4 merges ATA-3 and ATAPI into a single integrated standard and formalizes Ultra-ATA DMA/33 as a part of that standard.

ATA/ATAPI-5

Work began on ATA/ATAPI-5 in April, 1998, but has not yet been issued as an official standard as of June 2000, although the current draft standard is accepted and used as a *de facto* standard by component manufacturers. ATA/ATAPI-5 will formalize Ultra ATA/66 and may add support for Ultra ATA/100. ATA/ATAPI-6 is currently in development.

Although these formal standards define the ATA interface, the hard drives and interfaces you can actually buy are marketed using the following *ad hoc* standards:

Enhanced IDE (EIDE)

A Western Digital IDE implementation that incorporates and extends the ATA-2 and ATAPI standards. EIDE supports two devices each on primary and secondary ATA interfaces, for a total of four devices: fast transfer modes (PIO-3 or better and multiword DMA-1 or better), Logical Block Addressing (LBA) mode, and connecting ATAPI devices such as CD-ROM and tape drives to the ATA interface. EIDE includes the Western Digital Enhanced BIOS, which eliminates the 504/528 MB limitation under DOS. Recent Western Digital hard drives and EIDE interfaces support some or all of the ATA/ATAPI-4 and proposed ATA/ATAPI-5 standards, including Ultra-DMA/16 and /33 (UDMA modes 0 and 1), and Ultra-DMA/66 modes 2, 3, and 4.

Fast ATA

A Seagate IDE implementation, later endorsed by Quantum, that counters the Western Digital EIDE initiative. Fast ATA and Fast ATA-2 are based on ATA and ATA-2, but not on ATAPI. Fast ATA supports fast transfer modes (PIO-3 and multiword DMA-1); LBA mode, and Read/Write Multiple commands, also called Block Mode. Fast ATA-2 adds support for PIO-4 and multiword DMA-2. Recent Fast-ATA hard drives support Ultra ATA/33 and the nascent Ultra ATA/66 standard.

Ultra ATA

An extension to ATA-2, first proposed by Quantum and Intel, and now a part of the ATA/ATAPI-4 standard (as Ultra ATA/33 for UDMA modes 0 and 1) and the proposed ATAPI/ATA-5 standard (as Ultra ATA/66 for UDMA modes 2, 3, and 4). Ultra-ATA enhances the earlier SDMA and MDMA modes by adding CRC error detection to prevent data corruption during fast DMA transfers.

To benefit from the increased data transfer rates provided by Ultra-DMA, the drive, the BIOS, the ATA interface, and the operating system must all support it. By late 1997 some PCs and motherboards included embedded Ultra ATA/33 support, and most shipped later than late 1998 support Ultra ATA/33. Ultra ATA/66 drives and interfaces began shipping in early 1999. As of summer 2000, systems and motherboards based on earlier chipsets that support only Ultra ATA/33 are still shipping in volume, but those based on more recent chipsets that support Ultra ATA/66 are beginning to supplant them. You can implement Ultra ATA/33 or /66 on older PCs by installing an add-on IDE interface card like the Promise Ultra66 (*http://www. promise.com*) and upgrading the system BIOS.

ATA Multichannel Support

The original ATA specification defined one dual-channel ATA interface that supported one or two ATA devices. ATA-2 defines a second interface, with the *Primary Interface* using standard ATA IRQ and base address, and the *Secondary Interface* using the alternate IRQ and base address that had always been set aside for that purpose. Any modern motherboard or interface card provides dual-ported ATA support.

Windows 9X and Windows NT/2000 recognize and use the secondary interface automatically. DOS and 16-bit Windows are not dual-port ATA-aware, so installing more than two ATA drives with these operating systems requires either BIOS support for the secondary port or supplemental drivers. If BIOS Setup allows you to enter drive parameters for four drives, you already have the BIOS support you need. If BIOS Setup lists only two drives, you must (in order of desirability) install an updated system BIOS *or* use a dual-ported bus-mastering ATA adapter with an on-board dual-port BIOS *or* install dual-port device drivers.

In addition to the well-standardized primary and secondary ATA interface, some devices support semi-standard tertiary and quaternary ATA interfaces. In theory, at least, you can support up to 8 ATA devices on one computer by adding a dual-ported interface card that can be configured as tertiary/quaternary to a system that includes a standard dual-ported ATA interface, assuming that you have the four IRQs needed to support all four ports. We have not seen a BIOS that includes direct support for ATA Ports 3 and 4, although the current Phoenix BIOS specification allows ATA ports beyond 1 and 2 to be defined arbitrarily. Table 13-3 lists the IRQs and Base Addresses for AT Ports 1 through 4.

Table 13-3: ATA Port IRQ and Base Address Assignments

ATA Port	IRQ	Hex Base Addresses (Channel 0/Channel 1)
Primary	14	0x1F0–0x1F7 and 0x3F6–0x3F7
Secondary	15 or 10	0x170–0x177 and 0x376–0x377
Tertiary	12 or 11	0x1E8–0x1EF and 0x3EE–0x3EF
Quaternary	10 or 9	0x168–0x16F and 0x36E–0x36F

Compatibility Between Old and New IDE Devices

With only minor exceptions, there are no compatibility issues when using new ATA devices with old ATA interfaces or vice versa. Newer drives cannot yield their highest performance when connected to an ATA interface that does not support the fastest transfer modes the drive is capable of, just as a new interface can't improve the performance of an older drive. But you can connect any ATA drive to any ATA interface with reasonable assurance that it will function, although perhaps not optimally.

Nearly all modern ATA interfaces—including the ubiquitous Intel PIIX3 and PIIX4—support independent timing for master and slave devices. This means that you can safely put an old, slow ATA or ATAPI device on the same cable as a new, fast hard drive without concern that the older device will cripple the throughput of the newer one.

IDE Capacity Limits

Various IDE capacity limits exist, which depend on the BIOS, interface hardware, operating system, and other factors. There's a lot of information and misinformation about these limits, so it's worth getting the facts straight before you accept unnecessary limitations. Most of these limits are a result of interactions between the methods that the BIOS and the ATA interface use to address sectors on a hard disk. Even the oldest BIOS or ATA interface can address large hard disks. In combination, however, interactions between the BIOS and the interface may limit the number of addressable sectors to a fraction of the number either could address alone. Table 13-4 summarizes these limits.

Table 13-4: ATA Addressing and BIOS Addressing Limitations

Maximum Addressable	ATA Limit	Int13 Limit	Shared Limit
Cylinders	65,536 (2^{16})	1,024 (2^{10})	1,024
Heads	16 (2^4)	256 (2^{16})	16
Sectors per track	255 (2^8-1)	63 (2^6-1)	63
Disk size (bytes)	136,902,082,560	8,455,716,864	528,482,304

ATA addressing uses four registers that total 28 bits. ATA numbers cylinders starting at 0. The *cylinder address* is a 16-bit value, divided as a least-significant 8-bit *Cylinder Low* register and a most-significant 8-bit *Cylinder High* register, allowing up to 65,536 cylinders to be addressed. Each cylinder has a number of heads, also numbered starting at 0, which are addressed using a 4-bit value stored in the lowest four bits of the *Device/Head* register, allowing up to 16 heads to be addressed. Sectors are numbered starting at 1, and are addressed using an 8-bit value stored in the *Sector Number* register, allowing up to 255 sectors to be addressed. These capacities mean that ATA can address up to (65,536 × 16 × 255) 512-byte sectors, which equals 136,902,082,560 bytes.

BIOS Int13 API addressing uses three registers that total 24 bits. *Cylinder Low* is an 8-bit register that stores the least significant eight bits of the 10-bit cylinder address. *Cylinder High/Sector Number* is an 8-bit register whose least significant two bits store the most significant two bits of the cylinder address and whose most significant six bits store the sector number. In conjunction, these addresses allow up to 1,024 cylinders and 63 sectors/track to be addressed. *Head Number* is an 8-bit register, which allows up to 256 heads to be addressed. These capacities mean that Int13 can address up to (1,024 × 256 × 63) 512-byte sectors, which equals 8,455,716,864 bytes.

The impact of these limits depends entirely on the addressing method used by the BIOS. From the oldest to the newest, here are the methods used by various BIOSes:

Cylinder-Head-Sectors (CHS)
   Cylinder-Head-Sectors (CHS) is the access method used by early BIOSes to address individual sectors on a hard disk by identifying them directly by the

cylinder, head, and sector where they reside. CHS in an ATA/Int13 environment is subject to the maximum common address register size supported for each element by ATA and Int13 addressing. This means that CHS can address at most 1,024 cylinders, 16 heads, and 63 sectors per track, which results in the 504/528 MB limit.

Extended Cylinder-Head-Sectors (ECHS)

Extended Cylinder-Head-Sectors (ECHS) is the most popular of several access methods (others being *Large* and *Big IDE*) used by so-called enhanced or translating BIOSes to support hard disks larger than those supported by CHS. ECHS or *bit shift translation* works by lying about disk geometry, translating an unsupported physical geometry to a supported logical geometry whose address will fit the available registers. For example, ECHS translation may represent a 1 GB drive whose physical geometry is 2,048 cylinders, 16 heads, and 63 sectors per track as having a logical geometry of 1,024 cylinders, 32 heads, and 63 sectors per track, allowing the full 1 GB to be recognized and used. The problem with ECHS translation is that it is nonstandard, and different BIOSes handle it differently.

Logical Block Addressing (LBA)

Logical Block Addressing (LBA) dispenses with CHS addressing entirely, and addresses each sector sequentially. With LBA addressing, all 28 address bits (16+4+8) are used as one LBA address, allowing up to 2^{28} (268,435,456) sectors or 137,438,953,472 bytes to be addressed. Note that, with LBA addressing, sector numbers start at 0. LBA assist translation can be used only with BIOSes and drives that support LBA addressing. With LBA translation, the drive reports its actual geometry to the BIOS, which then multiplies the cylinders, heads, and sectors reported by the drive to determine the total number of sectors to be used for LBA translation. All modern BIOSes support LBA.

Various environments may enforce the following limits:

504/528 MB

Results from the interaction between ATA addressing and CHS Int13 addressing, which allows 1,024 cylinders, 16 heads, 63 sectors/track, limiting drive capacity to 528,482,304 bytes, or 504 MB. To get around this limit, you may upgrade the PC BIOS to one with LBA support, disable the embedded interface and replace it with one that has LBA support, or install a BIOS extender card that provides LBA support with the existing interface. If a hardware solution is not feasible, installing a third-party driver such as Ontrack Disk Manager allows using large disks, but with some limitations relative to the hardware solutions.

2.0/2.1 GB (hardware)

Various manufacturers attempted to solve the 504 MB limit by various methods, including modifications to the way registers were manipulated. One such method was to "steal" the two previously unused high-order bits assigned to the head register and assign them to the cylinder register, expanding it from 10 to 12 bits. This increased the number of addressable cylinders to 4,096, but in doing so limited the number of heads that could be addressed to 64. Because this translation method was not commonly used, the two high-order head bits cannot safely be assumed to be assigned to either the head count or the cylinder count, which allows 1,024 cylinders, 64 heads, and 63 sectors/track. Multiplying these numbers yields 2,113,929,216 bytes, usually stated as 2.0 or 2.1 GB. You've encountered this limit if the system hangs during POST when the BIOS attempts to translate the cylinders and heads. The solutions are the same as for the 504 MB limit.

2.0/2.1 GB (software)

This limit derives from how the FAT filesystem tracks hard disk space. FAT16 cannot use clusters larger than 32,768 bytes, or 64 512-byte sectors per cluster, and can track at most 65,536 clusters. Multiplying the numbers yields 2,147,483,648 bytes, or 2 GB. The only solution is to use multiple partitions, each no larger than 2 GB. The FAT32 filesystem used by Windows 95B/98/2000 and the NTFS filesystem used by Windows NT/2000 are not subject to this limit.

3.27 GB

Some BIOSes do not properly handle cylinder counts over 6,322, enforcing a limit of about 3.27 GB. A BIOS has this limit if the PC hangs when you enter a value of 6,322 cylinders or more. The solutions are the same as those listed for the 504 MB limit.

4.2 GB

Some interfaces store the number of heads reported by the BIOS as an 8-bit number, calculated modulo-256. If the BIOS reports 256 heads, these interfaces fill the 8-bit register with zeros (the least significant eight bits), assume that the drive has zero heads, and refuse to allow it to be configured. This problem occurs if the drive reports 16 heads and 8,192 or more cylinders to the bit shift translation, effectively limiting drive size to 1,024 cylinders × 128 heads × 63 sectors/track × 512 bytes/sector = 4,227,858,432 bytes. Because LBA translation never reports more than 255 heads, this problem does not occur with BIOSes that use LBA translation. A BIOS has this limit if the computer hangs at boot after you create partitions on the drive. The solutions are the same as those listed for the 504 MB limit.

8.4 GB

LBA translation uses ID words 1, 3, and 6 of the Identify Drive command. These three 8-bit words allow maximum LBA values of 16,384 cylinders, 16 heads and 63 sectors/track, for a total capacity of 8,455,716,864 bytes. Exceeding this limit requires BIOS support for Extended Int13 functions, which is available with recent BIOSes. Extended Int13 functions no longer transfer disk addresses via host registers. Instead, they pass the "address of an address" by placing a 64-bit LBA *Device Address* packet in host memory. The least-significant 28 bits of this packet contain a standard 28-bit LBA address. If the drive uses LBA addressing, the least-significant 28 bits of this packet may be passed directly to the ATA registers. If the drive does not support LBA addressing, the host translates the full LBA address to a CHS address, allowing the full capacity of the disk drive to be used, within overall ATA and LBA limitations.

The BIOS may have this limit if: (1) the PC hangs during POST when it tries to translate cylinders and heads; (2) the total disk capacity reported to the operating system is 8.4 GB or less; or (3) strange things happen when you partition or format the disk. For example, *fdisk* may refuse to partition the drive, claiming that it is read-only, or *format* may report a huge number of bad sectors. The solutions are the same as those listed for the 504 MB limit.

 The *atapi.sys* driver provided with Windows NT 4 does not recognize hard disks larger than 8 GB. To install Windows NT on a larger disk, follow the instructions in the Microsoft Knowledge Base article at *http://support.microsoft.com/support/kb/articles/q197/6/67.asp*.

32 GB

An Award BIOS dated earlier than June, 1999 does not recognize drives larger than 32 GB. Current versions of the Award BIOS no longer have this limit. Many motherboard manufacturers have posted updates for their products that use an Award BIOS.

137 GB

This is an absolute limit that results from the 28-bit addressing used by ATA, which limits the total number of sectors to 268,435,456. With standard 512-byte sectors, 137,438,953,472 bytes is the largest drive that can be supported by ATA.

BIOS upgrades for extended Int13 support

The best solution for all of these capacity limits (except the absolute 137 GB limit) is to update the BIOS or to buy a motherboard with a more recent BIOS. The best (and possibly only) place to get an updated BIOS is from the manufacturer of your computer or system board. This is true because, although many manufacturers use BIOSes based on the Phoenix, Award, and AMI core BIOS code, they may have made changes to it that render an updated generic BIOS unusable and may have also impacted the extended Int13 support present in the core BIOS code. That said, here are the BIOS levels that eliminate limitations through the 8.4 GB limit:

American Megatrends, Inc. (AMI)

AMI BIOSes dated January 1, 1998, or later include extended Int13 support. Contact AMI directly for update information. (*http://www.ami.com* or 800-828-9264)

Award

Award BIOSes dated after November 1997 include extended Int13 support and can be used with disks larger than 8.4 GB. Award recommends contacting Unicore for BIOS updates. (*http://www.unicore.com* or 800-800-2467).

Phoenix

All Phoenix BIOSes are Version 4. It's the revision level that counts. Phoenix BIOSes at Revision 6 or higher have extended Int13 support. Phoenix recommends contacting Micro Firmware for BIOS updates. (*http://www.firmware. com* or 800-767-5465)

ATA and RAID

RAID (*Redundant Array of Inexpensive Disks*) is a means by which data is distributed over two or more physical hard drives to improve performance and increase data safety. A RAID can survive the loss of any one drive without losing data. Until recently, RAID was a SCSI-only technology largely limited by cost to use on servers. That changed when Promise Technology (*http://www.promise.com*) introduced a line of ATA-based RAID controllers that combine the benefits of RAID with the low cost of ATA, making RAID a realistic alternative for small servers and individual PCs.

We've been using a $100 Promise FastTrak66 card for some time now to mirror two large ATA drives. Anything written to one drive is automatically mirrored to the other drive. If either drive fails, the other drive continues to function without loss of data. Although such an array leaves only 50% of the installed disk space visible to the operating system, the low cost of ATA drives means this is a small price to pay for improved performance and greatly enhanced data safety. If you're building a small server, or even if you just want to protect the data on your standalone PC, look into the Promise RAID products.

SCSI

We'll devote less space to SCSI than IDE, because IDE drives dominate the PC platform but we will try to hit the high points of SCSI. *SCSI (Small Computer Systems Interface)* is a general-purpose I/O bus that is used in PCs primarily for connecting hard disks and other storage devices, and secondarily for connecting a variety of devices, including scanners, printers, and other external peripherals. Although common in the Apple Macintosh world, SCSI has remained a niche product in PCs, limited primarily to network servers, high-performance workstations, and other applications where the higher performance and flexibility of SCSI are enough to offset the lower cost of ATA.

SCSI Standards

SCSI is confusing because of the proliferation of terms, many of which refer to similar things in different ways or to different things in similar ways. There are actually three SCSI standards, each of which refers not to any particular implementation, but to the document that defines that level.

SCSI-1
> The SCSI standard was adopted in 1986 and is now obsolete. Originally called simply SCSI, but now officially SCSI-1, this standard defines a high-level method of communicating between devices, an *Initiator* (normally a computer) and a *Target* (normally a disk drive or other peripheral). SCSI-1 permits data to be transferred in *asynchronous mode* (*unclocked mode*) or *synchronous mode* (*clocked mode*), although commands and messages are always transferred in asynchronous mode. SCSI-1 uses the low-density 50-pin connector for both internal and external connections. The external low-density 50-pin connector is also referred to as the Centronics SCSI connector. SCSI-1 is a single comprehensive document that defines all physical and protocol layers, and is published as ANSI X3.131-1986.

SCSI-2
> SCSI-2 was adopted in 1994, and many current SCSI devices are SCSI-2 compliant. SCSI-2 updated the SCSI-1 standard to include faster data rates and

to more tightly define message and command structures for improved compatibility between SCSI devices. SCSI-2 devices use various connectors, depending on the width and speed of the implementation. SCSI-2 is a single comprehensive document that defines all physical and protocol layers, and is published as ANSI X3.131-1994.

SCSI-3

The monolithic documents that describe SCSI-1 and SCSI-2 became too unwieldy for the greatly expanded SCSI-3 specification, so beginning with the SCSI-3 specification the document was separated into multiple layered components, each defined by an individual standards document. Together, these individual documents comprise the SCSI-3 standard, which is now officially referred to as simply SCSI.

For more information about SCSI standards, visit the SCSI Trade Association (*http:// www.scsita.org*).

SCSI Implementations

SCSI implementations are characterized by their width (bits transferred per clock cycle), clock rate, and by their overall throughput, which is the product of those two figures. Bus width determines how much data is transferred per clock cycle, and may be either of the following:

Narrow SCSI

Narrow SCSI transfers one byte per clock cycle, using a one-byte wide data bus on a 50-pin parallel interface, which is defined by SCSI-1.

Wide SCSI

Wide SCSI transfers two bytes per clock cycle, using a two-byte wide data bus on a 68-pin parallel interface, which is defined by the SCSI-3 SPI document. Although SCSI-3 allows bus widths greater than two bytes, all current Wide SCSI implementations use two bytes.

The *signaling rate* (or *clock rate*), properly denominated in *MegaTransfers/Second* (*MT/s*) but more commonly stated in MHz, specifies how frequently transfers occur. Various SCSI implementations use signaling rates of 5 MHz, 10 MHz, 20 MHz, 40 MHz, and 80 MHz, which are given the following names:

SCSI

SCSI when used without qualification to describe a transfer rate refers to the 5 MT/s transfer rate defined in SCSI-1. Because SCSI-1 supports only narrow (8-bit) transfers, SCSI-1 transfers 5 MB/s (5 MT/s × 1 byte/transfer).

Fast SCSI

Fast SCSI describes the 10 MT/s transfer rate defined in SCSI-2. Used with a narrow interface (called Fast Narrow SCSI or simply Fast SCSI), transfers 10 MB/s (10 MT/s × 1 byte/transfer). Used with a wide interface, called Fast Wide SCSI, transfers 20 MB/s (10 MT/s × 2 bytes/transfer).

Ultra SCSI (Fast-20 SCSI)

Ultra SCSI, also called Fast-20 SCSI, describes the 20 MT/s transfer rate defined in an extension to the SCSI-3 SPI document (ANSI standard X3T10/1071D revision 6). Used with a narrow interface (called Narrow Ultra SCSI or simply Ultra

SCSI), transfers 20 MB/s (20 MT/s×1 byte/transfer). Used with a wide interface (called Wide Ultra SCSI), transfers 40 MB/s (20 MT/s×2 bytes/transfer).

Ultra2 SCSI (Fast-40 SCSI)

Ultra2 SCSI, also called Fast-40 SCSI, describes the 40 MT/s transfer rate defined in SCSI-3 SPI-2. Used with a narrow interface (called Narrow Ultra2 SCSI or simply Ultra2 SCSI), transfers 40 MB/s (40 MT/s×1 byte/transfer). Used with a wide interface (called Wide Ultra2 SCSI or U2W SCSI), transfers 80 MB/s (40 MT/s×2 bytes/transfer).

Ultra3 SCSI (Fast-80DT SCSI)

Ultra3 SCSI, also called Fast-80DT SCSI or Ultra160 SCSI, describes the 80 MT/s transfer rate defined in SCSI-3 SPI-3. Only wide interfaces are defined for speeds higher than Ultra2 SCSI, which means Ultra3 SCSI transfers 160 MB/s (80 MT/s×2 bytes/transfer).

In addition to being differentiated by bus width and signaling speed, SCSI devices may be one of two general types, which are incompatible with each other:

Single-ended

Single-ended SCSI (SE SCSI) devices use *unbalanced transmission* (one wire per signal), which minimizes the number of wires required in the connecting cable, but also limits maximum bus length and maximum data rates. Until recently, all PC-class SCSI devices were SE, but SE SCSI devices are now obsolescent.

Differential

Differential SCSI devices use *balanced transmission* (two wires per signal, plus and minus), which reduces the effects of noise on the SCSI channel. This requires a more expensive cable with additional wires, but extends the maximum allowable bus length and allows increased data rates. Originally, differential SCSI was used only on large computers, where the greater bus length of differential SCSI allows connecting mainframes and minicomputers to external disk farms. In modified form, differential SCSI is now commonplace on PCs. Two forms of differential SCSI exist.

High-Voltage Differential

High-Voltage Differential SCSI (HVD SCSI) was originally called simply *Differential SCSI* before the advent of Low-Voltage Differential SCSI. HVD SCSI is very seldom used in the PC environment.

Low-Voltage Differential

Low-Voltage Differential SCSI (LVD SCSI) devices use differential transmission, but at lower voltage than HVD SCSI devices. LVD is where the action is in high-performance PC SCSI drives now, and where it is likely to remain for the foreseeable future. Although they are technically unrelated, LVD and U2W are often used as synonyms because most U2W hard drives use LVD transmission.

Table 13-5 summarizes implementations of SCSI you may encounter. For Narrow SCSI implementations, the word "Narrow" in the name is optional, and is assumed unless Wide is specified. The Clock column lists the signaling rate in MT/s. The DTR column lists the total Data Transfer Rate, which is the product of the signaling rate and the bus width in bytes. The Devices column lists the maximum number of SCSI devices that may be connected to the SCSI bus, including the host adapter. The maximum number of devices supported on any Narrow SCSI bus is 8, and on a Wide SCSI bus is 16. Because a longer bus results in signal degradation, the number of devices supported is sometimes determined by the length of the bus. For example, Wide Ultra SCSI supports up to eight devices on a 1.5 meter (~4.9 foot) bus, but only four devices (host adapter plus three drives) on a bus twice that length.

Table 13-5: SCSI Implementations

| Name | Clock | Width | DTR | Bus Length (meters) | | | Devices |
				SE	LVD	HVD	
(Narrow) SCSI-1	5 MHz	8 bit	5 MB/s	6	o	25	8
Fast (Narrow) SCSI	10 MHz	8 bit	10 MB/s	3	o	25	8
Fast Wide SCSI	10 MHz	16 bit	20 MB/s	3	o	25	16
(Narrow) Ultra SCSI	20 MHz	8 bit	20 MB/s	1.5	o	25	8
(Narrow) Ultra SCSI	20 MHz	8 bit	20 MB/s	3	o	o	4
Wide Ultra SCSI	20 MHz	16 bit	40 MB/s	o	o	25	16
Wide Ultra SCSI	20 MHz	16 bit	40 MB/s	1.5	o	o	8
Wide Ultra SCSI	20 MHz	16 bit	40 MB/s	3	o	o	4
(Narrow) Ultra2 SCSI	40 MHz	8 bit	40 MB/s	o	12	25	8
Wide Ultra2 SCSI	40 MHz	16 bit	80 MB/s	o	12	25	16
Ultra3 SCSI (Ultra160)	80 MHz	16 bit	160 MB/s	o	12	o	16
Ultra320 SCSI	160 MHz	16 bit	320 MB/s	o	12	o	16

SCSI Cables and Connectors

SCSI devices use a variety of connectors. Until recently, there was little standardization, and no way to judge the SCSI standard of a device by looking at its connector. For example, current U2W devices use the 68-pin high-density connector, but that connector has also been used by old Digital Equipment Corporation (DEC) for single-ended devices. By convention, all SCSI devices have female connectors and all SCSI cables have male connectors. This rule is generally followed by modern SCSI devices intended for use on PCs, although it is frequently violated by very old PC devices and by devices intended for use outside the PC environment. Mainstream SCSI devices use the following cables and connectors:

DB25 SCSI connector
> Some scanners, external Zip drives, and other Narrow SCSI devices use the DB25 SCSI connector, also called the Apple-Style SCSI connector. Unfortunately, this is the same connector used on PCs for parallel ports, which makes it easy to confuse the purpose of the connector on the PC. Devices are linked using a straight-through DB25M-to-DB25M cable.

50-pin Centronics SCSI connector
> The 50-pin Centronics SCSI connector is also called the Low-density 50-pin SCSI connector or the SCSI-1 connector and resembles a standard Centronics

printer connector. Male SCSI-1 connectors are used on external cables for SCSI-1 devices, and by internal ribbon cables for both SCSI-1 and SCSI-2 devices.

Micro DB50 SCSI connector

The Micro DB50 SCSI connector is also called the Mini DB50 SCSI connector, the 50-pin High-density SCSI connector, or the SCSI-2 connector. Male SCSI-2 connectors are used on external cables for SCSI-2 devices.

Micro DB68 SCSI connector

The Micro DB68 SCSI connector is also called the Mini DB68 SCSI connector, the 68-pin High-density SCSI connector, or the SCSI-3 connector. Male SCSI-3 connectors are used on external cables and internal ribbon cables for SCSI-3 devices.

Ultra Micro DB68 SCSI connector

The Ultra Micro DB68 SCSI connector is also called the Very High-density condensed 68-pin SCSI connector or the VHDCI SCSI connector, and is also often incorrectly called the SCSI-4 connector or the SCSI-5 connector. The VHDCI SCSI connector is used by Ultra160 SCSI devices.

Single Connector Attachment (SCA)

The SCA interface, originally used primarily in large IBM computers, uses a standard 80-pin connector that provides power, configuration settings (such as SCSI ID), and termination of the SCSI bus. SCA was designed to allow hot-swappable drives to connect directly to the SCSI bus via an SCA backplane connector, without requiring separate power or interface cables. SCA interface drives can be connected to a standard 50- or 68-pin connector on a PC SCSI host adapter by using an SCA-to-SCSI adapter, which is readily available from most computer stores and mail-order sources.

SCSI IDs and Termination

SCSI uses a logical bus topology, which means that all SCSI devices on a single SCSI bus connect to and share that bus. The logical bus is implemented with a daisy-chain, whereby the first device connects to the second device, which connects to the third device, and so on. The physical cabling used to implement this daisy-chain varies with the type of SCSI device, as follows:

- Many external SCSI devices and some older internal SCSI devices have two narrow SCSI connectors. To build the daisy-chain, you use a cable to connect the "out" SCSI connector on the first device to the "in" SCSI connector on the second device, the "out" SCSI connector on the second device to the "in" SCSI connector on the third device, and so on.

- Some external SCSI devices and most recent internal SCSI devices have only one SCSI connector. These devices connect to a cable that contains multiple device connectors, similar to a standard IDE cable. You can connect as many devices to these cables are there are positions. In effect, the daisy-chaining is done within the cable itself.

Each SCSI device on a bus is identified by a unique *SCSI ID*. On a Narrow SCSI bus, the SCSI ID must be in the range of 0 through 7, inclusive. By convention, the SCSI host adapter is assigned SCSI ID7, the primary hard disk (if present) is assigned SCSI ID0, and the secondary hard disk (if present) SCSI ID1. A Wide SCSI bus doubles the number of supported devices from 8 to 16, using SCSI IDs 0 through 15, with the same default assignments.

A SCSI bus must be terminated on both ends to prevent *Standing Wave Reflection* (*SWR*). When a SCSI signal on an unterminated bus reaches the end of the cable, it is reflected back toward the source, which causes errors because SCSI devices cannot differentiate between the reflected wave and the original signal. Two types of terminators exist:

Passive SCSI terminator

A *passive SCSI terminator* is simply a resistor pack that roughly matches the impedance of the SCSI bus. It is connected to the end of the bus, where it absorbs signals before they can be reflected, preventing SWR. A passive terminator relies on the SCSI host adapter to provide consistent voltage to the bus. If that voltage fluctuates, an impedance mismatch occurs between the cable and the terminator, which allows SWR and may cause errors on the bus. Passive terminators are used by SCSI-1 and some SCSI-2 devices.

Active SCSI terminator

An *active SCSI terminator* uses a live electronic circuit (a voltage regulator and associated circuitry) to maintain constant impedance at the end of the SCSI bus. Because active termination can regulate impedance much more accurately than a simple resistor, voltage fluctuations from the host adapter cannot cause the wide impedance swings that may occur with a passive terminator. More tightly controlled impedance translates into a more stable SCSI bus that allows higher speeds without errors. Many SCSI-2 and all SCSI-3 devices use active termination.

The method used to terminate the SCSI bus depends on the type of cable and devices used on the bus, as follows:

Standalone termination

Some external SCSI devices and a few internal SCSI devices have two SCSI connectors, which allows those devices to be physically daisy-chained by using separate cables to connect to the previous and next devices in the SCSI chain. Although some of these devices can be terminated by setting a switch or jumper to activate an internal terminator, many require instead using a separate SCSI terminator pack, which is connected to the unused SCSI connector on the last physical device in the chain.

Device-based termination

Most SCSI devices other than LVD/U2W drives contain internal SCSI terminators, which are activated by setting a switch or jumper. When connecting such devices, activate termination for the last physical devices on each end of the chain, and make sure that all intermediate devices have termination disabled. On most drives, disable termination by connecting the jumper labeled Terminator Disable (or similar) or disconnecting the jumper labeled Terminator Enable (or similar). On some older drives, the terminator is a resistor pack that you physically install or remove to enable or disable termination.

Cable-based termination

LVD/U2W drives make no provision for manual termination. If those devices are used as the last device on an SE SCSI bus, termination must be supplied by external means. For this reason, special cables are available that have built-in terminators.

Automatic termination

Some SCSI devices, particularly host adapters, sense whether they are the last device on the bus, and enable or disable termination automatically as appropriate.

Technically, in addition to terminating the last physical device on the bus, you should also terminate the cable itself if unused positions exist beyond the last device. In practice, we have never bothered to do so and have never experienced problems attributable to not doing so. Usually, we just connect the last device to the last cable position, which sidesteps the problem.

When configuring SCSI devices, do not confuse *termination* with *termination power*. The former specifies which is the last device on the bus. The latter specifies the power source for termination, which may be the device or the SCSI bus. Configuring termination power incorrectly may cause various symptoms, including the system failing to boot or locking up immediately after boot.

A special case exists when you have both internal and external devices connected to a single SCSI bus. In this case, the host adapter, which is ordinarily on the end of the bus and therefore terminated, is instead in the middle of the bus and must not be terminated. In this situation, turn off termination for the host adapter, and terminate the last physical device on the internal chain and the last physical device on the external chain.

Incorrect termination is one of the three most common causes of problems when installing SCSI devices (the others being assigning duplicate SCSI IDs and using poor-quality cables). Failing to terminate one or both ends of the SCSI bus may cause various symptoms, including one or more devices not being accessible, frequent errors and retries, slow throughput, or a complete failure of the SCSI bus. Another common error is terminating the bus at both ends *and* in the middle. This usually occurs when someone adds a terminated device to an existing bus and forgets to disable termination on one of the existing devices. If the new device is added to the end of the chain without disabling termination on the device that formerly ended the chain, the new device is not recognized. If the new device is added to the middle of the chain, the new device is recognized, but all existing devices downstream of the new device disappear.

On older SCSI devices, SCSI IDs and device termination are usually assigned manually by setting jumpers or switches on the devices, or, on external devices, by turning a small dial. Most newer SCSI devices support *SCSI Configured AutoMagically* (*SCAM*), which is essentially Plug-N-Play for SCSI.

SCAM-compliant devices

SCAM-compliant SCSI devices automatically report their current SCSI ID and termination status to the host adapter, and allow the host adapter to change those settings dynamically. In a system with a SCAM-compliant host adapter and all SCAM-compliant devices, you never need to set SCSI ID or termination manually.

SCAM-compatible devices

SCAM-compatible SCSI devices automatically report their current SCSI ID and termination status to the host adapter, but do not allow the host adapter to change those settings. In a system with a SCAM-compliant host adapter and a mix of SCAM-compliant and SCAM-compatible devices, you ordinarily do not need to set SCSI IDs manually, because the host adapter works around the IDs in use by SCAM-compatible devices by assigning unused IDs to the SCAM-compliant devices. You may, however, need to set termination manually, because SCAM cannot reset an improperly terminated SCAM-compatible device.

Non-SCAM devices

Non-SCAM SCSI devices neither report their current SCSI ID and termination status to the host adapter, nor allow the host adapter to change those settings. In a system with all non-SCAM devices, you must set SCSI ID and termination manually for each device. In a system with a SCAM-compliant host adapter and one or more non-SCAM devices, you must disable SCAM on the host adapter and configure all devices manually to avoid conflicts that may occur if SCAM unwittingly assigns the same SCSI ID to a SCAM-compliant device that is already being used by a non-SCAM device.

SCSI Interoperability

SCSI host adapters and drives used in PCs are in theory interoperable whatever their age and level of standards compliance. That is, if you have the proper cable, you can connect a new Ultra Wide SCSI hard drive to an old SCSI-1 host adapter and it will work, albeit at only the 5 MB/s transfer rate supported by the old host adapter. Similarly, you can connect an elderly SCSI-1 CD-ROM drive to a U2W host adapter and expect it to work. But just because you can do something doesn't mean you want to. Keep the following in mind if you mix SCSI device types:

- All devices on a SCSI bus communicate at the speed of the slowest device. For example, if you connect a U2W (80 MB/s) hard disk and a Fast SCSI (20 MB/s) CD-ROM drive to the same bus, the hard disk operates at 20 MB/s, which may significantly degrade hard disk performance. In general, assuming that your hard disks are all of the same type, the best practice is to place all hard drives on one host adapter or channel and put other SCSI devices (like CD-ROM drives, tape drive, and scanners) on a another, slower channel or host adapter.

- Although you *can* connect both wide and narrow devices to the same channel on a wide host adapter, you must install the wide devices physically closest to the host adapter, and use a cable converter that terminates the wide portion of the cable between the last wide device and the first narrow device.

- The presence of one SE device on the SCSI bus forces all other devices on the bus to operate in SE mode.

- Most LVD drives make no provision for setting termination on the drive and hard code termination power to Drive Supplies the Bus, both of which are standard practice for LVD host adapters, but may be incompatible with earlier host adapters. If you need to mix SE and LVD devices on one channel, construct the daisy-chain such that the final device is an SE device, which allows you to use its built-in terminator to terminate the channel. If for some reason the only choice is to put an LVD device as the final device on the cable, the only option is to use a cable with built-in termination.

ATA Versus SCSI

Relative to ATA, SCSI has the following advantages:

Performance
ATA drives simply cannot compare to SCSI drives in performance. In our testing, the *slowest* SCSI drives we tested were faster than the *fastest* ATA drives, particularly under Windows NT/2000, Linux, and other multitasking operating systems. This held true across the board, even when we tested an elderly, mid-range Seagate Fast Wide SCSI drive against the fastest of the current crop of ATA/66 drives. SCSI is simply faster. Don't let anyone convince you otherwise.

Bandwidth and concurrency
SCSI provides usable bandwidth at the nominal value stated. For example, an 80 MB/s U2W SCSI channel in fact provides usable bandwidth of 80 MB/s, which may be shared among the devices on the channel. And given the actual 20 MB/s to 30 MB/s throughput of current hard disks, that means you can run two or three hard disks on a U2W channel—all of which can read and/or write data simultaneously—without bandwidth becoming an issue. This is not true of ATA, because ATA allows only one device to use the channel at a time, regardless of how much bandwidth may be going unused. For example, if you connect two ATA/66 drives to an ATA/66 interface, and each drive has actual throughput of 25 MB/s, the data rate on that channel will never exceed 25 MB/s.

Reliability
In our experience, SCSI devices are simply more reliable than equivalent ATA devices, both in terms of the robustness of the devices themselves and the reliability of communication on the channel. For example, with some effort, an ATAPI CD burner can be configured to run reliably without generating excessive coasters, whereas an equivalent SCSI burner simply works. We also believe that most SCSI devices are better-built than many ATA devices, although we have no hard evidence to prove this speculation.

Number of devices supported

A standard embedded dual-channel ATA interface supports at most four ATA/ ATAPI devices, two per channel. A Narrow SCSI interface supports seven devices (besides the host adapter itself), and a Wide SCSI interface supports up to 15 devices. Many PCs now include a second hard disk, a tape drive, a CD burner, and so on. The ATAPI 4-device limit may force trade-offs that you'd prefer not to make, such as removing the CD-ROM drive when you install a CD burner, or replacing a hard disk rather than adding a second hard disk. SCSI avoids this problem.

Resource demands

ATA uses system resources relatively inefficiently. An ATA interface requires one interrupt per two-device channel, whereas a SCSI host adapter supports as many as 15 devices on one bus, using only one interrupt. On older systems with PIO hard drives, the difference in CPU utilization can be immense. PIO mode drives under load may demand 80% to 95% of the CPU, whereas SCSI drives (or ATA drives operating in DMA mode) may require from 0.5% to 2%.

Cable length and support for external devices

ATA is limited to 1.5 foot (0.46 m) cables and officially supports only internal devices (although various workarounds are available that allow using ATA devices outside the main system enclosure). Depending on the version, SCSI supports cable lengths from about five feet (1.5 m) to 39.4 feet (12 m) or more. Adding external SCSI devices is no harder than installing internal ones—less so, actually, because you don't even need to open the PC case.

New technologies ship first in SCSI

Interface issues aside, the simple fact is that manufacturers treat ATA products as mass-market items, whereas their SCSI products are premium items. That means that new technologies always arrive first in SCSI. For example, 7,200 RPM hard disks were available in SCSI long before the first 7,200 RPM ATA drive shipped. Now, with 7,200 RPM ATA drives the fastest available, 7,200 RPM SCSI drives are the entry-level and mid-range, with 10,000 RPM drives readily available and 15,000 RPM drives on the near horizon. The same is true for such things as very fast head actuator mechanisms. They ship first in SCSI, sell at a premium there for a while, and then gradually make their way into mass-market ATA drives.

SCSI also has the following disadvantages:

Cost

More than any other factor, the cost of SCSI keeps it from becoming a mainstream PC technology. SCSI hard disks typically sell at a significant premium over ATA drives with similar specifications. For example, as of June 2000, 20 GB Seagate Barracuda ATA II drives sold for about $150, while 18 GB Barracuda U2W drives sold for about $300. Buying a SCSI host adapter bumps the cost higher still, with good host adapters costing $100 to $250.

Complex installation and configuration

ATA devices are simple to configure—set one jumper to specify Master or Slave, and connect the device to the Primary or Secondary ATA interface. Before the introduction of ATA/66, which requires a special 40-pin, 80-wire cable, ATA devices all used the same cables and connectors. Even with this change, installing and configuring ATA devices remains a straightforward task. SCSI, conversely, can be quite complex. The diversity of SCSI standards, cables, and connectors, along with the need to specify SCSI IDs and to terminate the SCSI bus properly means there is more confusion and more room for errors when installing and configuring SCSI. For example, it is quite possible to buy a SCSI host adapter and a SCSI drive that are, if technically compatible, functionally mismatched. It is also possible to buy a SCSI cable that will not physically connect to the host adapter, the drive, or both. In practice, however, the widespread use of SCAM and the *de facto* standardization of cables and connectors has simplified installing and configuring SCSI to the level of ATA, at least for recent host adapters and devices.

Limited support by BIOSes and operating systems
   Whereas ATA interface is rigidly defined and supported natively by all BIOSes and operating systems, SCSI remains an add-on technology. In practice, this is a smaller problem than it might seem, as SCSI host adapter manufacturers provide loadable supplemental BIOSes, ROM-based configuration and diagnostics utilities, and solid drivers for all common operating systems.

On balance, the overriding issue is cost. If you can afford SCSI, get it. For shared disk volumes, SCSI drives stand up to much higher loads without bogging down. For PCs that run multitasking operating systems such as Windows NT/2000 and Linux, SCSI provides much snappier response. Before you spend several hundred dollars buying the fastest processor available, consider buying a slower processor and spending the extra money on SCSI drives. If most of your work is processor-bound, get the faster processor and ATA drives. But if much of your work is disk-bound, you'll find that the system with the slower processor and SCSI drives will provide better performance.

Our Picks

Here are the IDE and SCSI host adapters we use and recommend:

IDE host adapter
   Promise Technology Ultra66. Current motherboards and systems provide embedded ATA/33 and/or ATA/66 interfaces, but you need an add-on IDE adapter to upgrade a system with an older motherboard or one in which an embedded ATA adapter has failed. We use an Ultra66, for example, in our SE440BX-based test bed system, which supports only ATA/33 natively. Also, because the Ultra66 can be configured as tertiary and quaternary ATA interfaces, it allows you to use up to four IDE devices in addition to the four supported by the embedded motherboard ATA interface. If you need an add-on IDE host adapter, buy the $30 Promise Ultra66. (*http://www.promise.com*)

IDE RAID host adapter
   Promise Technology FastTrak66. RAID has historically been limited to SCSI-based systems—usually servers or high-end workstations—but the $100 Promise FastTrak66 brings the advantages of RAID to systems that use inexpensive IDE drives. The FastTrak66 supports RAID 0 striping for performance, RAID 1 mirroring for data security, and RAID 0+1 to provide both. With fast

IDE hard disks selling for well under $10/GB, using this inexpensive RAID adapter with a second hard disk allows you to build a fully-redundant disk subsystem at minimal cost, making data loss due to drive failure a thing of the past. We use the Promise FastTrak66 in RAID 1 mode in one of our storage servers, where it has operated for months under heavy load without problems. We have extensively tested all supported modes—RAID 0, RAID 1, RAID 0+1, and spanning—and found that all work exactly as advertised. We consider the FastTrak66 an excellent solution for high-end personal systems and small workgroup servers.

SCSI host adapter (single hard disk)

Adaptec 2930U2. For systems with one LVD SCSI hard drive and other SCSI devices such as CD-ROM, DVD-ROM, and CD-R(W) drives, choose the $225 Adaptec 2930U, which is optimized for use with one LVD hard disk, and supports multiple supplementary SCSI devices like CD-R drives, tape drives, scanners, and so on. Barbara uses an Adaptec 2930U2W in her main system. (*http://www.adaptec.com*)

SCSI host adapter (multiple hard disks)

Adaptec 2940U2W. For small servers or workstations with multiple SCSI hard disks, choose the $260 Adaptec 2940U2W, which is optimized to support multiple LVD hard disks, and also supports multiple supplementary SCSI devices. Robert uses an Adaptec 2940U2W in his main system.

Finally, for times when you use an ATA hard disk, but need an inexpensive 10 MB/s (SCSI-1, SCSI-2, Fast-SCSI) host adapter to support other peripherals, we recommend the following:

PCI SCSI host adapter (non-hard disk peripherals)

Adaptec 2906. This $50 bus mastering PCI SCSI host adapter is perfectly adequate to support non-hard disk SCSI peripherals such as a CD drive, tape drive, or scanner.

ISA SCSI host adapter (non-hard disk peripherals)

Adaptec 1505A. This $40 ISA SCSI host adapter is a good choice when you need to connect external SCSI devices to an ISA-only PC. Note that this host adapter supports neither Plug-N-Play nor DMA transfers, so pay close attention to the instructions when installing it.

We constantly test and review new equipment. For the latest information about what we currently use, visit:

http://www.hardwareguys.com/picks/harddisk.html

CHAPTER 14

Hard Disk Drives

Replacing the original hard disk or adding a hard disk is one of the most common upgrades. It's easy to do and a very cost effective way to extend the life of a PC. This chapter explains what you need to know to choose, install, and configure hard disks and interfaces.

How Hard Disks Work

All hard disks are constructed similarly. A central *spindle* supports one or more *platters*, which are thin, flat, circular objects made of metal or glass, substances chosen because they are rigid and do not expand and contract much as the temperature changes. Each platter has two *surfaces*, and each surface is coated with a magnetic medium. Most drives have multiple platters mounted concentrically on the spindle, like layers of a cake. The central spindle rotates at several thousand revolutions per minute, rotating the platters in tandem with it.

A small gap separates each platter from its neighbors, which allows a *read-write head* mounted on an *actuator arm* to fit between the platters. Each surface has its own read-write head, and those heads "float" on the cushion of air caused by the Bernoulli Effect that results from the rapid rotation of the platter. When a disk is rotating, the heads fly above the surfaces at a distance of only millionths of an inch. The *head actuator assembly* resembles a comb with its teeth inserted between the platters, and moves all of the heads in tandem radially toward or away from the center of rotation.

The small separation between the heads and surfaces means that a tiny dust particle could cause a catastrophic head crash, so these components are sealed within a *head/disk assembly*, or *HDA*. The sealed HDA contains air filters that allow air pressure to equalize between the HDA and the surrounding environment. Opening an HDA other than in a factory clean-room is a certain way to destroy a disk drive.

Each surface is divided into concentric *tracks* that can be read from or written to by that surface's head. Each surface on a modern disk drive contains thousands of tracks. Each track is divided into many *sectors*, which store 512 bytes of data. Old drives used the same number of sectors on every track, typically 17 or 26. Modern drives take advantage of the fact that tracks near the outer edge of the platter are longer than those near the center by storing more sectors on the outer tracks.

All tracks that are immediately above and below each other form a *cylinder*. If a drive has eight surfaces, each with 2,048 tracks, that drive contains 2,048 cylinders, with eight tracks per cylinder. The concept of cylinders is important because it determines how data is written to and read from the drive. When a drive writes a file that is larger than one track, it fills the current track and then writes the reminder of the file sequentially to the next available track within that cylinder. Only if the capacity of the current cylinder is exceeded does the drive move the heads to the next available cylinder. The drive writes data in this fashion because selecting a different read-write head is an electronic operation, which occurs quickly, while moving the heads to a different track is a mechanical operation that requires significantly more time.

The heads write data to the surfaces in exactly the same way that data is written to a floppy disk or magnetic tape. Each track contains myriad discrete positions, called *magnetic domains*, that can each store a single bit of information as a binary 0 or 1. When writing, the head exercises a magnetic flux to alter the state of a domain to a 0 or 1, as appropriate. When reading, the head simply determines the existing state of a domain.

Because they reside in such close proximity, it is non-trivial for a head to locate the correct track and sector. Early drives used a stepper-motor assembly similar to that still used on floppy drives. A stepper motor simply moves the heads to where the track is supposed to be, without reference to its actual location. On stepper-motor drives, thermal expansion and contraction gradually cause the expected locations of tracks to drift out of alignment with their actual physical location, which requires frequent low-level formatting of the drives to return them to proper alignment. This is the main reason that stepper-motor actuators are no longer used on current drives.

Later hard disk drives used a voice-coil actuator mechanism in conjunction with a dedicated servo surface. For example, a drive that had eight surfaces used only seven of these to store data, and dedicated the eighth surface to servo information that helped locate the correct track. A voice-coil drive does not seek to an absolute track position. Instead, the head actuator assembly seeks to the approximate position where it expects the track to be located. The servo head then fine tunes the positioning by locating the servo track that corresponds to the desired track. Because all tracks in a cylinder must necessarily be aligned, locating the correct servo track automatically also locates the correct data cylinder. Early voice coil drives were effective and not subject to thermal drift, but designers hated wasting an entire surface on servo data. All current drives use *embedded servo* information, which means that no surface is dedicated to servo information. Instead, it is interspersed with data on normal data tracks, which allows every surface to be used to store data.

The hard disk drive connects to the PC via a controller interface. Early hard disk drives used a separate controller card that installed in an expansion slot and connected to the drive via ribbon cables. All modern disk drives, IDE and SCSI, have the controller embedded in the drive itself. A ribbon cable connects the drive to a connector located on the system board or to an expansion card that provides a connection point. Hard disk interface cards are not actually disk controllers, and are properly referred to as *host adapters*. They do not contain disk controller circuitry, but simply provide a connection point between the system bus and the disk controller embedded in the drive.

The disk controller serves as an intermediary between the system and the hard drive. When the system needs to read data from or write data to the drive, it issues commands to the controller, which translates those commands into a form understandable by the drive. The drive then supplies data to the controller during read operations, and accepts data from the controller during writes.

Choosing a Hard Disk

The good news about choosing a hard disk is that it's hard to choose a bad one. All major drive manufacturers—IBM, Fujitsu, Maxtor, Quantum, Seagate, Western Digital, and others—make high quality drives at similar price points for a given type and size drive. When you buy a hard disk in today's competitive market, you get what you pay for.

All drives are not the same, though, because manufacturers often have different lines of drives that vary in several respects, all of which affect performance and price. Within a given grade of drive, however, drives from different manufacturers are usually closely comparable in features, performance, and price. Neither is compatibility an issue, as it occasionally was in the early days of ATA. Any recent ATA hard disk coexists peacefully with any other recent ATA/ATAPI device, regardless of manufacturer. The same is generally true of SCSI drives. All of that said, we use Seagate and Maxtor IDE drives and Seagate SCSI drives when we have a choice.

Use the following guidelines when you choose a hard disk:

Choose the correct interface and standards
> The most important consideration in choosing a hard disk is whether to use ATA or SCSI, based on the issues we described in the preceding chapter. Once you make that decision, choose a drive that supports the proper standards.

> *ATA*
>> Any drive you buy should support at least ATA/ATAPI-4 UDMA Mode 2 (Ultra-DMA/33). Drives that support UDMA modes 3 and 4 (Ultra-DMA/66) sell for little or no price premium *per se*, although some economy drives support only Ultra-DMA/33, as much for market differentiation as anything. Ultra-DMA/33 and Ultra-DMA/66 drives are backward compatible with earlier modes, including PIO modes, so choose an Ultra-DMA/66 drive if one is available in the size and price range you want.

> *SCSI*
>> Buy only Ultra2 Wide SCSI (often labeled "U2W" or "LVD") hard disks, which cost little more than drives that use earlier SCSI standards, and provide higher performance. Ultra3 (160 MB/s) drives provide little advantage in standard PCs and are expensive. Purchase only SCAM-compliant drives.

Buy the right size drive

It's tempting to buy the largest drive available, but that's not always the best decision. Very large drives often have a much higher cost per megabyte than the mid-size drives. Also, the largest drives may have slower mechanisms than mid-size drives. So, in general, decide what performance level you need and are willing to pay for, and then buy a drive that meets those performance requirements, choosing the model based on its cost per megabyte. All of that said, it sometimes makes sense to buy the largest drive available despite its high cost per megabyte and slower performance, simply to conserve drive bays and ATA channels.

Choose the best rotation rate for your application

Rotation rate specifies how fast the drive spins. For years, all hard drives rotated at 3,600 RPM. Several years ago, drives that rotated at 5,400 or 7,200 RPM started to become available, initially for servers. This higher rotation speed has two benefits: first, a drive that rotates faster moves more data under the heads in a given amount of time, providing faster throughput. Second, the higher the rotation speed, the lower the latency. Nowadays, inexpensive ATA drives rotate at 5,400 RPM and mainstream ATA drives at 7,200 RPM. Although a few entry-level SCSI drives rotate at 5,400 RPM, mainstream models rotate at 7,200 RPM, and high-performance models at 10,000 RPM, with 15,000 RPM models on the immediate horizon. All other things being equal, drives with higher rotation speeds provide faster data access and transfer rates, but with correspondingly higher noise and heat. We recommend using 7,200 RPM models (ATA or SCSI) for all mainstream applications. Choose a 5,400 RPM ATA model only when cost is an overriding concern, and even then you'll save only a few dollars by buying a 5,400 RPM drive rather than a 7,200 RPM unit. Choose a 10,000 RPM SCSI model only if getting the highest possible performance outweighs the $100 to $200 additional cost of the drive relative to a 7,200 RPM model.

Give average seek/access times heavy weight if you work mostly with many small files

Seek time is a measure of how quickly the head actuator can reposition the heads to a different track. Statistically, for a random access, the drive heads on average have to move across one third of the disk surface. The time they require to do so is called the *average seek time*. Once the head arrives at the proper track, it must wait until the proper sector of that track arrives under the head before it can read or write data, which is called *latency*. Average latency is one half the time that the disk requires to perform a full revolution. A 7,200 RPM drive, for example, turns at 120 revolutions per second and requires 8.33 milliseconds (ms) for each full revolution. The *average latency* is one half of that, or 4.17 ms. The sum of average seek time and average latency is called *average access time*, and is the best measure of a drive's access performance. Do not compare average *seek* time of one drive to average *access* time of another. Because average latency is a fixed value that is determined solely by the drive's rotation speed, you can easily convert back and forth between average seek time and average access time to make sure you're comparing apples to apples. For an entry-level ATA drive, look for an average access time of 15 milliseconds (ms) or less. For a mainstream ATA drive, 12.5 ms. For a mainstream SCSI drive, 10.5 ms. For a high-performance SCSI drive, 9 ms.

Give data transfer rate heavy weight if you work mostly with large files

In most applications, *Data Transfer Rate* (*DTR*) is usually less important to overall performance than average access time. DTR does become crucial if you work primarily with relatively few large files (sequential access) rather than many smaller files (random access). DTR is determined by several factors, the most important of which are disk rotation speed, cache size, and the onboard circuitry. When comparing advertised data transfer rates, be aware that there are several possible ways to list them, including internal versus external and burst versus sustained. The various transfer rates of drives are normally well documented on the detailed specification sheets available on their web sites, and less well documented in typical marketing materials. Overall, the most important basis for comparison is the sustained transfer rate. Note that on drives that use more sectors on the larger outer tracks, transfer rates can vary significantly between inner and outer tracks. For example, a fast drive may specify transfer rates of 15 MB/s on inner tracks and 25 MB/s on outer tracks. For an entry-level ATA drive, look for average (inner and outer track) sustained transfer rate of 7.5 MB/s or higher. For a mainstream ATA drive, 15 MB/s. For SCSI drives, 20 MB/s or higher. Note that none of these sustained transfer rates are fast enough to saturate even ATA/33, let alone ATA/66 or U2W SCSI.

Get a model with large cache if it doesn't cost much more

Disk drives contain cache memory, which in theory provides benefits similar to those provided by L2 cache on a CPU. Low-end drives may have 64 KB or 128 KB cache, whereas mainstream drives typically have 256 KB to 512 KB cache, and high-performance SCSI drives may have 2 MB or more. Some manufacturers sell the same model drive with differing amounts of cache, often indicated by a different letter on the end of the model number. In our experience, larger caches have a relatively small impact on overall drive performance, and are not worth paying much for. For example, given two otherwise identical drive models, one with 128 KB cache and one with 512 KB cache, we might pay $5 or $10 more for the 512 KB model, but not more. Adding cache is cheap, but it doesn't provide the benefits of a fast head mechanism and a fast rotation rate, both of which are more expensive to implement.

Make sure the drive fits your computer

All drives use standard width/height dimensions and screw hole positions to allow them to fit standard mounting locations. Drives for standard PCs are available in two nominal widths, named for the size of the platters they use. Each width is available in different heights. Together, the width and height describe the form factor of the drive, as follows:

5.25"

Some drives, typically of large capacity, use the 5.25" form factor. These drives actually measure 6" wide and come in three heights. *Full-height* devices measure 3.25" vertically, and are relatively uncommon these days. About the only 5.25" full-height drives you may encounter are very large capacity SCSI hard disks intended for use in servers. *Half-height* drives measure 1.625" vertically, and are far more common. A few 5.25" drives have been made in *third-height* form, which measure 1" vertically. Any of these drives fits in standard 5.25" drive bays. All cases except some low-profile cases have at least one full-height 5.25" drive bay, which can also be used instead to hold two half-height 5.25" drives.

3.5"

Most hard drives use the 3.5" form factor. These drives actually measure 4" wide and come in two heights. Most drives are third-height, or 1" high. Some high-capacity 3.5" hard drives use the 1.625" high half-height form factor.

Pay attention to how much current the drive draws

Here's one that few people think about, but that can be critical. A drive that requires only five or six watts at idle or during read/write operations can easily require 30 watts or more when it spins up. Spinning up three or four ATA drives (or even one high-performance SCSI drive) may draw more current than your power supply can comfortably provide. Nearly all modern drives and BIOSes automatically support staged spin-up, whereby the Primary Master ATA drive (or Drive 0 on the SCSI chain) spins up first, with other devices spinning up only after enough time has passed to allow each earlier device to complete spin-up. However, not all drives and not all systems stage spin-up, so note the startup current requirements of a drive before you add it to a heavily loaded system. The current requirements of a drive are normally detailed in the technical specification sheets available on its web site.

Here are some things that you can safely ignore when shopping for a drive:

MTBF

Mean Time Between Failures (MTBF) is a technical measure of the expected reliability of a device. All modern ATA drives have extremely large MTBF ratings, often 50 years or more. That doesn't mean that the drive you buy will last 50 years. It does mean that any drive you buy will probably run for years (although some drives fail the day they are installed). The truth is that most hard drives nowadays are replaced not because they fail, but because they are no longer large enough. Ignore MTBF when you're shopping for a drive.

MTTR

Mean Time to Repair (MTTR) is another measure that has little application in the real world. MTTR specifies the average time required to repair a drive. Since nobody except companies that salvage data from dead drives actually repairs drives nowadays you can ignore MTTR.

Shock rating

Drives are rated in gravities (G) for the level of shock they can withstand in both operating and non-operating modes. For drives used in desktop systems, at least, you can ignore shock rating. All modern drives are remarkably resistant to damage if dropped. All of them break if you drop them hard enough.

Installing a Hard Disk

The following sections describe the steps required to install ATA and SCSI hard disks.

Installing an ATA Hard Disk

To install an ATA/IDE hard disk, you first physically install the drive in the PC and then configure CMOS Setup to recognize the drive. Each of these steps is described in the following sections.

Physical installation

The general procedures for installing any hard drive are similar, but the exact steps required vary according to the specific drive and case. Most cases contain *drive bays*, which form a part of the chassis structure designed to secure drives in place. Others use removable *drive cage* or *drive tray* arrangements, in which you first secure the drive to a removable carrier and then attach the carrier to the chassis. Whatever the arrangement, once you've removed the cover it will almost certainly be obvious to you how to physically secure the drive within the case. If not, refer to the hardware documentation.

On a well-designed case, the screws that secure the drive will be readily accessible on both sides. Some cases are so badly designed that you may have to remove the drive bay assembly itself, or even the system board to access the screws on one side of the drive. Once you have removed the cover and decided where and how you will physically install the drive, take the following steps:

1. If you are also installing an enhanced ATA interface card, configure that card per the maker's instructions, attach the IDE cable(s) to it, and install the card in an available slot. If that card will replace one or both embedded system board ATA interfaces, restart the system and use CMOS Setup to disable the system board ATA interfaces before you install the card.

2. Ground yourself, open the anti-static bag that contains the drive, and place the drive flat on top of the antistatic bag. Recent systems automatically determine the proper drive parameters by querying the drive directly. However, if you are installing the drive in an older system, write down the drive parameters listed on the drive in case the BIOS fails to identify the drive.

 Most manufacturers print the drive geometry and jumper settings on the drive itself, but some drives are not labeled. The manufacturer's web site is usually the best source for this information. If you can't find the information there, the Micro House SupportSource page (*http://www.supportsource.com/hdfind/hd.htm*) has settings for thousands of obsolete and current drives from every manufacturer we could think of except Rodime.

3. If necessary, visually examine any existing drives to determine how they are jumpered and to which IDE interface they connect. On recent systems, there's an easier way. BIOS Setup identifies ATA-3 (or later) compliant ATA/ATAPI devices by name, the channel to which they connect, and whether they are jumpered master or slave. Depending on the existing configuration, you may choose simply to add the new drive to a free channel, or you may need to rejumper

existing drives and/or move them to another interface. Use the following guide-lines to set master/slave jumpers when connecting ATA/ATAPI devices.

4. Make the hard disk from which the PC boots the Master on the Primary ATA channel.

   – To connect only one device to an ATA channel, configure it as Master (or Only), whether it is an ATA hard disk or an ATAPI CD-ROM or tape drive. Note that most ATAPI CD-ROM drives and many ATAPI tape drives are jumpered Slave by default on the assumption that they will be connected to an ATA channel that already has a Master hard drive on it. On most systems, an ATAPI Slave works properly as the only device on an ATA channel, and some BIOSes do not support ATAPI Masters, but the Master-less Slave configuration is technically not permitted. If an ATAPI device is not recognized after you change operating systems, suspect this as the cause.

   – To connect two ATA drives to an ATA channel, jumper one drive as Master and the other as Slave. The controller on the drive jumpered as Master controls both devices on the cable, so it usually makes sense to jumper the newer and presumably faster device as Master.

   – To connect two ATAPI devices to an ATA channel, jumper one drive as Master and the other as Slave. It doesn't matter which is which.

   – To connect an ATA hard drive and an ATAPI device to one ATA channel, jumper the ATA drive as Master and the ATAPI device as Slave. The reverse usually works, but is technically not permitted, and may cause problems if you later make changes to your system.

   – On an IDE cable with two device connectors, it doesn't matter which device you connect to which connector, so long as you make sure that pin 1 on the interface and each device is connected toward the red stripe on the cable. If you are connecting only one device to a cable with dual connectors, good practice suggests that you connect that one device to the end connector and leave the middle connector unused.

5. After you have jumpered the new drives (and rejumpered existing ones, if necessary), but before you mount the drive in the bay, connect the IDE cable to the new drive, making sure that the red stripe on the cable connects to pin 1 on both the drive and the adapter. It may or may not be easier to connect the power cable as well at this point.

6. Slide the new drive into a drive bay, but don't secure it with screws just yet. If you've set a jumper incorrectly, you may need to remove the drive to correct the problem. If you didn't connect the power cable earlier, do so now, making sure that it seats fully.

7. Leaving the cover off for now, give the system a quick visual check to make sure everything is connected properly. Connect the keyboard, mouse, and monitor if you'd previously disconnected them, then flip the power on to start the smoke test. You should hear the new drive spin up. If it's difficult to tell (which it often is with newer drives), you can put your fingertip against the drive and feel it spinning up. Watch the screen as the system starts, and invoke CMOS Setup.

CMOS Setup

After you've physically installed a new ATA hard drive, the next step is to get the PC to recognize it by configuring CMOS Setup. New BIOSes automatically detect and query attached ATA devices during boot. If your system has such a BIOS, it will display installed ATA devices by type, name, and model during the normal boot sequence as it detects them. If this occurs, it's generally safe to assume that the PC has automatically configured BIOS settings for optimum performance. If you have an older BIOS, you have to configure it manually to recognize the new drive. The exact steps required to do so vary according to the BIOS type and revision level, but the following general guidelines should suffice:

1. Display the BIOS Setup screen that lists installed devices. Any modern BIOS should list four devices—Primary Master/Slave and Secondary Master/Slave. If Setup has space for only two devices, you badly need a BIOS update. With recent BIOSes, all ATA drives—including the one you just installed—should be listed by device name, size and (perhaps) geometry, and ATAPI CD-ROM drives should be listed by name and type. If the drive you just installed is listed, the PC has configured that drive properly and you can use the operating system to partition and format the drive.

2. If the drive you just installed is not listed, try changing Drive Type for the channel where the new drive is installed from None or User to Auto, if that option is offered. The BIOS may or may not recognize the drive. If it doesn't do so immediately, try restarting the computer. If that doesn't work, but if the BIOS Setup main menu offers an option named IDE HDD Auto Detection (or something similar) invoke that option and then view BIOS Setup again to see if your new drive appears. If it does, you can use the operating system to partition and format the drive.

3. If the new drive still isn't listed, you'll have to configure it manually. Examine the options available for Mode, enter the drive parameters recommended by the manufacturer for that mode, and choose one of the following modes:

   Normal
   > Configures the drive to operate in CHS addressing mode, which limits the drive to 504 MB.

   Large
   > Configures the drive to use ECHS translation mode. Select this mode, which may instead be labeled Large, ECHS, Translation, or something similar, only if the BIOS does not offer LBA mode or if you are installing an older, non-LBA capable drive. Note that, because translation modes are not necessarily compatible between different BIOSes, you cannot safely move a hard drive configured to use translation mode on one machine to another machine, whose translation mode may be incompatible. If the two machines use compatible translation modes, everything may work properly. If not, the data will be scrambled beyond recovery when the second computer writes to the drive.

   LBA
   > Configures the drive to use Logical Block Addressing (LBA) mode, which allows you to use the full capacity of the drive. Select this option unless

you are installing an older, non-LBA drive. LBA mode is standardized, and it should be safe to move a drive configured for LBA mode from one machine to another. We have done so many times, but your mileage may vary, so back up before you attempt this.

4. For BIOSes that require you to enter drive geometry manually, you should also examine the CMOS Setup screen that configures the embedded ATA interfaces, if available. Use this screen to configure the interface to use the fastest transfer mode common to the interface and the drive itself. For example, if you have just installed an Ultra-DMA/33 drive in a system with an older BIOS, you may find that the fastest mode supported by that interface is PIO-4 at 13.3 MB/s. If the embedded interface does not support modern high-speed transfer modes, consider replacing the interface. Enhanced ATA interfaces are relatively cheap, and allow you to take advantage of the faster throughput and greater safety of UDMA-0 or –1. If the drive is configured to use LBA, you can safely use the existing interface temporarily and replace it later with a faster interface. The drive will function properly as is with the upgraded interface, but will simply begin using the fastest transfer mode common to the drive and new controller.

5. Once the drive is installed, recognized by the system, and configured properly in CMOS Setup, turn off the system. Align the screw holes in the drive with those in the bay. If screws were supplied with the drive, use them. If not, you can use any standard drive screw, but first verify that it is not too long by using your fingers to tighten the screw into the bare drive, making sure that no resistance is felt before the screw is fully seated. Insert four screws to secure the drive, two on each side. Some drives and some bays also allow screws to be inserted from beneath. Once you have all four screws loosely secured, tighten each of them gently. Good practice (seldom seen nowadays) suggests using a lock washer or a small dab of fingernail polish to prevent the screws from vibrating loose.

6. With the drive secured, start the system again, and use the operating system to partition and format the drive.

Installing a SCSI Hard Disk

When installing and configuring a SCSI hard disk, use the following guidelines:

- Avoid mixing different types of SCSI devices on the same bus, if it is possible. For example, if your system has a Wide Ultra2 SCSI hard disk and Ultra-SCSI CD-ROM, CD-RW, and tape drives installed, put the fast hard disk on its own SCSI bus and install the slower SCSI devices on a separate SCSI bus. If necessary, purchase and install an inexpensive SCSI host adapter to support the slower devices.

- For easiest installation and configuration, use all SCAM-compliant devices. SCAM-compliant drives allow a SCAM-compliant host adapter to set the drive's SCSI ID and termination status automatically. SCAM-tolerant drives report their SCSI ID and termination status to the adapter, but you must manually change settings on the drive if SCSI ID and/or termination need to be altered. Non-SCAM drives neither report their current settings to the adapter nor allow the adapter to reset them automatically. When using non-SCAM devices, you must manually verify settings and change them as necessary.

- Many SCSI problems are cable-related. The cables supplied with SCSI hard disks and host adapters are usually decent quality, but we've seen some truly horrible ones. Good SCSI cables aren't cheap, and the $3 ones you find in the bin at computer stores should be avoided. If you install SCSI devices frequently, consider purchasing a "good set" of SCSI cables. Use them to get the system working, and then replace them with lesser cables once everything works. For that purpose, we like Granite Digital cables (*http://www.scsipro.com*), but be prepared for sticker shock. Their least expensive 18" Wide Ultra2 SCSI cable, for example, costs $63, and prices go up quickly from there. But they are excellent cables.

 If you plan to boot the system from a SCSI hard disk, that disk must connect to a *bootable SCSI host adapter*. Inexpensive SCSI host adapters, especially those bundled with CD burners and similar SCSI devices, are usually not bootable because they are intended merely to provide an inexpensive way to connect SCSI devices to a system that boots from an IDE hard disk.

Installing a SCSI drive may be more complicated than installing an IDE drive, particularly if your drive and/or adapter are not SCAM-compliant. The following steps illustrate the general procedure for installing a SCSI hard disk with a PCI SCSI host adapter. The exact steps vary depending on which components you use.

1. If you have not already done so, install the SCSI host adapter. To do so, turn off the system, remove the cover, and locate an available bus-mastering PCI slot. Recent systems support bus-mastering on all slots. Some older systems support bus-mastering on only some slots. In that case, bus-mastering slots are normally light colored and non-bus-mastering slots are dark. Remove the slot cover for the selected slot, align the bus connector with the slot and press down firmly to seat the adapter. Use the screw that secured the slot cover to secure the adapter. If you have a spare drive activity indicator LED, connect it to the appropriate pins on the host adapter.

2. If both drive and host adapter are SCAM-compliant, proceed to step 5. If the host adapter is SCAM-compliant but the drive is non-SCAM, the system may hang if you leave SCAM enabled on the host adapter because the adapter is unable to determine current settings for the non-SCAM device. Disable SCAM on the host adapter by starting the system and running the ROM-based Setup utility for the adapter.

3. Set SCSI IDs manually using the jumpers or switches on the adapter and drive. If the host adapter supports seven devices (plus the adapter itself), the adapter is normally configured as SCSI ID 7, leaving SCSI IDs 0 through 6 available for drives. Higher-numbered IDs have priority. ID 0 is normally reserved for the boot hard disk and ID 1 for a second hard disk. Set the hard

disk jumpers for the appropriate SCSI ID, according to whether the hard disk is the primary boot drive or a secondary drive.

4. Terminate the SCSI bus. Exactly two devices must be terminated on each SCSI bus, and these devices must be those at each end of the bus, as follows:

 - If the SCSI adapter has only internal devices attached to it, the adapter itself and the final device on the internal SCSI chain must be terminated.

 - If the SCSI adapter has only external devices attached to it, the adapter itself and the final device on the external SCSI chain must be terminated.

 - If the SCSI adapter has both internal and external devices attached to it, *do not* terminate the SCSI adapter itself. Instead, terminate the final device attached to the internal chain and the final device attached to the external chain.

 SCAM-compliant SCSI host adapters detect terminated SCSI devices on the bus and set their own termination status automatically. On Adaptec models, which we recommend exclusively, this option can be enabled or disabled by using SCSISelect to set Host Adapter Termination to AutoTerm, which is the default setting. Also note that some internal SCSI cables have a built-in terminator at the end of the cable. If you use such a cable, make sure that termination is disabled on all drives connected to that cable.

---

5. Once SCSI ID and termination are configured correctly, physically install the drive and connect the cables. Most adapters are supplied with a standard two-device cable. If you need to connect more than two drives, replace the cable before proceeding. Otherwise, connect the cable to each drive, making sure to align pin 1 on the cable (indicated by a red stripe) with pin 1 on each device (indicated by a small number, triangle, or dot on the connector). It doesn't matter which drive connects to which cable position, so mix and match drives and cable positions in whatever way makes it easiest to route the cable. Don't forget to connect the power cable.

6. After verifying all settings and connections, turn on any external SCSI device(s) first, and then turn on the PC. If the SCSI hard disk is to be the boot drive, run CMOS Setup and verify that the entry for IDE Primary Master is set to None or Not Installed. If necessary, change it, save the new entry, and restart the system. On most systems, the PCI bus assigns IRQs and port addresses automatically. If your system requires setting PCI bus parameters manually, do so during this restart, using the system or motherboard documentation for guidance. Save the new settings and restart the system again.

7. The SCSI BIOS displays its own splash screen while initializing, which normally displays adapter and BIOS information and a list of installed SCSI devices. Ordinarily, default settings are fine, but in some cases you may need to change settings to get the drive to work at all or to optimize its performance. If this is the case for your system, press whatever key sequence is

needed to invoke the SCSI setup routine and make the necessary changes, as recommended by the documentation for the host adapter and/or drive.

8. Once the drive is installed and recognized by the system, use the operating system to partition and format the drive.

Enabling ATA DMA Mode Transfers

Enabling DMA transfers usually provides no increase in disk performance, but it is worth doing nonetheless because it greatly reduces the burden that PIO transfers place on the processor. If a computer has 75% CPU utilization using PIO transfers, that same computer using DMA transfers may provide the same or better disk performance at perhaps 1.5% CPU utilization. With multitasking operating systems, those extra free CPU ticks translate into faster system response.

To use DMA transfers, your drive, BIOS, and chipset must explicitly support DMA, and your operating system must have DMA drivers installed, loaded, and enabled. All versions of Windows 95, Windows 98, and Windows NT 4.0/2000 support DMA transfers, but DMA is disabled by default in some environments, as follows:

Windows 95B, Windows 98, and Windows 2000
A fresh install automatically installs DMA-capable drivers and tests the system for DMA support. Setup queries the chipset to determine if it supports DMA. If it does, Setup queries the drive itself to determine what DMA level, if any, it supports. If the drive is also DMA-capable, Setup does a series of reads and writes to determine if system reliably supports DMA. If any of these tests fail, DMA is disabled. If all three succeed, DMA is enabled automatically at the fastest DMA mode common to the drive and interface. Upgrading an existing system to Windows 95B, Windows 98, or Windows 2000 automatically enables DMA only if the DMA was previously enabled.

Windows 95 and Windows 95A
These operating systems do not install DMA support automatically. If your ATA interface and drives are DMA-capable, you can install and enable DMA-capable drivers manually.

Windows NT 4.0
Does not install DMA support automatically, but SP3 and higher includes DMA-capable drivers that you can install and enable manually.

Enabling DMA transfers is always an adventure because the only way to determine if your system works properly with DMA is to try it. Therefore, before you enable DMA, make sure you can recover if it doesn't work as expected. Always do a full backup and verify, including the registry, before you attempt to enable DMA.

For Windows 9X, have a known-good Startup diskette available before you try to enable DMA. If DMA does not work properly, you can recover by booting with the floppy, starting Windows in Safe Mode, disabling DMA, and restarting the system.

For Windows NT, the process is more perilous. If problems are immediately obvious when you restart the Windows NT system after enabling DMA, you can restart the system and choose the Last Known Good configuration to revert to the earlier, non-DMA drivers. Just don't log on before you do this, or the non-DMA

Last Known Good configuration will be overwritten by the flawed DMA configuration.

When you restart the PC, immediately check the current DMA status. Windows 9X and Windows NT both automatically disable DMA transfers at boot and revert to PIO transfers if they detect an obvious DMA problem. A DMA checkbox that won't stay checked when you restart the system is a good indication that your computer does not support DMA properly. Unfortunately, this is not foolproof. DMA may appear to install successfully, but may have intermittent problems anyway. Any of the following symptoms may (or may not) indicate a DMA problem:

- You cannot access the hard disk at all, or you notice corrupt or missing files.

- The drive sometimes hangs briefly or seems to speed up and slow down during file access.

- The keyboard or the foreground application sometimes stops responding for short periods, or the mouse becomes jerky or non-responsive.

- Windows 9X locks up during the Plug-N-Play detection phase of Setup.

- Windows 9X will only start in Safe Mode.

- Windows 9X or Windows NT shutdown takes a lot longer than before you enabled DMA.

If any of these problems occur, it does not necessarily mean that you cannot use DMA with your computer. The following are likely causes of the problems:

Cable

According to the ATA standard, cables can be no longer than 18" (0.45m), but we often see IDE cables of 24" and even 36". These long cables simply will not work reliably, if at all, with high-speed DMA modes. Cables also vary greatly in quality. The ones you see for $3 in bins at the computer store are less likely to work reliably at high speeds than those that are supplied with a new DMA drive. When you're installing a DMA drive, always replace the old IDE cable with the cable that comes with the drive. If you don't have a known-good cable, one source of high-quality IDE cables is the UltraCable ATAS, which can be used to connect both Ultra-DMA/33 drives and Ultra-DMA/66 drive, which require a special 40-pin, 80-wire cable. You can purchase this cable at *https://www.ultracable.com/html/orderatas.cgi*. If you have problems with DMA, simply replacing the cable with a better cable may solve them.

Drive

Any new drive should support DMA properly, but some early Ultra-DMA/33 drives did not implement fast DMA modes correctly. If you reconfigure an older drive to use DMA, first check the manufacturer's web site for details on that model. Software patches for some models are available.

BIOS

Some early BIOS implementations that nominally provide DMA support do not do so correctly. If a more recent BIOS revision is available for your computer, downloading it and installing it may resolve intermittent DMA problems. If your current BIOS does not support DMA, you may find that a revised version is available to add that capability.

Determining if a drive supports DMA

The easiest way to determine if a drive supports DMA transfers is to check the specifications in the manual or on the web site. You can also use *debug* to query the drive directly to determine what level of DMA, if any, it supports. To do so, boot the PC using a DOS floppy that contains the *debug* utility. (Running *debug* under Windows NT does not allow you to access the registers needed to perform this test.) At the DOS prompt, type debug and press Enter. At the debug hyphen prompt, type the following commands, ending each line by pressing Enter. Note that the first character in each of the first four lines is the lowercase letter o rather than zero.

```
o 1f6 a0
o 1f2 22
o 1f1 03
o 1f7 ef
i 1f1
```

The first line selects the drive to be tested. The a0 argument selects the master drive. Use b0 to select the slave drive. The second line specifies the DMA mode to be tested. The 22 argument specifies DMA Mode 2. If the test fails for this mode, you can retest using 21 to test for DMA Mode 1. The 03 argument on the third line programs the disk timing. The ef argument on the fourth line is the Set Feature command for the drive. The final line reads the error status and returns either the value 00, which indicates that the drive supports the DMA mode being tested, or the value 04, which indicates that the drive does not support the DMA level being tested. To exit *debug*, type the letter q at the hyphen prompt and press Enter.

Enabling DMA mode transfers with Windows 9X

To determine if your system board and ATA interface support DMA, right-click the My Computer icon and choose Properties to display the System Properties dialog. Display Device Manager and expand the Hard disk controllers item. You do not have DMA-capable hardware if you see only one or two entries that read "Standard IDE/ESDI Hard Disk Controller." If the first entry is "Intel 82371SB PCI Bus Master IDE Controller" or similar, the system board and interface provide DMA support. The critical words are "PCI Bus Master." The exact model number is less important.

Windows 98 and Windows 95B automatically load DMA-capable drivers if they detect DMA hardware. To install DMA support for the initial Windows 95 release, download and execute the file *http://support.microsoft.com/download/support/mslfiles/remideup.exe* and follow the prompts.

After you restart the system, enable DMA transfers by right-clicking My Computer and choosing Properties to display the System Properties dialog. Display the Device Manager page and expand the Disk drives item. Double-click the drive in question to display its Properties sheet and display the Settings page, shown in Figure 14-1. If a DMA-capable driver has been loaded, a DMA checkbox appears in the Options section. Mark that checkbox to enable DMA transfers for that drive. Exit the dialog, restart the system, and redisplay the dialog to verify that DMA remains enabled after the restart. If rebooting clears the checkbox, Windows has decided that some problem exists with DMA transfers, and has reverted to using PIO. If the checkbox remains marked, DMA transfers are enabled and should work, subject to the provisos listed earlier.

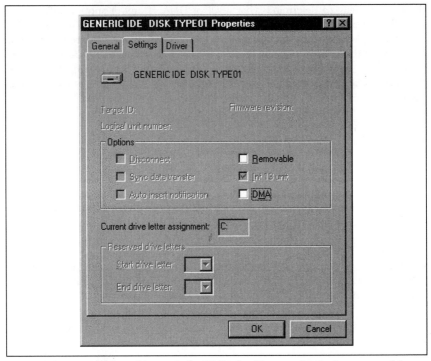

Figure 14-1: In Windows 98, mark the DMA checkbox on the Settings page of the disk Properties dialog to enable DMA transfers

Enabling DMA mode transfers with Windows NT

Windows NT 4.0 Service Pack 3 and later includes *Dmacheck.exe*, shown in Figure 14-2. This utility displays DMA detection status and usage on your computer. You can copy *Dmacheck.exe* from the SP3 or higher CD (the Intel version resides in *\Support\Utils\i386*), or download and expand the file *http://support.microsoft.com/download/support/mslfiles/Dmachcki.exe*.

Current DMA Usage displays one of three values for each DMA channel. "DMA in use" indicates that that channel is currently configured for and using DMA transfers; "DMA not in use" indicates that that channel is currently using PIO mode transfers; "No IDE/ATAPI Devices detected" indicates either that *Dmacheck* could not read the status of that channel from the registry, or that the current user has insufficient privileges. DMA transfers are disabled by default even if the drive and adapter are DMA-capable.

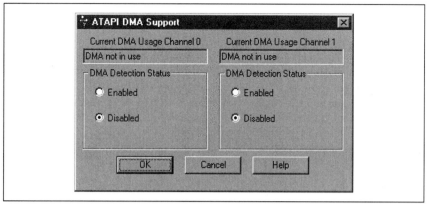

Figure 14-2: Use Dmacheck.exe to view and set DMA options for Windows NT

DMA Detection Status for each channel indicates whether the ATAPI driver will attempt to detect and use DMA on that channel. If DMA is disabled for a channel, that channel uses PIO transfers, at a level negotiated automatically by the drive and interface. Marking the Enabled option button for a channel causes the ATAPI driver to query the hardware to determine if it supports DMA, and enables DMA transfers if the hardware allows it. If the hardware does not support DMA transfers, PIO is used even when the Enabled option button is marked. If DMA transfers are used, the mode is determined by the drive and interface. Once DMA is enabled, Windows is not concerned with the particular DMA mode and speed being used.

Our Picks

We use various hard disks in our systems, including models from Seagate, Maxtor, Western Digital, Quantum, IBM, and others. Here are the ATA hard disk drives we recommend:

Economy IDE hard disk

Seagate U10 series. To build or upgrade a low-end system at the lowest possible cost, use a Seagate U10 series hard drive. They're the best of the current generation of 5,400 RPM drives—inexpensive, reliable, quiet, and quite fast for 5,400 RPM drives. But before you buy any 5,400 RPM IDE drive compare prices against 7,200 RPM units, which often sell for only $5 to $30 more than otherwise comparable 5,400 RPM units and provide noticeably better performance in applications that access the disk frequently. (*http://www.seagate.com*)

Mainstream IDE hard disk

Seagate Barracuda ATA II series. For mainstream systems, we use and recommend the Seagate Barracuda ATA II series of 7,200 RPM drives. In addition to the faster spindle speed, which contributes most to higher performance, these drives have higher areal densities, faster seek times, and larger buffers than lesser drives. They provide top-notch performance, under both Windows 9X and Windows NT, which has historically been a Maxtor stronghold. Although we prefer the Seagate Barracuda ATA II, we also like the Maxtor DiamondMax Plus 40 series of 7,200 RPM drives, which would be our close second choice.

IDE hard drives are ideal when performance takes a backseat to cost. With cost no object, SCSI hard drives are the equally clear choice. It's in the middle range, when cost and performance must be balanced, that we believe SCSI is given too little consideration. For example, as we write this in June 2000, mainstream systems use 600 to 866 MHz processors. High-end systems use 933 to 1,000 MHz processors, but cost $300 to $1,000 more. Based on our tests, we believe that most people would be better served by putting that additional money into SCSI components rather than a marginally faster processor.

As a component of overall performance, disk performance is at least as important as processor performance to most people, and SCSI hard disks beat the pants off even the fastest IDE hard disks, particularly if you run a multitasking operating system like Windows NT/2000 or Linux. We have found, for example, that even an elderly 5,400 RPM SCSI drive outperforms the best 7,200 RPM IDE drives in our real-world tests. Before you spend an extra $500 on a faster processor, consider spending that money on a good SCSI host adapter and SCSI hard disk.

Here are the SCSI hard disks that we use and recommend:

Mainstream SCSI hard disk
> **Seagate Barracuda series**. The 7,200 RPM Barracuda series, formerly Seagate's mid-range SCSI line, has become their entry-level/mainstream SCSI drive with the discontinuation of their 5,400 RPM SCSI drives. The Barracuda blows the doors off the fastest ATA drives, compares favorably in our testing to competing models from other makers, and is appropriate for high-end personal workstations and low-end to mid-range network servers. The latest Barracudas run cooler and much quieter that previous models, although we still use a drive cooler. Barbara's main system uses an ST318275LW Barracuda 18LP, and our primary server uses an ST150176LW Barracuda 50.

High-performance SCSI hard disk
> **Seagate Cheetah series**. The 10,000 RPM Cheetahs are Seagate's fastest SCSI drives, at least until their 15,000 RPM drives start to ship in quantity. The Cheetahs are the fastest drives we have ever used, and are appropriate for high-performance personal workstations and mid-range to high-end network servers. Recent Cheetahs are quieter and cooler-running than earlier models, although "quiet" and "cool" are relative terms for any 10,000 RPM drive. Compared to lesser drives, the Cheetahs run hot and loud, albeit no worse than other 10,000 RPM drives, and better than many. If you buy a Cheetah, you'll definitely want to install a high-end drive cooler and place the system on the floor. Robert uses an 18 GB Seagate ST318203LW Cheetah in his personal system.

Some might question our choice of U2W (80 MB/s) drives and host adapters rather than Ultra160 components. The reason for that choice is that, for now at least, Ultra160 drives typically cost $50 to $100 more than equivalent U2W drives, and Ultra160 host adapters $100 to $150 more than U2W host adapters. On standard PCs, Ultra160 provides no discernable advantage over U2W, because the fastest current drive models cannot saturate even a 40 MB/s channel. Also, although 32-bit PCI Ultra160 adapters are available, realizing the performance potential of Ultra160 requires using a 64-bit PCI adapter, which doesn't fit a standard PC. We recommend 80 MB/s U2W simply because U2W drives and host adapters sell at little or no premium over comparable UW components. If when you read this Ultra160 drives and components are selling at little or no premium over U2W components, go with the Ultra160 versions of the products we recommend.

We constantly test and review new equipment. For the latest information about what we currently use, visit:

http://www.hardwareguys.com/picks/harddisk.html

CHAPTER 15

Video Adapters

A video adapter accepts raw video data from the CPU, processes that data, and supplies it to the monitor in a form that the monitor can display. In DOS text-mode days, that wasn't a demanding job. Early video adapters simply interfaced the CPU to the monitor, did little or no manipulation of the raw data, and depended on the CPU itself to render the data into a form usable by the monitor. When Windows arrived, the emphasis shifted from text mode to graphics mode, which increased video processing demands dramatically.

That made it impractical to use the CPU to perform video processing, and a new generation of video adapters, called *graphics accelerators*, was born. A graphics accelerator off-loads the video processing burden from the main CPU by serving as a dedicated video co-processor. In doing so, it not only frees up the main CPU, but also reduces the amount of video data that crosses the system bus, which also contributes to faster system performance. All modern video adapters are also graphics accelerators.

Formerly, all video adapters were separate expansion cards, a form in which they are still readily available today. However, demand for reduced costs has resulted in motherboards with embedded video circuitry becoming much more common, a trend that is likely to continue. Although they are inexpensive and tightly integrated, the problem with embedded video adapters is that upgrading the video may require replacing the motherboard. But all current video adapters are so good that anyone other than a hard-core gamer is likely to find them more than good enough to get the job done.

Video Adapter Characteristics

The following sections describe the important characteristics of video adapters.

2D Versus 3D

The first graphics accelerators were 2D models, designed to provide hardware acceleration for the common display tasks (drawing and moving windows, scaling fonts, and so on) needed when running standard business applications under Windows. 2D accelerators essentially treat your display as a flat, two-dimensional workspace. Although one window may overlay another window, the top or foreground window always has focus.

Conversely, 3D accelerators treat your display as though it had depth. For example, when you play one of the new generation computer games, an on-screen character may walk in front of a table. The video adapter must determine the relative positions of the character and the table as seen from the viewer's position and display that portion of the character that is in front of the table rather than that portion of the table which should be concealed by the character. 3D video cards also support a variety of supplemental functions to enhance realism, for example, adding textures to the surface of concrete or adding reflections to a pool of standing water. Adding these minor but visually important enhancements consumes a great deal of memory and processor power, so high-performance 3D video adapters are relatively expensive devices, with typical street prices of $175 to $300 or more.

Note that 3D performance is merely a matter of degree. That is, even an elderly 2D-only adapter can be used to play 3D games, but because it does not incorporate 3D acceleration features in hardware, the main system CPU itself must do all of the calculations that would otherwise be done by a 3D adapter. The result is very high CPU utilization (with the associated system sluggishness) and jerky or poorly rendered 3D video without the modeling nuances provided in hardware by the 3D accelerator.

In fact, pure 2D accelerators haven't been manufactured for years. In the early 90s, two distinct types of video adapters were available: moderately priced ($50 to $200) 2D accelerators intended for mainstream use with standard Windows programs, and very expensive ($500 to $2,000) 3D adapters intended for niche markets like animation and video production. As 3D applications (particularly games) became more common, old-line 2D manufacturers like Matrox and ATI incorporated a limited subset of 3D functions in their mainstream adapters. There it stood until a few years ago, when upstart companies like 3dfx and nVIDIA caught the old-line makers napping by releasing graphics accelerators with a full range of 3D functionality.

That led to the current situation, where 3D performance is the only aspect of a graphics card that interests most people. Reviews talk of little but how video cards compare in various 3D benchmarks. That's unfortunate, because in reality 3D performance is unimportant for most users. In fact, unless you are a serious gamer, 3D performance should probably be your last consideration when choosing a video card. Such factors as 2D display quality and availability of stable drivers are actually much more important for most users.

All video cards and embedded video chipsets currently available provide at least reasonable 3D support. The important thing to remember is this: just as there is not really much absolute performance difference between a $50 Intel Celeron and a $500 Intel Pentium III, neither is there is much real difference between a $50 video card and a $500 one. Benchmarks aside, the $50 card does everything that 99% of users are likely to need. Yes, the differences are there, just as they are between the Celeron and the Pentium III, but unless you push your hardware to the limit you're not likely to notice much difference in day-to-day use.

Components

A video adapter comprises the following components:

Graphics processor
> Rather than depending on the main system CPU to create each video frame, a graphics accelerator contains a graphics processor, which is optimized to perform in hardware low-level video functions like transferring bitmaps, doing color and pattern fills, scaling fonts, sizing and positioning windows, and drawing lines, polygons, and other graphics primitives. An accelerated video adapter also requires much less data to be transferred between the system bus and the video adapter. For example, to draw a circle with a frame grabber, the system CPU must create a bitmap of that circle and transfer it to the frame grabber. Conversely, given only the center and radius of the circle, a graphics accelerator can render the circle directly.

> Early accelerators were optimized for 2D graphics operations, which are still most important when running standard business and personal software such as word processors and web browsers. More recent accelerators, including all current models, provide 3D acceleration, which is primarily useful for playing graphics-intensive games like Quake. Unfortunately, some recent 3D adapters are so heavily optimized for 3D that they provide mediocre 2D performance. Our venerable Matrox Millennium II adapters, for example, are useless for playing 3D games, but provide better 2D performance (especially text quality) than most current 3D accelerators.

Video memory
> Video adapters use memory for several purposes. A portion of video memory called the *frame buffer* stores the image as it is constructed by the graphics processor and before it is sent to the monitor. Available memory not occupied by the frame buffer caches fonts, icons, and other graphic elements to improve video performance. Some video adapters also allocate memory not being used by the main frame buffer as a second frame buffer, allowing the next frame to be created in the background while the current frame is being displayed. The most important characteristics of video memory are its size, type, and speed. Video adapters use one of the following memory types:

> *DRAM (Dynamic Random Access Memory)*
>> First- and some second-generation graphics accelerators used standard DRAM, which was not ideal for the purpose. DRAM is no longer used in mainstream video adapters because it is so slow, mainly because it is *single-ported*, which means that it does not allow data to be read and written simultaneously.

EDO DRAM (Extended Data Out DRAM)

EDO provides higher bandwidth than DRAM, can run at higher speeds, and manages read/write access more efficiently. EDO is single-ported, typically operates with 50 to 60 ns access times, is typically 64 bits wide, and yields overall bandwidth of 400 MB/s. EDO was commonly used in video adapters before the advent of SDRAM and the various specialized types of video memory described later in this section, and is still used in some inexpensive video adapters. Purchase an EDO-based video adapter only if you are upgrading an old ISA- or VLB-based computer.

VRAM (Video RAM)

A special type of DRAM, used only in video adapters, and designed to overcome the limitations of the single-ported arrangement used by DRAM and EDO. VRAM is *dual-ported*—which allows the next frame to be written while the last frame is being read—operates at 50 to 60 ns access times, is typically 64 bits wide, and yields overall bandwidth of 400 MB/s. Because it requires less frequent refreshing than DRAM or EDO, it is much faster, and correspondingly more expensive. VRAM was commonly used in mid- to high-end video adapters through about 1997, but has now been superceded by SDRAM and SGRAM.

WRAM (Windows RAM)

WRAM, first introduced by Matrox with their Millennium series of video adapters, is an enhanced version of VRAM that is somewhat less expensive to produce and provides about 20% higher performance than VRAM. Like VRAM, WRAM has been superceded by SDRAM and SGRAM.

SDRAM (Synchronous DRAM)

A step up from EDO, SDRAM runs the memory and graphics processor on a common clock reference, allowing faster access times and higher throughput. SDRAM is single-ported, operates at 8 to 15 ns access times, is typically 64 bits wide, and yields overall bandwidth of 800 MB/s. SDRAM is used in most current low-end and mid-range and a few high-end video adapters. Any video adapter you buy today should use either SDRAM or the superior SGRAM described.

SGRAM (Synchronous Graphics RAM)

An enhanced form of SDRAM, used only on video adapters, that supports write-per-bit and block writes, both of which improve performance over SDRAM when used with graphics accelerators that explicitly support SGRAM. SGRAM video memory is single-ported, operates at 6 to 10 ns access times, is typically 64 bits wide, and yields overall bandwidth of 800 MB/s. SGRAM is used on mid-range and high-end video adapters.

RAMDAC (Random Access Memory Digital-to-Analog Converter)

The RAMDAC examines video memory many times per second, using a look-up table to translate the digital values it finds in memory to the analog voltages that the monitor requires to display the corresponding colors. The RAMDAC contains three Digital-to-Analog converters (DAC), one each for the red, green, and blue signals that the monitor uses to display the full spectrum that it supports. The architecture and speed of the RAMDAC (along with the graphics processor itself) determine the combinations of resolutions, color depths, and refresh rates that the video adapter supports. All other things being equal, an adapter with a faster RAMDAC outperforms an adapter with a slower RAMDAC. Many current video adapters are sold in two versions that differ only in the speeds of the RAMDAC and in the type and amount of memory installed. The faster versions, often described as "Ultra" or "Max," usually sell at a substantial premium, run hotter, and provide little or no real benefit for most users.

Drivers

Drivers translate the display data generated by an application or operating system into the specific instructions needed by the graphics processor to create the image that will be displayed on the monitor. The driver decides how to present data to the graphics processor so as to optimize the hardware acceleration functions available on the graphics processor. That means that a mediocre graphics processor with an excellent driver may outperform an excellent graphics processor with a mediocre driver, so the availability of robust, well-optimized drivers for whatever operating system you run is a crucial factor in choosing a video adapter. Drivers are often optimized for particular combinations of resolution and color depth, so it's often worthwhile to experiment with different settings.

In the past, video drivers had to be written for a specific application running on a specific operating system using a specific video adapter. If you wanted to run UltraCAD 5.1 on a FastPix SuperVGA adapter with a 2.03 BIOS under ABC-DOS 3.3, you had to have a driver written specifically for that combination of hardware and software. The flood of 3D software titles and 3D accelerators made that situation untenable. The solution was to use an intermediate hardware abstraction layer (HAL) to isolate the graphics processor from the operating system and applications, and to develop standardized APIs to communicate with that HAL. Two 3D APIs are dominant in the PC environment:

OpenGL

OpenGL was originally developed by Silicon Graphics, Inc. (SGI) as a general-purpose 3D API. OpenGL found its first niche in high-end CAD systems running on Unix X terminals, and was later implemented on PC workstations running CAD and other 3D graphics-intensive environments. With the release of a Windows version in 1996, support for OpenGL began to migrate downward to mainstream 3D applications, including games. OpenGL is widely supported by software developers because it offers better low-level control over 3D graphics operations and was perceived as being an easier API to write to than the competing Microsoft standard. OpenGL support can be implemented in two ways: *Mini Client Drivers* (*MCDs*) are relatively easy to write, but provide limited functionality. *Installable Client Drivers* (*ICDs*) are much more difficult to write, but provide additional functionality.

Direct3D (D3D)

D3D is the 3D acceleration part of DirectX, Microsoft's umbrella multimedia standard, which also includes DirectDraw (2D acceleration), DirectSound (audio), DirectInput (support for joysticks and similar input devices), and DirectPlay (Internet gaming). Versions through 5.0 were slow, buggy, and feature-poor when compared to OpenGL and proprietary 3D APIs. Microsoft refined and tuned D3D by reducing dependence on the main system CPU and incorporating OpenGL features. With version 6.0 D3D could finally compete on a reasonably equal basis with OpenGL and proprietary APIs, although it was still somewhat slower and less feature-laden. Although 3D software manufacturers had been burned by D3D 5.0, they recognized the improvements in 6.0, and most incorporated D3D 6.0 support immediately. The convergence between D3D and OpenGL continued with version 7.0, and applications that support only D3D are no longer at a significant disadvantage relative to those that support OpenGL and/or proprietary APIs. D3D and OpenGL may eventually merge. Fahrenheit, a joint initiative between Microsoft and SGI, was originally intended to result in a unified standard, but has since become moribund. Some elements of Fahrenheit are already in place, however, and many enhancements planned for Fahrenheit will be incorporated in subsequent releases of D3D.

For now, any video card you choose should support the latest release of D3D, which is used by most current 3D games and other 3D applications. Many 3D applications, including some games, also support OpenGL for its higher performance and additional functionality, so ideally the card you choose should also have an OpenGL ICD. Support for the proprietary 3dfx Glide API, which dominated 3D gaming through about 1999, is no longer important because nearly all current games support D3D and/or OpenGL.

Interface

Early video adapters, including the first generation of graphics accelerators, used the ISA bus, which soon proved inadequate to carry the high volume of video data required by graphical operating systems and applications. *VESA Local Bus (VLB)* adapters, shipped with many 486 systems and a few early Pentium systems, greatly improved throughput. ISA and VLB video adapters, although no longer mainstream products, are still available for those who need to upgrade the video on older systems, although they are now increasingly hard to find and generally use a video chipset that is three generations or more out of date. Still, if you need to upgrade the video in an older PC, installing a recent ISA or VLB video card can dramatically improve performance at low cost. Current video adapters use one of the following interfaces:

PCI
> The PCI bus is 32 bits wide and runs at 33.3 MHz, providing peak throughput of 133 MB/s. The fact that a PCI video card shares the bus with other PCI devices means that heavy transfers of video data reduce the bandwidth available to other PCI peripherals, such as hard disk controllers and network cards. This concern is still largely theoretical because PCI bus saturation is very rare with current systems and software

AGP (Accelerated Graphics Port)
> Intel's concern about PCI throughput limitations and the increasing amount of data that new generations of 3D video adapters would demand led it to

introduce AGP. Although AGP supports 2D operations, it provides no real benefit over PCI in 2D. As the name implies, AGP is a port rather than a bus, which means that it connects only two devices. AGP provides a direct unshared channel between the AGP device and chipset, which allows the CPU to transfer data to the AGP card without the 133 MB/s limitation of the PCI bus. On a 66 MHz FSB, standard 1X AGP transfers 32 bits per clock cycle, for total peak base throughput of 264 MB/s. AGP X2 mode, called 2X AGP, transfers data on both rising and falling edges of the clock cycle to yield peak throughput of 528 MB/s. 4X AGP, introduced with the AGP 2.0 specification, doubles throughput again to just over 1 GB/s by transferring data four times per clock cycle.

The AGP bus has two other throughput advantages relative to PCI: AGP supports pipelining, which allows it to sustain throughput at 80% of theoretical, and AGP uses Sideband Addressing, a process that allows queuing up to 32 commands and allows data and commands to be sent simultaneously. One highly touted benefit of AGP is *Direct Memory Execute* (*DIME*), which allows the AGP adapter to use system memory as though it were locally installed video memory. DIME is implemented with a device called a *Graphics Aperture Remapping Table* (*GART*), which can claim small, widely distributed areas of main memory and present them to the adapter as a large, contiguous area of virtual "local" video memory. In theory, DIME allows an AGP adapter with limited local memory to store large texture bitmaps and other graphic elements in main memory. In practice, DIME is of little real benefit, because most high-end video adapters (PCI or AGP) are equipped with enough memory (16 MB to 32 MB or more) to store textures locally. Also, although DIME is faster than accessing main memory across the PCI bus, DIME is still slower than accessing local memory on the video card, particularly if that local memory is DDR memory, which many current high-performance video cards use.

In short, for now at least, AGP is a solution in search of a problem, particularly for those who use primarily 2D applications. Windows NT users have no reason to buy AGP, because NT treats AGP cards as standard PCI cards, as do early releases of Windows 95. Only Windows 95 OSR2 or higher, Windows 98, and Windows 2000 have operating system support for AGP.

However, AGP is still the best choice if your motherboard has an AGP slot because AGP adapters sell at little or no price premium over equivalent PCI adapters. 1X AGP cards are no longer sold and should be avoided, not because they are slower than 2X or 4X AGP cards, but because they use obsolete graphics processors and have functional and feature limitations. In fact, many 1X AGP cards were really simply PCI cards with an AGP interface substituted for PCI, and did not support AGP features. 2X AGP is the sweet spot. Although makers tout the huge throughput of 4X AGP, current hardware cannot exploit even 1X AGP, and only the latest motherboards support 4X AGP, so paying extra for 4X versus 2X makes no sense.

You may have little choice but to buy AGP, however, and 4X AGP at that. Video card makers are beginning to abandon PCI in favor of AGP (and 2X in favor of 4X) for their latest adapters. For example, 3dfx ships the Voodoo3 2000 and 3000 in both PCI and AGP, but ships the Voodoo 3500 only in AGP. Similarly, Matrox supplies their flagship G400 adapters only in AGP, but continues to ship both PCI and AGP versions of the older G200 adapters.

Embedded video adapters may be either PCI or AGP. If you buy a motherboard with embedded video, keep in mind that you may one day want to upgrade the video in that system. Doing that requires both that you can disable the embedded video (which is not possible on all motherboards) and that you have an available slot for the new video card. Ideally, choose a motherboard with embedded AGP 2X video circuitry that also contains an unused AGP 2X (or 4X) slot. Note that many motherboards with embedded AGP video have no AGP slot. These can be upgraded only by installing a PCI video adapter. That's not a problem now, because competent PCI video adapters are widely available. However, that is likely to change as AGP continues to supplant PCI.

Display Settings

The following display settings determine how much information a video adapter and driver display and how often that information is updated:

Resolution

> Resolution, also called *addressability*, refers to the maximum number of pixels the video adapter can display, listed by vertical columns and horizontal rows. For example, a standard VGA adapter can display at most 640 columns by 480 rows of pixels, abbreviated as 640×480 resolution. Video cards do not support continuously variable resolution, but instead provide standard "prepackaged" combinations of vertical and horizontal resolution, e.g., 1024×768. Using higher resolution permits more information to be displayed. Also, for any given size of an object on-screen, using higher resolution allocates more pixels to that object, avoiding "jaggies," "stair-stepping," and other video artifacts that degrade image quality. Conversely, using too high a resolution for the monitor size results in individual display elements becoming too small to be readable. The best resolution to use is determined by monitor size and quality, video adapter capabilities, and personal factors like visual acuity.

Color depth

> A *pixel*, also called a *pel* or *picture element*, is the smallest individually addressable display element, and comprises three sub-units, one each for red (R), green (G), and blue (B). *Color depth* refers to the number of discrete colors that can be displayed, and is determined by the number of bits allocated to each primary color, quantified as *bits-per-pixel* (*BPP*). Standard VGA allocates 4BPP, which allows at most 16 (2^4) colors to be displayed simultaneously from a total palette of 256 available colors. Current video adapters support 256-color mode (8BPP); High Color or 64K Color mode (16BPP, 65,536 colors, 5 bits each allocated to Red and Blue, and 6 bits to Green); and True Color or 16.7 Million Color mode (24BPP, 16,777,216 colors, 8 bits each allocated to Red, Green, and Blue). Note that, although True Color requires only 8 bits each on the Red, Green, and Blue channels (24 bits total), some adapters add a fourth "alpha" channel, and therefore require 32BPP. Although 256 colors are adequate for standard business applications, displaying continuous-tone High Color or True Color images with only 256 colors results in posterization

effects that reduce realism. Any recent graphics accelerator can run True Color mode at commonly used resolutions, and that is usually the best choice.

Refresh frequency

A video card displays the screen image as a series of images that is replaced many times per second, even when the screen image is unchanging (e.g., your desktop). As with movies or television, a phenomenon known as persistence of vision allows the human brain to recognize a rapid sequence of still images as continuous smooth motion. In order for this phenomenon to occur, screen updates must occur very frequently. The number of times per second that the video card replaces the current screen image with a new image is called the *refresh frequency*. The refresh frequency necessary to provide a stable image varies with the individual, monitor size, persistence of monitor phosphors, ambient lighting, the image being displayed, and other factors, but is typically somewhere between 60 and 90 images per second. Setting refresh frequency too low results in visible flicker. Setting it too high for any given combination of monitor and video adapter may limit you to using a lower resolution and/or color depth than you would prefer, so make sure that the monitor and video adapter you buy support reasonable refresh rates for the resolution and color depth you intend to run. We generally use a refresh rate of 75 Hz or higher on 15" monitors running 800×600, 75 to 85 Hz on 17" monitors running 1024×768, and 85 Hz or higher on 19" and larger monitors running 1280×1024 or higher. Most people find these settings suitable for running typical office productivity applications, web browsers, graphics packages, and so on. Note, however, that some special applications, such as medical imaging, may require very high refresh rates and accordingly expensive monitors.

Resolution and color depth settings together determine how much data must be stored for each image, and so the amount of video memory required. Refresh frequency determines only how often the image is updated, and as a result has nothing to do with the amount of video memory needed. Table 15-1 lists the amount of video memory required for various combinations of resolution and color depth in 2D mode.

Table 15-1: Video Memory Required to Support Standard Resolutions and Color Depths in 2D Mode

Resolution	BPP	Colors	1 MB	2 MB	4 MB	8 MB
640×480	8	256	•	•	•	•
640×480	16	64 K	•	•	•	•
640×480	24	16 M	•	•	•	•
640×480	32	16 M	○	•	•	•
800×600	8	256	•	•	•	•
800×600	16	64 K	•	•	•	•
800×600	24	16 M	○	•	•	•
800×600	32	16 M	○	•	•	•
1024×768	8	256	•	•	•	•
1024×768	16	64 K	○	•	•	•
1024×768	24	16 M	○	○	•	•

Table 15-1: Video Memory Required to Support Standard Resolutions and Color Depths in 2D Mode (continued)

Resolution	BPP	Colors	1 MB	2 MB	4 MB	8 MB
1024×768	32	16 M	○	○	•	•
1152×864	8	256	•	•	•	•
1152×864	16	64 K	○	•	•	•
1152×864	24	16 M	○	○	•	•
1152×864	32	16 M	○	○	•	•
1280×1024	8	256	○	•	•	•
1280×1024	16	64 K	○	○	•	•
1280×1024	24	16 M	○	○	•	•
1280×1024	32	16 M	○	○	•	•
1600×1200	8	256	○	•	•	•
1600×1200	16	64 K	○	○	•	•
1600×1200	24	16 M	○	○	○	•
1600×1200	32	16 M	○	○	○	•

Throughput

The overall throughput of a video adapter is constrained by the speed and architecture of its RAMDAC and video memory, and the number of bits that it processes per operation. The throughput required at any given combination of display settings is the product of four factors: resolution (how many pixels per frame), color depth (how much data per pixel), refresh rate (how many frames per second), and number of planes (one for 2D modes, and typically three or four for 3D modes). When a video adapter reaches its throughput limit, you can increase any of these factors only by reducing one or more of the others.

For example, a video adapter may have a RAMDAC that can process at most 225 million bytes/sec. Operating in 2D mode, that adapter supports 1024×768 resolution at 24 bits/pixel (BPP) and 85 Hz refresh. With those settings, the video adapter processes (1024×768×24BP×85 Hz = 200,540,160 bytes/sec), well within the RAMDAC limits. Increasing resolution to 1152×864 requires (1152×864× 24BPP×85 Hz = 253,808,640 bytes/sec), well beyond the capacity of this RAMDAC. To run 1152×864, you can either continue using 85 Hz refresh, but reduce the color depth from 24BPP to 16BPP (1152×864×16BPP×85 Hz = 169,205,760 bytes/sec), or continue using 24BPP, but reduce the refresh rate from 85 Hz to 75 Hz (1152×864×24BPP×75 Hz = 223,948,800 bytes/sec). Similarly, when the adapter runs in 3D mode, the requirement for three (or four) planes forces lower resolutions, color depths, and/or refresh rates. This RAMDAC, for example, is at its limit in 3D mode when running 800×600 resolution at 16BPP and 78 Hz (800×600×16BPP×78 Hz×3 planes = 224,640,000 bytes/sec). This is why, relative to 2D cards, 3D video cards are equipped with a much faster RAMDAC (to process the additional data) and much more memory (to store the additional planes as well as supplementary information such as texturing data). In practice, you'll never need to calculate these numbers, because video drivers support only those combinations of display settings that are within the ability of the video hardware.

Although conventional wisdom says increasing resolution and/or color depth slows performance, because more information must be processed and transferred, this is not invariably true. Some video adapters run faster at 1024×768 than at 800×600, for example, or faster at 16.7 million colors than at 256 colors. Why? Because the driver is optimized for the higher resolution or color depth. Don't assume that increasing either resolution or color depth will slow down your video. Test each usable combination and pick the one that works for you.

Choosing a Graphics Processor

In the past, people bought graphics cards primarily based on manufacturer brand name. The graphics processor any given card used was identified, if at all, by an anonymous part number. Nowadays, the name of the manufacturer is less important to knowledgeable buyers than which graphics processor the card uses. There's not much debate any more on newsgroups about which manufacturer makes the best graphics cards; instead, people debate which is the best graphics chipset. Buyers choose a card because it uses a particular 3dfx chipset or a particular nVIDIA chipset, giving only secondary consideration to whose name is on the box. To choose wisely when purchasing a 3D accelerator, it's helpful to understand something about the competing products. Here are the major players:

3dfx (Voodoo series)

3dfx basically invented the consumer 3D graphics card market with their original Voodoo chipset. By 1997, they dominated that market, selling their Voodoo chipset to several OEM graphics card makers, including Creative Labs and Diamond, two major players in the retail channel. The proprietary 3dfx GLIDE API was almost univerally supported by game software makers, and most serious gamers used a Voodoo card, although the nVIDIA RIVA TNT was beginning to make inroads. The second-generation Voodoo2 graphics processor was a major step forward, but 3dfx began to see serious competition from nVIDIA. Although the follow-on Voodoo3 was a significant improvement in some respects, it failed to meet the expectations of many gamers and allowed nVIDIA to begin grabbing major market share. In what may have been their worst decision ever, 3dfx acquired old-line graphics card maker STB, thereby at a single stroke assuming the difficulties and costs of developing retail distribution channels while angering existing OEM customers, including Creative Labs and Diamond, with whom they had just gone into direct competition. 3dfx now faces major challenges from both distribution and technical perspectives. The success or failure of the Voodoo4, in development as this is written, will likely determine the long-term viability of the company. Our take:

Voodoo3

Excellent 3D performance; mediocre 2D display quality, especially at higher resolutions; the second- or third-best choice for a serious gamer; not the best choice for general use.

Voodoo2

Essentially obsolete, though it still provides very good 3D performance; mediocre to poor 2D display quality; much better alternatives are available.

nVIDIA (TNT series and GeForce/NV10)

nVIDIA has returned from the edge. After flirting with bankruptcy just a few years ago, nVIDIA has become a major player in the 3D graphics processor market. Unlike 3dfx, which attempted to play an active role in how OEMs used and marketed their technology (and ultimately went into direct competition with their OEMs), nVIDIA sees their role as simply providing very fast graphics processors to OEMs, who are free to develop products around those processors and market them as they see fit. While 3dfx spent huge amounts of money on ad campaigns to promote Voodoo, nVIDIA focused their resources on making technical improvements to their products, leaving advertising to the OEMs. As a result, many OEMs (including Creative Labs and Diamond) adopted the TNT chipset and its follow-ons, the TNT2 and TNT2 Ultra. The GeForce 256 (formerly known as the NV10) has just begun shipping as this is written, and appears poised to inherit the 3D performance crown. Our take:

GeForce 256

Superb 3D performance; mediocre 2D display quality at higher resolutions; the first- or second-best choice for a serious gamer; good to very good for general use on mainstream and high-end systems.

TNT2 and TNT2 Ultra

Excellent 3D performance; mediocre 2D display quality at higher resolutions; a good choice for a gamer on a budget; good for general use on mainstream and high-end systems.

TNT and Riva 128

Now found primarily as embedded video in integrated motherboards; good to very good 3D performance; mediocre to poor 2D display quality at higher resolutions (except the TNT implementation on the Intel SR440BX motherboard, which has good to very good 2D quality); adequate for all but the most graphics intense games; good to very good for general use on low-end and mainstream systems.

Matrox (Millennium series)

Matrox has been making graphics cards since before PCs existed, and has always been the driving force in the 2D graphics market. They shipped the first 64-bit 2D graphics accelerator in 1993, stealing a two-year march on the competition, and their Millennium series has been the standard in 2D graphics since it was introduced. But Matrox was very late to the 3D party, not recognizing that a consumer market for 3D graphics cards existed until late-comers like 3dfx and nVIDIA had already gained a strong foothold in that market segment. Matrox responded with the G200, a competent 3D graphics card whose acceptance by gamers was hampered by their very late delivery of OpenGL Installable Client Driver (ICD) support for that card. The Matrox G400 series, shipped in mid-1999, levels the playing field between Matrox and its competitors for the 3D performance market, while retaining the advantages that Matrox cards have always had in 2D display quality. Our take:

G400 and G400 Max

Excellent 3D performance; superb 2D display quality; the first- or second-best choice for a serious gamer; the best choice for general use on mainstream and high-performance PCs.

G200

Good 3D performance; superb 2D display quality; adequate for all but the most graphics intense games; very good for general use on mainstream systems.

ATI (Rage series)

ATI is another old-line maker, formerly known as an OEM supplier of competent if unexciting graphics cards like the Rage Pro. ATI is caught in the middle, unable to compete equally with nVIDIA and others in 3D, and without the fabled 2D quality of Matrox. ATI models with TV and DVD support are a good choice for those who require those functions, but Matrox is a very strong competitor in those niches. Our take:

Rage Fury

Very good 3D performance; adequate 2D display quality; the fourth- or fifth-best choice for a serious gamer; good to very good for general use on mainstream PCs.

Rage Pro

Mediocre 3D performance; adequate 2D display quality; fair to good for general use on mainstream PCs; better alternatives are available.

S3 (Savage series)

Long known as an OEM supplier of single-chip video solutions, S3 has only recently attempted to enter the performance video market. Their earlier Trio64 and ViRGE chipsets were used primarily for embedded video and low-end graphics adapters. Their first attempt at a mainstream 3D chipset, the Savage3D, was not competitive with existing 3D accelerators, and disappeared quickly from the market. Like other OEM chipset suppliers, S3 decided they needed retail distribution channels, and attempted to purchase Diamond. That purchase, which is still up in the air as this is written, would saddle S3 with the same problems as 3dfx assumed by purchasing STB. In the meantime, S3 3D technology is competent if unexciting. That may change with the introduction of the Savage2000, although that remains to be seen.

Savage4

Very good 3D performance; adequate 2D display quality; the fourth- or fifth-best choice for a serious gamer; good to very good for general use on mainstream PCs. Better alternatives are available.

Intel

Intel attempted to enter the video adapter market with cards based on their i740 graphics processor. Although the i740 provides acceptable 3D performance for low-end systems and very good 2D performance, rapid developments in 3D graphics processors from 3dfx, nVIDIA, and others quickly overwhelmed the limited 3D capabilities of the i740. In 1999, Intel abandoned the standalone video adapter market when they discontinued the i740 and cards based on it. Intel remains a factor in video adapters, however, because they ship millions of motherboards, many of which have embedded video based on the Intel i752 chipset, the follow-on to the i740. Like the i740, the i752 is not a high-end graphics solution. Also like the i740, the i752 has excellent 2D characteristics and is more than good enough for most users.

Choosing a Video Adapter

Use the following guidelines when choosing a video adapter:

- Remember that video is just one part of your system. If your system has only a Pentium II/233 and 32 MB of memory, you're likely to be disappointed if you install a cutting-edge $400 graphics card. Buying a $150 mid-range graphics card instead and spending the other $250 on a CPU and memory upgrade will yield much better video performance, and increase general system performance as well.

- Unless you spend most of your computing time running Quake or other resource-intensive games, performance is probably the *least* important selection criterion. Any current video adapter, and many older models, is more than fast enough to run standard 2D business applications at normal resolutions and refresh rates (e.g., 1024×768 at 85 Hz). Previous-generation 3D adapters (such as, when this was written, the ATI Rage Pro, the Intel i740, or the nVIDIA RIVA 128 and TNT) are discounted deeply when their replacements ship, and are excellent choices for most users. These older video chipsets are often used for embedded video on integrated motherboards, and will suffice for nearly anyone. Don't forget that today's obsolescent chipset was the leading-edge barn burner not long ago. Don't get caught up in the horsepower race, and don't waste money buying performance that you'll never use.

- Choose the correct interface.

  - If you have an AGP slot, buy an AGP adapter. Depending on the motherboard, the AGP slot may be 1X, 2X, or (soon) 4X. Most current AGP adapters are 2X, although 4X models are becoming more common. Any AGP adapter can be used in any AGP slot, although performance will be limited by the slower of the slot or the adapter. With current hardware and software, even 1X AGP has little or no real-world performance advantage over PCI, and that is likely to remain true for some time. The performance advantages of 2X and 4X AGP are likely to remain theoretical (except when using some graphics-intensive games) for the next several years. Note that Windows NT 4 does not recognize AGP, and treats an AGP adapter as a PCI adapter. The best course is simply to make sure any motherboard you buy contains at least a 2X AGP slot (4X is better, when available), and any AGP card you buy is 2X. Older 1X AGP cards support fewer features than 2X cards, and 4X cards are not worth their higher cost until systems catch up with the need for 4X AGP throughput.

  - If you have no AGP slot, buy a PCI adapter. PCI adapters are still widely available, and likely to remain so for some time. You may have to settle for a graphics chipset that is one or two generations out of date. For example, Matrox sells its older G200 adapter in both AGP and PCI versions, but the flagship G400 is available only in AGP. Still, if the video adapter in your system is more than a year old, installing even an inexpensive current model PCI video adapter can provide dramatic improvement for 3D applications.

- If you have only ISA or VLB slots, purchase a video adapter that fits an available slot, choosing VLB if that is an option. ISA and VLB video adapters are hard to find nowadays, and the supply will likely dry up completely in the near future. Although installing a newer video adapter in such an old system may improve video performance somewhat, you are likely to be disappointed with the overall results. Consider instead replacing your system or motherboard.

- Display quality is subjective and very difficult to quantify, but a real issue nonetheless. The consensus, with which we agree, is that Matrox video adapters provide the highest 2D display quality. Many other adapters provide reasonable 2D quality, but the fastest 3D adapters sometimes compromise 2D quality.

- Before you purchase a motherboard with embedded video, verify that the embedded adapter can be disabled, allowing you to replace the adapter in a year or two, when even inexpensive adapters will greatly outperform your embedded adapter. If possible, choose a motherboard that has an available AGP slot. The availability of PCI adapters is waning, and you may have few or no choices in PCI video adapters by the time you're ready to upgrade.

- Unless the system you are building or upgrading has no AGP slot available, buy an AGP video adapter that supports at least 2X AGP. 4X AGP is not necessary for current systems, but many newer adapters are available only in 4X.

- Buy a card with enough memory. PCI video cards can use only memory that resides on the card itself. AGP video cards can also use main system memory, but for performance and other reasons it's always better to have the necessary memory on the video card itself.

- For a video card used primarily for business software and other 2D applications, 4 MB is marginally adequate, allowing up to $1,600 \times 1,200$ resolution at 64K colors. You're better off with 8 MB or more, which is enough to run 32-bit color at up to 1280×1024—adequate for all but 20" and larger monitors. Note that 16 MB adapters often sell for little more than 8 MB ones, and that additional 8 MB is useful for caching fonts and other graphics elements.

- If you run hardware-intensive games like Quake, consider 16 MB the absolute minimum. Some low-end consumer-oriented 3D accelerators still ship with only 8 MB, which is adequate for running 3D at 800×600 resolution. Running 32-bit color at 1024×768, however, requires nearly 8 MB just to store the x-, y-, and z-buffers, leaving no memory available on an 8 MB adapter for storing textures and other elements. Although AGP adapters can use main system memory as video memory, for performance reasons most gamers prefer to have a large amount of video memory physically installed on the video card.

- Make sure that the adapter you choose has drivers available for the operating system you intend to use. This is particularly important if you run Windows NT/2000, Linux, BeOS, or another OS with limited driver support. The best vendors, like Matrox, provide frequent driver updates. Matrox offers better driver support than any manufacturer we know of. They provide three levels of driver: Microsoft-certified (slowest, but stable), Matrox-certified (faster, but not certified by Microsoft), and beta (fastest, but not certified by anyone).

Some video card manufacturers (we won't name names to avoid being sued) focus most of their driver development resources on Windows 98, and provide only primitive, low-performance, feature-poor drivers for less popular operating systems. Consider the manufacturer's history of providing frequent driver updates and supporting new operating system versions, which you can determine by examining the manufacturer's web site, checking the Usenet newsgroups, and cruising the hardware enthusiast web sites.

- Make sure the video card has a good warranty. Video cards used to be among the most reliable components of a PC. This is changing, not because manufacturers are cutting corners, but because new high-performance video cards are pushing hardware technology to the limit. Having a video card die after only six months or a year is now relatively common, particularly for those who push the card past its limit by overclocking it in pursuit of the highest possible performance.

Installing a Video Adapter

Physically installing most video cards is very straightforward. Simply choose an available expansion slot—PCI or AGP, as appropriate—seat the video card, and connect the monitor. Nearly all video cards are standalone devices, with the 3dfx Voodoo 1 and Voodoo 2 as notable exceptions. The Voodoo 1 and 2 are 3D-only video cards. Because they do not provide 2D functions, you must also have a standard video card installed in the system in which you install the Voodoo. The Voodoo serves as a kind of "3D coprocessor," relieving your standard video card of 3D processing duties, but using it for 2D functions.

 Many video adapters now come with heat sinks on the graphics chipset. Some whose chipsets run at very high speeds go further, adding a fan to the heatsink. If your adapter has a fan, make sure to connect power to that fan before you use the adapter. We received mail from a reader who didn't realize that connecting the fan was mandatory and as a result literally burned up his expensive new video adapter.

Video
Adapters

Configuring Video Under Windows 98/2000

Windows 98/2000 video is configured from the Display Properties → Settings dialog, shown in Figure 15-1, and the Display Properties → Settings → Advanced dialog, one page of which is shown in Figure 15-2. To view Display Properties, run the Display applet from Control Panel or right-click on a vacant area of the desktop and choose Properties. The following sections describe how to use Display Properties to configure Window 98 video settings. Windows 2000 is similar, with minor differences in the appearance, names, and functions of the dialogs. To configure specific settings for the adapter and monitor, enable or disable video acceleration settings, and choose Color Management options. The exact pages in this dialog vary according to the video adapter and driver installed.

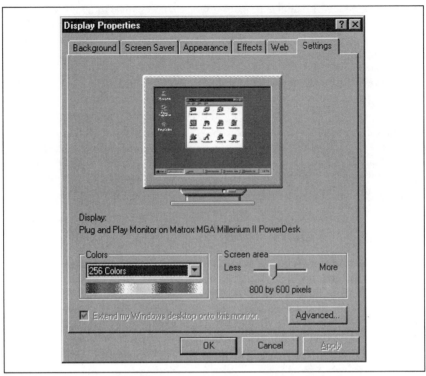

Figure 15-1: *The Display Properties Settings page*

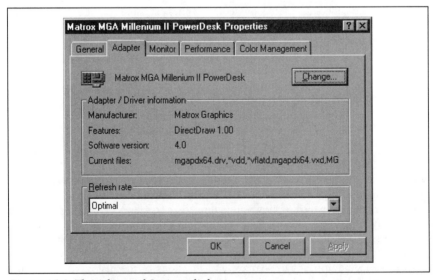

Figure 15-2: *The Advanced Settings dialog*

Installing or Changing Video Drivers

Windows 98 does reasonably well at detecting common video adapters and installing the proper drivers for them. However, you may need to install a video driver manually in one of the following circumstances:

- Windows 98 does not have a driver for your adapter. This situation is more common than you might expect. For example, Windows 98 does not provide a driver for the ubiquitous Intel i740 video adapter. This situation may also arise if you install a new video adapter in an existing Windows 98 system.

- Windows 98 has a driver for your adapter and recognizes the hardware, but you have a more recent driver supplied by the adapter manufacturer. Manufacturers often provide enhanced drivers that are faster or support more features than the vanilla drivers included with Windows 98.

- Windows 98 has a driver for your adapter, but fails to autodetect the presence of the adapter, or autodetects the adapter as a different model than is actually present. This situation also arises more often than it should.

To install a new or updated video adapter, first visit the video adapter manufacturer's web site and download the latest Windows 98 drivers for your adapter. Get the most recent release version of the driver, avoiding beta or unsupported versions. To install the driver, display the Settings page, click Advanced, choose the Adapter tab, and click Change to start the Update Device Driver Wizard.

Also use this dialog to set Refresh rate. Available options depend on the combination of monitor, adapter, and driver being used. When using a PnP monitor, the usual choices are Optimal—which selects the highest refresh rate supported by both the monitor and adapter at the current resolution—and "Adapter default," which simply uses the (usually low) refresh rate that the adapter defaults to. Some configurations allow you to specify actual refresh rates, e.g., 60, 70, 72, 75, and 85 Hz. Before you specify a refresh rate manually, make sure your monitor supports that refresh rate at the resolution and color depth you have selected. Some configurations do not allow changing Refresh rate, in which case the Refresh rate drop-down list does not appear.

 Some manufacturers supply video drivers as executable files. Running the program installs the driver and may add a custom tab to the Display Properties dialog that allows you to set properties for that driver and adapter. Such drivers also often put a video management utility in the system tray, which you can use to change settings on the fly.

When you change resolution or refresh rate, some monitors automatically adjust to the new settings and display a properly centered image. Others require changing vertical and horizontal size and centering adjustments on the monitor to display the image properly. If you select a resolution and refresh rate that the monitor cannot display, the screen may be blank or filled with wavy lines. To correct this problem, restart the computer in Safe Mode by pressing F8 during boot and choosing Safe Mode. Choose the Standard VGA driver, restart the system normally, use Display Properties to select the proper driver and display settings that your monitor supports, and then restart the system normally.

Choosing a Video Driver

Deciding which video driver to use is nontrivial. If Windows 98 supplies a driver for your video card, you can assume that it is at least stable and provides the basic functions, although it may well be slower or have fewer features than the latest driver from the video card manufacturer. The alternative is using a driver from the adapter manufacturer, which may or may not be a good idea.

Some manufacturers have become famous for the "driver of the week." Each new release adds features, improves speed, kills old bugs, and (usually) introduces new bugs. Use such drivers at your own risk, and be prepared for a lot of crashes. Other manufacturers, notably Matrox, treat video drivers with the seriousness they deserve.

Our advice: choose a video card from a manufacturer, like Matrox, that treats drivers with respect. For clients and standalone PCs, use the latest release driver certified by the adapter manufacturer. For servers and other critical systems, use either the vanilla Microsoft driver or a later Microsoft-certified driver supplied by the adapter manufacturer. In either case, avoid subsequently upgrading video drivers unless there is a compelling reason to do so. Avoid beta and other bleeding-edge drivers unless you enjoy having your system crash unpredictably.

Changing the Screen Area Setting

The Screen area setting determines how much information is displayed on the screen by specifying the resolution of the image that the video adapter delivers to the monitor. The default resolution installed by Setup will be within the capabilities of your video adapter and monitor, but may not be optimum. Use the Screen area slider in Display Properties → Settings to change resolution. Note that the selection range is not continuous. If your monitor is Plug-N-Play compliant and recognized by Windows 98, Windows 98 allows you to select only those discrete values that are supported by both the video adapter and monitor.

Although Windows 98 itself supports changing resolution on the fly, doing so requires that the video adapter and driver support that feature. Changing resolution with some older video adapters and drivers requires shutting down and restarting Windows 98. If so, Windows notifies you that a shutdown is required to put the change into effect and allows you to shut down immediately or defer doing so. If you choose the latter, configuration changes do not take effect until you later restart the system manually.

If the monitor type is not recognized by Windows, be careful when changing resolution settings. Depending on the default monitor setting, Windows may allow you to select a resolution setting higher than the monitor actually supports. At best, this results in an unreadable display. At worst, it may overdrive and damage the monitor. A seriously overdriven monitor may begin whining like a Star Trek phaser about to self-destruct, with similarly catastrophic results likely. If this happens, turn off the monitor *immediately.* More than a few seconds of this abuse may turn a monitor into scrap.

If you find yourself with Windows set to a resolution that the monitor cannot display, shut down and restart Windows in Safe Mode. Use the procedure described at the end of the preceding section to reconfigure Windows to use a video driver and display settings that are supported by your hardware.

Enabling and Using QuickRes

If you frequently need to change resolution or color depths, the preceding procedure gets old fast. Enabling the Windows 98 QuickRes utility allows you to change resolution and color depth on-the-fly. To enable QuickRes, choose Display Properties → Settings → Advanced. On the General page of that dialog, mark the "Show settings icon on task bar" checkbox. With QuickRes enabled, clicking its icon in the system tray displays a menu that displays all combinations of resolution and color depth supported by the video adapter and monitor, and marks the active settings with a check mark. Change resolution or color depth by clicking on the combination you want to use. The Adjust Display Properties menu item provides a one-click method for invoking Display Properties when you need to change properties other than those shown on the QuickRes menu.

QuickRes was first released as one of the unsupported Windows 95 Power Toys utilities, but is integral to Windows 98. If you installed QuickRes under Windows 95 and then upgraded to Windows 98, the Windows 95 version of QuickRes may still appear in your system tray. If so, you can continue to use it. If you prefer to remove the older version and install the Windows 98 version, you'll have to edit the Registry. To do so, start Registry Editor and open the key HKEY_ CURRENT_USER\Software\Microsoft\Windows\CurrentVersion\Run. Double-click the value entry Taskbar Display Controls to edit the entry. Change the value entry, which should be "RunDLL deskcp16.dll, QUICKRES_RUNDLLENTRY" to "RunDLL deskcp16.dll" and save the change. Then enable QuickRes 98 by marking the checkbox as described previously.

Changing Performance Setting

By default, Windows 98 configures the video driver it installs to use all accelerator functions. Ordinarily, this setting works properly and can be left as is. If you experience video problems, including a mouse pointer that is jerky (check that your mouse is clean first) or disappears entirely, odd video artifacts, or program crashes, Windows 98 permits you to selectively disable some video acceleration functions (Display Properties → Settings → Advanced → Performance). Before you use this feature, first attempt to locate and install an updated video driver. Otherwise, choose an accelerator setting as follows:

Full
> All accelerator functions enabled.

High
> Most accelerator functions enabled. Use this setting if you experience minor video or mouse problems. Performance will be degraded somewhat but may be acceptable, particularly for simple 2D applications such as word processing.

Low
> Most accelerator functions disabled. Use this setting if you experience severe video problems or have one or more programs that routinely hang. With this setting enabled, performance may be marginally acceptable for text applications, but little else. Make getting a better video card a high priority.

None
> All accelerator functions disabled. Use this setting only if it is required to allow your system to run without crashing. When this setting is enabled, your video card is acting as a simple frame grabber, and its performance will almost certainly be unacceptable even for text applications. If you find this setting is required, replace your video card as soon as possible.

Setting Font Size

Windows uses Small Fonts by default, but allows you select predefined Large Fonts, or to specify a custom font size by choosing Other. The font size setting you select provides a "baseline" value from which the size of vector-based fonts used in applications is calculated. Choosing one of the predefined settings also installs a set of raster fonts that are used for such things as icon labels. A common reason to use Large Fonts is to enable running higher than standard resolution, e.g., 1024×768 on a 15" monitor. Using Large Fonts or a custom font size allows you to make the text large enough to be readable. Be cautious, however. Many applications do not display properly using anything except Small Fonts. Note that instead of changing font size directly (Display Properties → Settings → Advanced → General), you can achieve similar results by selecting a different Scheme in the Appearance page of the Display Properties dialog.

Using Color Management

Getting consistent color across a wide range of peripherals, including monitors, scanners, and printers, is nontrivial, a task made more difficult by the diverse means used for producing color. Monitors produce color by illuminating phosphors. Printers may produce output that uses transmitted or reflected light to produce color by means of dyes or pigments. Scanners may capture either transmitted or reflected images. The color temperature of the lighting used to produce or view an image differs according to its source, and the gamma (in simple terms, contrast) varies with the device. With so many variables in play, the colors on your monitor are likely to be only an approximation of the original colors you scanned, and printed output is likely to differ substantially from both the original and the image on your monitor.

The different methods used to produce color mean that it is impossible to render color with complete consistency. A printed copy, for example, simply does not have the dynamic range that a transparency or monitor image has. But for those doing pre-press work, some means of minimizing those differences is needed. To address this problem, Microsoft introduced *Image Color Management (ICM)* with Windows 95. ICM organizes the characteristics of each device (e.g., for a scanner, the color temperature of the light source and the gamma of the image sensor; for a printer, the reflectivity characteristics of its various inks) and uses those stored characteristics to make color reproduction as consistent as possible across different devices.

Windows 98 includes the ICM V 2.0 API, which improves on the limited capabilities of ICM V 1.0. Previously, you had to define color characteristics for each combination of application and device. Windows 98 allows you to define color management profiles that take into account the specific imaging color characteristics of each input and output device and allow all installed applications to use that shared profile to maintain color consistency. ICM characteristics for scanners and printers are set in the drivers for those applications. Those for monitors are set in Display Properties → Settings → Advanced → Color Management.

Color management is an extremely complex issue. For more information, read the Microsoft ICM whitepaper, available online at *http://www.microsoft.com/windows/ platform/icmwp.htm*. This whitepaper also contains links to various other color management resources.

Configuring Video Under Windows NT 4

Like Windows 98, Windows NT 4 centralizes video configuration functions in the Display Properties Settings page, shown in Figure 15-3. Two key differences are that Windows NT 4 does not support PnP (although it automatically detects some video adapters via a different mechanism) and that Windows NT 4 never knows what monitor type is connected unless you tell it. The implications of these differences are that you may have to choose the proper video driver and that using the optimum settings for a monitor requires either you know the detailed specifications for that monitor or you use trial and error to determine the best settings.

Viewing or Changing Adapter Information and Video Drivers

To view information about the currently installed video adapter and its drivers, click Display Type. Windows NT 4 does not support PnP, but it attempts to detect

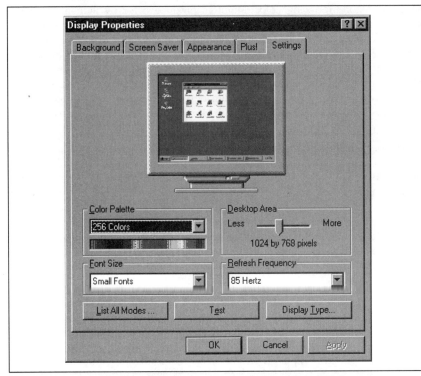

Figure 15-3: The Display Properties Settings page in Windows NT 4

the installed video adapter by searching BIOS memory space for strings contained in the adapter BIOS and comparing the strings it finds against a database of known adapters. Although not as effective as PnP, this method allows Windows NT 4 to detect many common video adapters successfully and install the proper drivers for them. But detection is not perfect, and you may need to install a driver manually, for the same reasons listed in the preceding section for Windows 98.

To install a new or updated video adapter, first visit the video adapter manufacturer's web site and download the latest Windows NT drivers for your adapter. Get the most recent release version of the driver, avoiding beta or unsupported versions. To install the driver, click Display Type. Although the resulting dialog includes a Detect button that causes Windows NT to attempt to detect the adapter, we recommend avoiding that process. Instead, click the Change button and follow the prompts to install the new driver you downloaded from the display adapter manufacturer.

Setting Resolution, Color Depth, and Refresh Frequency

Although you can change individual settings for Color Palette, Desktop Area, or Refresh Frequency by using the associated drop-down list or slider, we recommend using the List All Modes button instead, which sets all three of these settings at once and guarantees that the combination you choose is one supported by the installed adapter and driver.

Before you accept a new group of settings, always click Test to verify that the new settings are compatible with your monitor. If your monitor does not display the image properly with the new settings, but you accidentally click Yes to enable them—as we have done more than once—you could simply turn off the power to the computer, but that risks data corruption. Better practice is to recover using the following procedure. You won't have video for the first three steps, so you'll have to do them blind:

1. Press Ctrl-Alt-Del to invoke the Windows NT Security dialog.

2. Pause briefly, then press Alt-S to begin the Shut Down process.

3. Pause briefly, then press Enter to shut down the computer. Depending on the last shut down action you took, the computer may Shut Down or it may Shut Down and Restart.

4. After the Shut Down completes, restart the computer if necessary. When the OS Loader startup menu appears, start Windows NT in VGA only mode. Windows loads the current video driver (not its vanilla VGA driver), but sets the display to 640×480. After you log on, Windows displays an information box to tell you that the current display settings are invalid. Clear that display and continue.

5. Bring up Display Properties Settings and choose new settings that your monitor can display properly.

This procedure works if you have the correct video driver installed, but what if you've somehow installed the wrong video driver entirely? If that happens, repeat this procedure to shut down Windows NT gracefully. When the system restarts, choose Last Known Good configuration to restart Windows with the original video driver and then choose a proper set of new settings.

Setting Font Size

Windows NT 4 allows you to select between Small Fonts and Large Fonts by using the Font Size drop-down list on the Settings page of Display Properties. Unlike Windows 98, Windows NT 4 does not allow you to specify an arbitrary font size. The same caveats apply to using Large Fonts in Windows NT 4 as in Windows 98. To change font size in Windows NT, choose the other font size and follow the prompts. If the new font size was installed previously, Windows NT offers to use the existing font files on disk. Otherwise, you'll be prompted to insert the distribution CD so that Windows can load the new fonts. Once the files are loaded, restart the system to put the font size change into effect.

Troubleshooting Video Adapter Problems

If you experience video problems, first check the obvious things—that the monitor has power and is connected properly to the adapter, that no one has changed settings on the monitor, and so on. If you have another monitor handy, try connecting it to the problem system to eliminate the monitor as a possible cause.

Once you eliminate those possible causes, the next consideration is whether you've made any recent changes to your video hardware, software, or configuration. If so, that is a likely cause. Sometimes, problems caused by such a change don't manifest immediately. We have, for example, seen an updated driver function perfectly until one particular program was loaded or another piece of hardware was installed, which caused the system to crash and burn horribly.

That means the next step is to change video drivers. If a later driver is available, download and install it. If no later driver is available, try reinstalling the current driver. If problems manifest soon after installing an updated driver, try reinstalling the older driver.

Once they are installed and running properly, video adapters seldom fail, short of something like a lightning strike or abusing the adapter by overclocking it. Over 20 years' experience with hundreds of systems, we remember only a few instances when a functioning video adapter just died. Hardware failures are more likely today, not because newer video adapters are inferior to their parents, but because they're now pushed harder. High-end video adapters nowadays come with at least a heat sink for the graphics processor, and it's not unusual to see a video adapter on a gamer's system with a fan or even a Peltier cooler installed. If you install a high performance adapter, make absolutely certain that the fan, if any, has power, and that there is free air flow to the heat sink. Many video problems on systems so equipped are due to simple overheating.

Here are some specific problems you may encounter and how to remedy them:

Windows 9X displays only 640×480 with 16 colors, with no higher options available
Windows is using the standard VGA driver. If Windows 9X cannot detect the display adapter type when it is installed, it installs the vanilla VGA driver. Windows may have been installed or reinstalled improperly, or the display adapter may have been deleted in Device Manager, and Windows did not successfully detect the video adapter the last time it was restarted. If Color palette has options above 16, but Desktop area is fixed at 640×480, the monitor type may be incorrect or missing. To solve this problem, install the correct drivers for the video adapter and/or monitor.

The Windows 9X startup splash screen displays properly, but the desktop does not
This problem is also caused by incorrect video drivers or configuration errors. The startup screen is a low-resolution image that is displayed at standard VGA settings. To solve the problem, restart the system in Safe Mode, and reinstall or reconfigure the drivers for the video adapter and/or monitor.

Icons display incorrectly or as black squares
One likely cause is a corrupted ShellIconCache file, a problem that occurs frequently on systems running IE4 and TweakUI, but is by no means limited to that environment. To solve this problem under Windows 9X or NT, uninstall TweakUI (if it is installed), then delete or rename ShellIconCache (in the Windows directory) and restart the system, which automatically rebuilds the ShellIconCache file. Alternatively, view Display Properties → Appearance. In the Item drop-down list, select Icon. Use the Size spinner to change the icon size one step up or down and click Apply to save the change. Change the icon size back to its original value and click OK to save the change and exit

the dialog. This process forces Windows to rebuild ShellIconCache. Icon display problems also occur sometimes on Windows NT 4 systems running early builds, a situation that is easily solved by installing the latest service pack. Finally, we have seen this behavior caused on one system by overheating. In that case, the icons displayed normally for some time after the system was started, but turned into black boxes after the system had been running for some time. Cleaning the dust out of the system and installing a supplemental cooling fan made the problem go away, and it has never returned.

The monitor displays random black or parti-colored blocks

These screen artifacts may appear only when using certain combinations of resolution and color depth, and are not affected by mouse movement or by running a different application. They may be persistent or may appear and disappear seemingly at random. This problem is a result of malfunctioning video memory. Possible causes include: upgrading an adapter with slow or mismatched memory, overclocking an adapter, improperly seated memory modules or corroded connectors, and the video adapter not being fully seated. If you are overclocking the adapter, stop doing so and see if the problem goes away. If the adapter is out of warranty and at least a year or two old, consider replacing it. Even inexpensive current adapters greatly outperform anything of that vintage. If you decide to troubleshoot the problem, observe anti-static precautions. Remove and reseat the adapter in its original slot. If it is a PCI adapter, try moving it to another slot. Use your thumb to press gently on each chip or memory module to ensure it is fully seated. If the adapter uses memory modules, remove and reseat each of them, although this may be impractical if the modules require special tools. Use rubbing alcohol or a commercial contact cleaning product to clean accessible connectors and slots, both for memory and for the adapter itself. If you have recently installed a memory upgrade on the adapter, remove it temporarily to see if the problem disappears.

Text is scrambled, incomplete, or appears in an odd font

If this occurs when you build or upgrade a system, the most likely cause is incorrect video drivers. Download and install the most recent stable video drivers for your adapter. If it occurs on a system that had been working correctly, there are several possible causes. If text entered in an application appears in a strange font, but menus and other system fonts are correct, use preferences or options within the application to choose another font. If menus are scrambled only within one application, uninstall and then reinstall that application. If the problem occurs in multiple applications and system applets, system font files may have been corrupted or replaced with older, incompatible versions. The easiest cure is to reinstall the operating system, using its repair option. If you run Windows 9X, the hardware acceleration setting may be too high. Decrease it, as described in the preceding section on Windows 98. Although this problem usually is obvious when the system is first brought up, we have seen it occur on a system that had been running perfectly at the highest setting. In that case, installing a DVD drive broke the system. As it turned out, reducing hardware acceleration by one level allowed the video card and DVD drive to co-exist, but we ultimately replaced the video card with a later model that would run with full hardware acceleration.

Under Windows NT 4, you replace a PCI video card with an AGP card, and another card stops working
Windows NT does not support AGP, but treats an AGP card as a PCI card. If the motherboard maps the IRQ assigned to the AGP slot to the same IRQ used by the first PCI slot, installing the AGP card creates an IRQ conflict. Move the affected PCI card to a different slot, or use BIOS Setup to remap IRQ assignments.

Video is usually fine but becomes jerky during DVD playback
This is often caused by insufficient system resources (such as a slow processor, aging video adapter, inadequate memory), by having too many other programs running, or by attempting to display DVD video at too high a resolution and/or color depth. If you use software MPEG decoding, rather than replacing the processor, consider adding a dedicated DVD decoder card. If the DVD drive is ATAPI, configure it for DMA mode rather than PIO mode (see Chapter 12, *DVD Drives*). Finally, Windows 9X IRQ Steering may configure the video card to share an IRQ with another card, such as a network card. Use Device Manager to check IRQ assignments and verify that the video card is not sharing its IRQ. If so, relocate the PCI card to a different slot.

When using an overlay DVD MPEG decoder card, one particular color (often magenta) doesn't display properly
This is an artifact of how some DVD MPEG decoder cards function, mapping the DVD video to one particular overlay color. As a temporary fix, connect the monitor directly to the video card except when you are displaying DVD video. The only real fix is to replace the DVD decoder with one that does not do such mapping.

Our Picks

Here are the video adapters we use and recommend:

Gaming video card
Card of the Month. If you spend most of your time playing Quake, check enthusiast sites such as AnandTech (*http://www.anandtech.com*) for news about the best current gaming video adapters (and be prepared to replace your adapter every few months). As we write this in mid-2000, cards based on the nVIDIA GeForce 256 are the fastest gaming cards readily available, but that will likely change before you read this.

High-performance video card
Matrox G400. The Matrox doesn't win all the benchmark comparisons on enthusiast web sites, but it wins some and is in the running on the others. The $175 G400 offers an excellent combination of price, performance, display quality, robust drivers, extra features (including dual-head support for using multiple monitors), and good support. If games are only part of what you use your computer for, buy the G400 or its faster and more expensive sibling, the $225 G400 Max. (*http://www.matrox.com/mga/products/mill_g400/home.htm*)

Business video card

Any reasonably recent adapter. We have a motley collection of aging video cards around here, and they're all more than good enough for normal business use. You're likely to find any recent video adapter adequate for undemanding 2D applications like word processors and web browsers, including embedded adapters and video cards that are one or even two generations out of date. That said, we still use Matrox cards whenever possible for their excellent display quality and driver support.

Video card with TV/DVD support

ATI All-In-Wonder 128. We like Matrox video cards a lot, and their Marvel G400-TV provides competent TV capture and editing features. We almost picked it, but we found something better. The ATI All-In-Wonder 128 ($150 to $250, depending on memory) includes built-in DVD decoding hardware, whereas the Marvel G400 uses software decoding unless you purchase an add-on hardware decoder. The ATI card stores video natively in MPEG-1 or MPEG-2 format, which results in smaller files at any given image quality than the MJPEG format used by Matrox. ATI also makes the similarly named All-In-Wonder 128 Pro, which we did not receive in time for review. That card uses the faster Rage 128 Pro chipset rather than the Rage 128 chipset, but is otherwise comparable. Note that TV cards function as ordinary video cards under Windows NT. Their special TV features are available only under late releases of Windows 95, Windows 98, and Windows 2000 (once drivers are available). (*http://www.ati.com/na/pages/products/pc/aiw_128*)

We constantly test and review new equipment. For the latest information about what we currently use, visit:

http://www.hardwareguys.com/picks/video.html

CHAPTER 16

Monitors

Like a television set, a monitor comprises a *Cathode Ray Tube* (*CRT*) and supporting circuitry that processes the external video signal into a form that can be displayed by the CRT. Monitors use a different video interface than televisions, have much higher bandwidth, and can display much finer detail. In fact, with the proper interface adapter, computer video signals can be displayed on a standard television, but only at low resolution. Conversely, a monitor can be used to display television video at very high quality, although doing so requires using a video card with TV input, a tuner, and other electronics that are built into television sets but not monitors. The quality of the CRT and supporting circuitry determines the quality of the image a monitor can display. Because of their higher bandwidth and resolution, computer monitors cost much more than televisions with equal screen sizes.

Monitors comprise the following major elements:

CRT

The CRT is essentially a large glass bottle, flat or nearly so on one end (the screen), tapering to a thin neck at the back, and with nearly all air exhausted. The inside of the screen end is covered with a matrix of millions of tiny *phosphor* dots (or stripes). A phosphor is a chemical compound that when struck by electrons, emits visible light of a particular color. Phosphors are organized by groups of three, collectively called a *pixel*. Each pixel contains one phosphor dot that emits each of the additive primary colors, red, green, or blue. By choosing which dot(s) to illuminate and how brightly to illuminate each, any pixel can be caused to emit any one of thousands or millions of discrete colors. For example, 24-bit color allocates a full 8-bit byte to each of the primary colors, allowing it to be set to any of 256 levels of brightness. Three colors, each of which can be set to any of 256 brightness values, provide a total color palette of 256^3 colors, or about 16.7 million colors. The distance between nearest neighbors of the same phosphor color on adjacent rows is called the *dot pitch* or *stripe pitch*. A smaller pitch results in a sharper image and the ability to resolve finer detail.

Electron guns

The phosphor dots are excited by one or more electron emitters, called *electron guns*, located in the neck at the back of the monitor. A gun comprises a heated cathode, which emits electrons, and circuitry, which focuses the free electrons into a thin beam. Most CRTs use three separate guns, one for each primary color. Sony Trinitron CRTs use only one gun. There has been much debate about the relative display quality of single-gun versus triple-gun CRTs, both of which have theoretical advantages and disadvantages. In practice, we find the images indistinguishable. The quality of the electronics used to control the shape and positioning of the electron beam is very important to image quality, because the relative position of pixels to electron gun varies with the position of the pixel on screen. Pixels near the center of the screen are oriented at 90 degrees to the gun, and are struck dead-on by the beam. Conversely, pixels near the corners of the screen are struck by the beam at an angle, which, in the absence of correcting circuitry, causes the beam to assume an oval rather than circular shape. High-quality guns correct this problem by changing the shape of the beam according to the position of the pixel being illuminated. Lower-quality guns used in inexpensive monitors do a much poorer job of adjusting the beam, resulting in images blurring near the edges and corners of the tube.

Deflection yoke

The *deflection yoke* is located around the tapered portion of the CRT, between the guns and the screen. This yoke is actually a large electromagnet, which, under the control of the monitor circuitry, is used to steer the electron beam(s) to impinge on the correct phosphor dot at the correct time and with the correct intensity.

Mask

The *mask* sits between the the electron guns and the phosphor layer, very close to the latter. This mask may be a sheet of metal with a matrix of fine perforations that correspond to the phosphor dot triads on the screen or a series of fine vertical wires that correspond to phosphors laid down in uninterrupted vertical stripes. The perforations or stripes permit properly aimed electrons to impinge directly on the phosphors at which they are aimed, while blocking excess electrons. This blocking results in a cleaner image, but blocked electrons heat the mask. To prevent differential heating from distorting the mask, it is often constructed of Invar (an alloy with an extremely low coefficient of thermal expansion) or a similar material. Although the mask improves image sharpness, it also dims the image, because areas blocked by the mask cannot emit light, so design efforts focus on minimizing the percentage of screen area blocked by the mask.

In practice, and despite the marketing efforts of manufacturers to convince us otherwise, we find that the mask type makes little real difference. Good (read expensive) monitors produce good images, regardless of their mask type. Inexpensive monitors produce inferior images regardless of their mask type. Monitors from the best makers—Hitachi, Mitubishi, NEC, and Sony—produce superb images using different masking methods. That said, however, there's no substitute for looking at the monitor yourself. You may have a strong preference for the type of picture produced by one of the following mask types.

Aperture grill

The Sony Trinitron television tube appeared in the 1960s as the first alternative to standard shadow mask tubes and has since been used in most Sony monitors. Rather than using the standard dot triads, aperture grill monitors use uninterrupted vertical stripes of phosphors, alternating red, green, blue across the width of the screen. Masking is done by an aperture grill, which consists of a series of very fine vertical wires covering the full width of the tube, and corresponding to the phosphor stripes. In any given vertical phosphor stripe, no mask separates individual pixels vertically, so the top and bottom of each pixel must be delimited by the accuracy of the scanning electron beam. The advantages of the aperture grill are that it allows more electrons to pass than any other masking method, which makes for a brighter, saturated, high-contrast image on screen, and that the absence of "hardcoded" vertical boundaries on pixels allows using any arbitrary vertical resolution. A minor disadvantage is that the fine vertical wires that comprise the grill are easily disturbed by mechanical shock such as bumping the monitor, which results in a shimmering effect that may take a few seconds to stabilize. Also, the vertical wires are supported by one fine horizontal wire in 14" and smaller Sony monitors, or two such wires (which divide the screen roughly in thirds) on 15" and larger Sony monitors. These horizontal damper wires cast a shadow that some users find objectionable, particularly when they are visible on a light background. The Mitsubishi Diamondtron tube, used in their mid-range and high-end monitors, uses similar technology.

Shadow mask

The *shadow mask* is a perforated sheet of metal whose holes correspond to *dot triads*, groups of three colored phosphors, which may be arranged in various ways. Three distinct variants of this masking technology are used.

The *standard shadow mask* is still used, particularly in inexpensive generic monitors and in the "value" models from name-brand manufacturers. The standard shadow mask perforations are arranged at the apices of an equilateral triangle. The advantages of the standard shadow mask are that it is inexpensive and provides a reasonably sharp image. The disadvantage is that it blocks more screen real estate than other methods, resulting in a noticeably dimmer image, lower color saturation (muddy colors), and less contrast. Also, its triangular pixel arrangement means that vertical lines may show noticeable "jaggies." Standard shadow mask monitors are suitable for casual use, but are not the best choice for intensive use.

The *slotted mask*, developed by NEC, is a hybrid that combines the stability and sharpness of the standard shadow mask with most of the brightness, contrast, and color saturation of the aperture grill. The slotted mask is essentially a shadow mask in which the small round holes are replaced by larger rectangular slots. Like a standard shadow mask, the slotted mask uses discrete phosphor trios, although they are arranged as rectangular stripes and cover more of the screen surface. The slotted mask design is physically more stable than an aperture grill, while the larger slots allow many more electrons through than does a standard mask. The resulting picture is brighter than a standard shadow mask monitor, but less so than an aperture grill monitor.

The latest masking technology, *Enhanced Dot Pitch* (EDP) from Hitachi, improves on the standard shadow mask by increasing the size of the phosphor dots and changing their shape from an equilateral triangle to an isoceles triangle. The larger phosphor dots result in a brighter image with more contrast and color saturation, and the changed shape provides a better image that resolves finer detail. For example, a standard shadow mask monitor with a 0.28 mm diagonal dot pitch actually uses a 0.14 mm vertical pitch and a 0.24 mm horizontal pitch. A corresponding Hitachi EDP monitor uses a 0.27 mm diagonal dot pitch with a 0.14 mm vertical pitch and a 0.22 mm horizontal pitch. The smaller overall dot pitch renders finer detail, and the smaller difference between vertical and horizontal pitch results in subtle but very noticeable differences in image quality.

Monitor Characteristics

Here are the important characteristics of monitors:

Screen size

    Screen size is specified in two ways. The nominal size—the size by which monitors are advertised and referred to—is the diagonal measurement of the tube itself. However, the front bezel of the monitor conceals part of the tube, making the usable size of the monitor less than stated. Various consumer lawsuits have resulted in monitor manufacturers also specifying the *Viewable Image Size* (*VIS*), which is the portion of the tube that is actually visible. Typically, VIS is an inch or so less than nominal. For example, a nominal 17" monitor may have a 15.8" VIS. Small differences in VIS, e.g., 15.8" versus 16" make little practical difference. The smallest monitors commonly available are 15", although a few 14" models can be found. 17" models are currently the most popular, but the rapidly falling prices of 19" models means they may soon overtake 17" models in popularity. 20" and larger monitors are still quite expensive, and are used primarily by graphics artists and others who require huge displays. Table 16-1 lists monitor size and resolution combinations that most people with 20/20 vision find optimum. An entry of ++ indicates optimum conditions, + indicates suitable, – is generally unsuitable, and – – indicates completely unsuitable conditions.

Table 16-1: Monitor Size and Resolution Quality

Resolution	Monitor Size			
	15"	*17"*	*19"*	*21"*
640 × 480	+	–	– –	– –
800 × 600	++	+	–	– –
1024 × 768	–	++	+	–
1152 × 864	– –	++	+	–
1280 × 1024	– –	–	++	+
1600 × 1200	– –	– –	+	++

People with less-than-perfect vision often use the next size larger monitor (e.g., running 800×600 on a 17" monitor or 1024×768 on a 19" monitor), but we recommend instead using the optimum settings listed and configuring Windows and applications to display larger-than-normal fonts, e.g., set Display Properties to use the "Windows Standard (large)" or "Windows Standard (extra large)" scheme; set Internet Explorer font size to Larger or Largest; set Word to display text at 150% or 200%, and so on. Using high resolution provides finer-grained images, which are easier on the eyes.

Dot/stripe pitch

Dot pitch or *stripe pitch* is measured in millimeters, and specifies the center-to-center distance between the nearest neighboring phosphor dots or stripes of the same color. Smaller pitch means a sharper image that resolves finer detail. Unfortunately, dot pitch, which is used to describe shadow mask monitors, cannot be compared directly to stripe pitch, which is used to describe aperture grill monitors. For equivalent resolution, stripe pitch must be about 90% of dot pitch. That is, a 0.28 mm dot pitch monitor has resolution similar to a 0.25 mm stripe pitch monitor.

Maximum resolution

Maximum resolution specifies the maximum number of pixels that the monitor can display, which is determined by the physical number of pixels present on the face of the tube. The maximum resolution of many low-end monitors is identical to the optimum resolution for that monitor size. For example, 1024×768 is optimum for 17" monitors, and so many low-end 17" monitors provide 1024×768 maximum resolution. Conversely, mid-range and high-end monitors may have maximum resolutions higher than practically usable. For example, a high-end 17" monitor may support up to 1600×1200. There is no real benefit to such extreme resolutions, although it can be useful to have one step higher than optimum (e.g., 1280×1024 on a 17" monitor or 1600×1200 on a 19" monitor) available for occasional use for special purposes.

Synchronization range

The *synchronization range* specifies the bandwidth of the monitor, which determines which combinations of resolution, refresh rate, and color depth can be displayed. Synchronization range is specified as two values:

Vertical Scanning Frequency (VSF)

The inverse of the time the monitor requires to display one full screen. VSF (also called *refresh rate*) is measured in Hz and specifies the number of times per second that the screen can be redrawn. To avoid screen flicker, the monitor should support at least 70 Hz refresh at the selected resolution. Within reason, higher refresh rates provide a more stable image, but rates beyond 85 or 90 Hz are necessary only for specialized applications such as medical imaging. Most monitors support a wide range of refresh rates, from very low (50 Hz) to very high (120 to 160 Hz).

Horizontal Scanning Frequency (HSF)

The inverse of the time the monitor requires to display one full scan line. HSF is measured in kHz, and specifies the overall range of bandwidths supported by the monitor. For example, a monitor running 1280×1024 at 85 Hz must display 1024 lines 85 times per second, or 87,040 scan lines per second, or about 87 kHz. In fact, some overhead is involved, so the actual HSF for such a monitor might be 93.5 kHz.

Resolution, refresh rate, and color depth are all interrelated parts of synchronization range. For example, increasing the refresh rate increases the number of screens (and accordingly the amount of data) that must be transferred each second. Similarly, increasing color depth from High Color (2 bytes/pixel) to True Color (3 bytes/pixel) increases the amount of data to be transferred by 50%. To increase resolution, refresh rate, or color depth, you may have to decrease one of the others to stay within the HSF limit on total bandwidth.

Note that manufacturers often specify maximum resolution and maximum refresh rate independently, without consideration for their interrelatedness. For example, specifications for a 19" monitor may promise 1600×1200 resolution and 160 Hz refresh. Don't assume that means you can run 1600×1200 at 160 Hz. 160 Hz refresh may be supported only at 640×480 resolution; at 1600 ×1200, the monitor may support only 70 Hz refresh.

Tube geometry

Monitors use one of three geometries for the front viewing surface. *Spherical* tubes are used in older monitors and some inexpensive current models. The viewing surface is a section of a sphere, rounded both horizontally and vertically, which results in apparent distortion at normal viewing distances. This geometry keeps the center and corners of the screen close to the same distance from the electron guns, allowing the use of less expensive shadow mask materials and less sophisticated and cheaper electronics. *Cylindrical* tubes, first introduced with the Sony Trinitron, use a section of a cylinder as the viewing surface, and are vertically flat but horizontally rounded. This keeps the distance from gun-to-center and gun-to-corners similar, while reducing apparent distortion of the viewing area relative to a spherical tube. *Flat Square Tubes* (*FST*) are actually spherical in section, but form a sphere with a radius so large that they appear nearly flat. The advantage to FST is that the image area is effectively flat, minimizing viewing distortion. The disadvantage is that the electron guns are much farther from the corners than the center, which in turn demands a relatively costly Invar mask and more expensive electronics to provide even coverage. Other than some "value" models, all current monitors, including Sony Trinitrons, use an FST. Don't consider buying a monitor that is not FST.

Controls and stored settings

All monitors provide basic controls—brightness, contrast, horizontal/vertical image size and centering. Better monitors provide additional controls for such things as screen geometry (pincushion and barrel distortion adjustments), color temperature, and so on, as well as an on-screen display of settings. Changing display settings such as resolution and refresh rate may also change the size and position of the image. If you frequently change resolution, look for a monitor that can store multiple settings so that you will not have to read-just the monitor manually each time you change display settings.

Neck length

As 19" monitors become increasingly mainstream, monitor depth also becomes an increasing problem. Historically, most monitors were about as deep as their nominal screen size. With 15" monitors, depth was usually not a problem. With 17" monitors, depth began to be an issue, and with 19" monitors many people find that their desks are not deep enough to allow using a 19" monitor. Manufacturers have responded by producing reduced-depth or "short-neck" monitors. A short-neck 17" monitor is about the depth of a standard 15" monitor, and a short-neck 19" monitor is about the depth of a standard 17" monitor. That shorter neck involves some trade-offs, however. Foremost is the fact that achieving that shorter depth requires changing the deflection angle from the standard 90 degrees to 100 or even 110 degrees. Increasing the deflection angle requires more expensive electronics to compensate and results in reduced image quality. In effect, you pay twice for a short-neck monitor, because it both costs more and provides an inferior image.

Choosing a Monitor

Use the following guidelines when choosing a monitor:

- Remember that a monitor is a long-term purchase. Even with heavy use, a high-quality monitor can be expected to last five years or more, whereas inexpensive monitors may fail within a year or two. We have several 17" monitors that were purchased with one system and have been moved to two or three successor systems over the years. Good large monitors are inexpensive enough now that it makes sense to buy for the long term.

- Make sure the monitor is big enough, but not too big. Verify that your desk or workstation furniture can accommodate the new monitor. Many people have excitedly carried home a new 19" or 21" monitor only to find that it literally won't fit where it needs to. Check physical dimensions and weight carefully before you buy. Large monitors commonly weigh 50 lbs. or more, and some exceed 100 lbs. That said, if you find yourself debating between buying one monitor and another that's the next size up, go with the larger monitor. But note that if your decision is between a low-end larger monitor and a high-end smaller one for about the same price, you may well be happier with the smaller monitor. A $350 17" monitor beats a $350 19" monitor every time.

- Avoid reduced-depth monitors whenever possible. Space constraints may force you to choose a short-neck model. Just be aware that you will pay more for such a monitor, and its image quality will be lower.

- Stick with good name brands and buy a mid-range or higher model from within that name brand. That doesn't guarantee that you'll get a good monitor, but it does greatly increase your chances. The monitor market is extremely competitive. If two similar models differ greatly in price, the cheaper one likely has significantly worse specs. If the specs appear similar, the maker of the cheaper model has cut corners somewhere, whether in component quality, construction quality, or warranty policies.

Deciding which are the "good" name brands is a matter of spirited debate. Our opinion, which is shared by many, is that Sony makes the best monitors available, although they sell for a significant premium. Hitachi, Mitsubishi, and NEC are very close to Sony. EIZO/Nanao, Nokia, and (lately) the better Samsung models are well thought of by many. You're likely to be happy with a monitor from any of these manufacturers, although we still recommend choosing one from the first group of four. A step behind those are the immensely popular ViewSonic monitors, which we have been told by industry sources are actually manufactured by other companies in bid lots and simply relabeled by ViewSonic. ViewSonic did not confirm this when we asked them.

Further down the ladder are "value" brands like Mag Innovision, Princeton, Optiquest, and others. Our own experience with value brands, albeit limited, has not been good. A Princeton monitor we bought died a month out of warranty, as did an OEM Mag Innovision model that we bought bundled with a PC. Two Mag Innovision monitors developed severe problems after only a year or two of use. In our experience, which covers many hundreds of monitors purchased by employers and clients, the display quality of the value brand monitors is mediocre, and they tend not to last long. The same is generally true of monitors bundled with systems. Although there are exceptions, bundled monitors tend to be low-end models from second- and third-tier makers. If you purchase a computer system from a direct vendor, we recommend you order it without a monitor and purchase a good monitor separately. You may be shocked by how little you are credited for the monitor, but that indicates just how inexpensive a monitor is typically bundled with systems. Also, make sure to request that the shipping cost be reduced accordingly. Direct vendors typically charge about $100 to ship the system and monitor, and perhaps $35 less to ship only the system unit. However, some credit the shipping only if you request it.

- Buy the monitor locally if possible. You'll pay more than you would buying mail order, but, after shipping costs, not as much more as it first appears. Monitors vary more between examples than other computer components. Also, monitors are sometimes damaged in shipping, often without any external evidence on the monitor itself or even the box. Damaged monitors may arrive DOA, but more frequently they have been jolted severely enough to cause display problems and perhaps reduced service life, but not complete failure. That makes the next point very important.

- If possible, test the exact monitor you plan to buy (not a floor sample) before you buy it. If you have a notebook computer, install DisplayMate on it (the demo version is adequate and can be downloaded from *http://www. displaymate.com/demos.html*) and use it to test the monitor. If you don't have a notebook, take a copy of DisplayMate with you to the store and get permission to run it on one of their machines. In return for the higher price you're paying, ask the local store to endorse the manufacturer's warranty—that is, to agree that if the monitor fails you can bring it back to the store for a replacement rather than dealing with the hassles of returning the monitor to the manufacturer. Mass merchandisers like Best Buy usually won't do this (they try to sell you a service contract instead, which you shouldn't buy), but small local computer stores will often agree to endorse the manufacturer's warranty. If the monitor has hidden damage from rough handling during shipping, that damage will ordinarily be apparent within a month or two of use, if not immediately.

- Most mainstream monitor manufacturers produce zero or one 15" model (there's no profit in them), and usually three—Good, Better, and Best models—in 17", 19", and 21". In general, the Good model from a first-tier maker corresponds roughly in features, specifications, and price to the Better or Best models from lower-tier makers. For casual use, choose a Good model from a first-tier maker, most of which are very good indeed. If you make heavier demands on your monitor—such as sitting in front of it 8 hours a day—you may find that the Better model from a first-tier maker is the best choice. The Best models from first-tier makers are usually overkill, although they may be necessary if you use the monitor for CAD/CAM or other demanding tasks. Best models often have generally useless features like extremely high resolutions and unnecessarily high refresh rates at moderate resolutions. It's nice that a Best 17" model can display 1600×1200 resolution, for example, but unless you can float on thermals and dive on rabbits from a mile in the air, your vision is likely to make that resolution unusable. Similarly, a 17" monitor that supports 115 MHz refresh rates at 1024×768 is nice, but in practical terms offers no real advantage over one that supports 85 or 90 MHz refresh.

- Decide which makes and models to consider (but not the specific unit you buy) based on specifications. Any monitor you consider should provide at least the following:

Controls

Power; Degauss (if not automatic); Contrast; Brightness; Horizontal Size; Horizontal Position; Vertical Size; Vertical Position; Pincushion/Barrel Distortion Adjustment. Better monitors may add some or all of the following: On-Screen Display; Focus; Individual Red, Green, Blue Color Control (or Color Temperature); Tilt; Align; and Rotate.

Warranty

Inexpensive monitors often have a one year parts and labor warranty (although 90-day warranties, particularly on labor, are not unheard of). Better monitors usually warrant the tube for two or three years (often excluding labor after the first year) with one year parts and labor on the remaining components. Warranties on high-quality monitors may be for three years parts and labor. In reality, the value of a long warranty on a good monitor is less than it might seem. The few times we've seen a good monitor fail, it's either been soon after it was taken out of the box or after many years of use. Conversely, a two- or three-year warranty on an inexpensive monitor would be useful indeed, because such monitors frequently fail after a couple of years. That's why you seldom find a good comprehensive warranty on a cheap monitor.

Other specifications vary according to monitor size. Note that shadow-mask dot pitches are not directly comparable with aperture-grill stripe pitches. A 0.28 mm diagonal dot pitch corresponds roughly to a 0.25 mm stripe pitch. Also, not all dot pitches are specified in the same manner. Some manufacturers specify the diagonal dot pitch. Others, such as Hitachi, specify individual horizontal dot pitch and vertical dot pitch. A monitor specified as having a 0.22 mm horizontal dot pitch and 0.13/0.15 mm vertical dot pitch corresponds roughly to a monitor with a 0.27 mm diagonal dot pitch. The minimum specifications are listed, with preferable values in parentheses:

15"

> 13.8" viewable image size (VIS); flat-square tube (FST); 0.28 mm diagonal dot pitch; maximum resolution 1024×768 (1280×1024); 75 Hz (85 Hz) refresh rate for standard 800×600 resolution. Automatically synchronize at 31 to 69 KHz (31–80 KHz) horizontally and 55 to 120 Hz (50–130 Hz) vertically. As of mid-2000, a high-quality, brand-name 15" monitor can be had for less than $200.

17"

> 15.6" (15.8") VIS; FST; 0.28 mm (0.27 mm) diagonal dot pitch; maximum resolution 1280×1024 (1600×1200); 85 Hz (100 Hz) refresh rate for standard 1024×768 resolution, and 75 Hz (85 Hz) refresh rate at 1280×1024. Automatically synchronize at 31 to 69 KHz (31–95 KHz) horizontally and 55 to 120 Hz (50–160 Hz) vertically. As of mid-2000, a high-quality, brand-name 17" monitor can be had for less than $300.

19"

> 17.8" (18.0") VIS; FST; 0.28 mm (0.27 mm) diagonal dot pitch; maximum resolution 1600×1200 (1920×1440) at 85 Hz (100 Hz) refresh rate for standard 1280×1024 resolution, and 75 Hz (85 Hz) refresh rate at 1600×1200. Automatically synchronize at 31 to 94 KHz (31–110 KHz) horizontally and 55 to 160 Hz (50–160 Hz) vertically. As of mid-2000, a high-quality, brand-name 19" monitor can be had for less than $500.

21"

> 19.8" (20.0") VIS; FST; 0.28 mm (0.27 mm) diagonal dot pitch; maximum resolution 1600×1200 (2048×1536) at 85 Hz (100 Hz) refresh rate for standard 1600×1200 resolution, and 75 Hz (85 Hz) refresh rate at 1856×1392. Automatically synchronize at 31 to 96 KHz (31–125 KHz) horizontally and 55 to 160 Hz (50–160 Hz) vertically. As of mid-2000, a high-quality, brand-name 21" monitor can be had for less than $900.

- Choose the specific monitor you buy based on how it looks to you. Comparing specifications helps narrow the list of candidates, but nothing substitutes for actually looking at the image displayed by the monitor. For example, monitors with Sony Trinitron tubes have one or two fine horizontal internal wires whose shadow appears on screen. Most people don't even notice the shadow, but some find it intolerable.

- Make sure the monitor has sufficient reserve brightness. Monitors dim as they age, and one of the most common flaws in new monitors, particularly those from second- and third-tier manufacturers, is inadequate brightness. A monitor that is barely bright enough when new may dim enough to become unusable after a year or two. A new monitor buy should provide a good image with the brightness set no higher than 50%.

Monitors

Installing and Configuring a Monitor

Physically installing a monitor requires only connecting its video cable to the video adapter and plugging the monitor into the wall receptacle. The steps required to adjust the monitor for proper screen size, best image quality, and so on vary according to the specific monitor you use. See the monitor manual for specific instructions.

 We recommend using DisplayMate (see Chapter 2, *Working on PCs*) when you install a new monitor or change video settings. In our experience, most monitors are not set for best image quality. Most people either use the default manufacturer settings or make a few arbitrary changes to brightness and contrast and let it go at that. Unless you've used DisplayMate to optimize it, chances are your monitor could be displaying a better picture than it is right now.

The steps required to configure the video adapter to use the monitor optimally vary by operating system, as described in the following sections.

Configuring a Monitor Under Windows NT 4

Windows NT 4 understands the capabilities of the installed video adapter, but has no knowledge of what monitor is connected to the system. Accordingly, it will permit you to configure video adapter settings that the connected monitor cannot display. In the worst case, you may configure the video adapter to use video settings so far beyond the ability of the monitor to display that using those settings for even a few seconds may physically damage the monitor.

Therefore, when installing a monitor on a Windows NT system, the first step is to check the monitor manual to determine the combinations of resolution, refresh frequency, and color depth that the monitor can support. Choose the optimum combination for your own needs from among the supported combinations, and then configure the video adapter to use those settings (see Chapter 15, *Video Adapters*).

Configuring a Monitor Under Windows 9X/2000

Windows 9X/2000 detects PnP monitors and automatically configures the correct settings for them, both when that monitor is present during Setup and, at the next restart, when you install a new PnP monitor. For non-PnP monitors, Windows uses the Standard Monitor, which displays only standard VGA resolution. Monitor type is configured from Display Properties → Settings → Advanced → Monitor. Changing monitor type manually uses the same Update Device Driver Wizard described in Chapter 15 but the search options are less useful for monitors than adapters.

Windows enables "Automatically detect Plug & Play" monitors by default. With some display adapters, enabling this setting causes the monitor to flicker during detection each time the system starts. This is harmless, but some people find it disconcerting. If that's the case, once your monitor is installed properly you can safely clear this checkbox.

Windows also enables "Reset display on suspend/resume" by default. This setting causes Windows to send a reset to the monitor each time you resume from Suspend mode. This causes annoying flickering with most video adapters, but disabling it can cause problems with some monitors, including inability to resume because the monitor never "wakes up" from Suspend mode. If you decide to disable this function and this problem occurs, the only option is to restart the computer and re-enable this setting. Note that even with this setting enabled, some configurations fail to resume from Suspend mode. If that occurs, the only solution we know of is to disable power management for video functions.

If Windows does not detect the monitor model (or detects the wrong model), use the Update Device Driver Wizard to select the proper monitor model from among those supported by Windows or to install a driver provided by the monitor manufacturer.

 Note that we refer to monitor "drivers" only for convenience. In fact, there is no such thing as a monitor driver in the same sense as a driver for a video adapter. The monitor "driver" is simply an information file that tells Windows the capabilities of that monitor—e.g., what refresh rates it supports at a given resolution—which allows Windows to choose optimal settings for that monitor for the video card in use.

Troubleshooting Monitor Problems

Monitors seldom fail outright without obvious signs, such as a loud snap or a strong odor of burning electrical components. Most monitor problems are really problems with the power, video adapter, cable, or hardware/software settings. To eliminate the monitor as a possible cause, connect the suspect monitor to a known-good system, or connect a known-good monitor to the suspect system.

If the monitor is the problem, it is often not worth repairing. If the monitor is out of warranty, parts and labor may cost more than buying a new monitor, which also gives you better specs and a warranty. About the only monitors we'd even consider repairing out-of-warranty are 19" and 21" models, and even there the economics are dubious.

Even if the monitor is in warranty, the shipping costs may exceed the value of the monitor. For example, shipping a monitor both ways can easily cost $75 or more. If that monitor is a two-year old 15" model, you're probably better off spending $150 on a new 15" monitor than paying $75 to fix the old one. Monitors have many components, all of which age together. Fixing one is no guarantee that another won't fail shortly. In our experience, that happens more often than not.

Never disassemble a monitor. At best, you'll likely destroy the monitor. At worst, it may destroy you. Like televisions, monitors use extremely high voltages internally, and have large capacitors that store that energy for days or even weeks after the monitor is unplugged. Robert once literally burned a screwdriver in half when working inside a color television that had been unplugged for several days. Also, the large, fragile tube may implode, scattering glass fragments like a hand grenade. People who repair monitors and televisions for a living treat them with great respect, and so should you. If you must repair a monitor, take it to someone who knows what he is doing. You have been warned.

Here are some common monitor problems:

Monitor displays no image
Check the obvious things first. Verify the monitor is plugged in (and that the receptacle has power), the video cable is connected to the video card, the computer and monitor are turned on, and the brightness and contrast settings are set to the middle of their range. If none of these steps solves the problem, your monitor, video card, or video cable may be bad. Check the suspect monitor on a known-good system or a known-good monitor on the problem system.

 If you have ACPI or APM power management enabled, it may be causing the problem. Some systems simply refuse to wake up once power management puts them to sleep. We have seen such systems survive a hardware reset without restoring power to the monitor. To verify this problem, turn off power to the system and monitor and then turn them back on. If the monitor then displays an image, check the power management settings in your BIOS and operating system and disable them if necessary.

Monitor displays only a thin horizontal line or a pinpoint at the center
This is a hardware problem. Take the monitor to be repaired, or replace it.

Monitor snaps, crackles, or pops when powered up, or emits a strong electrical odor
Catastrophic monitor failure is imminent. The noises are caused by high-voltage arcing, and the smell is caused by burning insulation. Unplug the monitor from the wall before it catches fire, literally.

Monitor emits a very high pitched squeal
There are two likely causes. First, you may be driving the monitor beyond its design limits. Some monitors display a usable image at resolutions and/or refresh rates higher than they are designed to use, but under such abuse the expected life of the monitor is shortened dramatically, perhaps to minutes. To correct this problem, change video settings to values that are within the monitor's design specifications. Second, the power receptacle may be

supplying voltage lower than the monitor requires. To correct this problem, connect the monitor to a different circuit or to a UPS or power conditioner that supplies standard voltage regardless of input voltage.

Monitor displays some colors incorrectly or not at all

This is usually a minor hardware problem. The most likely cause is that the signal cable is not connected tightly to the monitor and/or video card, causing some pins to make contact intermittently or not at all. Verify that no pins are loose, bent, or missing on the cable or the connectors on the monitor and video card, and then tighten the cable at both ends, If that doesn't fix the problem, open the computer, remove the video card, and reseat it fully. Another possible cause is your DVD decoder card: some hardware DVD decoder cards "steal" one color (usually magenta) and use it to map the DVD video signal onto the standard video signal. Short of replacing the DVD decoder card with another model that doesn't do this, the options are to live with the problem or to connect the monitor directly to the video card for normal operations and connect the monitor to the DVD decoder card only when you want to watch a DVD.

Image rolls or a horizontal line scrolls constantly down the screen

The most likely cause is that the monitor is receiving inadequate power. Connect it to a different circuit.

Image flickers

The most likely cause is that the refresh rate is set too low. Change the refresh rate to at least 75 Hz. Flicker also results from interaction with fluorescent lights, which operate on 60 Hz AC and can heterodyne visually with the monitor. This can occur at 60 Hz (which is far too low a refresh rate anyway), but can also occur at 120 Hz. If you're running at 120 Hz refresh and experience flicker, either use incandescent lighting or reset the refresh rate to something other than 120 Hz.

Image is scrambled

The video card settings are likely outside the range supported by the monitor, particularly if you have just installed the monitor or have just changed video settings. To verify this, restart the system in VGA mode. If the system displays a VGA image properly, change your display settings to something supported by the monitor.

Image displays rectilinearly, but is incorrectly sized or aligned on screen

Most modern monitors can display signals at many different scan frequencies, but this doesn't mean that the monitor will necessarily automatically display different signals full-screen and properly aligned. Use the monitor controls to adjust the size and alignment of the image.

Image displays other than rectilinearly (trapezoid, parallelogram, barrel, or pincushion)

Depending on the monitor, video card, and video settings, this may be normal behavior, adjustable using the monitor controls. If the distortion is beyond the ability of the controls to correct, the problem may be with the video card, the monitor, or the driver. First try changing video settings. If the problem persists at several settings, move that monitor to a different system (or use a different video card) to determine whether the problem is caused by the monitor or video card. Repair or replace the faulty component.

Image wavers or shimmers periodically or constantly

This is usually caused by RF interference from another electrical or electronic device, particularly one that contains a motor. Make sure such devices are at least three feet from the monitor. Note that such interference can sometimes penetrate typical residential and office walls, so if the monitor is close to a wall, check the other side. Such image problems can also be caused by interference carried by the power line. To rectify this, plug the monitor into a surge protector. Better still, plug it into a UPS or power conditioner that supplies clean power at constant voltage.

Colors are "off" or smearing appears in some areas

The monitor may need to be degaussed. A monitor that sits in one position for months or years can be affected even by the earth's very weak magnetic field, causing distortion and other display problems. Exposing a monitor to a strong magnetic field, such as unshielded speakers, can cause more extreme image problems. Many modern monitors degauss themselves automatically each time you cycle the power, but some have a manual degauss button that you must remember to use. If your monitor has a manual degauss button, use it every month or two. The degaussing circuitry in some monitors has limited power. We have seen monitors that were accidentally exposed to strong magnetic fields, resulting in a badly distorted image. Built-in degaussing did little or nothing. In that case, you can sometimes fix the problem by using a separate deguassing coil, available at Radio Shack and similar stores for a few dollars. We have, however, seen monitors that were so badly "magnet burned" that even a standalone degaussing coil could not completely eliminate the problem. The moral is, keep magnets away from your monitor, including those in speakers that are not video-shielded.

Our Picks

Here are the monitors we use and recommend:

15" Monitor

Sony CPD110GS or the NEC MultiSync A500+. We recommend 15" models only if spending $75 more for a 17" model busts the budget. If so, choose either of these monitors. Both provide superior images, and you can buy either for less than $175. (*http://www.ita.sel.sony.com/products/displays/gs/ cpd110gs.html* and *http://www.nectech.com/monitors/product_info/product. cfm?PDDProdIdx=250*)

17" Monitor

Hitachi SuperScan 640. For about $250, this monitor provides a very good image at 1024×768 and 85 Hz, which are ideal display settings for a 17" monitor. Hitachi also makes the more expensive 641 and 643 models, which have a slightly smaller dot pitch than the 640, support resolutions up to 1600 ×1200 (overkill for a 17" monitor), and support 115 Hz refresh at 1024×768, which is of little practical advantage over 85 Hz. If for some reason the Super-Scan 640 (or its successor) were unavailable, we'd buy a Mitsubishi, NEC, or

Sony model with similar price and specifications. (*http://www.hitachidisplays.com/products/17_elite640_641_643.htm*)

19" Monitor

Hitachi SuperScan 751. This monitor has topped most best-seller charts since it was introduced, and for good reason. It's reasonably inexpensive ($450 or so), supports 1280×1024 at 85 Hz and 1600×1200 at 75 Hz, and displays a superb, rock-solid image. This is the monitor that Robert uses on his main personal system. If you want a 19" monitor for general use, buy this model. For those who need to run 1600×1200 resolution at higher refresh rates, Hitachi manufactures the 752 and 753, which support 80 and 85 MHz refresh respectively, and the 769, which is a short-neck version of the 753. All are overkill for general use, but may be useful for those with special applications. (*http://www.hitachidisplays.com/products/19_751_752_753.htm*)

21" Monitor

None. We don't have a 21" monitor, have never had one, don't want one, and don't see the point to having one. These monitors are too large and too heavy for most desks, provide only about 20% more viewing area than a 19" model, and cost two to three times as much. For graphics artists, CAD workers, and others with similarly demanding graphics needs, a 21" monitor may be worthwhile. Even then, however, it may be better to use two monitors, perhaps a 19" main and a 17" supplemental. If for some reason we had to buy a 21" monitor, we'd compare specs and pricing on models from Hitachi, Mitsubishi, NEC, and Sony and buy whichever offered the features we needed at the best price.

We constantly test and review new equipment. For the latest information about what we currently use, visit:

http://www.hardwareguys.com/picks/video.html

CHAPTER 17

Sound Cards

Because no one envisioned sound as a business necessity, the only provision early PCs made for sound was a $0.29 speaker driven by a square-wave generator to produce beeps, boops, and clicks sufficient for prompts and warnings. Reproducing speech or music was out of the question. Doing that required an add-on *sound card*, which were quick to arrive on the market as people began playing games on their PCs. The early AdLib and Creative Sound Blaster sound cards were primitive, expensive, difficult to install and configure, and poorly supported by the OS and applications. By the early 1990s, however, sound cards had become mainstream items that shipped with most PCs. By the late 90s, many motherboards incorporated embedded sound functions. With a sound card and appropriate software, a PC can perform various tasks, including:

- Playing audio CDs, either directly or from compressed digital copies of the CD sound tracks stored as MP3 files on your hard disk.

- Playing stereo music, sound effects, and voice prompts in games, education, training, and presentation software, as well as for operating system prompts, warnings, and other events.

- Capturing dictation to a document file, adding voice annotations to documents, or controlling applications using voice/speech recognition software.

- Supporting audio conferencing and telephony across a LAN or the Internet.

- Supporting text-to-speech software that allows the PC to "read" text aloud, aiding children who cannot read and people who are visually impaired.

- Creating music using MIDI software and hardware.

Although this chapter focuses on sound cards, because MP3 has become increasingly popular and generates much reader mail, it also covers the basics of MP3— what it is, and how to use it to extract digital audio from CDs and store it on your hard drive in compressed form. The following sections describe what you need to know to choose, install, configure, troubleshoot, and use a sound card effectively.

PC Audio Types

Sound cards support two categories of audio, which are detailed in the following sections:

Waveform audio

> *Waveform audio* files, also called simply *sound files*, store actual audio data. When you record waveform audio, the sound card encodes the analog audio data in digital format and stores it as a file. When you play waveform audio, the sound card reads the digital audio data contained in the file and converts it to analog audio, which is then reproduced on speakers or headphones. Waveform audio files can store any type of audio, including speech, singing, instrumental music, and sound effects. The playback quality of waveform audio depends primarily on how much detail was captured in the original recording. Waveform audio files are large, requiring as much as 10 MB per minute of audio stored.

MIDI audio

> Rather than storing actual audio data, *MIDI (Musical Instrument Digital Interface)* files store instructions that a sound card can use to create audio on-the-fly. MIDI audio files store only instrumental music and sound effects, not speech or singing. Originally used almost solely by professional musicians, MIDI is now commonly used by PC games for background music and sound effects, so MIDI capabilities have become an important sound card issue. Because MIDI sound is created synthetically by the sound card, playback quality of MIDI files depends primarily on the features and quality of the MIDI support in the sound card. A MIDI file of an orchestral concert, for example, may sound like a child's toy when played by a cheap sound card, but may closely resemble a CD recording when played by a high-end sound card. MIDI audio files are small, requiring only a few KB per minute of audio stored.

Waveform Audio

Waveform audio files are created using a process called *sampling* or *digitizing* to convert analog sound to digital format. Sampling takes periodic snapshots of the instantaneous state of the analog signal, encodes the data, and stores the audio in digital form. Just as digital images can be stored at different resolutions according to their intended use, audio data can be stored at different resolutions to trade off sound quality against file size. Five parameters determine the quality of digital sound files and how much space they occupy:

Sample size

> *Sample size* specifies how much data is stored for each sample. A larger sample size stores more information about each sample, contributing to higher sound quality. Sample size is specified as the number of bits stored for each sample. CD audio, for example, uses 16-bit samples, which allow the waveform amplitude to be specified as one of 65,536 discrete values. All sound cards support at least 16-bit samples.

Sampling rate

> *Sampling rate* specifies how often samples are taken. Sampling rate is specified in Hz (Hertz, or cycles/second) or kHz (kilohertz, one thousand Hertz).

Higher frequency data inherently changes more often. Changes that occur between samples are lost, so the sampling rate determines the highest frequency sounds that can be sampled. Two samples are required to capture a change, so the highest frequency that can be sampled, called the *Nyquist frequency*, is half the sampling rate. For example, a 10,000 Hz sampling rate captures sounds no higher than 5,000 Hz. In practice, the danger is that higher frequencies will be improperly sampled, leading to distortion, so real-world implementations filter the analog signal to cut off audio frequencies higher than some arbitrary fraction of the Nyquist frequency, for example by filtering all frequencies above 4,500 Hz when using a 10,000 Hz sampling rate. CD audio, for example, uses 44,100 Hz sampling rate, which provides a Nyquist frequency of 22,050 Hz, allowing full bandwidth response up to approximately 20,000 Hz after filtering. All sound cards support at least 44,100 Hz sampling, and many support the Digital Audio Tape (DAT) standard of 48,000 Hz.

Sampling method

Sampling method specifies how samples are taken and encoded. For example, Windows WAV files use either *PCM* (*Pulse Coded Modulation*), a linear method that encodes the absolute value of each sample as an 8-bit or 16-bit value, or *ADPCM* (*Adaptive Delta PCM*), which encodes 4-bit samples based on the differences (delta) between one sample and the preceding sample. ADPCM generates smaller files, but at the expense of reduced audio quality and the increased processor overhead needed to encode and decode the data.

Recording format

Recording format specifies how data is structured and encoded within the file and what means of compression, if any, is used. Common formats, indicated by filename extensions, include WAV (Windows audio), AU (Sun audio format, commonly used by Unix systems and on the Internet), AIFF or AIF (Audio Interchange File Format, used by Apple and SGI), RA (RealAudio, a proprietary streaming audio format), and MP3 (MPEG-1 Layer 3). Some formats use *lossless compression*, which provides lower compression ratios, but allows all the original data to be recovered. Others use *lossy compression*, which sacrifices some less important data in order to produce the smallest possible file sizes. Some, such as PCM WAV, do not compress the data at all. Some compressed formats, such as MP3, allow selectable compression ratios, while others use fixed ratios.

 The large size of uncompressed audio files means that most common waveform audio formats use some form of compression. An algorithm used to compress and decompress digital audio data is called a *codec*, short for coder/decoder. Windows 98, for example, includes the following codecs: CCITT G.711 A-Law and μ_-Law, DSP Group TrueSpeech™, GSM 6.10, IMA ADPCM, Microsoft ADPCM, and Microsoft PCM (which is technically not a codec). You needn't worry about which codec to use when playing audio; the player application automatically selects the codec appropriate for the file being played. When you record audio, the application you use allows you to select from the codecs supported by the format you choose.

Number of channels

Depending on the recording setup, one channel (*monaural* or *mono* sound), two channels (*stereo* sound), or more can be recorded. Additional channels provide audio separation, which increases the realism of the sound during playback. Various formats store 1, 2, 4, or 5 audio channels. Some formats store only two channels, but with additional data that can be used to simulate additional channels.

Table 17-1 lists the standard Windows recording modes for PCM WAV files, the most common uncompressed waveform audio format, and three commonly used MP3 recording modes. MP3 at 256 KB/s uses little more storage than Windows' AM radio mode, but produces sound files that are near-CD quality. MP3 bitrates are approximate.

Table 17-1: Comparison of Storage Modes

Quality	Size	Sample Rate	Channels	Bytes/min	Compression
Telephone	8-bit	11,025 Hz	1 (mono)	661,500	PCM (1:1)
AM radio	8-bit	22,050 Hz	1 (mono)	1,323,000	PCM (1:1)
CD audio	16-bit	44,100 Hz	2 (stereo)	10,584,000	PCM (1:1)
MP3 (64 KB/s)	16-bit	44,100 Hz	2 (stereo)	~500,000	MP3 (~20:1)
MP3 (128 KB/s)	16-bit	44,100 Hz	2 (stereo)	~1,000,000	MP3 (~10:1)
MP3 (256 KB/s)	16-bit	44,100 Hz	2 (stereo)	~2,000,000	MP3 (~5:1)

MIDI Audio

A MIDI file is the digital equivalent of sheet music. Rather than containing actual audio data, a MIDI file contains detailed instructions for creating the sounds represented by that file. And, just as the same sheet music played by different musicians can sound different, the exact sounds produced by a MIDI file depend on which sound card you use to play it.

 Three PC MIDI standards exist. The first, General MIDI, is the official standard, actually predates multimedia PCs, and is the oldest and most comprehensive standard. The other two standards are called Basic MIDI and Extended MIDI. Both are Microsoft standards and, despite the name of the latter, both are subsets of the General MIDI standard. In the early days of sound cards, General MIDI support was an unrealistically high target, so many sound cards implemented only one of the Microsoft MIDI subsets. All current sound cards we know of support full General MIDI.

MIDI was developed about 20 years ago, originally as a method to provide a standard interface between electronic music keyboards and electronic sound generators like Moog synthesizers. A MIDI interface supports 16 channels, allowing up to 16 instruments or groups of instruments (selected from a palette of

128 available instruments) to play simultaneously. MIDI interfaces can be stacked. Some MIDI devices support 16 or more interfaces simultaneously, allowing 256 or more channels.

The MIDI specification defines both a serial communication protocol and the formatting of the MIDI messages transferred via that protocol. MIDI transfers 8-bit data at 31,250 bps over a 5 mA (milliamperes) current loop, using optoisolators to electrically isolate MIDI devices from each other. All MIDI devices use a standard 5-pin DIN connector, but the MIDI port on a sound card is simply a subset of the pins on the standard DB-15 gameport connector (see Chapter 21, *Game Controllers*). That means a gameport-to-MIDI adapter is needed to connect a sound card to an external MIDI device such as a MIDI keyboard.

MIDI messages are simply a string of ASCII bytes encoded to represent the important characteristics of a musical score, including instrument to be used, note to be played, volume, and so on. MIDI messages usually comprise a *status byte* followed by one, two, or three *data bytes*, but a MIDI feature called Running Status allows any number of additional bytes received to be treated as data bytes until a second status byte is received. Here are the functions of those byte types:

Status byte
> MIDI messages always begin with a *status byte*, which identifies the type of message, and which is flagged as a status byte by having the high-order bit set to 1. The most-significant (high-order) four bits (nibble) of this byte define the action to be taken, such as a command to turn a note on or off or to modify the characteristics of a note that is already playing. The least-significant nibble defines the channel to which the message is addressed, which in turn determines the instrument to be used to play the note. Although represented in binary as a 4-bit value between 0 and 15, channels are actually designated 1 through 16.

Data byte
> A *data byte* is flagged as such by having its high-order bit set to zero, which limits it to communicating 128 states. What those states represent depends on the command type of the status byte. When it follows a Note On command, for example, the first data byte defines the pitch of the note. Assuming standard Western tuning (A = 440 Hz), this byte can assume any of 128 values from Csharp/Dflat (17.32 Hz) to G (25087.69 Hz). The second data byte specifies *velocity*, or how hard the key was pressed, which corresponds generally to volume, depending on the MIDI device and instrument. The note continues playing until a status byte with a Note Off command for that note is received, although it may under programmatic control decay to inaudibility in the interim.

MIDI Synthesis Methods

The process by which sounds cards produce audio output from MIDI input is called *synthesis*.

FM synthesis
> *FM synthesis* combines multiple sine waves of differing frequency and amplitude to produce a composite wave that resembles the native waveform of the

instrument being synthesized. How close that resemblance is depends on the instrument and the quality of the FM synthesizer circuitry, and may vary from reasonably close to only a distant approximation. Even the best FM synthesis sound cards produce artificial-sounding audio, particularly for "difficult" instruments. Until the mid-1990s, most consumer-grade sound cards used FM synthesis. Today, only the least expensive sound cards use FM synthesis.

Wavetable synthesis

Wavetable synthesis uses stored waveform audio samples of actual instrument sounds to reproduce music. The sample may be used as is, or modified algorithmically to provide a sound for which no sample is stored. For example, the wavetable may contain a stored sample of an actual violin playing an A at 1760 Hz. If the MIDI score calls for a violin playing that A note, the sample is used directly. If the MIDI score calls for a violin playing an A note one octave higher (3520 Hz) and that note is not available as a stored sample, the synthesizer creates the 3520 Hz A note based on the data it has stored for the 1760 Hz A note. The quality of wavetable synthesis depends on the number, quality, recording frequency, and compression used for stored samples, and on the quality of the synthesizer hardware. Early wavetable sound cards were limited to the samples stored on their on-board ROM, which was typically 512 KB to 4 MB. Many current wavetable sound cards have, in addition to samples residing on on-board ROM, the ability to use additional samples stored on disk and loaded into main system memory as needed.

Some FM synthesis sound cards accept daughter cards that add wavetable support. Avoid these cards, which typically have limited functionality and are relatively expensive. Rather than upgrade an FM synthesis card to wavetable, simply replace it with a wavetable sound card.

Waveguide synthesis

Although good wavetable sound cards produce music quality an order of magnitude better than FM synthesis sound cards, they are still limited by the finite number of stored samples, and so still must simulate much of their output rather than using samples directly. For example, whereas most wavetable sound cards store a total of perhaps 4 MB of samples for all instruments, fully sampling just a piano would require 10 MB or more of samples. That means that some piano sounds must be interpolated from existing samples, which in turn means that the piano emulation is not as good as it might be, because interpolated sounds are less realistic than sampled sounds. The latest synthesis method, *waveguide synthesis,* also called *physical modeling synthesis,* creates a virtual model of an instrument and produces sounds based on calculations made against that model. Full waveguide synthesis for all instruments is beyond the hardware capabilities of any current PC. Some current high-end sound cards, however, use waveguide synthesis in conjunction with wavetable synthesis to improve the realism of emulation for some instruments.

Sound Cards

Downloadable Sounds

Downloadable sounds (DLS) is an extension to General MIDI that allows customizing the available MIDI sounds by temporarily replacing standard ROM-based MIDI wavetable instrumental sound samples with sound samples loaded from disk. DLS samples can be instrumental sounds, sound effects suitable for games (e.g., lion roars, tire squeals, or a machine gun firing), or even voice clips. In addition to customizing the available sounds, DLS allows software developers to ensure consistency across different sound cards and platforms, for example, by replacing ROM-based piano samples with DLS piano samples to make sure everyone hears the same piano. DLS Level 2 is supported by the DirectMusic component of Microsoft DirectX 7.0 and later running on Windows 95/98/2000, and is used by an increasing number of games, education packages, multimedia encyclopediae, and similar software.

Sound Card Components

The key function of a sound card is playback—accepting a digital data stream or MIDI instructions from the PC and converting them to an analog audio signal that can be reproduced on speakers or headphones. Most sound cards can also do the converse—accept an analog audio signal and convert it to a digital data stream that can be stored on a PC. Sound cards use the following components to support these functions:

Converters
Sound cards contain at least one *Digital-to-Analog Converter (DAC)* and one *Analog-to-Digital Converter (ADC)* for each of the two stereo channels, and some contain more. A DAC converts a digital audio stream into the analog audio delivered to the Line-out port. An ADC digitizes analog sound received from the Line-in or Microphone port. CD-Audio sound, generally the highest quality supported by sound cards, requires 16-bit resolution. The converters used in better-quality sound cards usually support higher resolution, typically 18- or 20-bit. Resolution sometimes differs between the DAC and ADC. For example, a card might use an 18-bit DAC and a 20-bit ADC. Internal resolution is often higher than that supported by the DAC/ADC, typically 24- or 32-bit.

Sample rate generator
The *sample rate generator* provides the clock for the converters under the control of the PC. While nothing prevents using arbitrary or continuously variable sample rates, most sample rate generators instead support discrete sample rates, which are usually even fractions of 44,100 Hz and 48,000 Hz. A sample rate generator might support sample rates of 48,000, 44,100, 32,000, 24,000, 22,050, 12,000, 11,025 Hz, and 8,000 Hz. Many sound cards support differing rates for record versus playback. For example, a card may support playback rates of 48,000, 44,100, 22,050, 11,025, and 8,000 Hz, but record only at 44,100 Hz.

Processor
The *processor* (also called the *sound generator* or *synthesis engine*) creates analog output from MIDI input by reading, interpolating, and combining wavetable samples into the composite audio waveform represented by the

MIDI instructions. Most sound cards use a custom *Digital Signal Processor* (*DSP*) like the E-mu Systems EMU10K1 or the Aureal Vortex2. The processor used directly or indirectly determines several key capabilities of the sound card, including how many MIDI channels, voices, hardware-accelerated sound streams, and so on it supports. DSPs provide useful supplementary capabilities in hardware, such as reverb and chorus effects, text-to-speech processing, and compression. Because a DSP is programmable, some DSP-based sound cards support related functions, such as faxmodem or TAD functionality.

Connectors

Sound cards typically provide at least the following connectors:

Line-out

> Line-out is a line-level (unamplified) stereo output intended to be connected to line-in on amplified speakers, headphones, home audio equipment, or a tape or DAT recorder. Most sound cards provide one stereo Line-out port, but some provide two mono Line-out ports, designated Left and Right. Sound cards that support four speakers usually have two stereo Line-out ports, one each for front and rear speakers. The PC 99 standard color code for Line-out is lime, although for this and other color codes makers often pay scant attention to the exact hue. The standard icon usually stamped into the card bracket is three concentric circle segments (to represent audio vibrations) with an outward-pointing arrow anchored in the center.

Line-in

> Line-in is a line-level stereo input intended to be connected to Line-out of external analog audio sources such as a CD player or VCR. Some microphones can also be connected to Line-in. The standard color is light blue. The standard icon is the same as for Line-out, but with the arrow head pointing to the center.

Microphone-in

> Microphone-in, sometimes labeled *Mic*, is a monaural input that supports inexpensive microphones for recording voice. The standard color is pink, although red is commonly used, and the standard icon resembles a microphone.

MIDI/gameport

> MIDI/gameport is a DB-15 connector whose primary purpose is to connect a game controller. However, the standard gameport (see Chapter 21) also supports connecting external MIDI devices such as keyboards and synthesizers. Doing so requires a special octopus cable, available from the manufacturer, which extends the MIDI signals present on the gameport to MIDI-standard 5-pin DIN MIDI-in and MIDI-out connectors, which resemble standard AT keyboard connectors. The gameport should fully support analog and digital game controllers, including force feedback and DirectInput devices. Standard color is Gold.

MPC-3 CD-in

> Although some recent CD-ROM drives can deliver CD audio digitally across the bus to the sound card, for most CD-ROM drives, listening to CD audio requires connecting the line-level Audio-out connector on the

back of the CD-ROM drive to the Audio-in connector on the sound card. Older CD-ROM drives and sound cards used a chaotic mix of proprietary and nonstandard connectors, which sometimes made it very hard to find the right cable. Recent CD-ROM drives and sound cards all use a standard cable. The sound card uses a shrouded, keyed, four-contact header-pin MPC-3 connector, often called a Molex or ATAPI connector. The CD-ROM drive uses an unkeyed version of the same connector, sometimes called a Sony connector. MPC-3 CD-in is usually color-coded black to differentiate it from other connectors that use the same physical connector.

Some sound cards also provide some or all of the following connectors:

Speaker-out/Subwoofer

Speaker-out/Subwoofer is an amplified stereo output intended to be connected to unpowered speakers, or to some powered subwoofers that expect a high-level input. Do not use this output to connect to standard powered speakers. Although it will usually work without damaging the speakers or the sound card, sound quality will be noticeably inferior to that provided by the Line-out connector. Standard color is Orange.

MPC-3 Aux-in

MPC-3 Aux-in uses the same physical connector as MPC-3 CD-in, described ealier in this section, and is usually color-coded white to differentiate it. This connector accepts any line-level input, although it is most commonly used on a system that already has one CD-ROM drive to connect audio from a second CD-ROM, CD-R(W), or DVD drive.

MPC-3 Modem-in/out

MPC-3 Modem-in/out uses the same physical connector as MPC-3 CD-in and MPC-3 Aux-in, and is usually color-coded green to differentiate it. MPC-3 Modem-in is a line-level audio input/ouput intended to be connected to a line-level connector on a modem. This allows modem tones to be played through the speakers, and also supports such functions as Internet telephony and audio conferencing via the modem.

Daughtercard connector

Some sound cards include one or more daughtercard connectors, which usually take the form of a large header pin connector similar to an IDE connector. Daughtercards, which are proprietary to the make and model of the sound card, may be used to add wavetable support, to extend ROM-based wavetable samples, or for other similar purposes.

S/PDIF

Sony-Philips Digital InterFace (S/PDIF) is an RCA coax jack that provides a direct digital connection between the sound card and an external device with an S/PDIF jack (typically, a DAT deck). All S/PDIF ports support 48,000 Hz. Most support 32,000 Hz; some support lower rates. S/PDIF is a standard feature on most high-end sound cards, and may be an option on mid-range sound cards. Some sound cards have both S/PDIF input and output ports, but others have only a S/PDIF output. Because of limited room on the expansion bracket of the sound card, S/PDIF ports are often present as header connectors on the sound card, which uses an extender cable to a cliffhanger bracket where the S/PDIF connectors reside. Some sound cards use a proprietary connector that joins the sound card to a remote head, which often contains S/PDIF connector(s), line-in connector(s), and MIDI connector(s).

CD interface connector

Some older sound cards include interface connector(s) for a CD-ROM drive, which made it easier and cheaper to upgrade older systems to multimedia capability. These connectors may be any of five types: the three proprietary interfaces used by early-model Mitsumi, Panasonic, and Sony CD-ROM drives; a second ATA interface, intended for use on early ATA systems that had only one embedded ATA interface; or a SCSI interface. Using any of these interfaces is a bad idea. The proprietary interfaces are used only by CD-ROM drives too old to be usable. The IDE interface is normally slow and conflicts with the second ATA interface present on all modern motherboards. The SCSI interface is slow, probably supports only one SCSI device, and often causes conflicts. Indeed, the presence of any of these connectors indicates that the sound card is so old that it should be replaced.

Amplifier

Early sound cards were intended for use with unamplified speakers, and so included an on-board amplifier. Nearly all modern computer speakers have built-in amplifiers that require only line-level input. Sound card amplifiers usually produce inferior sound, because they are inexpensive, underpowered, poorly shielded, and must operate in the electrically noisy environment inside a PC. Some modern sound cards include an amplifier, primarily for use with devices (like some powered subwoofers) that expect an amplified rather than line-level signal. A sound card that lacks an amplifier is not necessarily low quality. In fact, the converse is often true. Many inexpensive sound cards include amplified outputs, and many high-end sound cards do not.

Sound Card Characteristics

Here are the important characteristics of sound cards:

Interface

Discrete sound cards are available in ISA and PCI models. All recent embedded sound adapters use PCI. The much smaller bandwidth of ISA limits ISA cards in many respects, including generally requiring that wavetable data be stored locally, placing an upper limit of about 16 on simultaneous sound streams, and making effective 3D audio support impossible. The first PCI audio chipsets that emerged in the mid-90s were quite expensive, but current PCI cards are generally less expensive than ISA cards with similar functionality, primarily because they require little on-board memory.

Synthesis type

FM synthesis is used only for the least expensive current sound cards, typically those that sell for $25 or less. All mid-range and higher sound cards use Wavetable synthesis. The quality and features of that synthesis varies depending on both the processor and the quality and size of the wavetable samples, with more expensive cards producing better synthesis, as you might expect.

Channels

Each MIDI interface supports 16 channels, each corresponding to one instrument. Low-end sound cards use a single MIDI interface, allowing up to 16 instruments to play simultaneously. Mid-range and some high-end sound cards provide dual MIDI interfaces, allowing 32 simultaneous instruments. Some high-end sound cards, such as the Creative Labs SoundBlaster Live! Platinum, use a triple MIDI interface, which allows up to 48 simultaneous instruments. In general, 16-channel cards are suitable for most uses, 32-channel cards are useful for playing MIDI instrumentals realistically, and 48-channel cards are necessary only for the most complex MIDI environments.

Polyphony

Polyphony refers to the ability of a sound card to generate multiple simultaneous voices when playing MIDI. A *voice* corresponds to one note generated by one instrument. Do not confuse number of voices with number of channels. The 16 channels of a standard MIDI interface allow 16 instruments to play simultaneously. However, some instruments require multiple voices. For example, a piano occupies one MIDI channel, but if the musician is playing a single-note melody with one hand and three-note chords as accompaniment with the other hand, that channel requires four voices. A large number of voices is important for reproducing complex MIDI scores accurately. Voices may be hardware-based or software-based, and some sound cards use both types. For example, the Creative Labs SoundBlaster AWE64 sound card supports 64-voice polyphony, 32 in hardware and 32 in software. High-end sound cards support 64 hardware voices, and add software voices for a total of from 256 to 1024 voices.

Frequency response

The range of human hearing is usually stated as 20 Hz to 20 kHz. All current sound cards nominally support this range or close to it, which is in fact required for PC99 compliance. However, few cards state ±dB for that range, which specifies how flat the frequency response curve is. A good card may have frequency response of 20 Hz to 20 kHz at 3 dB down. A professional-level card may have frequency response of 20 Hz to 20 kHz at 1 dB down. Inexpensive cards may claim frequency response of 20 Hz to 20 kHz, but that range may turn out to be stated at 10 dB down or some similarly absurd number, which in effect means that actual usable frequency response may be something like 100 Hz to 10 kHz.

Sampling rate

All current sound cards support waveform audio playback at 44,100, 22,050, 11,025, and 8,000 Hz. Many also support various intermediate playback rates and the DAT-standard 48,000 Hz. Some cards record only at 44,100 Hz, although most also offer other standard rates.

Signal-to-Noise ratio

Signal-to-Noise ratio (S/N ratio), stated in dB, measures the amount of signal (data) relative to noise, with higher numbers indicating better performance. A low S/N ratio translates to audible hiss. The best sound cards have 95 dB or greater S/N; mid-range cards about 90 dB; and inexpensive cards may have 85 dB or less. In a typical PC environment, noise level (both ambient external audible noise and the electrically noisy inside of the PC) and the typical use of low-quality speakers or headphones make it unlikely that anyone could differentiate between cards with S/N ratios of 80 dB or higher if that were the only difference. However, cards with higher S/N ratios are generally better shielded and use better components, which translates to better sound and less hiss.

Duplex mode

Half-duplex sound cards can either play sound or record sound, but not both at the same time. *Full-duplex* sound cards do both simultaneously. For simple tasks—listening to CDs or playing games—a half-duplex card is adequate. More advanced audio functions, such as Internet telephony and voice recognition, require a full-duplex card. Most mid-range and all high-end sound cards support full-duplex.

Standards compatibility

In the past, software wrote directly to the sound card. That meant compatibility with proprietary standards—initially AdLib and later SoundBlaster—was important, because if your game or application didn't explicitly support your sound card you simply couldn't use sound with that software. Microsoft took the initiative away from sound card manufacturers by incorporating standard sound APIs into Windows. Here are the standards you should be aware of:

SoundBlaster

SoundBlaster compatibility, formerly a *sine qua non* for any sound card, is now largely immaterial except to those who still use DOS software, including DOS games. True SoundBlaster compatibility requires fixed IRQ, I/O port, and DMA assignments, whereas PCI cards are assigned resources dynamically. Within those constraints, all Creative Labs sound cards and most competing cards boast (nearly) full SoundBlaster compatibility. If you still use DOS applications, though, it's worth verifying whether or not real-mode drivers are available for a sound card before you purchase it.

Microsoft DirectSound

Microsoft DirectSound (DS) is a component of DirectX. Developers can write to the DS API, rather than to the underlying hardware, with the assurance that their software will function with any DS-compatible sound card. DS compatibility has replaced SoundBlaster compatibility as an absolute requirement for any sound card.

Microsoft DirectSound3D

Microsoft DirectSound3D (DS3D) is an extension to DS that supports 3D positional audio, which is a technology that manipulates sound information to extend stereo imaging to full surround sound, allowing sounds to appear to come from any position around you. For example, when in an air combat game your missile hits a bandit in front of you, the sound of that explosion comes from the front. But if you didn't notice his wingman on your six, the sound of his missile blowing off your tail comes from behind. The realism of DS3D imaging in any given situation depends on the means used to reproduce the sound (two speakers, four speakers, or headphones) and the hardware capabilities of the sound card. But whatever the physical environment, DS3D provides noticeably better imaging than older 2D technologies. If you intend to use DS3D-enabled software, it's important to have hardware support for DS3D in your sound card, because DS3D positional effects that cannot be processed in hardware are processed by the main CPU, which can bog down system performance.

Aureal A3D

Aureal A3D is a proprietary 3D positional audio standard that is available only on sound cards based on the Aureal Vortex and Vortex2 chipsets. Such cards are widely available, however, from manufacturers like Voyetra/Turtle Beach, Diamond Multimedia, Aureal itself, and others. A3D is available in two versions. A3D2.0 is supported only by the Vortex2 chipset, whereas the earlier and less capable A3D1.0 is supported by both the Vortex and Vortex2 chipsets. A3D1.0 provides realistic 3D imaging even on dual speaker systems or headphones. A3D2.0 provides extraordinary 3D effects, particularly on quad speaker systems. A3D has achieved broad support from game software manufacturers. For software without A3D support, A3D hardware drops back to using DS3D.

Creative Labs EAX

Creative Labs EAX (Environmental Audio Extensions) is basically a proprietary Creative Labs extension to DirectSound3D. EAX is technically less ambitious than A3D2.0, but provides reasonable 3D imaging. Given the dominance of Creative Labs, EAX is widely supported by game software.

 Windows 95, 98, and 2000 fully support DirectX, currently version 7.0. Windows NT supports a subset of DirectX 3 functions, including DirectSound (but not DirectSound3D). That means that, although DirectSound-compatible sound cards can be installed and used under NT, 3D functions are not available.

Hardware acceleration

Mid-range and high-end sound cards have an on-board DSP, which is a general-purpose CPU optimized for processing digital signals, such as audio. In 2D mode, the DSP provides enhanced audio effects like chorus, reverb, and distortion. In 3D mode, it processes 3D-positional audio (A3D 1.0/2.0, DirectSound3D, or EAX) algorithms locally, removing that burden from the main CPU. Inexpensive sound cards use the host CPU, which reduces performance significantly, particularly during complex operations such as 3D rendering. How many and which types of sound streams are hardware accelerated is an important specification, depending on how you will use the card. Aureal A3D2.0-based cards should provide hardware acceleration for 16 or more A3D2.0 and 64 or more A3D1.0 sound streams. A Creative Labs AEX card should accelerate 64 or more EAX sound streams. Any accelerated sound card should accelerate 64 or more DS and DS3D sound streams.

Choosing a Sound Card

Use the following guidelines when choosing a sound card:

Choose embedded sound, if available, for general use

If you are building a new system or replacing the motherboard on an existing system, choose a motherboard that includes embedded sound, unless you need features like 3D or enhanced MIDI functions. Embedded sound is inexpensive (typically $10 more than the same motherboard without sound) and well integrated, which minimizes installation and configuration problems. Embedded PCI sound also typically provides better SoundBlaster emulation than an add-on PCI card, if that is an issue.

Don't buy too much sound card

When you add or replace a sound card, don't pay for features you won't use. Don't buy an expensive sound card if you'll use it only for playing CDs, listening to system prompts, light gaming, Internet telephony, voice recognition (on a fast system), and so on. High-quality sound cards available for $35 or so, such as the Turtle Beach Montego A3DXstream and the Creative Labs SoundBlaster PCI 128, do not include enhanced MIDI support, 3D hardware acceleration, and other advanced features that expensive cards provide, but are more than adequate for most purposes.

Don't buy too little sound card

If you use a sound card extensively for purposes like 3D gaming, reproducing DVD sound, voice recognition (on a slow system), complex MIDI rendering, and so on, buy a sound card with hardware acceleration and other features that support what you use the card for. Capable consumer-grade high-end sound cards like the Turtle Beach Montego II, the Diamond Monster Sound 3D, and the Creative Labs SoundBlaster Live! sell for $75 to $150, and are suitable for anything short of professional audio production.

Consider replacing an older sound card

If a sound card is more than two or three years old, replace it. Even inexpensive current sound cards like the $20 Creative Labs Ensoniq AudioPCI are likely to provide better sound reproduction than high-end models that are a few years old, particularly for games and other MIDI applications.

Avoid ISA sound cards

Unless your system has only ISA expansion slots, choose a PCI sound card. PCI sound cards are faster and provide more voices, and are usually less expensive than equivalent ISA cards because PCI cards can use main system memory while ISA cards can use only on-board memory. One exception to this rule: if your system has barely adequate memory—less than 16 MB for Windows 9X or 32 MB for Windows NT—do not use a PCI sound card. The demands it makes on main system memory may slow performance and reduce system stability. If expanding memory is not an option, install an ISA card instead.

Avoid no-name sound cards

Stick to name-brand sound cards. We frequently hear horror stories from readers who have purchased house-brand sound cards—outdated drivers, missing or inadequate documentation, poor (or no) tech support, shoddy construction, incompatibility with Windows 98 or NT, and on and on. What's particularly ironic is that you may pay more for a house-brand sound card than for a low-end name-brand card. You can buy a decent sound card for $20 to $35 from reputable companies like Voyetra/Turtle Beach, Creative Labs, Diamond Multimedia, and others. There's no reason to buy anything less.

Make sure the sound card you choose has drivers available for your operating system
Nearly all sound cards are well-supported under Windows 95/98. Most mainstream cards have adequate Windows NT 4 drivers (although installing a PNP/ISA sound card under NT4 requires some extra steps). Windows 2000 includes drivers for most popular sound cards, but we have experienced conflicts and limited functionality with some of these drivers. Make sure any sound card you use with Windows 2000 has a certified Windows 2000 driver supplied by the manufacturer. Linux supports relatively few sound cards, although its support is much broader than it was only a year ago. If you run Linux, verify that drivers are available for the exact model sound card you plan to use.

Bundled software
We admit it. We've never bothered to install any of the plethora of applications that are bundled with many sound cards, particularly high-end models, and we probably wouldn't know what to do with them if we did. But that's because all we use sound cards for is to play back audio or to record audio from within other applications. The software supplied with a sound card varies according to the market focus of that card. Cards targeted at gamers often include a game or two intended to show off the features of that card, although such games are often demos, feature-crippled, or older versions. Similarly, cards with high-end MIDI features often include a competent MIDI sequencer and editor, although again it's likely to be a "Lite" version, intended primarily to convince you to upgrade to (and pay for) the "Professional" version. But if you do need one of these functions and your needs are moderate, bundled software may do the job you need and allow you to avoid spending more money on individually purchased applications.

 Embedded audio is destroying the standalone sound card market, so manufacturers are desperate to find new ways to sell cards. One popular means is to use packaging and bundled full-featured software to target a product at different niche markets. For example, Creative Labs markets their SoundBlaster Live! in several packages, including the MP3+ and the X-Gamer, which are targeted at music collectors and gamers respectively. Turtle Beach sells their Montego II card alone, or as the Voice Xpress or Home Studio versions, aimed at people who need voice recognition or audio mastering functions respectively. Same sound card, different software, different accessories, different markets. If you need a particular sound application, check the models available in such "families." One may have exactly the software you need at a lower combined price than you can buy the card and software for separately.

Installing a Sound Card

A sound card physically installs just as any other expansion card does. Some sound cards require many system resources, so keep the following guidelines in mind:

If you are installing an ISA sound card

Before proceeding, use Windows 9X Device Manager or Windows NT Diagnostics to determine which resources (IRQ, DMA, and I/O ports) are already in use and which are available. If installing the card using its default settings would cause a resource conflict, either reconfigure the card to use resources that are not already in use, or (better) leave the card configured at its default settings and reconfigure other system components to free the resources that the card wants.

 In particular, if you run DOS games, make sure the following resources are available and assigned to the card: IRQ 5, DMA 1, DMA 5, and I/O ranges 0220-022F, 0330-0331, and 0388-038B. DOS games often expect these exact resources, and fail to work if others have been substituted.

If you are building a new system

Install the PCI sound card before you install other components such as network adapters or SCSI host adapters, allowing the sound card to make first claim on system resources. Although PnP usually does a good job of juggling resources, we have sometimes experienced resource conflicts when installing a sound card in a system that was already heavily loaded with other adapters. If that happens, the best course is to disable all adapters in Device Manager (except essential ones like the video card and IDE interface), physically remove those adapters, then install and configure the sound card, and finally reinstall the other adapters one by one. If your CMOS Setup program allows you to assign an IRQ to a particular PCI slot, use that feature to assign IRQ 5 to the slot where you plan to install the sound card.

If you are replacing an existing sound card

Before you remove the card, delete it in Device Manager (if you are running Windows 9X) and delete all its drivers from the hard disk. Turn the PC off, take off the cover, physically remove the old sound card, and start the PC. Verify that all vestiges of the old sound card are gone. If the sound card is embedded, run CMOS Setup and disable it in BIOS. With all that done, turn off the PC again and physically install the new sound card. Start the system again and install the drivers for it.

Except for physically removing and replacing the sound card, we recommend following the same procedure when updating sound card drivers. That is, never upgrade sound card drivers. Instead, remove the old ones and install the new ones as a clean install. We have encountered problems more than once when attempting to upgrade existing drivers. A clean install avoids those.

If you are installing a sound card in a motherboard that has embedded sound

Before you install a sound card in a system with embedded sound, disable the embedded sound adapter either in CMOS Setup or by changing a jumper on the motherboard (or both). Every motherboard we know that includes embedded PCI sound allows you to disable sound in BIOS. Enabling or disabling sound usually has no effect on interrupts, because embedded PCI sound uses one or two shareable PCI interrupts. Older motherboards, however, may have embedded ISA sound adapters, which may use fixed ISA interrupts. Such motherboards may or may not allow sound to be disabled and the interrupt made available for other adapters. If it is possible to disable the interrupt, doing so usually requires removing a physical jumper on the motherboard.

When installing a sound card, remember to connect the CD audio cable from the Audio Out jack on the back of the CD-ROM drive to the CD Audio jack on the sound card. If you have two CD or DVD drives installed, you can connect Audio Out from the second drive to the Aux In jack on the sound card, if present. We always forget to connect these cables, which is a good reason to test the system before putting the cover back on.

Configuring a Sound Card Under Windows 95/98/2000

Configuring a sound card requires similar steps in Windows 95, 98, and 2000, with minor differences in the names and sequence of dialogs. To configure a sound card under Windows 9X or 2000, take the following steps:

1. After removing the existing sound card and drivers, if any, verifying all vestiges of the old sound card drivers are gone, and physically installing the new sound card, restart the system. Note that the drivers supplied on CD-ROM with some sound cards must be present in the CD-ROM drive when you start the system.

2. Windows should recognize that the new sound card is present and display the Add New Hardware Wizard. Although Windows 9X includes drivers for many sound cards, you are usually better off using the Windows 9X drivers supplied by the sound card manufacturer. To do so, mark the "Search for…" option button and click Next.

Windows 2000 includes drivers for relatively few sound cards. Even those drivers it does include often have limited functionality, such as supporting only two-channel sound on a four-channel card. We strongly recommend downloading Windows 2000 drivers from the sound card maker rather than using those provided with Windows 2000. Install Windows 2000 drivers in the same manner described for Windows 98 drivers.

3. When Windows displays the next dialog, either specify the location of the drivers, or tell it which drives to search for them. Click Next to continue.

4. Windows should locate the proper drivers and load them. When the process completes, reboot the system. Most sound cards include an automated installation procedure for bundled applications, which usually autoruns immediately after the system restarts. Follow the prompts, and provide any necessary information to complete the installation.

5. For Windows 98, right-click the My Computer icon, choose Properties, and then click the Device Manager tab. For Windows 2000, right-click My Computer, choose Properties, click the Hardware tab, and then click the Device Manager button. For either version, then expand the "Sound, video and game controllers" branch and verify that the sound card is installed properly and that no conflicts exist. Most sound cards also have a test utility that you should run to verify that all aspects of the sound card hardware and drivers are operating properly.

6. From Control Panel, double-click Multimedia to display the Audio page of the Multimedia Properties dialog (Windows 9X) or the Sounds and Multimedia Properties dialog (Windows 2000). If you have more than one audio device in your system, use the "Preferred device" drop-down lists in the Playback and Recording sections to select one of the installed audio devices as the default for each. Click the Advanced Properties buttons in the Playback and Recording sections to configure driver-specific options for such things as degree of hardware acceleration to be used, sample rate conversion settings, the type of speakers you are using, and so on.

Configuring a Sound Card Under Windows NT 4

The procedure required to install and configure a sound card under Windows NT 4 depends on the type of sound card. Before you can install drivers and configure the card, Windows NT must recognize it as present. Resources for PCI sound cards are configured automatically by the BIOS. Non-PnP sound cards must be configured manually, but present no other problems. PnP ISA sound cards are a problem, because Windows NT 4 does not recognize that they exist unless you take the following steps:

1. Insert the Windows NT 4 distribution CD and browse to the *Drvlib\Pnpisa* *i386* folder.

2. Highlight the file *Pnpisa.inf*, right-click it, and choose Install from the context-sensitive menu.

3. Restart the system.

When the system restarts, Windows NT 4 should display a New Hardware Found dialog. If it does, continue with the following steps to configure the sound card. If it does not, the file *\Drvlib\Audio\Sbpnp\Readme.txt* contains additional information that may be helpful. Once the sound card is recognized by Windows NT, take the following steps to configure it:

1. Before starting, verify that the sound card is physically installed, that the BIOS is set to Non-PnP Operating system, and that all applications are closed.

2. From Control Panel, double-click Multimedia to display the Multimedia Properties dialog. On the Devices page, click Add to display a list of available drivers.

3. Select "Unlisted or Updated Driver" and click OK. Windows NT prompts you to enter or browse to the location of the driver you want to install. Do so, and click OK.

4. Windows NT displays the "Add Unlisted or Updated Driver" dialog, with one or more drivers listed in the pane. Highlight the driver you want to use and click OK. Windows NT installs the driver and prompts you to restart the system. Do so.

5. After the system restarts, run Start → Programs → Administrative Tools (Common) → Windows NT Diagnostics. View the Resources page to verify that the sound card is recognized properly and using resources that do not conflict with any other device. If the sound card has a test utility, run it to verify that all functions are operating properly.

6. If you have more than one audio device installed, display Control Panel and double-click Multimedia to view the Audio page of Multimedia Properties. Use the "Preferred device" drop-down lists in the Playback and Recording sections to select one of the installed audio devices as the default for each.

Troubleshooting Sound Card Problems

Most sound card problems are a result of improper, defective, or misconnected cables, incorrect drivers, or resource conflicts. Sound card problems that occur with a previously functioning sound card when you have made no changes to the system are usually caused by cable problems or operator error (such as accidentally turning the volume control down). Sound card problems that occur when you install a new sound card (or when you add or reconfigure other system components) are usually caused by resource conflicts or driver problems. Resource conflicts, although relatively rare in a Windows 98/PCI/PnP environment, are quite common on machines running Windows NT and/or ISA, because sound cards are resource hogs.

To troubleshoot sound problems, always begin with the following steps:

1. Verify that all cables are connected, that the speakers have power and are switched on, that the volume control is set to an audible level, and so on. In

particular, if the sound card has a volume wheel on the back, make sure it is set to an audible level. It's often unclear which direction increases volume, so we generally set the wheel to a middle position while troubleshooting.

2. Shut down and restart the system. Surprisingly often, this solves the problem.

3. Determine the scope of the problem. If the problem occurs with only one program, visit the web sites for Microsoft, the software company, and the sound card maker to determine if there is a known problem with that program and sound card combination. If the problem occurs globally, continue with the following steps.

4. Verify that the sound card is selected as the default playback device. If you have more than one sound card installed, verify that the default playback device is the sound card to which the speakers are connected.

5. If your sound card includes a testing utility, run it to verify that all components of the sound card are operating properly.

6. If you have another set of speakers and/or a spare audio cable, substitute them temporarily to eliminate the speakers as a possible cause. If you have a set of headphones, connect them directly to line-out on the sound card to isolate the problem to the system itself.

If the problem is occurring on a new system, or one in which you have just added or replaced a sound card, take the following steps in order:

1. Verify that the speakers are connected to the Line-out or Speaker jack, as appropriate, rather than to the Line-in or Microphone jack. Connecting speakers to the wrong jack is one of the most common causes of sound problems. We still do it ourselves from time to time.

2. Verify that the CMOS Setup settings are correct for OS type. If you are running Windows 95/98/2000, OS type should be set to PnP Compatible (or similar words); if you are running NT4, it should be set to Non-PnP OS.

3. Use the procedures described in Chapter 1, to verify that no resource conflicts exist. If conflicts exist, remedy them and restart the system.

4. Check the troubleshooting sections of the Microsoft web site and the web sites for your motherboard and sound card manufacturer. Some sound cards, for example, have problems with motherboards with certain Via chipsets, while other sound cards have problems with AMD K6-family CPUs when used with certain AGP video cards.

5. Remove the drivers, restart the system, and reinstall the drivers from scratch.

6. Remove the drivers, shut down the system, and relocate the sound card to a different PCI slot. When the system restarts, reinstall the drivers from scratch.

7. If none of that works, suspect either a defective sound card or a fundamental incompatibility between your sound card and the rest of your system. Remove the drivers, shut down the system, remove the sound card, install a different sound card, and reinstall the drivers for it. If the replacement sound card is the same model and exhibits the same symptoms, try installing a different model of sound card.

Sound Cards

If the problem occurs on a previously working system, take the following steps in order:

1. If you have recently added or changed any hardware, use the procedures described in Chapter 1 to verify that no resource conflicts exist.

2. If you have recently installed or uninstalled any software, it's possible that Setup installed DLLs that are incompatible with your sound card, or removed DLLs that your sound card or applications require. Remove the sound card drivers and reinstall them from scratch.

3. If sound still does not function properly, suspect a sound card failure.

Here are some specific common sound problems and their solutions:

No sound

This is probably the most common sound problem, and can have many causes. Following the troubleshooting steps previoulsy listed should resolve the problem.

Scratchy or intermittent sound

This problem can also have many causes. Perhaps the most common is the fault of the sound card itself. Older and inexpensive sound cards often have poor audio quality, particularly FM synthesis models. Other common causes include a defective or low-quality audio cable, speakers placed too close to the monitor or other source of electrical noise, and the placement of the sound card within the system. If you have a choice, locate a sound card as far as possible from other expansion cards. Another possible cause is that some video card drivers are optimized for benchmark tests by causing them to keep control of the bus. The result can be intermittent drop outs and scratchiness in the sound.

Computer sounds are audible but audio CDs are not

Computer sound is digital, and is delivered directly to the sound card via the bus. Audio CDs produce analog sound, and require a separate internal cable joining the audio out connector on the back of the CD-ROM drive to the CD Audio connector on the sound card. If you do not have the necessary cable, you can temporarily fix the problem by connecting a standard stereo audio cable from the headphone jack on the front of the CD-ROM drive to the Line-in jack on the sound card. Note that recent motherboards and CD-ROM drives can deliver CD audio as a digital signal directly to the sound card, obviating the need for a separate CD-Audio cable.

Only one channel is audible

If you have another set of speakers or headphones, connect them directly to the sound card Line-out port to isolate the problem to either the sound card or the speakers. Roughly in order of decreasing probability, the most likely causes and solutions are:

– The Windows audio balance control is set fully in one direction. Double-click the speaker icon in the System Tray and verify balance settings in the Volume Control dialog (or the replacement applet installed with your sound card drivers).

- The balance control on your speakers, if present, may be set fully in one direction. This happens commonly when someone blindly attempts to change volume or tone and turns the wrong knob. Center the speaker balance control.

- The audio cable is defective. Many audio cables, particularly those supplied with inexpensive speakers, are constructed poorly. Replace it with a high-quality, shielded audio cable, available for a few dollars from computer stores, audio specialty stores, and mass marketers like Circuit City.

- The audio cable is not fully seated in either the sound card jack or the speaker jack. Verify that the cable is fully seated at both ends.

- You are using a mono rather than stereo audio cable to connect Line-out on the sound card to the speakers. Replace the cable.

- The sound card driver is not installed, is installed improperly, or is the wrong driver. Some sound cards may function partially under these conditions, and the most common symptom is single-channel audio. Uninstall any driver currently installed, and then reinstall the proper driver.

- Although it is rare, we once encountered a set of amplified speakers that one channel had died on while the other continued working properly. Replace the speakers.

After installing a sound card, your PC speaker no longer works
This is by design in some sound cards. Installing the card and driver intentionally disables the PC speaker and routes sounds that would ordinarily go to the PC speaker to the sound card instead.

You install a sound card on a Windows NT system but the drivers won't recognize it
This problem occurs only because Windows NT does not recognize PnP ISA cards unless you have installed *Pnpisa.inf.* To correct the problem, follow the directions earlier in this chapter for configuring sound cards under Windows NT 4, restart the system, and install the drivers.

Windows NT suddenly loses sound
On Windows NT systems with properly configured and functioning sound cards, sound may disappear entirely for no apparent reason. This has happened to us on many different NT systems, using different motherboards and sound cards. The sound card still shows as installed, and everything appears perfectly normal, but the system simply stops sending audio to the speakers. This problem may or may not be accompanied by the speaker icon disappearing from the system tray. We have no idea what causes this, and we've never been able to get a satisfactory explanation from Microsoft. Restarting the system normally solves the problem, until next time. On systems where "next time" is all too frequent, we have occasionally had some success by removing and then reinstalling the sound drivers.

The system locks up when you boot or bluescreens immediately after booting
This problem normally results from a severe resource conflict or an improperly installed card. Verify first that the card is seated fully. If so, boot the system in Safe Mode (Windows 9X: press F8 during boot) or using the Last Known Good Configuration (Windows NT: press the space bar when

prompted). With the system booted, determine which devices and resources are conflicting, resolve the conflict(s) and restart the system.

MP3

We get so many questions about MP3 that we felt compelled to explain briefly what MP3 is and how to use it. Here seems as good a place as any. *MP3* is short-hand for *MPEG-1 Layer 3 audio compression*. MP3 has quickly become the most popular format for storing audio on computers. Although the music industry, concerned about piracy, has done its best to kill MP3 by filing lawsuits and intro-ducing competing secure digital music formats, MP3 thrives and is likely to continue doing so.

The *raison d'être* for MP3 is that it compresses audio data significantly while main-taining acceptable audio quality. CD-Audio is recorded in stereo at 44.1 kHz with 16-bit sampling, and stored uncompressed as a 150 KB/s bit stream. Storing one minute of CD-Audio therefore requires 9,000 KB. A standard CD stores up to 74 minutes of audio, which translates to about 650 MB. Current hard disks are huge and cheap but, at about 1.6 hours/GB, storing even a small CD collection on hard disk in CD-Audio format is impractical.

Enter MP3. MP3 uses lossy variable compression, which means that it stores impor-tant data—such as foreground sounds in the middle ranges to which the human ear is most sensitive—using moderate compression, but uses high compression for less important data, such as very high and very low tones and quiet background tones that are overlaid by louder foreground tones. Some data is discarded entirely, such as audio that is identical on both stereo channels and audio that is below the human hearing threshold. MP3 allows encoding at different bit rates which correspond to different overall compression levels. The most commonly used bit rates are:

64 KB/s (19.2X compression)
> At this bit rate, often called AM radio quality or voice quality, a one-hour CD compresses to only about 30 MB. Sound quality, however, is noticeably sub-par, even when played on inexpensive computer speakers. Use this bit rate only for encoding voice-only audio, for which it is perfectly acceptable.

128 KB/s (9.6X compression)
> At this bit rate, often inaccurately called FM radio quality, a one-hour CD compresses to about 60 MB, or 1 MB/min. Sound quality may be indistin-guishable from a CD when played on inexpensive computer speakers, but the difference is readily apparent with good speakers or headphones. Most pirated music on the Web is encoded at 128 KB/s. We think this bit rate falls unfortunately in the middle—not good enough to be "good," and not small enough to be "small." We would never use it to encode classical music, but many people find it good enough for rock.

256 KB/s (4.8X compression)
> At this bit rate, which really is FM radio quality, a one-hour CD compresses to about 120 MB. Sound quality is, for many people, nearly indistinguishable from a CD, even when played on good-quality computer speakers or headphones.

We recommend this bit rate for all but the most discerning listeners using top-quality computer speakers in a quiet environment

320 KB/s (3.8X compression)

At this bit rate, usually called CD quality, a one-hour CD compresses to about 150 MB. Nearly everyone finds 320 KB/s MP3 files effectively indistinguishable from CD audio. Discerning listeners with top-notch equipment can usually discriminate between them, often describing the MP3 audio subjectively as "lacking sparkle in the highs" or something similar. We can't tell the difference, though, and recommend this bit rate for those who listen to MP3s on good home audio equipment.

In addition to these "standard" bit rates, some people striving to optimize audio quality versus storage space use intermediate bit rates, like 160 KB/s and 192 KB/s. Not all MP3 players support all bit rates, so make sure the player you want to use supports the bit rate at which you encode your CDs. If you're undecided between two bit rates, use the higher. Many people encode their entire CD collection at a lower bit rate only to find that the quality is unacceptable and they have to re-encode at a higher bit rate.

MP3 Software

Transferring music from CD to MP3 files requires software to perform the following functions:

Digital Audio Extraction

The process of copying the original digital audio data from a CD—properly termed Digital Audio Extraction (DAE)—is usually called *ripping*. The software used to do it is called a *ripper*. Ripping extracts an exact digital copy of the audio data and stores it as a *.wav* file on the hard disk. These are the same size as the original data—650 MB or so for a full CD. Rippers vary greatly in speed, features, and interface, but using any competent ripper produces the same result—an exact copy of the audio data in *.wav* format. Although ripping speed is partially dependent on the ripper, the major determinant is the speed at which the CD-ROM drive performs DAE. Not all CD-ROM drives can perform DAE, and many that do rip at 1X or less. That is, ripping one hour of music may take one hour or more. We use the ripper bundled with our Plextor CD-ROM drives, which typically rip at 14X to 20X and require only a few minutes to rip an entire CD. Numerous rippers, many of them free, are readily available on the Net (*http://software.mp3.com/software*).

MP3 encoding

The process of compressing *.wav* source files and storing them as *.mp3* files is called *encoding*. The software used to encode MP3s is called an *encoder* or *compressor*. Encoding is CPU-intensive, so although the specific encoder used and the degree of compression both affect performance, CPU speed is the main determinant. A slow PC may encode at 0.25X, taking four hours to encode one hour of music. A fast PC may encode at 1X or faster. Many encoders allow batch processing *.wav* files overnight. We like to use BladeEnc (*http://bladeenc.mp3.no*), which, although it has a minimalist text-based interface, is free, reasonably fast, supports a broad range of compression levels, and produces clean MP3 files. As with rippers, numerous free or inexpensive encoders are readily available for download.

Although ripping and encoding are distinct processes, some software combines the two. One such product we've used successfully is Media Jukebox (*http://www. musicex.com/mediajukebox*).

Playing MP3 files requires MP3 player software. The Microsoft Windows Media Player, bundled with recent versions of Internet Explorer and downloadable from *http://www.microsoft.com/windows/mediaplayer,* suffices for casual use. To download a more capable MP3 player, visit *http://software.mp3.com/software*, where numerous inexpensive or free MP3 players are available. The most popular MP3 player, WinAmp, formerly shareware but now free, is one we've used successfully.

MP3 Hardware

Depending on how you use MP3, you may need little or no additional hardware:

- Listening to MP3 files requires nothing more than a sound card and speakers or headphones.

- Creating MP3 files from Audio CDs requires a CD-ROM drive that supports Digital Audio Extraction. Most CD-ROM drives made after 1998 are DAE-capable, although more recent and better-quality CD-ROM drives provide both faster and cleaner extraction. That last may seem an odd statement. After all, isn't a digital copy always an exact duplicate of the original? Not necessarily. CD-Audio discs lack the second level ECC code that CD-ROM discs include. That means that the copy may differ from the source. A few flipped bits usually cause no audible differences in the copy, but we prefer to extract source files as cleanly as possible. For that, we have found Plextor SCSI CD-ROM drives to be the best available.

- Creating CDs from MP3 files requires a CD-R(W) drive, with which you can create two distinct types of CD. First, you can decompress the MP3 files and write them in CD-Audio format to the CD. This results in a normal CD-Audio disc—albeit with degraded sound quality relative to the original CD-Audio source—which is playable in any CD-ROM drive or CD player that supports multisession, which is to say all recent CD-ROM drives and most recent players. Second, you can write the MP3 files directly to CD, which allows creating a CD with four to ten hours of music on it. You can play these MP3 files on any computer, just as you would if they were stored on the hard disk. Although MP3 CDs are not playable in standard CD players, some new home and car CD players can play them.

Our Picks

Here are the sound cards we use and recommend:

General purpose sound

    Buy a motherboard with embedded audio. Many recent motherboards include embedded audio standard or as an option. These audio chipsets, usually from Creative, Crystal Audio, or Yamaha, don't include the cutting-edge features of standalone sound cards, but are more than Good Enough for standard business audio, listening to music, and casual gaming. The tight integration of embedded audio also makes compatibility problems and resource conflicts much less likely.

Basic PCI sound card

Voyetra Turtle Beach Montego A3DXstream. We recommend this card for new entry-level and mid-range systems without embedded audio and for upgrading PCI systems. It's full-duplex, has 18-bit converters and a 92 dB S/N ratio. It provides 64-voice wavetable sound, A3D (1.0, not 2.0), 48-stream DirectSound hardware acceleration, and good compatibility with DOS games. At $35, this is all the sound card most people need. (*http://www.voyetra.com*)

Basic ISA sound card

Creative Labs SoundBlaster AWE64 Value. Although we recommend avoiding ISA sound cards whenever possible, sometimes you must use one. For those times, this $30 wavetable card does everything you can reasonably expect from an inexpensive ISA card. Its MIDI support is not as good as the more expensive cards, and it can load down the main CPU, particularly in slower, older systems, but we don't know of a better basic ISA card. (*http://www. soundblaster.com*)

Enhanced PCI sound card

Voyetra Turtle Beach Montego II Quadzilla. At $75 or so street price, this sound card will probably do anything you need to do. It supports four speakers, and provides superior sound quality, excellent MIDI support, and A3D2.0 3D hardware acceleration. With A3D2.0-enabled software, the effects this card produces are extraordinary, making otherwise impressive Creative Labs EAX cards pale in comparison. For software that is not A3D2.0-enabled, this card falls back to DirectSound and DirectSound3D, which are pretty impressive themselves. This is the sound card we install when features and sound quality matter.

Enhanced ISA sound card

None. If you need 3D, hardware acceleration, enhanced MIDI support, and other features common to higher-end sound cards, buy a Turtle Beach Montego II PCI card.

We constantly test and review new equipment. For the latest information about what we currently use, visit:

http://www.hardwareguys.com/picks/audio.html

Sound Cards

CHAPTER 18

Speakers and Headphones

No matter how good your sound card, it's useless unless you have speakers or headphones to listen to the audio it produces. Extreme high-fidelity is usually unnecessary in PC speakers, both because system fans and other ambient noise tends to overwhelm minor differences in sound quality and because most PC sound applications do not use or require high fidelity. That said, inexpensive PC speakers, with their 3" drivers and low-power amplifiers often provide surprisingly satisfactory sound, and inexpensive headphones can produce sound rivaling the best consumer-grade audio equipment.

Speaker and Headphone Characteristics

Here are the important characteristics of speakers:

Number
> Computer speakers are sold in sets. Two-piece sets include two small speakers intended to sit on your desk or attach to your monitor. Three-piece sets add a subwoofer, which resides under the desk and provides enhanced bass response. Four-piece sets include four small speakers, and are useful primarily to gamers who have a 3D-capable sound card installed. Five-piece sets add a subwoofer to that arrangement. Most headphones use only two speakers, one per ear, but some use two horizontally-offset speakers per ear to provide true four-channel support.

Frequency response
> *Frequency response* is the range of sound frequencies the speaker can reproduce. The values provided for most speakers are meaningless, because they do not specify how flat that response is. For example, professional studio-monitor speakers may provide 20 Hz to 20 kHz response at ±1 dB. Expensive home-audio speakers may provide 20 Hz to 20 kHz response at ±3 dB, and 40 Hz to 18 kHz response at ±1 dB. Computer speakers may claim 20 Hz to 20 kHz response, but may rate that response at ±10 dB or more. A reduction of

about 3 dB halves volume, which means sounds below 100 Hz or above 10 kHz are nearly inaudible with many computer speakers. The only sure measure of adequate frequency response is that the speakers sound good to you, particularly for low bass and high treble sounds.

Amplifier power

Manufacturers use two means to specify output power. *Peak Power*, which specifies the maximum wattage the amplifier can deliver instantaneously, is deceptive and should be disregarded. *RMS Power* (*Root Mean Square*), a more accurate measure, specifies the wattage that the amplifier can deliver continually. Listening to music at normal volume levels requires less than a watt. Home audio systems usually provide 100 watts per channel or more, which allows them to respond instantaneously to transient high amplitude peaks in the music, particularly in bass notes, which extends the dynamic range of the sound. The range of computer speakers is hampered by their small amplifiers, but computer speakers also use small drivers that cannot move much air anyway, so their lack of power is not really important. Typical dual speaker sets provide four or five watts RMS per channel, which is adequate for normal sound reproduction. Typical subwoofers provide 15 to 40 watts, which, combined with the typical 5" driver, is adequate to provide flat bass response down to 60 Hz or so (although subwoofers often misleadingly claim response to 20 Hz). Headphones are not amplified, but use the line-level output of the sound card.

Connectors

Most computer speakers place the amplifier in one speaker, which has connections for Line-in (from the sound card), Speaker (to the other speaker), and DC Power (to a power brick). Many speakers also provide an output for a subwoofer. Some speakers also provide a second line-in jack. This is quite useful if you want to connect both your PC and a separate line-level audio source, such as a CD player or another PC, to the amplified speakers, allowing you to listen to either source separately or both together.

 USB speakers are becoming more common. Their advantages are that they receive audio data as a digital bit stream directly from the PC and process it away from the noisy environment inside the PC—which in theory allows cleaner sound—and that they can be controlled directly from the PC. Their disadvantages are that they can be used only with operating systems that support USB, like Windows 98 and Windows 2000, and that the sound they provide is generally not as good as that provided by a good sound card and traditional speakers.

Choosing Speakers and Headphones

Use the following guidelines when selecting computer speakers or headphones:

Choose speakers appropriate for your listening preferences and sound card capabilities

Picking suitable speakers requires considering what you listen to, how you listen to it, and the features of your sound card. For example, if you listen mostly to classical music at low to moderate volume, powerful bass is less important than flat, transparent frequency response in the midrange and highs. A high quality set of dual speakers with frequency response from 90–18,000 Hz and four or five watts RMS per channel will serve. Conversely, if you listen to rock or heavy metal, or if you play games and want to shake the walls, crystalline highs are less important, but bass is critical. You'll want speakers that include a powerful subwoofer. Similarly, if you have a 3D sound card, it makes little sense to couple it to a two-piece or three-piece speaker set. Buy a four-piece or five-piece speaker set to take advantage of the 3D capabilities of the card.

Avoid cheap speakers

The very cheapest speakers, those that sell for $15 or less or are bundled with inexpensive computer systems, have sound quality noticeably inferior to speakers that sell for even a little more. Speakers in the $25 range and above use better (and more powerful) amplifiers, better quality drivers (typically separate midrange/woofers and tweeters), and provide additional features, such as the ability to connect more than one sound source or a separate subwoofer.

Stick with name brands

Altec-Lansing and Labtec are the best-known names in computer speakers. Each produces a broad range of speaker sets, one of which should be appropriate for almost any requirements. Creative Labs, Sony, Yamaha, and others also produce good computer speakers, although their range of models is smaller. Increasingly, well-known names in home audio—such as Bose, JBL, and Polk Audio—are entering the computer speaker market. Ironically, their background in high-quality home audio means they tend to publish realistic specifications for their computer speakers, which make them look inferior to lesser speakers for which the makers publish inflated specifications.

Consider using headphones instead of speakers

Even inexpensive headphones often provide a better listening experience than good computer speakers, both because the cushions isolate you from ambient noise and because it's easier to render very high fidelity sound with the small speakers and tiny power levels used by headphones. Headphones also allow you to work (or play) without disturbing others. If you're going to buy headphones, consider instead buying a headset, which adds a microphone to support such functions as voice/speech recognition, Internet telephony, and adding voice annotations to documents. The only drawback to headphones is that most are not well suited for use with 3D sound cards, although some specialized four-channel headphones are available.

Get a no-questions-asked money-back guarantee

With speakers more so than any other computer component except perhaps input devices, personal preference must rule. Speakers that sound great to us may sound mediocre to you, and vice versa. The only way to know for sure is to listen to the speakers in your own environment. If they turn out to be unsuitable, you don't want to be stuck with them, so make sure you can return them without a hassle.

Our Picks

Here are the speakers and headphones we use and recommend:

Basic speakers

Labtec LCS-1030. You're likely to be happy with any name-brand speakers you choose in the $25 to $40 range, but these $35 speakers are our favorites in this group. They provide five watts per channel, which is more than adequate, and their frequency response makes them suitable for anything from casual gaming to listening to classical music. You won't mistake them for home audio speakers, but they provide very good sound at a reasonable price. (*http://www.labtec.com*)

Dual speakers with subwoofer

Labtec LCS-2422. If you play a lot of games or listen to rock music, you'll appreciate the extra bass that a subwoofer provides. At $65 or so, these speakers provide decent bass and clear mid-ranges and highs without breaking the piggy bank. These are the speakers we'd choose for a mainstream system.

Quad speakers with subwoofer

Creative Labs (Cambridge SoundWorks) FourPointSurround FPS2000 Digital. At $130 or so street price, these speakers sound as good as any computer speakers we've ever heard. Short of spending hundreds more for home audio gear, you're not likely to find better sound on a PC. These are the speakers we'd choose for a high-end system, or for any system for which sound quality was a primary consideration.

USB speakers

None. Although USB speakers are attractive in many respects, not least in that they permit purely digital delivery of audio and can be controlled from an on-screen window, we have yet to find any that deliver the sound quality of a good traditional sound card and speakers.

Headphones

Labtec C-324. At $18, this headset comprises stereo headphones with 20–20,000 Hz frequency response, and a noise-canceling boom microphone with 100–16,000 Hz response, which is adequate for voice annotations, voice/speech recognition, Internet telephony, multiplayer games, and so on.

We constantly test and review new equipment. For the latest information about what we currently use, visit:

http://www.hardwareguys.com/picks/audio.html

CHAPTER 19

Keyboards

A keyboard is a matrix of individual switches, one per key. Pressing a key closes its switch, generating a signal that the dedicated *keyboard controller* built into the keyboard recognizes as the *make code* for that key. Releasing the key opens the switch, which the keyboard controller recognizes as the *break code* for that key. Using a firmware lookup table, the keyboard controller translates received make code signals to standard *scan codes*, which it sends via the *keyboard buffer* to a second keyboard controller located in the PC, where they are recognized as specific characters and control codes.

Because releasing a key generates a break code, the local keyboard controller can recognize when two keys are pressed together (e.g., Shift-A or Ctrl-C) and generate a unique scan code for each such defined key combination. For undefined key combinations (e.g., pressing "a" and then pressing "s" before releasing "a"), the keyboard controller recognizes that, even though a break code for "a" has not been received, the user's intent is to type "as," and so generates the scan code for "a" followed immediately by the scan code for "s."

Communication between the two keyboard controllers is bidirectional and asynchronous, which allows the PC to illuminate and extinguish keyboard indicator lights and set Typematic parameters such as delay and repeat rate. The keyboard interface was standardized with the 1984 introduction of the IBM PC/AT, which means that any AT-class keyboard works with any 286 or higher PC.

In addition to basic functions, the local keyboard controller may support various programmable functions, using either or both of these methods:

Keyboard-based

The local keyboard controller may support creating custom definitions for specific keys and key combinations and storing those definitions in the keyboard itself. When a key with a custom definition is pressed, the local keyboard controller generates the necessary scan codes directly and sends them to the PC. Because this method uses only standard scan codes, it has the advantage of not requiring a driver on the PC—which means the programmable functions can be used with any operating system—but the disadvantage of being limited to functions that can be performed using standard scan codes. This method was commonly used with early programmable keyboards, but is less common nowadays.

PC-based

Programmable functions may require a driver running on the PC. That driver recognizes nonstandard scan codes generated by the local keyboard controller and takes whatever action the driver defines for "hard-wired" special keys. For keys with custom definitions, the driver uses stored user configuration data to determine what action to take. This method has the advantage of supporting programmable functions that would be clumsy or impossible to implement using only standard scan codes (such as opening your web browser or email client), and is the method used by most current programmable keyboards. If the driver is not installed, such keyboards function as ordinary keyboards, with special purpose keys and programmable features disabled.

Keyboard Switch Types

Underneath each key is a switch. When the key is pressed, the switch closes. Three types of switches are used in keyboards:

Mechanical

These keyboards use standard spring-loaded momentary-on switches, most of which are made by Alps Electric. Pressing a key compresses a spring and causes a plunger on the bottom of the key to make physical contact to close the connection. When the key is released, the spring forces it back into rest position. These keyboards provide the clacky feel typical of the original IBM Selectric and PC keyboards, are quite durable, and are usually relatively expensive ($75 to $125).

Capacitive

These keyboards are unique in that pressing a key does not make electrical contact to complete the circuit. Instead, movement of the plunger on the bottom of a key alters the state of a capacitive circuit, which the keyboard controller recognizes as a key press. Keyboards with capacitive switches provide clacky feedback, are even more durable than mechanical keyboards, and are quite expensive ($100 to $200). As far as we know, only IBM and Lexmark have produced such keyboards.

Membrane

Most current keyboards use membrane switches. Unlike mechanical and capacitive keyboards, which use discrete physical switches for each key and are correspondingly expensive to produce, a membrane keyboard combines all key switches into one unit comprising three membrane layers. The bottom layer has printed conductive traces that correspond to the individual key switches. The middle layer is a spacer, with holes that expose each underlying switch. The top layer is an array of rubber domes, against each of which the bottom of a key impinges. When a key is pressed, it forces the conductive bottom of the rubber dome through the spacing layer and into contact with the switch traces on the bottom layer, completing the circuit. When the key is released, the rubber dome forces it back into rest position. Early membrane keyboards were known for mushy feel and lack of tactile feedback. Current production models are better in that respect, so much so that it is often difficult to tell by feel alone whether you are using a mechanical keyboard or a modern membrane keyboard. Membrane keyboards are also inexpensive ($15 to $50), and nearly as durable and reliable as the best of the mechanical and capacitive keyboards.

Switch type as it related to durability was an important factor when keyboards cost $200. With high-quality membrane keyboards now selling for $25 or so, that distinction is much less important.

Keyboard Styles

Keyboards are available in two distinct styles:

Traditional keyboard
> A *traditional keyboard* is rectangular and has a constant slope, from highest at the rear to lowest at the front. These keyboards are available in various footprints, including standard (19"×8"); mid-size (18"×7"); and space-saver (17"× 6.5" or less). Size is important to the extent that large keyboards occupy considerable desk space and may not fit some keyboard drawers.

Ergonomic keyboard
> An *ergonomic keyboard* uses a split face and variable slopes which allow more natural and comfortable hand and wrist positions. Most ergonomic keyboards are as large or larger than standard traditional keyboards, not least because they include a built-in wrist rest. Some claim that ergonomic keyboards help reduce Repetitive Stress Injury (RSI) problems such as Carpal Tunnel Syndrome (CTS), but we have seen no credible evidence to support these claims. The secret to avoiding such problems, regardless of what keyboard style you use, is to take frequent breaks and to avoid using the keyboard continuously for more than an hour or so at a time.

Keyboard Interfaces

Keyboard interfaces are well standardized, and have been for years. This means that, with the exception of antique PC and PC/XT keyboards, you can plug any keyboard into any PC to which it physically connects and expect it to work. The following sections detail the three keyboard interfaces currently in use.

AT Keyboard Interface

The AT keyboard interface was introduced with the IBM PC/AT in 1984, and is still used by current production AT and BAT motherboards. AT keyboards use the 5-pin DIN connector (female at the PC), shown in Figure 19-1, whose pinouts are described in Table 19-1. On the PC side, the AT keyboard uses an Intel 8042 or equivalent interface chip, which is assigned IRQ1 and I/O base address 0060.

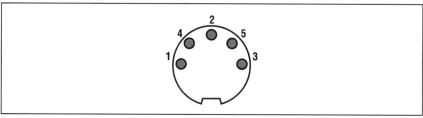

Figure 19-1: The AT keyboard connector

Table 19-1: AT Keyboard Interface Signals and Pinout

Pin	Signal Name	Description
1	CLOCK	Keyboard clock; open collector CLK, CTS
2	DATA	Keyboard data; open collector RxD/TxD, RTS
3	RESERVED	Reset (usually not connected)
4	GROUND	Signal ground
5	VCC	+5VDC

The pin descriptions are self-explanatory, other than pin 3. The 83-key IBM PC/XT keyboard, and some 84-key IBM PC/AT keyboards used an early keyboard protocol that did not include a software reset command. For these keyboards, the PC uses pin 3 to send a hardware reset to the keyboard. All systems and keyboards made in the last 15 years use a keyboard protocol that includes a software reset command, and nearly all recent keyboards leave pin 3 unconnected.

PS/2 Keyboard Interface

The PS/2 keyboard interface was introduced with the IBM PS/2 series in 1986, and is now used by all ATX and ATX-variant motherboards. PS/2 keyboards use the 6-pin mini-DIN connector (female at the PC) shown in Figure 19-2, whose pinouts are described in Table 19-2. On the PC side, the PS/2 keyboard uses the same Intel 8042 or equivalent interface chip as the AT keyboard, which is also assigned IRQ1 and I/O base address 0060.

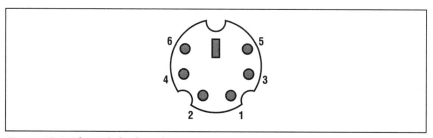

Figure 19-2: The PS/2 keyboard connector

Table 19-2: PS/2 Keyboard Interface Signals and Pinout

Pin	Signal Name	Description
1	DATA	Keyboard data
2	RESERVED	No connection

Table 19-2: PS/2 Keyboard Interface Signals and Pinout (continued)

Pin	Signal Name	Description
3	GROUND	Signal ground
4	VCC	+5VDC
5	CLOCK	Keyboard clock
6	RESERVED	No connection
Shield	o	Ground

The AT and PS/2 keyboard interfaces use incompatible connectors, but are electrically and functionally identical. You can connect an AT keyboard to a PS/2 keyboard port or *vice versa* by building or buying an adapter that uses the pinouts listed in Table 19-3. Many new keyboards come with an adapter to allow their use with the other style connector. Such adapters can also be purchased at most computer stores.

Table 19-3: Pinouts for an AT-to-PS/2 or PS/2-to-AT Adapter

PS/2 Pin	AT Pin	Description
1	2	Keyboard data
2	3	No connection
3	4	Signal ground
4	5	+5VDC
5	1	Keyboard clock
6	o	No connection

USB Keyboard Interface

Some recent keyboards can be connected to a USB port. For now at least, few keyboards are USB-only. Most USB-capable keyboards also provide a standard PS/2 connector. To use a USB keyboard, the PC BIOS must support USB keyboards, *and* you must run an operating system, like Windows 98 or Windows 2000, that supports USB. BIOS support is needed so the keyboard can be used before the operating system loads to do such things as changing Setup parameters or choosing options from a boot menu. Operating system support is required for the keyboard to be accessible after the system boots.

Our USB keyboard experience, which to date is limited to casual testing with Windows 98, suggests that USB keyboards are not ready for prime time. Testing several systems—all with the most recent BIOS updates available—with several USB keyboards, we have experienced numerous lockups and other oddities, including situations where the PC continued to run normally but the keyboard was no longer recognized. We recommend using the PS/2 interface rather than USB until some of the bugs are worked out.

Choosing a Keyboard

Use the following guidelines when choosing a keyboard:

Consider layout

The position of the primary alphanumeric keys is standard on all keyboards other than those that use the oddball Dvorak layout. What varies, sometimes dramatically, is the placement, size, and shape of other keys, such as the shift keys (Shift, Ctrl, and Alt); the function keys (which may be arrayed across the top, down the left side, or both); and the cursor control and numeric keypad keys. If you are used to a particular layout, purchasing a keyboard with a similar layout makes it much easier to adapt to the new keyboard.

Give personal preference top priority

Keyboards vary both in obvious ways—layout, size, and form—and in subtle ways like key spacing, angle, dishing, travel, pressure required, and tactile feedback. People's sensitivity to these differences varies. Some are keyboard agnostics who can sit down in front of a new keyboard and, regardless of layout or tactile response, be up to speed in a few minutes. Others have strong preferences about layout and feel. If you've never met a keyboard you didn't like, you can disregard these issues and choose a keyboard based on other factors. If love and hate are words you apply to keyboards, use an identical keyboard for at least an hour before you buy one for yourself.

Make sure your operating system supports extended keyboard functions

Some keyboards provide dedicated and/or programmable function keys to automate such things as firing up your browser or email client or to allow you to define custom macros that can be invoked with a single keystroke. These functions are typically not built in to the keyboard itself, but require loading a driver. To take advantage of those functions, make sure a driver is available for the OS you use.

Consider weight

Although it sounds trivial, the weight of a keyboard can be a significant issue for some people. The lightest keyboard we've seen weighed just over a pound, and the heaviest was nearly eight pounds. If your keyboard stays on your desktop, a heavy keyboard is less likely to slide around. Conversely, a very heavy keyboard may be uncomfortable for someone who works with the keyboard in his lap.

Avoid multifunction keyboards

Keyboards are low-margin products. As a means to differentiate their products and increase margins, some manufacturers produce keyboards with speakers, scanners, and other entirely unrelated functions built-in. These functions are often clumsy to use, fragile, and have limited features. If you want speakers or a scanner, buy speakers or a scanner. Don't get a keyboard with them built-in.

Consider a wireless keyboard for special purposes

Various manufacturers make wireless keyboards, which are ideal for presentations and TV-based web browsing. Wireless keyboards include a separate receiver module that connects to the PS/2 keyboard port on the PC. The keyboard and receiver communicate using either radio frequency (RF) or infra-red (IR). IR keyboards require direct line-of-sight between the keyboard and receiver, while RF keyboards do not. Most IR keyboards and many RF keyboards provide very limited range—as little as five feet or so, which limits their utility to working around a desk without cables tangling. Some RF keyboards and a few IR keyboards use higher power to provide longer range, up to 50 feet or more. These are often quite expensive and provide relatively short battery life. Whichever type of wireless keyboard you get, make sure it uses standard (AA/AAA/9V) alkaline or NiMH batteries rather than a propri-etary NiCd battery pack, which is subject to the infamous NiCd memory effect, whereby NiCd batteries soon begin to lose the ability to hold a charge.

The Northgate OmniKey keyboard, with its function keys down the left and a satisfyingly clacky feel, has attained nearly cult status among some users, although Northgate itself is long gone. Original OmniKey keyboards haven't been produced for years, so remaining working examples are sought after like Old Masters. Fortunately, there's an alternative. Creative Vision Technologies, Inc. (*http://www.cvtinc.com*) makes the Avant Stellar keyboard, which is more or less a clone of the Northgate OmniKey Plus. It isn't cheap, but it's as close as you'll find to the OmniKey in a current keyboard.

Configuring a Keyboard

Windows 95/98/2000 and Windows NT allow you to customize some aspects of keyboard behavior. To do so, run the Keyboard applet (Start → Settings → Control Panel → Keyboard) to display the Keyboard Properties dialog, which includes the following pages:

Speed (Windows 95/98/NT/2000)
Includes settings for how long a key must be held down before it begins repeating and how quickly it repeats. Also allows setting cursor blink rate, which controls how fast the virtual cursor blinks in Windows applications. Change any of these settings by dragging the associated slider. Changes take effect immediately when you click Apply or OK.

Language (Windows 95/98) or Input Locales (Windows NT/2000)
These pages are nearly identical except for their names. They are used to install additional keyboard languages and layouts. Windows 95/98/NT allow specifying a key sequence (either Left Alt+Shift or Ctrl+Shift) to rotate through available languages from the keyboard. Windows 2000 provides the same choices, and adds an optional second key sequence to jump directly to the default language using the same key sequences listed above, with the addi-tion of one character, 0 through 9, tilde or grave accent. Windows 2000 also allows specifying the method used to turn off Caps Lock, either by pressing the Caps Lock key or by pressing the Shift key.

General (Windows NT only) or Hardware (Windows 2000 only)

These pages display the type of keyboard installed. Clicking the Change button on the Windows NT General page allows you to select among alternative installed keyboard drivers, or to install a new keyboard driver from a disk supplied by the keyboard manufacturer. The Windows 2000 Hardware page instead provides a Troubleshoot button, which invokes the Keyboard Troubleshooter Wizard, and a Properties button, which simply displays Device Manager properties for the keyboard.

Installing a programmable keyboard and driver may install a separate management application, or may simply add pages and options to the standard Keyboard Properties dialog. For example, Figure 19-3 shows one of the additional pages of the extended Keyboard Properties dialog that results from installing the Microsoft Natural Keyboard driver under Windows NT. If you install a programmable keyboard, make sure to locate and explore the options its driver provides. The default driver installation for some programmable keyboards leaves some very useful options disabled or set to less than optimum values.

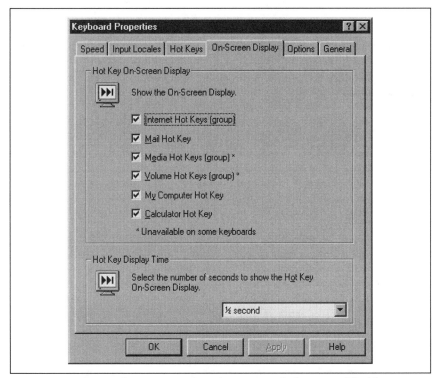

Figure 19-3: The Windows NT 4 Keyboard Properties dialog as modified by installing the Microsoft Natural Keyboard Pro driver

Finally, do not overlook the Accessibility Properties dialog, shown in Figure 19-4 (Start → Settings → Control Panel → Accessibility Options). This dialog is available in both Windows 98 and Windows NT. Although intended primarily to aid people with various disabilities, some options available here may be useful for anyone. In particular, anyone who has accidentally toggled Caps Lock on will appreciate the audible warning provided by ToggleKeys.

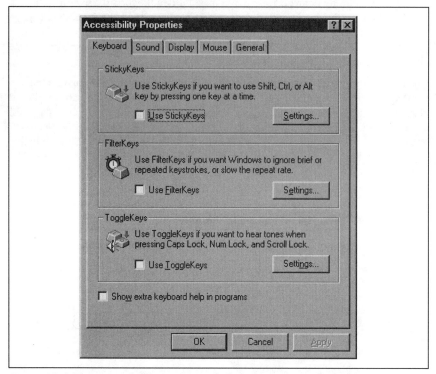

Figure 19-4: The Accessibility Properties dialog

Cleaning a Keyboard

Keyboards collect all manner of dirt, dust, and sticky spills, particularly if you smoke or drink near them. For routine cleaning, simply turn the keyboard upside down and shake it vigorously, which causes an incredible amount of stuff to fall out. Monthly, use your vacuum cleaner to do a thorough job. It's a good idea to shut down the system (or at least close all files) before you start vacuuming. Otherwise, the random series of keystrokes that vacuuming generates can have some unexpected results. In one case, we deleted a document. Formula 409 and similar commercial cleaners do a good job of removing grunge, but make sure the system is turned off while you use them, and try to avoid allowing too much to run down inside the keyboard. It's better to spray cleaner on a paper towel and then wipe than to spray the cleaner directly on the keyboard.

All of that presupposes that your keyboard is just normally dirty. For cleaning seriously dirty keyboards, we've been using the dishwasher method for more than 20 years. Most people think we're kidding when we recommend it, but it works for us. We've used it successfully with both mechanical and membrane-based keyboards. Proceed as follows:

1. Disconnect the keyboard from the computer. We probably shouldn't have to mention this step, but we don't want to get sued by someone who didn't realize it wasn't a good idea to run his system unit and monitor through the dishwasher.

2. Place the keyboard, keys down, in the top rack of the dishwasher. Secure the keyboard cable with a rubber band to keep it from becoming entangled in the moving parts of the dishwasher. Set the dishwasher for gentle cycle and coolest water temperature, if those options are available. Make sure to select the option for air dry rather than a heated drying cycle.

3. Run the keyboard through an entire wash cycle, using dishwasher detergent. When the cycle finishes, remove the keyboard and douse it with at least a gallon of water, making sure to repeatedly flood the keys themselves. For safety's sake, we always recommend using distilled or deionized water, but in fact we always use ordinary tap water and have never had a problem. After rinsing, turn the keyboard this way and that and shake it to drain as much water as possible. Use a towel to dry the accessible parts.

4. Set your oven to 150 degrees (or its lowest setting). We have no idea what the melting point of the plastic used in keyboards is, but we haven't melted one yet. Bake keyboard until done, usually one to two hours. Let the keyboard cool, remove, and serve.

We generally put the clean keyboard back in our stock of spares, where it may have another month or three to air dry naturally, but we've also reconnected a keyboard immediately after such treatment without any problems. We used to be concerned that puddles might still be lurking inside the keyboard, so we'd disassemble it and dry it thoroughly before reconnecting it. But we've found that a couple hours inside a 150 degree oven does a pretty good job of evaporating any residual water. Your mileage may vary. If you hear a sloshing sound after drying, it's probably a good idea to disassemble the keyboard and check further.

Troubleshooting and Repairing Keyboards

Good keyboards are so cheap that spending much time troubleshooting or repairing them is counterproductive. Membrane keyboards are irreparable in practical terms. Mechanical and capacitive keyboards can be repaired, but with parts expensive and difficult to find and technicians charging $50+/hour it's cheaper just to buy a new one. The same goes for repairing a keyboard yourself, unless your time is worth nothing an hour.

If a keyboard stops working or behaves strangely, check to make sure the cables are connected properly. If everything appears to be correct, it's worth doing a simple swap to verify whether the problem is the keyboard or the PC. If a known-good keyboard also fails to work, the problem is most likely caused by a defective keyboard interface on the motherboard, for which the only realistic solution is to replace the motherboard. If the known-good keyboard works, replace the defective keyboard.

Our Picks

The choice of keyboard is above all a personal matter, but unless you have very strong preferences you'll probably find one of the following keyboards suitable. Here are the keyboards that we use and recommend:

Standard keyboard

Microsoft Internet Keyboard and Internet Keyboard Pro. If you want a standard straight keyboard, give these serious consideration. The Internet Keyboard includes dedicated hot keys to control browser functions and email, as well as two programmable hot keys and a Sleep key. The Internet Keyboard Pro adds dedicated multimedia keys (volume, play functions, etc.) and two USB ports. Barbara uses the $40 Internet Keyboard Pro on her primary system and the $20 Internet Keyboard on her other systems. (*http://www.microsoft.com/hardware/keyboard*)

Ergonomic keyboard

Microsoft Natural Keyboard Elite and Natural Keyboard Pro. You'll either love or hate these "melted" keyboards. Robert loves them; Barbara hates them. The Natural Keyboard Elite is their basic ergonomic model. The Natural Keyboard Pro adds eight dedicated hot keys for browser functions and email, eight dedicated multimedia hot keys, two programmable hot keys, a Sleep key, and two USB ports. Robert uses the $45 Natural Keyboard Pro on his primary system, and the $30 Natural Keyboard Elite on his other systems.

 Some say that getting used to the Natural Keyboard layout takes a long time. That was not Robert's experience. He is a touch typist, and became completely comfortable with the Natural Keyboard in an hour or less. He uses Internet Keyboard models on some of his test-bed systems and switches back and forth without difficulty. The major adjustment is that the Natural Keyboard errs in putting the 6 key above and to the right of the T key, where it must be struck with the left index finger. Touch typists learn to strike the 6 key with the right index finger, and the change is a bit disconcerting at first.

Cordless keyboard (short-range)

Logitech Cordless series. If your keyboard cord gets in the way or you like to work with the keyboard in your lap, a short-range cordless keyboard may be just the thing. Logitech Cordless series keyboards are the best we've seen for that purpose. The $50 Cordless iTouch is a straight keyboard. The $75 Cordless Desktop iTouch adds a separate cordless mouse. The $100 Cordless Desktop Pro is an ergonomic version with separate ergonomic cordless mouse. (*http://www.logitech.com*)

Cordless keyboard (long-range)

Wombat Wizard. For presentations, controlling PC/TV digital systems, and other applications that require cross-the-room range, the best cordless keyboard we know of is the IR-based Wombat Wizard, which uses a compact 86-key layout, includes an integrated trackball, and provides a nominal 30 foot range. At $160 list, this is an expensive cordless keyboard, but we know of no less expensive long-range unit. As an alternative to using the compact key layout, Wombat offers an optional connector for using a standard keyboard and mouse. Wombat also manufactures the $130 Wizard Jr. which offers similar features except the optional connector. (*http://www.pckeyboards.com*)

We constantly test and review new equipment. For the latest information about what we currently use, visit:

http://www.hardwareguys.com/picks/input.html

CHAPTER 20

Mice and Trackballs

Mice and trackballs are members of a class generically described as *pointing devices*. All pointing devices have the same purpose—allowing you to move the cursor (or pointer) around the screen and to click to select items or perform other functions. A great variety of fiendishly clever pointing devices are built into notebook computers, but nearly all desktop systems use mice. Those few that don't use a trackball, which is essentially a mouse turned on its back, with the roller ball accessible.

Mice Versus Trackballs

As with any input device, personal preference should rule choice. That said, relative to mice, trackballs have the following advantages:

- A trackball remains in place, and requires less free desk space than a mouse.

- The trackball roller ball contacts your thumb rather than the desktop or mouse pad, which means it is less likely to require frequent cleaning.

- A trackball is often the better choice for 3D gaming and similar programs, where pointing and clicking are the most important functions.

- Some evidence suggests that using a trackball is less likely to cause RSI than using a mouse.

And the following disadvantages:

- Most trackballs are designed such that you guide the pointer with your thumb, which is the least dexterous digit. Accordingly, many users find it harder to position the cursor exactly with a trackball than with a mouse.

- Most people find a trackball clumsier than a mouse for operations that depend heavily on click-and-drag, such as creating and editing documents.

- Some evidence suggests that using a trackball is more likely to cause RSI than using a mouse. (Yes, we know . . .)

Mice and trackballs are both inexpensive enough that you should try both if you spend much time at a computer. If you have never used a trackball, doing so requires some adjustment. Many people find the Microsoft Trackball—which looks just like a mouse with the roller ball coming out the top—to be the easiest trackball to adjust to.

Mouse Characteristics

Here are the important characteristics of mice and trackballs.

Mechanism

Mice are available that use the following mechanisms:

Mechanical

Mechanical mice use a rubber-coated ball that contacts the mouse pad. Moving the mouse causes the ball to move, which in turn causes one or both of the internal cylindrical rollers with which the ball is in contact to move. These two internal rollers are oriented at 90° to each other, which allows one to respond to horizontal mouse movement and the other vertical mouse movement. Connected to the end of each roller is a wheel with many small notches around its circumference. As the wheel rotates, these notches alternately pass or block light from an LED aimed to impinge on a sensor. The rate at and duration for which the sensors see the light flickering correspond to how fast, how far, and in what direction the ball is moving. Most mice and all trackballs are mechanical. Modern mechanical mice are inexpensive and reliable, but require frequent cleaning.

Optical

Early mechanical mice provided limited resolution, were relatively unreliable, and required very frequent cleaning. Manufacturers addressed these problems by introducing optical mice, which substituted an optical sensor for the mouse ball. Reducing the number of moving parts greatly increased reliability. Because the optical mouse was a sealed unit, cleaning was needed much less often. The sole drawback was that the sensor of an optical mouse required a special mouse pad that contained an embedded mesh of very fine wires and was easily damaged. Improvements in mechanical mice and the requirement for a special mouse pad have made optical mice less popular than they once were.

IntelliEye

Microsoft recently introduced a new line of mice that use what they call IntelliEye technology. IntelliEye mice are essentially optical mice but with a much more sensitive sensor. By using a relatively high-power laser diode, IntelliEye mice are able to illuminate any mousing surface sufficiently well to detect very minor variations in surface texture, allowing them to work on nearly any surface from a standard mouse pad to a bare desktop. In fact, they work on everything we've tried except a mirror. We've even used them successfully on the featureless beige surface of a computer case and on an unmarked sheet of white copy paper. Because they are sealed units, they do not require routine cleaning, which is a blessing for people who eat, drink, or smoke at their desks. The sole drawback of IntelliEye mice is that they are more expensive than mechanical mice.

Number of buttons

Unlike the Macintosh world, where one-button mice are the rule, PC mice typically have two buttons, and some have three or more. In addition, many recent mice have a scroll wheel, which can function as another button. Using anything beyond the standard two buttons requires that both the driver and the application support the additional buttons. For example, the extended functions of the Microsoft Wheel Mouse are available only in applications that are specifically written to implement those extended functions, and only then if the enhanced mouse driver is installed to replace the standard mouse driver.

Interface

Mice have been produced in four interfaces. In relative order of current popularity, these interfaces include:

PS/2

The PS/2 mouse uses the same mini-DIN physical connector as the PS/2 keyboard, and interfaces to the PC using a second msi8042. But the mouse port uses IRQ12—versus IRQ1 for the keyboard port—which means that the mouse port and keyboard port are not interchangeable. All ATX motherboards provide a PS/2 mouse port on the I/O panel. Modern AT and BAT motherboards provide a PS/2 mouse port in the form of header pins on the motherboard, and use a port extender cable to jumper the header pins to a port connector on the back panel. The arrangement and pinouts of that header pin connector are not standard. We have seen motherboards that use five-pin in-line connectors, six-pin in-line connectors, and 2×3 rectangular connectors. Even motherboards that use the same physical connector may use different pinouts. Most AT motherboards include a matching port extender. If yours does not, verify the pinouts in the motherboard manual before purchasing an extender.

Serial

Most AT and Baby AT motherboards from 1995 and earlier do not include a PS/2 mouse connector. With these systems, you normally use a serial mouse. A serial mouse uses a standard DB9F connector, and connects to a DB9M serial port connector on the PC. A serial mouse uses no special resources other than the standard serial port resources for the port to which it is connected (IRQ4 and base address 03F8-03FF for COM1, or IRQ3 and 02F8-02FF for COM2). You can connect a serial mouse to either serial port. When the mouse driver initializes, it detects which port the mouse is connected to and uses the appropriate IRQ and base address to access it.

USB

A USB mouse uses no special resources beyond those claimed by the USB host controller itself. Unlike USB keyboards, USB mice do not require BIOS support because they need not be accessible until the operating system has loaded. They do require an operating system, such as Windows 98 or Windows 2000, that supports USB. Many current mice offer the USB interface, and usually include an adapter to allow the mouse to be connected to a standard PS/2 mouse port.

Bus

A bus mouse (also called an InPort mouse) is so-named because it connects to an adapter that plugs into the expansion bus. Bus mice were introduced to allow connecting a mouse to a PC that had no free serial ports. The adapter card is an 8-bit ISA card that provides selectable IRQ (usually 2, 3, 4, or 5) and base address settings. However, as an 8-bit card, it is limited to using 8-bit IRQs, most or all of which are already in use on a PC with two active serial ports, which is the reason for using a bus mouse in the first place. Ordinarily, the only available choice is IRQ5. If the system has an 8-bit sound card installed, IRQ5 is also occupied, which leaves no alternative unless you are willing to disable the IRQ for LPT1.

None of these interfaces are compatible with any of the others, although some mice are designed with autosensing circuitry to allow them to work with more than one interface. Dual compatibility is usually listed on the bottom of the mouse, e.g., "Serial and PS/2 compatible." In particular, be careful about interchanging PS/2 and bus mice, which use the same connector. Connecting a PS/2 mouse to a bus mouse port or vice versa can damage the mouse, the PC, or both.

Choosing a Mouse

Use the following guidelines when choosing a mouse or trackball:

Get the right size and shape

Mice are available in various sizes and shapes, including very small mice intended for children, the formerly standard "dovebar" size, the mainstream ergonomic mouse, and some very large mice that have many buttons and extra features. Most people find nearly any standard-size mouse comfortable to use for short periods, but if you use a mouse for extended periods small differences in size and shape often make a big difference in comfort. Although oversize mice like the Microsoft IntelliMouse Explorer provide attractive features and functions, people with very small hands often find such mice too large to use comfortably. Pay particular attention to mouse shape if you are left-handed. Although Microsoft claims that their asymmetric ergonomic mice are equally usable by left- and right-handers, many lefties find them uncomfortable and so resort to right-handed mousing. Other manufacturers, including Logitech, produce symmetric mice for which chirality is not an issue.

Get a wheel mouse

Although few applications support the wheel, those that do are the ones most people are likely to use a great deal—Microsoft Office, Internet Explorer, and so on. Using the wheel greatly improves mouse functionality by reducing the amount of mouse movement needed to navigate web pages and documents.

Consider a mouse with extra buttons

Standard two-button mice (three, counting the wheel) are adequate for most purposes. However, the new five-button mice are ideally suited to some applications, such as games and web browsing. For example, the two extra buttons can be mapped to the Back and Forward browser icons, eliminating a great deal of extraneous mouse movement.

Make sure the cord is long enough

We have seen mice with cords ranging in length from less than four feet to about nine feet. A short mouse cord may be too short to reach the system, particularly if it is on the floor. If you need a longer mouse cord, purchase a PS/2 keyboard extension cable, available in nearly any computer store.

Consider a cordless model

If your desktop is usually cluttered, consider buying a cordless mouse. The absence of a cord can make a surprising difference.

Try a trackball

Trackballs have never really caught on, probably because most require using the thumb to move the pointer. At least one newer model, the Microsoft IntelliMouse Trackball, resembles a mouse and allows using the index finger to point. In our experience, about one of every ten people who tries a trackball becomes a trackball convert. But trackballs sell probably only 1% the volume of mice, which says there are a lot of people who don't know what they're missing.

Configuring a Mouse or Trackball

Windows 95/98/NT/2000 allows you to customize how your mouse behaves. To do so, run the Mouse applet (Start → Settings → Control Panel → Mouse) to display the Mouse Properties dialog, which includes the following pages:

Buttons (Windows 95/98/NT/2000)

The Buttons page in Windows 95/98/NT allows you to configure the mouse for right- or left-handed use and specify the maximum duration between clicks that will still be recognized as a double-click. The Windows 2000 Buttons page has the same functions, and also allows you to specify whether a single-click or double-click opens a file or folder. Changes in this dialog take effect immediately when you click Apply or OK.

Pointers (Windows 95/98/NT/2000)

The Pointers page in Windows 95/98/NT allows you to change the appearance of the mouse cursor. If predefined mouse scheme(s) are installed, selecting one from the Schemes drop-down list defines all cursor types in one step. Double-clicking an individual pointer type displays a list of available cursor icons that can be assigned to that pointer type. Windows 2000 provides the same options, and adds a checkbox to enable pointer shadow.

Motion (Windows 95/98/NT/2000)

The Motion page in Windows 95/98/NT allows you to set the speed of the mouse pointer using the Pointer speed slider. Depending on the mouse driver installed, other options may also appear on this page, including Snap-to (automatically move the pointer to the default option button in dialogs);

Pointer trails (display a series of ghost pointers as the mouse is moved to prevent losing track of the pointer); and Vanish (hide the mouse pointer while typing). Windows 2000 provides the same options and adds standard Snap-to default and Acceleration settings.

General (Windows NT only) or Hardware (Windows 2000 only)
These pages display the type of mouse installed. Clicking the Change button on the Windows NT General page allows you to select among alternative installed mouse drivers, or to install a new mouse driver from a disk supplied by the mouse manufacturer. The Windows 2000 Hardware page instead provides a Troubleshoot button, which invokes the Mouse Troubleshooter Wizard, and a Properties button, which simply displays Device Manager properties for the mouse.

Installing a new mouse or an updated mouse driver may add pages and options to the standard Mouse Properties dialog. For example, Figure 20-1 shows one of the additional pages that results from installing the Microsoft IntelliPoint driver supplied with the Microsoft IntelliMouse with IntelliEye (where do they come up with these names?). If you install a new mouse driver, locate and explore the options it provides. The default settings for such things as wheel definition are probably useful, but one of the alternative options may better suit your work habits.

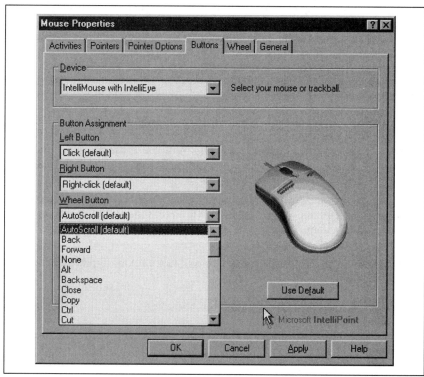

Figure 20-1: The Windows NT 4 Mouse Properties dialog as modified by installing the Microsoft IntelliPoint mouse driver

Cleaning a Mouse

No, we don't put mice through the dishwasher, although we may try that at some point. Optical mice are sealed units, and so require little more than an occasional wipe with a damp cloth. How often you need to clean a mechanical mouse depends on your working environment. Barbara, a true neatnik, needs to clean her mechanical mouse only every couple of months. Robert, who smokes a pipe, needs to clean his mechanical mice every few days.

The best sign that your mouse needs to be cleaned is when mouse movement suddenly becomes jerky or intermittent, particularly if the problem is limited to one direction. A mouse has two cylindrical rollers, one each to capture horizontal and vertical movement, and may also have one or more idler wheels designed to keep the ball in position. Dirt on these rollers and wheels is normally the cause of jerkiness and other movement problems. The best way we've found to clean a mouse requires only a soft cloth, an old toothbrush, and a bottle of rubbing alcohol. Take the following steps:

1. Dampen the cloth with alcohol and use it to wipe down the mouse cord and the exterior of the mouse.

2. Remove the plate that retains the ball and allow the ball to drop into your hand. Use the damp cloth to clean the ball and plate thoroughly and set them aside.

3. With the mouse upside down and using a strong light, look down into the hole normally occupied by the ball. Blow or shake out any large fluff balls or other accumulated trash.

4. Dip the toothbrush in alcohol and use it to scrub the rollers and wheels thoroughly, making sure to get them clean from end to end and all around their circumference. Because of the rolling action, hair and fibers can become knitted in a mat around the rollers, to the point where they're almost welded to the roller. If the toothbrush won't remove the mat, use the edge of a sharp knife *gently* to break up the mat without scratching the roller and then use the toothbrush to remove the freed junk.

5. If the mouse has a wheel, the bottom of the wheel is probably accessible from within the mouse housing. Use your finger to press the dampened cloth against the bottom of the wheel while you rotate the wheel from the top to remove accumulated grunge.

6. While you're at it, use the damp cloth to clean the mouse pad and the desk immediately surrounding it.

Troubleshooting a Mouse

If a mouse malfunctions, make sure the cable is connected properly and clean the mouse. If it still doesn't work, replace it.

Our Picks

We hate this. We really do. This section is a sweep for Microsoft. Before anyone accuses us of being in the pay of Microsoft and sends us marginally literate email complaining about Micro$oft and Windoze, please understand that we often get as mad at Microsoft as anyone else does. It just so happens we think Microsoft makes the best mice available.

Here are the mice and trackballs we use and recommend:

Inexpensive mechanical mouse

Microsoft Basic Mouse or Microsoft Wheel Mouse. We like to keep an extra mouse or two around so we'll always have a spare when we're building a system or need to replace a failed mouse. Either connects to a serial or PS/2 port. Both are straight-sided rather than the curved shape that Microsoft calls ergonomic, making them equally usable with either hand. The two-button Basic Mouse and the three-button Wheel Mouse are both so inexpensive—$15 or so for the Basic Mouse and $20 for the Wheel Mouse—that there's no point to using a no-name mouse. These mice are also excellent for building ultra low-cost systems. (*http://www.microsoft.com/products/hardware/mouse*)

Ergonomic mechanical mouse

Microsoft IntelliMouse. If you prefer the curved sides and humped back that Microsoft calls ergonomic, the IntelliMouse is an excellent choice. Other than the ergonomic style, it resembles the Wheel Mouse in features and functions. It connects to a serial or PS/2 port and costs $25 or so. Barbara uses a Microsoft IntelliMouse on her main system.

Optical mouse

Microsoft IntelliEye mice. Microsoft manufactures three versions of their optical IntelliEye mice, all of which are ergonomic and can connect to a PS/2 or USB port. The $45 three-button IntelliMouse with IntelliEye is simply an optical version of the IntelliMouse. The $60 IntelliMouse Explorer is an over-sized five-button mouse. By default, the two extra buttons are defined as Forward and Back for your web browser, although they can be programmed for other functions. The IntelliMouse Optical is simply a normal-size version of the IntelliMouse Explorer. Robert uses the IntelliMouse Explorer on his primary system, the IntelliMouse Optical on his secondary system, and IntelliMouse with IntelliEye mice on his other systems.

 The extra buttons on the IntelliMouse Explorer also make it an ideal gaming mouse for serious players of FPS games like Quake.

Cordless mouse

Microsoft Cordless Mouse. If you find your mouse cord is always getting in the way, the Microsoft Cordless Mouse may be the solution. This $35 mouse is simply a cordless version of the IntelliMouse. It includes a digital radio receiver that connects to either a serial or PS/2 mouse port. The receiver and mouse can use either of two channels, allowing two of these mice to operate in close proximity without interference. The receiver cord allows it to be placed several feet from the PC, and the mouse operates between 20 cm (8") and one meter (39") from the receiver, giving you a six foot or so range. The radio receiver is powered by the PC, and the mouse uses two standard AAA alkaline cells. We don't know how long they'll last, because our first set hasn't died yet.

Trackball

Microsoft IntelliMouse Trackball. Microsoft's $25 trackball is essentially an IntelliMouse with the ball sticking out the top. Unlike any other trackball we've seen, the IntelliMouse Trackball is designed to have the ball manipulated with the index finger rather than the thumb. If you've tried a traditional trackball and hated it, give this model a try.

We constantly test and review new equipment. For the latest information about what we currently use, visit:

http://www.hardwareguys.com/picks/input.html

CHAPTER 21

Game Controllers

A *game controller* is a specialized input device optimized for use with games. Unlike mice and trackballs, which are relatively standardized in form and function, game controllers run the gamut in shape, size, features, and purpose. Some game controllers sit on the desktop. Others clamp to the desk, and still others are held in both hands and manipulated directly. Game controllers may have a joystick, a steering wheel, a flight yoke, foot pedals, or may be what we call "grab, twist, and squeeze" controllers.

A particular game controller may be well-suited for one game and entirely inappropriate for another. For example, a game controller with a steering wheel may be perfect for playing NASCAR Winston Cup Racing, but unusable for a first-person shooter like Quake. Serious gamers who play diverse games often own several game controllers and use the one most appropriate for the game they are playing at the moment. Although you may have only one game/MIDI port on a PC, that port can support two game controllers simultaneously by using a splitter, which is supplied with many game controllers or can be purchased at most computer stores. Also, some game controllers have ports on the controller itself, which allow additional controllers to be daisy-chained from the controller attached to the PC.

Game Controller Characteristics

Here are the important characteristics of game controllers:

Type
> The first game controllers were *joystick controllers*, which are still available and still most appropriate for playing flight simulator and air combat games. Some are marginally usable for some driving, racing, action/adventure, and sports games. *Steering wheel controllers,* many of which include foot pedals, are ideal for driving/racing games and some flight simulators, but ill-suited to

other games. *Gamepad controllers* are suitable for action games, including first-person shooters, sports, and most arcade-style games.

Number of axes

An *axis* is a line drawn through the center of the joystick (or the D-pad on a gamepad) that defines the directions that one can move by manipulating the controls. All controllers have an *x-axis* (side to side movement) and a *y-axis* (front to back). Some controllers add a *z-axis* (up and down) and/or a *throttle axis*. Depending on the controller type, the third and/or fourth axes may also be called a *yoke control* or *rudder control*, for their intended function, or a *twist control*, for the method used to activate the axis.

Throttle

The *throttle* is a variable input, present on most joysticks and some gamepads, and normally assigned to the third or fourth axis on the controller. The throttle is usually used to control vehicle speed, and may be a slider, wheel, pedal, or variable-pull trigger, depending on the controller.

Response type

Motion along an axis can be tracked in two ways. *Proportional response* (common with joysticks) offers finer control, because small stick movement result in small incremental movement on screen. *Nonproportional response* (common with gamepads) is all-or-nothing—any movement of the control along an axis results in full motion on that axis, offering faster response at the expense of fine control. Some controllers are programmable to allow choosing between proportional and nonproportional modes.

Number of buttons

All controllers have buttons, which are momentary-on switches used to fire weapons and perform similar on/off functions. Pure analog controllers are limited to two or four buttons by the gameport itself. Digital controllers and the Microsoft DirectInput API allow using any number of buttons.

Hat switch

A *hat switch*, sometimes called a *POV hat*, a *Point of View hat*, or just a *hat*, is called that because it usually resides on the head of the joystick, where it's easily manipulated by the thumb. The hat switch is a directional rocker switch (usually four-way, but sometimes eight-way) that allows you to rapidly change your point of view to face front, rear, left, or right. Games that do not support POV may use the hat to provide four extra buttons.

Force feedback

Recent high-end game controllers have force-feedback technology, which uses small servo motors built into the game controller itself to provide physical feedback under the control of game software designed to use force feedback. For example, with a force-feedback joystick, as you pull a 7G turn you feel the joystick jerk and jitter as the aircraft control surfaces lose laminar flow, but as you extend to gain airspeed, the controls settle down again. When you come up on the six of a bandit and begin hosing him down with your 30 mm rotary cannon, the joystick stutters as the gun recoils.

Well-implemented force feedback greatly enhances the ambiance of games that support it properly, but the quality of force feedback hardware varies greatly between controllers. Even more important, games vary greatly in how well they integrate force feedback. Well-designed games use it elegantly to make the game more immersive. Many games, however, have simply grafted on minimal force feedback support, and use it in only the most basic ways. This problem will likely go away with new releases of such games. The only real drawback to force feedback at this point is that it is expensive. Typically a $60 controller without force-feedback might cost $120 with it. Interestingly, this same technology (in much enhanced form) is used in current fly-by-wire combat aircraft.

Programmability

All current game controllers include DirectInput drivers or are compatible with standard Windows 9X drivers. A DirectInput-compliant controller can be programmed within any DirectInput-compliant game. However, DirectInput provides only basic functionality, so many controllers come with their own programming software, which provides extended functionality, including:

Cross-game commonality

By default, games may use different buttons for similar purposes. For example, one air combat game may use button 1 to fire guns, button 2 to launch a Sidewinder, and button 3 to launch a Sparrow. Another air combat game may offer similar weapons selection, but use different buttons. Programmable game controllers allow you to redefine button functions, so the same button performs similar actions in different games.

Stored profiles

Many modern game controllers are quite flexible and may be used with diverse games. Optimal controller configuration for one game, however, may be less desirable for another. Better game controllers can store multiple groups of configuration settings, called *macros* or *profiles*, which allow you to quickly load whichever settings are most appropriate for the game you're about to play, rather than having to reprogram the controller manually each time. Most such controllers come with predefined settings for various popular games.

Interface

Analog game controllers connect to the gameport. Digital game controllers connect to the gameport or to a USB port. Analog controllers are obsolescent, because they provide limited functionality, require frequent calibration, and using them degrades system performance. Digital game controllers provide greater functionality, seldom or never require calibration, and do not degrade system performance, so nearly all game controller development now focuses on digital.

Gameport Interface

A standard PC gameport is actually a simple general-purpose analog data-acquisition port that supports four simple switched inputs and four variable-voltage inputs. A game controller connected to this interface uses one or more of the switched inputs to support buttons and one or more of the variable inputs to support a joystick, steering wheel, or similar device.

A *paddle* (originally used for Pong) is the simplest game controller. It uses only one switched input for a button and one variable input for a knob that controls movement in one direction. Accordingly, a gameport can support up to four paddles. A *joystick* uses one or two switched inputs for buttons and two variable inputs for a central stick that controls movement in both the horizontal (x-axis) and vertical (y-axis) directions. Accordingly, a gameport can support one or two joysticks. More complex game controllers use more of the switched inputs for additional buttons, and more of the variable inputs to control a third (z-axis) direction or for other purposes. This means that a gameport can support only one such controller.

Gameports do not require an IRQ, a DMA channel, or mapped memory, and occupy only one I/O base address. The downside of this small resource footprint is that gameports are not interrupt driven, so the CPU must constantly poll the gameport to detect when a button is pressed or a stick is moved. Polling can require as much as 10% of the CPU, which degrades performance when you least want the performance hit—as you're playing a shoot-em-up or trying to land a crippled fighter. The gameport connector on the PC is a DB-15F, shown in Figure 21-1. Table 21-1 describes the gameport interface and pinouts. Note that on MIDI-capable gameports (usually those on sound cards), Pin 12 is MIDI data out and Pin 15 is MIDI data in.

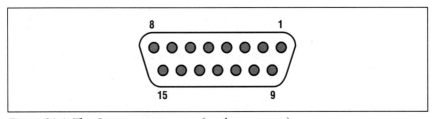

Figure 21-1: The Gameport connector (on the computer)

Table 21-1: Gameport Interface Signals and Pinout

Pin	Name	Joystick Function	Paddle Function	Direction
1	+5VDC	Joystick 1 power	Paddle A coordinate high	Out
2	Button 4	Joystick 1 button 1	Paddle A button high	In
3	Position 0	Joystick 1 x-coordinate	Paddle A coordinate wiper	In
4	Ground	Joystick 1 button 1 ground	Paddle A button ground	o
5	Ground	Joystick 1 button 2 ground	Paddle B button ground	o
6	Position 1	Joystick 1 y-coordinate	Paddle B coordinate wiper	In
7	Button 5	Joystick 1 button 2	Paddle B button high	In
8	+5VDC	(unused)	Paddle B coordinate high	Out
9	+5VDC	Joystick 2 power	Paddle C coordinate high	Out
10	Button 6	Joystick 2 button 1	Paddle C button high	In
11	Position 2	Joystick 2 x-coordinate	Paddle C coordinate wiper	In
12	Ground	Joystick 2 button 1/2 ground	Paddle C/D button return	o
13	Position 3	Joystick 2 y-coordinate	Paddle D coordinate wiper	In
14	Button 7	Joystick 2 button 2	Paddle D button high	In
15	+5VDC	(unused)	Paddle D coordinate high	Out

There are actually two types of gameport, single- and dual-port. Table 21-1 describes the dual-port type. The single-port uses the same connector, but does not support the Joystick 2 functions. In short, rather than supporting a total of four switched inputs and four variable inputs, a single-port gameport supports only two of each, and can therefore support only one two-button, two-axis game controller. All current sound cards and most older sound cards provide dual-port game ports. Only a few very old models are single-port devices.

Joystick coordinate signals are analog inputs. Pins 3 and 6 report the x- and the y-coordinates, respectively, for Joystick 1. Pins 11 and 13 do the same for Joystick 2. Moving the joystick alters the position of the slider on a 0 to 100 KOhm potentiometer, altering resistance, which in turn alters the voltage present on the pin. The gameport periodically samples the voltage on each coordinate pin using a monostable multivibrator. The gameport uses a base address of 201h. Writing to that address resets the monostable multivibrators and begins position measurement. Each byte subsequently read from 201h reports the status of the coordinate and button pins, as shown in Table 21-2.

Table 21-2: Gameport 201h Byte

7	6	5	4	3	2	1	0	Description	Pin
1	0	0	0	0	0	0	0	Joystick 2, button 2 (0=closed, 1=open)	14
0	1	0	0	0	0	0	0	Joystick 2, button 1 (0=closed, 1=open)	10
0	0	1	0	0	0	0	0	Joystick 1, button 2 (0=closed, 1=open)	7
0	0	0	1	0	0	0	0	Joystick 1, button 1 (0=closed, 1=open)	2
0	0	0	0	1	0	0	0	Joystick 2, y-coordinate (0=timed-out, 1=timing)	13
0	0	0	0	0	1	0	0	Joystick 2, x-coordinate (0=timed-out, 1=timing)	11
0	0	0	0	0	0	1	0	Joystick 1, y-coordinate (0=timed-out, 1=timing)	6
0	0	0	0	0	0	0	1	Joystick 1, x-coordinate (0=timed-out, 1=timing)	3

201h Byte Bitmask

Most game controllers introduced since mid-1999 use USB instead of or in addition to the legacy gameport interface. Because USB is a general-purpose digital interface, game controller designers can implement whatever custom functions they wish in the controller hardware and define support for those functions in the driver.

Choosing a Game Controller

More so than for any other input device, the "best" game controller is a matter of personal preference. If it feels right to you, it probably is right. If it feels wrong, it's probably wrong, no matter how much someone else may like it. Use the following guidelines when choosing a game controller:

Get the right type(s)

Make sure the game controller type is appropriate for the games you play most often. If you frequently play two or more games that are ill-suited to using the same controller, buy two or more controllers, and use the type most suited to whatever game you play. We make some suggestions as to appropriate types in the "Our Picks" section at the end of this chapter.

Avoid analog

All current game controllers worth having are digital models, although some analog models are still available. Note that many digital controllers use the analog gameport interface, including many high-end models. Digital gameport models are acceptable, but fully digital (USB) models are easier to swap in and out if you use multiple controllers.

Check compatibility

If you buy a model that connects to the gameport, verify that that controller is compatible with your gameport. Incompatibilities between PCI audio cards and digital game controllers are very common.

Buy a force feedback model

If an appropriate force feedback model is available and is within your budget, buy it rather than the cheaper model. More and more games support force feedback every month, and that support is of a higher quality with each upgrade of many games.

Solicit advice from friends

Friends are among the best sources of information about game controllers. You'll get a great deal of feedback from them, much of it conflicting, but valuable nonetheless. Not the least advantage of this method is that they'll probably let you play a few games with their controllers, giving you the opportunity to judge the merits for yourself in a realistic environment.

Installing a Game Controller

Physically installing a game controller is straightforward. Simply plug it into the gameport or a USB port, as appropriate. If the controller has both connectors, use the USB port unless the documentation suggests otherwise.

Before you connect the game controller, however, we suggest that you visit the Microsoft download site and update your copy of Windows 9X to the latest drivers, particularly DirectX.

Troubleshooting Game Controllers

It's impossible to provide comprehensive information about troubleshooting game controllers because both the controllers themselves and the problems you may encounter with them are so diverse. A cheap game controller is probably going to physically break or otherwise fail sooner rather than later. There's not much we can say about that, except to suggest that you buy a better quality game controller in the first place. If you experience problems with a good game controller, here are some actions to take:

Make sure the gameport is compatible with the game controller

Not all gameport game controllers are compatible with all gameports. Gameport conflicts frequently cause problems, particularly with digital game controllers connected to some models of PCI sound cards. We have also had reports of conflicts between some game controllers and some AGP video cards on specific motherboards, although we have not personally experienced or verified these. Most game controller vendors have detailed FAQ pages that list known incompatibilities for each model they sell.

Install the latest release of DirectX

DirectX (*http://www.microsoft.com/directx/homeuser/downloads/default.asp*) is a work in progress. If you experience problems with a game controller, particularly a new model, download and install the latest version of DirectX. For example, as this is written, Microsoft has just released DirectX 7.0a, which fixes problems that occur with several Microsoft game controller models under DirectX 7.0.

Install the latest drivers

Some game controllers provide basic functionality using the default drivers provided with Windows. If your game controller appears to be only partially functional, you may need to install a driver to support its enhanced functions. Most game controller vendors frequently update drivers to fix bugs, add support for new games, and so on, so it's a good idea to check the vendor support page frequently.

Make sure the game controller is configured for the game

If the game controller appears to work properly for one game but not others, make sure you've used the programmable functions of the game controller to configure it properly to support the other games. Most programmable game controllers include predefined profiles for popular games. If no profile is included for a game you purchase, check the vendor web site to see if an updated profile for that game is available.

Make sure the game is configured for the game controller

The default configuration settings for some games are inappropriate for some game controllers. For example, although many first-person shooter (FPS) games have freelook/mouselook disabled by default, the Microsoft SideWinder Dual Strike gamepad requires it be enabled for proper functioning. When you install a new game, check the game controller manual or web site to see if there are specific instructions to configure the controller optimally for that game.

Our Picks

Once again, Microsoft sweeps our recommendations, because they happen to make the best game controllers we've seen. We play games infrequently (and aren't very good at them), so the game controllers we prefer are likely not the models a serious gamer would choose. But serious gamers don't need our advice, while beginners may appreciate being given a starting point. So, although we won't tell you how badly we play Quake because it's embarrassing, here are the game controllers we use and recommend to people who are, like us, casual gamers.

Joystick controller

Microsoft SideWinder Force Feedback Pro. For flight simulators and air combat games you need a joystick. Although you can buy joysticks for $10, our experience with cheap ones has not been good. They drift, require constant calibration, and are quite fragile. We once unintentionally destroyed a cheap joystick the first time we used it, simply by overstressing it while playing the game. The best joystick we know of is the $115 SideWinder Force Feedback Pro (gameport). The $60 SideWinder Precision Pro (USB) is similar, but without force feedback. The entry-level $25 SideWinder Standard (gameport) is adequate for casual use. All three units are strongly built. (*http://www. microsoft.com/products/hardware/sidewinder*)

Steering wheel controller

Microsoft SideWinder Force Feedback Wheel. For driving and racing games you need a steering wheel controller. The $135 SideWinder Force Feedback Wheel (gameport) is an expensive wheel, but it's the best we've seen. Microsoft also sells the $70 Precision Racing Wheel (USB), which is similar but lacks force feedback. Both of these controllers are strongly built and durable, and include pedals that are actually usable.

Gamepad controller

Microsoft SideWinder Gamepad Pro. For sports and action games, a gamepad is the best choice. Again, although gamepads can be had for under $10, we recommend avoiding the cheapest ones. The best gamepad we've used is the $30 SideWinder Gamepad Pro (USB). Microsoft also makes the $60 SideWinder FreeStyle Pro (gameport/USB), which we have not used. For an entry-level pad, we like the $18 Logitech Wingman Gamepad (gameport/USB). Although to us it feels flimsier and sluggish compared to the Microsoft pad, it is quite usable. As a bonus, the Logitech profiling software is even better than Microsoft's latest, which is quite good itself. (*http://1164.224.37.201/*)

3D gamepad controller

Microsoft SideWinder Dual Strike. For playing FPS games like Quake or Rainbow Six and other 3D action/adventure games, you want a 3D gamepad, which combines mouse, keyboard, and joystick functionality in one device. A 3D gamepad is essentially a gamepad with a gimbal dividing it into two sections—what we call a "grab, twist, and squeeze" controller. It may be just our clumsiness, but the $40 SideWinder Dual Strike (USB) is the first 3D controller we've actually been able to use. All the others are so complex that we always get killed while trying to figure out how to make the controller perform basic functions (usually ducking, hiding, and running away, in our case). The Dual Strike probably won't appeal to Quake fanatics, who use the keyboard and mouse for look-and-aim, but it does give the rest of us at least a chance to perform respectably.

 The game controller market is extremely competitive, so manufacturers frequently offer significant rebates with their products. For example, the Microsoft SideWinder FreeStyle Pro sells for $60 or so, but Microsoft offers a $30 rebate throughout 2000, reducing your cost to $30 or less.

We constantly test and review new equipment. For the latest information about what we currently use, visit:

http://www.hardwareguys.com/picks/input.html

CHAPTER 22

Cases

Most people think of a case as just what holds a PC together. That view is reasonable for people who buy a PC and never open the case, but anyone who builds or upgrades PCs soon realizes that not all cases are created equal. The following sections describe what you need to know about cases.

Case Characteristics

PC cases are available in a bewildering array of sizes, shapes, and prices. Form factor is the most important thing about a case, because it determines which motherboards and which power supplies fit that case. Cases are available in the following form factors:

AT

> The 1984 IBM PC-AT introduced the AT form factor. AT cases accept full-size AT motherboards and reduced-size Baby AT motherboards. All AT-variant cases have a circular hole in the rear panel for the motherboard keyboard connector and knockouts for external DB connectors that mate to serial, parallel, and other ports present as header pins on AT motherboards. AT cases have been produced in two variants, which differ only in the power supply they accept. Desktop/AT cases use the original AT form factor power supply, with a paddle switch built into the power supply itself. Tower/AT cases use a modified AT power supply that instead has four main power leads that connect to a switch built into the case. Desktop/AT cases and power supplies are hard to find nowadays, but Tower/AT cases and power supplies are still readily available. AT cases of either type are a poor choice for building a new system.

Baby AT

> AT motherboards require large cases. The demand for smaller systems resulted in Baby AT (BAT) motherboards and cases. A BAT motherboard is simply a reduced-size AT motherboard, and uses the same connectors and

mounting hole positions. Like AT cases, BAT cases have been produced in Desktop/BAT and Tower/BAT form factors. Desktop/BAT cases accept only Desktop/BAT power supplies, which are smaller versions of the AT power supply, complete with paddle switch. Tower/BAT cases accept only Tower/ BAT power supplies, which are smaller versions of Tower/AT power supplies. Confusingly, many recent BAT desktop cases and systems were designed to use Tower/BAT power supplies. Adding to the confusion, BAT has become such a catchall term that some so-called BAT cases can in fact accept full-AT motherboards and power supplies. Desktop/BAT cases and power supplies are difficult to find new now. New Tower/BAT systems were still being sold as late as 1999, so Tower/BAT cases (in both desktop and tower styles!) are still widely available to upgraders, although they are a poor choice for building new systems..

LPX

Corporate demand for low-profile systems and the desire to reduce manufacturing costs led to the creation of LPX, a variant of BAT. LPX cases accept only LPX power supplies and LPX motherboards, which use a riser card to arrange expansion cards horizontally rather than vertically. Although it was for a while popular for mass-market consumer systems and low-profile corporate systems, LPX failed as a standard for several reasons: many manufacturers implemented proprietary variations of LPX; expected cost savings did not materialize, largely because most LPX implementations required expensive supplementary cooling fans; and the riser card made it difficult to work on the motherboard, increasing support costs. LPX cases are still available, although their distribution is very limited. The only reason to purchase an LPX case is to salvage components from an existing LPX system, which must by now be old enough that it is not worth salvaging anyway.

The preceding three form factors are obsolescent, although manufacturers continue to make them for the repair and upgrade market. The form factors of modern cases all derive from the *Intel ATX specification* (*http://www.teleport.com/ ~ffsupprt/*). ATX includes the following variants, whose dimensions and motherboard/case compatibilities are detailed in Table 22-1:

ATX

Both the lack of a formal BAT standard and some increasingly troublesome problems with BAT component layouts led Intel to develop the ATX form factor, which they introduced with the Advanced/ML "Marl" motherboard in 1996. ATX redesigned component layouts for easier access, improved cooling, and other factors, but the important aspect of ATX for cases is that it dispenses with the AT keyboard hole and port knockouts on the rear panel, replacing them with a consolidated I/O panel of standard size and positioning. Also, ATX motherboards control the power supply directly, which means that the "power" switch on an ATX system actually just notifies the motherboard to turn power on or off rather than doing so itself. The original ATX specification is often loosely termed "Full ATX" to differentiate it from smaller ATX variants. A full ATX case is usually the best choice for building a new PC.

Mini-ATX

As a part of the Intel ATX Specification, Intel also defines Mini-ATX, which is simply a reduced-size ATX motherboard. The primary motivation for Mini-ATX is manufacturing cost reductions, because four Mini-ATX boards can be produced from a standard blank, which yields only two ATX boards. Mini-ATX cases accept Mini-ATX (or smaller) motherboards, but are too small for ATX motherboards. It costs nearly as much to make Mini-ATX cases as full-ATX cases, which accept both ATX and Mini-ATX motherboards, so Mini-ATX cases are very uncommon.

NLX

NLX, introduced in 1997, is the ATX version of LPX, and is intended for inexpensive, low-profile corporate and mass-market systems. NLX cases accept only NLX motherboards, which use riser cards similar to those used by LPX cases, and a full-length I/O panel rather than the standard ATX I/O panel. About the only reason to buy an NLX case is to salvage an NLX system whose case is damaged. NLX cases are readily available from numerous sources, but are a poor choice for building new systems.

microATX

Smaller translates to cheaper. Intel released the microATX Motherboard Interface Specification in 1998 in response to the demand for low-cost consumer systems, for which expandability is not an issue. microATX motherboards have only four expansion slots (versus seven for ATX), which allows using smaller and less expensive cases. Some microATX cases accept only SFX power supplies (described in Chapter 23, *Power Supplies*) which are smaller, cheaper, less powerful, and less functional than standard ATX power supplies. Because such cases are too small to accept a standard ATX power supply, upgrade options are severely limited. Although microATX cases are available from third-party manufacturers, their distribution is limited and they are a very poor choice for building new systems.

FlexATX

Just as microATX is a smaller version of ATX, FlexATX is a smaller version of microATX, picoATX as it were. FlexATX is an addendum to the microATX specification, intended for even smaller systems, such as Web devices, set-top boxes, and novelty PCs such as the Barbie PC and the Hot Wheels PC (we are not making this up). If for some reason you want to know more about FlexATX, download the FlexATX Addendum Version 1.0 to microATX Specification Version 1.0 (*http://www.teleport.com/~ffsupprt/spec/FlexATXaddn1_0.pdf*).

WTX

Reversing the trend toward ever-smaller variants of ATX, the WTX Workstation System Specification Version 1.1 defines WTX as Intel's extension of the ATX standard to the requirements of mid-range workstations, with explicit support for dual processors, large memory configurations, AGP Pro graphics, dual-fan power supplies, and other workstation-oriented features. WTX-compliant cases, power supplies, and motherboards began shipping in limited quantities in Q1 2000. For additional information about WTX, see *http://www.wtx.org*.

Table 22-1: Maximum Motherboard Dimensions and Chassis Compatibility for ATX Form Factor Variants

Motherboard	Width$_{max}$	Depth$_{max}$	Fits ATX case style(s)					
			Full	Mini	micro	Flex	NLX	WTX
ATX	12.0"/305 mm	9.6"/244 mm	●	○	○	○	○	○
Mini-ATX	11.2"/284 mm	8.2"/208 mm	●	●	○	○	○	○
microATX	9.6"/244 mm	9.6"/244 mm	●	●	●	○	○	○
FlexATX	9.0"/229 mm	7.5"/191 mm	●	●	●	●	○	○
NLX	13.6"/346 mm	9.0"/229 mm	○	○	○	○	●	○
WTX	16.75"/425 mm	14.0"/356 mm	○	○	○	○	○	●

Some hybrid cases are available that accept either BAT or ATX motherboards and power supplies, and include both the AT-specific keyboard connector hole and port knockouts and the ATX-specific I/O Panel cutout. These cases may come equipped with a "universal" power supply that provides both AT and ATX motherboard main power connectors. These cases are popular with some upgraders, as they allow using an AT motherboard now and upgrading to an ATX model later without replacing the case. We don't much like universal cases, because they often focus on flexibility and low cost at the expense of quality.

Although form factor is the most important characteristic of a case, numerous other factors are worth considering:

Size and orientation

Cases are available in a variety of sizes and orientations, including low-profile desktop, standard desktop, micro-tower (for the new microATX boards), mini-tower, mid-tower, and full-tower. Low-profile cases are popular for mass-market and business-oriented PCs, but we see little purpose for them. They take up more desk space than towers, provide poor expandability, and are difficult to work on. Micro-tower cases take very little desk space, but otherwise share the drawbacks of low-profile cases. Mini/mid-tower styles—the dividing line between them is nebulous—are most popular because they consume little desktop space while providing good expandability. Full-tower cases are what we really prefer. They take up no desk space at all, and are tall enough that CD-ROM, tape, and other external drives are readily accessible. Their cavernous interiors make it very easy to work inside them, and they often provide better cooling than smaller cases. The drawbacks of full-tower cases are that they are more expensive than other cases, sometimes significantly so, and they may require using extension cables for keyboard, video, and/or mouse.

Drive bay arrangement

The number and arrangement of drive bays may be unimportant if the system is unlikely to be upgraded later. All current cases provide at least one 3.5" external bay for a floppy, one 5.25" external bay for a CD-ROM, and one 3.5" internal bay for a hard disk. That may change, however, as Microsoft and Intel strive to rid the world of "legacy" devices, including the venerable floppy drive. Table 22-2 shows typical arrangements for various case styles.

Table 22-2: Typical Drive Bay Configuration in Various Case Styles

	External Bays		Internal Bays		Total Bays
Case Style	3.5"	5.25"	3.5"	5.25"	
Low profile	1–2	1	1–2	0	3–4
Desktop	1–2	2–3	1–3	0–3	4–7
Micro-tower	1–2	1	1–2	0	3–4
Mini-tower	1–2	2–3	1–4	0–2	4–7
Mid-tower	1–2	3–4	1–5	0–3	5–8
Full-tower	0–2	3–8	0–8	0–8	8–14

Drive mounting method

Drives mount in most cases via screws driven directly through the chassis into the sides of the drives. This method is secure, provides good electrical grounding, and allows the drives to use the chassis as a heat sink. The drawback is that, for some chassis, it is difficult to access the screws on the right side of 3.5" drives. Some cases address this problem by using removable motherboard trays or removable drive bays. Others simply have access holes punched in the right side of the chassis. Some cases use mounting rails, which screw or snap onto the drive and fit slots in the drive bays. Rails are less likely to physically torque a drive, which can cause read/write problems, and make it easier to remove and replace drives. On the downside, rails provide inferior electrical and thermal contact compared to direct mounting, may rattle if they fit loosely, and sometimes cause vertical alignment problems where one drive that should fit an adjacent bay will not do so because the faceplate is a tiny bit too large. In practice, we've never much cared whether a case required securing drives directly or used rails. If you are building a system that you will seldom open, drive mounting method is relatively unimportant. If you are building a test-bed or other system in which you will frequently swap drives, either buy a case that uses rails or simply don't use screws to secure the drives.

Accessibility

Cases vary widely in how easy they are to work on. Some use thumb screws and pop-off panels that allow complete disassembly in seconds without tools, while disassembling others requires a screwdriver and more work. Similarly, some cases have removable motherboard trays or drive cages that make it easier to install and remove components. The flip-side of easy access is that, unless they are properly engineered, easy-access cases are often less rigid than traditional cases. Years ago we worked on a system that experienced seemingly random disk errors. We replaced the hard disk, cables, disk controller, power supply, and other components, but errors persisted. As it turned out, the user kept a stack of heavy reference books on top of the case. As she added and removed books, the case was flexing enough to torque the hard disk in its mounting, causing disk errors. Rigid cases prevent such problems. The other aspect of accessibility is sheer size. It's easier to work inside a full tower case than a smaller case simply because there's more room.

Provisions for supplemental cooling

For basic systems, the power supply fan and CPU fan normally suffice. More heavily loaded systems—those with dual processors, high-performance SCSI hard drives, lots of expansion cards, and so on—require adding supplemental fans. Some cases have no provision for adding fans, while others provide mounting positions for half a dozen or more fans. A few towers and hobbyist-oriented cases have supplemental fans as standard features, but most cases do not.

Construction quality

Cases run the gamut in construction quality. Cheap cases have flimsy frames, thin sheet metal, holes that don't line up and razor sharp burrs and edges that make them dangerous to work on. High-quality cases—like those from PC Power & Cooling and Antec—have rigid frames, heavy sheet metal, properly-aligned holes, and all edges rolled or deburred. One seldom-noticed specification is weight, which is largely determined by the thickness of the frame and panels, and can provide a good clue to case quality. Without power supply, for example, the PC Power and Cooling Personal Mid-Tower weighs 18 pounds (8.2 kg) and the similar Antec KS-288 weighs 23 pounds (10.5 kg). We have seen no-name cases of similar size that weigh as little as 12 pounds (5.5 kg). For cases, heavier is usually better.

Choosing a Case

Use the following guidelines when choosing a case:

Choose the correct form factor

If you are migrating an existing motherboard, buy a case to fit that motherboard. If you are building a new system, buy a case that accepts full ATX motherboards, even if you're installing a Mini-ATX or microATX motherboard. A full ATX case allows upgrading later to a full ATX motherboard, and provides more working space even if the system will never have anything larger than a microATX motherboard installed.

Plan for expansion

Choose a case that leaves at least one or two bays—ideally 5.25" external bays—free for later expansion. As the price of tape drives, DVD-ROM/RAM drives, and CD burners continues to fall, you're likely to want to install one or more of them in the future. That's impossible without free drive bays. A mini/mid-tower case with three external 5.25" bays, two external 3.5" bays, and perhaps one or two internal 3.5" bays is usually the best compromise between size, cost, and available bays, although a full tower may be the best choice if your current configuration fills or nearly fills a mid-tower. Some cases can be ordered with two or three optional internal 3.5" bays for very little additional cost, typically $5 to $8. If in doubt, always buy the next size up.

Avoid cheap cases

It's always tempting to save money, but cases are one place where it's easy to spend too little. The cheapest cases ($30 or $40 with power supply) are often unusable due to misaligned holes and so on. Even mid-range "name-brand" cases often have razor-sharp edges and burrs, which can cut you and short out wires. Expect to pay at least $35 (without power supply) for a decent mini/mid-tower case and $50 to $60 for a full tower. See the end of this chapter for specific recommendations.

Buy a case without power supply if possible

Most cheap and mid-range cases include a "throw-away" power supply that's of poor quality and undersized. Choosing case and power supply separately gets you both the case you want and a better quality power supply sized appropriately for your needs. Standard power supplies fit standard cases interchangeably, so compatibility is not an issue. See Chapter 23 for details.

Add supplemental cooling fans

Heat is the enemy of processors, memory, drives, and other system components. Cooler components last longer and run more reliably. A processor run at 50°C (122°F), for example, will last only half as long as one run at 40°C (104°F), but twice as long as one run at 60°C (140°F). The best way to minimize temperature inside the case is to move a lot of air through it. Although the power supply fan and processor fan may provide adequate cooling on lightly-loaded systems, adding supplemental fans can reduce ambient case temperature by 20°C (36°F) or more on more heavily loaded systems. Many cases can be ordered with optional supplemental fans. If the case you order offers optional fans, order them. Otherwise, add the fans yourself. You can purchase supplemental fans for a few dollars from local computer stores and mail-order suppliers. They are available in various standard sizes from 60 mm to 120 mm, so make sure to purchase the correct size. Note that many cases that accept multiple fans use different sizes in different locations.

 Make sure supplemental fans blow the right way, including those that arrive installed in a case. Some power supplies have intake fans, and others have exhaust fans. The ATX specification recommends but does not require using an intake fan on the power supply. Many (including us) prefer power supplies that use exhaust fans, and many manufacturers now supply exhaust fans on ATX power supplies. The danger arises when the power supply fan and supplemental fan(s) blow in the same direction. When that happens, the fans work against each other, either pressurizing the case or creating a partial vacuum. In either event, air flow is reduced or eliminated, which causes the processor and other system components to overheat. Supplemental fans can be mounted to blow either direction. If your power supply uses an exhaust fan, configure supplemental fan(s) as intake fans. If your power supply uses an intake fan, configure supplemental fan(s) as exhaust fans.

Consider accessibility

If you frequently add and remove components, consider purchasing a case with accessibility features such as removable motherboard trays and drive bays. If you tend not to open your computer case from one month to the next, you may be better served by a case with fewer accessibility features, which is likely to be less expensive for equivalent quality and rigidity.

Consider shipping costs

When you compare case prices, remember that the cost to ship a case can be substantial. Cases you find at local stores already have that factored in. Mail order companies may charge $20 to $40 to ship a case, or even more for heavy full tower cases.

Our Picks

Although we certainly haven't used every case available, we have used a lot of them over the past 20 years. Here are the cases we use and recommend:

Premium mini/mid-tower

PC Power & Cooling (PPC) Personal Mid-Tower. The PPC Personal Mid-Tower is what we use for many of our own systems. At $65 direct without power supply, this is not an inexpensive case, but it is the best mid-tower case we've seen. It is rigidly constructed of heavy-gauge metal. Everything aligns properly, and there are no sharp edges or burrs. This case provides eight (!) drive bays, two of which are optional, a removable motherboard tray, and accepts either AT or ATX motherboards and power supplies. (*http://www. pcpowercooling.com*)

Economy mini/mid-tower case

Antec KS-288 Value Line Mid-Tower. At about $65 street price including an Antec PP253X 250W power supply, the KS-288 is an incredible value. Unlike most inexpensive cases, the Antec KS-288 is well-built from very heavy-gauge metal. There are no sharp edges, everything aligns properly, and panels are easy to remove and replace. The right side panel is removable, which makes drive bay access easy. Antec also manufactures the KS-280 Premium Mid-tower case, which we have not reviewed. Frankly, their value line is so good that we didn't see the point. (*http://www.antec-inc.com*)

Premium full tower

PPC Solid-Steel Tower. Robert uses the PPC Solid-Steel Tower for his personal workstation. This is an industrial-grade case, as its weight of 40 lbs. (18.2 kg) without power supply indicates. It is big, heavy, and solidly-built. With ten 5.25" half-height drive bays, all of which are external and use drive rails, there's room for anything you're likely to add. This case accepts power supplies up to 600W, and redundant, hot-swappable power supplies of 600W or 850W. At $279 direct without power supply, this case is clearly intended for high-end workstations and workgroup/departmental servers. If that's what you're building, we don't know of a better case to use. (*http://www.pcpowercooling.com*)

Economy full tower case

Antec KS-180 Premium Full-Tower. At about $100 street price including an Antec PP253X 250W power supply or $110 with the 300W PP303X, the KS-180 is another incredible value. With six external 5.25" drive bays and four 3.5" drive bays (two of each), this case provides adequate space for all but the most heavily equipped systems. If even the optional 300W power supply is a bit light for your configuration, keep it as a spare and install one of the PC Power & Cooling units described in Chapter 23. (*http://www.antec-inc.com*)

We constantly test and review new equipment. For the latest information about what we currently use, visit:

http://www.hardwareguys.com/picks/cases.html

CHAPTER 23

Power Supplies

Power supplies lack glamour, so nearly everyone takes them for granted. That's a big mistake, because the power supply performs two critical functions: it provides regulated power to every system component and it cools the computer. Many people who complain that Windows crashes frequently understandably blame Microsoft. But, without apologizing for Microsoft, the truth is that many such crashes are caused by low-quality or overloaded power supplies.

If you want a reliable, crash-proof system, use a high-quality power supply. In fact, we have found that using a high-quality power supply allows even marginal motherboards, processors, and memory to operate with reasonable stability, whereas using a cheap power supply makes even top-notch components unstable.

The sad truth is that it is almost impossible to buy a computer with a top-notch power supply. Computer makers count pennies, literally. Good power supplies don't win marketing brownie points, so few manufacturers are willing to spend $30 to $75 extra for a better power supply. For their premium lines, first- and second-tier manufacturers generally use what we call mid-range power supplies, better than the Pacific Rim junk used by some garage shops and low-end assemblers, but not nearly as good as what you can get on the aftermarket. For their mass-market lines—like those sold at Circuit City, Best Buy, and Target—even name-brand manufacturers may compromise on the power supply to meet a price point, using what we consider marginal power supplies both in terms of output and construction quality.

The following sections detail what you need to understand to choose a good power supply.

Power Supply Characteristics

Here are the important characteristics of power supplies.

Form Factor

As with cases, the primary characteristic of a power supply is its form factor, which specifies dimensions and mounting hole locations, which in turn determine which case form factor(s) the power supply fits. Form factor also specifies the type of motherboard power connectors the power supply provides, which in turn determines the type(s) of motherboards the power supply supports. Table 23-1 lists compatibility of power supplies with cases.

Table 23-1: Power Supply Compatibility with Case Form Factors

	Accepts These Power Supplies								
Case Form Factor	*D/AT*	*T/AT*	*D/BAT*	*T/BAT*	*LPX*	*ATX*	*SFX*	*NLX*	*WTX*
Desktop/AT (D/AT)	●	○	●	○	○	○	○	○	○
Tower/AT (T/AT)	○	●	○	●	○	○	○	○	○
Desktop/BAT (D/BAT)	○	○	●	○	○	○	○	○	○
Tower/BAT (T/BAT)	○	○	○	●	○	○	○	○	○
LPX	○	○	○	○	●	○	○	○	○
ATX	○	○	○	○	○	●	●	○	○
Mini-ATX	○	○	○	○	○	●	●	○	○
microATX	○	○	○	○	○	○	●	○	○
FlexATX	○	○	○	○	○	○	●	○	○
NLX	○	○	○	○	○	○	○	●	○
WTX	○	○	○	○	○	○	○	○	●

AT-variant case/power supply issues are confusing because of the lack of standards. For example, many current BAT *desktop* cases use Tower/BAT power supplies instead of Desktop/BAT power supplies! See Chapter 22, *Cases*, for details.

Rated wattage

The nominal wattage that the power supply can deliver. Nominal wattage is a composite figure, determined by multiplying the amperages available at each of the several voltages supplied by a PC power supply by those voltages. Nominal wattage is mainly useful for general comparison of power supplies. What really matters is the individual wattages available at different voltages, and those vary significantly between nominally similar power supplies, as detailed later in this chapter.

Nominal voltage

Nearly all PC power supplies can use either 110/115V or 220/230V nominal. Some detect input voltage and adjust themselves automatically. Many, however, must be set manually for 110V or 220V, usually via a red sliding switch on the rear panel. Be very careful if your power supply is not autosensing. If the switch is set for 220V and you connect it to a 110V receptacle, no damage is done, although the system will not boot. But if the power supply is set for 110V and you connect it to a 220V receptacle, catastrophic damage to your motherboard and other system components is likely to occur.

Operating voltage range

The highest and lowest AC voltages that the power supply can accept while continuing to supply DC output voltages and currents within specifications. Typical high-quality power supplies function properly if the input voltage is within about ±20% of the center of the range, i.e., 90V to 135V when set for nominal 110/115V input, and 180V to 270V when set for 220/230V nominal. Less expensive, but still name-brand, power supplies may have a range of only about ±10%, i.e., 100V to 125V when set for 110/115V nominal, or 200V to 250V when set for 220/230V nominal. Cheap, no-name power supplies often do not supply power to specification even when provided with nominal input voltages, if indeed they even list nominal output specifications. Having a broad operating voltage range is particularly important if you operate without a UPS or line conditioner to ensure that the voltage supplied to the power supply does not vary due to brownouts, sags, and surges. It is less important if you do have a line conditioner or line-interactive UPS, except as an indicator of overall quality of the power supply.

Input frequency range

The range of AC frequencies over which the power supply is designed to operate. Most power supplies function properly within the range of 47 Hz to 63 Hz, which is adequate for nominal 50 Hz or 60 Hz input. In practice, this means that the power supply will operate properly on any nominal 50 Hz input voltage so long as it does not drop below 47 Hz and any nominal 60 Hz input voltage so long as it does not rise about 63 Hz. This is seldom a problem, as utilities control the frequency of the power they supply very tightly. Inexpensive power supplies usually do not list input frequency range, although we have seen cheap Pacific Rim units that list their requirements as "50 Hz to 60 Hz AC," implying that they have no tolerance for frequency variations.

Efficiency

The ratio of output power to input power expressed as a percentage. For example, a power supply that produces 350W output but requires 500W input is 70% efficient. In general, a good power supply is 70% efficient. However, calculating this figure is difficult because PC power supplies are *switching power supplies* rather than *linear power supplies*. The easiest way to think about this is to imagine the switching power supply drawing high current for a fraction of the time it is running and no current the remainder of the time. The percentage of the time it draws current is called the *power factor*, which is typically 70% for PC power supplies. In other words, a 350W PC power supply actually requires 500W input 70% of the time and 0W 30% of the time. Combining power factor with efficiency yields some interesting numbers. The power supply supplies 350W, but the 70% power factor means that it requires 500W 70% of the time. However, the 70% efficiency means that rather than actually drawing 500W, it must draw more, in the ratio 500W/0.7, or about 714W. If you examine the specifications plate for a 350W power supply, you may find that in order to supply 350W nominal, which is 350W/110V, or about 3.18 amps, it must actually draw up to 714W/110V, or about 6.5 amps. Other factors may increase that actual maximum amperage, so it's common to see 300W or 350W power supplies that actually draw as much as eight or ten amps maximum. That has planning implications, both for electrical circuits and for UPSs, which must be sized to accommodate the actual amperage draw rather than the rated output wattage.

One of the chief differences between premium power supplies and less expensive models is how well they are regulated. Ideally, a power supply accepts AC power, possibly noisy or outside specifications, and turns that AC power into smooth, stable DC power with no artifacts. In fact, no power supply meets the ideal, but good power supplies come much closer than cheap ones. Processors, memory, and other system components are designed to operate with pure, stable DC voltage. Any departure from that may reduce system stability and shorten component life. Here are the key regulation issues:

Ripple

A perfect power supply would accept the AC sine wave input and provide an utterly flat DC output. Real-world power supplies actually provide DC output with a small AC component superimposed upon it. That AC component is called *ripple*, and may be expressed as *peak-to-peak voltage* (p-p) in millivolts (mv) or as a percentage of the nominal output voltage. A high-quality power supply may have 1% ripple, which may be expressed as 1%, or as actual p-p voltage variation for each output voltage. For example, on a 5V output, a 1% ripple corresponds to ±0.05V, usually expressed as 50mV. A mid-range power supply may limit ripple to 1% on some output voltages, but soar as high as 2.5% on others, typically –5V, +3.3V, and +5V$_{SB}$. We have seen cheap power supplies with ripple of 10% or more, which makes running a PC a crapshoot. Low ripple is most important on +5V and +3.3V outputs, although 1.5% or lower ripple is desirable on all outputs.

Load regulation

The load on a PC power supply can vary significantly during routine operations, for example as a CD burner's laser kicks in or a DVD-ROM drive spins up and spins down. *Load regulation* expresses the ability of the power supply to supply nominal output power at each voltage as the load varies from maximum to minimum, expressed as the variation in voltage experienced during the load change, either as a percentage or in p-p voltage differences. A power supply with tight load regulation delivers near-nominal voltage on all outputs regardless of load (within its range, of course). A high-quality power supply regulates +3.3V to within 1%, and the ±5V and ±12V outputs to within 5% or less. A mid-range power supply might regulate +3.3V to within 3% or 4%, and the other voltages to within 5% or 10%. Regulation of +3.3V is critical, and should never exceed 4%, although many inexpensive power supplies allow it to vary 5% or even more.

Line regulation

An ideal power supply would provide nominal output voltages while being fed any input AC voltage within its range. Real-world power supplies allow the DC output voltages to vary slightly as the AC input voltage changes. Just as load regulation describes the effect of internal loading, *line regulation* can be thought of as describing the effects of external loading, e.g., a sudden sag in delivered AC line voltage as an elevator motor kicks in. Line regulation is measured by holding all other variables constant and measuring the DC output voltages as the AC input voltage is varied across the input range. A power supply with tight line regulation delivers output voltages within specification as the input varies from maximum to minimum allowable. Line regulation is expressed in the same way as load regulation, and the acceptable percentages are the same.

Transient response

If the load on the power supply varies momentarily from the baseline and then returns to baseline, it takes a certain period for the output voltages to return to nominal. *Transient response* is characterized in three ways, all of which are interrelated: by the percent load change, by the amount of time required for output voltages to return to within a specified percentage of nominal, and by what that percentage is. These figures are difficult to compare because different manufacturers use different parameters that are not directly comparable. For example, a high-quality power supply may state that after an instantaneous 50% load change, the power supply requires 1 millisecond (ms) to return to within 1% of nominal on all outputs. A mid-range power supply may specify the load change as only 20% and state that the ±5V and ±12V outputs return to within 5% of nominal within 1 ms. If the load change were 50% instead of 20%, that same mid-range power supply might require 2 or 3 ms to return to within 5% of nominal and 10 ms to return to 1% of nominal (if in fact it could control voltages to within 1% under normal conditions, which it probably couldn't). In general, a power supply with excellent transient response will specify (a) a load change of 50% or thereabouts, (b) a return to at or near its standard regulation range, and (c) a time of 1 or 2 ms. A decrease in the first figure or an increase in either or both of the second two are indicative of relatively poorer transient response. The major benefit of good transient response is increased reliability in disk operations, both read and write. A power supply with poor transient response results in frequent disk retries, which are visible to the user only as degraded disk performance. Many users who upgrade to a better power supply are surprised to find that their disk drives run faster. Hard to believe, but true.

Hold-up time

That period for which, during a loss of input power, the power supply continues to provide output voltages within specification. Hold-up time may be specified in ms or in cycles, where one cycle is 1/60 second, or about 16.7 ms. High-quality power supplies have hold-up times of 20 ms or higher (> 1.25 cycles). Lower-quality power supplies often have hold-up times of 10 ms or less, sometimes much less. There are two issues here: first, if you are running a stand-by power supply (commonly, if erroneously, called a UPS) that has a switchover time, hold-up keeps the PC running until the UPS has time to kick in. This is less of a problem with modern SPSs/UPSs, which commonly have transfer times of ~1 ms, compared to the 5 ms to 10 ms transfer times common with UPSes a few years ago. Hold-up time is even more important if you are not using a UPS, because about 99% of all power outages are of one cycle or less, many so short that you aren't even aware that they occurred because the lights don't have time to flicker. With such outages, a power supply with a long hold-up time will allow the PC to continue running normally, while one with a short hold-up time will cause the PC to lock up for no apparent reason. The first comment most people make who do not have a UPS and upgrade to a better power supply is that their systems don't lock up nearly as often. That's why.

Power Good signal

A power supply requires time to stabilize when power is first applied to it. When it stabilizes, the power supply asserts the Power Good (AT) or PWR_ OK (ATX) signal to inform the motherboard that suitable power is now available, and continues to assert that signal so long as suitable power remains available. The time a power supply requires before asserting Power Good varies between models, between examples of the same model, and even between boots with the same power supply. Some motherboards are sensitive to Power Good timing, and may refuse entirely to boot or experience sporadic boot failures when used with a power supply that has lengthy or unpredictable Power Good timing. A superior power supply may raise Power Good within 300 milliseconds (ms) plus or minus a few ms of receiving power. A mid-range power supply may require from 100 to 500 ms before asserting Power Good. Another aspect of Power Good that is seldom specified is how long the power supply continues to supply good power after dropping the Power Good signal. A good power supply should continue to provide clean power for at least one ms after deasserting Power Good.

Noise and fan air flow rating

The power supply fan produces air flow that cools both the power supply itself and other PC components such as processors and drives. In general, doubling the air flow reduces system operating temperature by about 50%, which in turn increases the life of system components. The old chem lab rule says that increasing the temperature by 10˚C (18˚F) doubles the rate of reaction, and reducing it by 10˚C halves the rate. That ratio holds roughly true for component life as well. A processor with a design operating temperature of 50˚C, for example, will last twice as long if run at 40˚C. But in the process of moving air, the fan generates noise. The amount and nature of that noise depends upon the number, design, size, pitch, and rotation speed of the fan blades, the size, design, and bearing type of the hub, the internal layout of power supply components, the depth and configuration of the venturi (air path), and other factors. In general, high cooling efficiency power supplies are noisier than those that move less air, and power supplies that use sleeve bearings are quieter (albeit less durable) than those that use ball bearings. Noise is measured on the logarithmic dB(A) scale at a distance of 1 metre from the fan. On the dB(A) scale, each 3 dB change indicates a doubling or halving of sound energy. A very quiet power supply may be rated at 34 to 36 dB(A), which is almost inaudible in a typical work environment, and provide 20 to 30 cubic feet per minute air flow. A typical power supply may generate 40 to 44 dBA, which is audible but not overly intrusive in most work environments, and provide 25 to 35 CFM. A high-performance power supply may generate 44 to 48 dB(A), which is distinctly noticeable, and provide 35 to 50 CFM.

Mean Time Between Failures (MTBF)

MTBF is a much-misunderstood way of specifying component reliability. MTBF for power supplies is a projected estimate based on a combination of operating data and calculated data as specified in MIL-HDBK-217. The MTBF projected failure curve for a particular model of power supply takes the form of a Poisson Distribution, with a few power supplies of that model failing very early, the vast majority failing from a year to a few years out, and (at least in theory) a tiny number surviving for decades, with that number tailing off as time passes to almost (but never quite) zero. A good power supply has an MTBF of approximately 30,000 to 100,000 hours; a mid-range power supply may have an MTBF of perhaps 15,000 to 35,000 hours; and a cheap power supply may have an MTBF of 10,000 hours or less. A 100,000 hour MTBF does not mean, however, that you can expect your power supply to last 100,000 hours, nor does it mean that that unit is "twice as reliable" as a unit with a 50,000 hour MTBF. Use MTBF only as a rough basis for comparison. It is safe to say that a unit with a 100,000 hour MTBF is probably more reliable than a unit with a 50,000 hour MTBF, which in turn is probably more reliable than a unit with a 10,000 hour MTBF, but don't attribute much more to it than that.

Another important characteristic of power supplies is the emissions and safety standards with which they comply. This information is useful both as it pertains specifically to the item being regulated and generally in the sense that power supplies that meet more and/or tighter regulatory approvals tend to be better built and more reliable.

Overvoltage protection, overcurrent protection, and leakage current

Properly-designed power supplies include *overvoltage* protection circuitry that shuts down the power supply if output voltage exceeds specified limits, and *overcurrent* protection circuitry that protects the power supply (and the PC) from excessive current. At minimum, overvoltage protection should be provided for +3.3V (if present) and +5V and should cause the power supply to trip to reset if either of these voltages exceed nominal by 25% or more. Better power supplies also provide similar protection for +12V. Overcurrent protection should prevent any level of overcurrent, including a dead short, from damaging the power supply or PC. A good power supply might provide latching protection (a level-sensitive cutout) for +3.3V at 60 Amperes (A), +5V at 50A, and +12V at 20A. *Leakage current* specifies the maximum current that can leak to ground during normal operation, and should be less than one milliampere (ma) at 220/240V.

Emissions approvals

Electromagnetic interference (EMI) is noise generated by the switching action of the power supply, and comes in two varieties. *Conducted interference* is noise of any frequency that the power supply places on the AC source line. Conducted interference may cause problems for other devices connected to the same circuit, and is controlled by means of capacitive and/or inductive line filters to isolate the power supply from the AC source. Radiated interference is *Radio frequency interference* (RFI) that may affect nearby electronic devices even if they are not connected to the same AC circuit (or any AC circuit at all). Radiated interference is controlled by physical shielding of the power supply, both by the power supply enclosure itself and by the shielding provided by the PC chassis. Both types of interference are regulated in the United States by the Federal Communications Commission (FCC), and in other countries by various regulatory agencies. A power supply should have FCC Class B approval (and/or the roughly equivalent CISPR22), although many inexpensive units have only the less restrictive FCC Class A.

Safety approvals

Various safety standards are promulgated by standards organizations in the U.S. and elsewhere. Any power supply you use should have at least UL certification (UL 1950). Other standards to look for include: CSA Std. C22.2, TUV EN60950, IEC950, KS, SEMKO, NEMKO, DEMKO, SETI, and CCIB.

Volts, Amps, Watts, and Regulation

Power supplies are rated in watts, but that cumulative figure doesn't tell the real story. Watts (W) are calculated by multiplying Volts (V) and Amperes (A). A power supply must provide specific amperages (or currents) at numerous voltages—how many and which depends on the type of power supply. All PC power supplies provide at least +5VDC, +12VDC, and −12VDC. Some power supplies also provide +3.3VDC, −5VDC, and/or $5V_{SB}$.

Another important aspect of voltage—one that varies greatly between power supplies—is *regulation*, which specifies how tightly voltages are controlled. For example, a memory module that expects +3.3V may work at +3.2V or +3.4V, but will probably not work at +3.1V or +3.5V. Regulation may be specified as a maximum percentage variation or as a maximum variation in absolute voltage.

No standards body produced a formal specification for all aspects of the AT power supply or its BAT and LPX variants. However, the ATX power supply—along with its variants, the NLX and SFX power supplies—is completely defined in a group of documents, many of which are referenced in the following descriptions, and can be downloaded from *http://www.teleport.com/~ffsupprt.*

ATX Power Supply Specifications

ATX Specification Version 2.03 and associated documents define the ATX voltage rails and tolerances shown in Table 23-2. V_{min} and V_{max} are calculated values, provided for the convenience of those testing power supplies with a DMM. An ATX 2.03-compliant power supply must provide these voltages at these tolerances or better. High-quality power supplies provide tighter tolerances, sometimes much tighter, such as 1% across all positive voltages. Cheap power supplies often do not meet the required tolerances for one or more voltages, and are therefore technically not ATX power supplies. However, they look like ATX power supplies, quack like ATX power supplies, and are sold as ATX power supplies. Avoid any power supply that does not meet the standards in Table 23-2.

Table 23-2: ATX Specification Version 2.03 Voltage Rails & Tolerances

Voltage Rail	Tolerance	V_{min}	V_{nom}	V_{max}
+3.3VDC	±4%	+3.168V	+3.300V	+3.432V
+5VDC	±5%	+4.750V	+5.000V	+5.250V
−5VDC	±10%	−4.500V	−5.000V	−5.500V

Table 23-2: ATX Specification Version 2.03 Voltage Rails & Tolerances (continued)

Voltage Rail	Tolerance	V_{min}	V_{nom}	V_{max}
+5V$_{SB}$	±5%	+4.750V	+5.000V	+5.250V
+12VDC	±5%	+11.400V	+12.000V	+12.600V
+12VDC (peak load)	±10%	+10.800V	+12.000V	+13.200V
−12VDC	±10%	−10.800V	−12.000V	−13.200V

Intel ATX Power Supply Design Guide Version 0.9 recommends (but does not require) the power distribution levels listed in Table 23-3. A_{min} specifies the highest minimum amperage load the power supply should require to function. A_{max} specifies the lowest maximum amperages the power supply should provide continuously. A_{peak} describes startup surge current required to spin up disk drives. The 250W and 300W units include the ATX Auxiliary Power Supply Connector, and may or may not include the ATX Optional Power Supply Connector, both of which are described later in this section.

Table 23-3: Intel ATX Power Supply Design Guide Version 0.9 Recommended Power Distribution

Voltage Rail	160W			200W			250W			300W		
	A_{min}	A_{max}	A_{peak}	A_{min}	A_{max}	A_{peak}	A_{min}	A_{max}	A_{peak}	A_{min}	A_{max}	A_{peak}
+3.3VDC	0.3	14.0		0.3	14.0		0.3	16.0		0.3	28.0	
+5VDC	1.0	18.0		1.0	21.0		1.0	25.0		1.0	30.0	
+3.3V&+5V	110W total maximum			125W total maximum			145W total maximum			220W total maximum		
−5VDC	0.0	0.3		0.0	0.3		0.0	0.3		0.0	0.3	
+5V$_{SB}$	0.0	0.72		0.0	0.72		0.0	0.72		0.0	0.72	
+12VDC	0.0	6.0	8.0	0.0	6.0	8.0	0.0	10.0	12.0	0.0	10.0	12.0
−12VDC	0.0	0.8		0.0	0.8		0.0	0.8		0.0	0.8	

NLX Power Supply Specifications

NLX Power Supply Recommendations Version 1.1 defines the NLX voltage rails and tolerances shown in Table 23-4. An NLX 1.1-compliant power supply must provide these voltages at these tolerances or better. Note that NLX has tighter requirements than ATX on some rails. This document also recommends (but does not require) the power distribution levels listed for a typical 145W sustained (160W peak) power supply. A_{min}, A_{max}, and A_{peak} are as described for Table 23-3. NLX power supplies may or may not include the NLX Optional Power Supply Connector described later in this section.

Table 23-4: Intel NLX Power Supply Recommendations Version 1.1 Voltage Rails, Tolerances, and Recommended Power Distribution

Voltage Rail	Tolerance	V_{min}	V_{nom}	V_{max}	A_{min}	A_{max}	A_{peak}
+3.3VDC	±4%	+3.168V	+3.300V	+3.432V	0.3	9.2	16.0
+5VDC	±5%	+4.750V	+5.000V	+5.250V	1.0	16.0	18.0

Voltage Rail	Tolerance	V_{min}	V_{nom}	V_{max}	A_{min}	A_{max}	A_{peak}
–5VDC	±5%	–4.750V	–5.000V	–5.250V	0.0	0.1	
+5V$_{SB}$	±5%	+4.750V	+5.000V	+5.250V	0.0	0.72	
+12VDC	±5%	+11.400V	+12.000V	+12.600V	0.0	1.4	4.0
–12VDC	±5%	–10.800V	–12.000V	–13.200V	0.0	0.2	

SFX Power Supply Specifications

SFX systems are designed to be low-cost, and the SFX specification reflects this with less stringent requirements than the ATX and NLX specifications. SFX power supplies are designed to provide 90W maximum continuous power, with peak power of 135W for 15 seconds duration on a 5 minute duty cycle. The *Intel SFX Power Supply Design Guide Version 1.1 Release* defines the SFX voltage rails, tolerances and power distribution shown in Table 23-5. An SFX 1.1-compliant power supply must provide these voltages at these amperages with these tolerances or better.

Table 23-5: Intel SFX Power Supply Design Guide Version 1.1 Release Voltage Rails, Tolerances, and Required Power Distribution

Voltage Rail	Tolerance	V_{min}	V_{nom}	V_{max}	A_{min}	A_{max}	A_{peak}
+3.3VDC	±5%	+3.135V	+3.300V	+3.465V	0.0	6.0	
+5VDC	±5%	+4.750V	+5.000V	+5.250V	1.0	10.0	12.0
+5V$_{SB}$	±5%	+4.750V	+5.000V	5.250V	0.0	0.72	
+12VDC	±5%	+11.400V	+12.000V	+12.600V	0.02	1.5	4.8
–12VDC	±10%	–10.800V	–12.000V	–13.200V	0.0	0.2	

Power Supplies

Although derived from the ATX and NLX specifications, SFX has several differences, all of which are oriented to the low-end focus of SFX, and allow lower-cost power supplies that still meet the needs of these systems. +3.3VDC is regulated to 5% rather than 4%; a peak current is specified for +5VDC; –5VDC, included in ATX for backward compatibility with ISA cards, is absent because SFX systems do not use ISA cards; +5V$_{SB}$, although specified, is optional; and the A_{min} for +12VDC, 0.0A for ATX and NLX, is now 0.02A.

Power Connectors

All power supplies provide two types of power connectors. The first powers the motherboard and differs according to form factor. The second powers drives and other internal peripherals, and comes in two varieties, which are described in the following section. Tower/AT and Tower/BAT power supplies include a third type of power connector—a high-voltage cable that connects the power supply to an external main power switch.

AT Main Power Connector

Table 23-6 lists the standard AT Main Power Connector pinouts used by all AT power supply variants, including Desktop/AT, Tower/AT, Desktop/BAT, Tower/BAT, and LPX. PC/XT power supplies use the same pinouts, except that pin P8-2 is unused. In addition to supplying various standard voltages, this connector includes a special-purpose pin. Pin P8-1, PG, carries the Power Good signal, which the power supply asserts once it has started and stabilized. The motherboard will not attempt to boot until the power supply asserts PG.

Table 23-6: Standard Motherboard Connector Pinouts for an AT Power Supply

Pin	Color	Signal	Pin	Color	Signal
P8-1	Orange (white)	PG	P9-1	Black	Ground
P8-2	Red	+5V	P9-2	Black	Ground
P8-3	Yellow	+12V	P9-3	White (blue)	–5V
P8-4	Blue (brown)	–12V	P9-4	Red	+5V
P8-5	Black	Ground	P9-5	Red	+5V
P8-6	Black	Ground	P9-6	Red	+5V

Note that P8 and P9 are separate connectors from the power supply, but mate to a combined connector on the motherboard.

The P8 and P9 connectors are individually keyed, but it is possible to connect P8 from the power supply to the P9 connector on the motherboard and *vice versa*, with potentially catastrophic results.

P8 and P9 were IBM's original designation for these connectors. Not all power supplies or motherboards label these connectors, so you may have to determine which is P8 and which is P9 by examining wire colors. The colors shown are those most commonly used, but some AT power supplies use the alternative (ATX) color coding shown in parentheses. We have also seen AT power supplies that use completely nonstandard wire colors, such as green for ground wires.

When installing an AT power supply, the key factor is to ensure that, regardless of wire colors or connector labels, the connectors are aligned so as to place all four ground pins contiguously. It's safer still to examine the documents for the motherboard and power supply. We have seen a few proprietary motherboards and power supplies that used standard connectors but with completely nonstandard pinouts. This was clearly done to force customers to purchase replacement components from the original vendor, and is happily not something you're likely to encounter on any recent system.

ATX Main Power Supply Connector

Table 23-7 lists the pinouts for the ATX Main Power Supply Connector of an ATX power supply and the recommended, but not required, colors. This is a 2X10 connector with pin 1 keyed. The motherboard connector is a Molex 39-29-9202 or equivalent. The power supply connector is a Molex 39-01-2200 or equivalent. All wires are 18 AWG, except pin 11, which is specified as 22 AWG. For power supplies 300W or larger, the specification recommends using 16 AWG wires for +3.3VDC, +5VDC, and COM (ground).

Table 23-7: ATX Main Power Supply Connector Configuration

Pin	Color	Signal	Pin	Color	Signal
1	Orange	+3.3VDC	11	Orange	3.3VDC
2	Orange	+3.3VDC	12	Blue	−12VDC
3	Black	COM	13	Black	COM
4	Red	+5VDC	14	Green	PS_ON
5	Black	COM	15	Black	COM
6	Red	+5VDC	16	Black	COM
7	Black	COM	17	Black	COM
8	Gray	PW_OK	18	White	−5VDC
9	Purple	$5V_{SB}$	19	Red	5VDC
10	Yellow	+12VDC	20	Red	5VDC

In addition to supplying various standard voltages, this connector includes four special-purpose pins:

Pin 8 (PW_OK)

PW_OK is the ATX equivalent of the AT Power Good signal, which the power supply asserts once it has stabilized. The motherboard will not attempt to boot until the power supply asserts PW_OK.

Pin 9 ($5V_{SB}$)

$5V_{SB}$ is the +5V standby circuit, which supplies +5V at low amperage to the motherboard even when the power supply is off. Any ATX power supply must provide at least 10 mA $5V_{SB}$, but motherboards with the Wake-on-LAN (WOL) feature require 720 mA, which all ATX 2.03-compliant power supplies and most good ATX power supplies of earlier vintage also provide.

Pin 11 (Remote Sensing)

On the critical +3.3V rail, small loads can cause large percentage shifts in voltage. This pin provides a means for the power supply to detect the actual voltage present on the +3.3V rail at the main power connector and modify its output to compensate for up to 100 mV of drop due to cable, connectors, and PCB traces, thereby maintaining +3.3V within tolerance.

Pin 14 (PS_ON)

PS_ON is used by the motherboard to turn the power supply on and off.

ATX Auxiliary Power Supply Connector

The ATX Auxiliary Power Supply Connector, shown in Table 23-8, is recommended by the ATX Specification Version 2.03 for motherboards that require 250W or 300W power supplies. Wire colors are standard. This is an in-line 6-pin connector with pin 6 keyed. The motherboard connector is a Molex in-line 6-pin 15-48-0412 header or equivalent. The power supply connector is a Molex 90331-0010 or equivalent. Few inexpensive power supplies provide this connector, but it is present on many better power supplies. Few motherboards include this connector.

Table 23-8: ATX Auxiliary Power Supply Connector

Pin	Color	Signal	Pin	Color	Signal
1	Black	COM	4	Orange	3.3V
2	Black	COM	5	Orange	3.3V
3	Black	COM	6	Red	5V

ATX Optional Power Supply Connector

In addition to the main and auxiliary power connectors, ATX 2.03 defines the ATX Optional Power Supply Connector, shown in Table 23-9. This is a 2X3 connector with pin 1 keyed. The motherboard connector is a Molex 39-30-1060 or equivalent. The power supply connector is a Molex 39-01-2060 or equivalent. All wires are 22 AWG. Wire colors are standard. The first color indicates the base color, and the second the stripe color.

Table 23-9: ATX Optional Power Supply Connector

Pin	Color	Signal	Pin	Color	Signal
1	White	FanM	4	White/black	1394R
2	White/blue	FanC	5	White/red	1394V
3	White/brown	Sense	6	NC	Reserved

ATX Optional Power Supply Connector signals perform the following functions:

FanM

> FanM is a two-pulse/revolution signal generated by the power supply fan that notifies the system of current fan speed. If this signal drops, the motherboard realizes immediately that the power supply fan has failed, and can shut down the system in an orderly manner.

FanC

> FanC is an optional signal generated by some motherboards to control fan speed for power supplies that are designed to allow this. The signal can range from 0VDC to +12VDC. A signal of +1V or less is recognized by the fan as an order to shut down, and a signal of +10.5V or more is recognized as an order to run at full speed. Intermediate voltage levels, which are supported by some motherboards and some fans, allow the system to instruct the fan to run at some intermediate speed. If this signal is left open (0VDC), properly designed fans run at full speed.

Sense

> This is a supplementary +3.3VDC *remote sense* line, which allows the power supply to monitor the actual voltage at the motherboard connector of the nominal +3.3VDC rail and adjust it to stay within specifications.

1394R

> 1394R provides an isolated ground return path for the 1394V voltage rail.

1394V

> 1394V is a segregated voltage supply rail for powering IEEE-1394 devices. The voltage on this rail depends on the IEEE-1394 implementation, may range between +8VDC and +40VDC, and is typically unregulated. If implemented, this rail should deliver voltage only while PS_ON on the main connector is asserted low.

NLX Power Connectors

The NLX Main Power Supply Connector uses the same pinouts, wire colors, and physical connectors as the ATX Main Power Supply Connector shown in Table 23-7. The NLX specification also defines the NLX Optional Power Supply Connector, shown in Table 23-10. This connector uses the same physical connectors and 22 AWG wire as the ATX Optional Power Supply Connector described in the preceding section, but uses different wire colors and a slightly different pinout.

Table 23-10: NLX Optional Power Supply Connector

Pin	Color	Signal	Pin	Color	Signal
1	White	FanM	4	NC	Reserved
2	Blue	FanC	5	Gray	1394
3	Brown	Sense	6	NC	Reserved

Pin 5 (1394) on this connector is analogous to pin 5 (1394V) on the ATX connector, and also supplies voltage to unpowered 1394 devices. However, rather than using pin 4 as a ground return path for 1394 voltage, this connector leaves pin 4 unconnected. It appears unwise to share the main system ground return path with the ground return path for unregulated 1394 voltage from pin 5, particularly with pin 4 sitting there so obviously unused. If you understand the reason for this difference, please let us know.

SFX Power Connectors

The SFX Baseboard Connector uses the same pinouts, wire colors, and physical connectors as the ATX Main Power Supply Connector shown in Table 23-7, with one or two exceptions:

- Pin 9 (+5V$_{SB}$) is an optional signal for SFX power supplies. If present, it allows the motherboard to control the power supply, just as with ATX and NLX. If pin 9 is not connected, the power supply must be controlled by a standard AC on/off switch.

- Pin 18 (–5VDC) is not connected on SFX power supplies, because –5VDC is required only by ISA expansion slots, which are not supported by SFX systems.

The SFX specification also defines the required SFX Control Connector, shown in Table 23-11. This connector uses the same physical connectors and 22 AWG wire as the ATX and NLX Optional Power Supply Connectors described in the preceding sections, but has only one connection, FanON/OFF, which corresponds to FanC. Wire color is standard.

Power Supplies

Table 23-11: SFX Control Connector

Pin	Color	Signal		Pin	Color	Signal
1	NC	Reserved		4	NC	Reserved
2	Blue	FanON/OFF		5	NC	Reserved
3	NC	Reserved		6	NC	Reserved

Power-Supply-to-Device Connectors

Power supplies provide two types of connectors to power disk drives and other internal peripherals:

Peripheral Connector

The Peripheral Connector, shown in Figure 23-1, is often called a Molex connector by technicians. The cable uses a Molex PS-8981-4P connector or equivalent, and 18 AWG wires. Pin 1, at left as you view the connector face, carries +12V and uses a yellow wire. Pins 2 and 3 are COM (ground) and use black wires. Pin 4 is +5V and uses a red wire.

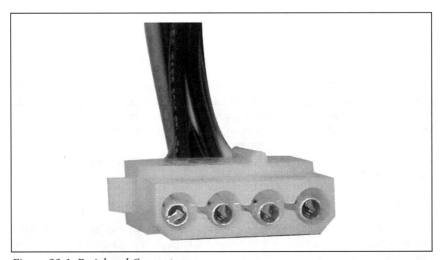

Figure 23-1: Peripheral Connector

Floppy Drive Connector

The Floppy Drive Connector, shown in Figure 23-2, is often called a Berg Connector, and is also used by other types of drives. The cable uses an AMP 171822-4 connector or equivalent. The wires are 20 AWG. Pin 1, at left as you view the connector face, carries +5V and uses a red wire. Pins 2 and 3 are COM (ground) and use black wires. Pin 4 is +12V and uses a yellow wire.

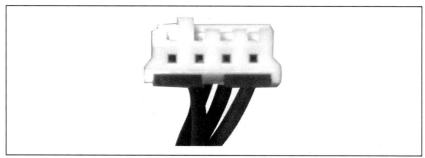

Figure 23-2: Floppy Drive Connector

 Note that wire colors map to the same voltages on the Peripheral Connector and the Floppy Drive Connector, but the pinouts are exactly reversed. While building a homemade cable, we once toasted a drive by assuming the pinouts were identical, thereby putting +12V on a +5V device.

The number and type of device connectors provided is loosely linked to the form factor and power rating of the power supply. Generally, power supplies with low power ratings and those designed for smaller cases provide fewer device connectors, sometimes as few as three. Power supplies with higher power ratings and those intended to fit large tower cases provide more device connectors, sometimes as many as a dozen. So long as you do not exceed the power supply capacity, you can freely clone device connectors by adding Y-splitters, which are available for a couple of dollars at any computer store.

Main Power Switch Power Connectors

Desktop/AT and Desktop/BAT power supplies have a built-in paddle switch to turn power on and off. ATX and ATX-variant power supplies seldom have a physical power switch, because they are turned on and off by the motherboard. Some ATX power supplies have a rocker switch on the back of the power supply that disconnects the power supply entirely from mains power. This can be useful because the alternative is disconnecting the power cable when you need to kill all power to the system, including +5V_{SB}, which is ordinarily always present.

Tower/AT and Tower/BAT power supplies have no built-in main power switch. Instead, they have four power leads that connect to a push-button or toggle switch on the case, as shown in Figure 23-3. These leads, which are usually white, black, blue, and brown, carry AC mains voltage to the power supply.

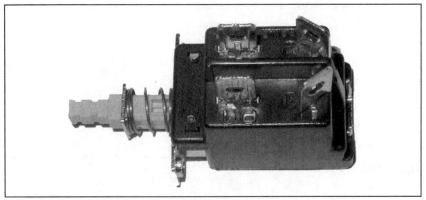

Figure 23-3: Typical connections for a Tower/AT or Tower/BAT power switch

 Although these four wire colors are relatively standard, different switches require connecting them differently. These wires carry full main voltage, which can kill you, so *never work on them without first disconnecting the main power cable from the power supply.* Connecting them improperly can also damage the power supply and the computer, so never use trial and error or guess about which wire goes where. Contact the case and power supply manufacturers to verify it. Because these wires carry high voltage, we recommend using electrical tape to insulate the connections.

Real World Power Supplies Compared

Table 23-12 lists the output by voltage of three nominally 300-watt power supplies. The PC Power & Cooling Turbo Cool 300 ATX is a premium unit, with a street price of about $90; the Antec PP303X is a name-brand unit that sells for about $40; the Astec SA302-3515-288 is not readily available to individuals, but is shown for comparison because many first-tier OEMs (such as Compaq, Dell, Gateway, and IBM) use Astec power supplies for at least some of their systems. We would like also to have compared a no-name Pacific Rim power supply, but finding technical specifications for such units is impossible, probably because they vary so much from one lot to another that no one bothers to test them.

The three key voltage rails are +3.3V (used to power processors and memory), +5V (used to power other electronic components and some drive motors), and +12V (used to power most disk drive motors). Note that, although all the power supplies list individual maximum outputs for +3.3V and +5V, they also note maximum combined output of +3.3V and +5V–150W for the PC Power & Cooling unit, 160W for the Antec, and 170W for the Astec unit.

Table 23-12: Output Comparison of Three Nominal 300-Watt Power Supplies

Rail	PC Power & Cooling Turbo-Cool 300 ATX			Antec PP303X			Astec SA302-3515-288		
	+/–	A_{max}	Watts	+/–	A_{max}	Watts	+/–	A_{max}	Watts
+3.3VDC	1%	14	46.2	4%	14	46.2	5%	23	75.9
+5VDC	5%	30	150	5%	30	150	+5/–4%	32	160
Maximum Combined Wattage			150			160			170
–5VDC	5%	0.3	1.5	5%	0.5	2.5	10%	0.5	2.5
+5V$_{SB}$	5%	0.85	4.25	5%	2	10	10%	0.85	4.25
+12VDC	5%	12	144	5%	10	120	5%	12	144
–12VDC	5%	1	12	10%	0.5	6	10%	1	12
Total Nominal Wattage			357.95			334.7			398.65
Total Deliverable Wattage			311.75			298.5			332.75

The main differences between these power supplies are as follows:

Total wattage

The most obvious difference is in total wattage deliverable. The PC Power & Cooling and Astec units can both deliver well above the nominal 300 watts, whereas the Antec unit falls a bit short.

Individual wattages

The wattages deliverable on various rails differ significantly. In particular, the Astec unit delivers up to 75.9 watts of +3.3VDC, much more than the 46.2 watts deliverable by the other two units. In practice, however, this difference is less significant than it might seem, both because 46.2 watts of +3.3VDC is adequate for normal systems, and because the combined wattage deliverable at +3.3VDC and +5VDC is only 10 to 20 watts more than the other units.

Another significant difference is at +12VDC, where PC Power & Cooling and Astec units deliver 144 watts, 20% more than the Antec unit. +12V is used primarily for drive motors and some fans, so this differential may or may not matter on any particular system. On a heavily loaded system (we have one with three high-performance SCSI hard drives, a CD-ROM drive, a CD-RW drive, a DVD-RAM drive, and a tape drive) the PC Power & Cooling and Astec units are likely to run without problems, while the Antec unit may be gasping to provide the +12V wattage demanded by all these drives. As the voltage drops, the current increases, which can cause overheating and damage to both the power supply and the drives.

Regulation

The PC Power & Cooling and Antec units are both within ATX specifications for regulation on all voltage rails. The Antec unit exactly meets the ATX regulation requirements on all rails; the PC Power & Cooling unit meets minimum ATX requirements on all rails, and greatly exceeds them on +3.3VDC (which runs processors and memory) and −12VDC. The Astec unit is not ATX-compliant, because its 5% regulation on +3.3VDC is less stringent than the ATX-required 4%.

A more subtle aspect of nominal wattage is component loading. A premium power supply may deliver its rated wattage while driving its components at only 50% of their rated capacity; a mid-range name-brand power supply may deliver near its rated wattage while driving its components at 70% of their rated capacity. A no-name power supply will likely deliver nowhere near its rated wattage, and will drive its components at 100% (or even more) of their rated capacity to do so.

Component loading has two important aspects. First, components driven at a fraction of their rated capacity are likely to exceed their design life significantly, while those driven at (or above) their designed limits are likely to be short-lived. Second, a component that is "loafing" is likely to perform much better than one that is being driven at or above its design capacity. For example, components designed to supply +3.3V and driven at 50% of capacity are likely to supply 3.3V bang-on; those driven at 100% of capacity may deliver 3.3V nominal, but the actual voltage may vary significantly. Unfortunately, short of disassembling the power supply (never a good idea) and checking the number, size, and quality of the components, about the only thing you can do to assure that the power supply you choose uses good components is buy a good name-brand power supply.

Comparing the full spec sheets for these three power supplies turns up other differences not shown in the table, of varying significance. For example, the PC Power & Cooling unit provides both the standard 20-pin ATX Main Power Supply Connector and the recommended 6-pin ATX Auxiliary Power Supply Connector, while the Antec and Astec units provide only the standard 20-pin connector. The hold time of the PC Power & Cooling unit is 20 ms, which is the minimum required for ATX compliance. The hold time of the Antec is specified as "< 20 ms" and that of the Astec as 17 ms at 115VAC input, which means that technically neither of these units is ATX-compliant.

In short, there are very real differences between power supplies, even if they have the same nominal rating. The PC Power & Cooling unit is a superb power supply, which will supply clean, closely regulated power even when driven at its rated wattage, and is unlikely to fail even if used 24×7 at its rated output power. The Antec unit is a very good power supply, likely to work reliably in less demanding applications. The Astec unit is robust, but relatively poorly regulated, particularly relative to the PC Power & Cooling unit. About the best you can say for no-name units is that power is likely to come out of them, although how much, how well-regulated, and for how long is in doubt.

Choosing a Power Supply

Use the following guidelines to choose a power supply appropriate for your system:

Choose the correct form factor
> Above all, make sure the power supply you buy fits your case and has the proper connectors for your motherboard. If your motherboard includes the ATX Optional Power Supply Connector, buy a power supply that provides

that connector. Consider buying such a power supply even if your current motherboard does not require that connector so that if you upgrade the connector will be available.

Match power supply to system configuration

Some sources recommend adding up maximum current draws for all system components and sizing the power supply on that basis. The problem with that method is that it can be nearly impossible to determine those draws for all components, especially motherboards and expansion cards. We recommend using the KISS method instead, as follows:

Basic system

For a desktop or mini-tower system with a Celeron or other low-end processor, 64 MB or less RAM, one IDE hard disk, one IDE DVD/CD-ROM drive, and zero or one expansion card, install a 230W to 250W power supply.

Mainstream system

For a desktop or mini/mid-tower system with a Celeron or FC-PGA Pentium III Coppermine processor, 128 MB RAM, one or two IDE hard disks, a DVD/CD-ROM drive, a CD-RW drive, perhaps a tape drive, and one or two expansion cards, install a 300W power supply.

High-performance system

For a mid- or full-tower system with one fast Pentium III or Athlon processor, 128 MB to 256 MB RAM, one or two fast SCSI hard disks, a DVD/CD-ROM drive, a CD-RW drive, a tape drive, and several expansion cards, install a 350W power supply.

Heavily loaded system

For a full-tower system with two fast Pentium III processors, 256 MB or more RAM, two or three fast SCSI hard disks, a CD-ROM drive, a DVD-ROM/RAM drive, a CD-RW drive, a tape drive, and all expansion slots filled, install a 400W power supply.

Obviously, individual configurations vary, but generally following these guidelines ensures the power supply is adequate for the current configuration and has some room for growth if you add components. If in doubt, buy the next size up.

Match power supply capacity to case style

Regardless of your current configuration, take case style into account. It is senseless, for example, to install a 200W power supply in a full-tower case. You might just as well buy a smaller case, because that power supply will never support even a fraction of the number of devices the case can hold. Neither does it make sense to install a 450W power supply in a mini-tower case, which simply does not have room for enough drives to require all that power.

Avoid cheap power supplies

Don't assume that the power supply bundled with an inexpensive case or a $20 unit you find on the sale table at the computer store is adequate. It probably isn't. A good power supply costs at least $35 for a basic system; $50 to $75 for a mainstream mini/mid-tower system; and $100 or more for heavily loaded, full-tower systems.

Avoid replacing proprietary power supplies

Some big-name computer makers (notably Compaq) have used proprietary power supplies in their systems, although this practice is fortunately less common nowadays. If a proprietary power supply fails, the only source for a replacement is the manufacturer, who may charge literally $500 for a power supply equivalent to a standard $50 unit. If you need to replace a proprietary power supply in a system that cannot physically accept a standard power supply, it may be cheaper to replace the PC than to buy a new power supply for it. Rather than pay proprietary prices, consider buying a new case and power supply and migrating the components from the failed unit to the new case. You may also have to buy a new motherboard, but you should be able to migrate the processor, memory, and other components.

A similar problem exists with some of the inexpensive systems sold by such retailers as Circuit City and Best Buy. Many of those use inexpensive, low-output SFX power supplies that are prone to fail quickly. For some of these systems, manufacturer policies make replacing a failed power supply quite expensive, even if the system is still under warranty.

 Instead of overpaying for a replacement power supply that's no better than the original, purchase a replacement power supply from PC Power & Cooling (*http://www.pcpowercooling.com*), which makes both a standard SFX power supply and a special SFX model for eMachines models. Better still, replace the power supply *before* it fails. Doing so improves the system's reliability, stability, and life expectancy. Put the original, still-functioning, power supply on the shelf as a spare, although you probably won't need it.

Installing a Power Supply

Standard power supplies are secured with four screws. To remove a power supply, disconnect the AC supply cord, the motherboard power cable(s), and all device power cables. Use one hand to hold the power supply in place while removing the four screws that secure it, and then lift it straight out. Some power supplies use a locking tab and slot arrangement, so you may have to slide the power supply a short distance to clear the tab before lifting it out. To install a power supply, slide it into place, making sure that the locking tab, if present, mates with the slot, align the screw holes, insert the screws, and reconnect all the cables.

Troubleshooting Power Supplies

Suspect a power supply problem if you experience any of the following symptoms, particularly in combination:

- Parity check errors. Such errors may also be caused by defective or poorly seated memory or by overheating, but insufficient or poorly regulated +3.3VDC or +5VDC (depending on memory type) from a failing or inadequate power supply is a likely cause.

- Sporadic or regular boot failures. Obviously, such errors may instead be caused by hard disk, cable, or disk controller problems, but inadequate or poorly regulated +12VDC (less commonly, +5VDC) is also a common cause of this problem.

- Spontaneous reboots or system lockups during routine operations, not attributable to running a particular program. Numerous other factors can cause this problem, but one common cause is insufficient or poorly regulated +3.3VDC and/or +5VDC being provided to the memory and/or processor.

- Lockups after installing a new processor, memory, disk drive, or expansion card. Driver issues and resource conflicts aside, this problem commonly occurs when new components overload a marginal power supply. This is particularly likely to occur if you make dramatic changes to the system, such as replacing a slow CPU with a fast, high-current CPU; if you expand memory significantly, e.g., from 32 MB to 128 MB; if you add a high-current expansion card such as a fast AGP video card or internal modem; or if you add a high-current drive, such as a high-performance SCSI hard disk or a CD burner to the system. Note that the power supplies provided with commercial systems, particularly inexpensive ones, often have very little reserve.

- Failure to function with a Wake-on-LAN (WOL) motherboard. The motherboard and power supply may both be operating properly, but incompatible. Many early ATX power supplies (and some current models) provide 100 mA or less of +5V$_{SB}$. Although that output met the ATX 2.01 requirements, WOL motherboards require +5V$_{SB}$ of at least 720 mA.

- Slow disk performance. Although this may seem an odd symptom to be related to power supply problems, inadequate voltage and current can cause disk retries on both reads and writes. The error correction circuitry built into hard disks and controllers means that this problem often (usually) goes undiagnosed. People often say to us something like, "I replaced the power supply as you suggested, and now my hard disk seems a lot faster. Is that possible?" Yes, it is.

 A very common source of problems is using a noncompliant ATX-like power supply. We say "ATX-like" because many power supplies that fit ATX cases are not ATX-compliant. Motherboards vary in their tolerance for voltages that are slightly out of spec, and a marginal power supply that works fine with one motherboard may not work with another, even of the same model.

Troubleshooting power supplies is difficult for several reasons:

- Other than an outright power supply failure, problems caused by an inadequate or failing power supply are likely to be subtle—occasional memory errors, lockups, slow disk performance, and so on—and easily attributable to something other than the power supply.

- It is difficult to "bench test" a suspect power supply because PCs use *switching power supplies* rather than *linear power supplies*. Unlike linear power supplies, switching power supplies by design do not operate unless minimum loads exist on specific voltage rails. The minimum load required varies from model to model, but in practical terms you must connect at least a motherboard, processor, and hard drive to most power supplies before they function at all.

- Systems draw varying amounts of current at different voltages during routine operations. For example, a drive spinning up draws down +12VDC, which in turn may cause another voltage rail to fluctuate, causing problems that are not clearly linked to the +12VDC load. Even processors use varying amounts of current, depending on what they happen to be doing at the moment. This constant variation in draw and the interdependency of currents on different voltage rails makes troubleshooting very difficult.

- Working inside a power supply is dangerous because high voltages are present, but testing only external connectors makes it difficult to troubleshoot effectively. Despite this, *we do not recommend removing the cover from a power supply for any purpose.* If you do so and electrocute yourself, don't blame us.

With the high cost of labor, it is usually more cost-effective in a business environment simply to swap out a suspect power supply for a new or known-good unit, particularly if the suspect unit is old and/or was inexpensive to start with. Paying for an hour or two of technician time makes little sense when the alternative is installing a new $50 power supply.

If you're working on your own system, however, and if you have a DMM, you can do a few quick tests that may isolate the problem to the power supply. These steps involve testing voltages on specific wires of the main power supply connector while it is connected to the motherboard. Some connectors have built-in probe contact points that provide easy access to each signal. If yours does not, slide the probe down inside the body of the connector until it contacts the crimp-on connector to which the wire is secured. Ideally, use a DMM that permits logging maximum and minimum voltages over a period of time while you use the system. If you're using an inexpensive DMM, you'll have to settle for instantaneous readings, but those often suffice.

To test your power supply, have a list of pinouts and signals for your power supply type (AT or ATX) handy, and take the following steps:

1. With the black probe touching the power supply case, touch the red probe in turn to each Ground/Common (black) wire on the main power supply connector, on any subsidiary connectors, and on the Peripheral Connectors and Floppy Drive Connectors. The DMM should show 0.00V. Significant voltage present on any ground wire indicates a serious problem in the power supply.

2. If the system is completely dead when it is plugged in and turned on, the power supply may not be asserting Power Good. Even if the system runs, check the Power Good voltage, because voltage variations on Power Good commonly cause subtle system problems. With the black probe of your DMM touching the power supply case or other grounding point, touch the red probe to the Power Good line. Power Good is nominally +5VDC. The DMM should indicate between +4.0V and +6.0V. Most motherboards trigger at from +2.0V to

+2.5V, so a reading below +4.0V may allow the motherboard to boot, but indicates a possible power supply problem. If the DMM indicates less than +3.0V or more than +6.0V, replace the power supply. If no voltage is present, the power supply is not asserting Power Good, and is likely defective.

3. Test each voltage rail against ground to verify that they are within specifications. If a particular voltage appears on multiple pins, test that voltage at each pin.

4. For each Peripheral Connector and Floppy Drive Connector, test each of the two voltages present against ground. That is, touch the red probe to +12V (yellow wire), and then touch the black probe to the adjacent ground pin (black wire). The DMM should read +12V within tolerance. Then touch the red probe to +5V (red wire) and the black probe to the adjacent ground pin. The DMM should read +5V within tolerance. Finally, touch each probe to one of the ground pins. The DMM should read 0.00V or something very near it.

If any of these tests fails, a defective or overloaded power supply is the most likely cause. In that event, replacing the power supply is usually the best choice. We have never attempted to repair a power supply ourselves, and do not recommend doing so. If the power supply is under warranty—good units often have three to five year warranties—call the vendor for an RMA number and ask if they are willing to cross-ship a replacement unit. If the power supply is not under warranty but is an expensive (high-wattage or redundant) and relatively new unit, contact the vendor about having it repaired. Some vendors quote a fixed price, while others charge time and materials. Be wary of the latter.

Our Picks

Although we certainly haven't used every power supply available, we have used a lot of them over the past 20 years. Here are the power supplies we use and recommend.

Premium AT and ATX power supplies

PC Power & Cooling Turbo-Cool series. These are simply the best PC power supplies we have seen, period. They combine high output with tight regulation and a powerful cooling fan. Their only drawbacks are that they are noticeably louder than standard power supplies, and they are not cheap. The Turbo-Cool 300 ATX, for example, sells for $99 as this is written, and the Turbo-Cool 425 ATX for $199. Still, if you can afford the best, these are the ones to buy. (*http://www.pcpowercooling.com*)

Quiet AT and ATX power supplies

PC Power & Cooling Silencer series. Silencer models are nearly inaudible in a normal office environment, provide the tight regulation typical of all PC Power & Cooling units, and are available in 235W ($75) and 275W ($99) versions. If noise is an issue and you do not require high output, you're likely to be pleased with a Silencer power supply.

Standard AT and ATX power supplies

PC Power & Cooling Economy series. When neither high output nor silent operation is required, we use a PC Power & Cooling Standard power supply. They're available in Standard 230 Slim ($45) and Standard 235 ATX ($55) models. Both provide the expected tight regulation, but are louder than the

Silencer models and provide lower power output and cooling air flow than the Turbo-Cool models. The Standard 230 Slim is a good choice to replace the power supply in an aging BAT computer, as is the Standard 235 ATX for building a no-frills basic PC.

Inexpensive AT and ATX power supplies

Antec and Sparkle Power Inc. (SPI). We use premium PC Power & Cooling power supplies in our personal systems. However, we recognize that some cannot afford or refuse to spend the extra money for PC Power & Cooling power supplies. For them, we recommend power supplies from Antec Inc. (*http://www.antec-inc.com*) and Sparkle Power Inc. (SPI) (*http://www. sparklepower.com*). They are not as well-regulated or strongly built as the PC Power & Cooling units, but these units are well-made and reliable, particularly if they are not heavily stressed, and are significantly less expensive, particularly for the higher wattage units.

Replacement SFX power supplies

PC Power & Cooling Standard 145 SFX. We do not recommend building systems with microATX cases and SFX power supplies, but if you need to replace an SFX power supply in a mass-market system, you can do no better than these units. Two models are available, which differ only in the location of the AC power connector. One fits standard SFX systems, and the other eMachines systems.

Replacement NLX power supplies

Sparkle Power, Inc. (SPI) FSP 300-60GN. Once again, we do not recommend building a new system with an NLX case and power supply, but many mass-market and corporate low-profile systems use such components. If PC Power & Cooling made an NLX power supply, we'd probably recommend it. They don't, and the best other source we've found for NLX power supplies is this SPI unit.

Replacement LPX power supplies

None. Although aftermarket LPX power supplies remain available, we have had no occasion to use them. The LPX standard was so loose that an LPX power supply may be physically incompatible with some LPX cases. Any LPX system is now old enough that replacing the power supply makes little sense, because something else is likely to fail soon after. Better to replace the entire system.

We constantly test and review new equipment. For the latest information about what we currently use, visit:

http://www.hardwareguys.com/picks/power.html

CHAPTER 24

Backup Power Supplies

There really is a difference between an Uninterruptable Power Supply (UPS) and a Standby Power Supply (SPS), but common usage now designates a unit properly termed a Standby Power Supply (SPS) as a UPS. We call a unit of either sort a Backup Power Supply (BPS), which neatly sidesteps the terminology problem.

A BPS comprises a battery and some supporting circuitry, and is designed to supply power to your PC for a short period if the utility power fails. This temporary reprieve allows you to save your work and shut down the PC in an orderly fashion. BPSes differ in the quality of the power they supply, and how much and for how long they can supply it. BPSes also condition the utility power to protect equipment against spikes, surges, drops, brownouts, and electrical noise.

What BPSes Protect Against

Most electric utilities supply consistent, well-regulated power. But as that power moves from the generating plant through the distribution grid to you, the power company gradually loses control of its quality. A good BPS protects against all of the following power problems:

Blackout

A *blackout* is a sudden, complete loss of voltage, which may be accidental (a tree falling on a power line) or intentional (the power company shedding load during a power emergency). Blackouts are the reason most people consider buying a BPS, but they are the least common power problem. Blackouts of very short duration, called *drops*, occur frequently and often pass unnoticed. Drops may be so short that the lights may not flicker. High-quality PC power supplies have enough inertia to continue supplying power to the PC during short drops. Lower-quality PC power supplies have much shorter hold-up times, so even very short drops may cause the PC to lock up. This is one of the most common causes of PC lockups, and installing a BPS eliminates them.

Brownout

A *brownout* is a significant reduction in voltage lasting from seconds to days. Short brownouts, called *sags*, are usually caused by a sudden load on the line, such as a high-amperage motor being turned on. Longer brownouts may be caused by the utility intentionally reducing voltage in response to demands heavier than they can meet. Utilities supply a nominal standard voltage, which in the U.S. normally ranges from 108V to 125V, with 110 to 115V most common. During a brownout, voltage may drop from nominal to 90V or less. Brownouts can damage equipment, because as voltage drops current increases, which increases heat production.

Surge

During a *surge*, delivered voltage is substantially (20% to 100%) higher than nominal. Surges may last from a fraction of a second to several seconds, and often result when a heavy load is suddenly removed from the circuit. Surges are relatively common, and all but the most extreme are relatively benign. Despite so-called "surge protectors," most equipment takes normal surges in stride. A good BPS does, however, prevent them from reaching the equipment in the first place.

Spike

A *spike*, also called a *transient*, is an extreme overvoltage of very short duration. Spikes originate from various sources, including voltages induced by remote lightning strikes, transformer failures, and non-brushless motors turning on and off. Although spikes may carry 50,000V or more, most are of such short duration (milliseconds or less) that they deliver very little electrical energy. PC power supplies themselves protect against most spikes. A good PC power supply smothers typical short spikes up to 5KV without affecting system operation. Spikes of higher voltage or longer duration are stopped by a good BPS. The worst spikes, those that result from a direct "bolt on copper" lighting strike nearby cannot be stopped by any power protection equipment.

Most people don't realize that damage from electrical problems, particularly spikes, is incremental and cumulative. That is, a computer may absorb a severe spike and continue to operate normally. But that spike may have caused invisible damage to the chips, down almost at the quantum level. Computer chips, including memory and CPUs, typically use 3.3V or 5VDC. A spike at even 5,000 times that voltage may simply lock up the system with no other obvious effects or apparent damage, but leave the system teetering on the edge. A subsequent spike, even a small one, may be the straw that broke the camel's back. Little Spike finishes the job that Big Spike started, causing the system to fail for no apparent reason. A good BPS prevents such problems.

BPS Types

All BPSes have three common elements: a *battery*, which stores electrical energy against power failures, an *inverter*, which converts DC voltage supplied by the battery to the AC voltage required by the load, and *charging circuitry*, which converts AC mains power to the DC voltage required to charge the battery. IEEE recognizes three categories of BPS, which they term UPS:

On-line

An on-line *UPS* (often called a *True UPS* to differentiate it from an SPS) connects the load directly to the inverter, which converts DC voltage supplied by the battery to standard AC voltage. The charging circuitry charges the battery constantly while the UPS is operating, and the equipment always runs from battery power supplied by the inverter. On-line UPSes are not often used on PCs because they cost substantially more than SPSes, described later in this section. An on-line UPS has two advantages. Because the PC runs on battery power all the time, there is no switch-over time and no switch to fail. Also, because the PC does not connect to mains power, it is effectively isolated from AC line problems. Against this, an on-line UPS has three drawbacks. Foremost is cost, which may be 50% to 100% higher than an equivalent SPS. Also, because the system runs from battery constantly, UPS batteries typically require replacement more frequently than SPS batteries, and UPS batteries are not cheap. Finally, UPS efficiencies are relatively low. An SPS runs at nearly 100% efficiency during normal operations, and at lower efficiency only during power failures. A UPS runs its inverter all the time. That results in efficiency as low as 70%, which translates to higher electric bills. This is of little concern to most home and office PC users, but is a major issue for data centers. An on-line UPS may also be called a *dual-conversion on-line UPS*, to differentiate it from a line-interactive UPS, described next.

Line-interactive

A *line-interactive UPS*, also called a *single-conversion on-line UPS*, differs from an on-line UPS in that the load normally runs primarily from utility power as long as that power is available. Rather than convert utility power to DC, use it to charge the battery, and then reconvert it to AC for the load (the "dual-conversion" part), a line-interactive UPS feeds utility power directly to the load under normal conditions. Minor variations in utility power are smoothed out by the inverter using battery power. The defining characteristics of a line-interactive UPS are that the inverter runs at all times, and that the load is always dynamically shared between inverter and utility power. During routine operation, utility power may support 99% of the load and the inverter only 1%. During a brownout, the inverter may support 10% or more of the load. Only during a blackout does the inverter assume 100% of the load. A true line-interactive UPS has no switch-over time, because the inverter and utility power dynamically share the load at all times, so a power failure simply means that the inverter instantaneously assumes 100% of the load. Although line-interactive units do not isolate the load from the AC line to the extent that an on-line UPS does, they are quite good at maintaining clean, steady AC to the load. Line-interactive UPSes are common in data centers, but uncommon in the PC environment.

Off-line

Any BPS used with a PC (or even a server) nowadays is almost certainly an *Off-line Power Supply*, sometimes called a *Standby Power Supply* (*SPS*). UPS marketers dislike "standby" and downright hate "off-line," so off-line power supplies are always described as "uninterruptable" power supplies, which they are not. The defining characteristics of an SPS are that it has a switch and that the inverter is not always running. During normal operation the switch routes utility power directly to the load. When utility power fails, that switch quickly disconnects the load from the utility power and reconnects it to the inverter, which continues to power the equipment from battery. SPSes are less expensive than on-line and line-interactive units because an SPS can use a relatively inexpensive inverter, one rated for low duty cycle and short run time.

Unlike on-line and line-interactive units, SPSes do not condition or regenerate incoming AC before supplying it to the load. Instead, they pass utility AC power through a passive filter similar to an ordinary surge suppressor, which means that SPSes do not provide power as clean as that provided by on-line and line-interactive units. In theory, SPSes have another drawback relative to on-line and line-interactive units. Actual switching time may be considerably longer than nominal under extended low-voltage conditions and with partially depleted batteries. Because the hold-up time of a PC power supply decreases under marginal low-voltage conditions, in theory an SPS may require longer to switch than the hold-up time of the PC power supply, resulting in a system crash. In practice, good SPSes have typical switching times of 2 to 4 ms, and maximum switching times of 10 ms or less, and good PC power supplies have hold-up times of 20 ms or longer at nominal voltage and 15 ms or longer during sustained marginal under-voltage conditions, which means this is seldom a problem. Several SPS variants exist:

Standard SPS

A *standard SPS* has only two modes—full utility power or full battery power. As long as utility power is within threshold voltage limits (which can be set on many units), the SPS simply passes utility power to the equipment. When utility power dips beneath threshold, the SPS transfers the load from using 100% utility power to using 100% battery power. Some standard SPSes also transfer to battery when utility voltage exceeds an upper threshold. That means the SPS switches to battery every time a surge, sag, or brownout occurs, which may occur quite frequently. This all-or-nothing approach cycles the battery frequently, which reduces battery life. More important, frequent alarms for minor power problems cause many people to turn off the alarm, which may delay recognition of an actual outage so long that the battery runs down and work is lost. Most entry-level SPS models are standard SPSes. The American Power Conversion (APC) Back-UPS series, for example, are standard SPSes.

Line-boost SPS

A *line-boost SPS* adds line-boost mode to the two modes of the standard SPS. Unlike line-interactive units, which use battery power to raise AC output voltage to nominal, line-boost units simply have an extra transformer tap, which they use to increase output voltage by a fixed percentage (typically, 12% to 15%) when input voltage falls below threshold. For example, when AC input falls to 100VAC, a line-interactive unit uses battery power to raise it 15V to 115VAC nominal. For 95VAC input, the line-interactive unit raises it 20V to 115VAC nominal. For 100VAC input, a line-boost unit uses the extra tap to raise output voltage by the fixed percentage (we'll assume 12%), yielding 112VAC output. For 95VAC input, the line-boost unit raises it by the same fixed percentage, in this case to 106.4VAC. That means that output voltage follows input voltage for line-boost units, with the resulting transients and current surges on the load side as the inverter kicks in and out. Most mid-range and high-end PC SPS models are line-boost SPSes. The American Power Conversion (APC) Back-UPS Pro and Smart-UPS series, for example, are line-boost SPSes.

Ferro-resonant SPS

A *ferro-resonant SPS* uses a *ferro-resonant transformer* rather than the tap-change transformer used by a line-boost unit. Its sole advantage relative to a line-boost unit is that it provides some power conditioning rather than allowing output voltage to vary with input voltage. Against that, ferro-resonant units have several serious drawbacks. First, as a high-output-impedance source, ferro-resonant units are inherently unstable with some loads, including the power-factor-corrected (PFC) power supplies that are relatively common in PCs. Second, a ferro-resonant unit can introduce severe oscillation into output voltage even when input voltage is relatively clean and stable. Most important, although ferro-resonant units are often claimed to have zero transfer time, their actual transfer time can be greater than 25 ms, which is larger than the hold-up time of nearly any PC power supply. We believe ferro-resonant units are a poor choice for use with PCs. Best is the best-known maker of ferro-resonant units.

BPS Characteristics

Here are the most important characteristics of a BPS:

Volt-Ampere (VA) rating

The *VA rating* of a BPS specifies the maximum power the UPS can supply, and is determined by the capacity of the inverter. VA rating is the product of nominal AC output voltage and the maximum amperage rating of the inverter. For example, Barbara's 120V APC Back-UPS Pro 650 can supply about 5.4A (650VA/120V). Connecting a load greater than the amperage rating of the inverter overloads the inverter and soon destroys it unless the BPS has current-limiting circuitry. Watts equal VA only for 100% resistive loads (e.g., a light bulb). If the load includes capacitive or inductive components, as do PC power supplies, the draw in VA is equal to Wattage divided by the Power Factor (PF) of the load. Most PC power supplies have Power Factors of 0.65 to 0.7. For example, Robert's APC Smart-UPS 1000 is rated at 1000VA, but only 670 Watts, which means that APC assumes a PF of 0.67 when rating wattage for this unit.

Run time

The run time of a BPS is determined by many factors, including: battery type, Amp-hour capacity, condition, and state of charge, ambient temperature, inverter efficiency, and percentage load. Of those, percentage load is most variable. The number of Amp-hours a battery can supply depends on how many amps you draw from it, which means the relationship between load and run time is not linear. For example, our APC Back-UPS 600 can supply 600VA for five minutes, but can supply 300VA (half the load) for 22 minutes (4.4 times longer). Doubling load cuts run time by much more than half; halving load extends run time by much more than twice.

Many people believe VA rating and run time are somehow related. There is no such relationship, except that units with larger VA ratings typically also have a larger battery, which provides longer run time for a given load, both because the battery itself is larger and because the unit is supplying fewer amps than its rated maximum. It is, however, quite possible to build a BPS with a very high VA rating and a tiny battery or vice versa.

Output waveform

Utility AC voltage is nominally a pure sine waveform, which is what power supplies and other equipment is designed to use. The output waveform generated by BPSes varies. In order of increasing desirability (and price), output waveforms include: square wave, sawtooth wave, and modified square wave (often somewhat deceptively called near sine wave, stepped approximation to sine wave, modified sine wave, or stepped sine wave—marketers are desperate to get the word "sine" in there, especially for units that don't deserve it). The cheapest units generate square wave output, which is essentially bipolar DC voltage with near zero rise-time, which allows it to masquerade as AC. Mid-range units normally provide pseudo-sine wave output, which may be anything from a very close approximation to a sine wave to something not much better than an unmodified square wave. The output waveform is determined by the inverter. The inverter is the most expensive component of a BPS. Better inverters—those that generate a sine wave or a close approximation—are more expensive, so the quality of the output waveform generally correlates closely to unit price. Astonishingly, we once saw specifications for a no-name BPS that listed output waveform as "pure square wave," presumably intending to confound buyers with "pure" (a Good Thing) and "square wave" (a Bad Thing).

We have heard reports of fires caused by connecting a surge suppressor between the BPS and the PC. Although we have not been able to verify the reports, it makes sense that feeding square wave power to a surge suppressor designed to accept sine wave input could cause it to overheat. On the other hand, there is nothing wrong with using a surge suppressor between the BPS and the wall receptacle. In fact, we recommend it, both to provide increased protection against spikes reaching the PC and to protect the BPS itself.

Battery replacement method

Although it sounds trivial, battery replacement method is one of the most important characteristics of a BPS. Batteries must be replaced periodically, perhaps as often as annually if you have frequent long power outages. Better units have user-replaceable batteries. Lesser units must be returned to the factory for servicing. It's both much less expensive and much more convenient to be able to replace batteries yourself.

Warranty

The length of warranty is a reasonably good indicator of the quality of the unit. Better units have a two-year parts and labor warranty, although the battery is usually excluded. Lesser units often carry a one-year warranty, and we have seen many of them fail not long past that time. The cheapest units may carry only a 90-day warranty.

Configuration options

Inexpensive BPSes may provide few or no configuration options. They may, for example, be permanently set to transfer to battery if the input voltage drops below 102VAC or rises above 130VAC. Better BPSes offer flexible options for setting such things as transfer voltage thresholds, warning type (audible, visual, email and/or pager notification, etc.), delay before warning, warning duration, and so on.

Status indicators

Inexpensive units provide few status indicators, typically only an LED that illuminates when the unit is operating on battery. Better units provide detailed LED or LCD status displays to indicate such things as load percentage, battery charge status, overload conditions, and battery replacement required.

Overload protection

All units include some form of overload protection. Less expensive units often use a fuse, and may need to be returned to the factory if that fuse blows. Better units use a circuit breaker that can be reset by pressing a button.

Receptacle configuration

Most units include two types of receptacle, often differentiated by color. The first sort are backed up by the battery; the second sort are surge-protected only, and are useful for connecting items (such as laser printers) that you want surge protected but do not want to run from the UPS. Also note that units vary greatly in how many receptacles they provide and how convenient they are to use. Inexpensive units mount a few receptacles on the back panel. Better units provide additional receptacles, and arrange them—either by spacing or by making the receptacle a female connector on a short extension cord—so that connecting a power brick or oversized plug does not block other receptacles.

Manageability

There are two aspects to BPS manageability:

Automatic shutdown

All but entry-level BPS units include a network interface port. By connecting that port to a serial port on the computer—which usually requires a nonstandard cable—and running automatic shutdown software supplied with the OS or the BPS, you can allow the BPS to shut down the computer in an orderly manner during a power failure before battery power runs out. If your computer runs unattended, automatic shutdown is a valuable feature. Some new BPS models support automatic shutdown via a USB link. If you have such a model, make sure the unit also supports serial connection, or it will be unusable with Windows NT 4 and other OSes that don't support USB. Note that if you share one BPS among computers, you will be able to shut down only one of them automatically unless you purchase expensive hardware designed to distribute the automatic shutdown signal to multiple computers.

SNMP manageability

Simple Network Management Protocol (SNMP) can be used to centralize monitoring and control of a large network. In that environment, having SNMP-capable BPSes is important, but in typical home-office and small business environments, SNMP support is a non-issue. Inexpensive BPSes do not support SNMP. Mid-range and high-end SPSes may include it as a standard or optional feature. If SNMP is an issue for you, make sure that the BPS manufacturer supplies a MIB that is usable by your management package. If you don't know what a MIB is, don't worry about it.

Here are some BPS characteristics that are promoted by marketers but largely meaningless:

Operating system certification

This item is pertinent only if you use shutdown software, either that bundled with the OS or that provided by the BPS manufacturer. The shutdown software provided with a modern OS recognizes most common BPS models, and can usually be configured to support odd-ball requirements from off-brand BPSes. Most people use the automatic shutdown software bundled with the BPS, as it is usually more functional and supports specific features of the BPS model. In that case, the only thing that matters is that it runs on your OS, which it is likely to do unless you're running something relatively uncommon like OS/2 or BeOS. Linux support, formerly rare, is becoming much more common. OS certification should be at most a checklist item.

Switching time

Typical BPSes have nominal switching times of 2 to 4 ms. That's best case. Under adverse conditions, such as an extended period of low-voltage, partially discharged batteries, and so on, transfer time can be longer. A typical BPS might list worst-case transfer time of 8 ms, which should be within the hold-time of any decent power supply, even operating under adverse conditions. Shorter is obviously better here, but don't give nominal switching time too much weight.

Connected equipment warranty

Most BPS makers include a connected equipment warranty, typically for $25,000. In theory, if your equipment suffers damage attributable to a fault in the BPS, the BPS company pays to repair or replace it. That sounds good, but the truth is that few people ever collect on such warranties. There are so many exclusions and limitations, including the fact that the coverage is often subrogated to your home or business insurance, that such warranties are all sizzle and no steak.

Choosing a BPS

Use the following guidelines when choosing a BPS:

Select BPS type according to application

On-line and line-interactive units are too large and too expensive for most PC applications. Consider them only for enterprise/departmental servers and other critical systems. For standard PCs and workgroup servers, buy an off-line unit. If your location is subject to frequent power problems and you can afford to do so, choose a line-boost unit, which greatly extends run time under brownout conditions.

Pick a unit with adequate VA and runtime

You can calculate VA requirements by checking the maximum amperage listed on the PC power supply and on each other component the UPS will power. Total these maximum amperages and multiply by the nominal AC voltage to determine VA requirements. The problems with this method are that it is time-consuming and results in a much higher VA than you actually need. For example, a typical 250W PC power supply that actually draws about 375 VA (250/0.67) when fully loaded may list 8A maximum draw, which translates to nearly 1000VA. A better method is to use one of the sizing tools that most BPS makers provide on their web sites. For example, the APC UPS Selector (*http://www.apcc.com/sizing/*) allows you to specify your system configuration, the run time you need, and an allowance for growth. From that information, it returns a list of suitable APC models, with the estimated run times for each. Or, for a quick and dirty selection, simply use the following guidelines:

Entry-level system

For a low-profile, desktop, or mini-tower system with a Celeron processor, 64 MB or less RAM, one IDE hard disk, zero or one expansion cards, and a 14/15" monitor, choose a 275VA to 400VA unit.

Mainstream system

For a desktop or mini-tower system with a Celeron or Pentium III processor, 64 MB to 128 MB RAM, one or two IDE hard drives, one or two expansion cards, and a 17" monitor, choose a 350VA to 500VA unit.

High-performance system/small server

For a mini-tower or tower system with a Pentium III or Athlon processor, 128 MB to 256 MB RAM, one or two U2W SCSI hard drives, several expansion cards, and a 19" monitor, choose a 500VA to 650VA unit.

Dual CPU system

For a mini-tower or tower system with dual Pentium III processors, 256 MB or more RAM, two or three U2W SCSI hard drives, several expansion cards, and a 19/21" monitor, choose a 650VA to 1000VA unit.

In each case, the smaller unit provides little reserve capacity for expansion, and may provide as little as five minutes run time. The larger unit typically provides 30% to 50% reserve capacity for expansion, and run times of 15 to 25 minutes.

Consider buying one BPS for multiple PCs

If you need to protect multiple PCs in close proximity, consider buying one or a few larger units rather than many inexpensive smaller units. The larger unit will probably cost less for the same cumulative VA and run time, and will likely provide superior features (e.g., line-boost and a better waveform). The only drawback to one large unit versus multiple smaller ones is that the larger unit will be able to shut down only one connected system automatically unless you also buy shutdown-sharing hardware, which is quite expensive.

Get the best waveform you can afford

The very cheapest units provide square wave output, which PC power supplies can use for short periods without damage. However, running a computer on square wave power for extended periods stresses the power supply and may eventually damage it. Also, square wave units are entirely unsuitable for other electronic devices, which they can quickly damage. Buy a square wave unit only if the alternative is not being able to afford a BPS at all. For general use, buy a unit that provides simulated sine wave if you expect to run the PC for ten minutes or less on backup power before shutting it down. Buy a true sine wave unit if you expect to run the PC for extended periods on backup power, or if you also plan to power equipment that is intolerant of pseudo-sine wave power (such as some monitors and external drives).

Make sure the BPS has user-replaceable batteries

BPS batteries are consumable items. Under normal conditions, a battery may be usable for between two and five years, but if you have frequent outages lasting long enough for the battery to undergo deep discharge, you may find that the battery needs to be replaced annually or more often. Many BPS units must be returned to the factory for battery replacement, which incurs very high shipping costs and leaves you without the BPS until it is returned. Better units have user-replaceable batteries, which allow you to stock a replacement battery, install it when necessary, and simply purchase another replacement. The advantage of user-replaceable batteries, both in cost and convenience, is difficult to overstate.

Our Picks

Over the last 15 years, we have bought scores of BPSes of every size and type for ourselves and our clients, nearly all of them from American Power Conversion (APC). We have had no significant problems with APC units, something we can't say for units we've used from some competitors. In the past, we'd simply have advised readers to buy the appropriate APC unit and be done with it. However, in late 1999 we came across a line of BPSes from a relatively new company, Smart Power Systems (formerly IEPSS, Inc.) Smart Power Systems manufactures a full line of BPSes that compete head-to-head with similar APC models. The only Smart Power Systems model we've tested is the SineSmart, which competes with the APC Smart-UPS. After six months' use, we have been very favorably impressed with the features and quality of the Smart Power Systems SineSmart, and can recommend it. We have not tested the other Smart Power Systems models listed, and so cannot formally endorse them. We expect that other Smart Power Systems models would also compare favorably with APC models. We would not hesitate to buy them ourselves, so we have listed them for comparison.

Here are the backup power supplies we use and recommend:

Inexpensive SPS

APC Back-UPS series. Available in sizes from 200VA to 650VA and street prices from $75 to $200, the Back-UPS is an excellent entry-level unit, suitable for standard PCs in environments where power problems are relatively rare. Back-UPS models provide pseudo-sine wave output, long run times, and user-replaceable batteries. We use Back-UPS 600 units for our test-bench systems. Smart Power Systems manufactures the BAK Series units, which compete feature-for-feature with APC Back-UPS models, but sell for somewhat less. Smart Power Systems also manufactures the BAK-AVR Series units, which add line-boost voltage regulation, and sell for about the same price as the corresponding APC Back-UPS models. (*http://www.apcc.com*; *http://www.iepss.com*)

Pseudo-sine wave line-boost SPS

APC Back-UPS Pro series. Available in sizes from 280VA to 1400VA and street prices from $125 to $500, the Back-UPS Pro is an excellent mid-range unit, suitable for PCs, workstations, and small servers in environments where power problems are more common and of longer duration. Like the Back-UPS, Back-UPS Pro models provide pseudo-sine wave output and user-replaceable batteries. They add longer run times, line-boost voltage regulation, faster switching times, and a network interface port for automatic shutdowns. Barbara uses a Back-UPS Pro 650 on her main workstation. Smart Power Systems manufactures the equivalent EconoPro Series units, which sell for significantly less than comparable Back-UPS Pro models, and the EconoPro +TBF Series, which add transformer-based voltage regulation, and sell for somewhat less than equivalent Back-UPS Pro models.

Sine wave line-boost SPS

APC Smart-UPS series and Smart Power Systems SineSmart series. Available in sizes from 420VA to 3000VA and street prices from $225 to $1,500, the Smart-UPS is an excellent high-end line-boost SPS, suitable for workstations and small servers in environments where power problems are common and long-lasting. Relative to Back-UPS Pro models, Smart-UPS models provide true sine wave output, longer run times, shorter recharge times, more extensive status displays, greater expandability, and various remote management options. Robert uses a Smart-UPS 1000 on his main workstation. Smart Power Systems manufactures the competing SineSmart Series units, which sell for somewhat less than comparable Smart-UPS Pro models, and the SineSmart +TBF Series with transformer-based voltage regulation, which sell for the same or slightly more than equivalent Smart-UPS Pro models. Robert uses a SineSmart 2000 VA unit to power everything on his desk except his main workstation.

On-line UPS

Smart Power Systems ULT series and ONL series (tentative). We haven't bought an on-line UPS for many years, nor do we have any recent experience with them, so we can't really make a recommendation based on our normal practice of recommending only what we find suitable via actual use. Relative to SPSes, the chief advantage of an on-line UPS is that it has bypass capability. That is, if you have problems with a standard SPS, you must shut down the load to replace the UPS or battery. On-line UPSes, as a result of dual-conversion, allow bypassing the load temporarily while the UPS or battery is swapped out. When you absolutely, positively can't afford to go down even for a minute, you need an on-line UPS. Otherwise, you're better off with a good-quality SPS. We have compared specifications of various on-line UPS units, and the Smart Power Systems ULT and ONL series appear to be as good as or better than any of them. Like all on-line UPSes, the Smart Power Systems units are hideously expensive (although less so than many of their competitors). We can't recommend what we haven't used, but if you need an on-line UPS we do recommend that you look at the Smart Power Systems units first. (*http://www.iepss.com*)

We constantly test and review new equipment. For the latest information about what we currently use, visit:

http://www.hardwareguys.com/picks/power.html

CHAPTER 25

Designing a PC

This chapter lets you look over our shoulders while we design PCs for various needs and budgets, and then buy the components to build them. Each section describes a project system we actually built in late 1999. By the time you read this, many of the prices may be laughable and many of the components we chose will be discontinued. Whatever replaces them will no doubt be better, faster, and cheaper. That's not the point. What is important is the process of selecting components and making trade-offs to meet a target budget. When you design a system, the most you can hope for is to choose good components at a good price at that moment in time. The following sections detail choosing components for four representative systems: Low-End, Mainstream, High-Performance, and Personal Workstation.

Low-End System

Low-end systems are typically sold by resellers like Best Buy and Circuit City for $500 to $1,000. At the mid- to upper-end of that range, they may include a small, entry-level monitor and perhaps an inexpensive inkjet printer. Most low-end systems include things you either don't want or will end up replacing, but have to pay for anyway: Winmodems, entertainment or edutainment titles of questionable value, no-name small business suites, mushy keyboards, bar-o'-soap mice, and really, really bad sound cards. These systems use slow, small, inexpensive IDE/ ATAPI drives, have barely adequate RAM (typically, 16 to 32 MB), and offer limited expandability. The least expensive systems use an AMD K6-2 processor. Better models use an Intel Celeron or AMD K6-III processor.

At first glance it may seem there's not much hope of matching the price of an off-the-shelf low-end system with one you build yourself. In fact, low-end systems have a fair amount of margin built into their prices. Not only does the manufacturer need to make a profit, but so does the store. As it turns out, you can do a lot better by building a low-end system yourself. For the same price, you'll get a system with much better quality components.

We designed this first system for a friend on a tight budget. She actually called us on her cell phone while standing in front of the computers at Best Buy. We convinced her to let us see what we could do for her before she decided to buy a packaged low-end system. She already had an HP DeskJet printer and an external U.S. Robotics 56 K modem. She also had an old 486 with licensed copies of Windows 95 and Office 97 that we could transfer to the new system. The original monitor was failing, so she needed a decent new monitor. Her budget was $1,000 with monitor. Here's what we came up with:

Case and power supply

We wanted to use a PC Power & Cooling case and power supply, but budget ruled that out. You can buy cheap cases for $50 or so, but those are shoddily constructed and have very poor power supplies. Instead we opted for an Antec KS-288 Mid-Tower case (*http://www.antec-inc.com*), which costs $15 more, but is built like a tank, has no sharp edges or other signs of cost-cutting, and comes with a decent 250W power supply.

Processor

The most CPU we could afford was a K6-2/III or PPGA Celeron. Celerons provide better performance for the price and use Socket 370, which is more stable than Socket 7. As a baseline, the Celeron/400 ($60) costs only $10 more than a K6-2/400, and is faster and more stable. The K6-III/400 ($110) has similar speed, and is Socket 7. The Celeron/433 ($75) and 466 ($95) run only 8.25% and 16.5% faster, respectively, not worth the cost. The Celeron/500 ($160) runs a barely noticeable 25% faster, and is certainly not worth $100 more. We chose the Celeron/400, which is more than fast enough. (*http://developer.intel.com/design/celeron/*)

Motherboard

Staying within budget forced us to use an integrated Socket 370 motherboard rather than buying separate video and sound cards. The best such motherboard is the Intel CA810E, which has embedded Intel 752 graphics (excellent 2D and adequate 3D performance) and Creative Labs SoundBlaster Audio PCI 64V sound. Neither is cutting edge, but both are good enough. The CA810E is also very flexible about the CPUs it can use. It supports the FC PGA Pentium III Coppermine processors, the forthcoming 100 MHz FSB Celeron processors, and 133 MHz FSB. All of this will allow an easy, cheap upgrade in a year or two, when 600+ MHz Celerons with SSE will likely cost $50 and 800+ MHz Socket 370 Pentium IIIs $175. (*http://developer.intel.com/design/motherbd/ca2/ca2_ds.htm*)

Memory

This system will run Windows 9X, for which 32 MB is usable and 64 MB ideal. The CA810E has only two DIMM sockets, and requires at least PC100 memory (even for a 66 MHz FSB Celeron). We had room in the budget, so we elected to install 64 MB, which will improve both speed and stability. Using commodity memory is never a good idea, so we chose a Crucial Technologies 64 MB module, leaving one free socket for later expansion. At the time we configured the system, a 64 MB PC100 DIMM cost $94.50, but the same module in PC133 form cost only $4.50 more. We elected to go with the PC133 module, which will allow upgrading to a 133 MHz FSB processor later. (*http://www.crucial.com*)

Hard disk

This system will be used mostly for creating documents and browsing the Web, so drive size was not a major issue. We've had good experience with recent Seagate IDE drives, so we chose a 4.3 GB DMA/66 drive from their value-line U series. The 5,400 RPM spin rate of this drive means it's not as snappy as a 7,200 RPM drive, but the price is right. (*http://www.seagate.com/disc/disctop.shtml*)

CD-ROM drive

We definitely needed a CD-ROM drive, and we wanted a tape drive for backup. But even inexpensive tape drives cost $300+ with tapes, a budget buster. We decided to kill two birds with one stone by installing a CD-RW drive. Although not the perfect backup device, a CD-RW drive can back up 500 MB or so to $3 CD-RW discs, which suffices for this system. We like Hewlett-Packard ATAPI CD burners, but they're a bit pricey for this system. Fortunately, we can recommend the Smart & Friendly CD*SpeedWriter Plus, an inexpensive ATAPI CD burner that does 4X writes, 2X rewrites, and 24X reads. That drive comes with Adaptec Easy CD Creator and DirectCD, which are the packages we would have chosen anyway. With only one CD drive, we'll have to dupe CDs by first creating a disk image, but the Seagate drive has plenty of space for that. We'll install this drive as Secondary Master to avoid coasters and to prevent the data corruption that occurs if the CD burner and hard disk are on the same channel. Once we've installed the OS and applications, we'll also use it to create a master restore CD-R disc. (*http://www.smartandfriendly.com/cdr_cdspeedwriter_plus.html*)

 When we originally designed this system, the Smart & Friendly SAF798 was the best CD burner for the money, and Plextor made only SCSI CD writers. By mid-2000, Smart & Friendly had ceased operations, we had become disenchanted with HP CD burners and with Adaptec Easy CD mastering software, Plextor had begun shipping excellent IDE CD writers, and we'd discoverd Nero Burning ROM mastering software. Accordingly, if we were designing this system today, we'd choose the $250 Plextor 12/10/32A or the $185 Plextor 8/4/32A CD burner with Nero software.

Monitor

Here's another place where it's a mistake to compromise on quality. Budget puts a 17" monitor out of reach, and the person we're designing this system for says she's happy running 800×600 on a 15" monitor. We tell people they won't go far wrong choosing a monitor from Hitachi, Mitsubishi, NEC, or Sony, so we'll take our own advice here. The best of that group is the Sony CPD110GS for about $175. It supports 1024×768 resolution at 85 Hz refresh, which is more than adequate, and provides Sony's typical very high display quality. It'd be hard to find a better 15" monitor. (*http://www.ita.sel.sony.com/ products/displays/corp/cpd110gs.html*)

UPS

Some consider a \UPS a luxury, but we won't run a system without one. We have power outages frequently around here, particularly during spring thunderstorms and winter ice storms. We've used scores of American Power Conversion (APC) UPSes over the years, and have never had a problem with them, something we can't say for some of APC's competitors. This is a lightly loaded system, so one of the small units will serve. We chose the $75 Back-UPS Office 280VA, a charcoal-grey device not much bigger than a surge protector that provides three battery backup outlets and three surge suppression only outlets, plus telephone protection. (*http://www.apcc.com/products/ back-ups_office/index.cfm*)

Miscellaneous components

As usual, we don't sweat the small stuff. We used a Teac 1.44 MB floppy disk drive (FDD), although any name brand drive would have done as well. The choice of keyboard and mouse is really a matter of personal preference. Microsoft makes both keyboards and mice in great variety, and we seldom use anything else. At $35 or so, the Labtec LCS-2414 speakers are a good step up from the cheap speakers bundled with most low-cost systems. We even find them acceptable for casual listening to classical music. Table 25-1 shows the component list for a low-end system.

Table 25-1: Component List for a Low-End System

Component	Model	Price
Case	Antec KS-288 mid-tower	$65
Power supply	Antec PP-253X 250W ATX (included)	
Processor	Intel PPGA Celeron/400	$60
Motherboard	Intel CA810E	$140
Memory	Crucial CT8M64S4D75, 64 MB PC133 SDRAM DIMM	$99
Hard disk	Seagate ST34311A 4.3 GB 5,400 RPM DMA/66	$79
CD-ROM drive	Smart & Friendly SAF798 SpeedWriter Plus 2×4×24 CD-R(W)	$150
Floppy drive	Teac 235HF 1.44 MB	$15
Keyboard	Microsoft Natural Keyboard	$18
Mouse	Microsoft Wheel Mouse	$20
Monitor	Sony CPD110GS 15" SVGA	$175
Speakers	Labtec LCS-2414	$35
UPS	APC Back-UPS Office 280VA	$75
	Shipping and miscellaneous	$42
	Grand Total	$973

Our home-built system compares quite favorably with the $1,000 system from Best Buy. The case, power supply, processor, motherboard, hard disk, floppy drive, keyboard, mouse, and speakers we used are as good or better, and we used brand-name retail components rather than the generic components used in the commercial system. But there are differences.

On the plus side for the commercial system, it includes a generic 56 K Winmodem, a dubious advantage at the best of times, and no advantage for us at all. Winmodems are a bad idea, and we already have a superior USR external 56 K modem. It also includes a low-end HP inkjet printer, which is less significant than it seems. We've seen that same printer advertised for $75 with a $50 mail-in rebate, yielding a net cost of $25. HP, like all other inkjet printer makers, gives away the razor to sell the blades. The commercial system also comes with Windows 98—which would cost us about $90 if we needed it, which we don't—and an off-brand office suite. We'll use our existing copies of Windows 95 and Office 97. Even if we didn't already have Office 97, we'd be more inclined to install the freeware StarOffice Suite from Sun than use the off-brand suite.

On the plus side for the home-built system, it has twice as much memory, and that memory is Crucial PC133 memory rather than the unspecified (but probably OEM or commodity PC66) memory used in the commercial system. We've used a motherboard that can be upgraded inexpensively to a much faster processor in a year or two, which is unlikely to be true with the motherboard used in the commercial system. Rather than a standard IDE CD-ROM drive, our system has a CD-RW drive, which we can use for backup. The Sony monitor is greatly superior in both performance and quality to the generic monitor supplied with the commercial system

Here, approximately in ranked priority order, are upgrades we suggested if the budget could be increased slightly:

- Get a larger monitor. The 15" Sony is a superior monitor, but it's still only 15". The price of 17" monitors has dropped dramatically over the last couple of years, and a decent entry-level 17" monitor doesn't cost all that much more than a 15" monitor with similar resolution and refresh rate. If we had another $75 or so available, we'd go with the 17" Hitachi SuperScan Elite 640.

- Get a larger, faster hard disk. The 5,400 RPM 4.3 GB Seagate drive is adequate for present needs, but one can never have too much hard disk space. Spending another $50 or so would buy a 7,200 RPM ATA/66 drive in the 10+ GB range.

- Upgrade the case and power supply. A PC Power & Cooling case and power supply costs about $50 more than the Antec unit. We recommend this upgrade because a system with a mid-range power supply is less stable and more prone to fail than one that uses a top-quality power supply, particularly as the system ages.

As it turned out, our friend decided upgrading the monitor and hard disk made sense, so she ended up spending about $1,100 rather than the $1,000 she'd originally budgeted. That extra $100 bought her a lot more computer, one that will probably last her a year or more longer before it needs to be upgraded or replaced. We still think she should have spent the extra $50 on the PC Power & Cooling case and power supply, but the Antec is a very good case, and if the mid-range Antec power supply fails in a year or two, it's easy enough to replace it with a PPC unit.

Mainstream System

Mainstream systems typically cost from $1,000 to $2,500. Relative to low-end systems, mainstream systems use faster Celeron or Pentium III processors, more memory, larger, faster IDE hard drives, better video cards, and larger, higher-quality monitors. Mainstream systems may also substitute a DVD-ROM or CD-RW drive for the CD-ROM drive, better speakers (with perhaps a subwoofer) for the $15 speakers supplied with low-end systems, and Office 2000 for the no-name suite. Many mainstream systems also offer Windows NT Workstation or Windows 2000 Professional as a low-cost upgrade to Windows 98. Most systems sold today fall into the mainstream category.

We designed this system for a writer who wanted a high-quality PC at a reasonable price. He wanted to use top-notch components throughout, but avoid "overkill." He uses the Web extensively for research, and wanted a large amount of fast disk storage to store documents and images, which he downloads via his new DSL line. He once experienced a catastrophic data loss due to a failed hard disk, and so insisted on having a reliable tape drive. He plays computer games occasionally for recreation, and so wanted something with competent 3D graphics. His budget was under $2,000 with monitor. Here's what we came up with:

Case and power supply

> With more room in the budget, we started with a PC Power & Cooling Personal Mid-Tower case. We use PPC cases whenever possible for their high quality and solid construction. PPC power supplies are the standard by which we judge other power supplies. We don't consider using anything else for our own systems. A quiet power supply was important, so we looked at PPC Silencer models, which are nearly inaudible. We'd like to have used the $75 Silencer 235 ATX. That was a bit light for this system configuration, so instead we opted for the Silencer 275 ATX. (*http://www.pcpowercooling.com*)

Processor

> Processor speed is less important to this user than other factors, especially 2D display quality. We could have simply specified a Matrox Millenium G400 video card for its superb display quality, which would have allowed us to use any standard motherboard. Instead, we decided to see what was available in an integrated motherboard (see the following list item). As it turned out, the best choice of motherboard used Slot 1, which made either a Celeron or Pentium III Slot 1 processor the obvious choice. Although Intel discontinued SEPP (Slot 1) Celerons in mid-1999, they were still available when we designed this system. We chose the fastest SEPP Celeron ever produced, the /433, which nearly matches 450 MHz Pentium II/III performance. Slot 1 processors will continue to be available for some time to come, so we can upgrade to a fast Pentium III once prices drop into the $150 range. For that matter, we can later upgrade this system to a fast Socket 370 processor like the Pentium III Coppermine or Celeron II by using a slocket adapter. (*http://developer.intel. com/design/celeron/*)

Motherboard

> This user doesn't need the latest video or sound adapters, so we once again opted for an integrated motherboard. This time, we picked the Intel SR440BX,

a top-quality Slot 1 motherboard with embedded nVIDIA TNT 128-bit graphics and Creative Labs ES1373 SoundBlaster Audio PCI 64V sound. 2D display quality is critical for this user, who spends most of his day working in Word and his web browser. Although TNT video is known for unexceptional 2D display quality, particularly at higher resolutions, Intel installed filtering on the SR440BX that brings the TNT 2D display quality up near that of the Matrox Millenium, the standard by which 2D video is judged. Although no longer cutting-edge, the nVIDIA TNT was the fastest 3D video adapter available only six months before we built this system, and will be more than good enough for this user for the foreseeable future. (*http://developer.intel.com/design/ motherbd/sr/sr_ds.htm*)

Memory

This system will run Windows 98, which is happiest with 64 MB or more. The SR440BX has only two DIMM sockets, so we chose a single 64 MB DIMM, leaving the other socket free. As always, we spec top-quality memory, in this case a Crucial 64 MB PC133 DIMM. Once again, the price difference between PC100 and PC133 was so small that it made no sense to save $5 by buying PC100 memory, even though this system does not benefit from PC133. If we swap out motherboard and processor in a couple of years, the PC133 memory will likely still be usable, whereas the PC100 memory might not be. (*http:// www.crucial.com*)

Hard disk

Budget ruled out SCSI, but IDE is no real drawback on a Windows 98 system, so we looked for a big, fast IDE disk. Maxtor, Seagate, IBM, and others all make drives in this class, but we think the best of the group is the Seagate Barracuda ATA. It stores 20.4 GB, runs at 7200 RPM with an 8 ms average seek, and supports DMA/66. That last is of little use to us, because the SR440BX supports only DMA/33, but there's no real-world performance difference between DMA/33 and DMA/66 anyway. (*http://www.seagate.com/disc/ disctop.shtml*)

CD-ROM drive

We considered installing a decent $50 ATAPI CD-ROM drive (like the Toshiba XM-6502B), but we had some room left in the budget. For $100 or so more, a CD-RW drive is worth having. Although our author will have a tape drive for routine backup, burning an archive CD once a week or once a month is good belt-and-suspenders insurance for his data. Once again, the Smart & Friendly CD*SpeedWriter Plus does the job and costs less than an equivalent HP burner. We've used both, and the Smart & Friendly is at least as fast and reliable as the HP. We'll install both the CD burner and the tape drive on the secondary channel to avoid problems transferring data from the Barracuda to either of them. Also, please see the note in the "Low-End System" section. (*http://www.smartandfriendly.com/cdr_cdspeedwriter_plus.html*)

Tape drive

We needed a fast, inexpensive, large-capacity tape drive. A Travan TR-4 drive meets the first two requirements, but not the third. Its 8 GB compressed capacity is nowhere near large enough to back up the entire Seagate hard drive to one tape, even if the assumed 2:1 compression ratio was achieved, which is unlikely with real-world data. Fortunately, the Onstream DI-30 ATAPI tape drive meets all requirements. It's faster than the Travan, costs only $300 or so with three tapes, and stores 15/30 GB on tapes that cost less than $30. (*http://www.onstream.com*)

Monitor

Once again, the monitor isn't someplace to compromise, particularly for someone like this author who spends eight or more hours a day looking at it. A good 19" monitor costs $450 or more, which busts the budget. Fortunately, the "big four" offer many good 17" monitors. The most cost-effective of that group is the Hitachi SuperScan Elite 640 at about $250. It runs up to 1024×768 resolution at 85 Hz, which is adequate. Better models run up to 1600×1200 resolution at higher refresh rates, but also cost $350+, which isn't justifiable for this system. (*http://www.hitachidisplays.com/products/17_elite641.htm*)

UPS

Once again, we don't consider a UPS an option. We wanted at least five minutes of run time and some spare capacity for later expansion. The automatic UPS model selector on the APC web site recommended the Back-UPS Pro 420, so that's what we chose. (*http://www.apcc.com/products/back-ups_pro/index.cfm*)

Software

The vendor from whom we purchased the motherboard, processor, and hard disk offered a full OEM version of Windows 98 for $90 additional with the purchase of those components. Although that vendor also offered a full OEM version of Microsoft Office, our writer friend has been using WordPerfect for more than a decade, and chose to migrate his existing copy to the new machine.

Miscellaneous components

In this case, the Teac 1.44 MB FDD was out of stock at our chosen vendors, so we substituted a Mitsumi, which will do as well. This user likes the "melted" Microsoft ergonomic keyboards, and chose the Natural Keyboard Pro, which has many dedicated (and reprogrammable) keys for one-touch access to various web browser functions, email, and so on. He is a smoker, and was tired of having to clean his mechanical mouse every few days, so he was happy when we told him about the Microsoft IntelliMouse with IntelliEye, a fully optical mouse that has no ball and does not require any special mouse pad. The same Labtec LCS-2414 speakers we chose for the preceding system are also adequate for this user's needs. See Table 25-2 for a list of the components of a mainstream system.

Table 25-2: Component List for a Mainstream System

Component	Model	Price
Case	PC Power & Cooling Personal Mid-Tower	$65
Power supply	PC Power & Cooling Silencer 275 ATX	$99
Processor	Intel Celeron/433	$75
Motherboard	Intel SR440BX	$150
Memory	Crucial CT8M64S4D75, 64 MB PC133 SDRAM DIMM	$99

Table 25-2: Component List for a Mainstream System (continued)

Component	Model	Price
Hard disk	Seagate ST320430A Barracuda ATA 20.4 GB 7200 RPM DMA/66	$200
CD-ROM drive	Smart & Friendly SAF798 SpeedWriter Plus 2×4×24 CD-RW	$150
Tape drive	OnStream DI-30 15/30 GB ADR tape drive with three tapes	$300
Floppy drive	Mitsumi 1.44 MB	$15
Keyboard	Microsoft Natural Keyboard Pro	$50
Mouse	Microsoft IntelliMouse with IntelliEye	$49
Monitor	Hitachi SuperScan Elite 640 17" SVGA	$250
Speakers	Labtec LCS-2414	$35
UPS	APC BP420S Back-UPS Pro 420 VA	$195
Software	Microsoft Windows 98	$90
	Shipping and miscellaneous	$53
	Grand Total	$1,875

This home-built system compares favorably to $2,000 systems from Gateway, Dell, or Micron. As an experiment, we configured a $1,900 Gateway Essential PC (they charge about $100 to ship), trying to match components as closely as possible. Dell and Micron do not offer configurations even close to what we've chosen. Neither, for example, offers a hard drive larger than 13.6 GB on a Celeron/400 or /433 system. The Gateway Essential is available with either a Celeron/400 or a Pentium III/450, but comparing specifications and options makes it clear that they're based on different motherboards. The Gateway Essential 400 appears to use the PPGA Celeron/400 on an Intel CA810 motherboard, which uses the same integrated sound as the SR440BX, but has the inferior Intel graphics rather than nVIDIA TNT. The PPGA motherboard also eliminates the possibility of upgrading later to a Pentium III, unless that particular Socket 370 motherboard supports the FC PGA Pentium III, which many do not.

Disgarding the minor difference in processor speed—we could have saved $5 by using the Celeron/400 instead of the /433—and comparing other components from the top down, the Gateway OEM case and power supply aren't as good as PC Power & Cooling. In particular, there is a huge difference in power supplies. We couldn't determine exactly which power supply (or even what size) the Gateway system uses, but our experience tells us that it's likely to be under 200W, probably well under. Gateway offers two 17" monitor options, and the better monitor has roughly comparable specs to the Hitachi we chose. We prefer the Hitachi name. Gateway offers a 27.3 GB 7,200 RPM hard drive upgrade, but doesn't say who makes it. Once again, we prefer the Seagate Barracuda. Other components, including the CD-RW drive and UPS are comparable, although Gateway uses a Sony CD-RW drive, which has had some reported problems with regard to compatibility with Adaptec DirectCD. The same holds true generally for the other components such as the keyboard and mouse. We're using top-notch branded retail products, while Gateway is using generic white-box versions.

The Gateway Essential 400 does have some extras, including Windows 98 and Works, which we'd have to buy separately. It also includes a non-optional OEM Winmodem and a year of gateway.net Internet service, which might be valuable for some, but not for us. What the Gateway doesn't include (even as an option) is the tape drive, which occupies $400 of our budget. Overall, we conclude that the home-built system offers better components (and choice of components) with full manufacturer warranties at $200 to $300 less than the cost of the Gateway.

One dirty little secret PC vendors won't tell you is that the components they use often differ significantly from the retail (or even "white box" wholesale versions of similarly named products. For example, a reader purchased a Dell Dimension XPS T500 Pentium III system in the summer of 1999. That system supposedly used Diamond Viper 770 TNT2 video and Aureal Turtle Beach II sound. The reader learned after numerous problems and support calls that the Viper was a special "D-for-Dell" OEM version that ran much slower than the retail product. The Turtle Beach sound card was another special Dell OEM version that couldn't use the standard Aureal drivers. He attempted to replace the OEM sound card with a Soundblaster Live! Value card, and found that the Dell system wouldn't boot without the original sound card installed! So, just because a packaged PC uses components with familiar names, don't assume they're the same as the retail versions. They're probably not.

The home-built system is ideally suited to the needs of the person who will use it. The only upgrades we might consider, approximately in ranked priority order, are:

- Use Windows NT Workstation. This user knows Windows 9X and is comfortable with it, but Windows NT is so much more stable (and faster, given 64 MB or more RAM) that it would be worth spending the additional $50 or so that NT costs.

- Buy a better monitor. The Hitachi 640 runs 1,024×768 at 85 Hz, which is about right for a 17" monitor. If we had a bigger budget, we might go with a better 17" monitor (add $100) or a Hitachi 19" monitor (add $200).

- Install more memory. Either Windows 9X or Windows NT Workstation is comfortable with 64 MB, but either uses more memory if it's available. Windows 9X seems more stable and better performing with up to 96 MB of RAM, although going beyond that shows decreasing returns. NT Workstation is rock-solid with 64 MB, but will hit its swap file a lot less often with 128 MB of physical RAM. Installing a single 128 MB DIMM would provide more than adequate memory for either operating system while leaving a DIMM socket free for later expansion.

High-Performance System

High-performance systems use Pentium III or AMD Athlon processors and substitute SCSI peripherals for the IDE/ATAPI drives used in mainstream systems. High-performance systems are not readily available from major vendors like Dell and Gateway. For some reason, people who willingly pay a $500 premium for the latest Intel or AMD processor seldom consider instead spending that extra $500 on

---

SCSI drives, even though using SCSI often boosts performance more than using a marginally faster processor. That means if you want a high-performance system, you either have to build it yourself or buy it from a smaller specialty vendor.

With minor configuration changes, this system is appropriate as either a high-performance personal PC or as a server for a small (10 to 20 client) network. In our case it does both, functioning as both Barbara's personal system and as the main file and print server for our SOHO network. We will transfer Windows NT Server 4.0 and Office 97 from Barbara's current system, which will be relocated to the server closet as a Linux box, so we didn't need to buy software. We didn't really set a budget, but our target was under $2,500 without monitor. Here's what we came up with:

Case and power supply

We considered using the PC Power & Cooling Full Tower case for its additional expansion room, but ended up going with the Personal Mid-Tower case. That case has three 5.25" external drive bays, two 3.5" external bays, and one 3.5" internal bay, with a $5 option to add two additional 3.5" internal bays. We'll use two of the 5.25" bays for a CD-ROM drive and a tape drive, leaving one free 5.25" bay that we may use later for a CD-RW or DVD-RAM drive. Should we need another 5.25" bay, we can remove the tape drive from its 5.25" chassis and install it in the other external 3.5" bay. For power supply, we considered using the Turbo Cool 350 ATX ($149) or the Turbo Cool 400 ATX ($199), but after adding up current draws, we decided that the $99 Turbo-Cool 300 ATX power supply was sufficient with room to spare. (*http://www.pcpowercooling.com/home.htm*)

Processor

We definitely wanted to use a Pentium III CPU for the dramatically increased performance it provides over the Celeron when running SSE-enabled applications. Also, some of the applications we plan to run on this system saturate the small 128 KB Celeron L2 cache, and so run noticeably faster on a Pentium III with its 512 KB L2 cache. When we were designing this system, the Pentium III was available in four speeds: 450 MHz ($180), 500 MHz ($250), 550 MHz ($400), and 600 MHz ($600). Using the MHz/buck test, those processors come in at about 2.5, 2.0, 1.4, and 1.0 respectively. In other words, the 600 runs 33% faster than the 450 but at 333% the price. For most people, a CPU must be 25% to 33% faster before they notice much difference, so it's clear that using anything faster than the Pentium III/450 will be of little advantage. (*http://developer.intel.com/design/pentiumiii/*)

Motherboard

This system won't be used for heavy gaming or anything else that requires leading-edge video and sound, so we decided to go with a motherboard with embedded video and sound. Again, the superb Intel SR440BX does what we need to do at a significantly lower cost than buying separate video and sound cards for a nonintegrated motherboard. (*http://developer.intel.com/design/motherbd/sr/sr_ds.htm*)

Memory

This system will run Windows NT Server 4, for which 128 MB is the sweet spot. The SR440BX has only two DIMM sockets, so we chose one Crucial 128 MB

DIMM, leaving the other socket available. This system is a server, so we decided to go with ECC memory, which costs a few percent more than nonparity memory and imposes a slight performance penalty. As always, we chose PC133 rather than PC100 memory for future flexibility. In this case, doing that cost only about $10 more. (*http://www.crucial.com*)

Network card

No question here. We run a 100BaseT Ethernet network, and Intel makes the best 100BaseT network cards we know of. They're reliable and come with rock-solid drivers. With Intel PRO/100+ network cards selling for $40 or so, there's no reason to save $10 or $15 by using a third-tier product. (*http://www. intel.com/network/products/pro100_dsktop.htm*)

Hard disk

There are two issues here, capacity and speed. In addition to storing local applications and data, this drive is the main data store for our network. After determining current requirements and then adding room for growth, we concluded that we needed a drive in the 20 GB range. There are any number of inexpensive ATA drives that size, but ATA is not appropriate here. A 7,200 RPM UDMA drive is adequate for a personal system and marginally acceptable for a small server, but not for a machine that does both. In a concurrent access environment, SCSI features like command queuing and elevator seeking give it a huge performance advantage over an ATA drive with similar seek time and spin rate. We'd like a 10,000 RPM drive, but the higher cost relative to a 7,200 RPM model probably isn't justified for the moderate performance increase it would provide for this system. Many manufacturers make 18 GB 7,200 RPM drives, but we consider the Seagate Barracuda 18LP series the best of those. We wanted U2W (LVD) for its high sustained throughput, and so chose the ST318275LW Barracuda 18LP. (*http://www.seagate.com/disc/ disctop.shtml*)

SCSI host adapter

We use only Adaptec SCSI host adapters, which have been the standard ever since SCSI was invented. Second-tier adapters cost a bit less, but we know the Adaptec will work with anything. And, as anyone who bought a Diamond FirePort learned, companies that challenge Adaptec in the SCSI market may depart that niche with little notice. We know there will always be driver updates for an Adaptec. We want a U2W host adapter to go with our U2W drive. Although 80 MB/s U2W may seem excessive for a drive with a 22.5 MB/s sustained transfer rate, using U2W leaves us unoccupied bandwidth that we'll need when we add drives to the system. The choice is between the $200 2930U2 and the $240 2940U2W. Both provide 68-pin U2W and 50-pin Ultra SCSI internal connectors and a 50-pin Ultra SCSI external connector. The 2940U2W adds a 68-pin Wide Ultra SCSI internal connector and a 68-pin U2W external connector. This machine will never need those additional connectors, so we choose the 2930U2. (*http://www.adaptec.com/products/overview/ aha2930u2.html*)

CD-ROM drive

Ordinarily, we would install a CD-RW drive, but this system doesn't really need one because we already have CD burners on other systems. It does need a high-performance CD-ROM drive, which we'll use to convert our audio CD collection to MP3. This is an all-SCSI system, and Plextor makes the best CD-ROM drives available. We choose the UltraPleX 32X Max, which rips audio CDs at three times the speed of the fastest ATAPI CD-ROM drive we've seen, processing a typical audio CD in about three minutes. (*http://www.plextor.com*)

Tape drive

This system is our main network data store, so backup is critical. We need a drive that will back up the 18 GB Barracuda to one tape. (If we install more drives on this system, they'll store things like copies of installation CDs and MP3 files that don't need to be backed up). We want a drive with read-while-write and hardware data compression, which effectively limits our choices to 4 mm DDS-3 or Travan NS20. DDS-3 stores 12/24 GB versus Travan's 10/20 GB and uses somewhat less expensive tapes, but DDS-3 drives cost considerably more than Travan NS20 drives. After evaluating price and features of NS20 drives, we choose a Tecmar TS520CSL drive. (*http://www.tecmar.com/product/travan/travan20/travan20.html*)

Monitor

Barbara is happy with her current 17" Trinitron monitor, so we don't really need a new monitor for this system. If we did need a monitor, we'd choose a 19" Hitachi, Mitsubishi, NEC, or Sony that supported 1280×1024 at 85 Hz and (for infrequent use) 1600×1200 at 75 Hz. The best in that group is the Hitachi CM751U SuperScan 751. More expensive models support the same resolutions at higher refresh rates, but cost $200 to $500 more. (*http://www.hitachidisplays.com/products/19_751_752.htm*)

UPS

We wanted extended run time (to allow for orderly shutdowns) and some over-capacity to support whatever we add to this system later. Although in theory VA rating and battery capacity are unrelated, in practice UPSes with higher VA ratings come with bigger batteries, so buying additional run time also buys some over-capacity. The APC model selector recommended the Back-UPS Pro 650, which provides 23 minutes of run time, running at 38% of capacity. (*http://www.apcc.com/products/back-ups_pro/index.cfm*)

Miscellaneous stuff

We chose our standard Teac 1.44 MB FDD. Barbara dislikes the ergonomic Microsoft Natural Keyboard series, and prefers a standard keyboard layout. She chose the Microsoft Internet Keyboard, which has a built-in wrist rest, several dedicated keys for one-touch access to various browser functions, email, and so on, as well as some programmable hot keys. She loves the Microsoft IntelliMouse on her old system, so we chose another of those for the new system. Barbara listens to CDs while she works, so we wanted a good speaker system with a subwoofer. The one we chose was the Labtec ATX-5820, which provides superior sound quality for music and is also suitable for gaming and other purposes. See Table 25-3 for a component list for a high-performance system.

Table 25-3: Component List for a High-Performance System

Component	Model	Price
Case	PC Power & Cooling Personal Mid-Tower	$65
Power supply	PC Power & Cooling Turbo-Cool 300 ATX	$99
Processor	Intel Pentium III/450	$180
Motherboard	Intel SR440BX	$150
Memory	Crucial CT16M72S4D75, 128 MB PC133 ECC SDRAM DIMM	$220
Network card	Intel PRO/100+ fast Ethernet adapter	$40
SCSI adapter	Adaptec AHA-2930U2 U2W (80 MB/s) LVD SCSI adapter	$200
Hard disk	Seagate ST318275LW Barracuda 18LP U2W 7,200 RPM LVD	$420
CD-ROM drive	Plextor PX-32TSi UltraPleX 32X Max SCSI	$90
Tape drive	Tecmar TS520CSL Travan NS20 SCSI	$380
Floppy drive	Teac 235HF 1.44 MB	$15
Keyboard	Microsoft Internet Keyboard	$19
Mouse	Microsoft IntelliMouse 3.0	$25
Speakers	Labtec ATX-5820	$125
UPS	APC BP650S Back-UPS Pro 650 VA	$230
	Shipping and miscellaneous	$46
	Grand Total	$2,304

If this system is to be used primarily as a workstation role, we'd consider making the following changes:

- Run Windows NT Workstation 4 rather than the more expensive Server version.
- If disk performance is critical, substitute a 10,000 RPM Seagate Cheetah for the 7,200 RPM Barracuda.
- If CPU performance is critical, substitute a faster Pentium III for the Pentium III/450.
- If video performance is critical, replace the Intel SR440BX with a noninte-grated motherboard that provides at least a 2X AGP slot, and install a Matrox G400 Max video card and a Turtle Beach Montego II sound card.
- Substitute a less expensive tape drive (e.g., the OnStream ATAPI DI30 or SCSI SC30).

If this system is to be used primarily as a SOHO file and print server, we'd consider making the following changes:

- Downgrade the Pentium III/450 to a Slot 1 Celeron.
- If this server will support numerous shared SCSI devices, upgrade the 2930U2 host adapter to a 2940U2W.
- Replace the ATX-5280 speakers with a $25 set of powered speakers.

Workstation System

Workstation systems (in the true sense of the word) are characterized by their use of multiple processors, multiple large, fast U2W SCSI hard drives, copious amounts of RAM, and large, high-resolution displays driven by high-performance display adapters. Workstations run Unix, Windows NT, or both. We set out to design a workstation-class system for Robert. Within reason, money is no object for this system, because it's the one he uses all day every day. We didn't waste money, for example by buying a component that was 10% faster at five times the cost, but neither did we allow cost to play much role in our decisions. Here's what we came up with:

Case and power supply

We chose the PC Power & Cooling Solid Steel Tower case. With eight external and two internal 5.25" drive bays, this case provides all the expansion room we'll ever need. It also provides excellent cooling, with the power supply fan at the top rear, two supplemental fans at the bottom front, and space to add two more fans at the rear. This system will contain several high-current drives, so we opted for the Turbo-Cool 400 ATX power supply. PPC manufactures larger power supplies, including a 600 watt ATX unit and dual units of 600 and 825 watts, but those would be overkill. (*http://www.pcpowercooling.com/ home.htm*)

Processor

The only realistic choice for a dual processor system is the Intel Pentium III. Enthusiasts build dual Celeron systems, particularly now that dual Socket 370 motherboards are readily available. That isn't an ideal solution, though. With Celeron/500 and Pentium III/450 processors selling for about the same price, the cost advantage of dual Celerons has almost been eliminated. More important, the larger Pentium III L2 cache significantly improves performance in SMP systems.

Choosing which Pentium III to use was a bit more difficult. When we designed this system, 100 MHz FSB Pentium III CPUs were available in four speeds: 450, 500, 550, and 600 MHz. We wanted pure speed, so we used 550 MHz processors. Why not 600 MHz? Because the Pentium III/550 was really the fastest standard CPU that Intel sold. As regular readers of our web site know, we're not fans of overclocking, whether it's done by the end user or the manufacturer. The truth is that the Pentium III/600 is overclocked. Officially overclocked, granted, but overclocked nonetheless. The Pentium III/600 requires 2.05 volts rather than the standard 2.0 volts used by other Deschutes-based processors, which incontrovertibly proves (to us, at least) that it's over-clocked. We'll sacrifice that 9% speed boost to have processors that run at nominal voltage. So it's two Pentium III/550 processors for this system. (*http:// developer.intel.com/design/pentiumiii/*)

Motherboard

We would prefer an Intel motherboard, but Intel does not make a workstation-class dual Pentium III board. Paradoxically, the primary selection criterion for a dual-CPU board is not performance. All dual-CPU boards are fast. Perfor-mance differences amount at most to a couple of percent. Stability running multiple processors is key, and boards do differ significantly in this respect. We have found Intel motherboards to be the most stable available, but EPoX boards come close. EPoX has two 440BX-based boards suitable for this system, the BXB-S, which includes embedded Adaptec U2W SCSI, and the

KP6-BS, which does not. We prefer using a separate SCSI host adapter, and so opted for the KP6-BS. (*http://www.epox.com/products/mboard/kp6-bs_1.html*)

Memory

This system will dual-boot Windows NT 4 Workstation and Windows 2000 Professional. For an SMP system, a good rule of thumb is to install the same amount of memory for each processor that you'd install for a single-CPU system, e.g., for a dual-CPU system, install twice the memory you would for a single-CPU system. Both operating systems are happy in 128 MB, so we decided to install 256 MB. It's usually better to install one large DIMM rather than two smaller ones. In this case we'll use two 128 MB DIMMs, because 256 MB DIMMs are problematic. Some motherboards do not support them at all, and even those that do sometimes exhibit stability problems. The KP6-BS has four DIMM slots, so we'll still have two slots available for future expansion. As always, we use memory from Crucial Technologies. (*http://www.crucial.com*)

Hard disk

This system will use two hard disks, a "small" fast disk to store the operating systems, applications, and working data sets, and a large "slow" disk to store data. For the system disk, we wanted flat-out performance, which means a 10,000 RPM U2W SCSI drive. The Seagate Cheetah has for years been the best high-performance disk drive, and it remains the best choice. We chose an 18.4 GB Cheetah 18LP for the system disk. For the data disk, we wanted sheer size, and were willing to take a small performance hit to get that. Here again, there's no contest. We chose a 50 GB Seagate Barracuda 50LP. At 7,200 RPM, it's a bit slower than the Cheetah, but it matches or exceeds the performance of competing 7,200 RPM U2W drives and is the largest drive available. (*http://www.seagate.com/disc/disctop.shtml*)

Video adapter

Robert spends 10 or 12 hours a day working in Word and browsing the Web, so the most important criterion by far is sharp, stable 2D image quality. Nothing compares to Matrox video cards in that respect, particularly at high resolution and color depth. The flagship Matrox G400 series run at 2048×1536 resolution in True Color in both 2D and 3D mode, with high refresh rates. With Matrox cards, extreme resolutions are actually usable if the monitor can handle them. That's not the case with most competing cards, which may support high resolutions but yield seriously degraded 2D image quality at more than 1024×768 or 1280×1024. Although nVIDIA and Voodoo cards may be marginally faster on some gaming benchmarks, we've never been able to see a difference in actual use. Overall the G400 is the best video card on the market. (*http://www.matrox.com/mga/products/mill_g400/home.htm*)

Sound card

The Creative Labs SoundBlaster series of sound cards have set the standard for PC sound for years, but to our ears their sound quality is slightly inferior to that of cards based on Aureal chipsets. Accordingly, we decided to go with an Aureal-based card. Such cards are available from several vendors, notably Diamond and Voyetra/Turtle Beach. Turtle Beach has a reputation for selling top-notch high-end sound cards for more than a decade, so we chose their flagship model, the Montego II QuadZilla. (*http://www.voyetra-turtle-beach. com/site/default.asp*)

Network card

We chose the Intel PRO/100+ 10/100BaseT network adapter for the same reasons described in the preceding section. (*http://www.intel.com/network/ products/pro100_dsktop.htm*)

SCSI host adapter

Although the Adaptec 2930U2 SCSI host adapter we used on the preceding system would perform credibly on this system, we wanted a host adapter that provided the highest possible performance. Adaptec recommends the 2940U2W for systems with multiple hard drives, so that's what we chose. (*http://www.adaptec.com/products/overview/aha2940u2w.html*)

CD-RW drive

This system is our main CD burner, so we wanted a fast, top-quality CD-R drive. Plextor is widely acclaimed as the best manufacturer of optical drives—nearly all commercial CD duplication houses use Plextor drives—and our experience bears that out. Plextor makes two 8X burners, the PlexWriter 8/20 recorder and the PlexWriter 8/2/20, which adds 2X RW support. Although we seldom use CD-RW discs, the rewriter costs only $25 more, so we opted for the PlexWriter 8/2/20. (*http://www.plextor.com/8220.htm*)

CD-ROM drive

For gaming and doing direct CD-to-CD dupes, we wanted the fastest SCSI CD-ROM drive on the market. That turns out to be the Plextor UltraPleX Wide, which is what we chose. (*http://www.plextor.com/40wide.htm*)

DVD-ROM drive

We planned to use no IDE/ATAPI devices in this system, but the DVD-ROM drive we really wanted to use, the fourth-generation Hitachi GD-5000, was available only in ATAPI when we were putting the system together. We considered going with another brand of SCSI DVD-ROM drive, but we really wanted the 8X speed of the Hitachi GD-5000 for games, databases, encyclopediae, and so on, so we elected to use it in ATAPI. The lower data rates of ATAPI are really not an issue for DVD, even running at 8X, and using the ATAPI version at least gives us a drive that the BIOS will recognize as an ATAPI CD-ROM, which can be quite useful when installing operating systems. Robert doesn't plan to watch many DVD movies on this system, so we decided not to add a hardware DVD decoder card. Software DVD decoding should work fine on a system this powerful for watching an occasional movie. (*http://www.hitachi. com/storage/products/dvd/dvdframe.html*)

Tape drive

With nearly 70 GB of disk space, it might at first appear that we need an equally huge tape drive. Such drives are available, and although cost is not a major issue for this system, reality dictates that we at least consider it. There are three realistic choices for backing up huge amounts of disk space on one tape. DLT tape drives and high-capacity 8mm tape drives can be ruled out—they can easily cost as much as a decent used car. The 25/50 GB OnStream ADR-50 might be a reasonable choice, but it has two drawbacks: first, it doesn't support hardware compression or read-while-write, which makes it too slow to do a full backup and compare overnight. Second, at $50 or thereabouts, its tape cartridges aren't cheap.

Thinking the problem through, we realized that we don't really need to back up 70 GB of disk. We need to back up the 18 GB Cheetah drive regularly, certainly, but the 50 GB Barracuda is another story. It contains data that if lost could easily be reconstructed—our CD collection converted to MP3s, copies of distribution CDs, archived data that has already been burned to CDs and stored off-site, etc. We could safely do a full backup of the Barracuda every month or two with periodic differential backups to pick up any changes between full backups.

Realizing that, we decided to look at two mainstream backup technologies, 10/20 GB Travan NS20 and 12/24 GB DDS-3. Either would do, but we'll need many tapes to back up this system, so the cost of tapes becomes a consideration. NS20 tapes cost $40 or so. We'd need at least six for a full backup rotation for the Cheetah. Backing up the Barracuda would require at least three tapes and probably four, plus at least a couple more for differential backups. Maintaining two full sets for the Barracuda would require ten or twelve tapes. With the six for the Cheetah, that totals 16 to 18 tapes, or about $640 to $720 worth. Assuming we replace tapes every two years on average, that puts the annual tape cost for an NS20 drive at between $320 and $360. A DDS-3 drive would require a similar number of tapes (perhaps somewhat fewer due to the 20% higher capacity of DDS-3), but DDS-3 tapes cost only $10 or $12. That means we'd have to buy less than $200 worth of tapes initially, and spend less than $100 per year replacing tapes. That differential is enough to overcome the higher cost of DDS-3 drives versus NS20 drives, so we decided on a DDS-3 drive. There are many good DDS-3 drives available, but we've been using Tecmar drives for more than a decade with universally good results, so we chose the Tecmar 3900 internal DDS-3 drive. (*http://www.tecmar.com*)

Monitor

Robert was satisfied with his existing 17" Trinitron monitor, but that monitor stays with his old system. As long as we were building a new system, it made sense to make the jump from 17" to 19". Robert will run his monitor at 1280×1024 most of the time, and wanted a monitor that would support 85 Hz refresh at that resolution. He will use 1600×1200 resolution infrequently, and was willing to accept a 75 Hz refresh at that resolution. We looked at 19" models from Hitachi, Mitsubishi, NEC, and Sony. The Hitachi CM751U SuperScan 751 is the least expensive of that group that meets all requirements, and its image quality is superb—at least as good as any of the other models. So that's what we bought. (*http://www.hitachidisplays.com/products/19_751_752.htm*)

UPS

We wanted extended run time for this system, which often runs long jobs that cannot be interrupted easily. Adding up the current draws on all components including the monitor told us that we needed at least a 650 VA unit. To provide extended run time and some over-capacity for future expansion, we elected to go with a UPS in the 1 KVA range. We've trusted our systems to American Power Conversion (APC) UPSes for many years, and have never had a problem with them. Accordingly, we checked the APC web site, and found that they make 1 KVA units in both the Back-UPS Pro and Smart-UPS lines. We chose the Smart-UPS 1000 VA model for its true sine-wave output and increased expandability over the similarly sized Back-UPS Pro model. (*http://www.apcc.com/products/smart-ups/index.cfm*)

Miscellaneous stuff

We chose our standard Teac 1.44 MB FDD. Robert prefers the ergonomic Microsoft Natural Keyboard series, and chose the Natural Keyboard Pro model, which has multiple dedicated keys for one-touch access to various browser functions, email, etc., as well as several programmable hot keys. Robert smokes a pipe, and so must clean his mechanical mice every week or so to remove ash and bits of tobacco. For this system, he chose the Microsoft IntelliMouse with IntelliEye, a purely optical mouse that has no ball and so does not require frequent cleaning. Robert listens to CDs while he works, and wanted a good speaker system with a subwoofer. He also plays some computer games that support the four-channel sound provided by the Quad-Zilla sound card, and so wanted something with four satellite speakers. The best 4-channel speaker system available is the Creative Labs/Cambridge SoundWorks FourPointSurround FPS2000, and that is what we chose. Table 25-4 shows the component list for a high-end system.

Table 25-4: Component List for a High-End System

Component	Model	Price
Case	PC Power & Cooling Solid-Steel Tower	$289
Power supply	PC Power & Cooling Turbo-Cool 400 ATX	$199
Processor	Intel Pentium III/550 BX80525U550512E (2 @ $360)	$720
Motherboard	EPoX KP6-BS	$150
Memory	Crucial CT16M72S4D75, 128 MB PC133 ECC SDRAM (2 @ $220)	$440
Video card	Matrox G4+MDHA32GR Millennium G400 (32 MB)	$170
Sound card	Turtle Beach/Voyetra Montego II Quadzilla	$85
Network card	Intel PILA8461 PRO/100+ PCI Management Adapter	$40
SCSI adapter	Adaptec AHA-2940U2W KIT	$300
Hard disk 0	Seagate ST318203LW Cheetah 18LP	$600
Hard disk 1	Seagate ST150176LW Barracuda 50LP	$900
CD-RW drive	Plextor PX-W8220Ti PlexWriter 8/2/20	$425
CD-ROM drive	Plextor PX-40TSUWi UltraPleX Wide	$110
DVD drive	Hitachi GD-5000 ATAPI DVD-ROM	$200
Tape drive	Tecmar TS3900I-D01 DDS-3	$825
Floppy drive	Teac 235HF 1.44 MB	$15
Keyboard	Microsoft Natural Keyboard Pro	$50
Mouse	Microsoft IntelliMouse with IntelliEye	$49
Monitor	Hitachi SuperScan Elite 751 19"	$470
Speakers	Creative Labs FourPointSurround FPS2000 Digital	$150
UPS	APC SU1000NET Smart-UPS 1000 VA	$450
Drive 0 cooler	PC Power & Cooling Bay-Cool drive bay cooler	$49
Drive 1 cooler	PC Power & Cooling Drive-Cool hard drive cooler	$15

Designing a PC

Table 25-4: Component List for a High-End System (continued)

Component	Model	Price
	Shipping and miscellaneous	$68
	Grand Total	$6,769

Purchasing Components

After you design the system, the next step is to order all the components. Rather than shopping for the absolute lowest price for each component, we try to order everything from just one or two vendors. Ordering piecemeal incurs additional shipping costs that often nullify small price breaks on individual items. Although we try to order everything from one place, we usually have to place two or three orders because one or another vendor doesn't carry a particular item or is out of stock.

We've had good experiences with Insight (*http://www.insight.com*), NECx (*http://www.necx.com*), and PC Connection (*http://www.pcconnection.com*). Their prices are often a bit higher than some competitors, but they're reputable and (in our experience, at least) they ship what they say they're going to ship when they say they're going to ship it. We've also never had a problem with them repackaging used items and selling them as new, something we can't say for some other vendors. Your mileage may vary, so do your own homework and don't expect us to be able to do anything if you have a bad experience with one of the vendors we like.

When evaluating vendors, take particular note of the following:

Shipping charges
> Make sure to factor the cost of shipping into your price comparisons. Some vendors advertise very low prices, but have ridiculously high shipping charges, particularly on monitors, cases, and other heavy or bulky items. We were once quoted $28 to ship a single hard drive by surface UPS, for example, and $63 to ship a 17" monitor. Many on-line vendors automatically calculate and display shipping charges, either per item or for your order as a whole. If a vendor doesn't mention shipping, regard that as a red flag.

Return policy
> Read and understand the vendor's return policy. Vendors differ greatly in what they regard as an acceptable reason for a return and how they handle returns that turn out not to be defective. One otherwise highly rated vendor, for example, Bunta Technology (*http://www.bunta.com*), includes the following in their Terms and Policies: "All return products will be tested by BTI technicians to verify the problem. If found to be non-defective, we may ship back to the customer at his/her cost and may charge for diagnostic fee ($60/hr)." Also look carefully for any mention of a restocking fee, which may be as high as 25%, and may be charged even if you are returning an item because it is incompatible with your system. Better vendors have a no-questions-asked return policy and do not charge restocking fees. Unless the product is defective, all vendors refuse returns of opened software (except in exchange for the same title) and printers that have had ink or toner installed.

Warranty policy

Better resellers endorse the manufacturer's warranty. That is, if you buy a product from them and that product fails, you return the product to them and they ship you a replacement. Most such vendors limit their endorsement of the manufacturer's warranty to 30 or 60 days. The very best vendors pay for shipping both ways, and will often cross-ship a replacement before they receive the failed product, although they will require you provide a credit card number to ensure that you actually return the defective product. Some vendors have no warranty policy at all. If a product from them arrives DOA, they require you to return that product to the manufacturer. Avoid those vendors.

Reseller Ratings (*http://www.resellerratings.com*) rates hundreds of mail-order vendors on a seven-point scale, based on feedback from people who have purchased from them. Unfortunately, many of the listed vendors have only a few responses, which statistically limits the validity of the ratings for those vendors. Also, as far as we can see, there is nothing to prevent a reseller from "stuffing the ballot box," so use ratings based on few responses at your own risk. Ratings for those resellers that are represented by 100 or more responses are probably reasonably reliable. Ratings for those resellers from whom we have purchased generally correspond with our own experiences, good and bad.

To make it easy to compare total price and the price for each item, we create a spreadsheet with one column for the items to be ordered and other columns for two or three of our favorite vendors. After we determine which vendor has the lowest total price, we then compare individual item prices and ask that vendor to match any lower per-item prices quoted by their competitors. "NECx has this SCSI drive for $18 less than you guys are quoting. Will you match that?" Most vendors will, or will at least reduce the price somewhat.

If you want to take that a step further, use the various price comparison services available on the Web to find really low prices. We use *http://www.shopper.com*, *http://www.killerapp.com*, and *http://www.pricewatch.com*. Some of the prices you'll find are so low that they should raise a red flag. We've learned not to buy from "bottom feeder" vendors. They may ship late or not at all, charge your credit card more than the price they quoted, add ridiculous shipping charges, sell OEM versions as retail boxed versions, ship repackaged or otherwise inferior merchandise, and do other things to raise your blood pressure. Most stop short of outright fraud, but many tread near that line. It's just not worth the hassle to buy from them, but you can use their prices to beat down your preferred vendor.

But recognize the TANSTAAFL principle: There Ain't No Such Thing As A Free Lunch. Reputable vendors can't match the prices offered by scum-sucking bottom feeders and still stay in business, but they can usually do better than the prices they advertise. Specifically, here's how to beat down your chosen vendor. The following is a typical transcript of a telephone conversation between a Smart Buyer (SB) and a Slimy Salesman (SS). (Actually, reputable vendors very often have quite good salespeople. We've encountered many honest ones.) SB plans to buy a Seagate hard drive and several other items. We've appended comments to indicate the reason for each thing SB says. SB checked three of his favorite vendors, who had the drive priced (with shipping) at $624.95 ($0.00), $693.99 ($6.99), and $699.00 ($5.00):

SB: Hi, I need to buy a bunch of stuff. The first item is a Seagate ST318203LW Cheetah 18LP. Do you have one in stock that you could ship to me today? (*It's important to let the salesman know that you're a buyer, not a tire-kicker, and that you're buying several items. Start with the most expensive item and work your way down.*)

SS: Yes, I have 837 of them showing as available. Which credit card do you want to use?

SB: Before we do that, I see on your web site that you want $624.95 with free shipping. Is that price correct? (*Always verify current pricing. We've been pleasantly surprised more than once to find that an item was on special or that its price had been misprinted.*)

SS: Yes.

SB: [The name of the cheapest vendor SB found on PriceWatch.com] is selling this identical drive for $589, including shipping. That's $35.95 less than you guys. Can you match that? (*He probably won't be able to, but you've put yourself in the dominant position. The salesman now knows that he's dealing with a Smart Buyer.*)

SS: Umm. I don't know. I'll have to talk to my manager. What other items are you buying? (*SS is hoping that he can quote you a lowball price on this item and make up the difference on the others.*)

SB: Let's just look at the drive first. If you can't do better, there's not a lot of point to wasting both our time on the other items. And if you can't match, please at least find out the best price you can possibly give me. I'd really rather buy from you guys, but not for $36 more. (*We've acknowledged that we know he probably won't be able to match, but left open the possibility that we'll buy from him anyway if he can come even close. And we've let him know that he's not going to make up the differential on the drive by quoting higher prices on the other stuff.*)

SS: Okay, my manager says I can sell you the drive for $600, including shipping. How's that?

SB: That's fine, assuming you can give me a similar break on these other items too. . .

The net result was that buying from the reputable vendor cost about 2% more than buying from the cheapest source. That's well worth it for peace of mind if nothing else. We've sometimes paid a 5% or even 8% premium (on smaller orders), but we try to keep it down to 2% or 3% on larger orders. Never pay more than a 10% premium. You can almost certainly do better with another good vendor, even if their advertised prices are higher than those of the vendor you're talking to. If you can't do better, assume that your low price benchmark is simply unrealistic.

When the items arrive, open the boxes immediately and verify their contents against both your original order and the packing list. Don't stop there, however. Open each individual component box and compare the actual contents against the proper contents as listed in the manual for that component. On one memorable occasion, we received a factory-sealed box that contained manuals, CD, and cables, but not the product itself! Check carefully.

Some vendors routinely ship used product but represent it as new. Regardless of who you buy from, make it absolutely clear that you will accept only new, factory-fresh product. Repackaged products are not acceptable. Someone returned them, perhaps for good reason. Vendors should ship returned products back to the manufacturer or distributor. Instead, many vendors simply put returned products back in inventory and ship them to the next buyer.

Don't accept the fact that a box is shrink-wrapped as evidence that it is factory-fresh. Many vendors have shrink-wrap machines, and use them to rewrap returned products. Most manufacturers have taken to sealing the product box with a sticker or other means to make it obvious if that box has been opened.

If, despite insisting on new product, you receive a product that shows evidence of having been opened (e.g., broken box seal, broken CD seal, slightly bent header pins, expansion slot contacts that show burnishing from having been installed, etc.) contact the vendor immediately and demand to know why they shipped you a used product as new. Demand that they replace it with a factory-fresh product at their own expense, including issuing a pickup slip to have UPS come and get the original product. If the vendor is obstinate, threaten to request a charge-back from your credit card company and to make a complaint for wire-fraud. That gets their attention.

CHAPTER 26

Building a PC

With all the components in-hand, it's time to start building the system. If you've built systems before, you may be able to complete a simple system in a couple of hours, and even a complex system should take only an evening to build. If this is your first system, plan to assemble, configure, and test it over a weekend. Choose a well-lighted work area (the kitchen table is traditional) and lay out all of your components. We use old towels to protect the surface of the table. Observe anti-static precautions throughout. (See Figure 26-1.)

Many of the following steps may be done in whatever order is convenient. You may, for example, install the motherboard before the drives (although, having once dropped a drive on an installed motherboard, we prefer to install the drives first). Case design and motherboard layout determine the most logical order of steps, and may mandate doing things in slightly different order than that listed here. Use your best judgment. Many of the complex steps, such as setting drive jumpers, are described in more detail in the relevant chapter.

Step 1: Prepare the Case

If you are recycling an old case, first remove all components and clean the case thoroughly, using a soft brush and vacuum cleaner to remove dust and a cleaner like Fantastic or Formula 409 to remove grime. We sometimes take really filthy cases outside and literally hose them down (after first removing the power supply). If you do that, use a hair dryer to make sure the case is dry before you begin installing components. If you're not in a hurry, it's better still to let it sit a week or two and dry naturally. If the power supply has been in use for some time, it will likely have accumulated a lot of dust inside it. Do your best to remove dust using a brush and compressed air (the air hose at the gas station works well), but do not remove the cover from the power supply. Whether the case is new or old, check it

Figure 26-1: Gather and organize all components before starting work

thoroughly for sharp edges and burrs and file down any you find. That saves a lot of bloodshed later. Once the case is clean, dry, and defanged, proceed as follows:

1. Verify that all components are present, including the power cord and the package of small mounting hardware and other incidentals.

2. Remove the cover(s) and set them aside. If it is not obvious how to do so, see the manufacturer's instructions. You want the case wide open while you work on it. (See Figure 26-2.) Some cases have a removable motherboard tray. If so, remove it also.

3. Remove all drive bezels from the front of the case to give you easy access later when you're installing drives. Depending on case design, you may have to remove the front case bezel before you can remove the drive bezels. Most cases use plastic drive bay bezels, which snap into place using a small hook on each side to secure them to the chassis. To remove these bezels, bow them slightly until the hooks are clear and then pull straight out. Better cases may use metal drive bay bezels, which are secured with a screw on each side.

   Most cases have metal plates at the front of each drive bay, immediately behind the bezel, to shield against RFI. On better cases, these plates may be discrete pieces, mounted with screws or spring-clip retainers. On cheaper cases, the plates are often stamped as a part of the chassis and may have to be twisted out with pliers. Doing that often leaves a sharp barb. File it down now or it will cut you later. Cases often arrive with the plates already removed from one floppy drive bay and one externally accessible 5.25" drive

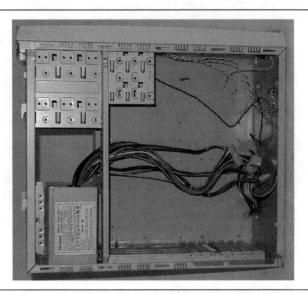

Figure 26-2: The Antec KS-288 mid-tower case with top and side covers removed

bay (for the CD-ROM drive). You need not remove the metal plates from positions where you will not be mounting externally accessible drives. To make the system easier to work on, we usually remove all anti-RFI plates, risking the wrath of the FCC. (See Figure 26-3.)

Figure 26-3: Removing a drive bay bezel—an anti-RFI plate is visible behind the bezel of the lower 3.5" drive bay

4. If you order a case and power supply together, the case usually arrives with the power supply installed. If so, verify that all screws securing the power supply to the case are tight and that the voltage selector (if present) is set to the proper input voltage. If you order a power supply separately, install it by aligning any locking tabs and slots, sliding the power supply into position, and securing the screws. (See Figure 26-4 and Figure 26-5.) Manufacturers often use cable ties to secure the wires coming from the power supply in a neat bundle. If so, carefully nip the cable ties with your diagonal cutters to free the wires. Better power supplies come with spare cable ties that you can use later to dress the wires. Electrical tape or one of those yellow plastic ties supplied with garbage bags work just as well.

Figure 26-4: Slide the power supply into position

5. Many power supplies are adjustable for 110/115V or 20/230V. Make sure to set the power supply for the correct input voltage. Some power supplies automatically sense inout voltage and adjust themselves accordingly. If there is no voltage switch on your power supply, check the manual rather than assuming that it is autosensing. (See Figure 26-6.)

6. If it has not already been done, install the power switch and connect the main power cables.

- Traditional AT power supplies for desktop cases have a built-in power switch (the "big red paddle switch"), and require no configuration.

Figure 26-5: Insert the screws (typically four) to secure the power supply

Figure 26-6: Power supply voltage switch

- Power supplies designed for AT mini-tower cases have four main power leads (usually blue, white, brown, and black) with spade lug connectors that attach to the power switch on the front of the case. If they are not already connected, connect them, being very careful to orient them properly. Note that these wires carry mains voltage; connecting them incorrectly may short the power supply and destroy it. Use electrical tape to insulate each of the four connections.

- In ATX cases, the power switch has only one light-gauge two-wire cable coming from it. You will connect this cable to the power switch header pins on the ATX motherboard during a later assembly step.

7. If the case has an LED to indicate CPU speed, change the jumpers on the back of the LED assembly to cause it to display the proper CPU speed. This step is entirely optional, because the LED display is informational only, and has no effect on system operation. We have one 300 MHz Pentium II system that still displays the CPU speed as 6 MHz, the default for that case, because we lost the instructions that tell us how to change the display.

8. Install supplemental case fan(s), if necessary. Not all cases can accept supplemental fans, and not all systems require them. Minimally configured systems with basic processors ordinarily do not require supplemental fans. Heavily loaded systems—those with multiple hard drives, fast (or dual) processors, most or all expansion slots occupied, and so on—should have supplemental fans installed. Fans are available in several sizes, including 60, 70, 80, 90, and 120 mm. Some cases have multiple fan mounting positions that require different fan sizes.

If you install supplemental fans, make certain they blow in the proper direction—aiding the main power supply fan rather than fighting it. We have seen processors destroyed by overheating in systems with supplemental fans blowing the wrong direction.

Standard AT power supplies and some ATX power supplies blow out from the power supply, exhausting air from within the case. For these systems, install supplemental fans to push air into the case.

Some ATX power supplies suck air into the power supply, pressurizing the case. For these systems, install supplemental fans to draw air out of the case.

Most supplemental fans can be installed to push air in either direction, either by simply reversing the fan assembly or by throwing a small switch on the fan itself. Some cases are supplied with supplemental fan(s) installed. Do not assume that these fans are necessarily configured correctly. We have seen more than one such case with power supply and supplemental fans both configured to push air into the case, or both configured to draw air out of it.

---

9. Install the feet on the case. Feet are usually plastic devices an inch or so in diameter and a quarter-inch thick. They may be secured to the case bottom via a bolt and nut or via small plastic spreaders that are inserted from inside the case. In all cases, the feet are designed to prevent scarring of the surface that the case rests upon. Some cases have vents in the bottom of the case, and must have the feet installed for proper cooling.

10. Most ATX cases are supplied with a standard I/O template already in place, which may or may not be suitable for your motherboard. Remove the motherboard from its anti-static bag and compare the I/O panel on the back of the

Building a PC

motherboard with the installed template. (See Figure 26-7.) If the template is appropriate for the motherboard, proceed to the next step. Otherwise, snap out the installed I/O template by pressing gently from the outside of the case. Install the new I/O template supplied with the motherboard from inside the case, and press gently toward the outside of the case until the template snaps into place. (See Figure 26-8.) If you do not have the correct I/O template, contact the motherboard or case manufacturer to obtain one. Running the system without an I/O template installed risks disrupting air flow.

Figure 26-7: The Intel CA810E motherboard I/O panel and the supplied I/O template

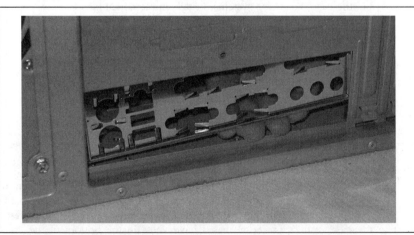

Figure 26-8: Insert the I/O template from inside the case and press gently until it snaps into place

11. Lay the motherboard flat in the case to determine which positions in the motherboard tray require standoffs. (See Figure 26-9.) Screw brass standoffs

into those positions, and verify that each motherboard mounting hole has a corresponding standoff installed. Also verify that no extra standoffs are installed, which might short the motherboard. Some cases use all mounting holes; others use a combination of holes and slots. If yours uses slots, lay aside the proper number of white nylon standoffs, which you will later snap into the bottom of the motherboard for each slotted position. Don't do that now, however, because it prevents the motherboard from lying flat while you install the CPU and RAM. If you need to remove a nylon standoff from the motherboard, use your needlenose pliers to squeeze the prongs on the front side of the motherboard gently while pulling from the back side of the motherboard.

Figure 26-9: Compare motherboard mounting holes against chassis standoff positions

Step 2: Configure the Motherboard

Motherboards differ greatly in how much configuration they require and exactly how it is done. Some motherboards use only one or two jumpers, or are configured through software during BIOS Setup. Others have dozens of jumpers to set such things as CPU voltage, FSB speed, and CPU multiplier. Refer to your motherboard manual to determine the proper settings for your processor and memory, and make any required changes before proceeding.

Step 3: Install the Processor

The exact sequence of steps required to install the processor depends on its packaging (slotted versus socketed) and whether it comes with a heatsink and fan installed. Regardless of processor type, always begin by laying the motherboard flat on a firm surface, padding it with the anti-static foam or bag supplied with it. Inserting the CPU (and memory) may require substantial force, so it's important to ensure that the motherboard is fully supported to avoid cracking it.

For an SECC or SECC2 Intel Celeron/Pentium II/Pentium III or an AMD Athlon processor:

1. Remove the processor from its packaging, and determine what additional cooling, if any, is needed.

   – Most retail-boxed processors have a heatsink and CPU fan already installed, which is perfectly adequate for normal operation. If your processor has a heatsink and fan installed, proceed to step 3.

   – Most OEM ("white box") processors have neither heatsink nor fan, so you will need to buy and install a third-party cooling solution, such as the heatsink/fan combinations sold by PC Power & Cooling.

   – Some Intel Pentium III processors come equipped with a massive heat sink, but no fan. These processors theoretically do not require a CPU fan, although it's a good idea to install either a supplementary CPU fan or a supplementary case fan that draws air directly across such processors.

2. Install the heatsink and fan, following the directions supplied. Always use thermal tape or compound between the processor and heatsink, and press the heatsink firmly against the processor to make sure good contact is made. If excess thermal compound has squeezed out, remove it before proceeding.

3. Some motherboards have a built-in folding universal processor support bracket that accommodates both SECC and SECC2 processors. If your motherboard has such a bracket, raise the arms to the vertical position until they lock into place. Other motherboards use separate brackets, which must be installed manually and secured with screws or pins. These brackets may be universal or may be specific to SECC or SECC2, so verify that whatever bracket you install fits your processor. Also note that some processor support mechanisms have a separate bracket to support the heatsink/fan assembly. If your motherboard is so equipped, install this supplementary support on the processor before proceeding to the next step.

4. Note that the card-edge connector on the processor has a key notch, as does the slot. Slide the processor into the support bracket, making sure that the key is oriented properly. (See Figure 26-10.) Press firmly until the processor seats in the slot, which may require substantial force. You should feel and hear the processor slide into place. (See Figure 26-11.) Most support brackets have locking tabs at the top that will snap into place to secure the processor once it is fully seated.

5. If the fan power lead is designed to connect to a motherboard power header, connect it now. If the fan power lead instead is designed to connect to a power supply power connector, you'll make that connection after the motherboard is installed in the case.

Figure 26-10: Guide the Slot 1 processor into place, making sure that the keys in the slot align properly with those in the processor's card-edge connector

Figure 26-11: Use both thumbs to press down firmly on the Slot 1 processor until it seats fully

Building a PC

For an Intel Celeron PPGA or Pentium III FC-PGA processor, or a Socket 7 processor:

1. Remove the processor from its packaging, and examine it closely to make sure that no pins are bent. A new processor should never have bent pins. If one or more pins are bent, that's certain proof that you were sold a used or repackaged processor. Do not attempt to straighten bent pins. Return the processor and insist on a replacement processor in original factory shrink wrap.

2. The processor fits a Zero Insertion Force (ZIF) socket on the motherboard. To prepare the socket to receive the processor, lift the small lever on one side of the socket to the vertical position.

3. Examine the socket to determine which corner is Pin 1. Pin 1 may be indicated by a small diagonal cutout on the socket, by a dot or arrow, by a number 1 printed on the socket or motherboard itself, or by other similar means. Once you have located pin 1 on the socket, locate pin 1 on the processor, which will also be marked clearly.

4. Carefully align the processor with the socket, making sure that pin 1 on the processor corresponds to pin 1 on the socket, and then drop the processor into place. (See Figure 26-12.) We say "drop" rather than "press" because the processor should seat fully in the socket with little or no resistance (that's why it's called "Zero Insertion Force"). If you encounter resistance, either the pins are misaligned or the ZIF lever is not fully vertical. Don't force the processor into the socket, because those tiny pins are very easy to bend, which effectively destroys the processor. When the processor is seated properly, its bottom should be flush against the top of the socket.

Figure 26-12: With the Socket 370 ZIF arm fully raised, carefully align the processor, making sure pin 1 on the CPU corresponds to pin 1 on the socket, and drop the processor into place

5. With the processor fully seated, pivot the ZIF lever down until it is parallel to the motherboard to lock the processor into place. (See Figure 26-13.) You may encounter noticeable resistance while closing the lever, which is normal. Continue pressing the lever down until it snaps into place. Don't press too hard, though. If the lever seems not to want to seat, you may have the processor misaligned.

Figure 26-13: With the processor fully seated, lower the ZIF socket arm until it seats parallel to the motherboard

6. Retail-boxed processors may include a fan and/or heatsink. OEM processors seldom do. Even if the package includes a fan/heatsink, you will have to install it yourself after installing the processor into the motherboard, because nearly all such devices attach to the socket rather than to the processor itself. Install the heatsink and fan, following the directions supplied. Use the supplied thermal tape or compound between the processor and heatsink, and press the heatsink firmly against the processor to ensure good contact. Clean up any excess thermal compound before proceeding. (See Figure 26-14 and Figure 26-15.)

 If no thermal compound or tape was supplied with the heatsink/fan, buy a tube at Radio Shack (it costs $2 or so) and use it. A processor installed without thermal compound may run as much as 20˚C hotter than one with thermal compound, which at best may merely shorten the life of the processor, and at worst may cause frequent system hangs. Thermal compound is frequently omitted, sometimes even on name-brand commercial PCs, so it's worth checking any processor that you didn't install yourself.

Figure 26-14: After applying thermal tape or compound, align the heatsink on top of the processor

Figure 26-15: Snap both heatsink support brackets over the matching connectors on the socket

7. If the fan power lead is designed to use a motherboard power header, connect it now. If it is designed to connect to a power supply power connector, you'll make that connection after installing the motherboard in the case. (See Figure 26-16.)

Figure 26-16: If the heatsink includes a fan, connect the fan power lead

Step 4: Install the Memory

Memory slots are always numbered, usually beginning with 0, but sometimes with 1. Always populate the memory slots from lowest to highest. That is, SIMM/DIMM slot 0 should be occupied before you install a module in slot 1, both slots 0 and 1 should be occupied before you install a module in slot 2, and so on. DIMMs may always be installed one at a time. SIMMs may be installed one, two, or four at a time, depending on the system and the type of SIMM. The exact procedure required to install memory modules differs slightly for SIMMs versus DIMMs:

- SIMMs: Align the SIMM so that the notch at one end of the SIMM matches the corresponding nub on the SIMM socket. Tilt the SIMM at about a 45-degree angle and slide it into the socket. When the SIMM will go no further in, pivot it toward the vertical until the locking clips on the SIMM socket snap into the holes on the top of the SIMM.

- DIMMs: Pivot the plastic arms on the DIMM socket away from the socket toward the motherboard. Align the offset notch in the card-edge connector on the DIMM with the corresponding nub in the DIMM socket. Insert the DIMM into the socket vertically, press it straight down until it snaps into place. Some DIMMs are easier to seat by pressing down evenly on the module with both thumbs. Others seat more easily if you press down first one side and then the other. Pivot the plastic arms fully vertical to lock the DIMM into place. (See Figure 26-17.)

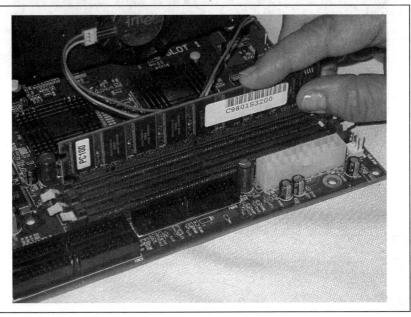

Figure 26-17: Installing a DIMM

After you finish configuring the motherboard and installing the processor and memory, lay the motherboard aside for the time being. Use the anti-static bag or foam packaging that came with the motherboard to prevent damage.

Step 5: Prepare Drives for Installation

Several steps may be required before installing some drives, including setting configuration jumpers, installing mounting hardware, and installing supplemental cooling. Some of those steps are difficult or impossible to perform after the drive is installed in the system, so plan ahead. If you are installing several drives, make a written plan of how each drive needs to be configured to ensure that there are no conflicts. As you configure each drive, check what you're doing against the list and mark off each drive as you finish it.

Many find it helpful to label each drive with its function and settings, e.g., ID-0, ID-1, and so on for SCSI drives, and Primary Master, Primary Slave, Secondary Master, Secondary Slave for ATA/ ATAPI drives. If you later upgrade the system, visible labels eliminate the need to remove drives to examine their settings.

1. In turn, remove each drive from its packaging and set jumpers as necessary to configure it. Leave unused jumper blocks connected to only one pin, which has the same effect as removing the jumper block entirely, but leaves that block conveniently available for future use. (See Figure 26-18.)

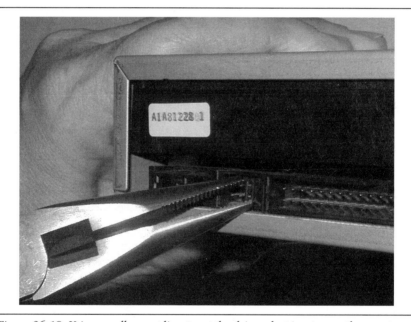

Figure 26-18: Using needlenose pliers to set the drive select jumper on the rear panel of the Smart & Friendly CD SpeedWriter Plus to Master

IDE/ATAPI drives

For each drive, set the jumper to designate the drive as Master, Slave, or Only, as appropriate. Some ATAPI drives, particularly tape drives, have jumpers to set other options, such as read-while-write or hardware compression. Set these jumpers as recommended by the documentation. A basic system uses one hard disk set as Primary Master and one CD/ DVD-ROM drive as Secondary Master. If your system has more IDE/ ATAPI devices, see Chapter 14, *Hard Disk Drives*, for more information.

SCSI drives

Some SCSI drives require setting jumpers or DIP switches to specify a unique SCSI ID for that drive and whether it is terminated. By convention, the SCSI host adapter is assigned SCSI ID 7. ID 0 is reserved for the boot hard disk, and ID 1 for a secondary hard disk. IDs 2 through 6 are available for use by other devices such as tape and optical drives. Make sure that the last physical device on each SCSI bus (and only the last device) is terminated. For most drives, you enable termination by setting a jumper or DIP switch, but some drives use a small resistor pack instead. Many SCSI drives have numerous other settings, e.g., parity, termination power, and delayed motor start. Set jumpers for these options as recommended by the documentation. If the host adapter and drives are SCAM-compliant (SCSI Configured AutoMagically), SCAM sets ID and termination automatically, but it does no harm to set parameters manually even on a SCAM-compliant system.

Floppy disk drives
Require no configuration.

2. If the drive is 3.5" form factor and will be installed in a 5.25" bay, install the drive in a chassis adapter.

3. For high-performance disk drives (some 7,200 RPM and all 10,000 RPM drives), install supplementary cooling to prevent overheating. Small supplementary fans (so-called "drive coolers") are adequate for most 7,200 RPM drives. For 10,000 RPM drives like the Seagate Cheetah 18LP we're using in the dual-CPU system, we recommend using a full bay cooling unit like the PC Power & Cooling Bay-Cool, which integrates a 3.5" to 5.25" chassis adapter with two fans and a filtered inlet. (See Figure 26-19.) The Seagate Barracuda 50LP runs cool for a 7,200 RPM and will be installed in the bottom drive bay, immediately above the two supplementary case fans. These provide adequate cooling for this drive, so we decided not to install a separate drive cooling fan.

4. Decide where to mount each drive, considering the following issues:

Convenient access
Place the externally accessible drives you will use most often where it is easy to reach them. For example, for a tower unit that will sit on the floor, place the CD drive in an upper drive bay.

Drive spacing
If you have more drive bays than drives, use that extra space to separate the drives, which improves cooling and makes it easier to connect cables or change jumpers.

Heat production
Some drives, such as CD writers and high speed hard drives, generate a lot of heat—hard drives constantly and CD burners intermittently. Heat rises, so install heat-producing drives above other drives whenever possible. For example, in the dual-processor system, we're installing one "hot" drive (the Seagate Cheetah) and three "warm" drives (the Plextor 8/2/20, the Tecmar DDS3 tape drive, and the Seagate Barracuda) in this system. We elected to put the Plextor 8/2/20 in the top drive bay (#1) with the Plextor UltraPleX CD-ROM drive and the Hitachi DVD-ROM drive (neither of which produces much heat) in bays #2 and #3 immediately below it. We elected to install the Seagate Barracuda in the bottom

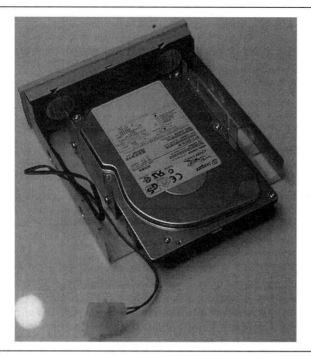

Figure 26-19: The Seagate Cheetah drive installed in a PC Power & Cooling Bay-Cool unit. The two small fans at the front bezel draw outside air through a foam filter and blow it across the drive.

bay (#10), immediately above the supplementary case fans. The bottom two drive bays in this case are not externally accessible, and the Cheetah installed in its Bay-Cool requires an external bay. We decided to install the Cheetah in bay #7, leaving bays #8 and #9 empty for additional isolation between the Cheetah and the Barracuda. (The last thing that Cheetah needs is more heat coming from the Barracuda.) We decided to install the floppy disk drive in bay #6, immediately above the Cheetah because, if we're going to overheat a drive, we'd rather it be a $15 floppy drive than an expensive drive. That leaves us with bays #4 and #5 available for the Tecmar DDS3 tape drive. Although we'd prefer to leave a free bay between the Tecmar tape drive and the Hitachi DVD drive above it, the Tecmar tape drive doesn't produce much heat, and we'd rather use the spare bay to keep the Tecmar further from the Cheetah. So we decided to install the Tecmar tape drive in bay #4, leaving bay #5 empty.

Cable routing

We've learned this one the hard way more than once. Make sure your cables will reach the positions where you install the drives. This is usually not an issue with desktop or mini/mid-tower cases, but with a full tower case it's easy to install two drives that must share the same cable so far apart that the cable won't reach. It's also less a problem with SCSI cables than with IDE cables, which are limited to 18". Take care even with SCSI, however. You may find that your SCSI cable is more than long enough, but the drive connectors are too close together to span two drives installed far apart.

Physical stability

If possible, avoid installing many heavy drives high in the case. This is not so much to prevent the case from tipping. Most cases are very stable. But tower systems with many heavy hard drives (and the power supply) all installed near the top of the case are very awkward to manipulate because all of the weight is at one end. In our case, the four drives installed in the top four bays are all relatively light, so this is not a problem.

5. Attach any required mounting hardware, such as drive rails, to the drive. Note that some cases have multiple locations where drives can be installed that use different mounting methods, so it's important to decide where each drive will be mounted before you attach the mounting hardware to it.

Step 6: Install the Floppy Disk Drive

Modern floppy disk drives have no user-configurable settings. All FDDs are set in hardware as B:. Whether the drive appears to the system as A: or B: depends upon which cable position you attach the FDD to and how the BIOS is configured. Install the FDD, noting the following:

- If the case has externally accessible 3.5" drive bay(s), use one of them for the floppy disk drive, saving the 5.25" bays for other purposes. If for some reason you must install the FDD in a 5.25" bay, you'll need to purchase an adapter for $5 or so.

- The 4-pin power connector is on the left, and the 34-pin data connector on the right. On some drives, including this one, pin 1 is not clearly marked on the data connector. Pin 1 is often (but not always) adjacent to the power connector, so try that first if in doubt. At worst, when you attempt to boot the system, the FDD light will come on and stay on. If that happens, reverse the cable.

- A standard FDD cable has three connector positions, one on each end and one in the middle. Between the middle and one end connector, a portion of the cable is twisted. The two connectors separated by the twisted portion are used to connect drives. The other end connector attaches to the motherboard FDD interface. Attaching the FDD to the connector on the far side of the twist makes that FDD A:. Connecting it to the middle connector (before the twist) makes it B:. Some cables have five connectors, with two connectors (one header-pin and one edge-card) at each drive position. These dual connectors can be used interchangeably, depending on which fits the drive. The edge-card connector was used by 5.25" FDDs, which are obsolete, but many adapters that allow a 3.5" FDD to be installed in a 5.25" drive bay use the edge-card connector.

- Most recent BIOSes support only one FDD, and have a BIOS setting that allows drives A: and B: to be swapped. This is important if the FDD cable supplied with your motherboard has only two connectors and no twist, as do some we have seen. In that situation, you can use the supplied cable to connect the drive, but make sure to use BIOS Setup to swap A: and B: so that the installed drive appears as A:.

Once you have determined where to install the drive and which connector you will use, slide the drive into the bay. Some drives and cases require that the FDD be installed from the front of the case, and others from the back. FDDs are inexpensive devices, and manufacturers don't spend much money on amenities such as shrouded connectors, so it's often easier to connect the data and power cables to the drive before you slide it into the bay. (See Figure 26-20.)

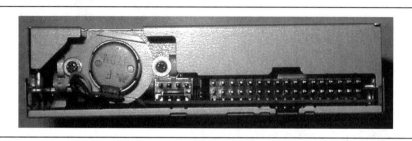

Figure 26-20: The rear panel of a typical 3.5" floppy disk drive, showing the lack of shrouded connectors

Although power cables are keyed, it can be difficult to line up the connection after the drive is installed. If the power cable is too short to allow connecting it to the drive while the drive is outside the case, you will have to connect it after the drive is installed. Depending on where the drive is mounted, it may be difficult to see the connector with the drive in place. If that's true for your system, connect the power cable to the drive temporarily to determine how it should be oriented, e.g., "red wire toward the data cable."

Step 7: Install Other Drives

How you mount hard disk drives, tape drives, and optical drives varies from case to case, and may depend on the drive itself and whether the drive is to be mounted in an externally accessible bay. Some cases use multiple mounting methods, as follows:

- With typical mini- and mid-tower cases, slide the drive into the bay and secure it with screws to the bay itself. (See Figure 26-21.) Depending on the particular case and drive, you may need to slide the drive into place from the front or from the back. Use the screws provided with the drive to secure the drive. If no screws were provided with the drive, make sure that the screws you use not only have the proper thread, but are the proper length. A too-long screw can project inside the drive enclosure and damage a circuit board or other component. Four screws—front and back on each side—are always adequate, although there may be room to install as many as eight. Although it is not recommended practice, we have sometimes secured a drive with only two screws on the same side when the case design made it difficult to drive screws into the other side. We have never had any problems result from doing this, but if you do it, do so at your own risk.

- Some cases use removable drive cages in which you install all drives and then mount the cage with installed drives as a single unit. Drive cages are in all other respects similar to the arrangement just described.

Figure 26-21: A typical mini-tower arrangement, where drives secure directly to the chassis

- Traditional desktop cases and high-end tower cases (such as the PC Power & Cooling Solid-Steel tower) use drive rails, which are secured to the drives and fit slotted channels within the case. (See Figure 26-22.)

Figure 26-22: The traditional arrangement, in which rails mounted to the drive slide into matching slots in the chassis, and are secured by a front screw or clips

The drive in the top bay of this Antec case has all four screw holes aligned with the corresponding holes in the chassis, which automatically aligns the drive front-to-back to be flush with the front bezil. Cases built with sloppier tolerance use slots rather than holes to make up for the loose tolerances, although some well-built cases also use slots.

Whichever mounting method(s) your case uses, verify that all externally accessible drives project the correct distance to ensure that they are flush with the front chassis bezel when it is installed. Some cases have alignment holes that make this job trivial. Others require trial and error. In the latter situation, we usually mount one drive, temporarily mount the front chassis bezel to ensure proper alignment, and then install all other drives flush with the first drive we installed.

You may have to depart from your planned arrangement of drives if you encounter vertical alignment problems. Some externally accessible drives have front bezels that are just enough oversize or with an incorrect vertical offset that you cannot install another externally accessible drive in the bay immediately above or below the problem drive. You can sometimes gently force such a drive to seat, but it's usually better to rearrange the drives to avoid such tight fits.

Before you install each drive, consider data cabling. If the drive is the only drive that will connect to a data cable, it's easier to attach the cable to the drive first and then feed the cable through the bay and into the chassis. If multiple drives will connect to the same data cable, choose the drive for which rear access will be most difficult after the drive is installed and connect the cable to that drive before you install the drive. After you install and secure each drive, connect the data cable (if you have not done so previously) and then the power cable.

Step 8: Install the Motherboard

1. Slide the motherboard into position, verifying each motherboard mounting hole aligns with its brass standoff, each nylon standoff slides properly into the corresponding slot on the motherboard tray, and the I/O connectors on the rear of the motherboard align with the I/O template (or the access holes in the chassis).

2. While maintaining continuous gentle pressure toward the rear of the chassis to keep the motherboard aligned with the mounting holes, insert one of the mounting screws, but don't tighten it fully. Continue inserting mounting screws loosely until all mounting holes are occupied. Finally, tighten each mounting screw gently. Finger-tight is adequate. We've seen people crack motherboards by applying too much torque to the mounting screws.

3. If you have not already done so, connect the CPU fan to the appropriate motherboard power header or to a spare drive power cable.

4. Connect the main power lead from the power supply to the motherboard. For ATX systems, the main power connector is a single 20-pin keyed connector. (See Figure 26-23.) AT systems use two main power cables, each with a 6-pin keyed connector (often labeled P8 and P9), which connect to one 12-pin connector strip on the motherboard. (See Figure 26-24.) It's possible to swap positions of these cables, which can destroy a motherboard, so be careful which you connect where. For nearly all AT power supplies, when both connectors are installed properly the black wires on each will be toward the center, but we have encountered AT power supplies with nonstandard wire

colors. Verify connector orientation with the documentation for your power supply and motherboard rather than making assumptions. Some power supplies have both AT and ATX power connectors, as do some motherboards. This 20-pin connector is keyed, preventing misconnecting the main power lead.

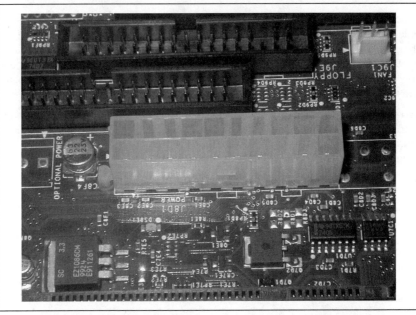

Figure 26-23: The light object in the center is an ATX power connector

Figure 26-24: The light object in the center is an AT power connector

5. ATX motherboards organize all I/O connectors in a block that matches the I/O template on the rear. AT motherboards use a permanently mounted keyboard connector that aligns with the keyboard hole in AT cases, but other I/O ports—serial, parallel, USB, and so on—exist only as groups of header pins on the motherboard. Those I/O ports are made accessible on the rear panel of the case by installing *port extenders*, which are cables with a header pin connector on one end and the appropriate I/O connector on the other. (See Figure 26-25.) Some port extenders are normally supplied with the motherboard, but many AT motherboards do not include port extenders for all ports. For example, the extenders for Serial 2 and USB are often optional items. These port extenders are relatively standard items. If you're missing any, you can buy them for a few dollars at any well-stocked computer store.

To install a port extender, align the header pin connector with the appropriate set of header pins on the motherboard, making sure that pin 1 corresponds to the red stripe on the cable, and press down until the connector seats. Most port extenders have the external connector mounted on an expansion slot bracket. The case may have more expansion slot cutouts than the motherboard has expansion slots. If so, mounting the port extender in an expansion slot cutout costs nothing. If your system has the same number of expansion slots and cutouts, mounting the port extender in an expansion slot cutout wastes that expansion slot. Most AT cases contain several precut holes for DB9, DB25, and other connectors. On better cases, the covers for these holes are secured by screws. On inexpensive cases, the covers are die-cut and need to be twisted out with needlenose pliers. Remove the covers for the ports you need to extend. Remove the port extender connector from the slot bracket and mount it directly to a matching cutout in the rear panel of the chassis.

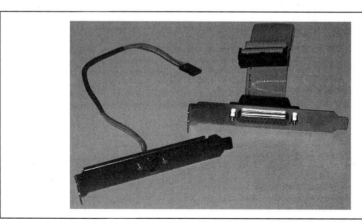

Figure 26-25: Typical port extenders for an AT motherboard: on the left is a PS/2 mouse connector, and on the right is a DB25 serial port connector

Step 9: Connect Cables to the Motherboard

All systems require connecting various cables to the motherboard. These include:

- Cables that connect floppy, hard, and optical drives to embedded motherboard interfaces

- Cables for miscellaneous functions, such as connecting audio out on the rear panel of a CD-ROM drive to the audio header on the motherboard, or connecting a CPU fan to a power header on the motherboard

- Cables that connect front panel switches (power, reset, keylock, etc.) and indicators (drive activity, power on, speaker, etc.)

It's usually easier to connect these cables before you start installing expansion cards. Proceed as follows:

1. Connect the drive data cables from the back of each drive to the appropriate connector on the motherboard, making sure to align pin 1 properly on both the drive and controller. Typical systems have at least two such cables: one 34-wire ribbon cable connecting the floppy disk drive to the FDD controller interface on the motherboard, and an IDE cable connecting the hard drive and CD- or DVD-ROM drive to the primary IDE interface connector on the motherboard. If the system has more than two IDE devices, you need to connect a second IDE cable from the third (or third and fourth) IDE devices to the secondary IDE interface connector on the motherboard. If the system has SCSI devices installed and the motherboard has an embedded SCSI host adapter, connect cable(s) from the SCSI device(s) to the SCSI connector(s).

2. If it has not already been done, connect a power cable from the power supply to the power connector on the rear of each drive. If you have more drives than power leads, use a splitter to allow two drives to share one power lead. Splitters may be provided with the case and power supply, or may be purchased inexpensively at any computer store. Although it's probably not a major issue, the power leads use relatively small gauge wires, so we try whenever possible to connect high-draw devices like fast disk drives and CD burners to separate power leads.

3. Connect any supplementary cables required, like CD audio, CPU fan, hardware management, temperature sensors, Wake-on-LAN, chassis intrusion, video-source line-in, aux line-in, telephony. Refer to your motherboard manual.

4. Connect the front-panel cables to the header pin connectors on the motherboard, which are usually arranged in a block near the front edge. Typically these connectors will include: power switch (ATX only), reset switch, hard disk activity LED, power-on LED, and speaker. Depending on the motherboard and case, you may also have connectors for keylock, Infrared port, and perhaps a secondary drive activity LED.

   Connectors may or may not be labeled. If not, you will have to trace each wire back to the front panel to determine which connector is which. Most connectors are two-pin. For those that connect to switches, polarity is immaterial. For those that connect to LEDs, polarity may or may not matter. Best practice is to orient the connector for proper polarity. Most cases use the black wire of each pair for ground. The ground pin for each connector may or may not be marked on the motherboard. If not, refer to the manual.

Pinout Mismatch Problem

One problem arises more often than it should. Sometimes, the pinouts on the motherboard do not match the pinout on the connector. Intel and other manufacturers are attempting to standardize the arrangement and pinouts for front-panel connectors, but many motherboards and cases still use their own arrangements. For example, we have encountered motherboards that have all four pins present for a standard four-position speaker connector (which actually needs only two wires anyway). If the four-position connector on the speaker wire has one position blocked, as is frequently the case, it is impossible to slide that connector onto the pins on the motherboard without some surgery. Sometimes you can penetrate the blocked position with a needle or sharp awl, or remove the plastic block with a small screwdriver or your needlenose pliers. If that doesn't work, you may be able to bend the extra pin far enough out of the way to slide the connector onto the three remaining pins. Other times, you must use your nippers to cut off the extra pin.

Even that's not the worst case. We have encountered some combinations of case and motherboard with oddball pinouts that are impossible to match up. For example, the case provides a single four-position connector that incorporates the Power LED and Reset Switch, whereas on the motherboard these functions are separated by several pins. In such cases, the only solution is to use a razor knife carefully to split the multi-position connector into separate one- or two-position connectors.

Some cases (oddly enough, usually the very inexpensive ones) avoid this problem entirely by using one-position connectors on all wires that lead to front-panel switches and indicators. That is, each wire is completely independent of every other wire, which allows you to connect individual wires in any fashion the motherboard requires. Dealing with individual connectors is clumsy and time-consuming, but it does provide complete flexibility.

The best way to avoid a situation like this is to verify ahead of time that the front-panel header pins on the motherboard match the connectors on the case.

Step 10: Install Expansion Cards

A modern motherboard includes some or all of the bus slot types shown in Figure 26-26. All motherboards provide PCI slots, most provide ISA slots (although the newest motherboards have no ISA slots), and many provide an AGP slot. You can install an expansion card only in a slot that is designed to accept it, either ISA, PCI, or AGP. The best rule to follow is to avoid installing any ISA cards if at all possible. If you have a choice between installing a PCI video card or an AGP video card, choose AGP. For everything else, use PCI.

To install expansions cards:

1. Decide where to install each expansion card. If you have more slots than cards, leave empty slots between cards to improve air flow and cooling. Video cards, particularly high-performance ones, generate significant heat, so

Figure 26-26: An Intel SE440BX "Seattle" motherboard showing, from left to right, one ISA slot, one combined ISA/PCI slot (which can accept an ISA or a PCI card, but not both simultaneously), three PCI slots, and an AGP slot

always leave an unoccupied slot between the video card and adjacent cards if possible. Sound cards are also significant heat sources, so give them second priority when juggling empty slots.

2. If your case came with slot covers preinstalled, remove and set aside the slot covers and screws for each position where you will install a card. You may find that removing all slot covers makes it easier to install cards.

3. If internal cables connect to the card (e.g., a SCSI host adapter or a sound card), connect those cables before installing the card.

4. Install each card, as follows:

   – Align the card bracket so its bottom tab will slide into position between the case and the motherboard.

   – Align the card edge connector on the bottom of the card with the expansion slot. Make certain that the card aligns with the slot both side-to-side and front-to-back. Well-designed motherboards, cards, and cases are built to close tolerances, and nearly always align properly. (See Figure 26-27.) Inexpensive components, particularly cases, are often built sloppily and may make it impossible to align the card with the slot front-to-back. If so, use your needle-nose pliers to bend the card bracket slightly to allow the connector to align with the slot. (See Figure 26-28.)

   – With the card aligned properly with the slot, use both thumbs to press straight down until the card seats fully in the slot. This may require significant pressure. You should be able to feel and hear the card seat. When the card is fully seated, the top of its bracket should be flush with the chassis and the screw slot in the card bracket should align with the screw hole in the chassis. When the card is fully seated and properly aligned, insert a screw to secure it.

5. Install a slot cover in each open slot position and secure it with a screw. Do not leave slot covers off unoccupied slots. Doing so damages cooling air flow.

Figure 26-27: With a high-quality case (this one a PC Power & Cooling mini-tower), expansion cards align properly front to back

 We usually install all expansion cards first, then install and configure the operating system. If you are building a heavily loaded Windows 9X system, it may be easier to configure if you install expansion cards incrementally. That is, install Windows 9X with only essential cards (video and perhaps SCSI) in place. Once the system is configured properly, shut it down and install the sound card. Sound cards are notorious resource hogs, and should be installed immediately following video to give them first choice of available resources. Once video and sound work, install the other cards one by one. Using this piece-meal method sometimes allows Windows 9X Plug-N-Play to configure the system properly when attempting to configure everything at once fails. Also note that some motherboards allow "locking down" specific IRQs to specific slots. If your motherboard supports this feature, you can use it to solve problems that may occur when Windows 9X IRQ Steering shares an IRQ with multiple devices. For example, slow video may be cured by making sure the video IRQ is not shared. Windows NT does not support Plug-N-Play, so there is no advantage to using this incremental method with it.

Figure 26-28: With a cheap case (this one a no-name Taiwanese product), expansion cards may misalign front-to-back with the expansion slots, sometimes by a quarter-inch (6.35 mm) or more

Step 11: Perform the "Smoke Test"

At this point, you're almost ready to turn on the PC for the first time. Don't replace the cover quite yet, though. You'll need to do a few more things inside the case before the system is complete. Proceed as follows:

1. Do a final check of the system, making sure that all cables are connected properly and that you haven't left any tools in the patient. Do not underestimate the importance of this final check. We have seen newly built systems shorted out and destroyed because a tool, screw, slot cover, or other conductive part was left where it shouldn't be. In fact, we always pick up the system and shake it gently to make sure no extraneous parts have been overlooked.

2. Connect the monitor, keyboard, and mouse to the appropriate ports on the computer. Connect the power cord to the PC power supply and then plug it into a wall receptacle. Turn on the monitor.

3. Turn on the PC. If all is well, the hard disk spins up, the BIOS screen appears on the monitor within a few seconds, and the system beeps to indicate a normal boot. If the system appears dead or beeps repeatedly, immediately disconnect the power and verify all cable connections and configuration jumpers. The most common problem is a floppy drive cable connected backward, which causes the floppy drive indicator to light and stay lit as soon as power is applied, or an IDE cable connected backward, which may cause the system to appear completely dead. In either case, check the cables, correct

any problems you find, and re-apply power. Repeat this process until the system boots normally.

4. Some motherboards require running BIOS Setup immediately to allow the system to self-configure. Doing that never hurts, so when the system prompts you "Press <key-name> to run Setup" (or words to that effect) press the indicated key to run BIOS Setup. Don't make any changes to BIOS settings now. Simply save the default settings, exit, and allow the system to restart.

5. Check the BIOS boot screens to make sure that all installed components are recognized properly. In particular, the initial memory check should display the correct amount of memory, and the screen(s) that list installed devices should show all installed ports and IDE devices. IDE/ATAPI devices should be listed correctly by name or model number. Devices that require drivers are not recognized at this point, which is normal. On fast systems, screens often flash by too quickly to read. Press the Pause key to interrupt the boot process long enough to read each screen. To continue, press the Space Bar.

6. After you verify that all devices are recognized, restart the system and run BIOS Setup again. With most systems, you need change only the time and date, and perhaps set the processor speed. Default values work perfectly well for other BIOS settings. Use the motherboard manual to determine which, if any, settings need to be changed. If you plan to delve deep into the BIOS settings to tune your PC for optimum performance, the motherboard manual may be of little use. Most provide only abbreviated descriptions of the most commonly changed BIOS settings. For detailed information about obscure settings, visit the web site of the BIOS manufacturer and download the full documentation for your BIOS version. Even with that information, however, you may find many BIOS options difficult to understand. We have found *The BIOS Companion,* by Phil Croucher (Advice), very helpful in deciphering obscure BIOS settings. You can order it directly from the author's web site at *http://www.electrocution.com/biosc.htm.*

7. If you have devices (such as a network card or SCSI host adapter) that have their own ROM-based setup programs, run those programs per the manufacturers' instructions.

8. When you complete BIOS Setup, save the changes and exit. Power the system down. Some motherboards, notably Intel models, have a configuration jumper that is set to one position for Configure and another position for Normal Operation. If your motherboard has such a jumper, move it to the position that sets the system for normal operation.

Step 12: Install Software

Install the operating system per the manufacturer's instructions. During installation or immediately thereafter, as appropriate, install any driver disks provided with hardware components. If possible, do this during installation to prevent problems. For example, when installing Windows NT 4, we first used the drivers provided on the NT CD for the Intel PRO/100+ Ethernet adapter. As it turns out, those drivers simply didn't support our more recent Intel adapter. We could have saved considerable time simply by supplying an updated drivers disk during installation rather than using the Microsoft-supplied drivers.

After you complete the installation and restart the system, connect to the Web and check the manufacturer's web site to locate the latest production drivers for each hardware component you have installed, particularly motherboard, video, sound, and network. If you've installed a CD burner, be sure to look for the latest firmware version for it. Once you've updated all drivers, restart the system and install your applications.

Step 13: Finishing Touches

At this point, the system should be fully functional, but a few things remain to be done:

1. Dress the cables. Many OEMs and most individuals neglect this step, but it's an important one. The typical rats' nest of cables that results when you build a PC can impede air flow, causing sporadic problems due to overheating. One system we saw ran fine for a few minutes and then locked up. As it turned out, a loose wire had fouled the CPU cooling fan, causing the CPU to overheat and crash. If you have them, use cable ties to secure individual wires—like those on power connectors—into neat bundles, and then secure those bundles to the frame. If you don't have cable ties, the little yellow plastic ties that come with garbage bags work about as well. Tape ribbon cables in flat bunches, and secure them to the chassis, well away from the processor and fans. We've used everything from masking tape to duct tape with equal success, although the heat inside a PC can make some types of tape gummy and hard to remove. Fold over a quarter inch or so at the end of the tape to provide a pull tab in case you need to remove the tape later.

2. If you have a tape drive or CD-ROM burner, run a full backup and stick it on the shelf. If your backup software allows you to make an emergency recovery disk, make one now.

3. If you have diagnostic software that provides a burn-in function, use it. Most hardware failures occur immediately. Those that don't are likely to occur within hours or days. When we're not in any hurry, we generally allow a system to burn in for a week or so before declaring it complete. Even when we are in a hurry, we generally insist on burning in the new system at least overnight. If you have hardware problems, it's better to find out now than later.

4. Re-install the cover on the case, and move the system to its permanent new location. Connect the monitor, keyboard, mouse, and any other external peripherals. Connect the power cord and start using the computer.

5. Enter a recurring to-do in your calendar to remind you to check every 30 to 60 days for updated drivers for the main system components, particularly video and sound. This is particularly important if you've built the system using newly introduced components, or if you're using a relatively new release of your operating system.

Index

C

P

S

S3 (Savage series), 288
sags (reductions in voltage), 413
sample rate generators, 326
sample size in audio files, 321
sampling sounds
  creating audio files, 321
  rates for, CD vs. analog, 193
Savage series (S3), 288
sawtooth waves, 418
SC242 sockets, 116
SCAM (SCSI Configured Auto
      Magically), 252
  CD-ROM drives, compliancy
      with, 202
  SCSI
    CD-ROM drives, configuring, 202
    devices, compliancy with, 252
    tape drives, configuring, 181
scan codes (keyboard signals), 350
SCAs (Single Connector
      Attachments), 249
screen area settings, changing, 294
screen size in monitors, 307
SCSI
  vs. ATA, 253
  cables/connectors, 248
  CD writers, installing and
      configuring, 213
  CD-ROM drives, 202
  differential devices, 247
  disadvantages of, 254
  as disk interface, 234
  drives, preparing for installation, 463
  DVD-ROM drives, 227
  fast, 246
  floppy disk drives, 170
  hard disk drives
    choosing, 259
    installing, 266–269
  host adapters
    for high-performance systems, 436
    recommended brands, 255
    for workstation systems, 441
  IDs and terminations, 249
  implementations of, 246–248
  interoperability, 252
  standards for, 245
  tape drives

communication problems and, 187
configuring Windows 9X for, 183
installing/configuring, 181
terminators, 250
SCSI Configured Auto Magically (see
      SCAM)
scuzzy disk (see SCSI)
SDRAM (see Synchronous DRAM)
SE SCSI (single-ended SCSI), 247
SECC (Single Edge Contact
      Connector), 116
  installing on PCs, 456
Secondary cache (see L2 cache)
Secondary Interface, 240
sector number registers, 241
sectors in hard disk drives, 258
SEPP (Single Edge Processor
      Package), 116
serial mice, 364
Serial Presence Detect (SPD), 76, 148
serpentine recording, 175
SFX Baseboard Connector, 401
SFX Power Supply Design Guide
      Version 1.1, 397
SGRAM (Synchronous Graphics
      RAM), 279
shadow masks in monitors, 306
side panel cases, 56
signaling rates, 246
Signal-to-Noise ratios (S/N ratios), 330
silver alloy in CD-R blanks, 219
SIMD (Single Instruction, Multiple
      Data), 114
SIMMs (Single Inline Memory Modules)
  form factors, 142
  installing, 461
  installing/removing, 152
  memory guidelines, 148
  rows and banks, 143
Simple Network Management Protocols
      (SNMPs), 420
sine waves, 418
Single Connector Attachments
      (SCAs), 249
Single Edge Contact Connector
      (SECC), 116
  installing on PCs, 456
Single Edge Processor Package
      (SEPP), 116

Z

About the Authors

Robert Bruce Thompson built his first computer in 1976 from discrete chips. It had 256 *bytes* of memory, used toggle switches and LEDs for I/O, ran at less than 1 MHz, and had no operating system. Since then, he has bought, built, upgraded, and repaired hundreds of PCs for himself, employers, customers, friends, and clients. Robert is the author or co-author of numerous online training courses and computer books, including *Windows NT Server 4.0 for NetWare Administrators* and *Windows NT TCP/IP Network Administration* (both published by O'Reilly & Associates). He is currently hard at work with co-author Jerry Pournelle on their next book project.

Barbara Fritchman Thompson worked for twenty years as a librarian before starting her own home-based consulting practice, Research for Authors (found at *http://www.fritchman.com*). Barbara, who has been a PC power user for fifteen years, researched and tested much of the hardware reviewed for this book. Barbara spends her working hours doing research for authors and her leisure hours reading, working out, and playing golf. She lives with husband Robert and their three Border Collie dogs, Kerry, Duncan, and Malcolm.

Colophon

Our look is the result of reader comments, our own experimentation, and feedback from distribution channels. Distinctive covers complement our distinctive approach to technical topics, breathing personality and life into potentially dry subjects.

The image on the cover of *PC Hardware in a Nutshell* is a scallop. The scallop is part of the pecten family, which includes other bivalve mollusks such as clams and oysters. Also called the fan shell or comb shell, scallops can be found on the sandy bottoms of most oceans, in both deep and shallow water. Scallops do not usually stay attached to rocks. Instead, they either rest on the ocean bottom or swim by rapidly opening and closing their shells. The water ejected by the movement pushes them forward and allows them a freedom of movement unusual in bivalves.

The scallop's shell is made up of calcium carbonate and other minerals embedded in an organic matrix secreted from a layer of tissue called the mantle. The upper and lower halves of the shell connect at a straight hinge line that can measure from one to six inches. The shell's paired valves have sharp edges and undulating ridges that radiate out in the shape of a fan, and range in color from red to purple, orange, yellow, or white.

Colleen Gorman was the production editor and proofreader, and Clairemarie Fisher O'Leary was the copyeditor for *PC Hardware in a Nutshell*. Melanie Wang and Jane Ellin provided quality control. Matt Hutchinson provided production support. Joe Wizda wrote the index.

Hanna Dyer designed the cover of this book, based on a series design by Edie Freedman. The cover image is an 18th-century engraving from the Dover Treasury of Animal Illustrations. Emma Colby produced the cover layout with QuarkXPress 4.1 using Adobe's ITC Garamond font.

Alicia Cech and David Futato designed the interior layout, based on a series design by Nancy Priest. Mike Sierra implemented the design in FrameMaker 5.5.6. The text and heading fonts are ITC Garamond Light and Garamond Book. The illustrations that appear in the book were produced by Robert Romano using Macromedia Free-Hand 8 and Adobe Photoshop 5. This colophon was written by Colleen Gorman.

Whenever possible, our books use a durable and flexible lay-flat binding. If the page count exceeds this binding's limit, perfect binding is used.

How to stay in touch with O'Reilly

1. Visit Our Award-Winning Site

http://www.oreilly.com/

★ "Top 100 Sites on the Web" —*PC Magazine*
★ "Top 5% Web sites" —*Point Communications*
★ "3-Star site" —*The McKinley Group*

Our web site contains a library of comprehensive product information (including book excerpts and tables of contents), downloadable software, background articles, interviews with technology leaders, links to relevant sites, book cover art, and more. File us in your Bookmarks or Hotlist!

2. Join Our Email Mailing Lists

New Product Releases

To receive automatic email with brief descriptions of all new O'Reilly products as they are released, send email to:
listproc@online.oreilly.com
Put the following information in the first line of your message (*not* in the Subject field):
subscribe oreilly-news

O'Reilly Events

If you'd also like us to send information about trade show events, special promotions, and other O'Reilly events, send email to:
listproc@online.oreilly.com
Put the following information in the first line of your message (*not* in the Subject field):
subscribe oreilly-events

3. Get Examples from Our Books via FTP

There are two ways to access an archive of example files from our books:

Regular FTP

* ftp to:
  ftp.oreilly.com
  (login: anonymous
  password: your email address)
* Point your web browser to:
  ftp://ftp.oreilly.com/

FTPMAIL

* Send an email message to:
  ftpmail@online.oreilly.com
  (Write "help" in the message body)

4. Contact Us via Email

order@oreilly.com
To place a book or software order online. Good for North American and international customers.

subscriptions@oreilly.com
To place an order for any of our newsletters or periodicals.

books@oreilly.com
General questions about any of our books.

software@oreilly.com
For general questions and product information about our software. Check out O'Reilly Software Online at **http://software.oreilly.com/** for software and technical support information. Registered O'Reilly software users send your questions to:
website-support@oreilly.com

cs@oreilly.com
For answers to problems regarding your order or our products.

booktech@oreilly.com
For book content technical questions or corrections.

proposals@oreilly.com
To submit new book or software proposals to our editors and product managers.

international@oreilly.com
For information about our international distributors or translation queries. For a list of our distributors outside of North America check out:
http://www.oreilly.com/www/order/country.html

5. Work with Us

Check out our website for current employment opportunites:
www.jobs@oreilly.com
Click on "Work with Us"

O'Reilly & Associates, Inc.
101 Morris Street, Sebastopol, CA 95472 USA
TEL   707-829-0515 or 800-998-9938
        (6am to 5pm PST)
FAX   707-829-0104

International Distributors

UK, EUROPE, MIDDLE EAST AND AFRICA (EXCEPT FRANCE, GERMANY, AUSTRIA, SWITZERLAND, LUXEMBOURG, LIECHTENSTEIN, AND EASTERN EUROPE)

INQUIRIES
O'Reilly UK Limited
4 Castle Street
Farnham
Surrey, GU9 7HS
United Kingdom
Telephone: 44-1252-711776
Fax: 44-1252-734211
Email: information@oreilly.co.uk

ORDERS
Wiley Distribution Services Ltd.
1 Oldlands Way
Bognor Regis
West Sussex PO22 9SA
United Kingdom
Telephone: 44-1243-779777
Fax: 44-1243-820250
Email: cs-books@wiley.co.uk

FRANCE

INQUIRIES
Éditions O'Reilly
18 rue Séguier
75006 Paris, France
Tel: 33-1-40-51-52-30
Fax: 33-1-40-51-52-31
Email: france@editions-oreilly.fr

ORDERS
GEODIF
61, Bd Saint-Germain
75240 Paris Cedex 05, France
Tel: 33-1-44-41-46-16 (French books)
Tel: 33-1-44-41-11-87 (English books)
Fax: 33-1-44-41-11-44
Email: distribution@eyrolles.com

GERMANY, SWITZERLAND, AUSTRIA, EASTERN EUROPE, LUXEMBOURG, AND LIECHTENSTEIN

INQUIRIES & ORDERS
O'Reilly Verlag
Balthasarstr. 81
D-50670 Köln
Germany
Telephone: 49-221-973160-91
Fax: 49-221-973160-8
Email: anfragen@oreilly.de (inquiries)
Email: order@oreilly.de (orders)

CANADA (FRENCH LANGUAGE BOOKS)
Les Éditions Flammarion ltée
375, Avenue Laurier Ouest
Montréal (Québec) H2V 2K3
Tel: 00-1-514-277-8807
Fax: 00-1-514-278-2085
Email: info@flammarion.qc.ca

HONG KONG
City Discount Subscription Service, Ltd.
Unit D, 3rd Floor, Yan's Tower
27 Wong Chuk Hang Road
Aberdeen, Hong Kong
Tel: 852-2580-3539
Fax: 852-2580-6463
Email: citydis@ppn.com.hk

KOREA
Hanbit Media, Inc.
Chungmu Bldg. 201
Yonnam-dong 568-33
Mapo-gu
Seoul, Korea
Tel: 822-325-0397
Fax: 822-325-9697
Email: hant93@chollian.dacom.co.kr

PHILIPPINES
Global Publishing
G/F Benavides Garden
1186 Benavides St.
Manila, Philippines
Tel: 632-254-8949/637-252-2582
Fax: 632-734-5060/632-252-2733
Email: globalp@pacific.net.ph

TAIWAN
O'Reilly Taiwan
No. 3, Lane 131
Hang-Chow South Road
Section 1, Taipei, Taiwan
Tel: 886-2-23968990
Fax: 886-2-23968916
Email: taiwan@oreilly.com

CHINA
O'Reilly Beijing
Room 2410
160, FuXingMenNeiDaJie
XiCheng District
Beijing
China PR 100031
Tel: 86-10-66412305
Fax: 86-10-86631007
Email: beijing@oreilly.com

INDIA
Computer Bookshop (India) Pvt. Ltd.
190 Dr. D.N. Road, Fort
Bombay 400 001 India
Tel: 91-22-207-0989
Fax: 91-22-262-3551
Email: cbsbom@giasbm01.vsnl.net.in

JAPAN
O'Reilly Japan, Inc.
Yotsuya Y's Building
7 Banch 6, Honshio-cho
Shinjuku-ku
Tokyo 160-0003 Japan
Tel: 81-3-3356-5227
Fax: 81-3-3356-5261
Email: japan@oreilly.com

ALL OTHER ASIAN COUNTRIES
O'Reilly & Associates, Inc.
101 Morris Street
Sebastopol, CA 95472 USA
Tel: 707-829-0515
Fax: 707-829-0104
Email: order@oreilly.com

AUSTRALIA
Woodslane Pty., Ltd.
7/5 Vuko Place
Warriewood NSW 2102
Australia
Tel: 61-2-9970-5111
Fax: 61-2-9970-5002
Email: info@woodslane.com.au

NEW ZEALAND
Woodslane New Zealand, Ltd.
21 Cooks Street (P.O. Box 575)
Waganui, New Zealand
Tel: 64-6-347-6543
Fax: 64-6-345-4840
Email: info@woodslane.com.au

LATIN AMERICA
McGraw-Hill Interamericana
Editores, S.A. de C.V.
Cedro No. 512
Col. Atlampa
06450, Mexico, D.F.
Tel: 52-5-547-6777
Fax: 52-5-547-3336
Email: mcgraw-hill@infosel.net.mx

O'REILLY®

O'REILLY®

O'Reilly & Associates, Inc.
101 Morris Street
Sebastopol, CA 95472-9902
1-800-998-9938

Visit us online at:
www.oreilly.com
order@oreilly.com

O'REILLY WOULD LIKE TO HEAR FROM YOU

Nineteenth century wood engraving
of a bear from the O'Reilly &
Associates Nutshell Handbook®
Using & Managing UUCP.

BUSINESS REPLY MAIL

FIRST CLASS MAIL   PERMIT NO. 80   SEBASTOPOL, CA

Postage will be paid by addressee

O'Reilly & Associates, Inc.
101 Morris Street
Sebastopol, CA 95472-9902